What Law School Doesn't Teach You . . . But You *Really* Need to Know

EXPERT TIPS & STRATEGIES FOR MAKING YOUR LEGAL CAREER A HUGE SUCCESS

Kimm Alayne Walton, J.D.

Printed in the United States of America.

Cover Design: Foster & Foster, Inc. (Fairfield, IA)
Interior Design: Desktop Miracles (Stowe, VT)

Harcourt Legal & Professional Publications, Inc., 111 West Jackson Boulevard, 7th Floor, Chicago, IL 60604. Phone: 1-800-787-8717. Fax: 1-800-433-6303.

"... the truth will set you free."

—John 8:32 NIV

"I can see clearly now, the rain has gone
I can see all obstacles in my way
Gone are the dark clouds that had me blind
It's gonna be a bright, bright, bright sunshiny day."

—Johnny Nash

"I'm a firm believer in luck.
The harder I work, the luckier I get."

—Thomas Jefferson

"Knowledge is good."

—Emil Faber, founder of Faber College

DEDICATION

I would like to dedicate this book to the people who make my life wonderful. After all, the work you do isn't as important as the people in your life.

To my family, my adorable husband Henry, Dad, Mom, Keir, Sherri, Ellie, Emmy and Hailey.

To my friends, Helene, Jody, Jackie, Lowry, Laura, Les, Rose, Arthur, Louise, and Joe.

And to the many, many wonderful career services people at law schools around the country, who have transcended the bounds of professional acquaintance to become true friends.

ACKNOWLEDGMENTS

My all-time favourite *New Yorker* cartoon features a well-to-do elderly couple sitting on armchairs, in front of the fireplace, in a very elegant living room. Their dachshund is standing looking at them, saying, "I once again find myself in the rather embarrassing position of having to ask one of you for a biscuit." Here's what reminded me of that cartoon. You're about to read a bunch of truly wonderful advice. None of it is from me. I'm in the rather embarrassing position of having to admit—once again!—that I've written a book with nary an original thought in it.

Instead, all of the credit goes to the many, many wonderful people who shared their insights with me, so that I could share them with you. When you nail down that permanent offer, when you see your career skyrocketing because of what you read in this book—take another look at this list, and think about the people who helped you get there!

Sharon Abrahams, Greenberg Traurig, P.A.
Eric Adams, Carlton, Fields, Ward, Emmanuel, Smith & Cutler, P.A.
Akin, Gump, Strauss, Hauer & Feld, L.L.P.
Carol Allemeier, Pepperdine University School of Law
Elizabeth Armour, Boston University School of Law
Arnold & Porter
Susanne Aronowitz, Golden Gate University School of Law
Drusilla Bakert, University of Kentucky School of Law
Diane Ballou, Quinnipiac University School of Law
Barnes & Thornburg
T. Jill Barr, American University Washington College of Law

William Barrett, Jr., Wake Forest University School of Law
Pat Bass, Mercer University School of Law
Anthony Bastone, University of Colorado School of Law
Mary Beal, Akin, Gump, Strauss, Hauer & Feld, L.L.P.
Joy Beane, Pace University School of Law
Laurie Beck, Brooklyn Law School
Gerald Beechum, University of Missouri at Columbia School of Law
Mary Birmingham, University of Arizona School of Law
Dan Boehnen, McDonnell Boehnen Hulbert & Berghoff
Elaine Bourne, Dickinson Law School at the Pennsylvania State University
Kathleen Brady, Milbank, Tweed, Hadley & McCloy LLP
Paul Bran, Dickstein Shapiro Morin & Oshinsky LLP
Carolyn Bregman, Emory University School of Law
Vickie Brown, Georgia State University College of Law
Brown, Todd & Heyburn PLLC
Joel Burcat, Kirkpatrick & Lockhart
Phyllis Burkhard, University of South Carolina School of Law
Lisa Smith Butler, Nova Southeastern University Shepard Broad Law Center
Carlton, Fields, Ward, Emmanuel, Smith & Cutler, P.A.
Nancy Carver, George Washington University School of Law
Bill Chamberlain, John Marshall Law School
Stephanie Rever Chu, Chicago-Kent College of Law
Carolyn Gentile Colangelo, DePanfilis & Vallerie
Rich Colangelo, Assistant State's Attorney, Fairfield County, Connecticut
Cowles & Thompson
Marcy Cox, Miami University School of Law
Gail Cutter, New York University School of Law
Anna Davis, Georgetown University Law Center
Davis Wright Tremaine L.L.P.
Bernice Davenport, Thomas M. Cooley Law School
John DeRosa, Brooklyn Law School
Joanne DeZego, Milbank, Tweed, Hadley & McCloy LLP
Tony Dowell, McAndrews, Held & Malloy, Ltd.
Claudia Driver, University or Arkansas School of Law
Grantland Drutchas, McDonnell Boehnen Hulbert & Berghoff

Alexandra Epsilanty, Syracuse University School of Law
Norah Faigen, McDonnell Boehnen Hulbert & Berghoff
Federal Defender Program—Chicago
Neal Fillmore, DePaul University School of Law
Cathy Fitch, Stetson University College of Law
Joni Coleman Fitzgerald, Willcox & Savage
Kay Fletcher, Texas Tech University School of Law
Kristin Flierl, Tulane University School of Law
Michelle Fongyee, St. Thomas University School of Law
Fowler, White, Gillen, Boggs, Villareal & Banker, P.A.
Vern Francissen, McDonnell Boehnen Hulbert & Berghoff
Norma Gaier, St. Mary's University School of Law
Susan Gainen, University of Minnesota Law School
Gardner, Carton & Douglas
Donna Gerson, University of Pittsburgh School of Law
Catherine Glenn, Carlton, Fields, Ward, Emmanuel, Smith & Cutler, P.A.
Goulston & Storrs
Gray, Plant, Mooty, Mooty & Bennett, P.A.
Gretchen Haas, University of Denver College of Law
Steven Hargrove, Emory University School of Law
Hillis Clark Martin & Peterson
Hodgson, Russ, Andrews, Woods & Goodyear, LLP
Skip Horne, Santa Clara University School of Law
Brad Hulbert, McDonnell Boehnen Hulbert & Berghoff
Sue Hunter, Baker, Donelson, Bearman & Caldwell
Monika Hussell, Jackson & Kelly
Jackson & Kelly
David James, Office of the San Diego City Attorney
Pat Jason, Nova Southeastern University Shepard Broad Law Center
Jolley, Urga, Wirth & Woodbury
Jones, Day, Reavis & Pogue
Jones Vargas
Laura Share Kalin, Harvard Law School
Scott Kaminski, Flaherty, Sensabaugh & Bonasso, P.L.L.C.
Robert Kaplan, William & Mary College of Law

Rebecca Katz-White, Hofstra University School of Law
Mary Kelkenberg, Hodgson, Russ, Andrews, Woods & Goodyear, L.L.P.
Dennis Kennedy
Joan King, Brooklyn Law School
Beth Kirch, University of Georgia School of Law
Kirkland & Ellis
Jill Kirson, George Washington University Law School
Nora Klaphake, University of Minnesota Law School
Audrey Koscielniak, SUNY School of Law at Buffalo
Joyce Laher, Hamline University School of Law
Laura Rowe Lane, O.C. Systems
Latham & Watkins
Lisa Lesage, Northwestern University Lewis & Clark College of Law
Steven Lesavich, McDonnell Boehnen Hulbert & Berghoff
Caroline Levy, Hofstra University School of Law
Lord, Bissell & Brook
Los Angeles Public Defender's Office
James Lovelace, George Washington University School of Law
Merv Loya, University of Oregon School of Law
Sarah Madden, Public Defender, Frankfort, Kentucky
Amy Berenson Mallow, UCLA College of Law
Pam Malone, Mcguire, Woods, Battle & Boothe, LLP
Markowitz, Herbold, Glade & Mehlhaf, P.C.
Mattel, Inc., Legal Department
Judy Mender, Benjamin J. Cardozo School of Law, Yeshiva University
Chris Miller, University of Pittsburgh School of Law
Jill Miller, Duke University School of Law
Suzanne Mitchell, The University of Chicago, The Law School
Morrison & Foerster LLP
Jason Murray, Carlton, Fields, Ward, Emmanuel, Smith & Cutler, P.A.
Kevin Napper, Carlton, Fields, Ward, Emmanuel, Smith & Cutler, P.A.
J.D. Neary, Akin, Gump, Strauss, Hauer & Feld, L.L.P.
Nancy Needle, Goulston & Storrs
Kelly Noblin, Southern Methodist University School of Law
Mary Obrzut, Northern Illinois University College of Law

Pam Occhipinti, Loyola University School of Law
Chet Olsen
Jacqueline Ortega, University of San Francisco School of Law
Matt Pascocello, American University Washington College of Law
Perkins Coie L.L.P.
Adam Perry, Hodgson, Russ, Andrews, Woods & Goodyear, LLP
Gail Peshel, Valparaiso University School of Law
Patricia Powell, University of Denver College of Law
Procter & Gamble, Legal Department
Proskauer Rose LLP
Jeanette Rader, Sanford University Cumberland School of Law
John A. Ragosta, Dewey Ballantine LLP
Stephanie Redfearn, Florida State University College of Law
Jane Reinhardt, Nassau/Suffolk Law Services Committee, Inc.
Susan Richey, Franklin Pierce Law Center
Hardy Roberts, Carlton, Fields, Ward, Emmanuel, Smith & Cutler, P.A.
Mary Karen Rogers, Suffolk University Law School
Joann Rothery, University of Tennessee College of Law
Gina Rowsam, Oklahoma City University School of Law
Kathryn Sanders, O'Melveny & Myers, LLP
Gina Sauer, William Mitchell College of Law
Rachael Schell, Mercer University School of Law
Diane Schwartzberg, Hofstra University School of Law
Karen Scully-Clemmons, University of Miami School of Law
Beth Sherman, Georgetown University Law Center
Shook Hardy & Bacon L.L.P.
Bart Showalter, Baker Botts, L.L.P.
Sidley & Austin
Jennifer Silverman, Nova Southeastern University Shepard Broad Law Center
Ann Skalaski, University of Florida College of Law
Dawne Smith, Rutgers University School of Law-Newark
Dorris Smith, Vanderbilt University School of Law
Snell & Wilmer, L.L.P.
Liz Stack, University of Miami School of Law
Jane Steckbeck, University of Oregon School of Law

Mary Brennan Stich, St. Mary's University School of Law
Steptoe & Johnson, West Virginia
Stites & Harbison
Strasburger & Price, L.L.P.
Debra Strauss, DMS Consulting
Brian Tanko, Jeffrey L. Burr & Associates
Jennifer Thomas, American University Washington College of Law
Vincent Thomas, Hamline University School of Law
Jane Thomson, UC Davis School of Law
Fred Thrasher, William & Mary College of Law
Kelly Toole, Gunstler, Yoakley, Valdes-Fauli & Stewart, P.A.
Marilyn Tucker, Georgetown University Law Center
Stefan Tucker, Venable, Baetjer, Howard & Civiletti, LLP
Jennifer Loud Ungar, University of Denver College of Law
United Mine Workers of America, Legal Department
United States Department of Justice
Karen Jackson Vaughn, Temple University School of Law
Anne Stark Walker, University of Denver College of Law
Waller Lansden Dortch & Davis, P.L.L.C.
Mark Weber, Harvard Law School
Barbara Weinzierl, Case Western Reserve University School of Law
Wendy Werner, St. Louis University School of Law
James Whitters III, Suffolk University Law School
Joyce Whittington, University of Mississippi School of Law
Abbie Willard, Georgetown University Law Center
The Williams Companies, Legal Department
Winston & Strawn
Pavel Wonsowicz, Vermont Law School
Writers Guild of America, west
Wyatt, Tarrant & Combs
Elizabeth Zabak, Carlton, Fields, Ward, Emmanuel, Smith & Cutler, P.A.

(P.S. For the law firms, government agencies, companies and other organizations on this list—obviously, an entity can't talk! Instead, people at these organizations were kind enough to survey their colleagues for advice. Throughout this book, when you see a quote from "a lawyer at . . . " those surveys were the source of those quotes.)

I also must thank my brother Keir, who, as always, encouraged, cajoled, and pushed me into finishing this book. Much of the advice I heard about dealing with people rang true to me because it reminded me of what Keir would do in any given situation. And he's funny and charming, too.

Many thanks to Tracy Hirsch, Stephanie Kartofels, Cathy Looney, Angel Murphy and Jennifer Payne of Harcourt who worked miracles with this book. They wouldn't have to be miracle workers if I were better about handling deadlines. But they are, and I am very grateful for that.

Rosemary Kocis of Oxford Bioscience Partners faithfully collected the many faxes I received from people all over the place. I could buy a fax machine, but then I wouldn't have a reason to visit Rose, so that's not a purchase I'm going to make.

I am eternally grateful to my sweet husband, Henry, who was such a trooper while I was working on this book. We were newlyweds of six months when I started working on this project, and he stoically stood by while I spent fourteen hours a day on the phone and computer. He also helped cut up and assemble all of the quotes I received from people—all 4,000 of them. I love you Lambchop.

INTRODUCTION—HOW TO USE THIS BOOK

You are in for such a treat. The people I interviewed for this book were incredibly generous in sharing terrific, hands-on advice for getting your career off on the right foot. If you do what I tell you to do in this book—and you avoid doing the things I tell you not to do—there's just no question that your career will take off like a rocket.

Apart from all of the "formal" interviews I did for this book, every time I met lawyers on a casual basis—at parties, in airports, wherever—I'd ask them, "What advice would you give to law students about how to handle their first job?" Once in a while, they'd answer, "Tell them—don't be a lawyer! Ar ar ar ar ar . . . " Jerks.

The fact is, to hear some people talk, you'd think that you weren't starting a new job but instead joining the Bataan Death March. There are always people who hate their jobs, in every field. But I think—no, I'm sure—there are strategies you can use, from Day One, to make your working life a whole lot happier, no matter where you work. In this book, I'm going to lead you through exactly what those strategies are.

As we'll see, one of the most difficult things about working is that there are lots of vague terms and no absolutes. People throw around terms like "maturity," "team player," "good judgment"—if you're like me, you ask yourself, "What exactly does that mean?" Well, in this book, we'll go through the practical behavior that exhibits maturity, a team player mentality, good judgment, and every other desirable trait. You won't be left wondering any more exactly what it is that team players do! And when it comes to avoiding absolutes, we'll discuss that, as well. For instance, you should limit chitchat, but small talk is an important technique for getting along with people in your office and learning the crucial information that travels via the "jungle drums." You should appear hardworking, but sacrificing your life for your work doesn't help the job—or you. You need to hand in flawless written work, but you need to meet deadlines—so you can't obsess over it. You need to appear confident, but not arrogant. I'm going to show you how to follow the "Golden Rule" on the job. And I'm absolutely positive that your career is going to be a lot happier and more successful as a result.

Now—how to use this book. When I sent the first couple of chapters to my editor, Stephanie, I waited a day or so and then called her, asking "So? How do you like it?" She replied, "I haven't had time yet to read everything you sent, so I just skimmed the text and really *read* the 'Career Limiting Moves.'" I'm not surprised that the "Career Limiting Moves" were the first things that caught Stephanie's eye, and I'm pretty sure you'll focus on them, as well (although I trust you'll also read everything in between!). The "Career Limiting Moves" and "Smart Human Tricks" that are peppered throughout this book highlight many of the points I make in the text, and if all you did was to read those, you'd probably save yourself from making any major mistake on the job. You'd be missing a lot of other great stories in the text, but you'd get a good flavour of what to avoid doing (and, with the Smart Human Tricks, what to do).

With some of the stories, you may say to yourself: "Did somebody really do this?" Yep, they did. However, the stories you read here do not reflect precisely the stories I heard—all except for three of the "Career Limiting Moves," which are my own, committed while I was a summer clerk at a law firm. Although the rest of the stories are accurate in every pertinent respect, I have changed the identifying elements so that the people involved needn't suffer the shock of seeing themselves in print. So if, as you read through this book, you think you recognize somebody in one of the stories—you don't. (Furthermore, some of the people who told me the most outrageous stories in this book did so only under the strictest anonymity. So if you try to match the stories with the acknowledgements—that won't work, either.) Incidentally, don't take those career limiting moves too seriously. There are plenty of people who commit career limiting moves and go on to stellar careers anyway.

If you are in a big rush, you can rely on the Table of Contents to tell you the pertinent points in every chapter, and then skim the headings in that chapter.

You'd have to be in a really big rush, though. Let's face it—this book doesn't exactly read like a dense physics text. You'll probably skate through a chapter in less time than it takes to watch an MTV Top Ten Countdown.

I am very excited for you! The career that is stretching in front of you is one of endless possibilities. It's my fervent hope that this book will help you fashion that career into everything you want it to be.

KIMM ALAYNE WALTON
WILTON, CONNECTICUT

HOW TO CONTACT THE AUTHOR

Maybe you've got a story of your own to share. I'd love to hear it! The fact that you're reading this book is a very hopeful indication that there'll be another edition of it at some point. I'll acknowledge you by name or preserve your anonymity, your choice. And if you e-mail or send me a story that I use in the next edition, you'll get a copy of that book as a thank you. Oh, boy!

Incidentally, I write a legal job search column that appears in law school newspapers all over the place, as well as on the Internet. It's called "Dear Job Goddess," and I think it's pretty funny and also very helpful, largely because, just as I did for this book, I don't rely on my own advice – I ask the experts for their take on every question. If you would like to read the Job Goddess column on-line, it's on several web sites (they change occasionally) but you can always find it on www.gilbertlaw.com. You can send job search questions to me there, or at my own address.

My e-mail address is: jobgoddess@aol.com. My snail mail address is: Post Office Box 1018, Greens Farms, CT 06436. And yes, Greens Farms is every bit as quaint as the name implies.

CONTENTS

Chapter Four

Chapter Five

Chapter Six

Handling Everybody Outside The Office— Clients, Opposing Counsel, Judges, Court Personnel . . . and the Media 383

Chapter Seven

When Your Boss Is A Judge: Handling Judicial Clerkships 431

Chapter Eight

Dealing With Jerks, Screamers, And Other Dwellers Of The Nether Anatomy 437

Chapter Nine

Handling Things You Don't Want To Handle: Mistakes, Too Much Work, Chimp Work, Ethical Issues, and Sexual Harassment. 453

Chapter Ten

Being Your Own Career Coach And Living The Life You *Want*. 497

CHAPTER ONE

The 1,640-Hour Interview: What Every Summer Clerk Should Know

Getting a great job is one thing. ***Doing*** a great job is another. It's not genius, it's not luck, and there's nothing intuitive about it. Successful people, whether they realize it or not, do exactly what I'm going to tell you to do in this book. If you follow the advice you read here, you will impress the heck out of people—and you'll enjoy yourself a lot more, because you'll know ***exactly*** what you have to do to succeed. That's all there is to it.

What we're going to do in this section is to make sure that you don't do anything that tanks your chances with your summer clerkship employer, no matter ***who*** you work for. In a lot of important ways, you should approach your summer clerkship the same way you'd approach your first "permanent" job after law school! Turning in the best possible work product, acting and dressing professionally, not getting crocked at employer social events—that's good advice whether you're going to be there for ten weeks, or ten years. So I'd strongly advise you to read the rest of this book before you go to your summer employer. Don't worry. It'll be fun. And when we get to certain topics in this chapter, like dealing with research assignments, I'll refer you to specific sections in the rest of the book.

But having said that, there ***are*** important differences between summer clerkships and permanent jobs. The summer is a kind of professional mating ritual. The employer is checking you out, and, just as importantly, you're checking out the employer. Let's see how you should handle it!

A. Keep Your Eye On The Prize: Remember The Goal Of Your Summer Clerkship.

You want to be invited back. That's it. You want an offer. Everything in this chapter steers you to that goal. If you don't like any of the individual things I'll suggest that you do, I recommend a trick that they teach people at Alcoholics Anonymous: Look past the drink. If you hate the idea of dressing to conform with people at work, or stopping with one beer at parties, or having to hold your tongue around clients, or putting in a late night now and then—look past your immediate preference to your ultimate goal: Getting an offer. If you get an offer, you can always make the decision not to come back if you decide you really don't want it. But to the extent you control the situation, put yourself in the driver's seat!

If your summer job won't result in an offer—it's for an employer with no permanent openings, for instance, or for an employer that doesn't hire new graduates—treat it the same way. What you'll be going after instead of an offer is a stellar reference, and perhaps even help and connections to a permanent job. So you'll want to follow the advice here as well!

B. Be Aware Of What Employers Are Looking For: The Top Eight Hit List.

1. Excellent "output"—whether it be written assignments or oral advocacy or dealing with clients. For written projects, show your ability not just to write but also to research and give strong legal analyses. For oral advocacy projects (typically for prosecutors), show your ability to think quickly on your feet and handle pressure.
2. Good judgment—the ability to act and dress appropriately and deal sensibly with situations as they arise. One lawyer told me about a firm

where a summer clerk house-sat for a senior partner while the partner was away on vacation, and the partner came back early to find that the associate had adorned statues in the garden with the partner's underclothes. I'm not suggesting that you need to be Solomon-like, but don't be an ***idiot***!

3. Enthusiasm for the projects you do and for the employer itself. When faced with choosing between summer clerks for permanent offers, employers will take the clerk who shows the most interest in ***them.***
4. Flexibility—the willingness to accommodate different work styles, personalities, and tasks.
5. Appreciation of the opportunity to work with the employer.
6. The ability to get along with support staff and colleagues—to "fit in."
7. An understanding of what the organization's goals are—whether it's a business (like a law firm) or any other kind of service provider (like a government agency or public interest employer), and respect the fact that even if your employer is a charity, it's not a charity for ***you***—you've got a role to play in helping the organization reach its goals.
8. Realistic expectations of what work is, and what you can expect from it. Show that you don't expect the employer to fulfill all of your expectations.

SMART HUMAN TRICK . . .

One career services director told me about a student of hers who made an unbelievable impression on his summer employer. He's a textbook example of how to be a great summer clerk, so much so that the firm he worked for called the career services director and thanked her for "sending us such an outstanding student."

What stood out about this particular clerk? The firm listed several things. "Number one, he had a shining personality, he was a very upbeat person. Even when he was down personally, he came in smiling. When we asked him, 'How are things going?' he'd respond,

'They're great!' He'd encourage **us**. He'd say, 'I know you've worked hard. Is there anything I can do to help you? Any research I can do for you?' We were amazed by his generosity of spirit. He'd offer assistance whenever he saw a busy person. Even though he didn't have to stay at night, he'd be willing to once in a while to help out.

"Then there was his great work product. It was just outstanding. But it wasn't so much that he was born a great researcher. He would go to older associates and ask, 'I know you worked for this person. What are they like? What do they look for?' He'd know in advance what every attorney wanted, what their styles were. It made his good work really stand out. He went the extra mile.

"When he got assignments, he'd get clarification, but not to the point of being a nuisance. He checked with each attorney and said, 'This is my understanding of what you want.' He got feedback that way.

"He particularly volunteered in areas that he liked, things he was good at. He was a chemical engineer, and coming to us, he knew he wanted to do some IP. He called associates who'd been with us the previous summer, and asked them for the inside scoop, which they were happy to share with him.

"As he moved from department to department at our firm, his reputation preceded him to the next department in his rotation. His whole attitude breathed, 'I'll do whatever it takes for all of us to succeed.'"

"Even though he's got two years of law school left, we'd take him back in a heartbeat."

C. Things To Do Before You Start Your Clerkship

1. A few weeks before you start . . .

   a. Don't treat your office like it has cooties. Get in there ahead of time and get to know people.

If you have the chance—for instance, you're going to school in the city where you're going to work in the summer, or you can spend Spring Break there—use a little bit of your time wisely, and get to know some of the people you'll be working with. One law school career services director told me about a student of hers who did this to brilliant advantage. "He got accepted into the summer program of one of the biggest, most prestigious law firms in the country. As soon as he got his summer offer, he called and scheduled a lunch with a partner he'd hit it off with in his call-back interview. He told the partner, 'I really like the firm. I want to get your guidance on some do's and don'ts before I start my clerkship.' The partner was ***very*** appreciative; he just loved it, and he spent the entire lunch giving the student tips on exactly what he ought to do during the summer. [This is Kimm talking. Everything the partner told this student, I'm going to tell you throughout this book.]

"Afterwards, the student contacted another partner with whom he had a similar background. They hit it off, and he asked this partner for the 'ins and outs' of the firm, telling him, 'I want to start my clerkship off right.' This partner was just as delighted as the first one. He told the student, 'Why don't you come in to the office. I'll have my assistant introduce you to more people.' He did that. He also called several other lawyers at the firm and asked if he could stop by for a casual visit. They all invited him in."

As the career services director commented, "This guy is all set. The partners all talked about him, commented on his initiative. He's coming in a step ahead of everybody else, because he's already shown them his enthusiasm for the job. That impression will take him a long way."

If you plan on doing something like this—and I ***strongly*** encourage you to try it!—there are a few things to keep in mind.

1) Think of the people you met during your call-back interviews to find a likely "target." In every set of interviews, there'll be people you connected with better than others. Call them. They'll be delighted to see you.

2) Don't assume that if you do lunch, it'll be their treat. It probably will be, but it's a serious faux pas to make that assumption. Instead, offer to take them out for coffee or explain that because you're still in school, you hope they won't be offended if lunch is Dutch treat. They'll appreciate your good manners.

3) Learn the names of support staff people when you visit the office, and repeat their names back to them. "It's great meeting you, Joe/Edith/Maureen." When the student in the anecdote did this, the support staffers told him on the way out, "We look forward to working with you." As I'll explain in great detail later in the book, the support staff at any employer can make you or break you. Be sure you are appropriately respectful and friendly with them!

4) Observe how the lawyers dress. We'll talk a lot about wardrobe later on, but the best way to answer the eternal "What do I wear?" question is by seeing what everybody there wears already. You want your wardrobe to fit in, not stand out, and looking to see what people wear to work is the best way to do that!

5) Write down everything you learn about the lawyers and support staffers you meet—their hobbies, spouse's and children's names, whatever you can find out. (Of course, don't do this during your visit. Wait until you get home.) Refer back to those notes during your summer, and ask them about little Johnny's school play, or the trout fishing in Alberta. When you take a personal interest in people you meet, you're exhibiting the kind of people skills that will make you a star.

6) When you get to the firm, let the lawyers who gave you the pre-clerkship advice know that you're heeding it. "Partners love it when they give you advice and find that you're following it," commented one recruiting coordinator.

b. Make sure your employer knows about any potential conflicts of interest you have.

One thing you ***have*** to do is to make sure you don't have any conflict of interest problems with your summer employer. I'm not talking about between you and the employer; you've got a big conflict there. You want to have a summer vacation, and they want you to work. I'm talking about legal conflicts of interest between your summer employer and anyone else you might have worked for during law school, or even before. As one recruiting coordinator said, "Conflicts of interest are a really big deal for law firms. Summer clerks don't often realize that. We ***must*** clear any conflicts before a summer clerk starts to work for us." William & Mary's Fred Thrasher points out that, "If the employer doesn't come forward with the issue, ***you*** should. It'll reflect on ***your*** professional judgment. If you've worked in a legal capacity previously, you have conflict potential. You can't say, 'Oh, I'd love to work on that. I worked on the other side at X.'"

If you don't tell your summer employer about all of your prior work before you start, you may find that your summer clerkship is delayed or suspended entirely. If they know about any potential conflicts well before you start, they can work on getting the appropriate waivers so that your summer will go smoothly. Not appreciating conflicts of interest is a big, bad judgmental boner. You don't want a strike against you before you ever set foot in the office!

One law firm told the story of a summer clerk who had spent the spring before his summer clerkship clerking for a small local law firm. It turns out that this little firm was working for the opposing party in a very litigious matter his summer employer was involved in. As the recruiting coordinator described it, "It was extremely unlikely that either side would sign a waiver. The summer clerk hadn't told us about his work during the spring, and worse than that, he hadn't told the other firm that he would be joining us for the summer, so that the conflict could have been avoided in the first place! It wasn't until the day he arrived that we learned about this other work. We couldn't let him start working for us until the conflict was resolved. He wound up sitting at home for two weeks while we scrambled to get the appropriate waivers from both sides. Fortunately, the case settled and the conflict resolved itself, so he could come to work for us."

Don't rely on matters settling in time for your clerkship. Be sure to keep your summer employer informed of any work you do before you start the clerkship—and tell any school year employers who you'll be working for this coming summer!

c. Think about what you want out of your summer—and write it down!

Kentucky's Drusilla Bakert has excellent advice for you: make out a list of questions and areas of interest before you start your clerkship, so you can refer to it over the summer to remind yourself of some of your goals. As she says, "You don't want to ruffle feathers as you gather information, but there's no question that you can learn everything you want in a subtle way over the entire summer. Among other things, you'll want to find out how the firm is governed, who its clients are, which are its vibrant practice areas. If you have a particular interest, you want to write it down so that you'll make sure to try and get assignments from partners and associates in that area and ingratiate yourself with them. And you want to pay attention to the culture. For instance, if you want to have a family, look and see how many people have children, and how issues of juggling the workday and parental leave are handled." It's easy to get wrapped up in a clerkship when you get to your employer, and forget all about why it is you wanted to be there in the first place. Having a list of "summer priorities" that you can check off ensures that you won't make that mistake!

d. Get administrative details straight.

Some time before you start, contact the employer—either the recruiting coordinator or the office manager or the person who hired you, depending on the employer—and ascertain the following:

(i) Your start date;

(ii) What time you should arrive;
(iii) How to get to the office;
(iv) Where to park, if you're driving;
(v) What you need to bring with you for your first day (for instance, valid Social Security card, driver's license, signed papers and/or documents);
(vi) Your salary or stipend (if any);
(vii) How you will get paid (that is, weekly? Or biweekly? Or monthly? You'll need to plan accordingly);
(viii) Any reimbursements for transportation to the clerking location. As Carlton Fields' Elizabeth Zabak points out, "Don't assume that the employer will pay for the car, train, hotels, and the like! Generally, firms will pay for legally-deductible roundtrip mileage."

If you haven't had a chance to visit the employer or you don't remember from your callback interviews—it's also worthwhile to ask what you ought to wear. With the onset of "business casual," no resource ***other*** than the employer you're going to work for can give you a definitive answer on what's appropriate to wear to work. Don't be afraid to ask! They'll be delighted that you cared enough to inquire. And they'll be impressed with your business savvy in realizing the importance of looking like you "fit in."

By the way, if you are spending your summer in a public interest work-study position, don't assume that your employer understands how work-study functions. One student arrived at her public interest summer job, figuring they knew they were responsible for half of her hourly rate. They refused to pay. She was left with having to volunteer for them or scramble for a ***new*** job with the summer already underway. Moral: Confirm logistics and work-study contracts early!

e. Get your personal stuff together—your finances and your housing.

Make sure you've got your personal life in order. You're probably going to be very, very busy. You don't want to worry about details of your private life while you're clerking. And just as importantly, you don't want to give your employer the impression that you don't have your life under control! One lawyer told the story of a summer associate who showed up the weekend before the summer clerkship started, without a dime in her pocket. When she tried to get into her apartment, she discovered that she needed to pay the first and last months' rent as well as a security deposit. She didn't have any cash, and she didn't have a local check to cover the rents and deposit. Frantic, her solution was to call the recruiting coordinator, at home, to ask to borrow a thousand dollars. The lawyer commented dryly, "She didn't make a very good first impression."

Apart from getting your finances in order, you also need to sort out where you'll live, if you're going to be clerking somewhere else. If you are clerking for a large firm in another city, call the recruiting coordinator to find out how housing is arranged. Do you have to find your own apartment, or does the recruiting coordinator help you find something suitable? If you're going to lean on the recruiting coordinator to help you find something, give them as much lead time as you can, because finding short-term leases in a lot of cities is pretty difficult. You don't want to get a reputation for being a pain in the neck before you even get there. (Actually, you don't want one ***ever***. But if you're going to get that reputation, put it off as long as possible.)

You also need to smooth the feathers of anyone in your personal life about the time commitment you're going to make. No matter whether you're working for a large, medium or small firm, government employer or public interest employer, your work has got to be your first priority for the summer. It will have to take priority over your other interests and commitments. You're probably not going to work huge hours, but there are going to be unexpected time commitments no matter where you work. If you go to a large firm, there will be social events that you'll be expected to attend, and if you have a significant other, that person will be invited, as well.

So if you have a family or a boyfriend or girlfriend, explain that it's very important to your career to make an excellent impression on your employer, and that may mean changed or cancelled personal plans. I realize this might make you cringe, and no decent employer will expect you to live your work, but they ***will*** expect a serious commitment from you for the summer. Arrange your private life so that you can show your employer, by your actions, that you value the opportunity to work with them.

If you find, during the summer, that the commitment you make isn't one you could make long term, then you've learned something very valuable: this isn't the employer for you! The time commitment for someone who's already graduated from law school is always considerably greater than it is for summer clerks. If it's a time commitment you aren't willing to make, what a blessing to find out before you're there on a "permanent" basis!

2. The day before you start . . .

Get plenty of sleep. You're going to have a big, big, big day tomorrow. You're going to learn a lot, and you're going to meet plenty of people—maybe more than you've ever met in a single day in your entire life. First impressions mean a lot. You want to be able to greet people bright-eyed and bushy-tailed. You need to be able to smile. A late night pounding kamikazes doesn't bode well. More than one recruiting coordinator lamented summer clerks who fell asleep during orientation. "People don't forget things like that," commented one of them.

Other than getting some rest, you should also call to find out if there's anything you need to know at the last minute. One firm tells the story of how, for one year's summer clerkship class, Queen Elizabeth's yacht arrived at the waterfront location where the firm's main office is located—on the very day the summer associate orientation was to take place! While almost all of the summer clerks made it into the office before traffic was totally jammed, one unfortunate summer clerk didn't realize the Queen was coming to town. She got caught in traffic, while the other clerks got to attend welcoming ceremonies for the Queen.

3. Your first day—a "Hair On Fire" day . . .

a. What to take with you

You'll want to refer back to your notes on how to get to the employer, where to park (if you're driving), and what to bring with you by way of identification and paperwork.

You'll also want a notepad or notebook to write on, because you'll certainly be going to some kind of orientation and you'll need to take notes. If you're a woman and you're wearing a skirt, take along a spare pair of pantyhose. Whether you're a man or a woman, carry your work stuff in an appropriate vessel. A backpack isn't appropriate for a professional job. You need a portfolio or computer-type bag that looks professional. (They don't have to be expensive. Nobody anticipates that you'll be walking into your summer clerkship with a thousand-dollar briefcase. Get a dark-coloured leather, vinyl, or nylon one.)

CAREER LIMITING MOVE . . .

One firm told a story about a summer clerk who showed up on his first day carrying a canvas bag with the word "VIAGRA" printed in large letters on the side, a promotional giveaway kind of thing. For all of the lawyers he visited that day, he made sure to sit with the bag on his lap, with the "VIAGRA" facing toward the other person. Needless to say, word of this spread around the office like wildfire. One of the lawyers was deputized to talk to the clerk about the bag. He called the clerk into his office, pointed to the bag, and said, "We know you didn't mean anything by it, but it's really kind of a questionable thing to bring to work." The clerk responded that he had debated about bringing it, but decided that "it would be a good ice-breaker." The lawyer commented: "It wasn't."

b. What to expect

1. A ***lot*** of administrative stuff. Read what you're supposed to read, and sign what you're supposed to sign!

You'll get an avalanche of information. You'll almost certainly get a copy of the employer's handbook, or some kind of a handout or notebook containing the employer's policies. Don't blow it off. Read it as soon as you can, so that you don't wind up asking a question you didn't have to ask.

You'll also have to sign a lot of things and handle a lot of details. It's routine. You'll get on to the "good stuff" soon enough!

CAREER LIMITING MOVE . . .

Summer clerk at a large West Coast law firm. He shows up on his first day two hours late, so everybody at the office is pissed off from the start.

The other summer clerks had already signed all of their paperwork without incident. When this clerk is given the same stack of papers to sign, he challenges one of the forms. "I'm not going to sign this." The problem is, it's a condition of employment. The recruiting coordinator looks over at the managing partner, who is clearly displeased. The form in question involves the Fair Credit Reporting Act. The firm has clerks sign it so that they can check to make sure that the clerk's name and Social Security number match—a practice shared by just about every large law firm in the country. But this clerk gets it into his head that they want him to sign the form so they can check his credit, and he won't sign it.

When the recruiting coordinator explains the purpose of the form, he demands that language is stricken from the form such that they can't check his credit report. Immediately the recruiting coordinator and managing partner are thinking, "What the heck is this guy hiding?"

He makes it through the rest of the forms without incident, but the managing partner is seething. The new clerk goes on to other orientation activities, and, thinking the better of it, visits the recruiting coordinator that afternoon.

He's a bit sheepish. "I guess I came off a little harsh this morning," he says. "The managing partner doesn't seem too happy with me." When the recruiting coordinator says that he's right, he nods and says, "Why don't I have my law school dean call him to smooth things over?"

As the recruiting coordinator says, "From day one, everybody has this picture in their mind: 'This kid's a pain in the butt.'"

2. Expect to feel overwhelmed

When you enter ***any*** new situation, ***expect*** to feel chaotic. You remember how you felt on your first day of law school. It's that same set of butterflies residing in your stomach now. It's normal. For many of us, our law school summer clerkships are the first time we've had a job that rises about the "you-want-fries-with-that?" level. It's important to remember a couple of things that will make you feel better.

First of all, every single person you meet, every person you work with, was once in your shoes. They ***know*** what it feels like to be you, and so on some very basic level they can empathize with you.

Secondly, ***don't*** put pressure on yourself to dazzle everyone you meet with your wit and intelligence from moment one. As one employer explained it to me, "Your most important first assignment is to ***listen carefully.***"

Thirdly, don't put your foot in your mouth from the moment you get there. Don't make any flip comments. At one firm, a summer clerk walked in, looked around, and loudly proclaimed: "So what does a person have to do to fit in around here?" He was stamped with the "arrogance" label before anybody had a chance to get to know him!

So—take a deep breath, smile, greet people in a friendly way, absorb what's told to you, and don't expect any more of yourself at the outset than that!

D. Handling The Work

You've probably heard that if you get a summer clerkship, the employer expects to make you an offer. In the cases where that's ***not*** true, the employer will typically let you know up front, and for them, you need to make a great impression to get an excellent reference. But even for the places where it ***is*** true—which would include large and medium-sized law firms—you don't have a free pass to ignore the work. Every summer program has ***somebody*** who washes out, and there are really only two mistakes you can make: you screw up with the work, or you screw up with the people. In this section, we're going to talk about screwing up with the work.

Up front you need to know that most research assignment issues are identical whether you're a summer clerk or a new permanent associate. Clarifying issues, ascertaining form, minding deadlines, asking questions—all the same. I've gathered all of that crucial advice in the section called "How To Crush Research And Writing Assignments." Read that!

At the beginning of your summer, pay attention to how you get your assignments. At some employers, all of your assignments will come through one person. At other employers, there'll be an assignment book where you get your own projects. At still other places, you're on your own. You'll get a desk and a file cabinet and you take it from there, seeking out projects. If nobody's spoon-feeding you, don't be afraid to go after the projects you want to do and the people you want to work for! They ***want*** to see you being entrepreneurial.

Here, we'll be focusing on issues about your research projects that are ***only*** relevant to your summer clerkship. If you spend your summer at any large- or medium-sized law firm and many small ones, you'll get assignments where your writing will be judged by stringent standards. In many firms that's about ***all*** you'll get. What do you need to know?

1. All appearances aside, it's not summer camp. Take your assignments seriously.

Summer clerkship programs can be very deceptive. If you're at a large firm with lots of social events, you can get the impression you're being shepherded into the practice of law on a sedan chair, with people peeling grapes for you and dropping them into your mouth. In that atmosphere it's very easy to overlook the importance of the work you do. But it ***is*** real work, for real clients, and you ***do*** need to pay attention to it. You might get some general memo-to-file projects, but you aren't in a position to make the assumption that your work isn't timely. Assume that every project you get is important. The opinion of the attorney you work for is ***certainly*** important, and if they don't think you're taking their work seriously, you're the one who'll suffer!

The fact is, most summer clerks do take their work seriously. And you probably would have without me reminding you of it. But sometimes people ***do*** blow off their work. They'll get busy with other things, or they'll have a vague deadline and forget about the project entirely. Don't let this happen to you!

CAREER LIMITING MOVE . . .

Summer clerk at a large New York firm. Senior associate gives him a research assignment, saying, "I need you to research an issue for a brief in support of a motion in federal court. Research it and get it back to me by next Monday, so I have a week to look at it before the brief is due the following Monday." When Monday comes, the senior associate doesn't receive anything from the summer clerk, and so she seeks him out. The clerk nonchalantly responds, "I'm not done." The senior associate says, "I'll give you until Wednesday then." Wednesday, the clerk's response is the same: "I'm not done." The senior associate, getting exasperated but hiding it, responds, "I'll give you until Friday. I'll work over the weekend to review it and incorporate it into the brief."

When Friday comes, the senior associate asks if the summer associate is done with the research. The summer associate sheepishly responds, "To tell you the truth, I haven't started it yet. I've been working on other projects for other people, and I didn't know how to tell you." The senior associate, her head reeling, cancels all of her plans for the weekend, and goes in early Saturday morning to research the issue from scratch, herself.

Late Saturday morning, the summer associate shows up, and the senior associate thinks, rationally enough, that the clerk showed up to help her out.

"Oh, no," the summer clerk responds. "I'm not here to work. I'm here to pick up baseball tickets."

2. Work for as many people as you can.

Put the numbers in your favour. As St. Louis University's Wendy Werner advises, "Try to work for more than one or two people. You want more opinions about you." Arizona's Mary Birmingham agrees, "Make sure all of your eggs aren't in one partner or senior associate basket. Give the firm more opportunities to review you!"

It's unusual to wind up glued to a partner or two for the entire summer at a sizeable firm, but it ***can*** happen. If you find yourself halfway through the summer with very narrow experience, inform the recruiting coordinator or hiring partner. Working for more people gives you a better opportunity to observe the firm and decide if you like it. You could easily work for the only partner or two that you wouldn't like in the entire firm. What a shame to blow off an employer you'd love just because you didn't get an accurate picture of the place! And of course, in the unlikely event that you screw up for one partner, you want a lot of strong "yes" votes to counteract it! So work for as many people as possible. The only caveat is this: Don't bite off more than you can chew ***really well.*** It's better to have a handful of great assignments under your belt than twenty mediocre ones.

3. Determine if there's a billable hours requirement for summer clerks.

If there's a billables requirement, governing how many hours of work for clients that you have to accomplish during the summer, you need to know what it is. Ask the hiring partner or recruiting coordinator for any hard requirements or expectations. Even if there isn't a billable minimum expected of summer clerks, Carlton Fields' Elizabeth Zabak recommends that you "ask what the billables requirement is for new associates. Go into any job with your eyes wide open!"

4. **Always carry a pad and a pen.**

   Whenever you leave your office, carry a pad and pen. Every single lawyer in the world will tell you this! As Milbank Tweed's Joanne DeZego explains it, "If you have a pad and pen in hand it'll help you in two ways. First, you're ready to take down any assignment, in case you happen to run into an assigning attorney in the hallway. And second, you always look busy. It's good for your image."

5. **If you're clerking for a medium-to-large law firm, your writing skills count. A *lot.***

   One lawyer, who'd gone to a ***very*** prestigious law school, said that his law school dean had advised him that, "Writing isn't so important." "He couldn't have been more wrong!" marveled the lawyer. "In a summer program it's ***incredibly*** important." Carlton Fields' Eric Adams advises that "You can't make up for poor quality work with enthusiasm." Georgetown's Beth Sherman agrees: "Not doing good work is the ***worst*** thing you can do. You need to be able to research and write!" Baker Botts' Bart Showalter adds, "It's rare for clerks to be able to do the work and not get offers due to social missteps. Not being a good writer is a career-killer at a large firm!"

6. **For summer clerkships in prosecutors' offices (like District Attorneys or State's Attorneys), be aware that your enthusiasm and ability to think on your feet is more important than your writing skills.**

   When you summer clerk for a prosecutor, you will be judged on how well you react to pressure and how quickly you can think on your feet. Unlike law firms, if you're working for a prosecutor's office, "writing assignments are no big deal," comments one prosecutor. "You might get one assignment, something like 'From this police statement, what five questions would you ask?'" (What does that tell you? If you clerk somewhere that gives you a lot of writing assignments and you find that they're an albatross around your neck, consider taking a permanent job as a prosecutor instead!)

As one DA's office noted, "We want to see people who are prepared and eager. The real stars in our summer program are people who actively go after the attorneys to ask if there are any motions or trials they can handle."

The flipside of this is that no prosecutor's office expects you to be a "polished attorney. We want desire, potential, and the personality that, win or lose, can hardly wait for the next trial."

7. In public interest clerkships, show compassion for constituents.

Public interest employers are particularly shocked when summer clerks seem unfeeling toward clients. When you work in public interest, you're not in law school anymore—these aren't hypothetical situations with names on a page. These are ***real*** people with ***real*** problems. While you don't want to appear an emotional wreck, take a compassionate and concerned tone. It's important to be sensitive to the suffering and situation of the people you serve. As lawyers in the Los Angeles Public Defender's Office say, "Many times clerks conducting intake interviews do so with a cold detached manner that is somewhat chilling to observe."

8. If you're doing a summer clerkship that is unlikely to result in a permanent offer, recognize the things that you *should* get out of it.

It may be that you're going to clerk for an organization that for whatever reason won't be hiring you back immediately after graduation. Maybe it's a firm that's not going to expand, and this is made clear to you before you start. Maybe you're clerking for the U.S. Attorney's Office, which doesn't hire anyone fresh out of school. There are myriad other situations where this might arise. The key here is to focus on what it is you can accomplish ***aside*** from getting a permanent offer. You should make it your goal to leave at the end of the summer with three assets:

a. Skills that you can transfer to other organizations or jobs, whether they be writing skills, handling certain kinds of transactions or clients, making presentations, or anything else.

b. Contacts that will be valuable to your job search. Remember that every single person you work with, from the most senior manager to the mailroom clerk, knows other people—people who may make wonderful employers for you. Cultivating the people you come in contact with during your summer not only makes your summer more interesting and fun, but it's a very wise career move. Remember that lawyers tend to be closely-knit with other people who do the same thing, and word travels fast. Take advantage of this!

c. An enthusiastic reference from your employer. Drawing a rave from your summer employer, even without the possibility of a permanent offer, will pave the way for a ***much*** easier transition to your career after law school.

9. If you are volunteering, behave as though you were being paid.

It's easy to take volunteer opportunities lightly. Because you aren't being paid, you might be tempted not to be as prompt, to dress more casually, and take your assignments less seriously. ***Don't do it!*** As one employer told me, "Regardless of whether you're paid or not, always act as though you are a professional employee of the organization." This means behaving as though it's your career, not just an unpaid clerkship. Be prompt, meet deadlines, cultivate your colleagues, treat support staff and clients with respect, and dress like a professional, not a student. The point of volunteering is to expand your professional possibilities, and the only way to do that is to create the image in the mind of your employer that you ***are*** a professional.

10. If you know what kind of work you want to try, get after it—but don't paint yourself into a corner.

Maybe your clerkship is at a place where there's only one kind of work—a prosecutor's office or a firm with one specialty, like medical malpractice or patent work. If that's the case, then you don't have to worry about making a choice—you're just deciding if you like what they do!

But maybe you're in a firm or a government job that gives you some choice of practice areas (like a state attorney general's office). Here's what you ought to do:

a. If you know definitely what you want to do, go in with a list of goals.

Valparaiso's Gail Peshel advises that "If you know what you want when the summer starts, talk to a very successful practitioner in that specialty to find out the qualifications they look for in a new attorney. Make a list, maybe ten to twelve things to accomplish in the summer, and check them off as you go."

b. Get experience with a department doing work that interests you.

Taking your dream for a trial run is an ideal use of at least part of your summer clerkship. Kentucky's Drusilla Bakert puts it best: "Keep your eye on the prize! If you chose a particular law firm because you were interested in a particular practice area, don't be distracted from asking for work in that area and finding out whatever you can about that department." And NYU's Gail Cutter advises, "If you hope to be given an offer in a particularly small or popular department, be sure you work closely with several lawyers in that department."

Apart from giving the attorneys in that area a chance to get to know you and your work, it's impossible to know for sure if you want to practice a certain kind of law in a certain setting (*e.g.*, large vs. small firm) unless you give it a try. As Carlton Fields' Kevin Napper says, "It's dangerous to go in thinking you know what you want. Law school doesn't tell you anything about the day-to-day of law. You can't learn how to represent a doctor sued for malpractice by sitting in a classroom. You ***need*** client conferences for that." Georgetown's Beth Sherman agrees. "The worst advice I ***ever*** got was, 'If you like mutually agreeable solutions, choose corporate work. If you like fighting, do litigation.' You can't rely on that kind of generalization. Instead, ***talk*** to people. See what they do. See what it's really like." One lawyer said that his firm had a summer clerk who commented, "I wanted to be a transactional lawyer—until I tagged along for a couple of depositions with the litigators!"

So, as Kevin Napper recommends, "Take advantage of what your firm offers you! Let people know you're interested in seeing a mediation, or bankruptcy hearings, or med mal defense work, or grand jury appearances, or depositions." Of course, you can't demand a steady diet of any one thing. The idea is to get to know the employer in general. But when you state an interest in getting to learn about something your employer does, you're exhibiting that very alluring trait: enthusiasm.

c. It's great to take an interest in something, but don't carve that interest in granite. Be flexible.

While you're going to enjoy some specialties more than others, it's important not to paint yourself into a professional corner by steadfastly demanding one specialty and one specialty only—***unless*** your summer experience shows you that that specialty is crying out for people and has job openings for new associates. Why? There are two reasons. One is that if you tell your employer "it's International Business Transactional work or nothing," it could well be "nothing." If the specialty you want doesn't need fresh blood, your employer may believe you wouldn't accept any other departmental assignment, and hence not make you an offer. You don't want ***that***. As Fred Thrasher says, "At some point in the summer they'll ask you what you want. It's a Catch-22. You want to be interested in something, but you don't want to be too narrow in your interests. If you want Sports and they have one lawyer in five hundred who does it, good luck. They're asking your interests to make sure you get exposure to what you want to see—they're not necessarily saying they have job openings in it." Gail Cutter agrees. "Being flexible in your choice(s) of departments will help to ensure that you get a permanent offer. Some students have lost permanent offers when their departmental choices didn't match the firm's needs."

The second reason to be flexible is that no matter what you start in at a large employer, there's always a chance to change later on. Once you're "in," you can maneuver for the work you want. (I talk about this topic a lot in "Being Your Own Career Coach" later on in the book.) So don't limit your career choices now. Even if you're dead set on a particular specialty, remember that your ultimate goal in the summer is to get an offer. Frame your interests appropriately!

11. Don't be too choosy about the assignments you take on.

If you're at a medium to large employer, you'll probably get your writing assignments from either an "assignments book" or from one designated attorney. Akin Gump's J.D. Neary warns that "If you're really choosy with writing assignments, you'll get a black mark against you—because you can't do that as a permanent associate!" As the hiring partner at a large West Coast firm points out, "We warn our summer associates the very first day of orientation that they'll get a mix of interesting and boring projects. We don't want to hear bitching if everything they do isn't fascinating, because we warned them it would be that way. And it will be that way when they're permanent associates."

Remember also that, especially if you work for a small firm, you might spend days doing work that has nothing to do with what you think of as "the law," but, as Bart Schorsch writes in *The Student Lawyer*, "Your work might have everything to do with a case. You might have to track down a medical model, climb around a client's burned building, fetch and carry large case files, console a distraught client, or get dirty and fix the office copier." When you get non-traditional tasks, you can do it moping, or you can do it smiling. But you'll impress people more—and have more fun—if you show you can handle ***anything*** with enthusiasm.

12. Even if you're really only working nine to five, you can't have a nine to five mentality.

During your summer clerkship, it's highly unlikely that you'll be expected to put in long hours on a regular basis. There really are employers who never require late hours. But if you clerk at a large-ish firm, or you work with litigators who are prepping for or conducting a trial, you can be sure that ***they're*** not working nine to five.

How do you know what hours to work? There are a couple of things to keep in mind.

a. **You don't score any points hanging around when you're not needed. But when you *are* needed, be willing to stay as late as the junior associates and/or partners you're working for.**

Most employers make a point of not loading down their summer clerks with work, at least much of the time. But it's dangerous to come to view a five o'clock quittin' time as a requirement. You'll torque off the permanent associates and partners if they feel as though you aren't willing to chip in when needed. To use the industry jargon, you won't be viewed as a "team player." As Georgia State's Vickie Brown advises, "Being willing to put in those few extra hours will make you seem like part of the team."

As Kentucky's Drusilla Bakert points out, "Law firm associates often develop a kind of 'bunker' mentality because of their heavy work load and long hours. When they see the big fuss that's made over summer associates, when they hear summer associates being told 'don't work too hard' by the partners and recruiting committee members, many of them wonder if the summer clerks can really cut it as permanent associates. You score a lot of points with these folks by demonstrating that you're there for the long haul. In other work environments as well, the attorneys will be impressed if they see you being willing to put in the long hours. If you are invited to participate in a closing or some other major project, stick around as late as the associates do. Whatever you do during those hours, your time will not have been wasted."

CAREER LIMITING MOVE . . .

Summer clerk at a medium-sized New York firm. She is in at nine and out at five every day. While the permanent associates work more than that, and so do most of the summer associates, no one is really bugged about it, even though the permanent associates are inevitably at work until seven, and the partners often until ten.

One day a partner goes to this summer associate's office at 4:45. He says to her, "I need you to do this project for me by 8:30 tonight for this client; we have to fax it out before 9 p.m."

She responds, in shock, "But it's 4:45!"

Immediately assuming that she's worried she won't have time to do a decent job on the project in three and a half hours, he assures her, "Don't worry. It's not a difficult question. You'll easily finish it by then."

She huffily responds, "I didn't mean that. It's 4:45. You don't honestly expect me to stay past five o'clock, do you?"

b. Follow the lead of people at the office to determine when you ought to show up.

I've already told you that you should call ahead to learn what time to arrive on your first day. When it comes to choosing a time to show up on a regular basis, ask the recruiting coordinator or hiring partner or a junior associate what time you ought to show up. It's part of fitting in, showing again that you're a member of the "team." As William & Mary's Fred Thrasher jokes, "If they're there at eight o'clock in the morning, you can't stroll in at 9:30 with coffee and a bagel!"

Don't feel like a chump for not knowing intuitively when to get to the office, and don't assume it's nine o'clock. Different cities tend to have their own cultures about when it's appropriate to show up. New York tends to be later than other parts of the country. One lawyer who'd clerked in New York went to a firm in the Midwest after he graduated. He wanted to show up early to impress people, and he walked in on his first day at 8:30. Everybody was already at their desks, working away. He was horrified to find out that in that particular city, most people are at their desks working by 8 a.m., and by 8:30 you're considered a slacker.

Finally, if the people you ask give you a range of times to show up, be at the early end of the range. For instance, if you're told

"The office officially opens at 8 a.m., but some people are here at 7:30," then you should show up at 7:30.

c. **If you *do* work late at night or on a weekend, make sure somebody sees you working.**

What we're talking about when we talk about the hours you work during the summer, we're talking about a matter of perception. It's like that old conundrum, "If a tree falls in the woods and nobody hears it, does it make a sound?" Well, if you put in the extra elbow grease at the office and nobody knows about it, you haven't done yourself a lot of good. If you're staying because there's a closing or a trial coming up, the attorneys will be there with you, so you're automatically seen. If you stay at night or come in on a weekend to work on a research project, walk around the office and say hello to whatever attorneys are working, so there's visual evidence you were there. It's not cheesy. It's marketing.

d. **If there's nobody looking over your shoulder, don't be tempted to slack off and leave in the middle of the afternoon on a regular basis.**

Not every summer program is highly structured. I talked with lawyers at several governmental agencies who had loosely structured summer programs, where there are "assignment books" for summer clerks. The clerks are supposed to take assignments from the book, and work on them diligently. As one government lawyer pointed out, "A system like ours depends on the integrity of the summer clerks. And when that's the case, some people are going to let you down. There are sometimes people who blatantly spend the whole day chatting with other clerks. The only person with a cubicle near theirs is a secretary. Sometimes the summer clerks assume that because she's not a lawyer who can hire and fire them, that she's invisible. She's not. She'll come to me and tell me 'They're making personal calls' or 'They're leaving at three in the afternoon.' She's incredulous. She says to me, 'Do they honestly think I'm not going to tell anybody?'"

e. If you are given "observation opportunities" to go to hearings or trials or other field trips, go—and work late to finish your research assignments.

Some summer associates, realizing the importance of research assignments, will turn down opportunities to get out of the office in favour of doing their work. Don't! Attorneys want to see you taking an interest in the practice, and that means watching them in action.

Clerk at a large firm down South, drafts a portion of a brief to be filed with the 11th Circuit. The partner who gave the clerk the assignment says, "You've done so much work, I'd love to have you come with me and watch me argue it."

The clerk responds, "You know, that time isn't billable, so I'd rather not go."

The partner, quietly fuming, leaves the clerk's office, only to return a few minutes later when he's regained his composure. He rests his hands on the clerk's desk, leans forward, and says, "Let me give you some friendly advice. When you're invited to sit in on something, don't **ever, ever** turn it down. You're missing the point. You don't learn how to be a lawyer in the library."

13. Gobble up formal training sessions if they're offered to you.

As Boston University's Betsy Armour advises, "Go to as many formal training sessions as you can, ***especially*** if they're led by important partners."

Similarly, if you're given mock trials to work on, "Prepare like you're prepping for the bar exam. Do a ***stellar*** job!" says Texas Tech's Kay Fletcher. Even during "dress rehearsals," your competence is being judged. Don't take casual learning opportunities casually!

14. The first cut is the deepest: Your first writing assignment for an employer is the most important project you'll do. Whatever you do, don't mess it up. And also . . . what to do if you d*o* mess it up.

Many, many lawyers stressed to me the importance of your first summer project. Your head may still be reeling from everything you're learning at work, but you've got to shake out the fuzziness and make your first writing assignment wonderful. It will set the tone for the summer, and you want that tone to be positive, so that it creates good buzz about you. As Georgetown's Abbie Willard advises, "You're setting a precedent for the summer. You want a halo effect—not a game of catch-up!" Texas Tech's Kay Fletcher agrees: "As a clerk going in, you want to make your first assignment untouchable intellectually. Blow them away. You want them to believe, 'This woman (or man) can ***think***!'"

If you have any doubts about your writing skills at all, one very easy way to ensure that your first project doesn't go awry is to take it to a junior associate with whom you've become friendly, or to the firm librarian (if you have one), tell them that you want to make sure you get off on the right foot, and ask politely if they wouldn't mind glancing over your work for you to make sure you're not way out in left field. Or you could go to the recruiting coordinator (if you have one) to check and see who might read over your writing assignment before you turn it in, to make sure you haven't made any glaring mistakes. If you're friendly with the assigning attorney's assistant, you might consider approaching him or her as well. Nobody is more familiar with what an attorney likes to see than his/her assistant. The important thing is that the person you approach should be someone you trust, because if your writing is truly horrendous, the person you show your work to will be tempted to mention it to other people at the firm. And regardless of who reviews your work first, you can't assume that the lawyer or other professional who glances over your work will have the same reaction as the assigning attorney. But a quick review like this will stop you from making any major mistakes.

The flipside of having a great first project is pretty ugly. One partner at a large firm observed that "Sometimes you'll get a first memo from a summer clerk and you'll think, this person can't write. They're ***really*** bad! Unfocused, badly organized. And the person you did it for won't keep a secret. Partners talk. People will say over lunch, 'Oh my God! How did so-and-so sneak in here? Was their writing sample any good?'" Vermont's Pavel Wonsowicz adds, "If your first writing assignment is bad, no one will trust you after that."

Having painted a pretty scary picture for you, I'll bail you out. What should you do if somehow your first assignment ***does*** go awry? Remember that you've got a lot working in your favour, for a start. Mostly that if you got the job, you've got the candlepower to do the work. What you need to do is this:

(i) Identify ***exactly*** what went wrong. Don't be defensive and don't point fingers.

(ii) Go back to the assigning attorney directly and ***beg*** for a second chance. That's right. Beg. Explain what you learned from your first screw-up and emphasize that you will do whatever it takes to ensure that it doesn't happen again.

Your entreaty ought to work. If it doesn't, go to your mentor and/or recruiting coordinator and/or the head of the department for which you did the work to ask for advice about how to redeem yourself, and follow that advice.

And for gosh sakes do yourself a favour . . . and don't let it happen again!

15. When they give you a deadline on a project, they *mean* it. *Obey* it. And—what to do if you blow a deadline.

It may well be that the project you get doesn't really have a "deadline" in the sense that it's not critical to a client, or the attorney you're working for isn't going to get the chance to review your work for weeks to come, or it's a slow time at the office and what you're getting is a bit of make-work. The problem is that as a summer clerk, it doesn't matter how pressing an assignment ***really*** is. If they give you a deadline for ***any*** reason, real or spurious, they will notice if you don't meet it, even if nothing is said to you about it.

One career services director tells the story of a student who returned to school after a clerkship with a large firm. She didn't get an offer. She fumed, "I don't know why they didn't like me. I turned in all of my assignments." After a little more digging, the career services director discovered that indeed she ***had*** turned in all of her work—a week late for every assignment. Indignant, she defended herself, "But I wasn't done! I had to fix them up." A missed deadline on occasion, fully explained to the assigning attorney and with a great excuse, ***might*** cut the mustard. But not on every project!

It's easy to understand why you'd be tempted to miss a deadline. Too much work, or you got bogged down in research, or you just can't stop revising it. ***Any*** writer can identify with the desire to endlessly re-edit! But you can't do it. Most importantly, your time is money. Clients will only pay for so much—and billing partners will only be willing to write off so much of your time. Being able to work under a deadline is a crucial skill your summer employer needs to see.

If you ***do*** get held up, don't stumble around in the dark, by yourself. Keep your assigning attorney apprised of your progress. ***Ask*** for extra time to see if it's OK to proceed. As Carlton Fields' Eric Adams says, "There's nothing wrong with going back to the assigning attorney and saying, 'I'd like to put some polishing touches on this and get it to you tomorrow at noon instead of today at five o'clock. Would that be OK?'"

CAREER LIMITING MOVE . . .

Small firm in California has two summer clerks, one from a local, not particularly distinguished law school, and the other with a stellar record from a top law school. At the beginning of the summer, everybody in the firm figures that the summer clerk from the distinguished law school will breeze through the summer and the clerk from the local school will struggle . . . including the clerk from the local school.

The clerk from the distinguished law school wants to be a patent lawyer, and immediately attaches himself to a prominent patent partner in the firm, volunteering to do a project for her. The partner gives him a research project with a deadline of two weeks, because she needs the issue he is researching resolved for a client. After two weeks he tells her, "I'm not done yet." She gives him an extension. Another two weeks go by. "I'm still not done." Lo and behold he never finishes the project the entire summer. He not only ignores the deadline, but he makes the partner look stupid in front of a client. The partner is so furious that she insists he receive no offer from the firm—and he doesn't. The other clerk—who'd looked a lot worse on paper—is invited back.

16. The two exceptions to the "Never Miss A Deadline" rule.

Having just told you that you should never miss a deadline, I've got to tell you about two important exceptions to that rule.

a. As Kentucky's Drusilla Bakert advises, "If a senior partner asks you to do a project, particularly a rush project, do ***not*** tell him or her that you must complete a project for an associate first. Try to do both within the time allotted, but if you must, delay the associate's work to complete the partner's, and tell the associate as soon as you can about your new assignment. Believe me, the associate would rather have their work be delayed than for you to tell the senior partner you are working on something more important for the associate. I've seen summer clerks actually say that, and it's not pretty."

b. If the due date arrives and you have not completed the project, do ***not*** turn in a rough draft, a memo you haven't completely cite-checked, or a piece of work with which you're not satisfied. One piece of poor work can haunt your entire summer. You are better off turning in a good piece of work late than turning in a shoddy one on time. If it appears that you won't be able to meet a deadline, let the attorney know that as soon as possible. Don't wait until the day the project is due to announce that you can't meet the deadline. And remember, it's better to work a few late nights or weekends than to miss a deadline or turn in a shoddy work product!

17. What to do about "squishy" deadlines—"Oh, whenever you get to it will be fine . . . "

Don't fall into the "whenever you get to it" trap. Act as though ***everything*** has a deadline, because it does. It's kind of like that saying "His days are numbered"—as though they aren't for the rest of us. ***All*** of our days are numbered, we just don't know what the number is. When it comes to your summer projects, they ***all*** have a deadline, whether you know what it is or not.

If you get a "whenever" project, or the assigning attorney tells you "there's no rush," here's what you should do:

a. "Be sure you understand what 'no rush' means," says Cardozo's Judy Mender. "Not due tomorrow, vs. next week, vs. this will just be a memo to file for general future reference so three months from now is OK?" Ask the attorney when you get the assignment to make it clearer!

b. Don't view the vague deadline as a "license to procrastinate," says Kentucky's Drusilla Bakert.

c. Drusilla Bakert also suggests that, "If you get tied up with other things, check back from time to time to let the assigning attorney make sure there's still no time pressure"

d. Also from Drusilla Bakert: "Regardless of a loose deadline, ***never*** leave your clerkship with a project uncompleted!"

e. Judy Mender also advises that you "Get enough of a start on a project with a vague deadline to be sure that you understand the assignment and are on the right track, and can ask the attorney for feedback and clarification of the assignment."

One lawyer tells the story of a summer clerk who got burned on a vague deadline. "A partner gave her an assignment at the beginning of the summer, and told her that anytime that summer would be OK for her to get it back to him. Since other assignments were more pressing, she worked on those first and returned to the partner's assignment toward the end of the summer. She relied on her notes from her original conversation with the partner and completed the assignment, doing what she presumed was her usual thorough, conscientious job on the memo. She was stunned and mortified when she was called into the partner's office—via the p.a. system!—and reprimanded for having missed the point of the assignment completely. She later had to explain her error to the summer associate supervisor. The whole thing could have been avoided if she had done at least an initial exploration of the topic when it was assigned, and checked to make sure she had it straight."

18. For difficult assignments, don't suffer alone.

It'll be unusual for you to be exposed to difficult attorneys during the summer. Here's why: firms know who their difficult attorneys are. They also know that they want you to like the firm, say good things about it to your classmates when you get back to school, and accept an offer if they make you one (which they almost certainly will, especially because you're reading this book).

Having said that, sometimes you may find yourself working for the Marquis de Sade. When that happens, don't think they're trying to "test" you. Go to someone for help: an attorney you trust or the recruiting coordinator. Don't suffer alone!

SMART HUMAN TRICK . . .

It's a summer clerk's first assignment of the summer, and it just so happens it comes from a very harsh partner. She walks into the partner's office. The partner doesn't even look up to acknowledge her presence, but instead immediately starts in: "I need you to look up a case in the FTCT, the case you need to find will say something like this . . . " The summer associate is totally confused; she has no idea what the FTCT even is. The partner's phone is ringing off the hook, and he immediately picks it up. The summer clerk doesn't have a chance to ask any questions and clarify the project, and she's too scared to ask any questions anyway. She skulks out of the office.

The one thing she thinks she heard and understood was the word "Securities." So off she goes to the firm library, where she looks up Article 9 of the UCC. In fact, it's not a secured transactions issue; it's a securities issue that's not in the UCC at all. She's convinced that she won't get an offer from the firm and in fact she'll never work again.

A second year associate is sitting next to her in the library. She looks over and sees this summer associate's angst, and asks, "Who are you working for?"

The clerk says, "Partner Torquemada" (not his real name).

The associate asks, "What did he ask you to do?"

The summer clerk sheepishly mumbles the few words she can remember from what the partner said. The second year associate nods, and says, "Could he have asked you to do this?" and she rattles off something about the FTCT.

The summer clerk brightens a bit and says, "Yeah, that sounds like it."

The associate continues, "Did he ask you to look for a case that says . . . ."

The summer clerk responds, "Yes! That's exactly it!"

The associate shakes her head, and says, "That idiot. He asked me to do exactly that same thing. I gave him that case two months ago." The associate rummages through her materials and pulls out a case. She hands it to the summer clerk, and says, "Here. Go give him this. Don't tell him I gave it to you. This'll fix his wagon."

The summer clerk thanks her profusely, takes the case and hands it to the partner, and asks casually, "Is this what you're looking for?"

The partner snaps "no" without even looking at the case, convinced there isn't any way the summer clerk could have comprehended what he wanted, and certainly not so quickly.

The summer clerk stands there for a moment, and the partner looks back down at the case, flips through it, and says, "Yes. Yes. This is it." The summer clerk turns to leave, and the partner stops her. "Wait! How did you find it so quickly?"

The clerk turns, smiles, and says, "Your directions were so explicit, you made it simple." The partner beams.

19. Do great work for *everybody*, regardless of whether they're a senior partner or junior associate.

Avoid establishing a pecking order in your mind, where you concentrate on performing well for senior people and cut yourself some slack on the more junior lawyers. First of all, you don't know who's got clout and who doesn't, and how seriously the firm will take a junior person's "no" vote on making you a permanent offer. Regardless of that, no firm wants you to blow off junior associates' work! As Kentucky's Drusilla Bakert advises, "***Always*** take the work seriously, no matter who it comes from. Even if the person asking for your help is a recent graduate, or someone you party with after work, don't assume that their low level in the organization, or your personal relationship, gives you the freedom to do a poor job on the assignment." One lawyer said that when he was a summer clerk, "At my evaluation I was stunned to find out that people who were only two years out of school were evaluating me. They ***blistered*** me. They said, 'His work doesn't show thought or attention to detail.' I'd been casual about it because in my eyes, they were peers, not superiors. Boy, was I wrong. You don't want the associate evaluation committee reading ***anything*** bad about you, from ***anybody***!"

One lawyer tells a story that happened at her firm: "This one summer associate had an assignment from an associate and another one from a partner. The summer clerk gave more attention to the partner and let the associate's assignment slide. What the summer clerk didn't know was that the associate was very well respected, and didn't appreciate that kind of treatment." Another summer clerk at another firm trumpeted loudly at an orientation social event, "I'm only going to work for partners, not associates." As one associate at the firm said, "That comment obviously made a big impression on associates!"

You get the point. Assume that every person you work for has the power to determine if you get an offer, and you'll be just fine.

20. Don't mistake quantity for quality.

Some summer clerks bog themselves down with work, believing that they'll overwhelm the firm with the sheer number of projects they complete. Don't fall into this trap! For one thing, no employer expects you to be a drone. They ***want*** you to come up for air and socialize, to get to know the attorneys. Apart from that, you don't ***need*** a ton of writing projects to get an offer. As Baker Botts' Bart Showalter explains, "Volume doesn't matter. Don't worry about getting ten projects under your belt. Attorneys care about horsepower and writing skills, ***not*** volume."

21. Keep a copy of every project you work on.

William & Mary's Rob Kaplan recommends that you keep a record of every single thing you work on during the summer. Record who it was for and what it involved. This is in addition to keeping a copy of all of your written work. Keeping this record will serve you in a number of ways. When it comes to your resume and future salability, you do yourself a ***huge*** favour by being able to recount in detail the kinds of experiences you have (without revealing confidential information, of course). Furthermore, it will help you get through future conflicts of interest reviews with other employers without tearing your hair out, trying to remember the clients you worked for and what you did.

22. Don't bitch about the work.

They're giving you the projects you're getting for a ***reason***. Either they (1) really need the work done, and/or (2) they're giving you a taste of the great-and-not-so-great work you'd get as a permanent associate.

If you aren't happy with the work you're getting as a summer clerk, ***volunteer*** to observe or help out with other things, ***on top of*** the work you're being assigned. Or go to the recruiting coordinator and, without complaining about the work you're being given, ask for the opportunity to try A or B or C. ***Complaining*** about what you get won't help you. As one partner at a large firm cautioned, "Nobody wants the 'grumbling clerk' who feels a project is beneath him. Not every project will be the most important. To ***you*** it may be a stupid pro bono assignment, but it's important to the client." Northern Illinois' Mary Obrzut adds, "Buy a punching bag for your home! Don't bitch and whine at work."

A recruiting coordinator at a large West Coast firm told of the summer clerk who, every time the assigning attorney gave him a project, would respond, "Don't you have anything more interesting?" The recruiting coordinator said, "In orientation they'd been ***told*** that they'd get some very interesting projects and some stinkers, but he ignored that. When I confronted him about it, he didn't realize he'd done anything wrong. 'I thought you guys ***wanted*** me to ask!' he responded. He took it well, but he was blackballed by that department."

23. Handling grunt work

The fact is, most employers will make a huge effort to get you a variety of projects during the summer, because they want you to come back after graduation. But sometimes they've got no choice; there's grunt work to be done, and somebody has to do it. What should you do if that somebody turns out to be you?

Now, when you become a permanent associate, getting stuck with a bunch of chimp work is something you ***can*** change, and I talk about that in the section called "Handling Chimp Work Without Going Bananas!" But as a summer clerk, you've got a fine line to walk. On the one hand, every employer wants to see that you're willing to pitch in and help, no matter how trivial or unglamorous the assignment might seem. But on the other hand, you've got to leave your employer with evidence that you can do more than sort documents, fax and make copies. Even if they don't have any permanent job openings, they need to be able to write something in your recommendation other than "She stacked papers very neatly."

As Emory's Carolyn Bregman advises, if you get mired in grunt work, "***Ask*** for more demanding projects. Let somebody know. Say, 'I'll do this, but I want more to bite off and chew.' Seek out projects you want and say, 'Ooh! Let me do it!' You can't avoid the bad work entirely—somebody's got to scoop the poop from the elephant cages—but you need to ask for more challenging work."

 CAREER LIMITING MOVE . . .

Large Northeastern firm. Summer clerk, sharing a secretary with several other people. The secretary doesn't have time to do some photocopying for the clerk, so the clerk has to go to the library and do it herself. The recruiting coordinator stops by to say hello. The clerk looks her in the eye, and says disdainfully, "I didn't go to Stanford to make photocopies." The recruiting coordinator nods and walks away, thinking, "You're going to be sorely disappointed in life."

CAREER LIMITING MOVE . . .

Medium-sized firm, one summer clerk is perfectly content to stand by the copier, never asking for anything else to do. The hiring partner marvels, "This guy completely slipped between the cracks. He should have hit the panic button at some point. At reference time, what could we say? He was a great copier?"

24. How to handle too much work without torquing anybody off.

Summer employers try to be good about not bogging you down with too much to do. Juggling multiple projects is the coin of the realm when you get to a job after law school, and I talk a lot about it in the permanent associates section under the title "Help! I'm drowning! What To Do When You've Got Too Much Work (Or Too Little . . .)" The issues are a bit different as a summer clerk. Here's what you need to know.

a. If you're at a small firm or government agency with very few summer clerks, speak to anyone you like and trust . . . but do it *right*.

If you don't have any one particular person assigning you projects, remember that lawyers are ***busy*** and won't be paying a lot of attention to your workload. If you're feeling overwhelmed, make a list of everything you've got to do (and who it's for), go to a lawyer you respect and feel comfortable with, and say, "Here's everything I've been assigned to do. Can you help me figure out how to prioritize this?" One of two things will happen. The lawyer will help you figure out what comes first and what to push off until later, so that you won't be accused of making a bad choice, or—here's that word again—exhibiting poor judgment. Or alternatively the lawyer will look at what's on your plate and say "Jesus Christ! What are they trying to ***do***? ***Kill*** you?" and help you take steps to lighten the load—without you ever having to complain. The watchword here: don't suffer in silence.

b. **If you're at an employer large enough to have an assignments partner or administrator for the summer program, let that person know if you're overloaded.**

As Miami's Karen Scully-Clemmons says, "Most big firms have structures in place, usually a partner who gives assignments. Students don't realize there are people outside of that structure who just dump things on summer associates. Don't stay quiet. It's not some kind of test! If they tell you at the beginning of the summer where work comes from and whom you report to, remember that somebody outside of that chain isn't supposed to give you work directly. Keep the communications line open with the proper assigning attorney. Ask that person, 'So-and-so gave me this assignment. What should I do?' Let them handle it between themselves!" Boston University's Betsy Armour adds, "Summer associates often have conflicting demands—work plus seminars plus social events plus observation opportunities at court. Don't resolve those conflicts yourself. Defer to a recruiting coordinator or mentor. Bounce it off them. They might tell you 'Partner X is more important' or 'That's one social event you really don't have to attend.'"

The most important thing is not to risk angering people yourself. As Kentucky's Drusilla Bakert says, "Sometimes it will seem as though you can't make one person happy without making someone else mad at you." The ***only*** way to avoid that is to offload your scheduling decisions on someone else. As a summer clerk, you can't afford to make enemies for any reason. So—don't!

c. **Most importantly, *never* take on more projects than you can successfully complete during the summer.**

If you go to work at a large employer, you may be tempted to overload yourself with work in order to get exposed to as many lawyers as possible. That's too much of a good thing, and it'll come back to bite you. If you take on too much, the quality of some project(s) will suffer—and you'll turn a neutral vote into a strong "no" vote against your getting an offer. As George Washington's Jim Lovelace says, "You need to leave behind a ***few*** good writing samples, not ***ten*** of them." Instead, he adds, the place to get to know people is "practice breakfasts, lunches, or social events."

At one firm, a summer clerk took on so much work during his last week with the firm that he ended up working until midnight on his last day—and missed his flight back to school. One lawyer at another firm warned, "If you're cramming in projects at the last minute, it won't be optimal work product. It might not even be complete. But the circumstances will be forgotten when the hiring committee meets a month later, when all they've got in front of them is your written work."

25. Don't knock yourself out trying to appear efficient—and don't write off any hours you work. Record *everything.*

Nobody expects you to be able to work efficiently as a summer clerk. You've never done this before. There's a steep learning curve. Take it easy on yourself! As the partner at one large firm commented, "Summer clerks don't get much grief over being inefficient. Everybody just wants good work product. Somebody might say, 'I can't believe it took that long,' but the important thing is for them to know you worked hard."

If you take a long time working on a project, you might be tempted to write off some of your time and not let anybody know about it. The problem is, you're not in a position to know how long is "too long." In the section on "Writing Assignments" in the permanent jobs section, I talk about what to do if a project you're working on is just taking way too long. Read that for advice, rather than writing off your time. If you ***do*** write off your time, you run the risk that people will wonder what you're doing at the office all day. As one hiring partner commented, "We expect inefficiency. That's not so bad. What ***is*** bad is when we start asking each other, 'What does he ***do*** all day long?' We wonder about some clerks. They'll be in the office every day and every night, and only write down a few hours. They're clearly not writing all of their hours down. We expect to have to write off some of the time summer clerks work. If we know you worked it and we had to write it off, at least we know you're a hard worker."

26. Keep accurate track of *all* the time you spend at work.

Whether or not you're at a private firm where you need to keep track of billable time, make ***sure*** that you accurately record ***all*** of your working time. Ask for help on specific procedures and expectations, if you didn't learn them at orientation or in a training manual. The time you should record includes meetings and telephone calls. If you have a secretary for the summer, get with him or her to figure out how your time should be recorded and who should do what.

Make sure that every project you do is recorded according to the client, the assigning attorney and any necessary billing information. You'll need to keep track like this as a practicing attorney. Start now!

27. Don't slack off as the summer drags on. Every project counts!

Stetson's Cathy Fitch advises that "In a summer program you have to prove yourself over and over again. You have to keep on giving." Joni Coleman Fitzgerald from Willcox & Savage adds, "You may only have one opportunity to work with any one attorney during the summer. It's difficult to redeem yourself if your work for that attorney isn't acceptable!"

Hamline's Vince Thomas compares summer clerkships to sports, saying that "Your summer clerkship isn't baseball! It's not three strikes you're out. It's ***one*** strike and you're out, until you've established some credibility and can strike out and get forgiven for it. That's the advice that a partner told me. He said that if you have only one strike, it reminds you that you've got to be on your toes and bring the same level of intensity and focus every day. You can't turn it on at the beginning and then coast off and on, as you did during semesters in law school. In law school, you'd turn it on at the beginning of the semester to see what's going on, then coast until the exam. There's no such thing in a summer program! Bring your best game to the office every day. You can't say 'I swung and missed it' even if it was a tough pitch to hit!"

E. YOUR THOUGHTS ARE YOUR EXCLUSIVE PROPERTY. YOUR EMPLOYER ONLY CARES ABOUT WHAT YOU SAY AND WHAT YOU DO. HERE'S HOW TO SAY AND DO THE RIGHT THINGS!

Whenever you talk to employers about what they look for in people they hire, the qualities you hear the most often are things like "teamwork," "maturity," "professionalism," "good judgment." You've probably heard them a bunch, even in school. I remember interviewing with a big firm in an on-campus interview, one of many interviews I bombed in law school. Actually it was with one of the firms in this book. OK. It was Jones Day. And the partner who was interviewing me asked, "So what do you consider your best trait?" I immediately responded, "My sense of humour." Ha ha! I was an idiot! Nobody wants a lawyer with a squirting flower boutonnière, but since I hadn't written *Guerrilla Tactics For Getting The Legal Job Of Your Dreams* yet, I didn't know that. Anyway, that answer clearly didn't go over very well with him, so I asked, "Just out of curiosity—what do you consider the most important trait for a lawyer to have?" He immediately brightened up and said, "Judgment. Good judgment. If you have good judgment, it cuts across everything you do."

He obviously gave me a great answer for every time I was asked that same question in other interviews, but to tell you the truth, when it comes to words like judgment and maturity and professionalism—they don't really mean a lot to me. When I think of the word "mature," I think of retirees—or cheese. I don't think that's what employers are talking about.

So when I interviewed people for this book, I asked them exactly what they meant when they used those kinds of words. What kinds of traits do they want summer clerks and new associates to exhibit? And I'll tell you some really good, I mean ***wonderful***, news. When it comes to your thoughts, they're your own. You can think anything you want. Now and for the rest of your life. Nobody cares about it. You're completely free. They only care about the manifestation of your thoughts. While you have no control over your thoughts—at least, your initial thoughts, your instincts—you have complete control over how you act on those thoughts. And that means that your behavior doesn't ever, ever have to drum you out of a job opportunity.

When it comes to what you do, remember first and foremost that your employer ***wants*** you to succeed. They want to like you, so that they can make you a job offer (if they have permanent openings) or give you an honest, rave review and help you find another job (if they don't). The table is set for you. The only person who can yank out the tablecloth and break all the china is ***you.*** But if you keep your wits about you and follow the rules I'm about to give you, that won't happen!

1. **Don't walk around like a grinning idiot—but it's important to *smile* and otherwise seem enthusiastic about the employer.**

   Part of what makes an employer want you is their feeling that you want ***them.*** If for any reason they get the impression that you don't want to be there, that ***one*** reason—on its own—can be enough to tank your chance at an offer. Not only that, but if you smile and seem generally happy, it can have a "halo effect" with your work. Dave James, of the San Diego City Attorney's Office, says that "Employers will see you as more proficient if you smile more. I've seen innumerable instances where people who generally smile and are upbeat get the benefit of any doubt about their performance."

   With that in mind, heed the following advice:

   a. Keep ambivalent feelings to yourself. As NYU's Gail Cutter advises, "If you verbalize your uncertainty about the firm's geographic location, practice, or atmosphere, your unhappiness may become a factor if the firm has to make some difficult offer choices."

   b. *Whenever* a partner casually asks how your summer is going, the answer has got to be a hearty "Great!" or "I love it here" or "I really appreciate being here" or something of that enthusiastic ilk. It's kind of like when you say "How are you?" to someone casually. You don't really want to hear about their aches and bumps and boils. You want to hear, "Great. How are you?" It's the same thing with a summer clerkship!

Summer clerk at a large firm. He was rather introverted. He was walking down a hallway at work one day when the managing partner came the other way. The partner asked the clerk how his summer was going. The clerk responded with a lukewarm "Fine." Later, the managing partner went to the firm's hiring partner and said, "Say, is so-and-so unhappy here?" Of course as this got around the firm it changed from a question to a statement, as these things do. "Is he happy?" became "He's not happy." The clerk had a heck of a time correcting the misimpression.

2. Be accommodating about your office set-up, no matter what it is.

If you work for a public interest employer or a government agency, you might get a steel desk and file cabinet. If you work for a small firm, your "office" might be the table in the firm library. At a big firm, you might have to share an office. No matter what you get, shut up about it. The idea of the squeaky wheel getting the grease applies to work assignments, and I talk about that in great detail in the section on being your own career coach. When the issue is offices, taking what you're given is part of what they mean by being a "team player." Whining about your space will make your employer question your priorities, and you don't want that!

CAREER LIMITING MOVE . . .

Summer clerk at a large firm. He was given his own office. He called the recruiting coordinator, and said, "These walls look ordinary. They need paint. I need pictures." It was one of a bunch of arrogant things he'd done during the summer. When the recruiting coordinator hung up, she grumbled at the phone: "What you **need** is a good spanking."

CAREER LIMITING MOVE . . .

Summer clerk at a medium-sized firm in the Southwest. Because of size constraints, the summer clerks had to double up in offices. The summer clerk went to see the recruiting coordinator, saying, "I need my own space so I can concentrate." It turns out one of the attorney offices was temporarily vacant because a junior associate was out sick; in fact, she had been in a very serious car accident and was undergoing intensive physical therapy, and her recovery was going agonizingly slowly. The recruiting coordinator reluctantly walked the summer clerk to the junior associate's office, explained the associate's situation, turned on the light, and said, "You can sit at this desk and use the phone if you have to, but you **cannot** turn on this computer. She wants to keep up with some of her work, and the only way for her to do it is to dial in to this computer. We don't want her to feel like she's out of the loop. So if you need to use a computer, go back to your own office." Sure enough, the junior associate called the recruiting coordinator later that day, frantic that she couldn't get into her computer. The summer clerk had ignored the recruiting coordinator's plea—and used the computer. Despite good work product, he didn't get an offer.

3. **Let your employer see only loyalty to *them* - no matter what other opportunities you're contemplating.**

Something that drives employers ***crazy*** is to see summer clerks "wheeling and dealing" offers. One large firm told me that "It's so important to focus on the organization as the place you intend to make a long-term commitment. When an employer can make offers to only 80% of their summer class, they tend to focus on people who have shown the most sincere interest in them. Don't make the common mistake of 'wheeling and dealing' alternative offers during your current clerkship!"

4. **Be tactful about things that are important to the firm.**

When anybody at your summer employer tells you about something that they're particularly proud of, the only reaction is something like, "That's great!" or "That's really impressive" or even better, follow-up questions to show that you're interested. Brushing off the sources of people's pride will make them question your tact and dislike you—and neither of those bode well for your future at that employer.

CAREER LIMITING MOVE . . .

Large firm in the Midwest. They are particularly proud of the fact that one of the associates made it on to *Who Wants To Be A Millionaire?* although he didn't make it into the hot seat. They talk about it a lot. The "Millionaire" associate and some of the other associates are at a summer function, and they're chatting with some clerks. One of the associates says to the clerks, "By the way, did you know that Fred got on *Who Wants To Be A Millionaire?*" When they mention that Fred hadn't made it into the hot seat, one of the summer clerks asks, "What was the question?" Fred tells him, and the clerk responds, "God, that was **easy**. I can't believe you didn't get **that**!"

The summer clerk's mentor is standing nearby, and hears this exchange. He blanches. Later on, he comments, "I had no idea how to clean up for him after that. He was tainted from that day forward. He showed no professional judgment whatsoever."

5. Be appropriately deferential to senior attorneys. You wouldn't treat your grandma the same way you treat your cousin. But don't be perceived as a "suck up."

There's a ***very*** important difference between sucking up and honest flattery. When you're an empty "yes person," people will smoke you out and think less of you—including the person you're sucking up to. As Pittsburgh's Chris Miller says, "Avoid compliments that don't seem genuine, offers to do tasks that are someone else's responsibility, being there every time somebody important turns around." Instead, seek out things that you can compliment sincerely about your superiors—and for that matter, everybody else as well. If you're telling the truth, people you flatter will like and trust you. It's a simple fact of human psychology that people like people who respect them.

By the same token, make sure you that while you show everybody respect, you're more deferential to the more senior attorneys at work. As Kentucky's Drusilla Bakert explains, "Some people are more equal than others. Know the status of every lawyer with whom you work. Associate?

Senior partner? Department head? Senior attorneys expect to be treated with more deference than new lawyers." She adds, "And if your firm has a hiring committee, be sure you know who the attorneys on that committee are—and that they know who ***you*** are!"

6. **Treat junior associates with respect, even though they're almost your age.**

   It's easy to think that as long as you butter up the senior partners, you'll get an offer. It's not true. Assume that everybody at the office has equal say over whether or not you get invited back—because in most places, they do.

CAREER LIMITING MOVE . . .

One junior associate reports that "My firm was running low on library space, and they had to store some old reporters on the bookshelves in my office. A summer clerk came to my office, looking for the reporters. I let him use my desk to do his research. When I came back, I found that he'd left books out all over the place, an empty Coke can on my shelf, and the furniture shifted around. When I tracked him down, he was very flip when I asked him to come back to my office to clean up after himself. It was almost as though he couldn't believe I'd dare say anything to him criticizing his conduct. If he'd apologized, come back and tidied up, I wouldn't have given it a second thought. But his reaction made me so angry that I reported the incident to the hiring committee. I subsequently found out that this guy had split his summer between two firms, and hadn't received an offer from either one."

If you're friendly with permanent associates, that's great. They want to work with people they like—and so do you! But don't take that familiarity too far, because they're your superiors first and your friends second, no matter how much you pal around after work. As Denver's Jennifer Loud Ungar says, 'You can be ***too*** cool and chummy. You aren't in yet."

CAREER LIMITING MOVE . . .

Male summer associate, gets friendly with a woman who is a mid-level associate at a large Midwestern firm. The mid-level associate is petite and has a very high-pitched, "girlie" voice. He does a writing assignment for her. When he goes to check on it, she says, in her Betty Boop voice, 'Oh, I'm sorry, I haven't had a chance to review your memo yet!' He pats her on the head, and says, 'Don't worry about it.' Even though they're friendly, she's none to happy about being patted on the head by a summer clerk.

7. Seek out associates who are well regarded, and emulate them!

You won't be at an employer very long before you hear through the grapevine that certain associates are regarded as superstars. Listen to what's said about those associates, observe them, and do as they do. If you have the opportunity, work with them and/or pick their brains, asking for their advice about doing well. It's a good idea to remember that lawyers ***inevitably*** like to give advice; when you ask someone for their advice, you're paying them a compliment. You'll not only learn what ***you*** need to do to get ahead at work, but you'll also gather some powerful allies—and you'll learn a lot about what the employer values, and whether those values match yours.

8. Punctuality counts. Don't keep lawyers waiting!

If you're the kind of person who's chronically late, your summer clerkship is the perfect opportunity to break yourself of the habit. You can infuriate lawyers if you keep them waiting. If you have an appointment with attorneys, whether it's to receive or go over an assignment, or to meet with clients or anyone else, set an alarm on your computer or electronic organizer to alert you a few minutes earlier. Or if you have a good relationship with your secretary, you might tell them about your tendency to be tardy and enlist their help in curing you of your bad habit! Carlton Fields' Elizabeth Zabak characterizes punctuality with attorneys as "internal marketing," and she says, "It will go a long way to advancing your career."

9. **Always carry a pad and a pen.**

It's worth repeating: *Whenever* you leave your office, carry a pad and pen. Every single lawyer in the world will tell you this! As Milbank Tweed's Joanne DeZego explains it, "If you have a pad and pen in hand it'll help you in two ways. First, you're ready to take down any assignment, in case you happen to run into an assigning attorney in the hallway. And second, you always look busy. It's good for your image."

10. **When they're looking for volunteers—volunteer.**

There will be times during the summer when some of the attorneys at work will be under a major time crunch. Maybe they've got to get a prospectus out tomorrow, and they need it proofread late at night. Or they have to collate and fax a bunch of documents to different parties in a suit. Or—you name it. If they're looking for volunteers and you don't have any ***very*** pressing assignments or engagements, chip in. When I talk about "teamwork" in the permanent associates section, you'll find that this kind of mucking in is what people really mean when they talk about teamwork. You can say all you want that you're a "team player," but your staying late one night to help out with something menial will have an incalculable effect on your reputation.

11. **Volunteer for "observation opportunities."**

If you're at a small firm or a government agency or prosecutor's office for the summer, you'll get plenty of opportunities to see—and help out—lawyers in action. If you're at a medium to large firm, those opportunities might not be as obvious. But the fact is, it can be tough to get juiced about your employer if all of your working hours are spent researching and writing. On top of that, attorneys will view your enthusiasm to go to court, client meetings, and the like as an indication of your enthusiasm for the work. As Carlton Fields' Eric Adams suggests, "Go to hearings, oral arguments, depositions, anything you can. If they circulate a docket sheet, look it over, and tell people what you'd like to see!"

12. **Stay awake during meetings and presentations . . . and here's how.**

"Well, duh," you're thinking. But you'd be surprised how many times summer clerks fall asleep during meetings, seminars, and presentations. One firm even told me about a summer clerk who fell asleep during ***orientation***. The fact is, things ***can*** get tiring. It's hot during the summer. You were out late the night before. What you're listening to is a real snoozer. Before you know it . . . zzzzzzz. How do you avoid it? One recruiting coordinator recommended that you "Take notes. Even stupid ones. It keeps you from rolling over."

13. When you are in the presence of clients, be observant—and be *quiet*.

If you are at a small firm or a public interest employer, you'll likely have "real" contact with clients during your summer clerkship. If that's the case, you should read the section on "Dealing With Clients" in the permanent associates section.

But at medium to large firms, you won't have a "real" role to play with clients. When you're around clients, there are three important rules to observe:

a. If you're the only clerk present with attorneys and client(s), and there is no support person there to take notes, volunteer to take notes. Or take them without even volunteering. That's one valuable role you ***can*** play.

b. You may not consider yourself a professional, but the client ***does***. Behave accordingly.

CAREER LIMITING MOVE . . .

Female summer clerk. She is invited by a partner to sit in on a hearing. During a lull in the hearing, in the client's and partner's presence, she takes her cell phone out of her purse and makes an appointment with her hairdresser.

c. *Don't talk* unless expressly and specifically told to do so by an attorney you work for.

CAREER LIMITING MOVE . . .

Large New York firm, partner takes a group of summer clerks down to Washington, D.C. to prep the CEO of a large corporate client for his upcoming testimony. One of the clerks has a Ph.D. in Psychology. After the partner finishes talking to the CEO, the clerk/psychologist pipes up, "Let me give you a few tips on how you should present yourself . . . " and goes on to advise the somewhat perturbed CEO. The partner says nothing—until they leave the client. Then the beet-red partner rips into the summer clerk, saying, "Don't you ever, ever, ever do that again!"

CAREER LIMITING MOVE . . .

Large D.C. firm, has a clerk who speaks fluent French. The clerk sits in on a client meeting with the executives of a French company, all of whom speak French more comfortably than English. The clerk listens to their conversations between themselves in French, and then cuts in and starts giving them advice in French. The attorneys in the room can't understand what he's saying. Subsequently, the French clients tell the most senior attorney that they were "a bit put off" about receiving advice from the summer clerk.

CAREER LIMITING MOVE . . .

As one partner recounted, "At law school, you are rewarded for speaking up. During your summer clerkship, don't offer your opinion in front of clients. On a first conference call with a client, don't offer a strategy or say, 'Oh, I did that last semester. Here's the answer.' You just cost the firm thousands of bucks. And if you get it wrong, you bought us a malpractice suit."

Finally, when it comes to clients, don't ***ever*** take the initiative of calling a client yourself. Or anyone associated with a client. Or worst of all, the opponent of a client. ***Always*** check with a supervising attorney first!

Summer clerk at a large East Coast firm. She gets an assignment involving performing due diligence for a company, which we'll call Alpha Company, involved in merger negotiations with a very large corporation. While culling through the files, she finds a letter from an attorney threatening to sue Alpha Company for infringing a patent this attorney's client held. Instead of simply highlighting the document for her supervising attorney to review, she decides to take the due diligence one step further and see if the attorney is intending to pursue the lawsuit. She calls the attorney who wrote the letter, and asks, "Are you still interested in suing Alpha Company for patent infringement? It seems to me that the statute of limitations hasn't run, and I need to sort this out because Alpha is in negotiations to be acquired." Yes, the attorney was interested in pursuing litigation. And no, the summer clerk wasn't invited back.

14. It may only be a summer job, but it's still confidential. Learn how to keep secrets!

Whether you're working for the government or for a corporation or for a law firm, you'll be exposed to confidential information during your summer. And it may be really juicy, good stuff. And you may be ***dying*** to tell people about it. ***Don't.*** If it's that good, save it for your first novel, when you can change the facts enough to protect the confidentiality of the client. In the meantime, be ***very***, ***very*** careful with information you learn at work. It's a secret.

Hardly any summer clerk dishes the dirt intending to hurt a client. It's just that the story is so exciting that you gotta tell ***somebody***. The problem is, the person you tell could be on the other side of the case or deal you're working on—particularly if it's a friend at another firm (in a civil case or business deal) or a prosecutor's office or opposing defense firm (on a criminal case). Or maybe the person you're talking to is A-OK, but you're sitting in a bar, or a restaurant, or a plane, or a train, or you're standing in an elevator or a public bathroom, and somebody who can overhear you turns out to be the "idiot client" you're laughing at—or their mother, father, friend, or 300-lb. bouncer of a brother, who's going to disconnect your head from your neck for telling tales out of school.

The fact is, if you disclose confidential information in the presence of others, you're jeopardizing the attorney-client privilege and that's a big, bad boner. (When I wrote the *Law In A Flash* cards, I covered this in a hypo set at a bachelor party, where the groom-to-be confesses embezzlement to the best man, while a stripper waiting to pop out of a giant cake listens to the whole thing. God I'm funny.)

Privilege isn't your only worry, by the way. As William & Mary's Fred Thrasher points out, "You could have valuable information. If you tell a friend something about a deal you're working on, you could be liable for insider trading."

Finally, don't ***ever*** use ***anything*** you write for work as a writing sample ***without getting permission first***, advises Gail Cutter. Even if you remove the parties' names, if it's still somehow identifiable, you're in trouble.

The bottom line—when it comes to confidential information, keep your mouth shut. Who knows. You might luck out. Maybe you'll overhear somebody opposing one of ***your*** employer's clients let something juicy slip, and ***you'll*** get to be the hero—while they get to be the goat.

CAREER LIMITING MOVE . . .

Two summer clerks, working for the same firm, sit on a train together. They discuss their work and projects so freely that by the end of their discussion, the name of their employer, their clients, and their clients' problems are all patently obvious—to the law school career services director sitting in the seat behind them. At the end of the train ride, the career services director leans forward, taps them on the shoulder, introduces herself, and says, "What you just did? Don't ever do that again."

CAREER LIMITING MOVE . . .

Summer clerk, large West Coast firm, uses a writing sample to apply for a job. The particular writing sample he chooses is the highly confidential memo outlining a client's strategy for dealing with an investigation by a federal agency. He thinks the memo will be a particularly effective writing sample, because he's applying for a permanent job with that very agency. "He removed the names," said a lawyer for the government agency. "But because we were familiar with the case we knew exactly who it was. The guy thought he was being clever, but I've never seen such a bad mistake."

15. Don't sit on your hands when there is downtime between (or during) assignments.

No matter how well organized a summer program you enter, there will be times when you're "at liberty." Maybe it will be between assignments, or maybe it will be when you're waiting for a document to be word-processed. No matter why it occurs, don't sit in your office waiting for your next assignment. Walk around, introduce yourself to people you don't know, see if there are any small ways to make yourself useful. This not only shows initiative and enthusiasm—two highly-prized traits—but also gives you more of a chance to get to know the employer, and determine whether *this* is where you want to start your career after law school.

16. Don't seem afraid or anxious. Project an attitude of humble confidence.

Your summer employer knows you've never done this before. They know that can be scary. As one recruiting coordinator points out, "Most clerks are more fearful than anything else." But as the old deodorant ad said, "Don't let them see you sweat."

If you're there in the first place, they assume you've got the raw material to be successful. As the lawyers at the firm Akin Gump advise, "Take for granted you belong there, that your credentials are fine. Relax! Interactions with anxious people don't inspire confidence."

One of the things that is a tip-off to anxiety is seeking constant reassurance. It's a good idea to seek out feedback (I talk about that elsewhere in this book), but that means asking for criticism—not the constant stroking of "Gee, you're great." If they're not telling you something is wrong, and you're not getting any subtle signals that something is wrong (like not having enough work when everybody else is very busy), then you can assume you're doing fine. As one recruiting coordinator at a large firm pointed out, "Your employer isn't going to conspire against you. We're not going to get five hundred lawyers in a room and say, 'Let's make sure Johnny doesn't get a job.'"

Anxious, high-maintenance summer clerks also seek validation for what they ought to be sure about. Again, this involves a bit of line drawing. There ***will*** be assignments with issues that are hard to tackle, and you need guidance on those. But some of your work will be straightforward. If you constantly ask "Have I got it right?" when you pretty obviously ***do***, your employer will resent the handholding.

Another dead giveaway of insecurity is turning a simple assignment into a Law Review note. In your summer clerkship, there ***can*** be too much of a good thing. And as with feedback and the complexity of issues, there's no clear rule here. On the one hand, your employer wants your research to be thorough and accurate, and they don't expect you to be as efficient as people who've been at it for a while. Assigning attorneys, especially if they've been practicing for a few years, quickly forget how long it takes to do an assignment when you've never done one like it before! But there's a limit. If you beat relatively simple issues to death, turning a two-hour assignment into a two-week ordeal, they'll question your judgment. If your research takes longer than the time estimate you were given when you received the assignment, check back with the assigning attorney to make sure you're on the right track.

17. Don't view the first couple of weeks as an acid test of your desire to be an attorney.

It's very easy to get impatient with your summer, and figure that if the first week goes badly, you weren't meant to be a lawyer. Even an entire ***summer*** isn't long enough to come to that conclusion, let alone an awful start. It could be that you're working with the one person in the organization with whom you'd just ***never*** be able to get along. Maybe you got a rotten or boring assignment. No matter what it is, don't ring down the curtain on your career before it's even started.

One law firm advised that "You have to expect a 'mood slump' toward the beginning of your summer. That is more likely related to the fact that it's summertime, you'd rather be outside, you haven't had a 'real job' in maybe two years, you're used to a flexible student lifestyle and not working ten-hour days in a suit, nylons, or uncomfortable shoes. Give yourself the whole summer to draw conclusions."

Another firm added that "Most people spend much of the summer battling overwhelming feelings of stupidity and incompetence. Remember that you aren't incompetent *or* stupid. Be patient with yourself! Law is a difficult profession and you have a lot to learn."

18. When they say "Be yourself," they don't mean it. What they mean is: "Be yourself *within reason.*"

Everybody will tell you to be yourself. Whenever I hear "Be yourself," I ask, "What if I'm a drunken, unethical, lecherous, sexist, racist, disrespectful boor who doesn't get going before noon?" Well, of course, you can't be ***that***, I'm told.

What they really mean when they say "be yourself" is, "Be yourself, as long as your behavior indicates that you are hard-working, respectful, ethical, friendly, enthusiastic, situation-appropriate, and smart."

During the summer, you actually have to bend a lot more than you do once you have a permanent job. Even if you're very shy, you simply have to go to social events, at least the most important ones. You don't have to talk to lots of people, but make a point of chatting one-on-one at big affairs. But it's important to remember that at most offices, there will be a whole range of personalities. If you tend to be more quiet and pursue more subdued social activities, there'll be some lawyers you can hang out with. If your idea of a good time is skydiving, well, you'll find your level, too. Don't convince yourself on the basis of just a few personalities that you don't "fit in," or that you've got to behave in an unnatural way to get along.

The areas where you really should feel free to "be yourself" actually concern whether you tend to be outgoing or reserved, serious or light-hearted—those kinds of things. Ultimately the most ***important*** thing for you to do is to find a work environment that makes you happy, where your personality meshes with your colleagues so that you all enjoy working together. If you pretend to be a hard partier to fit in, or you pretend to be serious and sober because the office is very formal, people will see through your act—and you won't be doing anyone a favour, least of all yourself.

19. When they say "Ask me anything," they don't mean it.

A lot of firms will encourage you to ask questions. And in some contexts, it's not only advisable, but extremely necessary. But no matter how appropriate questions are, you've still got to show tact, discretion, respect, and a lack of greed when you're told you can "ask anything."

CAREER LIMITING MOVE . . .

At one firm, the managing partner was a Vietnam War veteran. At a Q & A session with summer clerks, one of them asked him, "What's it like to kill people?" (His response: "Don't tempt me.")

CAREER LIMITING MOVE . . .

At one large-ish Midwestern firm, the managing partner would take out a few clerks every Friday for an "ask-me-anything" lunch. The firm paid its clerks the going rate for the area, considerably less than New York firms were paying. One of the clerks, from a prestigious East Coast law school, asked: "We can go back to the East Coast and make double what you're paying new associates. Why should we stay with **you**?" Once the managing partner regained the ability to speak, he sputtered, "I've got news for you. If I paid you what you're **worth**, you'd pay **me** for the first two years—then I'd pay you $150,000 a year!"

20. Take advantage of chances to have fun. But be careful with practical jokes!

Nobody wants to work with a stick in the mud. Yes, the work is serious and you should take it seriously. But people want to work with people they like, and you need to show them your relaxed side to encourage them to do exactly that.

Of course, there are limits to what's appropriate when you're around people from work. I go over a lot of those when we talk about handling social events a little later on. One area that's rife with potential pitfalls is practical jokes. Most of the time, they're fine. I've heard all kinds of stories, about people putting a velvet Elvis painting in another clerk's office, or sending a live lobster through the inter-office mail, or replacing a clerk's husband's photograph on her desk with a picture of Lurch. Pretty harmless stuff. Most people enjoy those kinds of diversions, and like working with people who come up with them. Humour is a great way to cut stress and keep people loose.

But use your—here's that word again!—judgment. If nobody else in the office is a joker, you might be stepping on thin ice. (And if you ***are*** a joker, it's telling you something important about the culture that might change your mind about working there after law school.) And sometimes even the most innocent practical joke can spin out of control!

CAREER LIMITING MOVE . . .

The partner at one large firm tells the following story: "When I was a clerk here, I thought my career was **over**. I go into my office one morning. It's a mess. I find a note on the desk that says, 'Keep your office neater.' It's signed by the firm's managing partner. I'm about to go and apologize to him, when I recognize the handwriting. It's another clerk's, a guy I'll call Carl. He's spending half his summer with the firm before moving onto another firm for the rest of the summer.

"At a clerk-versus-attorney basketball game the day before Carl is due to leave for his other firm, he decks a mid-level associate, sending him sprawling on the ground. I fake an e-mail to him saying, 'Sorry to hear about your conduct on the basketball court. Have your things packed up by five and security will walk you out.' I figure out how to remove my own name on the e-mail as the sender, and replace it with the managing partner's name. Carl immediately picks up on the gag, and shows it to people, saying ha ha, I'm fired.

"Carl moves on to his other firm. The maintenance guys come by his office to tidy up, and see the e-mail from the managing partner with Carl's writing across the bottom, reading 'I'm out of here.' The maintenance guys are concerned, and take it to the managing partner. He's confused, and asks the recruiting coordinator, 'Who wrote this?' As soon as I find out about it, I go to the managing partner to apologize. I explain it was a joke, but he doesn't get quite the laughs out of it that we had. The next few days are **very** uncomfortable.

If you do enjoy practical jokes, remember that you should never, ***ever*** do a practical joke that has a malicious element to it.

Large firm in New York has a summer clerk who pulled in a plum assignment: two weeks in Spain with a partner and associate from the firm, reviewing documents being produced for litigation. He developed a friendship with an associate from another firm who was also participating in the document review. They were both jokesters, and that's fine—but they seemed to spend more time talking and joking than reviewing documents. At one point during the review, he offered the partner a chair. The partner sat on it, and the chair promptly collapsed under his weight. The summer clerk's cohort from the other firm guffawed, saying, "Isn't that the chair **you** wouldn't sit in because it was too unstable?" The summer clerk just smirked. As one of the lawyers at the firm commented, "A career-limiting move if ever there was one!"

CAREER LIMITING MOVE . . .

Medium-sized firm. Mid-level female associate makes a point of inviting a different summer clerk to her house every few days, so she can get to know them. One of the male clerks is due to have dinner at her house one day. That day, flowers are delivered to her at the office. The card reads, 'I can't wait for our dinner tonight. I really want to get to know you better. Love—and the card is signed with the clerk's name. The mid-level associate is furious. She storms into his office brandishing the card, asking, "What the hell are you thinking about?" He stares at her, clueless—because he **is** clueless. The flowers aren't from him—they're from two other summer clerks, playing a joke on him. She could have a better sense of humour about it, but she doesn't. She fumes for days, and questions the summer clerks' judgment to anybody who would listen.

What if the tables are turned, and a practical joke is played on ***you***? Have a sense of humour about it, even if your feathers are ruffled. Realize that many times when people play a joke on you, they're telling you that they feel comfortable enough with you to be less formal. One junior associate told the story about her summer clerkship, where two associates told her, "Partner Harvey has a nickname. Not a lot of people know it. It's 'Spit.' He loves it when people call him Spit. You should call him that." Next time she ran into Partner Harvey—a rather formal man—she casually addressed him as "Spit." "Well, Spit, I'm almost done with the assignment you gave me . . . " She kept calling him that. He stared at her, incredulous. Finally, he said, "Why, might I ask, are you calling me 'Spit'?" She immediately realized that she'd been had. She explained what happened, without ratting out the names of the jokers, apologizing to him but not betraying any particular dismay about being the victim of a practical joke. The associates who'd pulled the wool over her eyes explained to the partner that it was their idea, and made sure he was OK with it. They spent the rest of the summer speaking glowingly of how she was a "good sport."

If the joke that's played on you is malicious, what you should do about it depends on who the joker is. If it's another summer clerk, drop word of it to other clerks or junior associates, without editorial comment. "Did you hear about what X and Y did to me? . . . " Leave it at that. If it's malicious, the firm will pick up on the inappropriateness and address it for you, so you don't look like the bad guy. If it's a lawyer or two who pick on you, and other people in the firm view the joke favourably, you've learned something very valuable about the culture.

21. What to do if you're swimming outside of your law school credential gene pool.

One of the beauties of interviewing a bunch of really great people when you write a book is that sometimes they'll come up with topics you never thought about. That's what happened here. I was interviewing a really delightful guy, and he was talking about the importance of making a strong first impression on your work assignments, and he added " . . . it's especially important if you're at a Harvard firm and you're not a Harvard guy." Hmm, I thought. I wonder if things are any different if you're either (1) not from a school your employer usually recruits from, or (2) your grades are lower than they usually demand?

Well, here's what I found out. Sometimes they care, and sometimes they don't. But what you have to do is the same regardless of how they feel.

First of all, you need to know that a lot of employers pointed out to me that clerks with lower credentials often turn out to be stars. As one hiring partner said, "Sometimes, if things come easily to people, they don't make an effort and they don't stand out. Last year we had a clerk who was a star from Day One. She wasn't the most brilliant clerk, but she sought out work, she was responsive and attentive and fun. She gave the proverbial 110%. She was our most successful clerk by far."

Also remember that even if you were #1 in the class at Harvard, if you turned in crappy work you still wouldn't get an offer. So don't tell yourself that anybody has a completely free pass—a little more wiggle room maybe, but not a lot. And the other thing to remember is that if you got the job in the first place by convincing the employer that your grades really don't reflect your ability, now's the time to put the pedal to the metal and prove it! Remember that you ***do*** have the candlepower to do the work or you wouldn't be there. As one career services director said, "You can't feel deficient and let it erode your confidence. You can get in your own way if you dwell on it. Go in there with your head held high!"

If you're surrounded by a whole bunch of fellow clerks who all went to distinguished schools and you didn't, give them credit. They did something you (and I, too) didn't do to get into those schools. And when I say give them credit I mean do it ***out loud.*** Say something like "Hey, I know you go to Harvard, you must have worked really hard to get in there." Which is true. You're paying an honest and well-deserved compliment. You're not suggesting they're smarter than you and certainly not that they'll be a better lawyer. But what you ***are*** doing is taking the possibility of one-upmanship off the table. Nobody will try to lord their credentials over you if you've already acknowledged how wonderful their credentials are. OK, maybe not nobody. But the kind of person who goes on ramming their superior grades and/or school down your throat after you've already said "uncle" is the kind of person who'll alienate everybody else, as well. So even if they're your colleague now, they won't be for long.

Needless to say, if your credentials aren't flawless, don't screw up at work. I mean ***really*** don't screw up. If they feel they're taking a chance on you, the first time you make a mistake, you won't get the benefit of the doubt. So prove them wrong, and do ***whatever*** it takes to turn in excellent work! After all, as one hiring partner dryly commented, "Clients don't accept C work."

One career services director summed up what you ought to do to overcome any preconceived notions about your grades or your school: "If they pay attention to your credentials once you get there, those in the firm who did not think they should hire from your school, or someone with your GPA, will be looking for something to carp on. They can't wait to say 'I told you so.' You have to be particularly conspicuous about working longer hours, turning in great product, and fitting in in every way, especially during the first four weeks of your clerkship, since much of this is an initial impression problem. After that, you can back off a little. You should also remember that whoever first interviewed you and recommended you to the firm will be looking for you to succeed, since their reputation is on the line as well. If that person gives you advice you need to ***follow it***, and if that person seems to be avoiding you, look out—they may be trying to put some distance between themselves and what may be perceived as a hiring mistake."

So if your credentials are wanting, go in and do what I would have told you to do anyway—blow them away with the quality of your work and your social savvy. Many lawyers told me that clerks they had who "felt they had something to prove" often turned out to be superstars, rather than people who felt they were so well qualified that they could coast through their summer clerkship on their resume as though it was a magic carpet. If you ***always*** feel like you've got to prove yourself, regardless of your credentials, you'll always be a better, more successful lawyer.

22. Being at the top of your class, and/or on Law Review, doesn't mean you can get away with doing anything you want.

No matter how sterling your resume is, trust me—law firms have rejected people who look better than you do on paper. It's possible to be great and ***still*** acknowledge your flaws, you know. Frank Lloyd Wright, the greatest architect of the 20th Century, freely admitted that the furniture he designed was hardly perfect. As he said in his autobiography, "I have been black and blue in some spot somewhere almost all my life from too intimate contact with my own furniture." Theodore Roosevelt said that even the smartest person in the world could only expect to be right seventy-five percent of the time. So even if you're a freakin' genius, a little humility would look good on you. "Humble confidence" is what employers want to see: You've got the raw material to be great, but you've got lots to learn.

A partner at one large firm said that "We've had clerks come in here figuring if they don't take a swing at the managing partner or make a pass at his wife they'll get an offer. It's not true. Park your sense of entitlement at the door." Another lawyer added, "Nobody's got room to be arrogant or smug. Your s*** ***does*** stink." Another partner at another large firm added, "When it comes to being a lawyer, summer clerks don't know ***anything***. Most summer clerks realize that and they're here to learn. But a few of them just don't get it. Don't come in thinking you're the cat's meow."

What's even worse is that if you've got great paper credentials and you get bounced by your summer employer, every other employer subsequently will look at you and think, "With those credentials, (s)he should have been a shoo-in. What's wrong with him/her that we need to know about?" Don't go there!

Follow the same rules that apply to everyone else as though they apply to you. Because they ***do***.

CAREER LIMITING MOVE . . .

Summer clerk, large firm, at the end of the summer he doesn't get an offer. He goes back to school on the West Coast, completely stunned. He goes to career services and sits down with a counselor. "I can't figure out what happened," he says. "I got great reviews on all my work, I didn't get drunk at social events . . . I just don't understand." She asks him, "What do you think **might** have happened?" He thinks a little bit about it, and then says, "I guess . . . I might have come off as a little bit . . . arrogant. But isn't that what they want? Don't they want to see that you're confident?" It turns out that when he got good reviews, he'd make comments like "I never expect anything less from myself" or "My work is always perfect." Not only did the employer find him arrogant, they found him **insufferably** arrogant—and it cost him an offer.

CAREER LIMITING MOVE . . .

Summer associate from a prestigious Midwestern law school, at a big firm in California. He's pretty pleased with himself. The first week he's there, he asks a senior associate out on a date. She turns him down. He's incredulous. He goes around saying unflattering things about her, how she was after him and he turned her down. He doesn't get an offer. Convinced that she had blackballed him, he gets his law school to call the firm and see what happened. They respond, "Sure, we weren't happy about that, but his work product wasn't all that great." He wasn't getting any other offers, and convinced himself that it was because this firm was badmouthing him all over town. He goes to his career services director and sits down to vent. He rants and raves, and finally says, "How dare they turn me down? I'm on **Law Review**!" At the end of her rope, the career services director blurts out, "Big f****** deal." He is ashen. He leaves her office. He returns two days later, and tells her, "Nobody ever talked to me like that before. But I thought about it, and . . . you were right." He'd been arrogant, but when he finally realized it, he turned around on a dime.

23. Don't assume that because you worked there last summer (or during the school year) that you're "in."

No, you're not. You're still being judged until the day you receive a permanent offer. Attorneys don't want to see you being an arrogant know-it-all with the "new" summer associates. You've got a leg up because you know how things work—but keep your confidence in check.

24. Greed may be good, but it doesn't play well when you're losing money for your employer.

If you're being paid more than a few hundred dollars a week for your summer clerkship, your employer isn't making money on you. They're making an investment in you. They hope that (1) you will go back to your school and say good things about them, and/or (2) You will come back to them permanently, and after a couple of money-losing years, you'll develop into a moneymaking asset. (I go into this in a lot more detail in the section of this book called "Econ 101.")

As I was interviewing lawyers for this book, I heard story after story about how ill-advised summer clerks occasionally abuse their firms' generosity. A piggy bank without a bottom! A credit card without payments! The lawyers went on and on and on. I would usually join in the lament.

"How could people be so short-sighted? What could they be ***thinking*** about? I would ***never***—" and then I thought back to my own summer clerkship with a large firm, and realized—not only ***would*** I. I ***did***.

The way I took advantage of my law firm's generosity was easily as stupid as any story I heard from anybody I interviewed. And since I'm going to tell you a lot of ***those*** stories, I might as well start with my own, the biggest, baddest boner of them all. And just to be fair, I'll treat it like all the rest . . .

CAREER LIMITING MOVE . . .

I spent my summer clerkship at a very large, incredibly generous law firm. Not only were we clerks paid more money than I'd ever dreamed of earning, the firm held fabulous social events and offered us all kinds of little perks. A cab home if we stayed at the office past five o'clock (five!). Dinner on the firm, anywhere in the city, if we stayed past six. Free tickets to any concert or sporting event in town. As many tickets as we wanted. It was an Aladdin's cave of goodies.

One of my summer clerk buddies, whom I'll call Buddy, and I couldn't believe the free tickets. We started out by calling the social director and asking for two tickets to the next day's baseball game. A messenger would come to our offices to drop off the tickets. We soon upped it to four. Then eight. Then sixteen. We were just doing it to see if they would really give us all of the tickets we asked for. We quickly learned that they meant it—we could have whatever we wanted.

Now, we were a little bit too thick to appreciate that the purpose of these tickets was for us to invite permanent associates and partners to baseball games so they'd have a chance to get to know us. We just thought—I don't know, we didn't think at all, I guess. It was like manna from Heaven.

Buddy came up with an idea we both thought was brilliant. "Hey—if they're just going to **give** us these tickets—why don't we go to the ballpark ahead of time and scalp 'em?"

And that's exactly what we did. We ordered sixteen tickets each, went to the ballpark, and scalped the tickets—all except for the two we wanted to use. We got a good price for them, because they were great seats, field boxes. When we went in to see the game, our section was full of the people to whom we'd sold the tickets. We glanced up at the firm's skybox, and saw some partners squinting in our general direction and nudging each other, as though trying to figure out who the heck was sitting in the firm's field box seats.

Aaah. Confession is good for the soul. We were never busted, but it was stupid anyway. Those baseball games would have been a perfect chance to get to know lawyers at the firm, and we blew it.

The bottom line is this: Be sensible with what your firm offers you. Whatever they're giving you by way of perks in the summer, it pales in comparison to an offer. If you blatantly abuse their generosity, you won't get that offer. And it's as simple as that.

CAREER LIMITING MOVE . . .

Summer clerks in the legal department of a Fortune 100 company. The company gives the summer clerks free housing that was very roomy and luxurious.

The clerks called and complained that they didn't get maid service.

CAREER LIMITING MOVE . . .

Summer clerk at a large New York firm. He goes to the recruiting department the day he arrives, and asks when he will be receiving his business cards. One of the recruiters explains to him as gently as she can, "Summer associates don't receive business cards. They are reserved for permanent hires." The summer clerk pitches a hissy fit and gives them a hard time. "But what about when I meet people at social events? What about when I'm at community functions? I **need** business cards!" The firm's recruiting coordinator pointed out, "He wanted to come off as hard-charging. He actually sounded like a spoiled brat."

CAREER LIMITING MOVE . . .

Summer clerk at a large firm. Takes her sister to a summer party hosted by a partner at the country club where he's a member. The clerk and her sister were too hungry to wait for the buffet to begin, so they both ordered food and charge it to the partner's account.

CAREER LIMITING MOVE . . .

Summer clerk at a large firm, wants to get all of the clerks together to discuss how their summer is going. Not a bad idea if it's conducted outside of the firm. However, this particular clerk reserves a conference room for the meeting, and orders lunch to be charged to the firm.

CAREER LIMITING MOVE . . .

Summer clerk at a large firm, finds out that other firms in town have just upped their summer associate salary. Sends e-mails on the office computer to the other summer clerks, rallying them to demand more money. "Just what we need," commented a lawyer at the firm. "A rabble rouser."

CAREER LIMITING MOVE . . .

Three summer clerks, large firm. They're researching in the firm's library. It's a hot day. They call the catering company that caters firm events, and order ice water to be delivered to the library. There is a drinking fountain in the hallway.

CAREER LIMITING MOVE . . .

Summer clerk at a large West Coast firm. Bragged to another associate, "I spent last summer at another firm in town so I could go through the restaurants that were rated 1-25 in the Zagat Guide. This summer I want to do number 26-50. I've already made it to number

37." The firms paid for all of these meals, of course. The summer clerk in whom he confided quickly spread it around, and soon the clerk was known solely as "the lunch guy." As the firm's hiring partner commented, "No matter how good his work was, he was just 'the lunch guy.' When we had a talk with him about it, he claimed other clerks were egging him on. He refused to take responsibility."

CAREER LIMITING MOVE . . .

Summer clerk at a Midwestern firm. One summer clerk had a birthday coming up. Another summer clerk wanted to take her out to lunch to celebrate. "A nice gesture," commented one of the lawyers in the firm. "We like to see that the summer clerks are making friends with each other." Problem: she came back with the receipt for the lunch, and tried to expense it. "Not such a nice gesture after all," the lawyer said. "We've got fifty summer clerks here. We have social events all the time. Birthday lunches aren't one of them. We offered to get one big birthday cake for every summer clerk with a summer birthday."

CAREER LIMITING MOVE . . .

Before the summer even starts, summer clerks-to-be for one large East Coast firm pelted the hiring partner with e-mails featuring salary information from other firms in town that they'd downloaded from the Internet. The hiring partner was so chuffed he sent them all an e-mail reading, "We've seen it, too. Please spend the rest of the semester paying attention to your studies." "Not the wisest move," he commented. "They come in with a mark against them before they even set foot in the door."

CAREER LIMITING MOVE . . .

One recruiting coordinator at a Southern firm complained, "Sometimes no matter what you offer clerks, it's not enough. We have a gym in our building. Last summer, it was being renovated, and it wasn't available. So we struck a deal with a local gym so that all of the summer clerks could have a free membership for the summer. One clerk called and beefed, 'That gym you got us isn't anywhere near where I live. Can you pick up the membership at a club closer to home?' When the hiring partner heard this, he said, 'If it's a close vote on this guy, he's not going to get an offer.'"

CAREER LIMITING MOVE . . .

Lawyer at a large West Coast firm: "We've got a huge summer budget. Huge. 'Do what you want!' is what they tell the summer clerks. But they don't mean it. Two summer clerks went out to dinner together and ordered a $700 bottle of wine. $700! Neither one of them got an offer."

CAREER LIMITING MOVE . . .

Partner at a West Coast firm, has to travel to the East Coast to prep the executive of a corporate client for a court appearance. The partner is going to take along a paralegal, and offers to take along a summer clerk so he can observe. "It's a real plum, that kind of trip for a summer clerk," the partner pointed out. The deal was that the clerk was to meet the partner and paralegal at the airport at seven o'clock Thursday morning to fly out. The partner and paralegal get to the airport on time. Seven o'clock comes and goes . . . seven thirty . . . the partner is frantic. He calls the firm. They track down the summer clerk, who has overslept after a hard night of partying. The clerk calls the partner on the partner's cell phone at the airport, telling him, "I'll get to the airport and take a later flight. I'll meet you there." The partner and paralegal take their flight as scheduled. The clerk shows up an hour later, books himself on the next flight—and upgrades himself to first class, on the firm's credit card. When he gets to the city, instead of taking the room that was assigned for him, he upgrades to a suite—again on the firm credit card. He cleans out the mini bar to the tune of $300. When the three of them are through with the client, the partner assumes the clerk will be flying back with him and the paralegal. The clerk says, "Oh, no. I want to stay a couple of extra days. I'll fly back separately." The partner is surprised, but says nothing. The clerk again upgrades himself to first class at firm expense. When the partner finds out about it, he's flabbergasted. "Sometimes," he ruminates, "you get the feeling that they're trying to tell us, 'Don't make me an offer. Please.'"

25. Don't think that the "one bite" rule applies to your behavior. One big bad boner can finish you off.

You know the old "one bite" rule about dogs. If you don't remember it, it's the rule that says you basically aren't liable for your dog's bites until you are on notice of the dog's "bite-y" propensity, which essentially gives you one "free" bite.

Well, when it comes to your summer clerkship behavior, don't make the same assumption. One ***really*** boneheaded maneuver ***can*** tank your offer. Now mind you, an awful lot ***can*** be smoothed over. But it's a mistake to take that too far. Turning in just one writing assignment citing a major case that's been overturned, offering your opinion to a client, one racist comment, anything that could be characterized as sexual harassment, a single disrespectful incident to a partner or even a partner's spouse—that's all it takes. As one hiring partner at a large firm says, "It doesn't take ten things to piss people off." And if you've done something horribly egregious to one partner, that partner may be willing to filibuster when the offering decisions are made, to make sure you aren't invited back. You ***do*** have a lot of latitude in the summer, but it's not boundless no matter who you are. Keep your behavior in check ***all*** the time.

26. Don't demand to be called "Mr." or "Ms."

It may be that the employer you're going to is quite formal, and ***everybody*** calls each other by their last names. If that's the case, you do the same. But let the attorneys decide for themselves what they'll call you. If you insist on formality, you'll rub lots of people the wrong way. As the hiring partner at one large firm commented, "We had a summer clerk who demanded that staff personnel address him as 'Mister.' That was an unforgivable mistake around here. We're an informal group."

27. Don't criticize attorneys, other clerks, or support staff.

"Joe is an idiot," "Sue never gets my work done on time," "Candy drinks too much." It's tempting to complain about the people you work for and the people who work for you. And it may seem as though you can make yourself look better by pointing out the inadequacies of other summer clerks. But as NYU's Gail Cutter advises, "It's inappropriate for you to comment on other people's work, habits or behavior. That kind of criticism reflects badly on you."

If you have a problem with a superior or staff member, and you can't resolve it yourself, approach the appropriate person and look for a solution. For instance, if you can't seem to please an attorney with your work, go to the recruiting coordinator, your mentor, or junior associates who've worked for the attorney, seeking advice on handling the situation in a positive way: "I don't seem to be giving Joe the kind of work he wants. You've worked with him in the past. Can you help me out?" They may come back with, "Oh, Joe's an idiot," confirming your original belief. But at least ***you*** didn't say it!

28. In the words of ZZ Top, "Keep your hands to yourself."

You may be a very friendly person, and that's a great quality to have. At the office, make sure that your friendliness doesn't express itself inappropriately. For instance, if you're in the habit of putting your arm around people you talk to, even if it's only a friendly gesture, you might ruffle feathers. One West Coast firm had a male summer clerk who lost out on an offer by putting a friendly arm around the shoulder of every woman he talked to.

It's even tougher if you have a naturally flirty personality. That can be very attractive socially but at the office, it can be poison. If people frequently misinterpret your friendly conversation as a come-on, go to your Career Services Office at school for help ***before*** you start your summer clerkship. They'll coach you on what's appropriate. If lawyers at work perceive that you're coming on to them, it can torpedo your chances there—even if you're totally innocent.

Finally, no matter how attractive a man you are and how many willing nubile young women fall at your feet, ***don't*** make passes at women at work. Maybe they'll respond positively, but if they don't, you're exhibiting really bad—here's that word again—judgment. No one wants to hire a potential sexual harassment suit.

29. Don't $*@($&#*%%!! swear.

It may be that around your friends, you swear like a sailor, and they don't care. There's nothing wrong with that. But it's a mistake to use foul language around anyone you work for, no matter ***how*** comfortable you feel with them. And if they swear, don't you join in! You're the one who's being judged, not them.

CAREER LIMITING MOVE . . .

Young female summer clerk. She got the job at the firm because she knew a partner socially. Before she joined the firm, whenever she saw him in a social setting, they'd be sitting around with a group of people, and a lot of times they'd tell lewd jokes and use bad language. When she got to work, she assumed that that kind of behavior was OK because it had always been OK around him socially. What she didn't realize that he was two different people, one person at work and one person socially, and she had to follow that lead. She told dirty jokes at firm events, and swore up a storm—f*** this and f*** that. As one lawyer at the firm commented, "We just couldn't take her seriously. We said to ourselves, 'Is this the type of person we want in the office? How will she seem around clients?' What students sometimes don't realize is that we're not just evaluating them on their work but also on their character and their judgment. The swearing, the jokes—you don't want a bad image! It's a mistake to jettison your good judgment for the sake of trying too hard to engage and fit in."

30. Think twice about the things you don't think twice about at home: the Internet, the phone, and e-mail.

The use of office goodies like the computer and the phone reflect heavily on your—here's that word again!—judgment. As a simple rule of thumb, assume that Big Brother is ***always*** watching you at the office and listening in on your phone calls. Don't say, send, or visit anything that you wouldn't want your employer to know about.

a. Internet usage

Your employer is a giant cookie. They have the ability to track your Internet usage, and according to the American Management Association, many of them do. You can't safely assume that your employer ***doesn't.*** What that means is: No visiting sites for yourself while you're on the clock. While a minute or two spent checking stock quotes or headlines is OK, hours downloading MP3 files or watching 24-hour Olgainherpanties.com is ***not.***

At one company's regional office, all several hundred employees were summoned to the cafeteria for a meeting. The President of the Company stood up and said, "It has come to our attention that some of you must not realize that we track Internet usage, and we consider hours spent at inappropriate sites a theft of company time." More than a dozen of the employees blanched. The offenders were fired on the spot and walked out of the building by security guards, in front of their stunned coworkers.

Inappropriate computer usage is particularly bad if you list as billable the time you spent visiting inappropriate sites or playing around. And I'm just as addicted to Solitaire as anybody else, but if an attorney you work with walks into your office and finds you playing on your computer, your reputation will suffer accordingly. Don't let it happen!

b. Phone calls

It's easy to think that with so many phones at the office and such a huge volume of telephone traffic, nobody will notice a long-distance call or two. But they will. Employers look at every long distance phone call to determine which client or account to bill. Many a summer clerk has been stunned to be presented with a phone bill for long-distance calls made at the office. It's not only expensive, but they'll be mad that you were chatting personally on ***their*** time. Everybody makes a ***few*** personal calls. But don't stretch the point!

c. E-mails

Assume that every e-mail you send and receive is being read by your employer. What does this tell you? First of all, pay attention to what other people at work use e-mail for. As William & Mary's Fred Thrasher says, "It's a cultural thing. Certain information is passed by e-mail at certain firms." Look and see what's sent, and ask if you don't know what's appropriate. It may be that the attorney you're working for doesn't check their e-mail regularly, and will be really furious if you send them an e-mail stating that you need a couple of extra days to complete the work you're doing for them. They'll just think you blew the deadline.

Secondly, ***never*** send a colleague an e-mail that you wouldn't want everyone in the office to read. There are plenty of stories about people pushing the "send to all" command when what they really want to do is say to Maria, "Can you believe what Cindy did to her hair?" Even if you ***don't*** "send to all," once you've sent an e-mail you have no idea who'll wind up getting it. You're releasing it to the world. It could be forwarded to anybody. So "be judicious with the use of the 'send' button," as Fred Thrasher recommends.

Thirdly—and this is going to seem really obvious, but you might need a reminder—if you send an e-mail from a certain account, people will assume it's OK to respond to that account. One career services director told of how she routinely gets e-mails from summer clerks asking about other jobs—from their employers' e-mail account! You don't want an e-mail coming to you at the office with a message line that reads "THAT JOB YOU WERE ASKING ABOUT . . . "

Finally, watch the funnies you receive and send, for a couple of reasons. It's very easy to glance at the first couple of lines of a joke and automatically forward it to someone else—or even worse, to forward it without even taking a look at it. I'm pretty sure that happens with at least some of the joke e-mails I get, because some of them are just appalling. I like raunchy jokes as much as anybody I know, but some of that Internet stuff—yikes, it's really disgusting. I know everybody who sends me jokes, and I know that a lot of what they send me is forwarded automatically, so they sometimes have no idea of exactly what they're sending me. You can't afford to put anybody you work with on the list of people to whom you automatically forward jokes. You need to be your own filter. More than one summer clerk has lost an offer by sending inappropriate e-mails.

Also, tell your friends to send you jokes and cartoons to your home computer, not your office. You don't want to be caught receiving raunchy stuff at work any more than you want to send it. On top of that, you might run into systems problems. One summer clerk told me he had a friend send him a cartoon file so large that it crashed the entire computer system at his office for several hours. "It took me days, and a lot of groveling, to get over that one," he said.

31. What to wear to work . . . and why "business casual" is a dirty word.

What you wear is a personal statement. At your summer clerkship that statement should be, "I want to work here, so while I'm here I'll dress the way you dress." As Kentucky's Drusilla Bakert says, "No matter where you work, you're more likely to get an offer if you dress like the attorneys for whom you work."

I talk about social dressing when I talk about handling social events. When it comes to choosing what to wear to work, on the other hand, here are a few rules to remember.

a. **Call before you start for guidance on what to wear.**

As William & Mary's Fred Thrasher says, "Ask! It won't be held against you. The whole idea of appropriate dress is out of control right now. Some employers are 'total casual.' Others don't have casual Fridays yet. The government has always been more casual than private employers other than litigators, but that means Dockers, not cut-offs. Nobody expects you to know any of this while you're still in school!" Don't flounder around in the dark. Call and ask. They'll respect the fact that you cared enough to find out before you showed up in your "I'm With Stupid" T-shirt.

b. **You don't have to blow your budget to fit in.**

Nobody expects you to stuff your closet with Armani just for the summer, no matter ***what*** the lawyers at work wear. Get a feel for the ***kinds*** of things that go over all right. There will be a range from casual to conservative, so head for the middle or err on the side of conservatism. Buy the best quality you can afford. At the end of the summer, you don't want what stood out about you to be your wardrobe.

CAREER LIMITING MOVE . . .

Summer clerk, large New York firm. He insists on wearing five-dollar suits from Goodwill to work . . . and they look like they're worth about that much. He shrugs off hints to "conform" by buying a "decent suit." Rather, he brags about how much money he's saving and how it's important "to be true to myself." As other summer clerks and junior associates grow more concerned about him, they offer to loan him suits. No luck. At the end of the summer, he's furious when he doesn't receive an offer.

c. **No matter what the dress code is, neatness counts.**

Everything's got to be clean, stain- and wrinkle-free. "Casual" never means "grunge."

d. Don't let your clothing sense slip as the summer slips away.

"Casual" doesn't mean "more casual" in August. As Drusilla Bakert warns, "Your employer will remember best how you looked at the end of the summer, not the beginning." Maintain your sense of what's appropriate until your very last day at the office. After that—heck, frost your naked body in chocolate, if you want. Just don't let anybody from work see you.

e. If your office is casual, bring in something formal and leave it at the office—just in case!

I've stressed to you the importance of taking advantage of "observational" opportunities, like client meetings and court-centered activities—and also the value of accepting social invitations from lawyers you work with. The rub with "business casual" dressing is that if you're dressed too casually, you can't meet a client or go to court or go to lunch at some ritzy places. The solution? "Have something at the office to change into when you need something more formal," says Carlton Fields' Kevin Napper. That way you need never miss ***anything*** you want to attend—and you'll be able to dress casually much of the time.

CAREER LIMITING MOVE . . .

Summer clerk, large Texas firm with "casual dress" Fridays. One female clerk took advantage of this policy to show up in ripped jeans. A female partner had arranged with the clerk to take her to a county women lawyers' lunch meeting that day. The partner was mortified. "I couldn't take her dressed like **that**," she said. "And apart from that, I felt as though it showed she had no respect for **me**."

f. If you clerk for a public interest employer, don't assume that casual dress is the norm.

Before your clerkship starts, take the opportunity—if your interview didn't present you with one—to observe the way your colleagues dress. As one public interest employer advises, "It's not unusual for public interest employers to expect jackets and ties. Pay attention to grooming! We expect you to dress appropriately, and to observe, or ask questions, to find out what the norm is."

g. **Don't assume that someone will tell you if you're wearing the wrong things.**

Unfortunately, lawyers are ***very*** reticent to say anything if they think you're dressing inappropriately. If what you're wearing is too tight, too bare, too bright, too casual or too cheap looking, don't tell yourself, "It must be all right, nobody at the firm has said anything about it to me." As South Carolina's Phyllis Burkhard says, "Unless you are ***way*** out of line, most lawyers won't say anything about it. They will just consider you unprofessional. They'll be disinclined to make you an offer or put you in a situation where you will meet clients."

32. Dealing with jerks, screamers, and other difficult people

If you're at a small office for the summer, you'll get to know all of the personalities, and whether they're nice or evil or a mixture, what you see is what you get. Decide if you can, and want to, work with them after you graduate. If you love the work or the location or ***some*** of the people so that you want to go back and work at the place regardless of a troublemaker or two, read the section on "Dealing With Jerks, Screamers, And Other Dwellers Of The Nether Anatomy" to learn how to handle people.

If you're at a large summer program, you'll find that the employer will make a special effort to keep you away from the jerks. As one recruiting coordinator commented darkly, "We know who the jerks are. We keep them far away from summer associates."

But sometimes you might find yourself working for a jerk in a large organization. They might circumvent the assigning attorney and come straight to you with work to do. Or, if your employer thinks you're cocky, your firm might throw you to a difficult partner "to take you down a notch," said one hiring partner. No matter how it happens, don't be too shocked if you wind up working with Simon Legree on a project. As one recruiting coordinator points out, "Be realistic. Not everybody is someone you want to spend a life with."

What do you do if you ***do*** get a real turd assigning you a project? First of all, read the section "Dealing with Jerks" that I mentioned a couple of paragraphs ago. If you can tame the evil beast, you'll look like a master of people skills. (In essence, the dealing with jerks section tells you to do your best, CYA, and keep calm.) On top of that, go to the hiring partner or recruiting coordinator, and ***wording it carefully***, ask for their help. ***Don't*** say, "God, X is such a buttmunch!" Instead, say something like, "Is it me, or is X challenging to work for? Can you give me some advice about doing work for him/her that (s)he'll like?" Their response will either be "Oh, grow up" or "Hmm. I didn't know. I'll investigate it." Either way, you've alerted other people to your plight without being negative, and that's exactly the way you want to handle it.

Never let a bad project with one attorney colour your impression of the entire office (unless the office is very small). Recruiting coordinators all know of summer clerks who endure a bad project and leave with negative feelings about the firm, and if they get an offer they reject it. Remember, your employer wants you to succeed and wants you to come back. As McGuire Woods' Pam Malone says, "The recruiting staff is invested in the success of the process. Give them a chance to help you!"

33. Don't let your partying interfere with your work.

Don't get the reputation as a partier. It's a fine line to walk. Your summer employer wants you to attend and enjoy social events—but not ***too*** much. They'll expect you to be at work, every day, fully functional. If this strikes you as a drag, remember it's not forever. As soon as you're back at school—party on, dude! But while you're there—everything in moderation.

CAREER LIMITING MOVE . . .

Hiring partner, large Midwestern law firm: "We had one summer clerk, a young woman, whose work product was fine. But when the hiring committee met to decide on offers, there were some questions about her. To be perfectly blunt, she was a party girl. We **all** like to have fun, but she was only willing to work if it didn't interfere with her party habits. For instance, she was working on a big case for a very senior partner. The partner asked her to show up at 9:30 a.m. on Saturday to help him out with a brief. She didn't come in until the middle of the afternoon, and even then, she was clearly hungover. She couldn't work at all. He told her to go home and dry out, and to meet him at eight o'clock on Sunday morning instead. He emphasized that he needed her help this particular weekend, because the brief in question was due in federal appeals court on Monday. That Saturday night, one of the partners ran into the summer clerk at a local nightclub. He took off at one a.m., and she was still there when he left. She didn't show up at the office at eight a.m. In fact, she came in at two o'clock. The partner was furious. "Sometimes," he commented, "an otherwise bright person just doesn't have the sense to figure it out."

34. You *can* maintain your personal social schedule during the summer—if you're *smart* about it!

During your summer clerkship, there's no question about it: you've got to fit your personal social schedule ***around*** your summer clerkship, not the other way around. But that doesn't mean you have to be married to your summer employer. It just means you have to be savvy about handling outside interests.

For instance, it may be that you have regular social activities of your own—maybe a bowling league, art classes, dance classes, whatever. There's no reason you can't do what you want ***as long as you arrange it so that your activities don't interfere with your work.*** It may be that you're facing a tight deadline and you miss a class or two or need a sub for your bowling league. You need to anticipate that. And even if you ***do*** have work that ***potentially*** interferes with something you want to do, it's not so much what you say to your supervisor but the way you say it.

Always approach your supervisor with requests to bail out as though they're doing you a favour. "I have a French class I usually go to on Thursday nights. Is it all right if I leave tonight by six o'clock?" It's the ***assumption*** of being able to leave that'll torque off your employer, not the fact of it.

CAREER LIMITING MOVE . . .

Summer clerk at a large West Coast firm. He's working in the corporate department, on a deal that is set to close. All of the attorneys are exceptionally busy. The clerk wants to play in a softball game. Instead of asking, he shows up, in his softball uniform, in the supervising attorney's office, and says, "I'm thinking of going to the game—is that OK?" The attorney, thoroughly aggravated, responds, "Fine. Go." He crucified the clerk in his evaluation. The attorney said, "I wouldn't have been so bothered, except he showed up in that goddamned uniform. And he didn't offer to come back after the game, knowing how busy we all were."

Social activities are one thing. Days off are another. Of course, if you have a wedding or funeral to attend, no one's going to argue with you taking time off to go. For graduations and events like that, Carlton Fields' Elizabeth Zabak advises you to "Give the firm as much lead time as possible." In other words, as soon as you know you're going, let ***them*** know.

As a general rule, you shouldn't plan on being able to take a week's vacation during your clerkship. You probably think that chomps, and if you've never worked during the summer before, maybe it does. But as Elizabeth Zabak points out, "Keep in mind that this is essentially a three-month job interview." Instead of risking annoying your employer with a request for time off during the summer, consider taking a week before school starts up again to satisfy your vacation jones.

If a particular week off is really important to you, it may be that if you approach your summer employer tactfully, you can do it. William & Mary's Fred Thrasher says, "If you've always spent a week at the beach house with your family in July, clear it with your employer before the summer even starts." Don't take the weenie way out and slink away unannounced. As Dave James of the San Diego City Attorney's Office advises, "There's a big difference between saying 'Would it be convenient if I were to be out of the office for these days?' instead of announcing 'This is when I'll be gone.'"

Similarly, if work comes up on the July 4th weekend—it's not ***likely*** to, but sometimes client crises arise and law is a client-driven business—you may find yourself canceling holiday plans. One law firm talked about a summer clerk who indignantly responded "'I can't work the holiday weekend. I have ***company.***' What she should have told us was, 'I have company flying in. Let me see how I can move them around.' If she'd said that, we probably would have scrambled to find a way to accommodate her. But her attitude made us not want to help her out."

CAREER LIMITING MOVE . . .

A small firm on the East Coast reports, "We had a summer clerk who made us ask ourselves, 'What's **with** this woman?' She had good credentials, but otherwise she was unbelievable. One of her antics was asking on Thursday if she could take off Friday and Monday to go to a beach house a couple of hundred miles away. We told her it was OK, but only reluctantly, because she had an assignment due Tuesday afternoon and we didn't think she could finish it in time if she took off for a long weekend. She called on Tuesday morning—from the beach house, no less—and said, 'Can I stay the rest of the week?' We wanted to tell her, 'You can stay the rest of your life!'"

35. Don't lie. Particularly about things that are easily verifiable.

Your reputation is the most valuable professional asset you have. Once people learn anything about you that impugns your integrity, you'll make them wonder, "What ***else*** are they lying about?" It's not worth it. Don't lie.

CAREER LIMITING MOVE . . .

Summer clerk, working for a large firm down South, mentions to a junior associate that he played football for a very prominent state university football team. She responds, "What a great fight song!" Throughout the summer she mentions the fight song to him. The summer clerk never sings it, and never even hums it, which she finds increasingly curious. At the firm retreat in August, the associate mentions to the firm's hiring partner that the summer clerk played football for X state university, but that he doesn't seem to know the fight song. The hiring partner is very curious and looks into the clerk's story. It seems he did play football at X state university, but not at its main campus—he played third string at a small satellite campus. The hiring partner didn't appreciate the deliberate misperception, and the clerk didn't get an offer.

36. As a summer clerk, don't choose sides in office politics.

We'll talk a lot about office politics later on. In short, no matter where you work, your office will be political. Unless you work alone, there's no way to avoid it.

As a summer clerk, the thing you need to know about office politics is this: "Don't choose sides," as William & Mary's Fred Thrasher advises. You don't know enough about the issues to make your own decisions. And besides that, you can't afford to make enemies as a summer clerk. You need all the support you can get to ensure that you get an offer!

37. Recognize that if you hate what you're doing, you only have to make the best of it for a few weeks.

Despite your best efforts in finding a great employer, you may in fact find that you've hitched your wagon to a slug, not a star. What should you do? Use it as a learning experience, and get what you can from it. And remember that the people you work with aren't fixtures. They could well go on to work at places you ***would*** enjoy, so if you make an effort not to alienate them no matter ***how*** bad a time you're having, you may find yourself open to opportunities down the road that you can't anticipate right now.

Comfort yourself with the thought that summers do end, so your agony is temporary. John F. Kennedy used to say that he could tolerate any pain if he knew it would come to an end. And in Alcoholics Anonymous, people are advised to "look past the drink"—look at the long-term benefits of restraint now. So if you're miserable at work, focus on a time when you *will* be happy, when the bad experience *will* be over. It's so much easier, and more productive, than wallowing in misery.

38. Be *careful* when you're asked to critique the summer program.

Don't think that if you make it unscathed to the end of the summer, you're home free. Many employers will have you fill out a critique of your summer experience. As NYU's Gail Cutter advises, "Be selective in the comments you make! Present any suggestions in a positive and constructive spirit. You are still under evaluation; here, your judgment, diplomacy and tact are under scrutiny. It's not unusual for firms to uncover disgruntled employees or people with perennially bad attitudes from critiques."

The same rule applies for critiques you are asked to do for any outside source. Be judicious about what you say; if your comments are too pointed or specific, they can easily be traced back to you. Remember where your bread is buttered. No outside source will decide whether or not you get an offer. Your employer ***will.***

F. Socializing—How To Get To Know People Without Shooting Yourself In The Foot

Work isn't all your summer clerkship is about. What you show your employer about your personality is just as important. They want to know a couple of important things in order to be comfortable making you a permanent offer. Do you get along with the people at the office? This query goes by a number of names. William & Mary's Fred Thrasher calls it the "Atlanta Airport" test—if they were stuck with you for hours at the Atlanta Airport, would they mind being with you? This compatibility is what employers are talking about when they talk about "fit." You've known all your life that you get along with some people more than others. When you're going to be spending lots of time at work, it's important not just for them, but for you as well, to feel comfortable.

Of course, there's more going on than "internal compatibility." Your employer will also be looking at your personality to see how well you'll represent them to clients, other lawyers, the outside world. Certain kinds of employers have even more specific requirements. If you're working at a prosecutor's office, they'll want to see how well you think on your feet. At a public defender's office, how do you interact with needy clients?

So when you interact with your summer colleagues socially, they're looking for a variety of traits and if you want to receive a permanent offer, you're going to exhibit those traits. Before you get chesty about this, I want to remind you of something very important: I'm not going to be telling you how you ought to behave ***all*** the time—only when you're around people you work with, whether it's lunch, a dinner at a supervisor's home, or an employer-wide event. Employers don't care about your personal life and whether or not you misbehave on your own time (although it probably wouldn't be a good idea to get arrested). If you want to put a sheep in a garter belt in the privacy of your own home, your employer doesn't care. The ASPCA might. And the sheep. But not your employer. So when I tell you how to behave socially, I'm not talking about your entire life—I'm talking about what's evident to your employer. So don't be resentful if you feel as though I'm trying to step on your freedom. I'm not. I ***am*** going to make sure that you don't do anything socially that stops you from receiving an offer.

1. Get to know as many people at work as you can!

You want to see if you'll like working with them, and you want them to know ***you***. It's hard to do that on the clock. Carlton Fields' Eric Adams said that as a summer clerk himself he made a point of highlighting every name in the firm phone directory of everyone he met. "I made a point of chatting with them at social events, weekly happy hours, observational groups with people I didn't know." If you're going to be a lawyer in a private firm, ultimately your business development skills depend on just this kind of behavior. Get a jump on it in your summer clerkship!

2. **Your employer will use social events to evaluate you. Don't *ever* let your guard down around colleagues.**

Don't ever, ever underestimate the value of socializing with your summer colleagues. Fred Thrasher advises that "just as many decisions are made about you socially as at work." John Marshall's Bill Chamberlain adds, "It's a bottom-line thing. They want to know, how will you deal with clients? In court? You're always being sized up." Kentucky's Drusilla Bakert agrees, "It's amazing how many students tank their summer not in the office, but at social events. Don't do ***anything*** that reflects poorly on your overall judgment or your interest in the organization."

McGuire Woods' Pam Malone points out that "The attorneys want to see how you interact with partners, associates, other summer associates, staff. They want to see if you'll be a team player. They want to see how you'll handle clients. Are you offensive? Too loud? Do you drink too much? Do you bother to show up at all? And if you do come, do you stand alone in a corner?" "Attorneys are forming opinions about you and evaluating you even in casual settings," agrees Willcox & Savage's Joni Coleman Fitzgerald. "If you're well known and well liked by the employer's attorneys, that can work in your favour," she adds. So the effect of attorneys' decisions about you socially can be the make-or-break element in whether you get an offer. That means that when it comes to socializing, "You don't want anybody to remember anything that stands out about you ***other*** than your work and your great attitude," says Milbank Tweed's Joanne DeZego.

SMART HUMAN TRICK . . .

Summer clerk at a large firm in Texas, goes to a party held at a partner's home, where there are a number of partners, associates, and all of the summer clerks. They engage in a lively game of charades, at which this particular summer clerk excels—he's quick with his guesses and acts out the phrases with great skill. After the game is over, one of the senior associates takes him aside and says, "Congratulations. You passed the creativity test." The summer clerk says, "What are you talking about?" The senior associate says, "The partners like to use the game to see how quick-witted the summer clerks are. You did great."

CAREER LIMITING MOVE . . .

Summer clerk at a large firm in the Midwest. The firm holds a lavish costume party, encouraging clerks to be creative with their costumes. There are pirates and people in togas, and one clerk even comes dressed as "Mrs. Palsgraf," from the famous Torts case, with a fake broken scale stuck to her head. Shortly after the party starts, one of the summer clerks walks in wearing a jacket on which he has written the words "F*** the Draft," just like in the freedom of expression case—but he didn't use the asterisks. Everybody at the party is in shock. The managing partner walks over to the recruiting coordinator and grabs her arm. "Don't let this guy out of your sight for the rest of the summer," he demanded. "God only knows what he might get it into his head to do."

CAREER LIMITING MOVE . . .

Female summer clerk at a large firm in a Southern city. She goes to a baseball game after work with a group of male clerks and associates. It's a very hot day. At the ballpark, the men get up to take off their jackets.

She stands up and, in full view of the crowd, removes her pantyhose.

Sometimes it's the employer that does something involving questionable judgment. The following story isn't really instructive at all—but I wanted you to see it. It's just too good to leave out.

STUPID EMPLOYER TRICKS

Large Midwestern law firm. Several years ago, they decided to give their summer clerks something a little "different," so they took them to a skeet-shooting range. Somehow, a gun went off accidentally and two of the clerks wound up having to be taken to the local emergency room to have pellets removed from their posteriors. Thereafter, the firm decided to eliminate from its summer schedule any events involving live ammunition.

3. **Don't treat social events as though they're typhoid carriers. Give your colleagues a chance to get to know you outside of assigning work to you.**

Your employer learns just as much about you by socializing with you as they do working with you. The fact is, if the only exposure a person has to you is in assigning you a writing project, they're not exactly getting a broad view of your personality. William & Mary's Fred Thrasher advises that, "they don't just want you to crank out briefs and memos." It's a mistake to tell yourself "I don't have to socialize. My work will speak for itself." You can't afford to lock yourself away in the library. As McGuire Woods' Pam Malone points out, "As a summer clerk, you aren't self-sufficient. Don't be self-focused. Get to know the other associates, both summer and permanent. They need to develop trust in you. Some summer associates come to work thinking, 'This is about me and proving myself. The other associates don't count.' They couldn't be more wrong!"

Hiding behind your work is also a cop-out. You don't have to be the most outgoing banana in the bunch to fit in. There are always personalities at work that you'll get along with. You've ***got*** to give them the chance to like you! One large firm rejected a summer clerk with very strong paper credentials. They said, "We do what everybody does. We look for a 'fit' in personalities. When you work the kinds of hours we work, you want to be around people you like. With this woman . . . we just didn't like her. Actually, it was more that she didn't seem to like us. So what was the point of making her an offer?" Another firm echoed that experience, talking about a summer clerk who was "Aloof. He didn't seem to enjoy it or want it. He avoided all of the social events. We didn't invite him back." A Midwestern firm talked about "Summer clerks who come in, they want to work twelve or fourteen hours a day. They get competitive. Being too competitive can hurt you! One summer clerk actually complained to our managing partner that he thought there was too much pressure to socialize. It was a strong black mark against him."

So whether you want to or not, you have to plan to spend at least ***part*** of the summer socializing with your colleagues, whether it's informal lunches or firm-organized social events. Whether you're not a social person, or you're loaded down with work, or you'd rather keep your social life private, bite the bullet at least ***sometimes*** so that people get an opportunity to know you and like you. As Hamline's Vince Thomas explains, "In a private firm, they won't get to know you on the clock. It's too expensive. It'll be at night or weekends. If you tell yourself 'I don't owe them time outside of work,' you're making a mistake."

Beyond giving lawyers a chance to get to know you, there are at least two other reasons to attend social events. First of all, as Betsy Armour explains, "Large firms spend ***lots*** of money to provide social events for summer clerks. They'll resent it if you seem ungrateful." Second, and most importantly, you need to get as many advocates as you can, so that when it comes time for the firm to make offers, you'll be a shoo-in. John Marshall's Bill Chamberlain stresses, "Don't just meet the people you work for! The more people you know, the safer you are. Some people are more powerful, and they'll shield you." Valparaiso's Gail Peshel agrees. "You can't keep your nose to the grindstone and avoid parties. You need to see partners so they know you and can vote for you."

CAREER LIMITING MOVE . . .

Summer clerk, D.C. firm. Very bright and capable, but he believed if he worked like a demon he could blow off everything else. He worked until the early hours of the morning on a regular basis on projects that didn't need it. He was very formal and serious, answering his phone, "Mr. Hale of Spade and Marlow" (not the real names). As the hiring partner said, "He overlooked the fact that the idea is to get to **know** people. You need to be a hard worker **and** a nice person, and give people a chance to get to know and like you."

4. If you work at an office with a huge number of social events, don't feel you have to go to *everything*. You don't . . . but ask for advice about what you can skip.

If you're at a large firm that puts an emphasis on entertaining summer clerks, you're going to be reminded of the fall of the Roman Empire. Parties, lunches, dinners, movies, concerts . . . it can be overwhelming. If you're not much of a socializer, you're bogged down with work, or you have a family, you may start wishing you were at a less generous employer. The good news is, you don't have to go to ***everything*** that your employer offers. But you do have to be savvy about what you turn down. As Arizona's Mary Birmingham advises, "Be up front! Don't be afraid to ask the question: 'If I can't do all of these, which should I attend?' Ask the recruiting coordinator directly, 'Does the firm expect us to go to everything?' If their schedule isn't overwhelming, they may expect you to go to everything. But if they go overboard, they're expecting you to pick and choose. Follow the recruiting coordinator's advice about which events you need to attend." The recruiting coordinator at one large firm told of a summer clerk who was told that the firm wanted to take her to the NFL draft. "That's the last thing I want to do!" she said. "I don't care about football. I want to be at home with my family." The recruiting coordinator told her, "There aren't a lot of events you really ***have*** to go to here, but this is one of them. It's a big deal to the partners."

If you are reluctant to socialize because of your workload, speak up about that, too. No large firm wants you to miss every social event because you've got too much work to do. By the same token, if you ***do*** have a pressing assignment, that comes first. Boston University's Betsy Armour advises that "The work does take precedence over play. There are real pressures and real deadlines. But when you're not sure about whether you can go to a social event or not, ***ask*** about it. Often a mentor or recruiting coordinator will run interference for you." The bottom line is, it's a mistake to miss social event after social event. For one thing, you'll miss out on a lot of fun. And secondly, you won't give attorneys a valuable chance to get to know you—and you'll deny yourself a chance to get to know them!

5. **If you play sports—tennis, softball, golf—play with your colleagues.**

   Many law firms participate in local softball leagues and/or charity golf tournaments. Employers recommend that you get involved in as many of these activities "as you have the energy for." Why? "Besides the schmooze value, you'll have fun and get to know the people you work with in a non-pressurized atmosphere. You'll be happier and you'll do better work."

6. **Don't continually blow off invitations to lunch or to the homes of lawyers.**

   Sometimes you may be tempted to turn down social invitations from associates and partners. After all, you can get tired of being on good behavior. You may want to go out with buddies from law school, your spouse, or other friends instead. But you shouldn't make a habit of saying "no." As Kentucky's Drusilla Bakert advises, "If you continually turn them down, they'll get the impression that you are not very interested in getting to know them. If you're asked out to lunch by one of the lawyers and for any reason can't accept, be sure and return the invitation later on."

   If a partner or associate invites you to their home, you might feel uncomfortable. You might feel you have nothing in common with them, and you've got other things you'd prefer to do with your time. Remember: it's just as much of a stretch for them. They don't know if you'll be a lot of fun or a real stiff. They're taking a risk, and you should, too. There are very, very few people who are truly unbearable socially, and you're unlikely to get a social invitation from one of them!

SMART HUMAN TRICK . . .

Large law firm and an African-American clerk. A partner in the firm invites the clerk over to his house. The clerk recalls, "The partner lives in a very white, very Irish Catholic town near the city where the firm is located. He wants me to have dinner with his family Friday night, and then go with them to a high school football game at a local Catholic high school.

"My first reaction is, 'Are you crazy? I couldn't care less about this game. I'm not Irish or Catholic. I'm not even crazy about the town where this guy lives. I already give the firm sixty hours a week. Isn't that enough?' But I think about it some more, and my better judgment takes over. So I accept the invitation. I show up with a hostess gift for his wife, I play with the kids. We have dinner, and then we leave the house to walk to the game.

"When we get to the stadium at the high school, I feel like I've stepped into a parallel universe. The only other African Americans at the game are the players. It's not my ideal night out on the town!

"But that night, they really made an effort to get to know me. They asked me about my family and where I grew up. They took an interest in me. That night taught me a valuable lesson: it doesn't pay to be aloof or reluctant. People will write you off. Don't give them a chance to leave a void where your personality ought to be. Create a reality for them. It'll pay off. That partner was a big supporter of mine after I spent that evening with him and his family. He invited me to a number of things during the rest of the summer. And when I had to turn him down for some of them because I had work to do or prior commitments, he knew I wasn't trying to avoid socializing with him."

7. Remember that employers are hierarchical. Be nice and respectful to everybody, but hang out with your fellow summer clerks and attorneys.

It's true that anyone's opinion of you at work can make or break you, so it's important to be respectful to, and appreciate of, everyone. As many lawyers point out, it's easier to replace a summer clerk than a treasured secretary. But having said that, watch who you hang out with on a regular basis. As South Carolina's Phyllis Burkhard says, "In an increasingly egalitarian society, it's upsetting to a lot of students to acknowledge that there are lines of status, particularly at large law firms. Although the runners may be the closest people in age to you, they shouldn't be your best friends at the firm. If you want the lawyers to see you as a lawyer and future colleague, you need to associate primarily with the other lawyers and summer clerks. Snobby? Probably. Realistic? Yes. If you keep your eyes open, you'll see that most of the time the lawyers lunch with each other or with the clerks, the secretaries lunch together, and the paralegals do the same."

8. Don't forget to RSVP invitations to firm events.

If you get a formal invitation to any employer-related event that requests an "RSVP," then make ***sure*** you respond in a timely manner—and that means a yes ***or*** a no. As Milbank Tweed's Joanne DeZego says, "Little things mean a lot. RSVP means 'no' as well as 'yes.' If you're asked to respond—respond!" There's a sound practical reason for this, which I happen to know because I was recently married. When you have a catered event, the caterer will charge you by the person. And it can get expensive, especially in the large cities. So having an accurate head count is crucial. If it's a party at an attorney's home, then it's just downright impolite not to give them an idea of how many people they need to provide for.

On that same note, if you say you're going to attend an event, go. If you don't, they'll pay for you anyway. And they won't be happy.

And if you need any further encouragement to make your social responses ship-shape, remember that the person you're torquing off if you ***don't*** respond is the recruiting coordinator, who inevitably has the partners' ears when it comes to considering offers. Not a wise person to annoy, ***especially*** not over something so easy to avoid!

9. If you're not sure what to wear to social events, ask someone at work. And if you *are* sure, ask someone at work anyway.

In an era when the words "business casual" strike fear in the hearts of young professionals everywhere, it's almost impossible to know what to wear to employer social events. There ***are*** a few hard and fast rules that I heard from lawyers everywhere. No flip-flops. No belly shirts. Nothing torn or cut off.

CAREER LIMITING MOVE . . .

One recruiting coordinator told me about a summer clerk who showed up at a firm event where the attire was "business casual" wearing a bowling shirt with an unusual pattern on the chest. The bowling shirt itself was out of place, but she was curious about the pattern, and asked him about it. "Oh, that," he said. "That's not a pattern. That's puke." "It was really bizarre," she said. "It was almost like he was **proud** of wearing this puke-stained shirt. Ugh."

CAREER LIMITING MOVE . . .

Summer clerk from California at a large firm in the Midwest. She wears flip-flops to a party at a partner's house. The partner, hugely offended (and vindictive), blackballs her, and she doesn't receive an offer.

CAREER LIMITING MOVE . . .

Female summer clerk, large Texas firm. At a firm party, the female lawyers showed up in tailored dresses or nice slacks and blazers. Clerk walked in wearing a big frilly pink dress, "perfect for a junior league tea, but not professional looking!" commented one of the lawyers. "She was bright and hardworking, but we couldn't make offers to everyone. In the end we chose the clerks, male and female, who looked like lawyers. She couldn't see that her 'little girl style' wasn't appropriate."

Aside from the obvious, there's nothing crystal clear about what to wear to events you've never been to before. One summer clerk told me about being invited to a boating event, where the invitation read "Attire: Casual." "So I showed up in what I considered casual wear—jeans, a T-shirt, beat-up tennies. I look around, and all of the lawyers are wearing pressed khaki pants, polo shirts, expensive top-siders. I thought to myself, 'They call that ***casual***? I'd dress like them for ***church***.'"

Don't make yourself miserable—and have people question your judgment—by showing up dressed inappropriately at a social event. Instead, ask a junior associate or the recruiting coordinator for what's appropriate. Nobody expects you to walk in the door knowing this kind of stuff, and it's actually a feather in your cap if you ask rather than show up looking out-of-place. As Kentucky's Drusilla Bakert says, "At social events, it's important for your appearance and behavior to be close to the norm. Don't underdress or overdress. ***Ask*** somebody! You'll feel more at ease if you're appropriately dressed."

10. **If you bring a date to an employer social event, make sure (s)he knows how to dress and act.**

As Temple's Karen Jackson Vaughn says, "As is the case in life, people at work judge you by the company you keep. As a general rule, if you don't have a spouse or significant other, it's best to go to these functions alone unless you know how your date dresses and behaves in social settings."

CAREER LIMITING MOVE . . .

Summer clerk at a large firm in the Midwest. He shows up at firm social events with a woman who wears very heavy makeup and tight, short dresses, and spike heels. She talks loudly and drinks enough to be noticed. Behind his back, the lawyers at the firm comment, "I wonder how much he pays for **her**?"

11. **Don't assume the employer will spring for *everything*.**

Particularly if you're spending the summer with a large law firm, you may get the feeling that they're a sugar daddy with a no-limit credit card. While formal firm events are obviously "on the house," when you go to lunch or dinner with partners or associates, don't make the same assumption. As Carlton Fields' Elizabeth Zabak says, "It may be that every lunch and dinner is paid for. But don't make that assumption. At least ***offer*** to pay. If nothing else, it's a good gesture."

12. Employer social events aren't the place to prove your beer-drinking capacity and your ability to belch the alphabet . . . and other alcohol-related advice.

Of all of the many thousands of stories I heard while researching this book, there were far and away more drinking stories than any other kind. I don't know if I've "heard it all," but I must have heard most of it. Summer clerks who get drunk at firm events and pass out. Or yak into the potted palms at a partner's house, or worse, directly onto a partner's lap. Or get so tanked they don't remember the event at all. Or have so much to drink that they have to be taken to the emergency room to get their stomachs pumped. One large West Coast firm recounted the story of a summer associate who got royally pissed at a firm social event, and decided to leave by himself. Unbeknownst to anybody else at the party, on his way home he tripped on the sidewalk, hit his head, developed temporary amnesia, and was picked up and taken to the hospital by a good Samaritan. "Of course, we were both embarrassed and concerned," said the firm's recruiting coordinator. "At the very least, if he was going to get that drunk, he should have gone home with a buddy."

I hate to be a party-pooper, but remember: these employer social events are parties in name only. You're still under the microscope. And there are a bunch of great reasons not to drink, other than the fact that in the morning you'll feel like there's a marching band in your head.

For one thing, as Georgetown's Abbie Willard points out, when you're drunk, you're out of control. A lot of the inappropriate sexual behavior I hear about (as will you, in the sections on Office Romances) is the result of demon rum. You might be able to corral your libido when you're sober, but after a few Kool-aid shots you're gazing into the eyes of a colleague's spouse and saying, "God, you're so f*****g hot!"

For another, you've got to take advantage of social events to meet the attorneys and their spouses, and to learn everything you can about what's going on at work, the good stuff that doesn't appear in official employer publications. You can't do that if you can't get your eyes to focus or your tongue to form itself around words.

Furthermore, as Gail Cutter suggests, you may be asked to go back to the office unexpectedly after a social event. So you want your fine motor skills in working order. And perhaps most importantly, what does getting drunk say about your judgment? It's hard to prove you're a responsible person capable of taking the fate of a client in your hands when you're stumbling around and plunging butt-first into the punch bowl.

"But Kimm," I hear you saying, "it's not that ***easy.***" I know the dilemma. You don't want to get blitzed, but you don't want to be a stick in the mud, either. No grown-up wants to feel like while they're having a beer or two, you're giving them the hairy eyeball. As one large firm hiring partner pointed out, "We wouldn't make an offer to someone who socialized every night and drank too much. But you ***do*** have to show you know how to enjoy yourself." At another large firm, the recruiting coordinator said that the junior associates egg on the summer clerks. "They'll say things like, 'I can't believe you're not drinking! What's wrong with you?'" Georgetown's Abbie Willard adds that "Even if the lawyers encourage you to party with them, they don't want you to be inappropriate." At one firm, some ***clients*** actually goaded the clerks into drinking at a firm event—and then complained to the firm when the clerks got stumbling drunk!

What you want to do is to hone some sleight-of-hand techniques so that people think you're matching them drink for drink, when you're not. Here's how it's done:

a. Confine yourself to one drink, and nurse it for a ***long*** time. Don't think that anybody's counting your drinks. As Hamline's Vince Thomas says, "It may be the finest gin you've ever had, but one is enough!" Abbie Willard agrees, saying "***You*** know your limits. You can have fun on one drink, without getting drunk."

b. If the alcohol is flowing ***really*** freely, and someone insists on bringing you another drink every few minutes, just take a sip out of the one in your hand, and when they're off retrieving another drink for you, surreptitiously ditch the one you've got now. "There's always a way to unload a drink without anybody noticing," commented one lawyer. "If it's an outside event, I just dump it on the grass. Or I put it on a table crowded with other glasses. If I'm really desperate, I'll knock it over, pretending it was an accident—but I make sure I don't spill it on anybody, of course!"

c. Get your own drinks from the bar. One summer clerk told of how he'd always go and get himself a sparkling water with a twist, because it looked just like a gin and tonic. That way, when anybody offered to get him a drink, he could point to the one in his hand, and say, "No thanks. Not now."

d. When they move on to doing shots, that's the time to excuse yourself. As Baker Botts' Bart Showalter advises, "Excuse yourself to talk to so-and-so when they start doing shots." There's no way to keep a clear head with even ***one*** turn at the vodka slalom.

e. You'll find that even if you use these techniques, the pressure may get more intense as the evening wears on. If you absolutely can't get away with just one drink, then alternate. As Georgetown's Beth Sherman suggests, "Have a beer then a water then a soda then a beer. Control yourself!" One recruiting coordinator commented that "When it comes to drinking, summer clerks start out with the best intentions. But then they're at a party, and the partners are drinking too much, the associates are drinking too much, and they start thinking, 'Everybody's drinking, why not me?' Don't fall into the trap!"

If you think this all sounds hopelessly dweebish, keep a couple of things in mind. One, it's not as though ***everybody's*** drinking. It might seem that way, but if you look around carefully, you'll find other people who are squeamish about getting drunk. So the overwhelming social pressure to drink is not as unanimous as you think. On top of that, what really bugs people if they're drinking and you're not is that they feel as though you're silently admonishing them. As Georgia State's Vickie Brown says, "You don't have to take part, but you ***do*** have to make them feel comfortable. Tell them, 'You go ahead!' in a hearty, encouraging voice. That'll alleviate the pressure on you."

13. Don't worry if you feel as though you don't "fit in." Personalities gravitate together. Give yourself time.

It's very easy to be intimidated toward the beginning of your summer clerkship, particularly if you're introverted. You might feel as though everybody around you is extroverted except for you. That's virtually never the case. It's just that noisy people are the ones you notice first. At any medium to large firm, you'll find a range of personalities. As Baker Botts' Bart Showalter says, "Personalities always tend to gravitate toward each other. Some clerks will get together and go to a baseball game. Others go to museums or to a steak dinner and bar-hopping until two in the morning." Look around for people who like the kinds of things you like—and you'll find them. Don't try hard to fit your personality into a mold that doesn't suit you. You won't like it, and other people won't feel comfortable around you. As Akin Gump's J.D. Neary advises, "If you tend to be yourself, you'll find your angels who will help you."

Of course, if you find that your social comfort zone is way out of whack with your summer employer, it may be that you're at the wrong place for you. In a large firm you'll find all kinds of attorneys, but if you're in a small office and everybody there is a boozer and you're not (or you are, and ***they're*** not), there's a cultural mismatch that might make it better for you to work somewhere else.

14. Don't forget who you're partying with when you go to firm functions.

It's easy to forget yourself at a firm function, even if you're ***not*** drunk. You might be at a country club or at somebody's house. People are laughing and joking and having a beer or two, and wham—all of a sudden you're feeling really comfortable, and you overlook the fact that the person you're talking to has some control over your career. Have a good time, but don't let down your guard. The most flagrant examples—other than drinking stories—involve playing games, where summer clerks let their competitive instincts drown out their common sense. If you're a professional-level card shark or championship athlete, ratchet it down a notch for firm events. And remember that while a desire to win is an excellent trait for an attorney, berating others for your losses doesn't fly.

CAREER LIMITING MOVE . . .

Summer clerk at a large firm. He goes to a partner's beach house, two hours from the office, for a firm event. He starts playing poker with the partners, and cleans them all out. High on his victory, he gets drunk as a skunk, pulls a cigar out of his pocket and starts to smoke it, and walks around jovially slapping partners on the back. As one partner commented, "Clearly at some point he'd decided he didn't want an offer."

CAREER LIMITING MOVE . . .

Male summer clerk, West Coast law firm. Goes to the firm's annual tennis outing, where he's scheduled to play against the managing partner's wife. He not only beats her, he whips her so badly—serving balls hard at her feet, bulleting balls toward her head when she's at the net—that she starts to cry.

CAREER LIMITING MOVE . . .

Summer clerk, firm event at a resort. At night, some of the clerks, lawyers and spouses get together for a game of charades. One summer clerk is on a team with a partner's wife. When he tries in vain to get her to guess a word, in exasperation he yells at her: "What are you? Stupid?"

15. Don't get chuffed if people don't remember your name. Help them out, and mention your name when you see them—even if you've met them before.

The recruiter at one large firm told me that "Summer clerks are way too sensitive about lawyers remembering their names. They have to remember that there are fifty of them, and when they go to a firm function, the managing partner might have met them once. I've had clerks come into my office after a firm party and say, 'I can't ***believe*** he didn't remember me!' I always want to say, 'When you guys first meet ***each other***, you have a hard time remembering names. Don't expect the lawyers to be better at it! Heck, the managing partner can't remember the names of all of the ***partners***, let alone the summer clerks!"

The fact that someone doesn't remember your name doesn't mean anything. Maybe they were preoccupied when they met you, or maybe they didn't catch your name the first time they heard it, or maybe they didn't use one of those memory cues designed to help you remember people's names (like repeating it back to them and using it in conversation to cement it in your mind). No matter what the reason, cut them a break. As Drusilla Bakert recommends, "When you meet lawyers at social events, make sure that they know who you are by introducing yourself if they do not greet you by name. For instance, when a lawyer comes up to you at a social event and gives you his or her name, that's a ***cue*** that (s)he's forgotten your name. Don't just say hello. Give them your name, also." Look at it this way: a lawyer can't give you a good review if (s)he doesn't know your name.

You could also try my trick. Whenever I see people that I've met before, if I notice that they seem to be struggling with my name, I tell a story that uses my name. "I was in this restaurant, and I said to myself, 'Now, Kimm, last time you were here the salmon smelled funny . . . ." There have been times when I've seen my conversational partner visibly relieved to be reminded of my name!

16. When you meet people, take a simple precaution to avoid embarrassing yourself in case you've met them before and forgotten about it.

Has this ever happened to you? You see someone at a social event, or a friend walks over with someone and asks if you know that other person, and thinking you've never met before, you say, "Nice to meet you." They respond with, "Oh, we've met before. Don't you remember? . . . ." ***Very*** embarrassing. It's happened to me a few times. And when you start at a new employer and you meet a whole ton of people in a hurry, it's ***very*** easy to forget whom you've met, and whom you haven't. Save yourself from embarrassment with a bit of wonderful advice from Boston University's Betsy Armour. "Instead of saying 'nice to meet you,' say 'nice to *see* you,'" she says. "That way, it's not specific to seeing them for the first time. It works whether you've met them before or not."

17. OK, I came to the party. What do I say? How do I approach people?

If you don't feel comfortable meeting people, you're not alone. It can be particularly intimidating when you're the summer clerk and everybody else is a "grown-up" lawyer. However, the way to handle social events is just the same whether you're a summer clerk or a new associate. I've gathered all of that advice together in Chapter Four, the section called "Social Graces, Or—How Not To Be Seen As A Pig, And How To Make Conversation With Anybody in Any Social Situation."

18. Remember that social events give you a *great* opportunity to help answer the question: Do I want to work here after I graduate?

When I ask law school graduates—and I've asked thousands of them—what they like about the place they work, the answer is almost always the same: the people. Interestingly enough, the people you work with, and how you feel about them, has a greater impact on your enjoyment than the kind of work you do. As Willcox & Savage's Joni Coleman Fitzgerald says, "Make no mistake about it—attorneys work very hard and put in a lot of hours at the office. You want to begin your legal career with a group of people whom you genuinely like and whose company you enjoy."

While working with people on assignments gives you some insight into their personalities, social events are ***tailor-made*** for that kind of research. Take advantage of those chances! As Georgetown's Jim Lovelace says, "When people relax and let their hair down a bit, that's the best time to get the inside skinny." Whether it's a firm event or a simple lunch or dinner with colleagues, ***listen*** to what they say, see whether the values they espouse agree with yours, and if they don't, see if they welcome diversity. If they're all hard partiers and you're a born-again Christian and they make fun of people who are "too straight-laced," you're not going to fit in. If they're all conservative Republicans, you're a liberal Democrat, and they uniformly deride "bleeding-heart liberals," your skin is probably going to crawl if you're around them on a regular basis. That's what lawyers mean when they talk about a "fit" between an employer and a new hire.

You can also learn a lot of valuable information about the employer. When people relax, they let slip all kinds of interesting information. Listen for tidbits about who's up and coming, and who's on the way out. Who's powerful and who's a blowhard. What the financial situation of the employer is. You need to be a sponge and absorb as much information as you can, so that when it comes to making ***your*** decision about where to work, you're making an ***informed*** decision.

19. Don't let the fact that they're telling dirty jokes seduce you into thinking you can do the same.

You know without my telling you that it's dangerous to tell dirty jokes around people you don't know. And if nobody else did it at your summer workplace, you probably wouldn't even ***think*** of doing it. The problem is when the lawyers themselves start telling off-colour jokes, and you know a whole flock of those.

Resist the temptation to chip in. Laugh your head off, ***even if you've heard the jokes before,*** and confine yourself to being a good audience. Nobody is checking out ***their*** judgment, but everybody's thinking about ***yours***. One recruiting coordinator told me about a summer clerk who matched ribald jokes with ribald jokes with a group of junior associates. "The very same guys who told the jokes with her blackballed her at the end of the summer!"

You get the point. Hold your tongue, and keep those jokes for your friends ***outside*** of work.

20. Don't ignore attorneys' spouses.

When you're at a social function with lawyers and you're trying to impress them, it's very easy to focus on the lawyers themselves to the exclusion of their spouses. Don't do it. Lawyers notice it and resent it. As Kentucky's Drusilla Bakert advises, "If you ignore a spouse while trying to impress the attorney, you'll do just the opposite."

21. Even if the event is really lame, at least act like you're having a good time.

Especially if your employer has arranged a lot of social events for the summer, some of them are going to be real dogs. Whatever you do, don't let on with your displeasure while you're there. It reflects poorly on your judgment. Why? For one thing, somebody who's got some say over whether or not you get an offer ***thought*** this event was a good idea, and if you loudly proclaim your disappointment, you're embarrassing them. For another, in a lot of situations, if you're bored, it's ***your*** fault. If you're at a party that doesn't take off, who's nailing your feet to the floor? Get an interesting conversation going with somebody. Make your own fun. And finally, your employer is always checking to see how tactful you will be when you have to deal with clients. You can't tell a client, "My God, this case is a loser!" You've got to put it more gently. Get into practice with social events that make you want to telepathically transport yourself anywhere but here. Laugh about it later if the event is a real bow-wow. But while it's going on, and while you're around people whose opinions count, keep it to yourself.

22. If you see inappropriate behavior by other summer clerks, think twice about reporting it.

There are naughty things to do, and then there are ***really*** naughty things to do. If you pal around with other summer clerks and they do something off the clock that does not impact their work, then keep your mouth ***shut.***

SMART HUMAN TRICK . . .

A group of summer clerks go out nightclubbing one Friday night. One of the clerks is from a very prestigious law school; the others are from a less distinguished school in the same city, and one of **them** is driving everybody else from club to club. As they are on the freeway going home, in the early hours of the morning, the clerk from the prestigious law school starts mouthing off about how good his school is. The driver swerves over to the breakdown lane, stops, and shouts at the braggart, "Get out of my f*****g car! You're an idiot!" The other guy responds, "But . . . but . . . " The driver will not be placated, and the other guy gets out. The other clerks in the car are stunned, and don't know what to do. They get out with the chastised clerk, and the driver drives away. So they're standing on the side of the freeway in the middle of the night. They start walking, and soon enough, a limousine driver with an empty limo comes along. He gives them a lift home. One of the clerks said, "We didn't know what to do. We talked a lot about it. But we figured, it doesn't have anything to do with the firm. It was outside office hours. It's just tensions between the schools. So we let it go."

G. Handling Secretaries, Recruiting Coordinators, And Anybody Else At The Office Who Isn't A Lawyer.

Everything in this section can be summarized in two sentences: Be nice to everybody at work. Assume that anybody's vote can make or break you, whether they're a lawyer or not.

In the permanent associates section, I talk an awful lot about support staff issues. Here we'll focus on issues relevant only to summer clerkships.

1. Handling support staffers in general. Remember: Their opinions *count.*

The last thing you want during your summer clerkship is to develop a reputation for being rude, abusive, demeaning, or demanding of the support staff. You may be better educated than they are, but every single employer I talked to said that if you can't play nicely at the office, you'll get bounced at the end of the summer.

For one thing, it's simple human decency to be nice to people. "Treat other people as you'd want to be treated," as William & Mary's Fred Thrasher says.

If the golden rule doesn't float your boat, there are a lot of selfish reasons to be nice to support staffers. At plenty of employers, support staffers get a vote on whether or not summer clerks will be invited back. As

Georgetown's Abbie Willard advises, "Secretaries will tell if a summer clerk has been abusive or demanding. And you ***won't*** get an offer. They value their support staff!" Willcox & Savage's Joni Coleman Fitzgerald agrees: "Support staff members won't hesitate to make their impressions and opinions of summer clerks know to attorneys and recruiting committee members." One hiring partner told me that at his firm, the partners make a preliminary decision about who they want to invite back, but before they make final choices, they call in the secretaries as a group, and ask, "Who do you think we should give offers to?" "Their vote is important," he said.

Beyond simple decency, acknowledge when a support staffer has gone above and beyond the call of duty for you. As William & Mary's Rob Kaplan points out, "If you're working your butt off on a tight deadline and you have paralegals and secretaries busting it for you, do something nice for them—give them candy or something like that." Stetson's Cathy Fitch agrees: "If someone at the office sets up a special reception or other social event, be it a support staffer or a partner's wife, send a thank-you note the next day. So many summer clerks treat social events as an entitlement. A ***lot*** of work goes into them, and a thank-you note recognizing that effort makes a big impression."

CAREER LIMITING MOVE . . .

Summer clerk at a large firm. He has occasional bouts of mistreating various staff members. The recruiting coordinator pulls him in and gives him a talking-to. He consequently turns on the charm and receives an offer. He decides to go somewhere else, but after a year or so, decides he wants to come back to the employer after all, and he reapplies for a job. The firm thinks about it, and remembering his temper problems with secretaries, decides not to reopen the offer.

CAREER LIMITING MOVE . . .

Summer clerk, splitting the summer between two firms. When he arrives at his second firm, he spends fifteen minutes with the recruiting coordinator, as she familiarizes him with the firm. He slouches in his chair, chewing gum, appearing totally disinterested in what she has to say. When she finishes, he gets up and spits his gum in her wastebasket, saying, "I gotta get rid of this before I meet anyone." She waivers on whether or not to report this to the hiring partner, but decides to do so. His response: "If they're going to treat you that way then we don't need them." His career at the firm was over before he worked on his very first project.

2. Handling secretaries/assistants.

It may well be that you don't get secretarial help at all during your summer clerkship. If you ***do***, it may be the first time in your life that you've ever had a secretary, and your first thought may be, "What the heck am I supposed to give him/her to ***do***?"

Relax. Nobody expects you to know how to handle a secretary. And anyway, it varies from office to office.

There are certain universal truths, however. No matter where you work, never ***ever*** expect a secretary to get you coffee! That ***really*** torques them off. Also, don't assume that they're called "secretaries" at all. In some offices, they're referred to as "assistants" and if you say "secretary," it'll get on their wick. When in doubt, it's always safest to call someone an "assistant" rather than a secretary. You won't offend anybody that way. The best way to figure out what to get your secretary to do is to ask around, either the recruiting coordinator or a trusted junior associate or any other mentor you have. McGuire Woods' Pam Malone says that "Secretaries generally help with time sheets, for instance. But it varies from firm to firm. Listen to the advice you get from people who are there already."

Incidentally, it's not always a good idea to figure, "If I do everything myself, I can't possibly misuse anybody." Some employers ***want*** you to learn the habit of relying on a secretary. They want you to get started delegating work, so that you focus efficiently on the work for which they can bill clients for your time.

When it comes to needing overtime help with secretaries, paralegals, word processing, or anyone else, NYU's Gail Cutter advises that you "Ask your mentor and/or a trusted permanent associate how much advance warning is typically needed to secure overtime secretarial help or word processing. The costs may vary widely, and you need to learn the firm's preference and policies. Ask your assigning attorney about the perimeters for using overtime or special support for a project. These additional costs will have to be borne by the client in most cases, and they can be substantial." If you run up a bill a client won't pay, it will reflect ***very*** badly on your judgment.

Also, keep in mind that if you ***do*** have a secretary, you're probably sharing that secretary with several other people, so you should be extra-careful about timing your requests. As Joni Coleman Fitzgerald advises, "Try not to make unreasonable demands, and provide plenty of time for a secretary to complete your work, keeping in mind those other demands your secretary has on his or her time."

SMART HUMAN TRICK . . .

Summer clerk finds out that both the firm's receptionist and his secretary have their birthdays during the summer. He brings in a flower for each of them on their birthdays. They're thrilled, and become strong allies of his. There's buzz all over the firm, "Pssst—where did the rose come from?" After that, he can do no wrong.

CAREER LIMITING MOVE . . .

Summer associate, large firm in New York. He breezes through the summer, on track for a certain offer. Throughout the summer he has shared a secretary with a senior partner.

Toward the end of the summer, on a Friday, he says to his secretary, "What are you doing this weekend?"

She responds, "I've got plans both days."

The summer associate nonchalantly responds, "I'll need you Saturday from nine in the morning until six o'clock." [Mistake #1—Never approach a secretary on your own initiative to do overtime. It's very expensive, and it's not your call to make! Ask a supervisor first.]

The secretary replies, "Well . . . my plans are pretty firm. Are you **sure** it's an emergency?" The summer associate assures her that it is.

She cancels her plans and shows up, as requested, on Saturday morning at nine o'clock. The summer clerk doesn't show up at nine . . . or ten . . . or twelve . . . or two. The secretary is terrified to leave, in case the summer clerk shows up. Finally six o'clock rolls around, and she gets up to leave. Just then, the summer associate rolls in. Without acknowledging her wasted day, he asks, "Are you leaving **already**?"

She sputters, "Yes. I've been here since nine o'clock."

He responds, "But I **need** you!"

She shrugs and says, "Too bad," and she leaves.

He calls her at home for the rest of the weekend. She leaves her answering machine on, refusing to answer his calls or call him back.

On Monday morning, the clerk races furiously to the recruiting coordinator's office and vents, "I can't get my work done around here. I'm getting no support from my secretary."

Just then, the recruiting coordinator's phone rings. It's the partner with whom the clerk shares the secretary. He says, "You wouldn't believe what happened." The partner has the secretary in **his** office, and he recounts the story over the phone to the recruiting coordinator. With the summer associate sitting right in front of her, the recruiting coordinator keeps a poker face, occasionally muttering, "Mm-hmm. Mm-hmm."

When the recruiting coordinator gets off the phone with the partner, the recruiting coordinator tells the summer clerk who it was, and gently explains to the summer clerk about the cost of bringing secretaries in on weekends, and general advice about the proper way of doing these things. She adds, "By the way, what was the emergency?"

The summer clerk responds, "I haven't done my time sheets"—the time he should have been recording on a daily basis the entire time—"all summer. I needed her help."

3. Walking a fine line with recruiting coordinators and mentors.

Recruiting coordinators and mentors are in a funny position. On the one hand, they're definitely there to smooth your way for the summer.

There is just about nothing you can't ask them: What to wear, who to talk to about a work-related issue, which summer events you can blow off and which you ***have*** to attend, tips for dealing with difficult personalities at the office, all the way to very serious matters involving ethics and harassment. As NYU's Gail Cutter points out, "The recruiting coordinator is an important ally and often has a strong 'informal' influence on whether or not you receive an offer."

But the fact that they're usually so friendly—for recruiting coordinators, it's a job that ***depends*** on great people skills!—often leads summer clerks to suspend their good judgment in talking to them. As William & Mary's Fred Thrasher says, "You can go talk to them, and they're often advocates for you. There are many issues they'll treat confidentially, but remember they still work for the firm!"

For instance, if you tell a recruiting coordinator about an incident of sex harassment, you're putting the firm on notice legally and the recruiting coordinator is ***not allowed*** to keep it a secret, no matter how much you may need a sympathetic ear (look for one ***outside*** of work to figure out your next move, unless you ***want*** the matter to be pursued). If for any reason you need to vent about anything involving your work, "Call your law school's career services office instead," says Gail Cutter. "Resist the urge to 'spill your guts' or 'let your hair down' with recruiting personnel."

CAREER LIMITING MOVE . . .

As one hiring partner reports, "Our recruiting staff members are told unbelievably personal things. 'I had an abortion,' 'I don't like this partner.' What the summer clerks don't realize is that the recruiting personnel are looking after the firm first and the summer clerks second. They're not appropriate confidants. You can't count on confidentiality. If you stayed out all night, and you came in in the same clothes you wore to the office yesterday, don't tell the recruiter, 'Hey, look! I was out partying all night!' Recruiters are very nurturing people, but they're not your Mom!"

4. Recognize the employer's law librarian is a *very* valuable resource.

If you go to an employer large enough to have its own law librarians, get out of your mind the image of a dowdy old lady in wing-tip glasses whose duties seem to consist entirely of putting a finger to her lips and saying "Shhhh!" Law librarians can make your life a ***ton*** easier, and make you look like a genius to your assigning attorneys. As Joni Coleman Fitzgerald says, "The firm's law librarian is a great resource for summer associates, especially in assisting with the proper use of computer research tools. Law librarians typically conduct a great deal of legal research for firms, and they can be invaluable to you in helping you get started with a research project."

Remember, you can't completely offload projects on librarians no matter how capable they are; you're there to be judged for ***your*** research skills. But when it comes to getting a push in the right direction, your law librarian can be a godsend.

H. Office Romances: Spend Your Summer Clerkship Getting To Know The Lay Of The Land, Not Getting To Be Known *As* The Lay Of The Land.

Aah. Summer and romance. They go together like—well, like "no" and "offer."

It's easy to see how office romance problems arise. ***Everybody*** understands temptation. Especially when it comes to summer clerkships. As one recruiting coordinator put it, "You can see why it happens. They're young. Many of them are very attractive. Sometimes they're in a new, exciting city for them. They've got money. They've got free time. If that doesn't get a person's libido going, I don't know what would." I've heard every combination you can imagine. Summer clerks with other summer clerks. With associates. With partners, single and married. With partners' spouses (a summer clerk at one firm ran off with a partner's wife and married her).

I hate to sound like a public service ad, but when it comes to sex and your summer clerkship, the overwhelming advice I heard from lawyers was: keep it in your pants. At least for the summer. As Hofstra's Rebecca Katz-White says, "If it's real, your feelings will last longer than the summer. Don't date attorneys. It'll complicate your offer." William & Mary's Fred Thrasher adds, "Recruiters always warn that there are so many factors involved in getting an offer, why take a chance on ruining your reputation with an ill-advised romance? You can create so much awkwardness, not just for you, but for the people around you." The "no dating" advice applies in spades if your employer has an anti-fraternization policy, forbidding intra-firm dating. It's not likely they will, but ***some*** employers do. If they do, don't let there be even a whiff of dating hovering around you. It's not because they can punish you for violating the policy—everybody agrees that those policies have no teeth—but it's a clear indication of their views on office dating, and how they'll look askance if you tiptoe through the tulips with a colleague.

If you can't (or don't want to) keep your gun in your holster for the summer, then resort to Option B: Do whatever you want, but be discreet about it. I've told you before, nobody cares what you do—they just care about what they see. If they're going to see you having a summer fling, make sure that they also see you showing good judgment about it.

With all of that in mind, let's go through the ABC's of Summer Clerkship Romances:

1. **Avoid spending too much time alone with another clerk or attorney. Even if you're not dating, people will assume you are.**

   Isn't ***that*** a bummer? You're good, you keep your hormones in check, but just because your summer buddy happens to be someone of the opposite sex, people at work think you're an item. It's like not getting to eat the chocolate cake and putting on the weight anyway. One former summer clerk told me that during her clerkship, she had hung around a lot with a male clerk from another school. "His girlfriend couldn't make it to the city for the summer, but he talked about her all the time, so there was no question there wasn't anything going on between us," she told me. "But one day I'm working with a partner, and he says to me, 'So has Dave proposed yet?' I couldn't believe it. But people had seen us together, and they'd put two and two together and gotten five. It taught me a lot about perceptions being everything."

2. If you *do* date somebody at the office, be discreet about it—but don't try to keep it a secret.

This may sound like contradictory advice, but it's not. What gets people into trouble with office romances isn't so much the fact of them, but rather their tendency to exercise what we'll call questionable judgment about the conduct of their romance. Remember, judgment is one of the primary elements employers want to see in you during the summer. That applies to the way you conduct every aspect of your life that you let them in on. Walk right down the middle: don't broadcast your love life, but don't hide it or lie about it.

I've heard about every kind of indiscretion you can imagine. Two summer associates going at it on the table in the library. Clerks getting their swerve on in a partner's private bathroom at the firm. In mail rooms. On copy machines. In cars in the parking lot. On a partner's desk during the firm's Christmas party. As Kentucky's Drusilla Bakert says, "If it's true love and you simply can't help but get involved with a lawyer or fellow clerk, be discreet about your relationship. Resist the urge to be conspicuous. Avoid any PDA's at the office or any social functions."

The flipside of being discreet is not being secretive. Don't even pretend that you'll be able to keep your romance a secret. People call it "water cooler osmosis." As one recruiting coordinator says, "Associates ***love*** gossip. ***Everybody*** will hear about it if you hook up." So what you're aiming for is the golden mean. If you're dating, don't tell anyone, but if they find out, or if they ***ask*** about it, don't deny it. As Drusilla Bakert says, "If you try to hide your relationship and you're found out, members of the organization may wonder what ***else*** they don't know about you."

CAREER LIMITING MOVE . . .

Large firm in the Midwest. The big summer social event is a camp retreat at a resort. The firm has one bunkhouse for female clerks, and one for male clerks. Two of the clerks bring a tent with them, pitch it between the two bunkhouses, and sleep there together.

CAREER LIMITING MOVE . . .

Large firm in the Southeast. Recruiting coordinator couldn't figure out why all of the male summer clerks were always fighting to take a taxi with one particular female clerk. Then one of the male summer clerks let it slip that the female clerk in question was in the habit of offering sexual favours to anybody who shared a taxi with her.

CAREER LIMITING MOVE . . .

Female clerk at a Midwestern firm. During the summer she has affairs with not one but three partners, all of whom are married.

CAREER LIMITING MOVE . . .

Male clerk at a East Coast firm. He has a fling with his secretary. She wants to continue the romance, he's not interested. She comes to work every day crying. The clerk is convinced that the firm will ask her to leave for behaving unprofessionally. Instead, the firm decides to get behind her, and doesn't extend an offer to him. "There are tons of law students," says the hiring partner. "But good secretaries are hard to find."

2. Make sure that you don't blow off other people at work to spend time exclusively with your honey.

Remember, you owe it to yourself and your career to get to know as many people as possible during your summer clerkship. If you are swept away on the wings of love, you'll be tempted to spend all of the social events gazing into your beloved's eyes. Don't succumb to that temptation. Treat social events as work that you have to get done ***before*** you can spend time with your sweetie. Apart from anything else, you don't know for a fact that your romance will last the summer. If you put all of your social eggs into your romantic basket, you won't have any friends for the rest of the summer.

I. You Can't Do Well Without Knowing How You're Doing: How To Get—And Handle—Feedback.

One of the biggest complaints summer clerks often have is the lack of feedback they receive from their employers. And that's understandable. When you're a student you get feedback on a regular basis in the form of grades. It's part of your professors' job to let you know, at least once a semester, how you're doing.

But your summer clerkship may not be the same. You may get a formal evaluation in the middle of the summer and just before you leave. You may have "readers" who give you detailed feedback on every writing project you do. Or you may get no feedback at all. At one firm, the recruiting coordinator told me that "If you're not told 'it's awful,' you're doing a great job." As William & Mary's Fred Thrasher points out, "A Post-It note on an assignment that says 'Good' is feedback, too!"

In the permanent associate section I'll talk a lot about feedback, because it has a huge effect on your career. Here, I'll focus on feedback issues that are critical to your summer job.

1. Remember that *all kinds* of evaluations determine whether you'll get an offer.

In Appendix B at the back of the book, I've included some formal evaluation forms to give you an idea of how your written work might be evaluated. What ought to strike you about those is the variety of elements that go into your evaluations. You should also know the evaluations cover more than just your work. As one recruiting coordinator points out, "The recruiting committee makes decisions on the basis of not just evaluations but any other information, as well. Senior partners may call and say 'At dinner last night so-and-so was very impressive' or 'X made a fool of himself. Watch him when he's around clients.' Or a secretary may say, 'I'm having real trouble getting what I need from this clerk.' All of those comments count as feedback as well."

2. Get feedback of some kind on every project you do.

It may be that your summer program is set up so that you get formal feedback on every project. But that's not common. And whether or not it's offered to you, you ***need*** to know how your work is being received, for ***every*** project you do.

3. If feedback isn't offered on every project, ask for it—the *right* way.

If you aren't offered feedback on everything you do, you need to take the initiative to get it. Here's the rub: You've got to ask for it appropriately. If you don't, you might find yourself worse off than if you didn't get any feedback at all.

First of all, watch your timing. As Kentucky's Drusilla Bakert recommends, "Catch the lawyer at a convenient time, not when (s)he's trying to meet a deadline." As Akin Gump's J.D. Neary suggests, "Try sending a simple e-mail that asks, 'Got ten minutes? I'd love feedback on my work.'" That way, when it *is* convenient to talk, the lawyer will let you know.

If you're at all worried about your timing—maybe the lawyer in question is ***always*** super busy, or just prickly to talk to—ask someone else at the firm how to approach him/her for feedback. As Fred Thrasher says, "Maybe you'll find that you'll get the best feedback from 'Bob' on the golf course as opposed to sending an e-mail."

Secondly, ask for ***specific*** criticisms. Say, "I really want to improve my skills. I know there's a lot to learn"—and go on to ask about whether you approached the issue correctly, researched everything necessary, whether the format was OK—you get the idea. Ask with a tone of voice that suggests you're looking for honest assessments, not a pat on the back. As Drusilla Bakert advises, "If you only ask generally 'Was my work OK?' the lawyer is likely to respond with a 'yes' and you won't have learned anything of value."

4. "Sound the ship" no later than halfway through your clerkship—so you can correct any problems that might sink your offer!

When a ship is "sounded," it's generally checked out to make sure the hull is intact. Well, when you're in a summer program, you can't wait until the end to see if everything is shipshape. If there's a problem—God forbid!—given enough time, you can almost certainly correct it. As

Drusilla Bakert recommends, "Early in the summer, consider approaching someone you know well—preferably a younger attorney, or your mentor if you have one—and ask if there's anything you could be doing to improve your performance. Ask the question in an open, positive way—"How could I improve?" or "What should I change?" That way you're more likely to elicit a helpful answer than asking in a way that makes it difficult for the attorney to be honest with you, like "I'm doing well, aren't I?" Or "I haven't made any mistakes, have I?"

5. Handling criticism

Ouch! It hurts. It ***always*** hurts. But the thing you've got to recognize is that the only way to improve is to have people tell you what you need to do better. You know that as a summer clerk you're not the best lawyer you'll ever be (at least, I hope it's not all downhill from here!). Incorporating improvements into your work is the ***only*** way to succeed.

Receiving criticism in a way that'll bolster your stock is an art, but it's an art that's easily learned. Here's what you need to know.

a. Remember that feedback only tells you one undeniable thing—someone's perception of you and your work. Don't take it personally.

Regardless of whether you agree with the criticism you receive, remember that it absolutely, positively shows one thing: The attitude of the criticizer toward you. And you can't argue with that. You're not an idiot, but if someone says to you, 'You're an idiot,' they're telling you what their perception is. Focus on ***that***, how that person might have gotten that impression, and how and/or whether you ought to change their opinion, rather than internalizing it as a statement of your personal worth.

b. Don't punish people who criticize you.

As Dave James of the San Diego City Attorney's Office says, "Universally, summer clerks say they want feedback, but many want only ***positive*** feedback. If you interrupt people who give you negative feedback and explain why their point is unwarranted, don't complain at the end of the summer that you didn't get as much feedback as you should have." If you're defensive, "your supervisors simply can't be fair, balancing constructive criticism and positive feedback. They have to accentuate the positive feedback and buffer the constructive criticism," he adds.

If this happens to you, not only will you be losing a valuable learning tool, but you'll make your employer think you're a cry-baby—to use the appropriate lingo, you "aren't mature." Instead, as Dave James recommends, "You can get more feedback by rewarding people who give it to you: listen intently, look them in the eye and nod affirmatively."

The recruiting coordinator at a large West Coast law firm: "We always sit down with summer clerks **immediately** if they've done anything wrong. We always tell them: if we have to sit you down and talk to you, don't get defensive! We'll say something like, 'We want to bring this to your attention now before it's a big thing . . . ' A few years ago we had a summer clerk who started yelling at us, blaming everyone including his mother and father for the way they'd raised him. He refused to take responsibility for **anything**. We were stunned."

c. Ask questions that clarify the criticism.

If you get a criticism like "This memo stunk," it's going to be hard to know how to un-stink the next one. Asking clarifying questions isn't being defensive. You need to ask for suggestions on what you should do differently so you don't make the same mistakes again!

d. Make a list of the criticisms you receive on each project and incorporate them into your next project.

Carlton Fields' Hardy Roberts says that "When you get criticized on your writing, write every criticism down on a list. You might hear 'You're splitting your infinitives,' for instance. Compare your next writing piece to the list, so you don't make the same mistake twice. The worst thing they'll be able to say about you is 'he learns well and responds to criticism,' and that's not bad. It means you have the raw material to be a great lawyer!"

e. How to respond to positive feedback.

Don't be arrogant! Instead, be aware that no matter how well you're doing, there's ***always*** a way to improve. Show that you ***recognize*** that! As Akin Gump's J.D. Neary suggests, "Even when you're told you're doing really well, ask, 'Anything I can do to improve? I'm glad I'm doing well, what ***else*** can I do?" You'll impress them with your graciousness, and your eagerness to learn.

f. Pay attention to *subtle* cues that tell you what's up!

It can be very easy to misinterpret criticism.

Sometimes you just don't want to know—or can't face it. But you ***have*** to. There's no such thing as a fatal mistake. There's almost always a way to resurrect an offer and even if you ***can't***, there's always a way to salvage a good recommendation from ***someone*** at work. So look criticism in the eye and deal with it.

One common mistake involves denial. As one recruiting coordinator says, "Sometimes when summer clerks hear a lawyer tell them something negative about their work, they'll say to themselves, 'Oh, they didn't really mean it.' That's dangerous. Lawyers don't ***like*** to criticize their clerks, so if you hear negative comments, assume they're for real."

And sometimes summer clerks hear a criticism but don't appreciate what it means. As one hiring partner says, "If they tell you halfway through the summer 'You need to do some great work' or 'You've got X number of weeks to improve' or 'We want to let you know about this before it gets serious,' what they're saying is, 'Right now, you wouldn't get an offer.'"

Listen also for casual comments in non-traditional settings. As Fred Thrasher says, "A comment in the car on the way back from court—that's feedback, too. Many lawyers don't like to give direct criticism. Listen to those comments!" Drusilla Bakert agrees. "If someone you work for makes an unsolicited comment about something you could improve, listen very carefully! (S)He's trying to tell you that you are making a mistake that you really need to correct in order to get an offer."

Pay attention to the source of a negative comment. Yeah, some people fell out of the wrong side of the crib and they've been crabby ever since. You still have to listen to their criticism, but filter it through the prism of their crummy personality. But if someone ordinarily very nice gives you some advice and/or criticism, take it ***very*** seriously. Many lawyers twist themselves in knots before they criticize, especially social behavior.

Sometimes the most effective feedback is never spoken at all. As the old saying goes, actions speak louder than words. If you're getting lots of interesting work and partners request that you work for them, that's the best feedback you can get—it may all be being said behind your back, but ***somebody's*** saying great things about you, says Hofstra's Diane Schwartzberg. By the same token, "If everybody else is busy and you're not, go to the recruiting coordinator and hiring partner and ask, 'What's going on?'"

J. What's *Really* In It For You? All Kinds of Tips for Figuring Out If This Is Really The Place Where You Want To Work

Your summer clerkship isn't all about you impressing the employer. Not by a long shot. It's your best opportunity for figuring out whether or not you want to work for this employer when you get out of school. As McGuire Woods' Pam Malone says, "It's a courtship. But ultimately, you're asking questions and making decisions. You shouldn't ever feel that your summer clerkship is one-sided. As a good consumer, you've got to do some judging as well!"

You need to use your summer to answer four basic questions:

(i) Will you like the work?

(ii) Will you like the people?

(iii) Are you comfortable with what will be expected of you?

(iv) Will this job help you get what you want out of your life?

If the answers to these four questions are all "yes," then congratulations! You've found the place to start your career. If the answer to any one of them is no . . . look ***very*** carefully at what you're giving up to make sure that you won't resent it. Because if you ***do*** resent it, you'll burn out quickly and perform badly.

We'll talk about all four of those questions. But we'll start out by talking about how you find the information you need to answer these questions—because it's not obvious!

1. Figuring out what the employer is really like

Inevitably, what you read in an employer's brochure or on their web site won't tell you what they're really like. All you find there is what they want you to know about them, the image they want to create. That's relevant, but it's far from the whole story. You've got to do a bit more digging to learn the truth.

If you're at an employer large enough to have a summer program, you've got a further impediment: You're not experiencing what life is really like working there. You can figure it out—I'm going to show you exactly how to do that—but it won't be laid out for you. Every employer with a summer program will tell you the same thing: they wish they were in a position to be honest with you during the summer, to give you the kind of work and the kind of hours and the kind of pressure you'd get as a new associate. They know full well that their retention rate for permanent associates would ***soar***, because new permanent associates would know what it's like and stay longer. But they're caught between the Scylla and Charybdis. If they're honest, they get slammed in outside reviews of their summer programs, which reward things like the interesting nature of the summer projects, reasonable hours and the social program, as opposed to the realism of the work. They ***want*** you to accept their offer, and just as importantly, go back to your law school saying good things about them, so future students will accept their offers as well. So that backs them into dishonest programs, which resemble summer camp more than a real lawyerly life.

The summer clerk at one prestigious law firm's summer program told me that at his firm, they made sure that the summer clerks never had to work past five o'clock or so. There were lots of social events to get them out of the office before dinnertime, and the junior associates at the firm joined them for some of these events. One day, there was a softball game between the summer clerks and the junior associates. After the game, everybody high-fived each other, saying things like "See you at the office tomorrow." The summer clerk said, "The clerks were given the definite impression that the junior associates were going home after the game. But it turns out that I'd left something at the office, so I headed back down there to pick it up. When I got there, all of the lights were blazing. I was confused. When I got to my hallway, I started noticing that a lot of the junior associates that I'd just played softball with were back at their desks, working away! One of them came out, and asked me nervously, 'What are ***you*** doing here?' I immediately got the impression that this was something the firm didn't want us to see—new associates working late at night. To tell you the truth, I was more angry with the deception than I was with the fact that they were there. It made me question what else they were lying to me about."

You could argue about this kind of deception, but there's no escaping the fact that sometimes it happens. No matter ***where*** you spend your summer, you rely on the same sources to get at the truth: your own observations, and what people there tell you when they're not speaking "officially."

a. To get the inside skinny, rely on the junior lawyers who work there.

In order to get the inside skinny, you've got to rely on the people who work there. As the law firm Wyatt Tarrant advises, "Establish relationships with associates. You can find out valuable, otherwise unattainable information about the firm from the junior associates." As this suggests, "You can't isolate yourself within the summer clerk group. A summer is a short time to learn the flavour of a place, but it can be done."

You have to watch and listen for cues when people don't realize they're giving them to you. Pay **special** attention when people have had a few drinks, or they're otherwise outside the office and relaxed. When people relax they let their guard down, and will frequently let slip things that they wouldn't say if they were sitting behind their desk at the office, fully alert.

b. **Watch what they do and how they behave. That tells you more than what they say.**

Almost any employer will tell you that they're collegial, that they're really just one big family, that they're interested in you balancing your life. Maybe they are. But if they tell you that, and then you observe that all of the lawyers call each other "Mr" and "Ms.," eat lunch in their offices alone, conversations at social events seem forced, they don't smile much, they work behind closed doors, and that the people who are applauded the loudest are the ones who bill 3,000 hours and make the most personal sacrifices, what do you suppose the truth is? Now mind you, I'm not saying that the truth is ***bad***. If you're more of a loner and you prefer formality—and some of us do—that might be your kind of place. My point is that you can't figure that out based solely on what people say. Watch what they do—because that will tell you what you'll have to do to fit in.

2. Will you like the work . . . and the clients?

Pay attention to the kind of projects that you ***would*** do as a permanent hire, your ability to change your specialty if you decide you don't like what you're doing, the kinds of clients you'll serve, and whether the work suits your emotional make-up.

When it comes to the projects themselves, be aware that at a medium-to-large firm summer program, the work you get is not the work of a permanent associate. As Dickstein Shapiro's Paul Bran says, "The summer program gives students an insight into the culture and atmosphere of a firm, but the work isn't realistic. It can't be. The goal is to give summer associates a variety of experiences. By necessity they get sound bytes. The work they do doesn't have the time pressure they'd have as permanent associates. So it's not a real working test."

To get an idea of what you'd be doing as a permanent hire, pay attention to people who are already in that role. Ask them about the projects they're working on. Find out about openings in specialties in areas that interest you, and find out how the permanent hires got there. Did they get hired directly into those areas? If they didn't like what they started out doing, how did they make the change—and were they allowed to change at all?

Another work-oriented issue to pick up clues about is the future viability of the employer. If you're working for the government, I'd say your odds are pretty good. But for private employers—if your employer isn't going to be around for any reason, then it doesn't matter how much you like the work. There isn't going to be any of it. No one will come out and tell you these kinds of things, but look for evidence of how vibrant the employer's business is. Are all of the major rainmakers getting long in the tooth? If so, who will replace them when they imminently retire? Do you hear rumblings that a major rainmaker is going to leave the firm? At one law firm, the atmosphere was so chaotic and the business was so out of control that they didn't even realize they had summer clerks who hadn't shown up for a week! If you start picking up clues like these, don't ignore them. They could have a significant impact on your early career.

When it comes to your employer's clients, pay special attention to whether these are the kinds of people/organizations you feel you can, or want to, represent. Remember: you take the king's dollar, you do the king's bidding.

CAREER LIMITING MOVE . . .

Hiring partner at large firm talks about a new associate: "We brought in a guy who'd been a summer associate with us. He expressed an interest in being a litigator, so we put him in the litigation department. One of his first assignments concerned a case that one of our clients, a gun manufacturer, was involved in. This guy refused to do the assignment, saying that he was morally opposed to guns. We couldn't believe it. One of my partners grumbled, 'He's not morally opposed to the paycheck.'"

SMART HUMAN TRICK . . .

Former summer clerk, large firm: "In law school, I bought everything we were taught about how everybody deserves representation, you have a professional duty to be a zealous advocate—I was down with that. Or so I thought. My first assignment was a contract case. The guy we were representing had been divorced several years earlier, and in his divorce, his wife had agreed to give up her claim to ten million dollars worth of stock that he owned as long as he would leave it in a will to their ten-year-old daughter. He was coming to us now and saying, 'Get me out of this. I want to sell the stock and spend the money.' Scumbag! But I bit the bullet and did the research, wrote up a memo with a strategy for him. Then my next assignment involved a school district that had fired a schoolteacher for refusing to do hall duty. It turns out that the real reason they fired her was because her husband, who had also been a teacher at the school, had brought in a teacher's union. They fired her to get back at him. So they wanted us to come up with an argument for them that her refusing to do hall duty was the same thing as being on strike. It was a pretty lame argument, but I did some research on it and wrote up something credible. Then we went to the hearing with an arbitrator, and I'm sitting there looking at this teacher. She's a nice woman, and clearly a dedicated teacher. And I thought to myself, 'What the hell are you doing?' I went to the john and cried and cried and cried. When we got back to the office, I told one of the permanent associates about it. He was totally shocked. He said, 'That bothered you?' I realized at that moment that to succeed there, I had to be more like him. I didn't think I could do it. When I got back to school in the Fall, I put a lot of time into looking at firms that did things I really thought I could get behind. I found a small civil practice and talked to them a lot before deciding to join them. I'm not always wild about the clients we have and the cases we take, but at least I don't feel like I'm doing something evil."

Before you take a permanent job with ***any*** employer, find out about the kinds of clients you'll be representing, the kinds of cases you'll take.

While I've heard very isolated instances when people have been able to be "conscientious objectors" with a particular client, you can't count on it. Even if your employer lets you opt out of a particular assignment, it'll call your judgment and commitment into question. This isn't just a matter of being selfish, by the way. It's human nature not to do well on things we don't like. If you hate your work, your performance will suffer, and that doesn't do any favours for you ***or*** your employer.

3. **Will you like the people?**

No matter where you work for the summer, you'll have an excellent opportunity to see whether or not you like the people you work with. As Dickstein Shapiro's Paul Bran says, "The real question for summer clerks to ask themselves is this: Do you like the people? Some people are constituted for doing battle, some for negotiating or researching. Find a practice where you fit in." The firm Hillis Clark agrees: "Although to a certain extent the type of work you do matters, it is largely who you work with that sustains you in the practice of law over time."

The kinds of questions you want to find the answers to are these: Are the people formal or laid-back? Are they hard partiers or not? Are they aggressive shouters or do they prefer a lower-key atmosphere? Are they the kind of people you'd like to chat with over the water cooler? Simply put—do you ***like*** them?

Keep a couple of things in mind. First of all, while some employers have a distinct "personality," there are offices where there's a huge range of personalities, and the key there is whether you're happy with that kind of diversity or whether you'd prefer to work with people who only think like you.

Secondly, be ***brutally*** honest with yourself about the kinds of people you like to be around, and how flexible you are. When I go around the country talking to law students for my *Guerrilla Tactics* job search seminars, I talk to a lot of students who say, "If I'm a Democrat and they're all Republicans, how am I going to convince them to hire me?" "If I'm gay and they're all conservative heterosexuals, how can I get a job with them?" "They all like to go out drinking together after work, and I'm a teetotaler. What should I do?" While there's almost always ***some*** way to get an offer, my first question back is: "Why would you ***want*** to work there?" Maybe you like heated political discussions and enjoy it when everybody is attacking you on your political beliefs, but if you don't, you won't like a place where everybody has values that are diametrically opposed to yours. And if you're gay, sure you can hide it—but are you going to ***want*** to do that in the long term? With the drinking—are you going to want to go to a bar every night with your cohorts, watching them get trashed while you sit nursing a Coke? Sometimes you've got to change your focus from "How do I make them want me?" and focus on "Do I want ***them***?" If you don't get along with the people, you won't enjoy working there. It's as simple as that.

While you're at work, pay attention to the little hints into how formal the place is. One lawyer told me about his first job, where he was sitting in the library in his suit and tie. It was a hot day, and he loosened his tie. A partner walking by admonished him, "***We*** don't loosen ties here." Do the name plaques on office doors say "Mr. Bunny" and "Mr. Duck," or "Bugs Bunny" and "Daffy Duck"? Do people formally address one another? Are the senior partners imperious and untouchable, or do they muck in? At one law firm, a woman who wound up being an associate there was walking through the office during her interviews, and came across a person she thought was a janitor, mopping up some spilled coffee from a hallway carpet. He got up and introduced himself. She was shocked to find that he was the firm's managing partner, and that since he'd spilled the coffee, he cleaned it up. Obviously ***not*** a formal place!

You should also watch for how people at the office treat each other. One lawyer told me that "I've worked for firms in the past where the attorneys would treat each other, associates, and staff members with disrespect. They were rude and discourteous. They'd shout and swear. If they're that way with each other, it's not likely they're going to treat you any better." On the same note, you might clerk at an office where everybody is very aggressive, and their normal mode of communication is to yell at each other. If you're not into that kind of verbal fencing, you'll hate it there. One lawyer told about starting his career at a firm that had high-tech clients and billed itself as a cutting-edge practice. But on his first day, he tried to run something through a laser printer outside his office, and was officiously warned by the secretarial pool manager that only secretaries were allowed to use the laser printer, and if he ever tried a trick like that again, he'd be fired. He got out of there in a hurry.

One lawyer told how "Our firm is a very introverted place. We don't wear our egos on our sleeves. We don't yell at secretaries. We had a summer clerk one summer who just flat-out ignored that. He stood out in all the wrong ways. He was abrasive. He'd make provocative, off-the-cuff comments. When we took the clerks on field trips, he'd make little comments under his breath. In a more freewheeling office, that would have been fine. But he wasn't paying attention. That's not the kind of behavior that got positive attention for the junior associates, and he should have paid attention to that, he should have gauged the environment before he started acting up. Partners started asking each other, 'Is this guy trying to deliberately jinx himself?' His mentor sat him down and said, 'Listen. You've got to ease up on this kind of behavior,' and explained to him what he'd done that had struck people the wrong way. The clerk was totally surprised. He said, 'I had no idea I was being perceived that way.' His only real mistake was not paying attention to the behavioral norms at the office and trying to fit in with those. Regardless, he didn't do himself a favor. He didn't get the benefit of the doubt on his work. He had one strike against him."

4. Are you comfortable with what will be expected of you?

Pay attention to what the new permanent hires in your office have to do. This is particularly true of business generation and hours.

With business generation, if you're at a private firm, you need to find out how soon you'll be expected to generate business. If you're at a large firm, business generation won't be an issue for several years; in the early days, hiring partners at large firms tell me that clients are more of a distraction than anything else! If you feel that your best asset is your sales ability and you're not so fond of researching and writing, you may find yourself strongly disappointed being a new associate at a large firm.

If you're at a smaller firm, you need to find out how soon they expect you to start developing your own book of business. Ask people there how they got started bringing in clients. Watch and see what they do, and see if you'd feel comfortable doing the same kind of thing. If you're very outgoing and you like being involved in community activities, you're born to bring in business and you stand to make a ton of money as a lawyer.

Another big expectation that you have to deal with is the chunk of time your employer will expect. In the section called "Econ 101," we will discuss the impact of huge salaries on hours. As a general rule of thumb, the more you get paid, the more you have to work. But that's hardly a hard-and-fast rule. Find out ahead of time, by listening to what people say and observing the hours they work, to see what the real time requirements will be. And be ***honest*** with yourself about the commitment of time that you're willing to make. This is an area where it's just excruciatingly difficult to be perfectly honest, largely because it's hard to tell the toll long hours will take on you until you actually work those hours. Your first reaction is probably what most people's is, when faced with the prospect of a big paycheck: "Hell yes! Count me in! Damn the torpedoes!" But working late nights and weekends wears you out faster than you realize. If you have children—or plan to have children—you won't have to miss many bedtimes with them to figure that you're making a sacrifice you don't want to make.

An issue related to hours is to check and see how much people at the office socialize together. If they go out a lot, do you like that idea, or do you prefer to keep your social life separate from your work? If you perceive that people at work spend a lot of time outside of work together, check with more people to make sure that you're getting an accurate snapshot of what's expected. It might be that the few people you've talked to are the primary socializers, or there are successful lawyers there who skip the socializing. What you most want to see is what's applauded—if people who keep to their own social lives get plum assignments and move ahead, then the socializing isn't a requirement.

5. **Will this job help you accomplish what you want to do with your life, whether it's professional opportunities or a good balance between your work and private life?**

You have to pay special attention to whether working with this particular employer after you graduate will give you the life you want. There are a few things to consider in relation to this.

a. **If you intend to have a family (or have one already), watch and listen to see how your employer deals with family issues.**

There's no question about it. Kids are demanding. Wonderful and demanding, but demanding. If you have them or intend to have them, will your employer work with you—or against you? No matter how you cut it, it's tough to balance work and family life, but some employers make it a lot easier than others. Look around the office to see how your employer feels about family issues. Do people speak in awe of the female lawyer who comes back to work two days after giving birth? How about the lawyer who rearranges his schedule to see his kid be the tooth in the school play? Do many of the women lawyers have children? (I hate to have to say this, but the number of men who have children isn't too relevant. Men have always had kids and jobs, so it doesn't tell you much about the family-friendliness of the employer—at least according to a lot of the female attorneys I talk to.) Do people on reduced schedules still get some choice projects? Do you see kids' art up in the offices of the lawyers? Do they have a room with toys in it where kids can play if Mommy or Daddy has to work on a weekend?

Listen to the lawyers there and see where they place their priorities. If they speak with favour of the lawyer who comes back to work right after a heart bypass operation, against the advice of his doctor, they're not going to look too favourably on you when you ask for paternity leave. Get a feel for whether what you feel important matches what your employer considers important! As a lawyer at the Williams Companies commented, "No matter how good a job looks on your resume and no matter how good the training, it's not worth it if you'll be unhappy. You can never get those years back—especially if you have a family!"

b. If you're considering coming back after graduation for particular professional opportunities, pay attention to what those opportunities really are.

Of course, it might be that what you want most from your job is opportunity, and the idea of hours or balance are things that you're willing to jettison. Then you want to look at the kind of responsibility you'll get, and when you'll get it. Look at what happens to lawyers who leave the employer. Where do they go? Does working for the employer enhance their future employability? If you want to be a politician, working as a prosecutor is an obvious steppingstone. Or perhaps there's a particular specialty that enthralls you. Get to know people in that specialty at your office, and see: Is that practice area vibrant and growing? Is it really what you thought it was like? If you're considering going back to your summer employer permanently because of the opportunities, make sure those opportunities are really there before you jump in!

K. WHAT TO DO IF YOU SPLIT YOUR SUMMER . . .

Employers are getting increasingly testy about letting clerks split their summers between two employers. Every employer wants a chance to get to know you and your work, and a ***whole*** summer is already short for that. If you've doubled down your bet for the summer, you've got to make an impression all the more quickly. Here are a few pointers to keep in mind:

1. Set the table to make a quick impression.

Talk to the recruiting coordinator and/or hiring partner and/or your mentor at each employer when you start to ensure that you get assignments from every attorney who really needs to see your work. And angle for shorter assignments so you get a lot of exposure quickly. As William & Mary's Fred Thrasher says, "The responsibility for getting broad assignments is yours, ***especially*** if you split your summer. Take the initiative!"

2. Don't let your second employer get a "diminished you."

As NYU's Gail Cutter advises, "Work to maintain your energy and enthusiasm during the second half of your summer, when summer associates typically begin to feel burned out."

3. Go into hyper drive to meet everybody you can.

Kentucky's Drusilla Bakert urges that you go to ***all*** social events at each of your summer firms, and circulate to introduce yourself to as many lawyers as you can. "Take the initiative and invite lawyers out to lunch," she says. Gail Cutter advises that you "Make a special effort to introduce yourself to a few more attorneys every day."

Particularly for your second half employer, "You want to be just as well-known and well-regarded as your summer associate colleagues who are spending the entire summer at the firm," says Gail Cutter. Drusilla Bakert agrees, adding, "Remember that at your second employer, the extra effort to get to know as many lawyers as possible is particularly important, because by then many of the lawyers will have stopped making an extra effort with the summer clerks." It's up to you to pick up the slack!

L. What To Do About Fall On-Campus Interviews If You Leave Your Summer Clerkship Without An Offer In Hand

It may well be that you leave your summer clerkship without knowing if you're going to be invited back or not. At many employers, offers don't go out until mid-September, when all of the clerks have finished their clerkship and the hiring committee (or other decision makers) have had a chance to meet. Particularly if you go to a law school with a pre-interview week, waiting to see if you've got an offer from your summer employer can make you miss a lot of on-campus interviews. What should you do?

It's a sticky situation. ***Everybody*** agrees that until you have an offer in hand, you should interview with other employers. No employer—at least, no employer who's speaking off-the-record—will expect you to cool your heels waiting for them to make a decision about you. As one career services director remarked, "I've seen firms push up their offer dates when they found out that their clerks were interviewing! And anyway, you never know when a firm will back off on the number of hires, or just be telling ***you*** 'September' because their first offers are going out to other clerks!" Paranoid yet? I hope not! You most likely will get an offer—especially if you spent your summer following all of the advice in this book!—but the point is, don't be a sap. Interview if you don't have an offer yet!

It's actually not the act of interviewing that will pose a problem for you. It's when your Fall interviewers ask you the question about your summer employer—and I promise you they will—"Will you accept their offer if they make you one?" This is the classic rock-and-a-hard-place dilemma! If you say, "Yes, I'd take it in a heartbeat," then the interviewer will wonder what you're doing in the interview, and won't appreciate being second best. If you say "No, I wouldn't," then you'd have to go into a long explanation of why not—running the risk that what you didn't like about the summer is also true for the interviewer's organization. On top of that, if you say you'd turn down the offer if you get it, that could well make its way back to your summer employer, drumming you out of an offer all by itself.

What you have to do is tread the middle ground. Milbank Tweed's Kathleen Brady suggests saying something like, "I don't know. I want to learn more about you. I'm here because I'm genuinely curious about your firm/company/agency." Hodgson Russ' Adam Perry agrees, suggesting wording like, "I haven't made up my mind yet. I really liked the particulars of your firm. That's why I'm interviewing with you."

Kentucky's Drusilla Bakert warns you not to say anything negative about your summer. Say, "I had a great summer at X but they haven't made offers yet. If I get an offer, I'd have to take it very seriously, but I'm interested in what you have to offer, as well." She says that if you get pushed on the genuineness of your interest in the interviewer's firm, "Say that you're dealing with the facts as they are right now, and the fact is, you don't have an offer yet and you're open to other options. What lawyer can argue with ***that***?"

M. You Drop The Ball, Or The Ball Is Dropped On You. You Don't Get An Offer From Your Summer Employer. *Now* What?

There's no question about it. Not getting an offer from your summer employer bites the big one. I know. It happened to me. I went from being perceived as one of the best and brightest at my school in the Spring of Second Year, to walking around with a professional Scarlet Letter on my forehead in the Fall. It just blew. There's very little that'll crush your ego like that kind of rejection. What made it even worse was the way they did it. One of the lawyers walked up to me, patted me on the head (!!), and said, "Kimm, some people just aren't good enough." Ow! Ow! Ow! Ow! Ow!

It sure seemed like the end of the world at the time, but in retrospect it really wasn't that big a deal. Of course, it's easy for me to say that now. It's kind of like talking about the extinction of the dinosaurs vis-à-vis the history of the Earth. We don't think about it much now, but it was pretty cataclysmic at the time. The point I'm making is that you have to get from the point you're at right now, to the point where you can put it in perspective. While I'm going to give you a bit of advice about that here, if you want to know more, check out my book *Guerrilla Tactics For Getting The Legal Job Of Your Dreams,* where I spend a whole chapter on it.

In a nutshell, here's what you should do:

1. Stay calm. This is not the time to tear people a new—ahem—excretory passage.

When you first get the word that you didn't get an offer, you're going to be massively pissed. If it's in the form of a letter, great. Go target shooting or drinking or running or vent with your best friend or whatever else you do to blow off massive steam. But if you get the news in the form of a phone call or person to person with your employer, ***stay calm.*** Take deep breaths. Don't betray ***any*** emotion to them, now or ever. For one thing, as NYU's Gail Cutter advises, "These people will serve as a primary professional reference for your third year job search, and even after graduation in your Character and Fitness affidavits for admission to the bar."

For another, don't let people who've rejected you see you crumble. No matter what went wrong during your summer, you can go a long way toward resurrecting your reputation by the way you handle the rejection.

Whether it's at the moment they reject you or after that, if you moan and scream and threaten and cry, they're going to think "Whew! Thank

God we dodged ***that*** bullet!" They'll pat themselves on the back for making the right decision.

But if you make a superhuman effort to suck it up, so they never see you sweat, you'll gain a lot of respect. And you'll make them wonder, what do ***you*** know that they ***don't*** know? It's kind of like breaking up with a boyfriend or girlfriend. If you've ever done it—and I'm sure you ***have***—be honest. When you break up with someone, don't you want them to be just a *little* upset? You don't want them to say, "OK, I understand, good luck." If you can manage your emotional response, you're outwardly acknowledging what the truth is: your future is within your control. I love the way Georgetown's Abbie Willard puts it: "When you're rejected, they're releasing you to the Universe!" The world is still full of wonderful jobs for you, minus one—that's all.

2. Take a deep breath, and talk to them to figure out what happened.

It may be that your employer isn't hiring anyone permanently, due to budgets or business prospects or ***whatever***. Or maybe they're not hiring anybody in the specialty you want. If that's the case, you're really not behind the 8-ball at all. No future employer could expect you to get an offer if ***none*** were forthcoming. You just need to make sure that the employer really will tell anyone you interview with in future that that was the reason you didn't get an offer.

But if your summer employer hired some or most of the summer clerks and you weren't one of them, you've got to find out what went wrong, whether it was a people-oriented problem or a work-oriented problem or exactly ***what*** it was. I'm not pretending this is ***easy***, mind you. As Gail Cutter says, "While it's very difficult under the circumstances, try to approach the situation calmly, rationally, and with a positive attitude. Try to understand what caused the firm's position. Don't confront those supervising attorneys who supplied negative reviews. Seek them out with an open-minded attitude and look at the situation as objectively as you can. Identify how you can learn from the experience. Regardless of who's right and who's wrong, if you approach a difficult situation in a positive way, you're most likely to secure the firm's cooperation and assistance going forward."

3. **If you missed the boat with a project or sparred with someone in the office, find references among people who *did* like your work, and did get along with you.**

   Drusilla Bakert calls this "damage control." She suggests that "If you didn't receive an offer because of a poor piece of work, or because you didn't get along well with people at work, find someone for whom you ***did*** good work, or ***did*** get along, and ask them to serve as a reference. You need to find at least two people. This is best done face-to-face. You should also confirm exactly what this person will say if called by a potential employer." Gail Cutter adds, "Getting a written reference on the employer's letterhead, though lawyers may be reluctant to give you one, gives you more control in later interviews than a telephone reference." She also recommends that you "seek out references that confirm your superior legal skills," because that's the primary concern future employers will have.

4. **Line up at least one other reference *outside* of your summer employer.**

   Stack the deck further in your favour by lining up another reference, from either a law school professor or another employer. What you want to do is to have references that are sufficient in number, and sufficiently glowing, to overcome any negative inferences of the non-offer.

5. **Acknowledge that what might have happened is that you just didn't want it.**

   Self-sabotage is a very common source of rejection. The fact is, if you really don't like something, it'll show. As B.U.'s Betsy Armour says, "If you seem indifferent to the employer, you won't get an offer. Sometimes it's just not the right place for you. Sometimes people respond to the royal 'should,' and take a job to fulfill other people's expectations." There's nothing wrong with that, but what you have to make sure is that you don't go back to that same well for another drink. If you're not emotionally suited to the work or you just don't fit in for any reason to a certain environment, don't go someplace else that has the same characteristics. If you didn't like it, be honest with yourself about it, and do some serious thinking about what you ***would*** like, now that you have the opportunity to explore anything you want. Go to your career services office and ask for help. They'll have a bunch of ideas for you. As Betsy Armour says, "Career services can help you pick up the pieces and move on."

6. **If you intend to be a lawyer somewhere else, don't *ever* say anything negative about your summer employer in *any* professional setting, be it an interview, a job, a professional function.**

   This is really, really easy to say and ***very*** hard to accomplish. Whenever you hear the name of an employer who rejected you, your temptation will be to chime in with a hearty "Those a**wipes!" Fight the urge if you possibly can, especially in job interviews. As one recruiting coordinator explains, "Sometimes things just don't work out, but remember that it is a small legal community and how you handle situations like this will be remembered for a long time. Don't burn any bridges."

7. **Do some practice interviews before you go for the "real thing."**

   When you've been rejected by your summer employer, it's easy to seem emotional and angry in subsequent interviews. To smooth out your interviewing skills, do some mock interviews with your career services office at school before you go out for the real thing. As Gail Cutter advises, "You have to be able to answer the question 'Did you get an offer?' easily and comfortably. You need to be confident and matter-of-fact in your interviews even though you may be feeling shocked, hurt and angry about the way your employer treated you. Work through those feelings with your counselor at school before you embark on any interviews."

8. **It's not the end of the world. It's the end of the summer. You've really only got one option: Get over it. And get on with it.**

   You can and will pick yourself up and have a happy life. My advice to you is to get on with it as soon as possible, instead of beating yourself up and ruminating about what might have been. For all you know, your future will be much brighter and much happier without working for your summer employer. It was certainly true for me, and it's been true for tons of other people as well. As Omar Khayyam wrote: "The Moving Finger writes; and, having writ; Moves on; not all your Piety nor Wit shall lure it back to cancel half a Line, Nor all your Tears wash out a Word of it." Accept what you can't change, and move on!

CHAPTER TWO

ECON 101—The Business Of Law

A. Understanding The Business of Law

When you become an associate at a law firm, you may not realize it, but your employer has a lot in common with a hot dog vendor. Why is that? They're both businesses. The hot dog vendor is peddling red hots, and your employer is selling ***time***: Your time and the time of every other lawyer who works there.

Maybe you've got the whole business thing down pat, and if so—skip ahead to the billables section of this chapter. I don't want to insult you. But from what I hear from partners at law firms everywhere, that's probably not the case, especially if you went straight from college to law school. ***Many*** partners complained that they felt new associates didn't understand the nature of the business they were getting into. If that sounds like you, well, here's everything you need to know. (I'm warning you up front that this is a drastic simplification, and as is always true in such a case, things won't match this at every single firm in America. But it's a pretty good approximation.)

OK. Here's how the business of law works. As a general rule, partners attract clients to the firm. When you, as a new associate, do work for those clients, the hours that you put on your time sheets generate reports which generate bills which generate revenue which pay overheads, associate salaries, and profits to the partners.

As you move up the food chain at the firm—faster, sometimes ***much*** faster at small firms, and slower at large firms—you are expected to shift your focus from work generation to business generation. At first, in a large firm, as one partner described it, your job is to "mine the ore." Clients are, in the words of another partner at a large firm, "kind of a distraction." You're a worker bee when you're a new associate at a big firm. At a small firm, on the other hand, the expectation for you to generate business might be almost immediate.

Those years when you're working your way up, you're said to be on the "partnership track," meaning that if all goes well, within a set amount of time you'll have the skills in place to become a partner. (If on the other hand, for instance, you're a contract attorney or staff attorney, you're not on the "partnership track," meaning that you'll always be on salary. You won't get work that's as sexy but you'll have less pressure and work fewer hours, and that can be very attractive.) After you've been on the partnership track for a while—again, longer at a large firm, shorter at a smaller firm—you'll be eligible for partnership. If the firm perceives you as a business generator, you'll be invited to become an "equity partner"—that is, you'll own a piece of the business and you'll be entitled to a commensurate piece of the profits. To become an equity partner, you have to buy your share. The price varies—at sizable firms it can be $35,000 to $100,000. If you aren't perceived as a business generator, you might be invited to become a "non-equity partner." In that case, everybody recognizes your value to the firm; perhaps you're an expert in a particularly useful area. Becoming a non-equity partner also gives you a chance to develop business generation skills. The big difference between an equity partner and a non-equity partner is that a non-equity partner isn't entitled to a cut of the profits. Of course, maybe you won't be invited to become a partner at all, but most firms will let you know that some time in advance so you can either polish your rainmaking skills, or—well, probably find a job someplace else.

What does this extremely simplified business model tell you?

1. As in all businesses, the people who bring in the business are worth more than the people who do the work.

Coaches of successful sports teams at colleges often make more, much more, than the college president. Why? Because big-time basketball and football teams bring in a ton of dough, and the big salaries are a recognition of that. It's the same in virtually every walk of business, including law. If you bring in business—you're a "rainmaker"—you'll do better than people who don't.

Does the idea of "selling" make your skin crawl? It shouldn't. You sell all the time without realizing it. When you convince anyone to do anything—whether it's to go on a date with you or to see the movie you want to see or go to dinner where you want to dine—you're selling. You're persuading. To get your job in the first place, you sold an employer on ***you***. Well, when you join a law firm, sooner or later those same skills are the ones that can rocket you to the top.

As the partner at one large firm put it bluntly, "If you want megabucks, generating money for the firm is the only way to do it. Bring the cash in! You're worth more money than the people who do the work. On top of that it's the only way to get autonomy. If you want independence, you need your own clients to be able to control your own schedule. And if you decide you want to leave, if you have a huge book of business, you can walk out any time you want."

Another lawyer, formerly an associate at a large firm, points out that "It's a mistake to think that 'if I just do good work every day, I'll make partner.' You're really a sole practitioner no matter where you work. If you can't make a book of business, you aren't profitable, you won't make partner no matter how much people or clients love you. They told me that after I'd been an associate for seven years. Until then, I thought, if I do a good job, I'll get rewarded with partnership. I had my head in the sand. You ***need*** to be economically self-sufficient as you move up. ***Pay attention*** as you progress. See what stars at your level are doing, in any year, whether it's your first or fifth or seventh. You'll find the people who succeed aren't smarter than you. They just pay ***attention***."

Another lawyer points out that "At bigger firms there are people with phenomenal technical skills but no people skills. You can't leave them alone in a room with a client. But there's a point where you reach the threshold of competency, and then it's about marketing. Because a brief is a brief is a brief. Clients don't want Hemingway (or Stein, for that matter)."

If this scares the tar out of you, remember that there's a bright side to it, as well. As one partner pointed out, "The way the business of law is right now, you can succeed in more than one way. It used to be that you needed to be a great lawyer to succeed. Now you can be a great businessperson and succeed tremendously. The scholarly aspect of it isn't so important. Good sales and social skills can make you great. There's room for people with a whole new set of skills."

The sooner you recognize that these are the skills that will ultimately be asked of you, the better off you'll be. A couple of years ago, after one of my *Guerrilla Tactics* job search seminars at a law school down South, a student came up to me to chat about an idea she had for becoming an entertainment lawyer. "Here's what I do," she said. "I go to the new talent night at local nightclubs. And when I see an act that seems pretty good, I'll go up to them afterwards, and say, 'Listen. I'm in law school. You can't afford a lawyer, and I can't represent you. But when you go to sign a contract, we can chat generally about the kinds of stuff you should watch out for. By the time I get out of school, maybe you ***will*** need a lawyer. And maybe it could be me." Did I think it was a ***good*** idea? I thought it was brilliant. She was thinking ten jumps ahead.

Do you ***have*** to think that way to be a successful lawyer? No. There are tons of jobs for all kinds of different people. But remember, law is a business—and the people who bring in the business are the most valuable.

2. Your firm has to make money on you to justify what they pay you, sooner rather than later.

I know that it's a popular pastime to get on-line and see who's paying what, who's handing out which goodies. It's a mistake to think that if somebody else is getting something you're not, that their employer is somehow more generous. These people you're working for, they're not Santa Claus. They're businesspeople. As Rhett Butler said in *Gone With*

The Wind, "I ***always*** get paid." Nova Southeastern's Pat Jason says, "The reality of work is not what you expect. If they're paying you, they're getting it out of you." A senior partner at one large firm said that "I got an e-mail from a student, saying he was turning down our offer and taking one in another city because they'd give him a new Rolex and $3,500 as a signing bonus, as though they were just doing it out of the kindness of their hearts. Then an associate came to me and said, 'I understand XYZ firm is paying new associates $10,000 more than we get.' I explained, 'Here's what you don't know. They're basing that starting pay on 2,200 billable hours and 300 quality non-billables, like bar work. We have a 1,800 hour billable requirement. For those last 700 hours they want out of you, you're getting $13 an hour. Think about what ***matters*** in your life."

A senior partner at another firm used a sports analogy. He said, "In the old days, if you were a top draft pick, if you had potential, they paid you a nice salary and you sat on the bench for two years learning the game. Now, with $5 million dollar salaries, they let you watch for two games and then boom, you're the man. It's the same with law firms. If they're paying you six figures to start, there's no honeymoon. You don't get to hand in a memo with even a typo on it. You've got to get out of the gate ***fast.***"

It's true that employers don't expect you to be a profit generator when you start out. At small firms, you've got to hit the ground pretty quickly; at large firms, they expect a two- to three-year investment in you. But they're not just throwing money at you in the meantime. As a rule of thumb, assume that unless you're bringing in business, the more money you make, the harder—meaning longer hours, not more efficiently—you'll have to work.

3. It's important that you understand *from the start* what's expected of you by way of business generation, and that you're comfortable with that.

At a big firm, you won't be expected to develop any business for years. It's not feasible with the kind of clients large firms serve. So you've got time to develop your skills without having to worry about netting business.

At a smaller firm, business generation is a much more immediate prospect. And while it can seem intimidating, it's very much a matter of getting involved in the community in a whole variety of ways, so that people see you and get to know you and like you and respect you.

In a nutshell, there are two ways to generate business: either bring in new clients, or get additional work from clients you already have. When it comes to bringing in new clients, "A lot of young lawyers say, 'I'll be active in the bar association,'" says Chicago-Kent's Stephanie Rever Chu. "But that's only useful if your business involves a lot of referrals. On the other hand, banks, investment companies, community groups, real estate brokers—those are more fertile sources. Serve on boards of community activities. Make presentations at senior community groups and nursing homes. Get to know real estate brokers with high net-worth clients who might get divorced if you've got a family law practice. Business can come from all kinds of sources."

Getting additional work from existing clients is something new lawyers don't often think about. The managing partner of one law firm talked about cross-marketing: "I worked my way through school at a shoe store. You can't make enough money selling shoes and nothing else. But if you can convince the person to buy the shoe polish or the laces, you can do a lot better. In a law practice, this kind of cross-marketing is a lot easier than bringing in new clients. Maybe you work for an entrepreneur doing their tax work. Then you see if they need estate planning. Other times, you use estate planning as a loss leader. You bring in big clients by giving them inexpensive estate planning, and then you talk about their business. There's more to selling legal services than glad-handing."

No matter how you bring in business, make sure that ***your*** expectations are in line with those of your employer before you start.

4. Billable hours count more than non-billables, no matter *what* the party line is.

Client matters are far from everything you handle at work. Pro bono, campus recruiting, panel participation, community activities, writing speeches for partners (or giving speeches yourself), penning articles for professional publications or the firm newsletter, organizing conferences for practice groups, working on committees—some firms consider those activities "billable" but they aren't, really. As one partner put it bluntly, "If one lawyer writes speeches and the other has pure billables, the billables rule." Another partner recounted that "As a junior associate I just focused on the 'total commitment' goal they gave me. I did a ton of community stuff and missed the billable goal. The harsh reality is that the billable hours number counts. Pro bono and bar activities are fine, but the hours you spend on billables and non-billables are not fungible. Billables are more valuable."

None of this is to suggest that you should ignore non-billable activities that your firm wants you to do. If you hog all of your time to focus exclusively on billables, you'll be viewed as selfish, a non-team player, and you'll be toast. But watch your ***balance***. If you're asked to join a committee to help pick out the furniture and carpeting for the firm's new office, it might be a lot of fun, but don't get swept up in it. The pro bono work you do may feed your soul, but watch how much of it you do; you can't ignore your moneymaking work at a private firm. One lawyer commented that "If the firm has a sixty-hour-per-lawyer pro bono target, you'd have to be an idiot to come in with two hundred pro bono hours, unless it's a ***very*** high-profile case or a senior partner is involved." The senior partner at one large firm told me, "If students think they're going to come here and make a six-figure salary representing the downtrodden, they're crazy. They're in denial."

The bottom line is this: no matter what your firm tells you about the value of non-billable work, look around. Look at the people ahead of you. See what they get rewarded for. And if you want to get ahead, do the same kinds of things.

5. There are *always* other options.

You may not believe it, but no law firm wants you to work for them if you're going to be miserable. There are millions of jobs you can get with your law degree. If you like the idea of being with a firm but don't want the hour and business generation pressure, be a contract attorney—you won't be on the partnership track and you won't get the sexiest assignments, but you'll have more time to yourself. Or go in-house or go to work in public interest. Or bag law altogether. Lots of law school grads find happiness being not-lawyers. Like—well—me, for instance. The bottom line is that nobody is looking out for your interests except for you. Just ***understand*** the nature of ***whatever*** job you get into—whether it's at a law firm or anywhere else. Look at what you'll get and the sacrifices you make to get it. It's the only way to be happy!

B. Everything You Never Wanted To Know About Billables, But You Have To Anyway: Including Squeezing Out More Billables Without Spending Even One Extra Minute Working

If you're in private practice, billables ***rule***. Your firm—and ultimately you—only gets paid if clients get bills reflecting the work done for them. As William & Mary's Fred Thrasher says, "Billables are a fact of life. You are peddling your time in a service-oriented business." Denver's Jennifer Loud Ungar points out that "No one cares that you used to be able to cram for an exam the night before and get an 'A'. In law, billable hours are the name of the game. You can't do that faster than anyone else."

Here's what you need to know about handling billable hours issues.

1. Clarify what's expected of you *up front*.

Virtually every private employer has a billable target for its lawyers. Smaller firms may not have a "quota" as larger ones do, but they ***do*** have some expectation of the hours they want you to bill. Ask what that is! Some employers say that their billable number for you is just a target, and not to worry if you don't meet it, they know that you won't be as efficient as a beginner. Well, you ***shouldn't*** worry, but you do have to be mindful of the fact that you ***do*** have to become a productive asset for your employer sooner or later—preferably sooner!

With billable targets, this is what you want to do. First of all, break the yearly target down so that you can see how many hours you are expected to bill on a monthly, weekly, and daily basis. Don't aim for the minimum;

go a little above it, for two reasons: One, you want to cover any contingencies you can't anticipate that may make your billable hours drop sometimes; and two, you don't want to develop the reputation for going for the bare minimum. At smaller firms, partners calculate minimum billables by looking at how much it takes to pay salaries, support staff, rent, other overheads, and allowing a 15 to 20% margin for uncollectables. They divide that by hourly rates, and come up with a break-even point. That's often what the minimum billables requirement represents. While a large firm isn't going to rise and sink on your particular hours, for a smaller firm, if you want to keep working, meet your minimum billables!

2. Find out up front what happens to the billable hours if clients don't pay.

Pepperdine's Carol Allemeier warns you to find out when you start what happens to your billable hours if the client whose work you're doing turns out to be a deadbeat. "At some firms, the associate takes the hit but the partner can still count the associate's hours for his/her bonus. At other firms, the partner and the associate split the loss."

3. Lunch isn't billable. Recognize that every hour you spend physically present is *not* a billable hour!

Maybe you'll do your billable target analysis and come up with a daily target of nine hours. You might figure, "OK. I'll come in at 8:00, take an hour for lunch, leave at 6:00. Cool!" Ah, but that it were true!

The fact is, there are lots of billable time killers, and sometimes there's nothing you can do about it—nor should you. Time that you spend in training sessions or recruiting for the firm or doing other administrative or community activities—these aren't billable hours, in the sense that no client is paying for them. Chit-chat with your colleagues is ***very*** important. You want to form good relationships with people at work, and you want to keep up with the inside skinny. But clients don't foot the bill for it.

What this means is that you'll work many more hours than you bill. Lawyers say that as a rule of thumb it takes between 10 and 12 hours to bill 8. If you find yourself consistently spending long hours at work and billing fewer than seven hours or so, NYU's Gail Cutter advises that you "try to get to the office early, by 7:30 or 8 a.m. That's well before most clients and their lawyers are open for business. You'll increase your uninterrupted work time while allowing for social events and conversation with people at the office."

4. **Keep track of your time with the ultimate goal in mind: Giving clients bills they'll pay.**

As Florida State's Stephanie Redfearn says, "The business of law firms is to bill hours and make money. If you don't bill it, they can't, either."

If you exhibit an early awareness of the importance of billables and accurate timekeeping, your reputation will soar. If on the other hand you keep sloppy or inaccurate records, you turn them in late on a regular basis, and you're generally cavalier about the importance of the billing function, you're toast. As Hofstra's Caroline Levy puts it bluntly, "If you're not vigilant about keeping your billing slips you're nothing more than a pro bono attorney." If you want to get paid, then dagnabbit make sure your employer gets paid! (Trust me, it's not easy to find a sentence where you can actually use the word 'dagnabbit'!)

Here's what you need to know about keeping track of your time.

a. **Keep track of every minute (yes, it's a pain in the butt). You'll find billable time you never realized you had.**

Every lawyer hates keeping track of billables. It drives some people to leave the business entirely. As a lawyer at Wyatt Tarrant points out, "Keeping track of every minute is very foreign—it's hard!" Boston University's Betsy Armour agrees: "Billable time is the single most difficult thing to get used to." And Georgetown's Marilyn Tucker adds, "Time sheets are a ***nuisance***!"

But the fact is you ***need*** to track your time, and the guiding principle is this: Don't put it off. We tend to procrastinate with things we don't want to do. As Stephanie Redfearn says, "Many attorneys ignore the drudgery, and two weeks after the fact find themselves trying to recreate what they did. It happens to everyone."

Everybody agrees that you should mark down your time ***at least*** once a day. If you only do it once a day, do it just before you leave, even if you've put in a long day. Think of it like brushing your teeth. You wouldn't go to bed without brushing your teeth (at least—I ***hope*** not). Don't leave work without marking down your time.

Keeping track more frequently is even better. Minnesota's Nora Klaphake says that "A wise partner once gave me a very helpful tip: At noon, before you go to lunch or leave for court or client appointments, take five minutes to account for your morning billing. Likewise, when you are ready to leave at the end of the day, account for your afternoon billing. If you are out of the office for the entire afternoon, when you get in the next day enter your billing for the previous day."

Betsy Armour suggests that you keep a pad on your desk and keep a running tally of your time (or keep your Palm Pilot handy).

The bottom line is this. If you keep an accurate tally of the time you work, you'll find that you actually wind up with ***more*** hours than you realized—without spending even one extra minute at work. If you wait, you'll forget a little time here and a few minutes there that are billable. It's the same thing that happens to overweight people who are asked what they eat in an average day. They forget about the broken cookies they "cleaned up" standing in front of the pantry. But when they keep a food diary of every bite that goes into their mouths, the truth comes out. You'll find the same thing with billables—you're cheating yourself out of the "broken cookie" billables if you delay recording your time!

Keeping track of your time isn't the only element of record-keeping that's time sensitive. You also have to turn in your hours on a timely basis. If your employer doesn't know about your hours, your minute-by-minute diary is useless. If you work on a real estate matter, for instance, once the closing takes place, that's it. If your time isn't in, the firm can't recoup. Even without a real-world deadline like that, you need to be timely with your billings. As Harvard's Mark Weber says, "Most firms run billing reports at the end of the month. It's near and dear to partners' hearts. Not getting them in on time will make people question your competence.

They'll think, 'If you can't do this little administrative chore, how will you get ***other*** things right?'"

CAREER LIMITING MOVE . . .

Junior associate at a medium-sized firm in California. She hates billing and puts it off as long as possible. She takes notes on what she's done, but she doesn't bother filling in time sheets and handing them in until the end of the month, when, in a panic mode, she gets it all done. She is bemoaning this to another associate, who says, "Didn't you know? Every senior partner gets a mid-month status report on billing." The associate realized, to her horror, that by failing to hand in billing reports promptly, she was getting a "zero" every month!

Incidentally, don't forget that copying, telephone calls, and faxes are billable items. NYU's Gail Cutter reminds you to ask about billing procedures for these services.

b. Don't mark it up, don't mark it down—just *record* it . . . but be aware of the hidden importance of efficiency.

As a new lawyer you'll probably be horrified by how long it takes you to do things. Relax. Everybody feels the same way when they start. As Stephanie Redfearn says, "If the senior attorney tells you, 'Oh, this is an easy issue' when she assigns it to you, and then you take twenty hours researching it, you'll feel stupid writing down all twenty hours. But bill it all anyway! Let your supervisors cut your hours if they think it's necessary."

If you're really concerned about taking too long on something, the best thing to do is to talk to the assigning attorney when you get stuck and look for more guidance. Remember, nobody expects you to be efficient when you start out. You're ***learning***. Carlton Fields' Jason Murray advises, "Go to the assigning attorney and say, 'You thought this would take two hours, I've spent four hours on it and I'm not close to done. Am I interpreting this right?'"

If you finish an assignment before the time problem strikes you, Carlton Fields' Kevin Napper recommends that you include a note with your time sheets saying, "It took me longer than I thought it would and here's why." If you went off on a tangent, say it. But bill all your time! At ***worst*** you'll be perceived as a hard worker.

If you don't bill all your time, a couple of things can happen. Number one, if people see you at the office all the time but you only bill five hours a day, they'll wonder what's up. For another, if your time sheets show low hours, they'll assume you're not overloaded and pile on even ***more*** work. Yikes! And if you feel so guilty about taking too long that you take work home with you without anybody knowing, you'll have ***no*** private life and you'll burn out in a hurry. ***Nobody*** wants that to happen to you!

The flipside of marking down your hours is even worse. You may get the idea that taking things slowly and running up your billables is a good idea. More billables, more money, right? Nope. Partners know that clients won't pay inflated bills. They'll just cut your time to what it should have been. As lawyers at Barnes & Thornburg point out, "Big billables where they're unnecessary is a negative, not a positive. Don't run up billable hours needlessly."

And don't ever, ***ever*** inflate your time, claiming you worked hours that you didn't work. ***Ever.*** It's a serious ethical breach and if you're busted, you will be cashiered on the spot. It's not worth the risk.

CAREER LIMITING MOVE . . .

Junior associate, whom we'll call Benedict Arnold, working at a large Midwestern firm. He and five other associates go out of town for a week on a document review. They work together all day and party together at night.

Shortly after they get back to the office, one of the other associates is called to the supervising attorney's office. "When you were in X city, did you work with Benedict Arnold every day?"

The associate says he did.

"Did he work by himself at all?" the supervising attorney continues.

The associate responds, "No, we all worked together."

The supervising attorney says "Thank you."

As the associate prepares to leave the supervising attorney's office, he says "Just out of curiosity—why do you ask?"

Supervising attorney: "Because all of the rest of you billed ten hours a day. He billed fourteen."

Busted!

Even if you're not expected to be efficient when you start, you need to know that it ***does*** count, and you should try to become efficient as soon as possible (don't worry—it gets much, much easier as you get more experience under your belt). There are two good reasons why: bonuses and "realization rates."

As the partner at one firm points out, "There's such a thing as 'quality' billing. A letter is worth 0.2 hours whether you took twelve minutes or an hour to write it. When you're new it can take you half an hour writing a letter to forward a pleading to a court, which should take five minutes when you're experienced." The partner doing the billing for your work will write down your time to the 'quality' billing level, no matter how long it took you. Another partner at another firm points out that "It may be that you work four hours and they get cut to one. Yes, you have four hours recorded. But someone is going to write off three of those hours. At the end of the year, the firm looks at the hours you actually worked to determine if you met your billing requirement; but for bonuses and raises and promotions, efficiencies count. They ***will*** look at how much they had to cut your hours." And another partner explains that "When your supervising partner writes off your time, it counts against ***them***, in the guise of their 'realization rate.' The realization rate reflects how many hours people who work for you have spent working on their files compared to what's collectible. If your associates work a hundred hours but only sixty are collectible, it's either a problem of slow-paying clients or inefficient associates. The higher your realization rate as a partner, say 80 to 90%, the better your compensation. So partners don't like writing off a lot of time—and they seek out associates who are efficient!"

c. **"But I dreamed about the case!"—figuring out what's billable.**

When you are filling out your time sheets, you have one goal and one goal only. As Carlton Fields' Jason Murray says, "You need to know: What I write down—will it help or hinder the billing attorney?" He adds, "If you do it wrong, the client will call and complain to the partner, 'Your associate wrote ***this*** on their time sheet. What were they ***doing***?'" The hours on your time sheets should be easy to sell. Make your supervisor's life ***easier*** and you'll be rewarded.

Hodgson Russ' Adam Perry recommends that "As a new associate, ask to look at client bills! Expressing an interest in seeing what clients will pay for and the form you should follow prepares you for being a billing attorney and makes people think you have rainmaking potential. If you think in that vein, when you become a billing attorney yourself, you'll be able to answer the question—Gee, will they pay for that? It makes you a better business developer." Keep in mind that once in a while partners will be territorial about their clients and not be willing to share their bills with you—and if you hear that about somebody, don't ask them!—but in general it's a good idea.

As a new associate, how do you figure out what's billable—and how to describe it? Let's see . . . .

1) Some things are never billable. *Ever.*

A partner at one large firm told me about an associate who asked him, "If I'm asleep on a plane and I have a dream about the case, can I bill it?" The partner responded, "When you woke up, had you propelled the case forward? Was it like the Kubla Khan?" The partner laughed and told me "The ironic thing is, ***I*** once had a dream about a something that was driving me crazy on a case, and when I woke up I had the problem solved. But I didn't bill for it. How do you explain to somebody that clients don't pay for dreams? You can't."

Lawyers have tons of stories about what new associates sometimes put on time sheets. Among the ones I heard:

- "Talked about assignment with a fellow associate at Friday ice cream social."
- "Packing for business trip."
- "Haircut." (The explanation: "My hair grows during the day on client time, so they should pay for it.").
- "Dry cleaning" at home. ("I wear the suits to work. . . .")
- Lunch. ("I think while I chew. . . .")
- "0.1 hours—bathroom."
- "Cleaning off desk." (Reports a supervising partner: "Soon we asked him to clean off his desk permanently.")
- "Nine hours in library spinning my wheels." (For this one, the firm's recruiting administrator said, "It would have been very funny, but the billing attorney didn't have time to review the entry and sent the bill directly to the client. Oops!")

One lamentable area that's not billable is professional reading. As one corporate associate said, "Out of school, you don't know anything about deals and how to structure them. PLI books, CLE books, they show you how deals are structured, from project financing to asset securitization to ADA issues. They're great books; they get down and dirty about how deals work. Reading them makes you immensely more efficient, but you can't bill the time you spend reading them; partners say, 'Read them in your free time.'"

And even though it's an outstanding idea to be familiar with your clients' industries, learning about them isn't billable. You need to do it on your own time. A partner at one firm said that "Our firm does a lot of work for companies that make equipment for airplanes. As a result, we subscribe to publications like *Aviation Week*. Nobody is required to read them; it's kind of like having the *Wall Street Journal* in your front lobby. Once, one of the partners was curious as to why the firm was not recapturing more billable time from our summer clerks, so he reviewed a printout of all their time. One of the clerks was putting down between an hour and two hours a day for activities like 'Reading *Aviation Week*.'"

2) Different firms bill differently. Ask for a "Billables 101" lesson at work.

   As Oregon's Jane Steckbeck advises, "Ask your mentor or an office administrator or a partner to put together a 'billable hour' workshop to explain the firm's billing policy, procedures, and proper vs. improper billing. Ask them to demonstrate with filled-out time sheets. The fact is, nobody comes out of law school knowing how to bill time, what's appropriate and what's not. Whether you're a summer associate or a new permanent associate, you need to take the initiative to find out how to do it right."

   You can also lean on your secretary for advice; as St. Thomas' Michelle Fongyee says, "Secretaries can be very helpful with billing questions because they handle it." Hodgson Russ' Adam Perry says that you can always ask another attorney as well. Nobody ***expects*** you to know intuitively what's billable; as John Marshall's Bill Chamberlain explains, "It's all unspoken policy."

   Among the areas that differ from firm to firm and client to client are:

   - Travel. Some clients negotiate up front that it won't be billable at all. For others, things like the time it takes you to get to the airport are billable, and sometimes they're not. When you're on the plane, if you're travelling for one client and doing work for another, you have to ask who gets billed? One—or split it?
   - Researching issues that impact more than one client—ask who pays for it?

One junior associate told me about putting an entry on her time sheet that said "0.1 hours—left message for client." Her supervising attorney said, "For my clients, you can't bill for leaving a message." She commented, "He wasn't mad that I wrote it down. I didn't know. Different clients have different sensitivities."

d. Realize that sometimes when it comes to billability, it's not what you say—it's the way you say it.

Remember, time sheets are documents with a particular audience in mind: the client. The days of quaint bills that had one line reading "For professional services rendered, $______" are gone. Clients sometimes even have their legal bills audited for fraud. So make ***sure*** your descriptions will fly. One lawyer said "Make sure every entry on your time sheet is meaningful by placing yourself in the client's position. Ask yourself: Would these time descriptions satisfy me if *I* were buying the time?"

One lawyer said that, "You can never tell what'll honk off a client. They can pay $100,000 for a month's legal work and then go ballistic over a $20 hotel breakfast. Think about that next time you want to send out a bill with excessive copier charges!"

CAREER LIMITING MOVE . . .

Partner at a large California firm: "In one of my early cases, I represented a large, wealthy company which was one of several defendants in the case. I got a terrific result in federal court on a motion to dismiss; the judge denied the plaintiffs the right to replead against my client, while denying other lawyers' motions to dismiss on behalf of the other defendants. It potentially saved my client from paying millions of dollars in damages. The judge's opinion read like he'd taken chunks of my brief verbatim, a fact that did not go unnoticed by the Assistant General Counsel of my client. I thought the General Counsel would be happy to see the decision as soon as possible, so I FedExed it to him. The next morning when the General Counsel called with what I was sure would be a grateful and congratulatory call, he reamed me out for spending money on FedEx without getting authorization from him first! A startling, but very useful, lesson about making assumptions—and **always** checking costs with your client!"

So on your time sheets, err on the side of giving too much detail rather than too little. As one partner puts it, "Don't write down things that clients won't pay! For instance, if you put '8 hours—reviewed file,' a client won't go for that. What in the world ***is*** that? Instead, put 'Reviewed this and this pleading and generated this report,' and the time you spent on each. 'Research' is another one that really bugs clients. They think it might be fluff. They want to get ***value*** for their time. Give a description: 'I researched X issue for _ hour, Y issue for one hour.' And copying cases! 'Copying XYZ cases' on your time sheet—the client will wonder, 'Why am I spending a hundred dollars an hour plus for ***you*** to copy cases? Why can't a secretary do that?'" He goes on to add that "Sometimes things are part of a bigger whole, and if you package it right it will fly. For instance, a necessary part of travel is getting to the gate at least half an hour before the flight takes off so you can check in. But anybody would be yanked at the idea of paying for 'Waiting.' So instead of saying 'Waiting at airport for flight,' make it part of a bigger 'Traveling to X destination.' Or let's say you're traveling to a deposition in another state. You need to prep for it, and review as you travel. Don't bill the time as travel; bill it as 'Prep for XYZ deposition, reviewing W document.' If you write 'Prep for deposition in X city, review documents and subpoena' for the time you were travelling, then the travel time is built in. Don't highlight the time as simply 'travel'! Another area that gets to some clients is conferences between attorneys in the firm. Conversations with opposing counsel, they have no problem with that. But each other—no. It's ridiculous for clients to think that way. You need to strategize. And asking a question of someone who handles a matter every day is

much more efficient—and much cheaper for the client—than having it researched from scratch. Batting an issue around will often lead to creative solutions to client problems. But clients don't see it that way, and you have to be sensitive to that. If a partner and an associate talk about something, a short quick conversation, then the junior person is the only one to bill it. For a longer conference, both the partner and associate will bill it, but word it as 'clarifying the issue' or something that the client will find more palatable." This is Kimm talking again. I read a story about how Xerox was putting tons of money into extensive manuals for copier repairmen. They found that it was a lot cheaper and more efficient if they just let the copier repairmen eat lunch together so they could swap ideas. So I guess the value of talking is an issue in more industries than just law!

Also be sensitive to billing large blocks of time in one day to one client. One lawyer points out that "There are clients who say that once they see more than eight hours on a given day billed to them, they scrutinize it very closely—they think, 'Gee, in that ninth hour, I wasn't getting the same bang for my buck as I was in the first hour.'"

e. Don't obsess with billables at the expense of your professional growth.

After all this talk about billables, you're thinking, 'Well, swell Kimmbo—now you're telling me to ***forget*** about billables?' No, of course not. But it's easy to be so focused on billables that you miss out on great non-billable opportunities. It's not just your time sheets. It's your ***career***. As Harvard's Mark Weber points out, "If you're obsessed with your billables, you miss out on tremendous opportunities to sit in on things and learn. If you tag along for negotiations, conference calls, the knowledge you gain is invaluable. The most valuable thing you can learn as a new lawyer doesn't have to do with research. See how more experienced attorneys handle situations. Learn how to deal with clients."

f. Even if you work for the government, for Legal Aid, or for a firm that works on a contingency basis, you *still* have time issues.

If you work for an employer for whom you don't have to keep detailed time sheets, thank your lucky stars. But check up front to see exactly how you ***should*** keep track of your time. It's a mistake to assume that because a client isn't paying for it, you don't have to keep track of your time!

If your public interest job is funded by the Legal Services Corporation, for instance, you have to keep track of your time the same as you would for paying clients. Government agencies don't strictly track your time, but they ***do*** watch to see how efficiently you handle cases. If you're a prosecutor, one prosecutor pointed out that "You're not doing billables, you're doing the job. If that means working the weekend, because you're going to trial on Monday and you have to spend the weekend organizing witnesses and reviewing exhibits and checking case law, you do it. You don't write it down, but you do it."

If you work for a personal injury firm that works on a contingency basis, don't make the mistake of figuring that since clients don't pay for your time, you don't have to keep track of it. Ask! A junior associate at one P.I. firm said that "When I worked at a plaintiff's P.I. firm during law school, I never had to bill to a file or track my time in any way. When I started practice after graduating, I went to work for another plaintiff's P.I. firm. You can imagine my horror when two and a half weeks had passed, I hadn't turned in a single time sheet, and a partner asked what I had billed for the past eighteen days. Unbeknownst to me, this particular firm billed against their contingency files to track their profitability!"

CHAPTER THREE

Getting Off On The Right Foot . . . Learning The Culture & Getting Organized

A. Today Is The First Day Of The Rest Of Your Career

That's a thought that's both scary and exciting, isn't it? If you've never had a real, full-time job that doesn't end when the Fall Semester starts again, it'll be quite a shock. If you ***have*** worked before, you know something of what to expect—but it's still a whole new world for you. Let's talk about what you ought to do!

1. Do the "prep" before you show up for work.

Read the section in "The 1,640-Hour Interview," on page 4, about things to do before you start work. Those all apply to your "after school" job as much as they apply to your summer position. In addition, as a new "grown-up" lawyer, there are a few other things you should do, and avoid doing:

a. Get out and meet your future co-workers.

Especially if you accepted your offer in September of your third year, Dickinson's Elaine Bourne recommends that you "Get together with attorneys in the group you'll be working for, for lunch or dinner. You're not a pest. You're just letting them know that you're eager to join them!"

b. If you're going to a medium to large law firm, don't leave your department and supervisor choices to "serendipity."

At every medium-to-large law firm, there are good partners to be assigned to, and bad ones. A lot of people will tell you that your assignment is serendipity—but it's not. At least, not if you do something about it ahead of time! As the managing partner at one law firm commented, "Before you start, ask the recruiting coordinator for future colleagues with whom you can go to lunch, so you can learn more about the firm. When you meet with them, ***listen*** to them. Tell them you want to get off on the right foot, and ask what they'd do differently—or the same!—if they started again. Get around to asking who they'd work for, perhaps who they'd avoid if the conversation goes that way. Go to the recruiting coordinator and request to be assigned to someone the associates recommended. That way, you'll avoid being stuck with a bad partner. Don't worry. You're not overstepping your bounds. We'd be ***delighted*** if our new associates showed that kind of initiative."

c. If you're going to be a litigator or a prosecutor, take time to go to the courthouse and watch your future colleagues work.

As Assistant State's Attorney Rich Colangelo says, "Going ahead of time to watch people work is a ***fantastic*** idea. There's no better way to figure out how to deal with judges and defendants, how to present a case, than to see somebody more experienced doing it. They'll be blown away if they see you show up ahead of time to watch them!"

d. Learn to play golf!

This is advice from lawyers at Akin, Gump, and even though they were kidding—at least, I think they were kidding—it's a good idea. Golf is a serious ritual at a lot of law firms, and you'll hear all kinds of things on the golf course that will benefit you in your career. You'll form a camaraderie with colleagues that you just can't forge as easily while you're on the clock. So if you have any attraction to the game at all—or think you might—hit the links while you're still in school.

e. Remember that while you're still in school, you're forming your professional reputation.

If you accept a permanent offer while you're still in school—and even if you don't!—remember that your law school classmates are going to be your professional colleagues, and the legal profession is a lot tighter than it seems from a law school perspective. People ***remember*** you. As the partner at one firm pointed out, "What people think of you in law school ***matters***. When we go to make lateral or new hires, we run the names of people we're considering by people we think might know them. That goes particularly for people who went to school with them. The last thing you want is for someone to say, 'Oh, yeah, I knew him. What a creep,' or 'Oh, her. She's a slut.' It'll catch up with you. So be careful how you interact with your classmates!"

f. Check in ahead of time to make sure your employer hasn't mutated.

Check in a month or so before you start work to see if anything significant has changed since you either interviewed or summer clerked with your employer. As San Francisco's Jackie Ortega recommends, "Call in before the bar exam to express your interest in hearing about firm news during the months prior to your arrival. And ***after*** the bar exam, do a little research to find out what may have happened during your study hibernation. Establish a contact with the firm (and your particular office, if the firm has more than one office) to stay abreast of what's happening."

CAREER LIMITING MOVE . . .

Former summer clerk, medium-sized New England firm. She received an offer of permanent employment and accepted it.

During her summer clerkship, she had identified the partner with whom she wanted to work—a big rainmaker at the firm. Unbeknownst to her, during the Spring of her third year at school, the partner got fed up with bringing in more business than everyone else and having to split the profits with the other partners, so he left the firm and started a new firm, taking several associates with him. The split got some media attention, but the former summer clerk didn't notice it because she was focusing on school. She had no contact with the firm during the year and no inkling the split might happen, and the firm didn't contact her to tell her about it. It wasn't until she showed up for her first day of work that she found the rug had been pulled out from under her. She was not pleased!

g. Get your financial act together.

Understand your salary and benefits before you start. As Minnesota's Sue Gainen explains, "Make sure you know what you will earn and what you will take home. Multiply your annual salary by two-thirds and divide that figure by twelve, and that roughly equals your take-home pay on a monthly basis. Budget accordingly! Also, read your insurance policies and understand what health coverage you have. Really, really understand it. You're a lawyer now!"

h. Don't touch that dial! *Do not* call ahead and see if your employer has raised the starting pay since you accepted your offer.

If the starting pay at your employer goes up between the time you accept their offer and you start work, it's manna from Heaven. Be grateful. But if you hear that other employers in town have raised their rates, ***do not*** call to see if your employer, in poker parlance, is going to "see" them. It starts you off on a ***very*** bad footing. Trust me, every employer knows what every other employer is paying. If they don't raise your pay commensurately, it's probably because they're giving you something else to compensate—like a lower billables target, or better benefits, or ***something***. They'll look after you. Don't worry. Plan on starting your job at the salary you accepted, and leave it at that.

i. **If you have children, have a plan B and C for childcare.**

The only certainty you have as a working parent is that somehow, sometime your childcare plans are going to break down. If you only have one nanny or sitter lined up, you won't seem as though you've got your life in order when you start work. Of course, ***every*** employer knows that emergencies come up when you simply can't hand off to somebody else, and people are understanding about that. But on a routine basis, make sure you have somebody other than your primary care giver to step in and help with the kids.

2. **Your first day . . .**

Make sure that you bring everything you'll need by way of documents and identification. And "Be early!" advises Georgetown's Anna Davis. You don't want to create the impression on the very first day that you're a slacker!

CAREER LIMITING MOVE . . .

Dan Boehnen, managing partner of McDonnell Boehnen Hulbert & Berghoff, tells the story of his first day at work: "I got off to a bad start by assuming the firm would know that I couldn't arrive until about 1 p.m. In this firm, the new grads usually worked through the summer while simultaneously taking the review course for the bar exam. They knew that I was starting the bar review course the same day that I was starting at the firm. They also knew that I was taking the morning sessions of the bar review course. Thus, I thought they would recognize that I couldn't arrive until about 1 p.m. **Wrong**! It seemed obvious to me, but they hadn't put two and two together, so they were confused and disappointed when I didn't show up at 9 a.m. The principal name partner had planned to take me around and introduce me to the other lawyers. Oops!" [P.S. This is Kimm talking. Since Mr. Boehnen is now a managing partner, this clearly wasn't much of a "career limiting move"!]

CAREER LIMITING MOVE . . .

Former junior associate, medium-sized Southern firm: "After accepting a position as an associate I told the firm I could not start until I returned from a vacation I had planned. Unfortunately, they asked me where I was going and unfortunately, I told them . . . Mardi Gras. Can you say "party girl"? To make a bad thing worse, two weeks after starting at the firm I flew to New York for St. Patrick's Day. Even though I left after work on Friday and returned to work bright and early Monday morning, the green beer entirely out of my system, I was and ever will be the "party girl" associate that once worked there. They may never again hire another young single woman associate."

3. Expect butterflies.

You're probably anxious about starting this new job, and that's natural. As Dickinson's Elaine Bourne says, "You'll be on information overload. You'll be dazed. 'Who was that?' 'What did they just tell me?'" You'll be buggin', but you don't want anybody to ***see*** that! As a lawyer, you want to exude confidence, and that starts with the first day. Your mind may be saying, "What the hell am I doing here?" but your smile and manner ought to say, "I'm happy and excited to be here."

4. Meet as many people as you can. Smile. Shake hands.

Somebody's going to show you around the office. You'll meet a lot of people. In a small to medium-sized office you might meet everybody. When you're introduced, "Greet people with a smile, a firm handshake and look them in the eye," says Carlton Fields' Elizabeth Zabak. "First impressions are really important!"

That handshake counts for a lot. Make it firm, but not a bone-crusher. When I travel around to law schools, I meet tons of people and they almost always have a good handshake. But when a handshake isn't good—either it's a wimpy wet noodle or a vise grip—it does stand out. If you don't have much experience shaking hands, practice on your friends and family and ask them for an honest assessment.

Incidentally, shake hands with women the same as you would with men. A female senior attorney at one large firm talked about how new male associates would sometimes "shake my fingertips." "It's a big turnoff," she said.

When you meet someone at the office, listen intently so that you get their name right, and repeat it back to them. "Hello, Mr. Jekyll/Ms. Hyde, Barney, Betty." If you are introduced to somebody by their full name—Bullwinkle Moose, Morticia Adams—whether it's a senior partner or a runner, return the greeting addressing them as "Mr. Moose" or "Ms. Adams." Leave it to them to correct you and say, "Oh, no, please, it's Bullwinkle." If for any reason it's not clear—for instance, a senior partner is introducing you around and the partner calls people by their first names but you shouldn't—ask people how they'd like to be addressed. Or ask your guide or anyone else in the office what the norm is. I might be making a big deal out of this, but if the managing partner has had the same secretary for the last thirty years, she may be the second most powerful person at work and command a lot of respect. If she expects to be called "Ms. Croft" instead of "Lara," you couldn't commit a bigger gaffe than assuming all support staff should be addressed by their first names.

If nobody takes the time to introduce you around, "take the initiative and do it yourself!" advises Florida State's Stephanie Redfearn. An attorney at one firm told of how a new associate had been at the office for two months, and because nobody had introduced her to the people in the office (and she didn't do it herself), a senior partner thought she was a runner, not a lawyer! Don't let that happen to you. Now's the time to meet people!

Incidentally, don't worry too much if you don't get everybody's name the first time around, especially if you're meeting a ***lot*** of people. Just ask somebody whose name you ***do*** remember, "This is embarrassing, but I forgot Aristotle's secretary's name. Could you tell me what it is?" People will understand and appreciate your asking.

5. **Pay attention at orientation—at least, stay awake!—and read the employee manual.**

OK, orientation for ***anything*** is usually a snooze. But remember, "It's not a blow-off," says Elaine Bourne. "You're making an impression on ***everyone*** you meet," including the people giving the orientation. Don't nod off! Have a pad and paper with you to take notes, as Milbank Tweed's Joanne DeZego advises. If you're busy writing you can't doze.

You aren't expected to remember everything at orientation. The most important thing to do is to "Figure out who you can go to afterwards. Nobody expects you to remember the fine points of working the office phone system," says St. Thomas' Michelle Fongyee. When it comes to asking questions at orientation, walk a fine line. If you have questions about office procedures, for instance, or you need to clarify something that's said at the orientation, that's fine. But remember that impressions are formed not just on the basis of what you say but also what you ask. If you ask questions like "How soon can I take a vacation day?" or "Who do I talk to about going part-time?" or "Who's in charge of the Employee Assistance Plan?" you're sending the wrong message. You don't want to come off as brown-nosing, arrogant, selfish, or neurotic. A ***lot*** of the inner workings of an office are best learned by observation and asking questions of people privately rather than in front of the group (I go into great detail in this shortly, in the section called "You Can Get Away With Just About Anything If You Learned How To Play The Game.")

6. Expect that things won't go as you expected.

It's impossible to go into any new job without thinking beforehand about what it will be like. I've already told you to expect to be busy and to meet a lot of people. But maybe it ***won't*** be like that. Maybe you'll be shown to an office with a desk . . . and that's it. At one firm the office was in such an uproar that for two weeks they didn't even notice that two new clerks hadn't even shown up!

And because the practice of law is unpredictable, the plans for your first day might have to be scuttled. Maybe Attorney Darrow was supposed to meet you but he's in litigation. As Anna Davis says, "Don't think, 'Oh my God, he doesn't want to talk to me!'" Instead, "Go with the flow," she advises. "Don't shut your door and put your head in your hands. Get out and talk to people. Introduce yourself. Ask to help out.

'Can I do some research for you?' Get yourself into the life of the office."

7. **What to do if you're starting work at the same employer as your boyfriend or girlfriend**

Sometimes people hook up in a summer program, and the romance lasts through the school year, through graduation, and—then what? When you're both going to go back to the same place, what do you say to the people at work—if anything? I asked a lot of people about this, and got a hearty "It depends" as a response. By and large, you want to do the same thing I recommended in the "1,640-Hour Interview" section for summer clerks. Namely:

a. If the employer has a "no dating" policy, then don't tell anyone at work you're seeing each other. Lawyers say that those policies have no teeth, but a "no dating" edict does tell you how your employer feels about lawyers seeing each other. So keep it to yourself.

b. If the employer doesn't have a "no dating" policy—and most don't—try to be assigned to different departments. "If you're in the same department, that raises conflict of interest concerns for your employer," says Hodgon Russ' Adam Perry.

c. In the absence of a "no dating" policy, virtually everybody agrees that you should keep your relationship low key, but not a secret. What that means is, "Go about your business, and if someone asks, say 'yes, we are seeing each other,'" advises Adam Perry. There's no point in trying to keep it a secret because "People figure these things out," says Kentucky's Drusilla Bakert. "If one other person knows, then the whole firm knows. If you try to keep it a secret, partners will wonder what else there is about you that you don't want them to know." Instead, go to the firm dinner-dance as a couple. Treat each other as you would anybody else you were dating ***outside*** of the office. At work, remember "no holding hands, hanging onto each other like a lifeline at every firm event, no going to lunch exclusively with each other," says Drusilla Bakert. "If you don't treat it like a big deal, people at work probably won't either. Don't violate other people's confidences to each other—it will get around that neither of you can keep a secret. And don't blab about your personal life to people you work with, any more than you would about any other romance."

B. You Can Get Away With Just About Anything If You Learn How To Play The Game. Learn The Culture!

If you think work is a meritocracy, ask yourself why some really smart people work really hard but never seem to get the recognition they deserve. If you think that everything you need to know about a place is written up in the policies and manuals, you're burying your head in the sand in a particularly dangerous way. As Dennis Kennedy says, "Your most important job from the time you accept the job is to learn the culture of the organization you are joining."

The fact is, if you want to maximize your effort—if you want to work hours that are as reasonable as they can be, if you want to have other people applaud you and give you opportunities and help you get ahead, if you want to smoke out the best work and best people to work for—you've got to learn how the game is played. If you don't want to be the one always saying, "How come ***she*** always gets the best projects?" and "What makes ***him*** so special?"—if you'd rather have people saying those things about ***you***—then pay special attention to everything I'm about to tell you. Because superstars at the office aren't born. They follow a subtle set of rules that you can apply, too.

Now all of this may strike you as kind of skeevy. You may think, I just want to be myself. They'll have to take me as I am. I'd say to you: No, they don't. When employers talk about finding a "fit," and only wanting people who "fit in," they don't mean it as a negative. They really mean: we want people who seem comfortable with our culture. I'm not telling you to do something totally against your nature. If you're at an office that's freewheeling, aggressive, and hard partying and where the lawyers believe in working twelve hours a day and then socializing together at night, and you're a more quiet, private person who wants to spend substantial time with your family, there's nothing wrong with either you ***or*** the office. But you don't agree with the culture, and it's probably not the place for you to work.

I think you'll find that there's a fairly substantial range of places where you fit into the culture. Your goal should be to figure out what that culture is, and in doing so identify where there's wiggle room, the extent to which you can "be yourself." There's no point in fighting it because you can't change the culture of an office all by yourself. Figure out how you can exploit it for your own benefit.

I'll give you an analogy from the world of science. Maybe you know about quantum mechanics, but if you don't, here it is: it's basically the science of really, really small stuff—atoms and subatomic particles. The problem is, these really small things don't behave like anything normal. For instance, subatomic particles don't have to be particles. Light, for example, behaves like a wave if it's measured like a wave, and as a stream of particles if it's measured as particles. And even more curious, the subatomic particles or waves don't necessarily exist at one point at a time. They can be at different points at the same time. Only measuring them makes them be anywhere specifically. When scientists first found this out they were totally flummoxed. But they learned to take advantage of the weirdness rather than fight it, and that led to a technology explosion and miniaturization of everything from motors to microchips.

At work, you should do the same thing. Take advantage of the weirdness rather than fight it.

What ***is*** that "weirdness"? What are we talking about when we talk about "culture"? When you think of the word "culture," you think of the rules, spoken and unspoken, by which a society lives. It's that way at work, too. What I'm going to do here is to teach you ***how*** to figure out what the rules are, and with those tools, what you ought to be looking for.

1. "Breasting Your Cards" Until You Know Who's Who and What's What.

Until you've figured out how the office works, you've got to tread very carefully. Soon enough you'll be in the swing of things. But when you start, you want to be very cautious about ***everything***.

a. Be *very* wary of people who try to "take you under their wing" from moment one.

You'll find at any office that there will be people you gravitate to more than others—and people who gravitate to you. And you'll find that you're the natural object of attention for your supervisor, the recruiting coordinator (if your office has one), and people like that. But if you notice somebody coming on strong to be your friend, tread lightly. It's tempting to fall into an immediate friendship when you're at a strange new place, but you can't afford to do that. A whole bunch of people I interviewed told me to warn you about this. Northern Illinois' Mary Obrzut says, "Keep your antenna up! Margaret Mead used to say that when she went into new environments, she didn't pay attention to the first few people out to meet the boat. The ones with power were the ones standing on the shore watching. People who reach out to you first may not have power." As Harvard's Mark Weber puts it, "The first person who tries to befriend you may be the jerk of the office." Instead of clinging to anyone as a buddy, wait first to see how other people react to them. As Mark Weber says, "Watch what other people say about them. How do they react when this person's name comes up? What kind of work do they get? Do other people seek them out? Does this person spend too much time chatting, passing along the latest office gossip, taking long lunches, or whining about things at work? You need to know how credible people are before you choose your friends at the office." Hamline's Vince Thomas adds, "You don't know who's important and who's not—and who'll stay and who won't! You can curry favour with someone, and six months later you're at their farewell lunch." If this sounds a bit cold, remember: your friends at work are your colleagues first, and your friends second. You can't afford to start off being associated in your superiors' minds with anybody who's got a bad reputation.

b. Don't establish a persona for yourself until you've got an idea of the lay of the land.

Elaine Bourne recommends that you "Watch, listen, and learn before you interject yourself into situations you know nothing about." As lawyers at Waller Lansden advise, "Don't try to be the funniest or the most clever or be too visible early on. Lay low for a little while!" You want to find out what goes over big at the office, and what you ought to save for your private life, until you figure out to what extent you can "be yourself" at work.

c. Keep your opinions to yourself until you know whom you can trust, and how your statements will go over.

As Minnesota's Sue Gainen says, "Bide your time. Find out who's who and what's what before you open your mouth about anything to anyone."

2. The "How" part—the tools you use to learn the culture

a. Listen to what people say when they don't think they're telling you rules.

If people are always saying "We should let Joe know about this," or "Let's see what Joe has to say," that means: Joe's got juice.

b. As Miami's Marcy Cox recommends, "Observe interactions."

See how people deal with each other, whether they're formal or freewheeling. If everybody at the office slinks into work every day without saying anything and you sail into the office every day with a singing "Good mo-o-o-o-orning!" you're going to stand out in the wrong way. (And you're probably at the wrong kind of office for your personality!) Some places love practical jokes and silliness. As Hofstra's Diane Schwartzberg says, "If your supervisor is very serious, don't crack jokes!" If they have a newsletter that publishes silly photos of people when they were children, that tells you about a lightheartedness at work. Maybe the managing partner won't mind if you paint a whipped cream beard on his face at the firm's annual summer bash, but don't count on it until you've observed other people joshing with him the same way. At meetings, watch how people respond to the person who's talking. Do they tap their pencils and roll their eyes? Or do they snap to attention and stop fiddling around?

c. Go out drinking with your fellow associates, and let them get hammered while you nurse a single beer.

As one new associate told me, "I made a point of going out for drinks with my colleagues when I first started. I'd nurse one or two while they'd down several. They'd vent and spill the beans about office politics and all of the goings-on at work. I gained invaluable information that saved my neck on several occasions."

d. Find a hobby that you share with colleagues at work, and use that as a source of bonding.

It can be ***anything***. Georgetown's Anna Davis found that when she was working at the FTC, a group of people would go jogging together. She liked to jog, so she joined them. One law firm told me about how some of the lawyers like to knit as a way to relieve tension, and several of the associates get together once a week to knit—and gossip. Hamline's Vince Thomas says that when he was a new associate, he went running every lunchtime with a group of associates and partners. He said, "We had a rule that nothing that we said would go any further than our running group. We'd run five or six miles, and while we were running, I heard a ***ton*** about what was going on in the firm. Partners would relax and talk about just about anything. They'd talk about who was going to make partner. A lot of times I knew who was going to partner before the people ***themselves*** knew it! I had colleagues who were jealous, knowing I was hearing a lot of inside scoop. I told them, 'Bring in your shoes and come with us!'"

On the other end of the "healthy habits" scale, one lawyer told me about how when he was a new associate, he and the other smokers in the office would all go out the same door to sneak a smoke a couple of times a day. "It turned out to be a great way to bond with my new colleagues," he said. "We'd all be out there huddling in the cold New England winters."

The point is, think about what ***you*** like to do, and integrate that into your work life. It's a great way to get to know people, make friends—and learn what you need to know about the culture!

e. Heed the "myths and legends" at the office.

As Dennis Kennedy recommends, "The 'myths and legends' at the office can help you out. If the managing partners of the firm shared a table in the library for their first few years in the firm, you can learn that you'll want to hesitate before you demand new furniture. An oft-repeated tale of the female partner who called into the office within an hour of giving birth can give you a clue as to what lawyers will think of your request for substantial paternity leave."

f. Pay more attention to what people do than what they say.

If they talk pro bono but reward huge billables, their actions are speaking louder than their words. If they say their office is open and collegial, but everybody works behind firmly closed doors, they've got a different interpretation of "collegial" than you do.

g. Ask questions, the *right* questions, of junior associates.

Encourage them to talk to you. "What do you wish you knew when you started here?" "How do you like what you're doing?" Those kinds of questions will give you all kinds of valuable tidbits. As lawyers at Jones Day point out, "Attorneys more senior than you can provide not just substantial legal advice but also insights into the 'ins and outs' of the firm."

h. Look at your employer's web site and brochures.

See what they brag about. Your observations at the office will be more relevant—for instance, every employer brags about family-friendliness, collegiality, whether or not that's accurate—but the way they present themselves to the outside world will give you a clue to how they like to think of themselves.

i. Ask the people at the top.

Lawyers at Steptoe and Johnson advise that you "Go to senior partners, make a conscious effort to seek them out, and ask them what they did when ***they*** started that got their career off to a good start." What they did will tell you what they'll appreciate seeing ***you*** do.

j. Identify positive role models.

Ask the recruiting coordinator or a mentor you trust, "Who's a superstar? Who should I try and emulate? What stands out about them?" Find positive role models and then do as they do!

k. Encourage people to talk to you.

Smile and look interested when they talk about work. Don't be judgmental, don't say "I would never have done that," or "She seems like the type who . . . " Just let them talk. You get to listen—and learn.

l. Watch how people treat their underlings.

If they treat them well, that's a big positive. On the other hand, no matter how nice they are to you, if they treat people badly who are in no position to talk back, then what they're telling you is that given the authority, they'd treat you like dirt, too.

m. Be nice to *everybody.*

It's not just the attorneys who can tell you valuable things. Secretaries, paralegals, and support staffers in general know ***tons*** of valuable information about the office. Encourage them to clue you in!

n. Listen to gossip!

That's right. I know that the standard advice you hear is "avoid gossip," but that's not what people really mean. Not entirely, anyway. Gossip is ***very*** valuable. The jungle drums teach you things you can't learn anywhere else. What people mean is, avoid being tagged ***as*** a gossip. Even senior partners listen to the grapevine. If you want to "think like a partner," you should stay plugged in, too! As Dewey Ballantine's John Ragosta says, "Malicious gossip has no place in business. But you have to stay informed about what's going on in the firm. Any partner would want to know immediately were a lateral coming to the firm, or an associate leaving. Why should you as an associate be any less interested? Don't sit in your office with your head in the sand!" Here's what you need to know about handling gossip:

1) Stay on the good side of office gossips.

You need to know the scoop. And you don't want malicious gossip to be circulated about ***you.*** That means that while you absolutely do not want to be considered a gossip yourself, you need to know what's being said! As Rutgers' Dawne Smith says, "You do need a gossipy acquaintance at work, especially if you're not much into office politics. You

have to tap into somebody who ***is***!" Harvard's Mark Weber adds, "People who ***are*** in the grapevine ***love*** to share!" However, you don't want to appear too buddy buddy with a gossip, because "you can lose credibility that way," says Denver's Jennifer Loud Ungar.

2) Pass along "constructive gossip"—gossip that will help the subject of the gossip or the person you're telling.

   As the recruiting coordinator at one large firm said, "I get a lot of good information from associates. I find out if somebody is unhappy or having a little trouble. If I find out that someone's always asleep, I can give them a gentle reminder about looking alert at work. Once a summer associate's father was really sick. He tried to keep it out of the office. Another associate told me about it, and I took steps to have the summer associate transferred to another office so he could be closer to his dad."

   I ***always*** make a point of telling people when I've heard good things about them. It's lovely being the bearer of good tidings, and people love to know that nice things are being said about them behind their backs. It also helps you be an office peacemaker. If you know two colleagues are at war and you can get one of them to say something nice about the other—"There must be ***something*** you like about Bluto"—passing that comment along to Bluto will go a long way toward smoothing things over and making your office a lot more harmonious for everyone.

3) Keep malicious gossip to yourself.

   This is the gossip people are talking about when they say "avoid spreading gossip." Don't pass along anything about anyone that is personally destructive. Lots of people spend time at work criticizing or making fun of other people. Don't succumb. It makes you look bad. As Jennifer Loud Ungar says, "Don't be the first to know who's crying, who's cheating, who got a bad review, or anything like that. Keep it to yourself, and if anyone asks you, 'Hey, did you know . . . ' say 'Oh, really?' Don't answer!"

4) Pay attention to the source *before* you act on gossip.

As American University's Matt Pascocello says, "Information isn't power. ***Acting*** on information is power. But only act on it ***after*** you validate it, and only if it impacts you." He suggests that you "put anything you hear through your filtration system." Let's say that you hear that your firm is in financial trouble. Pay attention to the departure of rainmaking partners, bonuses that are suspiciously small or nonexistent compared to prior years, changes in hiring patterns, those kinds of things.

When the gossip concerns what somebody in the office is like, file it away. ***Everybody*** speaks from his or her own agenda. When they recount conversations to you, they're remembering what's relevant to them, not necessarily what was said. As Ronna Lichtenberg says in her wonderful book *Work Would Be Great If It Weren't For The People*, "To figure out their agenda, remember that facial expressions are revealing, as is body language. A shrug. A lifted eyebrow. A roll of the eyes."

Also remember that everything you hear about someone else is an opinion. If someone tells you, "Alex is really a schmuck," and your own experience with Alex is pretty positive, all it tells you is that the person who made the schmuck assessment doesn't like Alex. That might be valuable information, but it shouldn't determine your own assessment. When people tell you their opinion of someone, ask ***why*** they think that. Maybe they'll say "He's arrogant" or "He never shuts up," which will give you valuable behavioral cues for yourself around the person giving you their opinion. The bottom line is, be careful about labeling people on the basis of other people's opinions, because if you start believing what they say, it may become a self-fulfilling prophecy. You get an assignment from Alex, and every time Alex does something you don't like, you say, "Aha! He ***is*** a schmuck!" As Georgetown's Marilyn Tucker says, "Listen to other people's opinions but form your own conclusions. While there are certainly difficult people in every organization, don't base your behavior toward anybody on someone else's view. Make your own judgments, and be open to each person. Don't get off to a poor start because of political naiveté!"

SMART HUMAN TRICK . . .

Female lawyer, wants to leave private practice and work for the state legislature. The only person who gives her an offer is somebody reputed to be a **terrible** screamer. After some thought, she decides to take the offer. For whatever reason, the "terrible screamer" takes a liking to her. He never screams at her, and after she's been working for him for a year, he says, "You're doing a great job for me, but to advance your career you really should move on to something else. I'll help you with it." As she says, "Reputation doesn't tell you for sure how things will be for you. People press each other's buttons differently."

o. Take note of physical evidence of what's acceptable.

Toys on people's desks, children's artwork in attorneys' offices (particularly female attorneys), cues like that can tell you a lot about how people at work feel about individuality and family issues. One recruiting coordinator points out that "If the prime reading material at the office is the novels of Pearl S. Buck, it's not exactly going to be forward-thinking on women's issues!"

p. Listen for euphemisms.

"We like to work hard and play hard" means "We put in lots of hours."

3. What to look for . . .

a. Hours! Law Is Not A Nine To Five Job, Unless You Work Part Time—In Which Case, It *Is* A Nine To Five Job.

As is true with ***everything*** else at work, when you're talking about the hours you have to put in, you're talking about a matter of ***perception***. It's not whether or not you're putting in the hours. It's whether or not the people you work for perceive you as working as much as they expect you to work. Image ***counts***.

SMART HUMAN TRICK . . .

Junior associate at a large Washington, D.C. law firm. He gets all of his work done and works pretty long hours. He knows that one particular partner, Partner Sundown —not one that he works for—makes a habit of strolling the halls at 10 p.m. every night, to see who's still working. One night, the junior associate has to race out of the office to help a friend at around nine o'clock, leaving a cup of coffee on his desk, his glasses next to the coffee, and his jacket on his chair. He never gets back to the office that night. The following morning, his supervising partner congratulates him, saying that "Partner Sundown said you were here working late last night." The junior associate is confused, knowing that he wasn't in the office for Partner Sundown's 10 p.m. "sweep." Then he realizes what happened: Partner Sundown saw his coffee, glasses, and jacket, and assumed that he was still there and had just stepped out of his office for a moment.

Thereafter, he makes a point of leaving a pair of glasses, a half-full cup of coffee, and a jacket on his chair every night.

SMART HUMAN TRICK . . .

Junior associate at a small firm. He's married and has a baby. He shares an office with a new associate whose wife is getting her pharmacist's degree out of state. The office mate is a really good guy, smart, funny, hardworking. Because the office mate is from out of town and has nothing else to do, his work is his life. He's at the office all the time. The partners start commenting on the disparity between the hours the two junior associates put in. When the junior associate mentions this to his career services director at school, she recommends, "Why don't you invite this guy to have dinner with you and your wife periodically? Introduce him to your friends? You'll never shine next to him otherwise." The junior associate does as she says, and it works like a charm.

CAREER LIMITING MOVE . . .

Female summer clerk at a large firm down South. The firm's library opens onto a large rooftop sun deck. She takes advantage of the sun deck for a tanning session every day at optimal tanning hours. She sits outside in a bikini, slathers herself with suntan lotion, and relaxes for two hours. The associates and partners who go through the library can clearly see the bathing beauty through large picture windows. When the recruiting coordinator gently suggested to her that perhaps the suntanning wasn't giving her the right image, she huffily replied, "Look at my time sheets. I'm meeting the billable hours you wanted me to work. I can manage my own time." She is not invited back.

1) Figuring out when you really have to be there. It's different from place to place, and supervisor to supervisor!

   I get a lot of questions for my *Dear Job Goddess* column asking me for places with "reasonable" hours. That's a tough question to answer, because although there are some generalities that are valid, they're not true a hundred percent of the time. For instance, it's ***generally*** true that if you work for the government, your hours will tend to be shorter than if you work for private firms. But if you're in litigation, whether it's for the Justice Department or the SEC or anywhere else, you'll work a lot. If you're an assistant district attorney with witnesses to interview, you'll be in on the weekend. It's also generally true that you tend to work shorter hours in a small firm than a larger one. But again, that's not always the case. In a nutshell, the hours you work are a ***cultural*** thing.

How do you figure them out? The same as with every other element of culture: Watch, learn, emulate. A big issue at law firms is the idea of "face time." "Face time" basically means, when do they have to see your face at the office? Some places swear that they have no such thing as face time. But you can't ***know*** that for sure until you see how they ***behave***. An employer might tell you "I don't care when you work as long as you get the work done," but I promise you, if you worked a graveyard shift from 7 p.m. to 8 a.m., you'd be out of there like—well, you know what. Here are a few guidelines to figuring out when you have to be at the office.

a) If you've got a deadline—or a partner—breathing down your neck, stay until the work gets done.

   Even places that genuinely don't seem to require any given set of hours agree about that. If it means an occasional night in the office until 3 a.m., that's what it means. If a partner walks into your office with a new assignment at 6 p.m. and says, "I need this tomorrow," then stay until it gets done. (Don't assume that your efforts won't be appreciated, by the way. One junior associate at one of the country's largest law firms told me that after putting in long hours on a court case, her partner walked into her office the day before Thanksgiving, and said, "See you next year." When she asked what he meant, he said, "You've worked hard enough. Take off. Go see your family. See you after New Year's." And he meant it.)

b) If you are assigned to a supervisor, be at the office when (s)he's there. That's it.

As you get more seniority, you'll have more control over your schedule. But when you're new, be there when the person you work for is there. "If your partner is looking for you at 7 p.m. and you're not there, your workload will suffer," commented one recruiting coordinator. The partner at one large firm talked about how when he was a junior associate, he was assigned to two partners. One of them would arrive at 7 a.m., and the other never left before 8 p.m. He made sure he was there for both of them. "It meant long days, but it paid off in the long run."

c) Watch how junior associate "superstars" handle their time, and emulate them.

Pay careful attention to how people react when a junior associate at the office brags about how "I spent the whole weekend here" or "I was here until midnight." It may be that people grumble behind the braggart's back, "He doesn't know how to manage his time," or "She's not impressing anybody with those hours. She doesn't have the work to justify it."

d) Err on the side of staying a little bit longer than you think you have to, at least at first.

If all of the junior associates leave between 6:30 and 7:30, then leave at 7:30. And when you're new, don't leave without walking around the office first. As Hamline's Vince Thomas recommends, "If most of the people are gone, go. If everyone is still there, don't leave without asking if you can help anyone before you go home."

e) Be aware of any "face time" requirements.

What I mean is, ask around to see if there are any times when you're expected to be at work regardless of whether you're busy or not—that is, when they expect to see your face. Talk to junior associates and/or your mentor to see what's appropriate. At one office, some junior associates told a new associate, "We have to stay until 6:30 or 7." When the new associate asked "Why?" they shrugged and said, "We just have to." If you get that response, then it means ***you*** have to stay, as well.

At a lot of firms, Saturday morning is "face time." As one lawyer recommended, "Saturday mornings are good for organizing, because no one is around. It's a good time to catch up." Another lawyer commented that "At our firm, the board members would come in on Saturday for board meetings. Junior associates would make a point of being at the office so the board members could see them. It didn't much matter if all you were doing was cleaning your desk or talking with people. But it was a risk. Sometimes you'd get a plum assignment because a board member bumped into you on a Saturday. Once in a while, you'd get handed something and they'd say, 'I need this Monday,' so you just gave up your weekend. But it was a good idea to be there at least some of the time."

At one large firm, the managing partner had a habit of coming in on Sunday mornings to see which associate mailboxes at the office had mail in them. The mail on Saturdays was delivered at 9 a.m., and if an associate had mail in his or her mailbox, the managing partner would know they hadn't been in—and he wouldn't be happy. So associates without any work to do would come in at 9:15, pick up their mail, and leave. Other firms have situations that echo that. At one firm, a "psychotic partner" would require that his associates come in on Saturday morning from 8:30 until noon. When one of them protested, "But if we have no work, why come in?" "Because there's so much to learn!" he'd respond. He himself didn't come in on Saturdays, but he'd sometimes call to see who picked up the phone. The associates would dutifully come in with their breakfast, eat together, read the paper, and leave.

f) If you're expected to show up once in a while on a weekend, try to be there when other people are there.

It doesn't really count as face time if nobody sees your face! But if you've made the effort and nobody was there, make sure to mention it to people. At lunch on Monday, you might want to work into the conversation, "When I was here on Saturday . . . " Remember, only do that if coming in on weekends is considered a good thing.

g) Don't routinely put in time when your supervisor isn't there just to say you did it.

After a while—and it's impossible for you to distinguish at first—you learn to tell the difference between real emergencies and false ones. If people expect you there every night and every weekend, you'll soon be loaded down with work because they figure you live there. As I talk about in the section called "Balance," over the long haul you just can't physically work those kinds of hours, and developing a reputation as a workaholic won't help you.

h) Don't make a habit of coming in late, even if you're a night owl.

If everybody else is in the office by 9:00 and you routinely wander in at 10:30, you'll be regarded as a slacker even if it's not true. A junior associate at one large firm said that "There's a perception here that people who come in after nine—the ones who work until midnight—are lazy. It's a mistake to think that people who come in the earliest are the hardest workers, but all of the partners seem to believe it. They all comment about it. So I make sure to come in before the partners arrive. They don't really care how late you stay; they don't comment about that. It's just your arrival time they notice. They're always telling me how productive and hard-working I am, even though I'm perfectly in line with everyone else. I've just moved my schedule up a few hours." At another firm, the junior associates were expected to work from 8 in the morning until 8 at night, which is when the partners were there. One junior associate had a horse, and wanted to leave at 5 o'clock every day to ride her horse. To compensate, she came in to work at 5 a.m. On her evaluations, her superiors dinged her for not being there three hours a day when everybody else was there.

i) If you work in an environment where the supervision is very lax, make a special attempt not to succumb to the luxury of bailing out early.

As one lawyer commented, "At our firm, we get a lot of freedom over when we come in and when we leave. Most senior associates and partners aren't on your back. We've had summer clerks who've taken that too far. We had one clerk who wouldn't bother to come back to work after lunch. Or he'd leave in the middle of the afternoon. Literally, he'd work maybe four hours a day and then show up at firm events. His mentor didn't even know. It's just a bad habit. Even if nobody's watching, you have to be a grown-up, because ultimately your career depends on what you do."

j) If you're unassigned (or you want to switch supervisors), find out when the person you *want* to work for is at the office, and make sure you're there, too.

As one junior associate said, "I was just dying to work for a sports lawyer at our office. I found out from his secretary that he regularly came to work between eight and ten in the morning on Saturdays. So I started doing that, too, and I made sure he saw me. We'd chat casually, and then, because I was just about the only associate there that early on Saturdays, he started giving me work. Now he's my supervisor."

k) Ignore the hours you worked as a summer clerk.

That wasn't real life. This ***is***. Pay attention to what junior associates actually ***do***, not what the party line is.

Junior associate at a large Midwestern firm: "In some firms, 'family friendly' means you get Christmas off. I clerked at this firm, and they sold me a bill of goods about how they're a 'lifestyle' firm, they're family friendly. That's really important to me because I have a wife and two small children. In fact, during the summer they would send me home at 6 p.m. even if I wanted to stay. When I came back as a permanent associate, I stuck with those hours. I was getting my work done. But then I heard through the grapevine that my supervising partner wasn't happy with me, not because of my work, but because of what he perceived as my poor work ethic. I was stunned. The lesson is this: Realize that even if a firm tells you it's 'family friendly,' that doesn't mean a 9 to 5 workday. No one will pay you more than $50,000 a year to start without expecting you to work the hours it takes to get the job done to **their** satisfaction."

2) How to be visible when you're invisible.

We live in a wired age—actually, a wireless one. It's possible to work from just about anywhere. If people at your office don't work on weekends and you take your work home with you, you run the risk of not getting sufficient credit for it because nobody ***sees*** you working. The solution? One Florida lawyer says, "Even if you're working at home, out on the deck, you can get the message across that you're putting in the hours in a lot of subtle ways. You can return e-mails on Saturday at noon. You can return voice mails on Sunday night. That way, people will know you're working even if they don't see you."

3) Make sense of the hours, and you won't resent them so much.

If you're expected to put in long hours, it's easy to become resentful. It helps to think about the ***why*** of those hours.

First of all, as many lawyers pointed out, law is a client-driven business. As lawyers at Carlton Fields suggested, "Typically, clients are not willing to pay lawyers until the problem has become severe, and then they expect their lawyers' undivided immediate attention." Carlton Fields' Hardy Roberts adds, "The word 'injunction' means 'they need it tomorrow.' It's a guaranteed all-nighter." Akin Gump's J.D. Neary echoes that, saying, "Nobody lies and tells you it's a 9 to 5 job. It's all client-driven. If they need stuff Saturday, they need it!" Florida State's Stephanie Redfearn adds, "There's a huge temptation to knock off at 3 p.m. on Friday, after working hard all week. But the problem is that that's when the big issues come in. It's often when the clients panic, so you have to be there." Despite your best-laid plans (and the best efforts of your supervisor), there may be times when you are called in to work unexpectedly because a client needs you. As Denver's Jennifer Loud Ungar suggests, "Be willing to change evening and weekend plans with no notice. Let people know where you can be reached when you're away for the weekend. Usually they won't bug you unless there's an emergency, but it makes you look good."

Secondly, remember that the hours you put in are "an investment in yourself," says NYU's Gail Cutter. "You need to put in the time not just to get the skills, but to earn your credibility. If you ever think you might want to work part time or get parental leave, you won't be able to if you haven't built up credibility with the firm, first. And that takes hard work." In your earliest days with an employer, you're building a reputation for yourself. As Minnesota's Nora Klaphake says, "If you show up early for work the first few months that you are there and drop in on weekends, you can ease up after that because you've established yourself as a 'weekend warrior' or an 'early bird.'"

Thirdly, when you're torqued about long hours, remember that "There's a relationship between what you're paid and what you have to produce," says Georgetown's Abbie Willard. As I explain in detail in the "Econ 101" section, if you want them to show you the money, you've got to show them the work.

Remember also that not all hours are created equal. Long hours don't necessarily mean that you're killing yourself from sun-up to sundown. As Georgetown's Beth Sherman points out, "As a new associate, a lot of what you do doesn't take a lot of thought. Those hours aren't as tiring because you aren't using as much brain power." And you can minimize your time at the office by making sure that when you ***are*** there, you're being efficient. As Carlton Fields' Eric Adams says, "The most important thing is that you give them high-quality work. If you spend two hours reading sports on the Internet and then realize you have tons of work to do, then you're spending more time at the office than you have to."

4) What to do when you're away from the office during the day.

When you leave the office during the day, Minnesota's Nora Klaphake recommends that you "Let others know what you're working on and where you are. Announce loudly enough for several people to hear that you are going to court or meeting a client outside the office. That way they don't assume that you are out playing golf or shopping for an afternoon."

b. Who's got the juice?

Many lawyers pointed out to me that at every firm, there are partners whose associates "never make partner." Some partners seem powerful but they really aren't; others may seem timid and out of the loop but they're actually highly valued and well respected. As Dickinson's Elaine Bourne says, "When you start, you may have a perception that so-and-so seems to be a lame duck. They don't seem to do a lot, they're quiet, not boisterous, and when they come to you, you may be telling yourself that their work isn't as important. But don't blow them off! You need to know what the power structure really is."

In every organization, some people will be more powerful than others, even if you can't identify them immediately. As one recruiting coordinator put it, "You can smell the fear when certain people walk down the hall." Use your "cultural tools" to find out who's really got the juice.

Hofstra's Rebecca Katz-White tells you to "Watch who hangs out with who, the social interaction." Miami's Marcy Cox tells you that "At meetings, see how people respond to the person who's talking. The one who talks all the time may not be respected, but people may really sit up and take notice when a person who's usually quiet takes the floor. Some lawyers are very quiet and ***very*** well-respected." Georgia State's Vickie Brown adds that you should "See who lawyers go to for advice and information. That shows you who they think has sound judgment." And of course, listen for people's comments about the people they work with!

How should you use this information? As Georgetown's Beth Sherman says, "If you don't know what you want to do, find a well-respected partner and work for him or her. You'll have a good experience." And as Chicago Kent's Stephanie Rever Chu advises, "You need to know who not to cross! It might be an attorney, an office manager, a secretary. The title doesn't count. The ***influence*** does."

Also, use your cultural tools to see if ***your*** supervisor is powerful. Watch when you mention his/her name to other people. Watch their reactions—enthusiastic? Noncommittal? Sympathetic? And listen to how they respond. If you haven't hitched your wagon to a star, you need to use tools to advance your career—you'll find those tools in the section called "How To Be Your Own Career Counselor."

c. Tips on working for your supervisor

In the "How To Crush Research And Writing Assignments" section, I tell you about the importance of gathering intelligence on working for a new supervisor—for instance, you need to get advice from other associates who've worked for your supervisor before. If your supervisor has likes, dislikes, quirks—you want to know that ***before*** you make a mistake.

SMART HUMAN TRICK . . .

Female associate at a small firm says, "I was warned shortly after starting my job that if one particular partner fired me I shouldn't pack my things—he fired every associate at one time or another. Sure enough, he stormed into my office one day and fired me over something stupid. I ignored it, and he calmed down. If I hadn't heard about his reputation ahead of time, I would have been devastated."

d. Socializing expectations

You need to fit in. As Harvard's Laura Share Kalin advises, "You can't lock yourself away. Be social!" You need to watch to see ***exactly*** what's expected of you. Minnesota's Susan Gainen tells you to "Watch for behavior cues at work. Do people eat lunch at their desks? Do they go out together? Do they work out together? Figure out what's going on by looking carefully around you. Don't isolate yourself and don't hang out exclusively in the company of support staff or your age peers!"

One career services director told of a student who called her, telling her he'd received an offer from a great firm. His only contact thus far had been interviews at the office. The managing partner had sent him a letter inviting him to the firm's annual golf outing. The letter included the line, "We know you may not golf, I don't, but I participate every year." The student asked the career services director, "Do I really have to go? I've got to study for the Bar exam. And I don't golf!" She responded, "Absolutely! You should tell them that you're really excited about it, but you've never held a golf club." He protested, but she continued, "You don't know if this is an event you can blow off. The tone of the letter suggests that every lawyer in the firm goes. If they all do it, you can't turn down the invitation."

e. The financial health of your employer

If you work for the government, we ***all*** fervently hope that your employer is financially sound. If you are at a private firm, you can never be sure. Your employer almost certainly won't say anything officially if things are going bad. You have to use your cultural tools—and your good sense—to figure it out for yourself.

If you start your career with a large firm where you're making six figures to start, you need to be ***especially*** vigilant about financial matters. Skyrocketing salaries are creating an upheaval in the entire business of law. *American Lawyer* even ran an article, under the headline "Eat Our Young," that proposed that the answer is not to hire first year associates at all. Yikes! The fact is, there are a lot of partners who are plenty pissed off about high starting salaries. You've got to keep your eyes and ears open to see their potential effect on ***your*** firm. As the senior partner at one firm told me, "If profits at a firm lag behind, if the compensation to partners gets reduced, partners leave and take their book of business with them. Yeah, they're making a lot of money anyway. But if they perceive they can make more without having to cut in new associates with big salaries, they'll jump." So don't be seduced by the mahogany paneling and lush surroundings into thinking that nothing can rock your world. Be vigilant!

One career services director told how she had two students spend the summer at a firm. Neither got an offer at the end of the summer. When she called the firm to ask why, the firm said, "Their skills were bad." She knew the students and was highly suspicious of this answer. On top of that, she knew that the firm had been shrinking for two years. Sure enough, six months later, it closed.

One of the people I interviewed for this book was an associate at Finley, Kumble—a firm that was the third largest law firm in the country in the 1980's. It collapsed in a spectacular fashion, described in the book *Shark Tank.* The former associate said, "The firm sent out press releases, held press conferences saying that 'The rumors are totally unfounded, the firm is not going under.' It sent a memo in October to all of the attorneys in the firm, denying the rumors, saying that 'Rumors that we are going to close are absolutely false,' all underlined and in caps. The firm closed two months later. The lesson I learned was this: Always make a point of knowing a nosy person in the know who can keep you abreast of things. Merger deals, financial status, the fact that partners are leaving. Even if you don't get involved, listen! If the firm is going under, they won't tell you officially because they're afraid you'll jump ship. But if you don't listen, you're stuck for two reasons: (1) you're stuck with more work because of the people who **do** know and **are** jumping ship, and with the extra work you don't have the time to look for another job, and (2) when you finally figure it out, all of the other people who didn't listen are figuring it out, too, and you've got a ton of competition for jobs."

SMART HUMAN TRICK . . .

Associate at a large East Coast firm in the early 1990's. It's a matter of "speculation"—a/k/a gossip—that "We're all getting fired." The firm line is, "We're not laying off anyone." The associate says, "I hear that, and then I look at my personal experience. I'm not billing enough to support my salary. Econ 101 tells me that I'm not staying." Some of the associates bring up the unsubstantiated rumour at the next firm-wide meeting. The partners angrily stand by their public statements, and view with displeasure being embarrassed by the associates who bring up the matter in public. The associate says, "Shortly after that, I get a review that's particularly ugly. The quality of my work hasn't changed, and I'm working for the same partner I've worked for in the past. I realize: they're setting me up. They're laying the groundwork for getting rid of me.'" He immediately found another job. And shortly after he left, many of the associates were, in fact, laid off.

f. The circumstances of associates leaving the employer before you got there.

Listen carefully when people talk about associates who were forced out before you arrived. The fact is, different employers have different sensitivities about different things. For some of them, getting drunk and passing out at a partner's party would get you cashiered on the spot. At others, it wouldn't. Even though firms are hyper-conscious of sexual harassment issues, there are certain partners at certain places who are so powerful that if they harass a female associate, the partner will stay and the female associate will be forced out. If you're a woman, it's ***extremely*** important to know if there are men like that at work, so that you can avoid them at all costs. The bottom line is, see what's killed others at the office, so that you can avoid the same death!

g. Attitudes about pro bono work.

Every law firm will publicly herald its dedication to pro bono work. As I discuss in "Econ 101—The Business of Law," the truth may be very different. The only way you can tell what your employer really thinks of pro bono is by using your culture tools.

Watch carefully and see how pro bono is treated. As one lawyer points out, "Pro bono commitment varies. Some firms are very committed. At others, it's your own personal obligation." Another lawyer added that, "At many big firms, there's really only one person who does all the pro bono, but the credit is spread out." The hiring partner at one large firm lamented that "We do a lot of pro bono work, and it makes new associates believe that in everything we do, we're on the side of the 'right.' That's not realistic, and if they looked more closely, they'd realize that."

h. Handling billables.

Recording your time is an art that varies to some extent from employer to employer. I could probably have told you about it here. It would fit. But because the whole idea of billables is so tied in with the business of law, I talk about it with those topics, instead—under "Econ 101—The Business of Law."

i. Handling expense reports.

You need to learn what's appropriate to charge to the office, and what isn't. This is very much a cultural matter; different employers feel differently about different items. The easiest thing to do is to ask the recruiting administrator, hiring partner, or your supervisor ***before*** you submit your expense report. As Carlton Fields' Elizabeth Zabak suggests, "Do not expect the firm to reimburse you for everything under the sun. If you exceed the budget for recruiting dinners and the like, don't just submit the expense statement and hope for the best. Do a little public relations. Go see the recruiting administrator to explain the situation and let her know that you don't expect to be reimbursed or why this particular dinner got out of hand. Being up front goes a lot further than hoping something will slip by. ***Someone*** will notice, and you don't want it to be the managing partner."

Georgetown's Abbie Willard recommends that "For long trips, ask—how many days can you travel before submitting a dry cleaning charge, or shoe shine, or haircut? Always err on the side of conservatism. And be aware that guidelines for meals are different for associates than they are for partners!"

CAREER LIMITING MOVE . . .

An associate files an expense report, asking for gas mileage reimbursement . . . for driving to a dinner party at a partner's home.

CAREER LIMITING MOVE . . .

A partner's wife asks the firm to pay for her new gas grill, arguing that "surely we will be hosting many outdoor parties for summer associates in the future."

j. Perceptions of you

As Vermont's Pavel Wonsowitz advises, "You need to keep your finger on the pulse of what's being said about you." When somebody brings you bad news, thank them. Don't shoot the messenger.

When people have a negative opinion of you, they will be loathe to say things to you directly—but they probably won't be as shy about saying things behind your back. Schmucks! When those comments come to your attention, keep two things in mind: 1) The messenger's motivation in telling you. Don't betray any emotion. Use your perceptions of your contact and of the original speaker to see how much credence to give to the comment. 2) Remember that anybody's perception is just that: It's only a perception. It tells you only what the speaker thinks of you at the moment they made the comment. Don't take it personally. You ***can*** change perceptions. (I talk about this in great detail in the section called "Use Evaluations And Criticism To Propel Your Career Forward.")

One associate at a firm in the Midwest talked about an experience he had when he started to work. "I had just finished the first client letter I ever wrote. My secretary, Tanya, brought it in, and I signed it. She asked, 'Would you like a copy?' She had a heavy Boston accent, and I thought she said 'Coffee.' So I responded, 'I'd love a coffee! Thanks. I take it light with sugar.' She angrily responded, 'I'm not your slave!' and stormed out of my office. I was totally confused. Another secretary came up to me fifteen minutes later, and said, 'How could you say that to Tanya? Secretaries here don't bring coffee to their bosses. Get your head out of the Fifties. Nobody will work for you if you have an attitude like that.' Thank God she said something to me! It gave me a chance to straighten things out with Tanya, and with all of the other secretaries who had daggers out for me."

k. How to Look the Part (. . . and Why Ally McBeal Is *Not* A Good Role Model)

Your clothes have always said a lot about you. When you become a lawyer, you want your clothes to say what your employer, your clients, and everybody else you have contact with professionally will ***expect*** them to say. Here's what to do to make sure you look the part:

1) Until you figure out the dress code at work, wear what you wore to interviews—as long as you dressed conservatively for those!

   Your temptation might be to buy a whole new wardrobe before you start working. That makes sense only if you've spent some time with the employer previously, either with a clerkship or with some casual visits or, in the case of prosecutors, by visiting the courtroom ahead of time and watching them work. You can also buy a wardrobe before you arrive at the office if you sit down first with the recruiting coordinator or hiring partner to ask about what's appropriate. Otherwise, have just a few "interview" outfits, and hold off on any major purchases. The reason you should do this is that if you buy ahead of time, you might be buying something, totally innocently, that's wrong for the office culture. Either that, or you'll buy an entire wardrobe that's too conservative, when you might find out that there's a lot more leeway for individuality at your office. You can always add livelier clothes to your conservative interview wear once you've learned the uniform at work. As Texas Tech's Kay Fletcher says, "You never get criticized for dressing too conservatively when you start! If you're too risqué you'll stand out for all the wrong reasons." Carlton Fields' Elizabeth Zabak points out that "Law is a conservative profession. Your initial impression will be a lasting one. You want to be remembered for your intelligence and ability, not the length of your skirt, your hairstyle or your make-up." "When you're new, you don't want to wear ***anything*** that will make people talk about you," adds Minnesota's Susan Gainen.

2) Watch what other people wear to work—and know what to watch for.

   Remember the movie "Men In Black"? When Rip Torn says to Will Smith, "Time to put it on. The last suit you'll ever wear," and hands him a black suit? Well, work isn't likely to be ***that*** strict. But as a new lawyer, you ***are*** going to be wearing something of a uniform. And that uniform will be decided by people in your office. Here's what you want to watch out for:

   a) I've already told you to keep an eye—and ear—out for the most respected junior associates. Wear what they wear.

   b) Be aware that different kinds of employers have different quirks. Georgetown's Anna Davis recounts her own experience as a new lawyer on Capitol Hill. She says, "I figured I couldn't go wrong if I wore a conservative blue suit to work. I didn't realize that on the Hill, ***pages*** wear blue suits. I couldn't figure out what was going on when everybody handed me envelopes. They thought I was a page, not a lawyer!"

   c) If you are working in a part of the country that's new to you, "Be especially adept at picking up clues about what the sartorial norms are," says Kentucky's Drusilla Bakert. People mentioned this to me all over the country. In

New York and Los Angeles, you can be more fashion-forward. At a lot of employers in those cities, a man can get away with a four-button suit that wouldn't fly in more conservative places. In Texas, women are expected to wear more makeup. In the Pacific Northwest, just the opposite is true; a more natural look is the norm. These are of course generalizations, but the point is this: be sensitive to geographic wardrobe styles if you're in a new place.

d) Be aware that some people in ***every*** office dress inappropriately. Be more conservative than the wilder dressers. And don't take your dress cues from the support staff! As Dave James of the San Diego City Attorney's Office says, "Figure that the shortest skirts are too short; the most casually dressed are too casual; the most rumpled suits are too rumpled. If your dress is at the outer margins of attire in your office, you need to move toward the center. When you find yourself defending your dress by comparing it favourably to what somebody else in the office wears, remember how impressed the highway patrol officer is when you say, 'But Officer, others were going faster than me.'"

   Furthermore, remember that more experienced lawyers have more leeway to dress more individualistically. Because they are powerful, they have a bargaining chip that you don't have as a new lawyer. When you've earned some juice, you can wear the red leather miniskirt, too (unless you're a man, in which case that's probably ***never*** a good idea no matter ***how*** powerful you get).

e) Pay more attention to what people in your office wear than you do to articles about what lawyers are supposed to wear. Mississippi's Joyce Whittington tells the following story: "I saw an article one day in a national legal magazine that said that men should only wear shoes that lace up, not slip-ons of any kind. It was during on-campus interview season. When a group of about six male interviewers came into my office the next day, the magazine was on my desk. As we all walked out of my office, one of the men asked me if I had read the magazine on my desk. I told him I had, and said, 'It was interesting to see that they said men should only wear tie-up, wingtip-like shoes.' We all found ourselves immediately looking down at everyone's feet. As it turns out, ***none*** of them were wearing the shoes the article had said were mandatory. All of them had on very nice slip-ons. I told them jokingly that since they weren't dressed appropriately, they should go home and change!"

Articles tell you only about what the reporter who wrote the article was told by whomever (s)he interviewed. If what people wear at your office belies any published source, follow what you see at work!

3) " . . . But Why Do I Have To Dress Like Everybody Else?"

The short answer is: you don't. Not all the time. At home, you can wear a tutu, scuba gear, and mukluks if it floats your boat. But at work, you're a lawyer. And there are a bunch of good reasons for dressing like everybody else.

a) You want to be taken seriously as a lawyer by the people at your office.

If you don't look the part, you won't be. As Georgetown's Abbie Willard says, "When people look at you, you don't want them to notice how short your skirt is or how expensive your suit is." Nova Southeastern's Pat Jason points out that "If you dress provocatively, you'll have a hard time being taken seriously. Not only that, but you'll be perceived as insecure. You can't put your best foot forward if it's clad in a shocking pink five-inch heel!"

CAREER LIMITING MOVE . . .

New female associate, large firm. She attends a meeting with other partners and associates. Everybody is shocked to see that she is wearing an "Ally McBeal" outfit with a **very** short skirt. She sits down, and to make matters worse, she doesn't cross her legs. When the meeting is over, the buzz behind her back is about her bright yellow underwear—visible to everybody in the room.

As DePanfilis & Vallerie's Carrie Colangelo says, "If you're a female litigator, you have to start out playing by the rules if you want people to view you as capable. I started out playing by the rules. In my mind, you earn the right to wear the candy apple red suit. Once you've been around and you know what you are doing, it's all right to stand out. But when you're new, and you have no clue what you're doing or sometimes even where the heck the courtroom you need to be in is located, your major objective is to survive. You don't want to be remembered as the incompetent lawyer in the pink suit. The rules only change once you know what you're doing."

b) If you don't dress appropriately, people will question your professional competence.

It doesn't seem fair, but people draw conclusions about your abilities based on what you wear. They'll think, if you can't get the clothes right, what else are you messing up? It influences their opinion in ways they themselves may not even realize. One older attorney described a young female attorney as being "just so incompetent. And everything she owns is the color of sherbet!" That's not the way you want to be viewed.

c) Your clients deserve to have a lawyer who dresses the way they expect lawyers to dress.

Even if your office has gone to "business casual" (and we're going to talk about that in a minute), remember that whenever you have contact with clients, casual wear ***doesn't*** fly. As Venable, Baetjer's Stefan Tucker says, "I always wear a tie when I meet with clients. It's a respect thing." Hofstra's Rebecca Katz-White points out that, "When you're young, your clients have a hard enough time taking you seriously. You need to see yourself as a professional, and that means looking like a lawyer. You act more professionally when you're dressed appropriately."

When you have paying clients, they expect you to look like a worthwhile investment. As Carlton Fields' Kevin Napper says, "If you were paying someone hundreds of dollars an hour, wouldn't you want them to look the part?" DePanfilis & Vallerie's Carrie Colangelo adds, "If you want to get a client to hire your firm and pay a ten thousand dollar retainer, your stockings shouldn't have runs in them, your makeup should be on, and your nails should be neat. If you look like a mess and can't present a good image, why should anyone think you could present a neat case?"

If you are a public defender or otherwise work with low-income clients, take special care in what you wear when you meet with them. You want to dress respectfully. As one public defender pointed out, "We have men who graduate from law school and come to our office, and think, 'Hey, here I am in this cool office in the public sector, there's nothing wrong with having a pony tail down to my waist.' It's not fair to their clients! They have a right to somebody who ***looks*** like a lawyer!" You also want to be careful about flaunting your comparative wealth to your low-income clients.

As Northern Illinois' Mary Obrzut says, "You can't dress like a Junior Leaguer if you're a public defender." And one female lawyer adds, "When I deal with workers' comp clients or I'm doing pro bono work, I don't wear my diamond engagement ring. I was once trying to explain to a client why he should accept a rather paltry sum of money for his not-so-great case. He looked at my ring, and said, 'Look—I don't expect you to understand my life.'"

4) Getting the hang of "business casual." It's not the same as "law school casual."

   The legal profession is in an uproar about the concept of "business casual." The fact is, ***nobody*** knows what it means. It differs from office to office. Here's some advice about how you should handle "business casual."

   a) Ask!

      The best advice on figuring out what to wear to a "business casual" office is to call ahead of time and ask the recruiting coordinator, hiring partner, or anybody who interviewed you about what exactly is appropriate. As Arizona's Mary Birmingham says, "Ask what to wear. They'll appreciate that you bothered to ask!"

   b) "Business casual" doesn't mean "law school casual."

      Sport shirts and jackets, khakis, sweaters, pantsuits for women—that's all fine. Flip flops, T-shirts, jeans, shorts, leggings, flashy jewelry are not. If you see it on MTV, nobody should see ***you*** in it at the office. Bras, definitely. Visible bra staps, no. Don't come to work in the outfit in which you went clubbing last night. Other outfits recruiting coordinators have seen new associates wearing to work: beach wear, gardening outfits, and pajamas. Don't go there!

   c) "Business casual" doesn't mean "cheap looking."

As Mary Birmingham says, "You still have to look great. You can get away with polyester, but it can't be plastic bag polyester." Shop at quality stores and see what their idea of casual is. Some firms even have in-house fashion shows from Brooks Brothers! Dickinson's Elaine Bourne says that if you go to "Talbots, Brooks Brothers, stores like that—they have people who deal with 'business casual' every day."

d) Even at a business casual office, *always* have something formal at work in case you're called out of the office on business at a moment's notice.

I've made this point several times throughout the book, but it's worth making again. If you're dressed casually, you will not be able to take up a senior attorney's offer to go to a client meeting, court function, or professional event. As Florida State's Stephanie Redfearn points out, "More senior attorneys tend to dress down on occasion, but that's because they know their schedules and know when they are going to be going to court or meeting with clients. As a new associate, you don't have that kind of schedule mastery. If you're new, dress professionally or have something at the office to put on. A lawyer may call and say, 'Who wants to come to this deposition with me?' or 'Who wants to come to court with me?' If you aren't dressed appropriately, you'll miss the chance." The lawyer at a county attorney's office commented that one day when she was wearing a dress and a shawl, her boss ran into her office, and said, "I need someone to argue this case in the Second Circuit. Our adversary will pick you up here." The lawyer was mortified; she was dressed completely inappropriately for a court appearance. After that, she ***always*** kept formal clothes at work.

5) Your appearance isn't limited to the clothes you wear.

"Dress" is really shorthand for "appearance." Your appearance in general should be professional. At the risk of telling you what you undoubtedly already know, there are ***lots*** of stylish accoutrements that don't fly when you're a lawyer. Body piercing? Don't have anything pierced that will show when you're wearing a suit. A pierced lip or tongue—no. Anything below your neck—fine. Nobody will see it.

For men and women—no backpacks. Briefcases. As Quinnipiac's Diane Ballou says, "You can bring in a briefcase even if it only contains lunch, sneakers, and a magazine!"

For men—"Watches, shoes, and ties say it all," says Ronna Lichtenberg in *Work Would Be Great If It Weren't For The People*. "Watches are basically sports cars on men's wrists." For women, watch what the other women at the office do with their hair, and don't stray far from that. One recruiter in the Northeast commented on a summer clerk who came in with huge pouffy hair: "She looked like a banshee." If everybody else at the office has big hair, that's fine. But if they don't—reduce the volume on yours. Also, nails. Keep them relatively short and well-groomed. No long, curved acrylics. No designs! Set up a regular manicure appointment for yourself. It's something that used to be an indulgence, but now that you're a professional, it's a necessity. For jewelry—nothing cheap or flashy. Makeup—natural looking, no lipsticks that take you anywhere on the colour wheel away from the red family. Save the blue lipstick for clubbing—or Halloween.

6) Figuring out what's *de rigeur* socially.

As is true with every other aspect of business dressing, you can't go wrong by asking what's appropriate. Whether it's the firm retreat or a semiformal affair, ***ask***. One lawyer talked about showing up at his firm's annual retreat at a resort wearing a college sweatshirt. "Everybody else was wearing khakis and polo shirts," he said. "I looked like I was there to swab the floors!"

At more formal parties, it's easier for men than it is for women. For men, formal means a tux. A ***black*** tux; you don't want to look like Tom Hanks in "Big." (Rent it. It's funny.) Semi-formal means a suit and tie. For a holiday party, maybe a Christmas tie. For women, formal means a long gown, and semi-formal means a headache.

As South Carolina's Phyllis Burkhard says, "Female attorneys are in a quandary when it comes to semi-formal wear. Do you 'look like a woman' in dressy attire, or do you 'look like a lawyer' in a suit?" Ask other female lawyers at the office what's appropriate; ask them what they wear to these kinds of events. Phyllis Burkhard recommends something like a tailored dress or "something a bit more flashy than what you wear to the office, but still businesslike." Stay away from something terribly sexy. As one lawyer commented dryly, "You don't want to go to a senior partner's party perceived as competition for his wife." If you wind up being overdressed, Greenberg Traurig's etiquette guru Sharon Abrahams suggests that you follow her mother's advice, and say, "Excuse me, but we have another function to go to"—and pretend you dressed for ***that***.

If you are going straight from work to a social function, Sharon Abrahams says that for men, you can wear exactly what you wore to work. For women, "You want to look a little more festive. Wear a shift under a suit coat to work. For the evening, add a bit of jewelry, remove the jacket, add a little more makeup, and change shoes."

7) Remember that you've *got* to rely on your powers of observation and answers to the questions you ask as guideposts to what to wear.

As Hamline's Vince Thomas says, "Lawyers won't tell you you've dressed wrong, but they ***will*** notice and they ***will*** talk about it." As one lawyer pointed out, "Dress isn't accidental. There are these wonderful things called ***mirrors***. Think about the image you're creating."

1. **Three situations where you should definitely *ignore* the culture and "do the right thing."**

   After telling you over and over again to follow the culture at work, there are three situations where you should absolutely, positively ignore the culture and follow your better instincts. They are:

   1) Ethics.

      It's the culture of your firm to "bend" the rules of ethics and/or they encourage you to do so, ***get out*** before you're led away in handcuffs. Under ***no*** circumstances "follow the herd" into ethical violations. (I address this in more detail under "Ethical Issues".)

   2) Racist, sexist behavior.

      Whether it's inappropriate jokes or discriminatory or harassing behavior, don't go there. Just don't. You don't want the racist and/or sexist tag to dog you for your entire career, even if you were just going along with the pack.

   3) Treating support staff badly.

      Maybe your superiors treat the support staff like a rented mule. Don't you do it. It's inhumane and wrong. And it tells you something very significant—and very bad—about the people you work for.

4. **If you're African-American, here's some advice about starting your career from an experienced African-American attorney.**

I'm not African-American. My heritage is British and Indian. So half of my ancestors oppressed the other half. The point is, I can't possibly know what it's like to be African-American. But many people I interviewed pointed out to me that new lawyers who are African-American face a host of issues that white lawyers don't.

For advice on this issue, I turned to an African-American senior associate at a large Midwestern firm. He is often called upon to address race and gender issues for groups of law students and new practitioners. Here's his advice for you.

"As an African-American associate at a large firm, realize that starting at a large firm is tough for ***everybody***. You can't sulk too much. You can't tell yourself, 'Everybody has it easier than me.' You're only making it harder for yourself. Don't be eaten up by feeling 'I'm not being treated fairly here.' In that sense color is no different than gender. You can't be bitter and make partner. You have to be serene. Don't draw energy away from what's already a difficult task. If you get swallowed up by anger, the firm won't care. They'll just say that you're another associate who didn't make it. You can't be distracted by things that will destroy you if you want to succeed.

"It helps if you find a social niche. Find a situation where color or gender isn't an issue. Find golf, tennis, aerobics, bowling, a book club. Get yourself into situations where distinctions disappear; get to know people on a fundamental level to break down the race and gender barrier.

"As an African-American lawyer, use warmth and candor to break down barriers. Speak candidly about your own life experience so people can say, 'In a lot of ways he's no different than me. He's middle class, he went to law school, he has dreams for his career—how different is he really?' Tell people about your parents' jobs, about your childhood. Let them get to know you. Let them see that you're struggling to make a success of your career, too. Don't be on pins and needles. Let them know they can joke around with you. Of course you have every right to be aloof, but it helps to be warm if you can!

"When I started at my firm, I was the first African-American lawyer they'd ever hired. There are many, many law firms with very few attorneys of color, maybe yours included. When you're in that situation it's very easy to have your head turned. I remember going to a furniture store to buy a desk for my apartment when I first started out. When I got talking with the salesman, he asked me what I did for a living. When I told him where I was working, he responded with genuine respect, 'You are with the finest law firm in this city.' I was pretty full of myself. Then I got invited to a county minority lawyers' association meeting. The speaker was the first African-American judge in the county. The room was full of guys who had graduated from law school in the 1960s and 70s, when a job like mine would have been closed to them. They were very talented but they were shut out without a chance. They had careers but not a lot of prestige. Seeing people who strived the way they did was a humbling experience. I had no pretentiousness after that. The fact that I was the first one at my firm instead of one of them was a historical accident. It should have been one of these older lawyers who broke the color barrier.

It doesn't pay to be arrogant no matter who you are. You don't have to pump yourself up. The fact is, if you win a big case or do great work or get elected to office, people will heap praise on you no matter who you are. You'll get your due."

C. Getting Organized . . . And Staying That Way!

Maybe you're a naturally organized person. But the number of books on the market about getting organized suggests that you're probably more like me. I've got a bunch of those books, and as soon as I can lay my hands on them in my office I'm going to get organized. I know they're in here ***somewhere***.

The fact is, life is a lot easier for you if you get organized and ***stay*** organized. This came home to me a couple of years ago, when my sweetie Henry and I were planning a trip to San Francisco and the Napa Valley. I was chatting with our neighbor Claudia, and when I mentioned our trip, she said, 'Oh, come into the house. I'm sure I have an article about the wine country.' I followed her into her den, where she opened a file cabinet that was meticulously organized. She flipped straight to "Travel" and under that topic, "Wine Country." She pulled out the article and handed it to me. The whole exercise took her about ten seconds. I was dumbfounded. Heck, if you asked me to borrow a book, it'd take me ***hours*** to find it. Even for a book ***I wrote***. Claudia saw the look on my face, and said, "I always say: if you can't find it, you might as well not have it." And by gum, she's right. In this section, we'll talk about everything you need to know to get organized—and why you should be that way!

1. Six great reasons to make your office hum like a well-oiled machine

As a lawyer, you've got a lot more riding on your organizational skills than your vacations. There are six excellent reasons to take the time to get organized ***right now***.

a. You'll save tons of time.

If you have to spend even a few minutes looking for a document or a phone number, the time quickly adds up. You can't bill your 'searching' time to anybody. Over the space of a year, you'll spend hours and hours at work that you could be spending having fun. If that's not motivation enough to get organized, I don't know what is!

b. You'll protect your ideas and your work product.

Sometimes you hear about unscrupulous people who will try to hock your work and claim it as their own. I hope it never happens to you. But the fact is, you can't just whine 'But *I* did that' without backup (actually, you can't whine ***at all***). If you keep meticulous records of what you do, you'll always be able to protect your work. In your time sheets, be detailed in your descriptions of your work. Keep accurate records of who you talk to and the issues you cover. Keep case logs. (And incidentally, when a more senior associate tries to swipe credit for your work, one associate recommends that you "Go to the partner in charge of the project and say casually, 'I hope my work on that issue was helpful.' It's sneaky, but it works.")

c. You'll cover your a—I mean, butt.**

Keeping accurate records of what you've done, what you're being asked to do, and what you're doing, will reap rewards in a ton of situations.

For instance, when you receive a research assignment, if you take accurate notes and show them to the assigning attorney, and you keep those notes where you can put your hands on them quickly, you can't ever be accused of getting the facts wrong because you missed something. You've got written proof of what you were told.

If you keep accurate records of the work you do for every client, you've got insulation from bar complaints and malpractice suits because you can prove your level of diligence. A lawyer at one firm told me about a group of doctors his firm represented in a medical malpractice case. He said, "There's an old saying that your client can become your worst enemy. When these doctors lost the case, they went to another law firm, looking to see if they could sue us for malpractice. We always keep meticulous records. When the firm they hired investigated us, they asked for all of our records in the case. They went back to the doctors and said, 'You have no case. They did everything we would have done.' If we didn't have careful records of our work and our conversations with these doctors and very complete correspondence, we could have had a nasty situation on our hands, ***regardless*** of how good our work was." As Northern Illinois' Mary Obrzut says, "Paper the world. It's the only way to protect yourself!"

SMART HUMAN TRICK . . .

Junior associate at a large Southern firm: "I was once asked to review a huge bulk of documents for incidents in which our client's products had caused injuries. After producing a ton of documents to the partner, he returned a huge portion of the documents to me, telling me that I had 'over-produced' them and they were irrelevant. Fast forward three months, when the partner came raging into my office screaming that I was going to get him fired, that I was incompetent in not producing documents properly, that he was facing sanctions for not disclosing all relevant incidents of injury.

In what was a wonderful stroke of luck, I opened my file cabinet in his presence, pulled out a stack of the 'unproduced' documents that he had returned to me, along with a nice clear memo to file that read, 'Attached to this memo are the documents I presented to [partner], but which he thought were irrelevant to the production and returned to me.' I have never seen this man eat crow like he did at that moment. What a great feeling! I hadn't made a habit of writing 'memos to file' until then, but I do it **constantly** now. They're easily dictated or even scribbled on a sticky pad, and I use them for everything from deadlines to project details."

 SMART HUMAN TRICK . . .

Assistant District Attorney. She works in a team with other prosecutors. One of her co-workers calls in sick, asking her to cover his calendar. "Can you write it out for me?" he asks. He tells her where his plea sheet is, stating what every plea should be. Their mutual supervisor comes to her subsequently, and says, 'Why did you ask for this plea? You should have asked for 150 days, not 50 days.' She says, 'He told me to do it.' The supervisor responds, 'I talked to him, and he said that's not the plea he asked you for.' She goes to her file cabinet and pulls out the plea sheet the guy had given her, in which he'd stated the pleas he wanted. Instead of throwing it out, she'd hung onto it. There, plain as day, is a plea request of 50 days, signed by the guy who'd called in sick.

d. You'll protect your reputation.

As a new lawyer, "Visual perceptions count!" says Syracuse's Alex Epsilanty. "If your office looks like a mess, you look like you don't know what you're doing. Later on, when you are more established, you have more leeway, but in the beginning, your office has to look controlled." One lawyer adds that "No law firm wants its clients seeing crap all over the floor. Make ***piles*** if you're that messy, so at least your desk ***looks*** cleaned up. At worst, hide stuff under your desk so it's not visible from the doorway."

Some people pointed out to me that some lawyers think if their office is messy, it implies that they're so busy and preoccupied with more important things that they have no time for "trifles" like tidying up. One lawyer commented that "You'll see offices that look like a Force-5 hurricane, with piles upon piles of loose papers, file folders, note-laden legal pads and miscellaneous office supplies on every surface." The problem is, all you need is one incident of losing a document in the turmoil for you to be cured of this perception. As Bart Schorsch writes in *Student Lawyer*, "If you ever want to commit suicide, just misfile or lose an important memo or copy of a judgment. Your death may be quick and painless, or it might come screaming out of the senior partner's office, but if you really lose something, you will have all the life expectancy of a gnat in a blast furnace. Bottom line: Learn the system and make backup copies of *everything*."

CAREER LIMITING MOVE (BY A PARTNER) AND SMART HUMAN TRICK (BY AN ASSOCIATE) . . .

Junior associate at a large West Coast firm: "There is a partner here who is known for having an office that looks like an explosion in a paper factory. He recently received a frantic call from a client saying, 'I lost the original of that agreement I just signed with X. I don't want to renegotiate the agreement with that son-of-a-bitch. Can you send me another copy of it as soon as possible?' The client knew that the firm had a copy of the agreement. The partner, claiming he could not locate the agreement in his office or files, sent out urgent voice mail and e-mail messages to other lawyers involved in the matter asking them to search high and low for a copy of the agreement. After a couple of days searching without success, the client was so desperate to retrieve the document that he offered to pay the firm to get a paralegal to spend full-time looking through our offices for the document until it was found, and this partner forwarded this request to the rest of us by e-mail on a Sunday when I happened to be at work. To satisfy a hunch I had—namely, that this partner was the most likely person to have the agreement because he was the one who was working on it—I went into his office to dig through the debris hunting for the agreement. I found it within ten minutes—on his **desk**! Needless to say, while the client was relieved, the partner was highly embarrassed that he had wasted a lot of his colleagues' time searching for something that had been less than two feet from him the entire time."

e. You'll be able to go into evaluations armed and ready.

If you keep complete records of all of your work, any written comments you've received on your work, and any verbal compliments that you've jotted down, you'll be able to go into annual or semi-annual reviews being able to defend yourself against any unfair characterizations of what you've done.

f. Being organized will help you get another job, if and when you want one.

If you keep a copy of all of your work, and a form file of your own, you're setting yourself up for the rest of your career. You'll be able to refresh your memory for what you've done if you can look through a file of your written work, and you'll be able to go into more detail on your resume about the types of experience you've had (which will make your experience look more substantial). And if you keep your own 'form file,' that is, copies of the types of documents you work on the most, you'll save tons of time when you revisit those kinds of projects whether at this employer or anywhere else.

2. What To Do To Get And Stay Organized: A stupendous all-around organizational system

One of the great things about researching a book like this is that people just overwhelm you with the quality of their suggestions. I asked everybody I talked to about their organizing tips, and the most incredible advice I got was from a lawyer at Goulston Storrs, who called what you're about to see the "fundamental rules of organization." I think if you follow this program, you can't possibly go wrong. As this lawyer pointed out, "Organization can make or break your experience as an associate because you are responsible for huge amounts of paper and data. If you handle it well, you earn a reputation within the firm and with clients for efficiency and thoroughness. If you handle it poorly, you will likely work longer hours and enjoy the work less." I can't imagine anyone being anything other than awed by this system. Here it is:

a. Anything that comes in (or goes out) by hard copy, fax, or e-mail is immediately cc'd to the appropriate client file so that you can find things later when the dust settles (be sure to include in such copies all attachments and backups). I bcc every e-mail to my secretary so she can print every message and attachment for the file.

b. I make heavy use of Microsoft Outlook to schedule meetings (every meeting has an automatic alarm to remind me to be there), maintain my Rolodex (that way addressing letters in Word or e-mail messages in Outlook is quicker through linking to my Rolodex) and maintain my task list. I reformatted the Outlook task list to be three columns: (i) for priority listing (1 for highest, must be done today, 2 for perhaps today, and 3 and 4 for even further back on the burner), (ii) client name and client code, and (iii) comments to remind me about the tasks. I review and revise the priorities every day, print priorities 1 and 2 each day, and keep them on my desk. It's handy to keep track of what I am doing, shows the work allocators how heavy my plate is, and makes an easy place to hand write the notes of the day such as telephone calls to return.

c. I set up a sidewise filing cabinet next to my desk and keep active matters in drop files in alphabetical order to be handy when clients call.

d. When communicating by electronic mail I always bcc myself and store a copy of the message in an Outlook electronic file folder for the particular client (this saves time when trying to find messages and documents).

e. When communicating documents within the office I always use e-mail because people get it more quickly and may not need to print out the document if review onscreen is available.

f. I have a handheld computer (an LG Electronics Phenom Express, although a Palm Pilot would work just as well) that allows me to synchronize calendar, contacts, and documents to my desktop. I can carry all this information with me to meetings.

g. I use our document management program (Imanage) to create lists of the most important documents by client so I can quickly access the principal agreements and the fax cover sheet for clients (as opposed to searching and searching for the key documents). I use the same technology to keep copies of form documents handy.

h. I am a heavy Internet user and am constantly obtaining government documents and information electronically. It is usually far faster and more accurate than photocopying from paper sources, particularly as I can cut and paste needed text into memoranda and other documents. I bookmark Internet sites by topic (federal government, state government, particular topics).

i. When managing a complex transaction with many documents, I create 3-ring binders to hold current drafts, disclosure schedules, and others.

j. Whenever possible, I try to answer voicemails, e-mails, or letters immediately upon receipt so that no time is wasted reading, putting in a to-do pile, and then re-reading later.

3. Everything else you need to know about getting organized

Here are other ideas I heard from other people about getting your act together at work!

a. Get with your secretary and/or office manager to learn the ropes at your office.

If there's a particular way that your office likes to keep track of matters and organize files, then by all means, use that system! You'll make it easier on yourself and everyone you work with if you all follow the same routine. Your secretary is a great resource for this; (s)he'll know exactly what the office routines are.

b. Keeping Track Of Your Work

The most important tracking function of all—your billables—is covered in "Everything You Never Wanted To Know About Billables . . . " on page 148. Other than billables, here's what you need to know:

1) Remember that other people may need to use your files, so make them readily accessible with that in mind.

   Whether you are working on a corporate deal or a litigation matter, whether you're a private practitioner or a prosecutor, other people may need access to your work, and you have to organize your projects with that thought in mind. As Alex Epsilanty says, "In a law firm, your boss will assume you'll have a file. You never know when (s)he'll come into your office looking for something, whether or not you're there." It's kind of like the rule your mom always taught you, about wearing clean underwear just in case you get into an accident. "You don't want the people at the hospital seeing you wearing dirty underwear."

   NYU's Gail Cutter recommends that you "Put all documents in clearly labeled folders, with client and matter numbers, or neat piles so that others can locate them in your absence. Also remember that all attorneys working on a case or deal have access to all files, so be mindful of what you keep in your 'office' files!"

   If you are a litigator, Loyola's Pam Occhipinti recommends that you "Keep a legal pad as a case log for every case, so that anyone who has to take over your case will know what you've done. On the right-hand side of each page, keep a history of any court documents. On the left-hand side, keep a detailed log of everything you do on the case: every meeting, phone call, what you were told, who you talked to, and summarize comments. If you're ever sued for malpractice, this case log can be vital because it shows your standard of care."

2) Create a form file of your own.

   As Nova Southeastern's Pat Jason recommends, "Develop a loose-leaf folder as a 'form file' of your own." In it, you want to keep documents that you often use or duplicate, like pleadings, leases, agreements—anything. It'll be an excellent reference tool and save you tons of time hunting around for a model from which to work. Not only that, it's ***yours***, so you can take it with you if and when you change jobs.

3) Keep track of phone calls and conversations with a "memo to file."

   As Dewey Ballantine's John Ragosta says, "Write a memo to file after every phone call or conversation in which substantive issues are discussed. Sometimes the most important memoranda are not those sent to anyone, but those kept in a file! Litigation attorneys taught me this mantra: 'memorandum to file' after every phone call or conversation. After a phone call in which substantive issues are discussed, prepare a memo while your memory is still fresh." Weeks later, you won't remember exactly who said what without being able to refer to your notes.

4) Record any time your supervisor rejects your stance on a matter.

   Your supervisor has a lot more experience than you do, and you can learn a lot from them. But sometimes things go wrong, and when they do, you don't want any finger-pointing to result in your lynching. To avoid this, keep track of such differences with a memo to file. The fact that you wrote the memo contemporaneously will prove that you weren't subsequently making up an excuse to save your neck.

5) Have a "to-do" list every day.

   Florida State's Stephanie Redfearn suggests that you come up with a daily to-do list, either at night before you leave work or in the morning before you get started. Cardozo's Judy Mender suggests that your to-do list might take the form of a "file, in which you keep nothing but your to-do list. That is, cases and projects on which you are working, possibly including relevant time frames and deadlines (deadlines should also be 'diaried' in a calendar/appointment book which is checked daily). This file should not include the actual paperwork, but just a list that should be updated weekly. Also, your supervising attorney may appreciate you keeping this list so that the two of you can readily discuss your workload at any given time. It may also help you handle those situations in which the partner is ready to give you more work and you need to demonstrate that you are already truly overloaded!"

6) Consider carrying around a small notebook.

I have a number of friends who swear by the 6" x 9¼" notebooks they constantly carry, and I use this system myself (along with a DayTimer). It's a great way to gather together in one place everything you want to keep track of: assignments you get, conversations, meetings, deadlines, promises, names, and phone numbers. You have everything in chronological order, and you just start each day on a new page with the date at the top. If you also want to keep certain things in files—like notes to meetings for a particular client—you can always copy the relevant page of your notebook and pop it into the file.

7) Keep a calendar. Duh!

You were going to keep a calendar even if I didn't mention it. But Stephanie Redfearn has two tips about your calendar that you might have overlooked. First, she suggests that you "Keep a calendar that gives you detailed lead times. 'For April 20th, reminder—discovery response due on April 25th.'" Second, she advises that you "Make sure that all of the dates on your calendar are on at least one other person's calendar, so you can be reminded of things." Also, if you keep your calendar in a Palm Pilot or in a DayTimer, and you lose it—God forbid—that other person will be able to bail you out.

8) Files you need to keep.

John Ragosta gives you a rundown on the files you ought to keep:

a) Every matter requires a chronological file, which is a master file containing the following types of information: a reverse chronological filing of pertinent letters, memoranda, notes, and the like (some lawyers keep incoming and outgoing chrons separately);

b) Subject matter files ("SS 751 research," "New Brunswick timber values," "debenture agreements," and the like);

c) Pleadings files, if you are a litigator (the file should include every piece of paper that is formally filed, none that are not formally filed, in reverse chronological order with each document numbered, tabbed and indexed); and

d) A detailed, accessible index of all files. He suggests that "Even if official 'firm' or 'case' files exist, keep your own backup of appropriate materials that you can readily retrieve."

e) Take care of paperwork every night.

Take a few minutes before you go home at night to sort through the mess and put things in their appropriate files, even if you're going to leave the folders on your desk. If you do this on a daily basis you'll tackle the paper monster, and when you come in in the morning, you'll be in a better frame of mind to tackle things if your desk doesn't look like a bomb hit it.

c. Keeping track of people

As a lawyer, you'll meet tons and tons of people, both at work and at outside events. Use a Rolodex or Palm Pilot to record phone, fax, mail and e-mail information on every person you think you might have to contact again. You should also keep notes of anything relevant you learn about them—names of spouses and children, hobbies, notable achievements, and the like. In addition, Greenberg

Traurig's Sharon Abrahams says that when you collect business cards, "you should catalog them alphabetically and by urgency, and also by contact (whether it's a referral, a future colleague, and so on)."

d. Organizational tips for prosecutors.

As a new prosecutor, you'll find yourself dealing with a ***ton*** of different cases and different kinds of cases, right off the bat. Texas Tech's Kay Fletcher—a former prosecutor herself—advises that "You need to be very regimented from the very start. If you miss deadlines, it's in the newspaper and you're embarrassed." Prosecutors I spoke to offered these general organizational tips:

1) Remember that several prosecutors will often work on the same file. Make notes of every conversation concerning the case and keep those notes in the file. "That way, if any defense attorney is tempted to lie about a plea bargain that was offered or about representations that were made to the judge, the file provides evidence of what you really said," said one prosecutor.

2) Make sure every file has relevant phone numbers written on the inside of the folder. "You don't want to have to hunt around for a phone number when you open a file. You need it to be ***right there.***"

3) Make up "cheat sheets"; that is, little cards or slips of paper showing the potential penalties for all of the crimes you prosecute. For instance, you might handle motor vehicle violations and drug cases. You'd want your "cheat sheets" to show the fines and jail time for each of these crimes, and whether or not the jail sentences are consecutive or concurrent. "That way, you have a quick reference when you're in court or dealing with defense attorneys."

CHAPTER FOUR

The "People" Part Of Work. It's Not What You're Like Or How You Feel—It's How You Seem That Counts. How To Come Off As The Person You Want Other People To See.

A lot of people will tell you that attitude is everything. In fact, it's ***appearances*** that count. It's what you ***project***. As I've said before, what you ***think*** and ***feel*** is your exclusive purview. It's the manifestation of those thoughts and feelings that count at work. This distinction is important, because while you have little control over your "gut" thoughts and feelings, you have complete control over what you do with those thoughts and feelings, what other people ***see***. You're not powerless to change your behavior. You don't ***have*** to badmouth anything or anyone. Even if your supervisor is a jerk, the catered food at lunch is disgusting, the support people are incompetent or stupid, you don't have to say anything. Even if you feel incompetent or better than anybody else, it doesn't matter. It's what other people ***perceive*** that counts, and you have total control over that. That's all I'm worried about. I want people you work with to see the best possible you, and I'm going to explain exactly how you accomplish that.

It's ***very*** dangerous to assume that your work will speak for itself, and if your work is good enough, it doesn't matter what people think of you. As Boston University's Betsy Armour says, "Just being a good memo writer is not enough." Law school doesn't teach you that ***at all.*** "Plays well with others" is the most valuable skill you could bring forward with you from your education into the real world. As Venable Baetjer's Stefan Tucker says, "Law school teaches you how to analyze the law, not deal with people." Chicago's Suzanne Mitchell agrees, saying that "Success doesn't depend on what you're good at in school!" Your ability to deal with people ***always*** matters. As Hendrie Weisinger points out in his book *Emotional Intelligence At Work*, empirical data shows that the relationship between IQ and work performance is non-existent. You can be smart and not succeed, and not as smart and succeed. You work with ***emotions***, and even if that doesn't come naturally to you, you can ***learn*** it (which is what we'll be dealing with in this chapter!).

We'll learn why it's so dangerous to think you can just "be yourself." As I explained in the "1,640-Hour Interview" chapter, at work you can be yourself . . . but only to a point. You can't be perceived as a huge partier, or the kind of person who talks first and thinks about it afterwards. You can't be disrespectful or indiscreet or lazy or dishonest or immature. But even given the parameters we're about to discuss, there's ***lots*** of room to be yourself, even at work. And of course, outside of work, you're free to be anything you want. Let's get started!

A. Qualities to Manifest

In this section, I'll tell you what to show people. I'm not terribly concerned here about the quality of your work product—I talk enough about that elsewhere! Instead, I'm talking about the "non-work" work that you've got to do to be a success. And I'll be as specific as I can be. I'll explain exactly what people ***mean*** when they use words like "maturity" and "team player." The qualities that I'm describing here all go toward having that elusive "good attitude" that every employer craves. If you're perceived as having a good attitude, your career will rocket ahead because people will think better of you and stumble over themselves to help you succeed. As Dennis Kennedy says, "Think of two new attorneys doing the identical work on a document and the documents have identical typos and mistakes. If you have a good attitude, communicate with the assigning attorney and show a willingness to learn, I guarantee that the worst comment you'll get is that it was a good effort. If you have a 'bad' attitude, act like you know it all and that the project is beneath you, you risk someone questioning whether you have the ability to be a lawyer."

So these "non-work" qualities count for a lot. Let's get started!

1. **Display humble confidence. And if you don't have it, fake it. Everybody does.**

   You wouldn't believe how many lawyers consider themselves frauds. Not in an ethically dishonest way, mind you. But just about everybody fakes more confidence than they really feel. One senior lawyer told me "Everybody feels like a fraud. Nobody feels like they're good enough. Including me." Carlton Fields' Hardy Roberts commented that, "Everybody's scared. Everybody has to get past the deer in the headlights feeling. ***Everyone*** is nervous, including big partners." One female lawyer said that "Whenever they ask me to do something, I'll answer with this big hearty, 'OK!' but inside I'm thinking to myself, 'Oh my God, how am I going to do ***this***?'" Loyola's Pam Occhipinti added that "Especially when you start, everything seems to take longer than it should, and you don't feel like you know what you're doing. It's natural." Minnesota's Nora Klaphake pointed out that "You should be prepared to feel utterly and completely stupid, incompetent, hare-brained, dumb—you name it. Shortly after I became an associate, I was watching an episode of *ER* where Carter had just graduated from medical school, and was now a doctor. As a patient was crashing, Carter looked at a nurse and yelled, 'Someone get a doctor!' The nurse looked at him and said, 'You ***are*** the doctor!' There are many times I wanted to tell people to 'Ask a lawyer!' only to realize that ***I*** was the lawyer. That's a very normal feeling. Everyone, even senior partners, feels unsure of themselves sometimes."

   So what do you do? First of all, as Arizona's Mary Birmingham points out, "Recognize that 'This Too Shall Pass.' Tell yourself, 'I ***will*** be able to manage my workload better. I ***will*** understand my work better.' You just plain get better, quicker, and more efficient, and that's when it gets fun. But be patient. It takes time to develop expertise!"

   Appearing confident is made even more difficult by the fact that it flies in the face of advice that you ***always*** get—namely, "Ask lots of questions." "How," you might be wondering, "can I ask lots of questions and still look confident?" The answer is in the manual that the firm Strasburger & Price gives to its new associates. The manual states, "Out of law school, you have a highly-inflated view of yourself, which quickly comes crashing down around your ears. Suddenly, you realize you don't know anything. There are 18 trillion practical things you don't know. The key? Alternate your questions between four to five people. Several good things will result: (a) You'll get your answers; (b) Four or five people will be flattered that you consider them knowledgeable enough to answer your questions; (c) No one person will feel pestered by your questions; and (d) Since you are alternating between four or five people, no one person will know how clueless you truly feel."

As Dewey Ballentine's John Ragosta points out, part of 'acting like a partner' is operating with a certain amount of self-assuredness. Hardy Roberts says that "You might be scared, but you can't let it show. There are no right answers. There are only the best answers under the circumstances." You don't want to come across as a know-it-all—I talk about that in the "Perceptions You Should Avoid" section when I talk about arrogance—but you've got to have the mental cajones to speak confidently about your research, your case, your opinions and your conclusions when you know you've done a competent and thorough job.

2. Don't just work hard—come across as a hard worker, as well.

Well, duh! Like some employer would say, "We love to hire slackers." But what I'm specifically referring to here is creating the ***impression*** of hard work. Employers expect you to work hard, and certainly things like billable hours and time sheets are not an area you can fudge at all—they're concrete evidence of the hours you put in. Instead, what I'm talking about here is how people ***view*** you.

In his book *The Man With The $100,000 Breasts*, Michael Konik talks about how to be comped all kinds of goodies by Las Vegas casinos, the goodies that are usually reserved for high rollers, without spending a bunch of money. The strategy essentially boils down to keeping an eye on when the pit boss strolls by your blackjack table. When he's watching, you bet $25 a hand. When he walks away, you go back to betting $5. I'm not suggesting that you slack off when nobody's watching—take some pride in your work, for chrissakes!—but I ***am*** telling you to pay attention to the impression you're making. Don't let people see you chit-chatting during the day too much. (If you have an office mate or coworker who is a big chit-chatter, say things like, "I'd love to talk, but I've got to get this done today—talk to you later," or even simply, "Sorry—can't talk now.") Don't write off hours you actually work. When you're going to stay late or come in on a weekend, make sure someone sees you. If you take a laptop home, you're working hard but nobody's around, and while it's admirable, it's less visible. So make sure you're mindful of doing what's necessary to create the image of a hard worker.

3. Show that you're enthusiastic.

America is a cynical place. An ***increasingly*** cynical place. Admitting that you like ***anything*** opens you up to scorn. But the fact is, employers need to see that you like your work, that you're eager to do it. You don't have to have a puppy dog personality—"I'll get the Frisbee!"—but your words, actions, and body language should say, "I'm down with this." It makes a huge difference in how you'll progress. Simply put, if you exhibit an interest in the employer, in the work you do, in the people you work with, it pays off. Don't believe me? There was a survey done by iSwag that showed that 37% of employees who had a coffee mug with their employer's logo on it had been promoted in the last six months; of people who didn't have those mugs, only 8% had moved up.

So—what should you watch out for?

First of all, don't offer a lukewarm response when people ask how your work is going. "When people at work ask, 'How are you doing here?' you can't say, 'OK.' There's no such thing as casual conversation," says Brooklyn's Joan King. When you are asked to do a project, lawyers at Wyatt Tarrant warn you not to say things or adopt an attitude that says, "This is boring," "I can't be bothered," "Okay, if I really have to," or "I'm not to busy to work for senior partner X, but I'm too busy to work for you, you're only a senior associate." You've ***got*** to respond with enthusiasm, or they'll question not just your happiness, but all of the things that flow from satisfaction with your work—productivity, dedication, all the good things. Remember the movie *Bull Durham*? In it, Kevin Costner plays a veteran catcher in the minor leagues, coaching Tim Robbins, a pitching phenom. Costner tells Robbins that when it comes to dealing with the press, stick with the following script: "We've gotta play them one day at a time. I'm just happy to be here. I hope I can help the ball club. I just want to give it my best shot, and the good Lord willing, things will work out." When you're talking with higher-ups at work about how you feel about the job, remember to keep it positive!

You also want to be aware of your body language. If you're enthusiastic, you sit (or stand) up straight, you don't slouch. You look people in the eye. You lean forward slightly when you're sitting. You look alert. If you're saying "Yeah! That sounds great!" while you're slouching and sighing, nobody's going to believe you.

If you honestly aren't thrilled—you're overloaded or questioning your own confidence or going through a sophomore slump or whatever—respond with a smile and say something that is both true and positive, like "I'm learning a ***lot***." Notice I didn't tell you to lie. You're just putting a very positive spin on how you really feel. I learned this trick from Miss Manners, the etiquette expert. Someone once asked her how you respond when somebody shows you their new baby, and it's a real toad. Miss Manners' response was basically that you can ***never*** make a negative comment about the relative cuteness of a baby to its parents. And you don't want to lie. So she suggested using something that people would misinterpret as a hearty endorsement. "Now, ***that's*** a baby!" comes to mind. Phrases like "I'll be delighted to do it. When do you need it?" "I'll stay as long as it takes to finish it." "Do you need help with anything?" "Is there anything else I can do?" are all hallmarks of enthusiasm. Make sure the right words are part of your vocabulary.

Many lawyers recommended that you get involved in the "life of the firm." As lawyers at Davis Wright Tremaine point out, "Successful associates take affirmative steps to become integrated." Boston University's Betsy Armour recommends that you "keep up with what goes on in the firm, either on the firm's Intranet or in its newsletter." Comment on them, and ask questions about them. Show that you're interested. By the same token, make sure that you attend employer social events and lend a hand with non-billable activities (recognizing that you can't shirk your billable activities in their favour, of course!). Actions speak louder than words, and taking part in the life and business of the employer shows you're enthusiastic.

Even if you don't play the sports all of your colleagues play, show up and cheer them on. Pass out the beers. Whatever. An associate at one firm told me a delightful story about this. She said, "When I interviewed with the firm, the interviewer asked me, 'Do you play softball?' I figure that must be the firm sport, so I say, 'Oh, sure, I love softball.' In reality I've never played softball before, I have no idea how to play. I get the offer, and my first week at the office, sure enough, there's a softball game Friday after work. I go along to the field, and I'm watching everybody warm up, trying to get an idea for how to play. They're soft-tossing balls back and forth, they're wearing mitts, I figure, hey, I can do this. I'm the first one up. I go over, pick up a bat, and walk over to the plate. I hear people tittering on the bench behind me, and I turn around and ask, 'What's so funny?' One of my new colleagues says, 'When you bat, it's customary to take off the mitt, first.' Everybody cracked up—including me. Now it's a legend at the office. I shouldn't have lied about it, but they respect the fact that I wanted to be a part of it!"

(By the way, if you're really not liking it at work, read the section called "What To Do If You're Hating Your Job." You still don't get to seem like a poop at work, but it'll help you out of a rut.)

CAREER LIMITING MOVE . . .

Medium-sized firm. An associate is asked to leave after six months on the job. One of the other associates asks a partner, "What happened? She seemed really smart!" The partner responds, "To tell you the truth, I always felt guilty giving her work. I felt like I was imposing on her. She always said she was busy, she always wanted to leave early. If you had something come up at 4:30 on Friday, you couldn't even **think** of asking her to work late or on a weekend to help out. She wouldn't even dream of doing it. I mentioned it when I was at lunch with a couple of the other partners, and they had the same reaction.

And one of them said, 'Wait a minute. We shouldn't feel guilty giving her work. It's her job!' It's a shame. She's a funny and delightful person, but she just made us feel bad giving her assignments."

4. **Exhibit an upbeat personality. Pointing out that "this grunt work sucks" doesn't help *anybody.***

If you've got a naturally cynical personality, this is going to be tough. But study after study shows that people who exhibit an upbeat disposition rise faster and higher than their smarter but more cynical peers. Smile, offer honest compliments, welcome the work assignments that you get, be helpful . . . gee, I feel like I'm about to tell you to learn how to tie three kinds of knots, just like a Boy Scout! But you get my point. If you still don't know what to do, mimic somebody who does. Every office has people who are considered upbeat. Make a point of getting to know them and hang around with them. Not only are they fun, but they're excellent role models, and you'll be "upbeat by association."

As Vermont's Pavel Wonsowicz notes, "So much of succeeding in a heavy work culture is being someone people enjoy working with." Carlton Fields' Elizabeth Zabak echoes that, saying, "People like to be around positive people!" Many, many people I've interviewed have said exactly the same thing. There are ***always*** negative things you can say about any situation, but don't you get into the habit of being the person who says them!

5. **Be a "team player"—and what the heck that *means.***

Every employer wants "team players." So it's important for you to know exactly what being a team player ***means***. Often when you hear the definition of "team player," it's replete with words and phrases like "sacrifice" and "putting the good of the organization over your own personal interests." Actually, I don't think that's what teamwork is about. I think those concepts run contrary to human nature. Instead, I think we're all hard-wired to work in our own best interests. When we do good things, when we donate our time for a good cause, for instance, we do it because it makes us feel like contributing members of the human race. Helping others makes us feel good. I've never seen formal research about this, but my hunch is that most people feel this way. I'll bet ***you*** do!

The good news is that when you think about being a team player, you similarly shouldn't think in terms of sacrifice. Being a team player is actually enlightened self-interest. You don't practice law in a bubble. You periodically need help. And if you're willing to help others when they need it, they'll help you in return. If on the other hand you're protective of your time, they'll cut you off at the knees. As Carlton Fields' Eric Adams says, "Don't be afraid to sacrifice something to ***get*** something!" Vermont's Pavel Wonsowicz puts it this way: "When you're a lawyer, you have a lot of brush fires. Good lawyers keep them under control without letting the forest burn. Everyone has out-of-control brush fires occasionally, and a 'team player' helps you put them out." Mark Weber makes an analogy to friendship: "Your colleagues are just like your friends. If you were arrested at three in the morning, who would you call? You'd call some of your friends and you'd avoid others. The team players are the ones you'd call."

Here are the kinds of things team players step up to the plate for:

a. Copying, faxing, answering the phone—activities that you might consider "beneath you"

No matter how well-staffed your office is, there will be times when you're there and support staffers aren't. You don't need a law degree to operate office machines—but if you show that you're not above such tasks when the situation calls for it, you'll be looked upon very favourably.

SMART HUMAN TRICK . . .

New associate, in the office at 6:30 a.m. He can hear the phone ringing at the reception desk, some distance from his office. He assumes he's the only one in the office. Rather than letting the call ring through to voice mail, he picks it up—figuring that at that time of the morning, it might be something important. It turns out to be a client who is calling from Sweden, wanting to speak to a partner, whom the associate knows is a "big rainmaker, with a reputation for being chilly with new associates." The associate tracks down the partner, who turns out to be sitting in his office waiting for this particular phone call; he doesn't realize that the call wasn't coming to his office directly. The associate reports that "After I did him this one favor, his whole attitude toward me changed. Answering the phone just once gave me an immediate rapport with one of the most influential people in the office."

CAREER LIMITING MOVE . . .

It's a Saturday night at a very large firm. A group of partners and associates are working on a big case. No support staffers are there. The partners don't know how to use the fax machine, which is relatively technical. One of the partner asks a junior associate to copy some cases and fax them out. The associate responds, "I don't think copying would be the best use of my time." The partner visibly fumes. One of the other associates quietly picks up the cases and does the copying and faxing herself. Afterwards, the partner tells all of the other partners about the incident, and the associate who'd been too good to do the copying finds he's suddenly not in much demand for choice work.

b. Accepting the work that's assigned to you

In the sections "Handling Chimp Work Without Going Bananas" and "Being Your Own Career Coach," I talk about how to position yourself for great projects. In "Help! I'm Drowning! What To Do When You've Got Too Much Work (Or Too Little . . .)," I tell you how to reject work without seeming to reject it.

When you read those sections you'll see that I ***never*** tell you to turn down work that you don't want to do. You have to be more subtle and clever than that. Harvard's Mark Weber advises that when your supervisor asks you, "Would you do this for me?" no matter what it is your response should be, "I'd be delighted to." As Suffolk's Jim Whitters says, "As soon as you say, 'I don't want to do that,' you're not a team player."

New associate at a large West Coast firm. He's an ardent environmentalist. He's asked to represent a big company who dumps a lot of toxic waste. He responds, "I'm sorry, my conscience won't let me work for them." As his supervising attorney comments, "Turning down work that way doomed him at the firm. He could have avoided it so much more diplomatically if he'd said something like, 'I'd be happy to do something else. I realize I'm creating a problem by turning down this work.' It might not have totally salvaged his reputation—after all, when you walk through the door and take the paycheck, you're implicitly agreeing to represent the firm's clients—but it would have been so much better than doing what he did."

c. Handling someone else's work so they can take a vacation

No matter what your employer's stated policy is concerning vacations, you have to make sure your work, your assignments, your clients are covered. This is virtually impossible to accomplish if you're not willing to cover for other people when ***they*** want to take time off, because they won't cover for you if you won't cover for them. That is, if you're not a "team player." One lawyer at Goulston Storrs describes his system: "A colleague and I cover for one another when we go on vacation. Before either one of us leaves the office, we write a memo to the other describing any loose ends that are out there and issues that may arise while we're out. That way, each of us can go away and enjoy ourselves knowing that our clients' needs are being addressed."

d. Giving credit where credit is due

When you get a pat on the back for something you've done well, accept the compliment—***and*** acknowledge anyone who was particularly helpful to you: "I'm glad you like the letter. Your secretary, Miss Crabtree, was a great help. She showed me the prior correspondence with that client." "Joe made the memo a lot easier. He directed me to a brief in the brief bank on a similar issue." These kinds of comments don't diminish you; you're the one who took the initiative to seek the help in the first place, and that's a very savvy move. When you give credit to others, your magnanimity will make you shine, and your compliments will inevitably get back to the people who helped you. They'll be delighted—and they'll be right there if and when you need to turn to them again!

e. Being willing to sacrifice your time to help others, even if it's at night or on a weekend (and how to look good even if you can't chip in)

Your free time is precious. When you're willing to give up some of it to help out, it ***really*** stands out. As lawyers at Fowler White point out, "Making yourself available to assist your colleagues in a crunch goes a ***long*** way."

Helping out inevitably means shifting around your own work. You shouldn't just cavalierly blow off a deadline to help colleagues in a jam. Then you're not a team player. You're not even the water boy. Instead, when you're asked to help—or you see people struggling—say, "I'd love to help out. Let me check with Partner Petunia to see if I can move back the deadline on the work I'm doing for her." One of three things will happen. The lawyers in a bind will say, "Oh, no, you've ***got*** to do that. But thanks for offering." And you'll be viewed as a team player for trying. Or Partner Petunia will say "No," and again, you made the effort. Or Partner Petunia says "Yes," in which case you chip in and you really ***are*** a team player. It's a win-win-win situation.

SMART HUMAN TRICK . . .

Junior associate gets a call from a partner in another office of his firm, who says, "My maid has an INS problem. Can you handle it?" The associate is swamped with work, and the last thing he wants is a pro bono project. But he does it anyway, and makes a point of whining only to his wife. As it turns out, the partner who gives him the project is on the firm's compensation committee. At the committee's next meeting, he speaks up, lauding this associate for helping him out. The associate is rewarded as a result.

SMART HUMAN TRICK . . .

New associate, gives up his weekend to help a partner on a rush project. Two weeks later, the partner has to go to Amsterdam on business. As a thank-you, he invites the associate to go along to observe.

SMART HUMAN TRICK . . .

An attorney has to get a lot of documents out to a client on the night of his firm's holiday party. When he gets up to leave the party early, the colleagues at his table—two partners, two associates, and two secretaries—ask where he's going. When he tells them about the work he has left to do, the six of them promptly get up and leave with him to help him out.

6. **Be tactful. That painting you're laughing at was probably painted by the managing partner's wife.**

We all sometimes suffer from a case of foot-in-mouth disease. It's never the end of the world. But remember, if your superiors see you being tactless around them, they'll be leery of exposing you to clients, worrying about what you'll say when it ***really*** counts. My favourite example is in the movie *Four Weddings And A Funeral,* in an early scene where Hugh Grant is trying desperately to make conversation at a wedding reception. He says, "Oh, I remember you! Didn't you used to date so-and-so?" The guy nods, and Hugh Grant goes on, saying things like, what a scag, a tramp, gee, I wonder whatever happened to her, and the guy responds, "I married her."

Oops!

So learn to keep your lip zipped when it comes to making boastful, critical, or completely blunt remarks at work. One new associate at a firm told of having a partner ask her where she went to law school, and when she told him, he asked, "Oh, how did you like Professor Nutwell?" Her response was, "He was impossible. I couldn't stand him." The partner responded, "Really? He's my neighbor. We're great friends."

Another associate talked about a conversation he had with a partner at his firm. The associate said, "My brother just got a new job, he's working on Bufort Street, in that really crummy area," and the partner responded, "No kidding? That's where I live." The associate said, "I fumbled around saying, 'Oh, I didn't mean ***there***. Not ***that*** part of Bufort Street . . . ' it was ***really*** embarrassing."

Assume that someone associated with the employer was responsible for the décor and the artwork. As Susan Gainen says, "If you make a smart remark about a sculpture in the lobby, you can bet it was donated by a major client."

If a coworker or superior clearly needs some emotional support, your tact will again be called into question. Being blunt when somebody is feeling down on their luck is just plain mean. Find ***something*** positive to say. "You obviously worked hard on this," "That must have been really tough"—something along those lines. I went to a play a couple of years ago with a friend of mine. It was written by a local woman, and while I sympathize with the whole creative thing—I write screenplays of my own, after all—there just wasn't a single good thing to say about this play. It was just sloppy and sentimental and dumb as a bag of wet mice. I tried to sneak out, but the playwright was blocking the door. My friend said, "You can't leave without saying something to her." I asked, "Can I be honest?" and my friend responded, "Of course not. You'll hurt her feelings." I tried to find another exit, but all of the other doors were locked, so I was stuck. When we got to the door, I immediately started commenting on this woman's beautiful outfit (it really was very nice). She might have known something was up—I can't imagine she hadn't gotten the sense from other people in the audience that this particular work wasn't Broadway-bound—but I said something nice and I satisfied my conscience, as well.

In the area of people's looks, it's especially important to be tactful. Years ago I remember seeing an episode of *Hollywood Squares*—a font of useful knowledge if ever there was one—where Dr. Joyce Brothers was asked, "What's the most tactful way to tell somebody they're overweight?" And the correct response was: There isn't one. A lawyer at one firm told me about how partners in the firm had been worried about an associate with an increasingly severe weight problem. One of the partners, in an attempt to be helpful, said to her in a gentle voice: "Have you ever considered liposuction?" She blew a gasket. If someone's looking older or they're losing their hair, they've got a mirror too. They don't need your input. Keep your comments to yourself!

Finally, tact has to do not just with negative situations, but positive ones, as well. If something good happens to you, show discretion with how you handle it around your coworkers. As Venable Baetjer's Stefan Tucker advises, "If you're a star and you get great bonuses, that's wonderful. Don't tell others what you got. Dodge the question!"

7. Be on time!

Don't keep lawyers waiting. Or ***anybody*** at the office. Everybody understands an emergency. But nobody will cut you much slack if you routinely keep them waiting. What it says to people is, "My time is more valuable than yours. I've got more important things to do while you cool your heels." It's an image you don't want, so don't do it!

8. Be an interesting person to talk to.

When I talk about prepping for social events, in the section called "Social Graces" a little later in this chapter, I talk about the importance of being an interesting conversationalist. I don't want to repeat myself, so check that section out!

9. Be politically correct.

The world is not a politically correct place. You know that. But nonetheless, "You've got to be politically correct in what you say," advises Tulane's Kristin Flierl. If you spout off at work about your negative opinions about minorities or women or gays or anyone or anything else that is politically sensitive, your colleagues will ***seriously*** question not just your intelligence, but also your judgment.

CAREER LIMITING MOVE . . .

Law student, interviewing for a job with a small firm at the firm's offices. The interviewer asks him, "How do you feel about doing immigration work?" The student responds, "I'd like to try that, as long as it's for . . . Europeans." The interviewer looked at him for a moment, before realizing exactly what he was saying. "It was everything I could do to finish the interview," the interviewer commented. "I just wanted to tell him to get the hell out!"

CAREER LIMITING MOVE . . .

New associate, small med mal defense firm. The senior partner comes back from a conference with plaintiff's counsel in a big case, and the associate asks, "So did you jew him down on the settlement amount?" The senior partner said, "**What** did you say?" The associate repeated it, and the senior partner asked, "Are you Jewish?" The new associate said no, and the senior partner said, "Well, I am. And I'm insulted."

Although you should be politically correct in every way, if you're a woman, try to make a special effort with older, male colleagues not to take offense where none exists. I know I'm treading on very thin ice here, because the point I'm going to make is the kind that sometimes makes people angry. But I heard this advice from so many lawyers—an awful lot of younger, female lawyers—that I thought I should pass it along to you. You need to know this: If you're a woman and an elderly partner or judge calls you "Honey" or "Dear," ***don't*** assume that they have no respect for your work. As Oprah Winfrey says, there is no discrimination against excellence.

People talk about the "good old days," but if you look at America in the 1940's and 50's, there were an awful lot of social mores that were totally unacceptable by our standards today. The elderly lawyers you work with grew up in that environment. Times have certainly changed and the vast majority of older lawyers make a real effort to adapt to enlightened attitudes about women. If elderly lawyers use a term of endearment with you that you would resent coming from a contemporary, remember for a moment who it is who's talking. Hamline's Joyce Laher, a former lawyer herself, warns that "Too many women go into the work place overly concerned about political correctness. People in the workplace may be two generations older than you, and you need to be tolerant. When the grandfatherly type says 'Dear,' don't ruffle your feathers!"

10. Show an interest in the people and things that interest your colleagues.

One of the classic "people skills" is showing people that you pay attention to them. As lawyers at Goulston Storrs point out, "Being good with people means making them feel liked. Remember colleagues' children's names. Pay attention to their hobbies and interests outside the office." Cardozo's Judy Mender echoes that advice, saying that "Even though you're very busy with your work and all the stresses of your own life, make a point of stopping and talking with people at work, including colleagues, support staff, and clients. Remembering what people tell you and asking follow-up questions impresses people with the fact that you care. Find out how a person's son's play turned out, or how his or her trip to the Amazon was."

11. Don't underestimate the value of the words "Thank You," and gestures that signify your gratitude.

As the associate at one firm said, "The people who work for you always like to hear that you appreciate them. Once, when I won a big case, the managing partner sent a 'job well done' note about my victory to everybody in the office. It meant more to me than a bonus would have!" At another firm, the managing partner makes a point of putting up a congratulatory poster on the office door of any attorney who does particularly meritorious work.

Start as a new associate to show appreciation for people who do good work for you. I've heard stories about new associates bringing in a flower for their secretary or a box of muffins or cookies for paralegals and/or word processors who helped them out in a jam. If you think this kind of thing sounds hokey, you're overlooking one of the great management tools: the value of a simple thank you.

12. Be involved in the community.

"Yeah, right!" you're thinking. "I work too hard as it is!" I realize that there are certain work settings where you're so overloaded that it's not feasible to do anything else. But keep a close eye on what goes on at the office to see whether or not people get applauded for their community involvement. My hunch is that you'll find, ***as long as you get your work done as well,*** that your employer loves to see you involved in the local bar association and other civic functions. Not only is it a potential source of future business, but it's also good for the reputation of the firm—and not for nothing, it's good for your own reputation, as well. If you ever think of making a job change, having a reputation in the community is a very valuable asset indeed.

13. Exhibit decorum.

This is what people are talking about when they talk about showing "maturity." It's basically the idea of recognizing that even though there are definitely times—at least, at most offices!—where cutting up is a great idea, ***most*** of the time you've got to respect the office as a place of business. ***Never*** let clients see you acting anything but decorously. And if you do trash the office—make sure to clear up before anybody sees it!

CAREER LIMITING MOVE . . .

New associate at a Midwestern firm. After very long days of working on a prospectus, he and his colleagues stay late at the office celebrating. The office occupies several floors of a very old office building. He decides to crawl into the dumbwaiter and hoist himself up a floor. He tumbles out of the dumbwaiter, laughing hysterically, at the feet of a senior partner. He is fired on the spot.

CAREER LIMITING MOVE . . .

Big party at a senior partner's house, including lawyers and summer clerks from the corporate department and personnel from a prominent client. Kegs are brought in. The clients begin prodding the summer clerks. "Chug! Chug! Chug!" The summer clerks don't notice that the permanent associates are nursing a single beer. Prompted by the clients, a few of the clerks get hammered and yakked in front of the clients.

CAREER LIMITING MOVE . . .

Junior associate at a large firm down South. A group of associates had been working all night on closing documents in the firm's conference room. They finally finished late Saturday night. The traditional means of celebrating at this firm was to take sharpened pencils and throw them straight up, so they'd stick into the ceiling tiles. They stuck dozens of pencils into the ceiling, figuring they'd get in early Monday morning and remove the pencils before anybody saw them. Unbeknownst to them, a senior partner had arranged to meet a client in the conference room on Sunday. The partner showed the client to the conference room. As he held the door open, he noticed a confused look on the client's face. He looked in himself to find the ceiling covered with pencil stalactites. "I understood the need to celebrate," said the partner. "But it's a place of business. A little decorum is appreciated."

14. Display an appropriate sense of humour.

Every employer proclaims a desire to hire people who have a sense of humour. This doesn't mean that they'll appreciate you putting a whoopie cushion in their office, or sending them mail with a return address reading "Nymphomaniacs Anonymous." What employers really mean when they say they want you to have a sense of humour is that they want you to have ***their*** sense of humour, both in terms of when it's appropriate to joke around, and what it's appropriate to joke ***about***. As Hamline's Joyce Laher points out, "If you have a sense of humor and you use it in the wrong way at the wrong time, you're dead meat. But definitely ***use*** it wisely—if artfully timed to relieve a tense situation, it can generate respect and appreciation. It often raises your credibility, because there is no one and nothing that doesn't deserve a dose of irreverence."

SMART HUMAN TRICK . . .

Small firm in the Northeast. One of the partners is asked to leave the firm because he sexually harassed a female associate. The rest of the lawyers at the firm undergo sensitivity training, even though the entire problem had clearly been the partner who left. The managing partner is told that he will have to remove from his office a birthday card that the entire staff had given him—a Sports Illustrated swimsuit model in a bikini, shaped like a paper doll. They had all signed it. The staff protests that they don't have any problem with the card, but the sensitivity trainer says, "It doesn't matter what you think. It could be the cleaning lady who files a complaint. It could be the person who comes in to water the plants. It could be anybody. The card has to go." The managing partner is sputtering mad and getting angrier by the minute.

One of the female associates excuses herself for a minute, and comes back with a piece of paper and some scissors. "I have a solution!" she says. She takes the card and disappears for a minute. When she comes back, she sticks the card back on the partner's bulletin board, and produces a white paper "minidress" that she just made for the card. "While you're in your office, leave the card the way it is," the associate says. "And when you leave, put her dress on!" She slips the minidress onto the card, hanging little paper tabs over its shoulders. The dress makes the card look like a fully-clothed nurse. Everybody in the room laughs, including the managing partner. "Thank you," he says. "That's just what I needed."

If people start tossing jokes around and you want to add one of your own, it's got to be politically correct. If you don't have any jokes of your own that qualify, memorize these two:

A guy takes his pet to the veterinarian. The vet looks over the poor thing, looks up at the guy, shakes his head, and says, sadly, "I'm sorry. He's not going to make it." The guy pleads, "Are you **sure**? Isn't there **anything** you can do?" The vet says, "Well—OK." He claps his hands once. A door behind him opens, and a cat calmly walks out. It jumps up on the examining table, and looks over the ailing pet. Then the cat looks at the vet and shakes its head, jumps off the table, and walks out. The vet claps his hands twice. Another door behind him opens up, and a big black dog walks out. The dog walks over to the examining table, stands up on his hind legs, and checks out the pet. He looks into its eyes, takes its pulse, and then looks at the vet, and shakes his head. He leaves. The vet looks at the guy and says, "I'm sorry. Nothing can be done. That will be six hundred dollars." The guy is astounded and says, "Six hundred bucks? Are you kidding? For what?" The vet responds, "Two hundred dollars for my fee. Two hundred for the cat scan. And two hundred for the lab tests."

A guy works as the marketing manager for a huge chicken company. One day the board of directors calls him in, and says, "Listen. We want you to go over to Rome, and talk to the Pope, and get him to change the Lord's Prayer from 'Give us this day our daily bread' to

'Give us this day our daily chicken.'" The marketing manager says, "Are you crazy? He'll never do it!" The chairman of the board says, "Tell him we'll donate a million dollars a year to the church if he'll just change that one word." So the marketing manager flies to Rome, gets an audience with the Pope, and makes his pitch. The Pope shakes his head, "No, no, never." He won't hear of it. So the marketing manager flies home and reports back to the board of directors. The chairman says, "Go back there and make it fifty million a year." The marketing manager goes back to visit the Pope, and tells him, "Your Holiness, we're willing to pay fifty million a year. Fifty million dollars!" The Pope is unmoved. Now the marketing manager is getting determined. He goes back to the board of directors and says, "If you let me offer a hundred million a year, I think I can convince him." The board says "OK," and he flies back over to the Pope. He tells the Pope, "Your Holiness, 'We are willing to pay one hundred million dollars a year. It's our final offer. Think of all of the poor people you could help with that kind of money! And all you have to do is have people say, 'Give us this day our daily chicken.'" The Pope is swayed by this argument, and agrees. The triumphant marketing manager leaves, and the Pope calls a meeting of the college of cardinals. He says, "Gentlemen, I have good news, and I have bad news. The good news is, we will be getting an additional one hundred million dollars a year in donations. The bad news is, I lost the Wonder Bread account."

Finally, another aspect of "sense of humour" is that employers don't want to see you taking yourself too seriously. An associate at a large firm told me a story that perfectly illustrates this. A law student came in for an interview, and the associate noticed that on the student's resume he listed two jobs: He had been a bouncer at the Playboy Mansion, and he had been a land title abstractor, which in this associate's words is "the most boring job in the world." About halfway through the interview, the associate said, "I saw your resume, and I couldn't help noticing your work experience. I know everybody must ask you the same question, but I can't resist. What's it like to be a land title abstractor?" The associate told me that "The guy didn't bat an eyelash. Didn't even crack a smile. I sat there cackling like an idiot, and—nothing."

You *know* that as you proceed through your career, people will tease you about things. Take it in good humor!

15. Make your office a welcoming place.

As one associate recommends, "Don't close your door! It implies you're doing something you shouldn't be doing, and creates an illusion you don't deserve." Instead, as Hamline's Vince Thomas advises, "Make your office a hospitable place to be. When I was a junior associate, there was a partner who showed up at my office every afternoon. He would put his feet up on my desk and talk sports. It was obvious he appreciated having a place where his secretary and clients couldn't bug him for five or ten minutes, where he could just talk about whether the Vikings should have thrown that pass." He adds, "You ***want*** people to bring you work. Let them visit you for a sanity break. Being a good sounding board is a valuable skill!"

If you find that your office is turning into social central, use some tried-and-true methods of limiting the interruptions. For instance, stack your extra chair with books and papers so that people can't sit down. If there's nowhere to sit, people tend not to linger. But if your supervisor shows up, you can quickly clear off the chair for him or her.

16. Be a "dynamic listener."

As a lawyer, you've got to do a ***lot*** of listening. To clients, to other lawyers, to judges—a whole raft of people. Although we all think we're good listeners, studies show that we really aren't. We're often too busy thinking of what we're going to say next to really pay attention to what's being said. As Syracuse's Alex Epsilanty points out, "In law school and when you're new to practice, the temptation will be to talk more than you should. Spend a lot more time listening than you do talking. You'll find that people with the biggest books of business [that is, the most clients] have the ability to engage other people. They're really good listeners." Loyola's Pam Occhipinti agrees. "You have to listen ***very*** carefully. As an attorney, you need to gather information from a variety of sources and ask pertinent questions about what you hear. That takes great listening skills."

How do you become a "dynamic listener"? In his book *Emotional Intelligence at Work*, author Hendrie Weisinger tells you to:

1. Ask yourself what the speaker is really saying. What does he really want?
2. Summarize the person's statements and repeat them back (in your case, this would often come when you're receiving a research assignment).
3. Acknowledge what's being said, using phrases like "I see" and "I'd like to hear more."
4. Acknowledge people's feelings with "I hear." For instance, if your secretary is overworked, acknowledge that by saying "I hear you're feeling stressed out and that you're worried about making that deadline."
5. Be mindful of your body language. Make eye contact with the speaker, lean toward the speaker, and nod your head.

Weisinger adds that people are often blocked from hearing what's really being said by "personal filters," like hearing only what we want to hear, letting our preconceived notions of what a person is like interfere with what they're saying, ignoring the emotional content of people's communication and only paying attention to the words, and being thrown by the fact that the speaker is boring. You can overcome ***all*** of these filters as long as you're conscious of them. For instance, if you have a lot of client contact, you can be sure that there will be a strong emotional element in what some clients communicate to you. If someone is going through a divorce or filing for bankruptcy or facing jail time, what they're saying emotionally is far more important than the actual words they're using, and you need to acknowledge and respond to that (we talk about this some more in the section called "Dealing With Clients, Judges, And Other Lawyers." And when you're in a boring meeting or presentation, I've told you elsewhere to keep yourself awake by taking plenty of notes.

The bottom line is, you're going to be doing a lot of listening as a lawyer. If you learn to be a ***great*** listener, you're on your way to being a great lawyer!

B. Perceptions You Should *Avoid* Creating—And How To Do That!

As lawyers at Latham and Watkins advise, "Nothing will sour your reputation quicker than a bad attitude!" In this section, we'll talk about exactly what goes into creating the image of having a "bad attitude." You'll notice something interesting about the traits you'll find here. First of all, the negatives are all "evil twins" of the positive traits we just talked about. If it's good to be tactful, it's bad to be tactless. If it's important to be viewed as a hard worker, it's bad to be tagged as a slacker. So think of the opposites of everything on the list we just discussed, and you'll have a good roadmap of traits to avoid.

Another interesting quality of the traits to avoid exhibiting: They're just extremes of behavior that's otherwise fine or even admirable. For instance, self-confidence. You ***need*** a healthy dose of self-confidence to be a great lawyer. You can't seem hesitant, insecure, or neurotic. But when you go overboard with self-confidence you're arrogant, and from what I heard from lawyers all over the country, that's career suicide.

Take another one—chatting with colleagues. You can't lock yourself away and refuse to socialize with your colleagues. You need to be seen as "fitting in," and you need to hear what's traveling the grapevine. But if you seem to spend too much time chatting, or you're seen as a gossip, or you have too good a time at parties and get absolutely wasted, your reputation will suffer.

How about being honest? Honesty is a trait that everybody values, until you say to a colleague "You're fat," your secretary "You're incompetent," your client "You're a liar and your case stinks." In other words, when your honesty crosses the line to tactlessness, you're paving the way out the door.

With that in mind, let's talk about the qualities you should avoid manifesting at work.

1. Arrogant? Who? Me?

People who are arrogant have the same problem that psychotics have: they tend not to be able to see it in themselves. What you regard as healthy self-esteem may be interpreted by other people as arrogance. You may be thinking that you're only pointing out the truth, but others will be shocked by your insensitivity.

I've met tens of thousands of law students all over the country, but I've only ever met one who was truly arrogant. I've heard about lots of arrogant people and how oblivious they are to their own arrogance, but I never believed it until I met this one guy. He came up to me after one of my *Guerrilla Tactics* job search seminars, and he said, "I know you went to school in Cleveland. I've been to Cleveland. I really hated it. No offense." *Well, OK,* I'm thinking. He goes on, "What did you think of Case Western? I guess it's an OK school, but I didn't see any point in going to a law school that wasn't a ***top*** law school. No offense." *Hmm. Where's this going?* "You know, I thought you were going to gather up our resumes and review them." *Boy, wouldn't **that** have been a fun-packed two hours,* I'm thinking. "So this seminar really wasn't what I expected. No offense." *Yeah. Where's the door?* "So—would you take a look at my resume?" *Buddy,* I'm thinking, *if you don't have a job, I'm pretty sure it's not your resume that's the problem. NO OFFENSE!*

Here's why having the arrogance tag pinned to you is so poisonous. Human nature is such that we don't like people for how great they are. We like them for how they make us feel. We seek out the company of people who make us feel good about ourselves. If you don't do that—if you feel it's your job to put people in their place, or you say things to them to let them know just who they're dealing with, they'll hate you. And when people hate you, they look for an opportunity to hurt you. As a new lawyer, you can't succeed on your own. You **need** other people. You've got a lot of ropes to be shown and a whole ton of skills to pick up that law school just doesn't teach you. OK, maybe you ***are*** the sharpest tool in the box. But nobody wants to hear how you outshine them. There's no such thing as a meritocracy. If you make it obvious that no matter how well you did in school or how confident you are in your abilities, that you've got a lot to learn and you're grateful to people who teach you and work with you, people will do ***anything*** to help you out. You'll take those stellar credentials and turn them into a fabulous career. If you don't, they'll have the daggers out for you, waiting for you to make a slip (and you will). They'll cut you no slack. And your career will be over before it's hardly had a chance to start.

What I'm going to do here is to explain the kinds of things that people you work with will take as arrogance. I don't care how you think of these actions and statements yourself. What's important is other people's perceptions.

a. Making a point of mentioning your law school and/or your accomplishments in school

Maybe you went to a fantastic law school, and you ***should*** be proud of that. Maybe you were at the top of your class. Congratulations. It's an accomplishment nobody will ever be able to take away from you. But for chrissakes, keep it to yourself. Your education is only as meaningful as what you do with it. If you went to a great school or you were on Law Review, trust me, everybody at the office knows about it. All that great credentials will get you are increased expectations of your performance, and a little wiggle room when you slip—people will assume you've got the ability, you just had a bad day. But great credentials don't carry you on a sedan chair to a successful career. The managing partner of a large firm tells of getting a summer clerk from a very prestigious law school. At the firm's very first social event, this clerk went up to him, threw an arm around his shoulder, and said, "So, Frank [not his real name], tell me why I should pick you all." The managing partner reports that "I was too stunned to speak. This kid was ***dead meat.***"

If you pay attention to people who really are powerful, you notice that they don't ***have*** to brag about it. You don't notice Bill Gates boasting about his billions. People who are truly secure in their accomplishments let what they've done and what they're doing speak for themselves. Focus your attention not on telling people what makes you so special, but instead on doing things that create that indelible impression in their minds. After all, they'll believe it if they ***see*** that you're terrific. They'll resent it if you ***say*** it.

A hiring partner told me a story about a guy who'd come out of school with a 4.0 g.p.a. and was new to his office. "This guy was earning a well-deserved reputation for being self-centered. He had been asked to share an office with someone and before the other person could move in, he arranged the furniture so as to appropriate two-thirds of the office to himself. I got down and dirty with him and told him he wasn't going to be successful unless he started treating others the way he would like to be treated. After twenty minutes of my most heartfelt coaching, his response was, 'Gee, that sounds good, but how do I know you're right?' The upshot of the story is that he jumped from our office before he could be pushed. After passing the bar, he went to work as an attorney for a firm in town and lasted about ninety days. That was more than ten years ago, and except for a stint as a sole practitioner, he hasn't worked as an attorney since. When he approached me several years ago about coming back to work for us, I wasn't the least bit interested."

After a very short while, people who brag about where they went to school start sounding pathetic. It's a "What have you done for me lately?" kind of thing. People will think, "Why does (s)he have to keep on bringing up school? What's (s)he trying to cover up?"

I remember dating a guy who'd gone to a truly fabulous school. You'd know it immediately. It's on the East Coast. Anyway, he really was a brilliant guy, and we went out for a while about five or six years after we'd graduated from college. I quickly noticed a pattern: Every time I met any of his friends from school, they'd make a special point of bringing up the school thing. It was pretty funny because after all, I knew they'd gone to school with this guy, and they knew that I knew where ***he*** went to school, so it wasn't really necessary to bring it up. I finally told him, "You know, whenever I meet any of your friends, I'm getting hit over the head with the school thing. It's like they're tomcats pissing on the furniture to mark off their intellectual territory. It's kind of arrogant, don't you think?" He immediately said, don't be ridiculous, they don't bring it up, it's your imagination, you're jealous, they're not like that. So I told him, "I'll bet you a dinner that the next time I meet one of your school friends, within thirty seconds he'll manage to squeeze into the conversation the fact that he went to X school." He took the bet.

Shortly after that, we arranged to have dinner with his roommate—whom I hadn't met yet—and sure enough, this guy had been a college classmate of his. We were supposed to meet at their apartment. I got there and met the roommate, and he was very nice. Immediately after we met, he excused himself, and came back into the room in less than a minute, saying to my date, "Hey, did you see what came in the mail today?" And he held up their college alumni magazine, with the name of the school emblazoned across the front. My date looked at me, his face reddening. He said, "So—where do you want me to take you?"

You get the point. Leave the pride thing unspoken. Let your parents brag about you. Let your sterling credentials permeate your work in the form of feeling that you've got to live up to those credentials by producing outstanding work and doing whatever it takes to show that you aren't just book smart!

b. **Allowing the words "I deserve . . . " to poison your attitude. Don't even *think* them, unless you precede them with the words, "I'll do what it takes to earn what I think . . . .I deserve."**

Every employer moans about new graduates emerging from law school with a "sense of entitlement." As O'Melveny and Myers' Kathryn Sanders says, "Manage your expectations!" If you're starting work now, you've got a view of the world your employer doesn't share. It's only been since the 1990's that the economy has been in good shape on a consistent year-in, year-out basis. "Dot-com millionaires" are a recent phenomenon, too. If you want to go off and start your own dot-com (and trust me, I've got friends who've done it—it's not the overnight success, stock option gravy train that the media would have you believe), the door is open—go ahead and do it.

But if you work for somebody else, you've got to reconcile yourself to the deal that you signed up for. You're getting whatever salary you agreed to, you're sitting in the office space they give you, you're accepting the support staff (or lack of it) that they provide. When it comes to money, recognize that somebody ***always*** makes more money than you. As I talk about in detail in "Econ 101," as a new lawyer you lose money for your employer. If you agreed to fifty or sixty or a hundred thousand dollars, don't ***ever*** let people at work hear you whine. Trust me, every law firm knows what every other law firm pays. You don't have to download stuff from websites and e-mail it to partners, as a "hint hint" about the competition. If you're at a governmental employer, you're probably making less money than you might in the private sector. But you've got benefits of your own—likely more livable hours, more job security, work that you find exciting and rewarding. That "psychic income" is priceless. If, on the other hand, you're at a small firm, you certainly don't make as much to start as new associates at large firms. But statistics show that within five years you're likely to be neck-and-neck with your brethren at large firms, and in the meantime you'll often have a more "livable" schedule.

The bottom line is this: Focus your energy on doing what it takes to prove that you deserve what you're getting and you're worth more. Take the initiative to make your superiors look good, to give great service to your clients, to bring business and prestige to your employer by making a name for yourself in the profession. Don't just ***talk*** about what you "deserve." ***Prove*** it!

c. Making sure that everybody who works with you appreciates your status as an attorney.

Don't lord your newfound status over the help at the office, and don't think that it gives you a free pass when it comes to getting your hands dirty. As Milbank Tweed's Kathleen Brady points out, "There's a balancing act going on. Part of lawyering is posturing. But that's for an adversary. You need to know when to turn it off—like when you're dealing with the receptionist."

If your employer needs you to learn a certain kind of equipment, don't respond, "Isn't that what the secretary is for?" If they need you to stay late and help fax and collate documents, don't get your knickers in a twist because they're asking you to do work that's beneath you. As I explain in great detail when I talk about the importance of being perceived as a team player, if you start behaving as though you're too good for certain kinds of tasks, you won't get the opportunity to do much else.

d. Creating the perception that you know how to be a lawyer when you're just starting out

As lawyers at the Writers Guild of America west point out, "When you get out of school, you're not as smart as you think you are. In law school we're taught that we are privy to a highly specialized body of knowledge, that we are special and brilliant people. There's a ***lot*** to learn, however, from other people and experiences. Be humble—you'll learn more, be respected more, and have more friends!" Dennis Kennedy agrees, saying, "An attitude that indicates that you've made it, that you're ready to reap the benefits of your education immediately, and a sense that you don't have something else to learn, will cause you nothing but problems. You want to be self-confident, but humble, willing to learn, respectful of your position and ready to work."

e. Behaving as though because you have excellent credentials, you should bypass your colleagues and socialize only with your superiors

Big mistake. A lawyer at one firm described the experience of a new associate who was "flavour of the month" in all the partners' eyes. "In that he is their golden child of the moment, he decides that he is just too good to mingle with the other associates, preferring to have lunch with a different partner each day. Unsurprisingly, he finds himself ostracized by the other associates and quickly gains the reputation among the partners as a "non-team player" in that none of the other associates even bother to acknowledge him, much less work with him."

Remember, you ***need*** friends at work. If your superiors have great expectations of you and favour you as a result, be humble about it with your colleagues. If they're jealous of your status they won't want to help you out when you need it, and you ***will*** need it.

2. Exhibiting a lack of self-confidence.

Every employer wants to believe they've made a wise hiring decision in bringing you on board. While I've emphasized the fact that when you enter the legal profession you've got a ton to learn, you don't want to say things that make your employer wonder whether you've got the raw material to make it. Part of that "raw material" is exhibiting a faith in your ability to learn what you don't know. A lawyer at one small firm said that "We hired a new female associate in a job where we really needed a go-getter. But with every new project, she'd give us this forlorn look, and say, 'I've never ***done*** this before.' We ***knew*** that. It would have been fine if she asked for examples and advice on projects. But she didn't. She was just tentative."

As Hamline's Joyce Laher says, "Employers go through a lot of expense and trouble hiring you, and they want to believe they've got the best of the bunch. Self-effacing comments make them feel like they were wrong! Self-deprecating or disclaiming statements like 'I'm not ready for this,' 'I don't know much about X,' 'I only did that once before,' shouldn't be part of your vocabulary. They make employers tremor! Remember that your first or second year you'll feel a lot of the time that you're 'whistling in the dark.' You ***can*** do it: they wouldn't have hired you otherwise! Don't be intimidated by the environment!"

Watch also ***how*** you speak. If you constantly say "I'm sorry"—"I'm sorry, but could you help me with this?" "I'm sorry, but could you tell me how to work the phone system?" Apologizing when you've made a mistake is not just appropriate, it's mandatory. But when you pepper your conversation with "I'm sorry's," you sound unsure of yourself and you'll make people uncomfortable.

Also delete the "ums" from your speech. If you pause frequently when you talk and fill the gaps with "ers" and "ahs," the person listening to you will perceive that you lack confidence—and you don't want that!

3. Appearing competitive with your colleagues.

It's easy to look at your colleagues as competitors for offers and promotions and great work. It's easy, but it's a mistake. If you cultivate your peers, you not only make your current work environment easier and more harmonious, but you're laying the groundwork for your future. As Denver's Anne Stark Walker advises, "Your first job is likely to be a stepping stone in a long line of career-building experiences. Remember that your fellow associates may be your partners some day, voting on your compensation and other partner perks. They may also move on to in-house positions and be in a position to provide you with client work. Make friends with people who may be your references or future sources of client and job referrals."

Almost *all* of the more experienced attorneys I interviewed for this book got their wonderful jobs *not* through job ads or headhunters, but because somebody who liked them tapped them on the shoulder and offered them their job. The moral here: *Don't* alienate your colleagues, in a twisted sense of it's-me-or-them. It *isn't.* As O.C. Systems' Laura Rowe Lane succinctly puts it, "Be nice to everybody else in the sandbox!"

4. Focusing on your work to the exclusion of ingratiating yourself with your colleagues

The actress Ethel Barrymore once said that "For an actress to be a success she must have the face of Venus, the brains of Minerva, the grace of Terpsichore, the memory of Macaulay, the figure of Juno, and the hide of a rhinoceros." Similarly, if you're going to be a great lawyer, you can't be a one-trick pony. It doesn't matter how great your work is if people can't stand you.

A lot of people start their careers thinking that if you do a bang-up job on the work assigned to you, your work will speak for itself. As the managing partner at one large firm said, "You can't be arrogant, smart, and lack people skills, and expect to get ahead."

The fact is that law is a service business. When you start out, unless you're a sole practitioner, your clients are your superiors. As your career progresses, you weave in skills like business generation (if you're in private practice) or grant writing or fund raising (in public interest) or faculty politics (if you teach), but in every single situation your success depends on *much more* than your actual work product. In fact, your value as a leader and/or business generator has much more to do with the way you deal with people than it does with your legal intellect. As one senior partner told me, "Standing out isn't always a matter of objective legal skill. How well do you work with others? If you are enthusiastic, you show a sincere desire to do well and work hard, you show a commitment to the law that shows that it's more than just a job, you always seem to welcome working with people, and as a bottom line you're simply fun to work with—you're going to stand out and attract good work."

So *don't* think you can closet yourself in the library and ignore everything else. People will resent you—and you won't succeed.

5. Conversational flaws: interrupting and swearing

Don't interrupt people. It says to people: I'm quicker than you, and what I have to say is more important. ***Nobody*** wants to feel that way. Recognize that if you speak and think quickly, it's often true that you can finish people's sentences for them, and you're impatient to get on to the next point. But it's just rude and people will resent it, even if they don't show it. If you ***are*** in the habit of interrupting, make a special point of saying, "I'm sorry, I interrupted," whenever you do it, and giving people a chance to finish their thoughts. You'll be liked and respected more if you learn to let people complete what they're saying.

When it comes to swearing, let other people swear, but don't do it yourself. Lots of lawyers swear, but when you're new, don't let yourself be one of them. It sends out the wrong signals, and it offends a lot of people who'll never speak up and say anything to you about it. You've got a great vocabulary. Use it.

6. Complaining about your work

Whether there's too much or too little of it, or it's too difficult or too mundane or too boring, keep your complaints out of the office. I'm not saying you shouldn't complain to ***anybody***. Just don't whine at work. It won't help you.

I discuss under "Handling Chimp Work Without Going Bananas" how to deal with grunt work, and how to minimize it. Here, I just need to make the point: complaining about your work doesn't get you ***anywhere***. It's easy to think that if you complain about doing a certain kind of work, that people will recognize that you really deserve better projects. That's kind of like trying to get an inattentive spouse to pay more attention to you by berating them and making them feel bad for ignoring you. Your behavior will have just the opposite effect you want it to have.

Similarly, if you're getting too much work, moaning about it won't help you. As I explain in "Help! I'm Drowning! What To Do When You've Got Too Much Work (Or Too Little . . .),," there are a bunch of ways to minimize your workload without ever complaining about it or saying "no" to a project. Complaining will just make you sound like you're not capable, and you don't want that.

7. Complaining about clients

OK, maybe you really do have clients who are chuckleheads. And maybe they get themselves into really boneheaded predicaments or they've got simply terrible ideas about how to handle their lives and businesses. Or maybe they're just nasty, nasty people. But remember, if they could do all this stuff themselves, you'd be out of work. Your clients, whether you're working for a government agency or a private firm, are what make it possible for you to have work and get paid. If a client really is that much of a buttmunch, all of your colleagues know it, as well. You don't have to chip in your two cents to point it out.

8. Behaving as though your personal life is more important than your work (even though—let's face it—that's true)

This is a tough one, because after all, your work isn't your life. Your work is a means of creating the life you want. You'll always have things that you want to do outside of work (at least, I hope so!). One of the things about being a lawyer that really bites is that your schedule is often not your own. Client problems come up at inopportune times. Criminals don't work according to a convenient calendar. Stuff happens when you don't want it to, and it conflicts with your personal life. What do you do?

Don't make it obvious that you value your personal life more than your work. That's all. You can balance your life much better than you think you can, if you just watch the ***way*** you say things. The partner at one firm told me about a new associate whom he approached Friday at 4:30 to work over the weekend on a client matter that had to be completed by Monday at 5 p.m. She whined, "I worked last weekend and I don't want to work this weekend. I want to go to the beach. Can't it wait until Monday?" It couldn't, and he wound up working all weekend to finish the work himself. He commented, "What got me wasn't what she said, it was the way she said it. If she had said, 'I'd love to work with you. Can I be flexible this weekend? Can I come in Saturday night or Sunday afternoon?' I would have been thrilled. As it is, I won't use her again."

Take that advice to heart. Instead of saying to people, "I have a dog. I have to leave by five every night," or "My family always goes on vacation to Cape Cod for a week in the middle of July, and I'm going with them," say, "I have a dog. If it's not inconvenient, I need to walk him around dinnertime every night. I'll take work home or come back to the office if you need me. And if it's not convenient, I can hire a dog walker. But I'd really like to do it myself if it's possible." Or with the vacation thing, say, "My family has always vacationed together on Cape Cod for a week in July. It's a tradition I'd really like to keep up. Is there any way I can schedule my work around that week? If not, is there some work I could take with me?"

You see what I'm doing. I'm wording your request such that you put your employer in the position of being benevolent. It's only the truly sadistic—or ***truly*** rushed or overworked—supervisor who won't respond to that kind of request. Give it a try!

9. Being giggly

This is probably not a problem for you if you're a guy. But I heard from more than one employer that women who giggle a lot make people think they're immature and girlish. Everybody likes a pleasant personality and they want to know that you're enjoying yourself at work. But giggling isn't like that; it makes people think you're unsure of yourself, and masking that with giggles. Smiling is fine. Laughing when something is funny is great. But a constant giggle will drive people nuts.

10. Comparing yourself to others and suggesting that you're better and deserve more as a result

You're not in school any more. You're not being graded on a curve. Degrading other people's work and/or conduct makes you sound insecure. As lawyers at Gray Plant point out, "Anytime an associate gets competitive—saying things like 'I worked this many hours' or 'I'm more senior than so-and-so' or 'It should be my turn for a bigger office,' the rest of the associate group tends to discredit that person." Let your work and your accomplishments speak for themselves, and make the assumption that your superiors are clever enough to figure out for themselves who deserves more responsibility and more goodies.

11. Creating the image of a brown-nosing suck-up

I discuss elsewhere the importance of honest flattery and how valuable it can be. But when you're willing to prostrate yourself for your boss, when you make empty statements that everybody can see are lies—"Hey, nice suit, Stan!" when it's obvious that the pinstripes are washing off at the laundry—get you nowhere. People may be suckers for flattery, but watch what you say in front of an audience—because it's the creation of a perception that we're concerned with here.

12. Attempting to control other people's behavior. You're not Geppetto and they're not Pinocchio

When you manage people, you by necessity have to guide their behavior, just as when you work for somebody else, they guide yours. That's not what I'm talking about here. I'm talking about value judgments that we all make—that are ***fun*** to make—about how other people ought to behave.

In his autobiography, former Senator and astronaut John Glenn says he believes that a dressing-down he once gave his Mercury astronauts about their skirt chasing—"I read them the riot act, saying that we had worked too hard to get into this program to see it jeopardized by anyone who couldn't keep his pants zipped"—might have prevented him from being the first American in space.

Statements starting with words like "You have to . . . " "She should . . . " "He should have . . . " "They ought to . . . " will make you sound like a perpetual victim or a perpetual nag. As my favourite radio shrink,

Dr. Joy Brown, is always saying, the only person whose behavior you can control is your own. Let other people learn their own lessons their own way. Don't let people hear you taking charge of areas you can't—and have no right to—change.

13. Suggesting that this employer is just a stepping stone to what you *really* want to do

Ambition is good. Ambition that suggests you're walking all over your employer is not. As a new prosecutor, your goal is to move from misdemeanors to felonies. At a private firm, your goal is to become partner. I don't care if you never have any intention of staying as long as it will take to move up—don't let that be obvious to your employer! As Baker Botts' Bart Showalter advises, "Don't ever convey the attitude that you're just using this job as a means to get what you really want. 'I'll do this stuff but I've got a dream of starting my own business,' 'I want to get back to the East Coast where my family is,' 'I want to get into venture capital' or 'I want to get trained and land a sweet corporate job' just isn't appropriate." If you've got dreams, I applaud you. Share those dreams with your family and your friends ***outside*** of work. Your colleagues at the office should only see your desire to learn and move ahead ***there***.

14. Succumbing to the influence of alcohol

I talk in the "1,640-Hour Interview" section about the importance of not getting drunk at social events, as well as later on in this chapter under "Social Graces." Most of the inappropriate behavior I've heard about is the result of the demon rum. A pop or two now and then won't make anybody think the worse of you. But if you routinely drink so much that people comment on your behavior, you've gone over the line—and you probably need help to quit.

CAREER LIMITING MOVE . . .

Partner, on the board of various corporate clients. He's to attend a board meeting in another city on a Saturday morning. On the flight, he gets hammered. When he lands, he takes a taxi to the company's headquarters, a mirrored building in a park-like setting. The taxi leaves, and he walks to the front door. It's locked. He walks around the building, and tries the rest of the doors. They're all locked, too. He figures that his secretary told him the wrong day for the meeting, or it's been cancelled and nobody told him. In fact, the board meeting is taking place inside; he arrived late, and they locked the doors as a normal security procedure, assuming he was a no-show. He doesn't know this, and he's furious. He walks back toward the front of the building, intending to call a cab on his cell phone.

As he makes his way around the building, he realizes that with everything he drank on the plane, he needs to relieve himself. Looking around to make sure nobody is watching, he unzips his fly and relieves himself on one of the mirrored panels of the building.

Unbeknownst to him, the mirror is two-way. The other side of the panel on which he's urinating is actually the window to the conference room, where the other board members, stunned, are watching him the whole time.

15. Doing too much pro bono

This is a fine line to tread. It may be that the pro bono work you do suffuses your career with meaning. The problem is, it doesn't make any money for your employer. As Emory's Carolyn Bregman points out, "If you do too much pro bono, they may think your heart is in pro bono." Keep a close eye on how pro bono work at your office is perceived, seeing who gets bonuses, promotions, and general applause. If you find that it's not the people who do the amount of pro bono you want to do, ramp back your pro bono commitment. Or alternatively, get a job that leaves you more time for pro bono, or with an employer that has a different attitude toward pro bono work, or consider a full-time job doing public interest work. It might not pay as much, but if it's truly where your heart is, you'll find ultimately that the financial sacrifice is worth it.

16. Racist or sexist behavior

As Dewey Ballantine's John Ragosta points out, "It should go without saying that you shouldn't undertake any behavior derogatory to a particular gender, religion, or ethnicity. It's not just morally intolerable but, in today's world, stupid and dangerous. Partners don't need loose cannons."

CAREER LIMITING MOVE . . .

Summer clerk, great credentials, large New York firm. At a restaurant, he gets drunk and says to another clerk, "Women shouldn't be lawyers. I couldn't work for a woman." He wants to be in the real estate department at the firm, and the head of the real estate practice is a woman! No offer. **Obviously**.

C. The Care and Feeding of Supervising Attorneys and Other Muckety-Mucks At Work

It's ironic. If you want to move ahead in your career, if you want to be in a position to give orders, you need to show how good you are at ***taking*** orders first. The way you handle your supervising attorney and other people in authority has a tremendous effect on your early career. Let's see what you need to know.

1. If you're working at a private firm, the partners are your first clients. Treat them accordingly.

Boy, is ***this*** an old chestnut. I heard it ***everywhere***. As a lawyer at Proskauer Rose commented, "When you start, your clients aren't just the companies and people who hire the firm to work for them. The partners who pay your salary are your clients as well." A lawyer at Wyatt Tarrant points out that "At a large firm in particular, your partner 'client base' provides the work that allows you to develop professionally and establish a reputation, first within the firm, and then outside."

With that in mind, what should you do?

First of all, lawyers at Wyatt Tarrant advise you to "Put yourself in the partner's shoes and think about how you would want to be treated and the quality of the work you would want to see. That's what you'd do for a client, and it's what you should do for a partner." The way to get great work is to ***do*** great work. Make your work product excellent (and I tell you how to do that in the chapter called "How To Crush Research And Writing Assignments). As Carlton Fields' Hardy Roberts says, "If you make your partner look good, they'll make you look good. Partners talk. They'll say, 'He's really good, use him.' It's a great way to develop your reputation and get great work."

The flipside of that is to make sure you avoid embarrassing your partner. If there are holes in your research, if you mistreat support staffers or act inappropriately in front of a client or at a social event, it will reflect badly on your supervising attorney. You want people's reaction to be that your supervisor is lucky to have you. Remember that next time people are banging kamikazes at the firm picnic, or you're too busy to shepardize!

You should also be mindful of cultural differences when you're dealing with very senior attorneys. They grew up in a very different world than you did, and you want to be mindful of what makes them comfortable. As Dennis Kennedy reflects, "As a new associate I gradually grew to realize that many older lawyers are uncomfortable with one-on-one lunches, especially with members of the opposite sex or with people young enough to be their children. It's a cultural thing, but it helps to respect it. Invite a group of people or include a peer."

Finally, treat your superiors with respect. Maybe you don't think much of somebody's intellect or you don't like their company a whole bunch. But the fact is, they've made it for years in a tough profession, and that merits at least ***some*** respect. And if they're partners, they're the ones who are bringing in the business that pays your check. Treat them as you'd want to be treated in the same position!

CAREER LIMITING MOVE . . .

Large firm in California. A female senior partner makes plans to take three junior associates to a professional women's group, a very exclusive organization, for a luncheon meeting where a national speaker is going to give a lecture. The partner springs for the tickets, which are

$75 each. Fifteen minutes before the four of them are due to leave the office, one of the associates calls and leaves a voice mail saying, "I can't make it." The other two are no-shows. The partner, concerned that the three associates are too loaded down with work to go with her, tracks down one of their secretaries to try and find out who the associate is working for. When the partner asks the secretary about the associate, the secretary responds, "Oh, she's not working. She went shopping for makeup with . . . " and she names the other two associates.

2. **How to work with your supervising attorney and make it easy on *both* of you!**

   a. **Get advice in advance of working with a new supervisor.**

   As I discuss in the chapter called "How to Crush Research And Writing Assignments," before you start to work for somebody new, check around to get tips on working with them. Ask other associates, secretaries, your mentor (if you have one), about what the supervising attorney likes to see, what his/her style is like. You can smooth over a lot of misunderstandings and false steps by doing a simple "audience analysis" first.

   b. **Be flexible in your working style.**

   A lawyer at Latham and Watkins points out that you need to be flexible and be able to adapt to a variety of working styles, especially in firms where you're unassigned for a while at the beginning. The hours you work, the way you write, how you communicate—you'll find that this varies for every supervising attorney. As Milbank Tweed's Kathy Brady says, "You may be touchy-feely, your supervisor may be very matter-of-fact. Talk to him the way he talks." As Georgetown's Marilyn Tucker says, you need to make yourself a "legal chameleon." Your supervising attorney will be more comfortable with you if you do.

   c. **Pay attention to your supervisor's hobbies.**

Look at the photos and memorabilia that (s)he keeps at the office. Pay attention to what your supervisor talks about with the most enthusiasm. With these interests in mind, pay attention when you hear something about those hobbies and interests on TV or on the radio, or when you see something about them in magazines or on web sites or in the newspaper. Clip articles that you find. Everybody appreciates people who take interest in them as a person, including your supervisor.

d. **Figure out the traits that your supervisor values most in himself/herself, and pay honest compliments in those areas.**

Everybody has something they're particularly proud of. If your supervisor is a great writer or an excellent speaker or a particularly creative problem solver, compliment them about that trait when you see evidence of it. Everybody appreciates sincere flattery. When you pay someone an honest compliment, you're not being a brownnoser. You're acknowledging something you respect, and people appreciate that.

e. **If your boss is normally nice and suddenly snaps at you for no apparent reason, don't take it too personally.**

Don't take every glare, sharp intake of breath, or harsh word personally. Remember, your supervisor has stresses on his life just as you do on yours. Don't try to read your supervisor's mind. You can't always know what's going on, and when your supervisor snaps at you out of thin air, it's a good idea to accept the fact that the outburst is the result of something you don't know about.

f. **Be sensitive to your supervisor's workload.**

No matter how much ***you*** have on your plate, it's safe to assume that your supervisor has more. When you have questions for them, get to the point. As Denver's Jennifer Loud Ungar says, "They don't want to hear the long version of anything!" Syracuse's Alex Epsilanty advises you similarly to "Leave your oratory skills at the door." When you write for your supervisor, make your prose spare (unless you know definitively that they like long, flowery writing—which they probably ***don't***). When you have questions to ask, make a list of them and think about exactly what you're going to say ahead of time, so that you don't wear your supervisor out. And when you've got an issue you want addressed, watch your timing. As Kathleen Brady points out, "You've got to pay attention to the signals you get. If you walk into your supervisor's office and they're frantic, assume that your issue is a lower priority. Don't drop it in their lap at that moment. Say, 'I've got an issue, you look crazed, let me know when you have five minutes to discuss it.' Otherwise you'll dump your problem on them, they'll be angry, and you won't get what you want."

g. **Send your supervisor a weekly memo.**

As Georgetown's Marilyn Tucker recommends, "Write a weekly memo to your group head, assigning partner, or supervisor listing all of the projects you've been assigned, their status, any deadlines, and your availability for the next week. By writing this memo, you and your supervisor will know exactly where your workload stands, and you won't miss any deadlines."

h. **Keep your supervisor informed of good, bad, and ugly news.**

The famous movie producer Sam Goldwyn had a very funny quote about this. He said, "I don't want 'yes men' around me. I want everyone to tell me the truth, even if it costs them their jobs." Ha ha. I probably shouldn't have told you that. Because I'm about to tell you that you have to give your supervisor the accurate scoop on the work you're doing for them, even if it's not what they want to hear. As Carlton Fields' Kevin Napper says, "If they think the law is one way and you research and find that it's not, you have to ***tell*** them." If you're not going to meet a deadline, don't switch your route around the office and play a game of "Mission Impossible" so you don't have to give them the bad news. Tell them immediately. They can deal with the truth, but if they catch you trying to snow them, they'll never trust you again.

i. **When your supervisor pays a visit to your office . . .**

Whenever your supervisor stops by to see you, ***immediately*** stop what you're doing, take your hands from the keyboard (or pen from paper) and look them in the eye. ***Listen***, and have a pad and pen ready in case they need you to take some notes. They deserve your full attention. Whatever you're doing will have to wait.

j. **Wait until your supervisor feels comfortable working with you before you start making suggestions.**

In an effort to take the initiative, it's very easy to commence looking for things your supervisor can improve the moment you start working together. Try to rein in that impulse. After you fully understand what you're doing and the reasons why you're doing it the way you're doing it, ***then*** you can look at things critically. Especially in the area of computers and Internet resources—where you undoubtedly know more than your supervisor does!—consider making suggestions, explaining the value of what you're proposing.

 CAREER LIMITING MOVE . . .

Junior associate is appointed as a junior member of the firm's management committee. At her first meeting, she pipes up with suggestions for changes in firm policies. When the meeting is over, the managing partner takes her aside, and tells her, "You're new, you're green, keep your eyes and ears open and your mouth shut for a while. So what if you don't get it. There's a reason for it. If you have to, talk to me separately and I'll explain it. Don't question me in public."

D. Mentors: "When The Student Is Ready . . . The Teacher Will Come."

I don't mean to brag, but in some ways, you're ***holding*** your mentor. You're reading it now. Everybody in this book is your mentor. But in more traditional terms, the whole idea of having a mentor is somewhat controversial, and even people who do believe you should have a mentor differ about the kind of mentor you need. For instance, some people say your supervisor is your natural mentor. Others point out, "Then whom do you go to for problems dealing with your supervisor? Are you going to say to your supervisor, 'Here's my problem. My supervisor is a jerk'?"

The bottom line about mentors is this: "Being a lawyer takes some guidance," in the words of Hofstra's Diane Schwartzberg. As we'll see—and as I've said throughout this book—you ***need*** to be able to learn from other people in order to succeed. That's at the heart of mentoring. I've sifted through everything I heard to give you some ideas about mentors that I think you'll find really useful. We'll talk about the kinds of mentors you need, how to identify and use them, and how to make yourself "mentor-able."

1. **If your employer has a formal mentoring program, at least give it a try.**

   Formal mentoring programs have mixed success. They're like arranged marriages: it's luck if they work out. The fact is, a mentor has to take a sincere interest in somebody else's career, and you can't ***tell*** somebody to do that. But if your employer has gone to the trouble of setting you up with a formal mentor, Hamline's Joyce Laher recommends that you "talk to them at least once or twice. You don't have to jump into their lap!" Ask for their advice about the employer, the work, find out what they've done that you can emulate, mistakes they wish they hadn't made. A true "organic" mentor ***can*** grow from a formal mentoring program if your personality meshes with the mentor's such that the mentor develops a sincere interest in your advancement. Otherwise—no hard feelings! We'll talk about seeking out informal "mentors" if the formal program doesn't work (and even if it ***does***, you should have other mentors, as well).

2. **So what am I looking for?**

   When you're looking for "mentor material," you're looking for mentors with two sets of—well—qualifications, for lack of a better word. One set involves professional attributes, and the other, personal qualities and views.

a. Professional attributes of mentors you want:

1) People *at your office* who will give you insights into the workings of your office; tips on your supervisor, who's powerful, who you shouldn't cross, who to seek out. As Joyce Laher points out, "Mentors at the office can be incredibly valuable. A mentor might tell you 'X is on Y's side and Y is instrumental to your future, so don't stand around the water cooler and say that X dresses funny.'" American's Matt Pascocello adds, "It's too easy to feel paranoid. You need to have someone to ask, 'Why am I getting so much grunt work?' 'Why don't I have more work?' Mentors help you sort things out."

2) People with enough juice that they are in a position to speak up for you when you need a champion—when you've made a mistake that needs smoothing over, or you're being considered for a permanent offer, a promotion, a partnership.

3) People you admire, who are models for you to emulate in their work habits and "people skills."

4) People doing the same basic type of work as you (transactional, litigation), "who will critique your work," says Suffolk's Jim Whitters.

5) People *outside* of your office, to give you objective advice when (and if) you want to make a career move. As one lawyer points out, "No mentor at your firm will ever say 'It's time for you to go to the U.S. Attorney's office.'"

b. Personal qualities and views of people you want:

1) "People who share your values, outlooks, and perspective," says Rob Kaplan. For instance, if a partner at the office believes that work is the only thing in life and men who spend time with their kids are wimps, and you believe in balance above all, you're not looking at the right mentor for you!

2) "Someone with whom you feel comfortable enough to speak frankly," says George Washington's Jim Lovelace. If you're always on pins and needles around a powerful person, you won't be able to relax enough to benefit from their mentoring.

3) "If you are a woman, a female mentor is ideal," says Georgetown's Beth Sherman. Another woman can more fully appreciate the issues you face, "and there won't be any potential sexual harassment issues," she adds. It's a sad fact that men can hang out together without any tongues wagging behind their backs, but if a man and a woman spend time in each other's exclusive company—well! You ***can*** have opposite sex mentors, but be aware of the potential issues.

Ultimately, as Dennis Kennedy says, "You want their stories, their insights, their faith in you."

If you think these qualities suggest that you ought to have more than one mentor—you're right. As one recruiting coordinator says, "You don't have to love everything about a person to learn from them." Ideally you'll have several mentors with whom you can discuss different aspects of your career and your life. And as you move on and perhaps change jobs, your mentor "group" evolves, too. ***Always*** keep your eyes open for new advisors, new people to emulate. How do you find them? That's what we'll talk about next.

3. Baiting the hook—making yourself "mentor-worthy"

As is true about everything else to do with mentoring, how you go about ***getting*** a mentor is the subject of some controversy. Some people tell you to actively seek them out, but here's the problem: you can't ***make*** someone take an interest in you and your career. Let's face it: in every tangible respect, there's more in it for you than there is for them. You get the advice you need to propel your career forward, practical advice and inside skinny. They get the pleasure of seeing their protégé succeed. That's not nothing, but it really is their call as to whether there's going to be a mentor relationship or not.

So finding a mentor is really a matter of positioning yourself so that people you want to have as mentors will want to mentor ***you***. The Eastern proverb that opened this section, courtesy of Dennis Kennedy, says it all: "When the student is ready . . . the teacher will come." How do you make yourself ready?

a. Ask questions!

When you identify people with "mentoring potential," ***talk*** to them. ***Ask***, "How did you do this or that?" Georgetown's Anna Davis suggests that you ask, "I see what you've done with your career, I'd like to be there. I'd love your advice." Matt Pascocello recommends that you say things like, "I'd like to learn how you do this particular practice or how you got this client," or ask "I've heard great things about your work. Can I see some of your memos so I can emulate them?" Overall, Georgetown's Abbie Willard advises that you "Let them know you want to learn from them. Be overt about it!"

b. Pay appropriate compliments.

It's rare for someone ***not*** to enjoy being told by a younger person, "I admire you. I want to be like you. It amazes me how you get along with everybody. People rave about your work."

c. Think of people you clicked with during interviews.

As Vickie Brown points out, if they liked you when they interviewed you, their recommendations helped bring you into the organization in the first place. That makes them potential mentors.

d. See who's been pleased with your work.

If someone tells you "Great job!" on something you do, you've got a potential mentor.

e. Take advantage of social events at work.

I've already told you about using social events to get to know as many people as you can. As Denver's Pat Powell advises, "Whether it's a social event at work or a community event, you need to be open and create a comfort zone around you. You can't build barriers. They don't want to help you if they don't know you." See who you click with best at those functions. An easy relationship is at the heart of mentoring.

f. **Get active in the legal community outside of work.**

Dickinson's Elaine Bourne recommends that you "Get active on a committee. Take on a project for the bar association. Co-chair a project. Don't just go to meetings. Show yourself so people will notice you."

g. **Don't jump at the first person who strikes you as a potential mentor.**

When you start in a new job, it's tempting to glom onto the first person who takes an interest in you. Remember, you have to "qualify" people as mentors before you align yourself with them. As one partner pointed out, "You don't know on the first day of school if you're hanging with a geek—until you see them make a jerk of themselves in class." Be cautious until you've had a little time to analyze the situation and make sure it will work for you.

4. **Listen and watch for *cues*. Mentoring springs organically from there.**

As Elaine Bourne says, "When people express an interest in you and your career, take them up on that." Vickie Brown advises that you "Listen for phrases like 'Feel free to come in and speak to me.'" Openings like that lead to mentoring relationships.

5. **Now that you have your mentors, handle them wisely!**

First of all, remember that you can be open with your mentor but if you work together, (s)he still a colleague first. Don't throw your discretion entirely to the wind. And if the mentor in question is someone from outside your office, remember confidentiality: "You have to speak about your cases with outside mentors in general terms to protect confidentiality," says Joyce Laher.

Second, "Be a sponge. Incorporate what people tell you and emulate them," says Milbank Tweed's Kathleen Brady. Golden Gate's Susanne

Aronowitz points out that "If you routinely don't heed their advice, they won't go to bat for you. Show them that you respect their advice, follow up, let them know what, and how, you did."

Third, as Matt Pascocello points out, remember that "Sometimes what you get from a mentor is criticism. The more you get, the more grateful you should be. They're trying to help you succeed."

Finally, remember that you're not married to your mentor(s). If the relationship turns sour, or you find the mentor isn't who you thought they were, move on!

CAREER LIMITING MOVE . . .

New associate at a large firm. He identifies his mentor target the day he arrives: a partner in the litigation department who seems powerful. He aligns himself with this partner, and in his words "pat myself on the back for choosing this guy." The partner gives the new associate some work, and they have a good rapport. At the new associate's first semi-annual review, nobody has anything good to say about him. The associate stammers, "But . . . but . . . didn't X have good things to say about me?" The reviewers roll their eyes, and say, "Frankly, we didn't ask him." The associate reflects, "It turns out this guy was dead wood. He had no political clout. In fact, he was the laughingstock of the firm. If you find out your mentor is no good, cut bait. I hadn't taken the time to figure out who to be aligned with before casting my lot with this guy. You're responsible for managing your own career!"

6. Giving back to your mentor—and people who follow *you* up the ladder

I've already told you that mentors get the pleasure of watching you progress. It reflects well on them. They're flattered by it. But don't be a hog. Take advantage of ways to help your benefactor in return. For instance, many senior attorneys don't feel comfortable with computers. Help them out! Or if you know they like hearing the inside skinny on what's going on among the junior associates, tell them (being mindful of secrets—don't violate confidences any more than you'd expect anyone else to violate ***yours***). Or maybe your mentor needs help with an article or a speech. Be willing to step up to the plate for them as they do for you.

As you progress, keep your eye out for people behind you. As soon as you're a first year associate, you're more senior than the summer clerks! As Kathleen Brady says, "If you miss out on watching protégés succeed, you're losing out on one of the true joys in life. And it helps the profession. You hand off the ball to the next generation."

E. Tapping Into The Hidden Power Structure: Support Staff Issues

If you've worked before, you know how valuable—and powerful—support staffers can be. If you ***haven't***, you may tell yourself, "Finally, ***I'm*** not the lowest person on the totem pole—I've got somebody I can boss around!" Don't kid yourself. As Vermont's Pavel Wonsowicz points out, "The support staff is the backbone of the place." Hofstra's Diane Schwartzberg adds that "You can't bully people and be arrogant and get your way!"

Handling support staff well reflects on you in a whole bunch of ways: your ability to lead, accept responsibility, and deal with all different kinds of people (including clients). As lawyers at Goulston Storrs point out, "Treating support staffers with respect will get a summer clerk or new lawyer further than almost anything else besides good, competent lawyering."

Minnesota's Susan Gainen gets this across with her "Five Stages Of Relations With Support Staff."

Stage One: On your first day of work, people are predisposed to think well of you. They are prepared to like you, to help you, and to invest in your success.

Stage Two: You acted like a jerk. Whether you were rude to a support staff person or to a colleague, you can almost always repair the damage if you are sincere in your apologies, and never, ever repeat the behavior.

Stage Three: You really ***are*** a jerk. Whether it's rudeness, incompetence, laziness or a tendency to make mistakes and blame others, you are riding for a fall. The support staff, which can smooth the wrinkles in your appearance, cover for your small mistakes and chuckle at your eccentricities, will now take three steps back and watch you fall on your face. Real-life example: After an Associate General Counsel at a bank had been working for more than six months, staff began asking themselves questions like "Just how long should the learning curve be for remembering that each foreclosure needs a $75 filing fee check attached to it, and that the lead time for a request is 24 hours?" and "When will he stop blaming us for his mistakes?"

Stage Four: Singly and in groups they begin to approach their boss and your boss, saying "I can't believe that he/she did/didn't do (whatever)." This becomes a chorus, and everything that you've ever done that you weren't supposed to do—or that you've never done that you *were* supposed to—becomes sheet music for this group.

Stage Five—The Piranha Stage: Not a pretty sight. Singly and in groups, they approach your boss and their boss and say "It's him/her or us." Now is the time to pack up your desk and sneak away into the night or stand on your desk and disembowel yourself with the Waterford letter opener you got as a graduation present. When weighing the value of a new *summa cum laude* graduate who quickly demonstrates an unerring ability to antagonize large numbers of valued employees against a group of irreplaceable experienced legal secretaries and paralegals, there is no choice. You're out.

As the "Five Stages" illustrate, mistreating the staff can be detrimental to your professional health.

Let's see what you have to do when it comes to dealing with support staff:

1. Remember that they can be helpful to you in a million subtle ways.

When you start out as a lawyer, there are a bunch of things you don't know about practicing law. It's fair to say that support staffers who've been with your employer for a while know more about being a lawyer than you do. Real estate paralegals, for instance, can handle closings themselves! The secretaries, receptionists, word processors, copy room staffers, office gophers and runners, the mailroom clerks—they can save your skin in a bunch of ways.

a. They can run interference for you.

"If your secretary likes you, and you tell them, 'I have to buy a 30th anniversary gift for my parents' or 'I have to run out for a cake for my husband's birthday party,' they'll often tell someone looking for you that you're in a meeting," says Denver's Jennifer Loud Ungar.

If you're working in a public interest job, if a secretary or intake worker likes you, they'll field your calls. For instance, if it's a Social Security matter, they can answer people's questions. They know a lot of the answers. In the private world, if a client calls you, you ***have*** to return their call. They're paying. In the public arena, secretaries and intake workers can field your calls. They can make you or break you."

b. They can help you meet deadlines that you'd otherwise miss.

Lawyers at Goulston Storrs point out that "When you ask someone to stay late or deliver or copy something for you on a rush basis, your relationship with that person is likely going to be the one thing that determines whether that person will help you out. Lawyers with poor relationships with support staffers will suffer." As Brooklyn's Joan King says, "If you're respectful to the word processing staff, it pays dividends at 2 a.m., when your documents get pushed ahead of someone else's." One lawyer talked about having to get some important papers out to a client. He was certain that he'd missed the FedEx deadline. He went to the mailroom to check. The mailroom guy smiled, and said, "Come on. I'll help you out." He drove the lawyer to the airport, and took him to a secret entrance and got the FedEx off, even though the "technical" deadline had passed.

If you're a new lawyer and you're sharing a secretary with a bunch of other people, Hofstra's Rebecca Katz-White reminds you that "your work has the lowest priority. Some new lawyers have to share a secretary with four other people! You're low person on the totem pole, and that means that if you aren't nice to the secretary, you won't get ***anything*** done."

c. They can save you from looking stupid.

When you're a new lawyer, there are a lot of details that you don't know—but support staffers ***do***. Pepperdine's Carol Allemeier points out that you have to "Understand the difference between power and authority. Staff members can have a lot of power even if they don't have much authority. If you're comfortable talking to the boss's secretary, she can tell you when it's a good time or a ***bad*** time to talk to the boss. This can be very valuable information. You can also find out when (s)he will be out of the office and what their pet peeves are. Many an alum has told me that they asked for raises and scheduled their time off based on this 'insider information.' In addition, Georgetown's Marilyn Tucker points out, "Experienced support staffers will know the format documents should take, the number of copies required for different courts, and many other similarly critical details." Georgetown's Anna Davis points out that "If you're nice to the mail room guys, they'll look out for you. When you go to send something out, they'll tell you, 'Hey—you forget this on the envelope!'" One lawyer talked about her experience working for a "very intimidating" litigation department head. "He told me, 'I need this memo for the court from you. I only want two pages. Make it brief.' I researched it and wrote it, but it came out four pages long. Instead of editing it, I thought I could just single-space it to meet the two-page cutoff. When I took it to his secretary, she said, 'Oh, no—pleadings have to be double-spaced. Go and redo it.' If she hadn't told me that, I would have been toast."

d. **They listen to the jungle drums.**

If you want to know what's going on at work, your secretary is your first line of offense. As Wendy Werner points out, "They'll know before anybody which clients are coming and going, who are predominant business getters, what department generates the most revenue, who loses the most (and least) associates."

SMART HUMAN TRICK . . .

New associate at a large New York firm. He gets to know the entire staff in the first two weeks he's at work. The other associates laugh at him, but through this network he finds out that the firm is thinking of adding an associate at its London office. He finds out who is doing the hiring, goes to them, and says, 'Take me." No other associate had even **heard** about the plum assignment. It pays off. He gets the job.

2. Support staffers can be powerful in ways you can't imagine.

As St. Thomas' Michelle Fongyee points out, "Don't start with a hierarchy in mind, 'Me lawyer—you secretary.' Secretaries have a lot of power that new associates don't appreciate." Kentucky's Drusilla Bakert echoes that, saying, "Don't be deluded into thinking that just because your time is billable and theirs isn't that you're better than they are." Gunstler, Yoakley's Kelly Toole says that "your secretary was there before you, and she'll be there when you leave. She can be a great resource, or your worst enemy." If you treat secretaries badly, your work will suddenly be on the bottom of the pile. If you're rude to word processing people, "That brief you need? Suddenly they've got a project that's more important than yours!" says Drusilla Bakert. Florida State's Stephanie Redfearn points out that "Many runners are the children of partners or big clients. Attorneys shoot themselves in the foot when they treat runners badly. The kid goes home, and over dinner tells Daddy, 'So-and-so is a jerk.'" One recruiting coordinator commented that "The managing partner's secretary is the most powerful person in our firm. He relies on her for the inside scoop on everything that goes on in the office. Attorneys on her bad side are toast. She has the managing partner's ear. In some ways, he's closer to her than he is to his wife!" At another firm, the secretary for the head of the litigation department had the same role. As an associate in the department tells it, "She'll tell him things like, 'I don't like that associate. He's sneaky.' And that associate will have a black mark against him. And on the flipside of that, she controls the goodies. If the partner can't make a basketball game, she decides who gets his season tickets. She's a smart person to befriend." McDonnell Boehnen's Brad Hulbert points out that "The arrogant lawyer who forgets that secretaries are an essential part of the team is inevitably punished. 'Oh, I didn't know that you wanted the attachments actually attached to the brief!'" At another firm, a senior associate was asked to leave because he lost two secretaries in a row.

Remember above all that secretaries ***talk***. What they say about you helps develop your reputation, not just with other secretaries but with lawyers as well. If you treat the john as a reading room and spend a lot of time in there, your bathroom habits will soon get spread around the firm. At one firm, one partner was notorious for having lunch at his desk and putting his dirty wrappers and plates in his out box for his secretary to dispose of, rather than just dumping them in his wastebasket. That reputation followed him for years; every time his name came up, that's what people would think of first.

The bottom line: mistreating the support staff can kill you. They really do have that much power.

CAREER LIMITING MOVE . . .

Rainmaking partner in a large firm. He is renowned for treating support staffers badly, but because he's such a great source of business, his behavior is tolerated for a long time. One day, he is having a meeting in the firm's conference room at lunchtime with some clients. He tells his secretary, 'Order a sandwich platter from the deli. For my sandwich, you know what I like. Tell them **no mayonnaise**. Got it? **No mayonnaise**." Well, duh, yeah—she's not deaf. She orders the sandwiches, making a special point to the deli to leave the mayonnaise off of this partner's sandwich. When the sandwiches are delivered to the conference room, sure enough—his sandwich has mayonnaise on it. He gets on the intercom with his secretary and says—in front of the clients—"My sandwich has mayonnaise on it!" She apologizes profusely and explains that she did give the correct directions to the deli. She tells him, "I'll go down there and get you another sandwich." He snaps, "No you won't. You'll come in here and wipe off the mayonnaise yourself." There is stunned silence in the conference room, and she is in shock. What she **thinks** is, "You better hang on to that mayonnaise, because if you make me go in there, you're going to need all the lubrication you can get." What she **does** is to calmly pick up her purse and leave the office.

It's the last straw. The other partners ask this partner to leave the firm.

3. Don't force your superiors to choose sides between you and a support staffer.

As Wake Forest's Bill Barrett warns, "Young associates will be out before the partner's secretary leaves. Secretaries and office managers run the office!" Baker Donelson's Sue Hunter adds that "It's a bad idea to get too big for your britches. It's a lot easier to find good attorneys than it is to find good secretaries!" Dennis Kennedy advises that you "Learn your place in the pecking order. I used to joke in the hiring process that we should hire military veterans because they knew that you started at the bottom and earned your way up the ladder. Everyone at the office plays a different role and the value of those roles is not determined by title. If you've been at a firm for a few months and get into a situation where you force a partner to choose between supporting you or the secretary (s)he's had for ten years and relies on in ways you can't even imagine (until ***you've*** had a secretary you've relied on for ten years), I guarantee that a hundred percent of the time the partner will support the secretary. It's a showdown you can't win. Don't try to force it."

CAREER LIMITING MOVE . . .

A summer clerk. His first day at his summer employer. He walks into the managing partner's office while the managing partner is talking with his secretary. The summer clerk interrupts, saying, "Hello, Sir. It's nice to meet you. It's my first day . . . " The partner gives him a cold look and says, "I am in the middle of talking to my secretary, Miss Hathaway. She is more important than you will ever be."

4. Don't think that your superiors will respect you for lording it over the support staff.

Don't worry. Everybody at work assumes that you're smart and capable. You don't have to treat support staffers like dirt to burnish your position. And if you ***do***, it'll hurt you. Lawyers at Lord Bissell point out that "No matter how smart someone is and how technically savvy they may be as a lawyer, if they treat the staff with disrespect, they won't succeed." A lawyer at Shook Hardy adds, "Nobody wants prima donnas." Denver's Anne Stark Walker points out that "A few instances of brow-beating a secretary, or berating an office messenger, can do permanent damage to your reputation at the office."

5. **If the firm culture is to treat staff badly and/or make sexist comments around them—for gosh sakes *ignore* the firm culture!**

Don't take your behavioral cues from people who behave badly. As Lewis & Clark's Lisa Lesage points out, "Don't pay attention to how senior partners treat ***their*** secretaries!" Hamline's Vince Thomas adds that "Lots of people are short with staff, and sexist in a frat boy kind of way. It ***always*** comes back to bite you."

Remember, if you see attorneys at work treating their staffers badly, it tells you something you really don't want to know about them. And if you get into the good ol' boy mentality when it comes to handling "the girls," you're not just being stupid—you're opening up your employer to the threat of a sexual harassment suit, and I don't have to tell you that that's ***really*** bad news. Furthermore, if you flatter partners and then treat support staffers badly, it will expose you to everyone at the office as a phony. That's a bad reputation to have.

So follow a simple rule: treat support staffers with respect no matter how anybody else treats them, and you can't go wrong.

6. **Remember that little things mean a lot.**

Treat the support staff well from day one. The very first day at work, "Introduce yourself to them immediately and be certain to learn each person's name," says Marilyn Tucker. At one firm, a new associate brought in a box of muffins on his first day for all of the support staffers. "Now he gets everything he wants ***immediately***," commented the firm's hiring partner.

When you're brand new, acknowledge to your secretary that you've got a lot to learn. As Arizona's Mary Birmingham suggests, "Say to your secretary, 'I'm gonna ask you a ton of dumb questions, and I hope that's OK, because I'm trying to learn the ropes.'" At one firm, on her first day of work an associate walked up to her extremely experienced secretary and said, "Look, I know you've been doing this longer than I have. I know I probably can learn a thing or two about practicing law from you." As a colleague of hers pointed out, "It set a tone of mutual respect from the outset." At another firm, a new associate recalls that "I was warned that I'd been assigned a crotchety secretary who resented working for someone who was one-third her age. Knowing this, I took her flowers, and said, 'I look forward to learning from you. I know that you know more about the practice of law and this firm than I do.' After that, I had no trouble getting my work done. The fact is, when you're dealing with your secretary you've got to put your inflated ego aside. You can't assume you'll win pissing contests with secretaries, because you won't."

If secretaries at your office are referred to as "assistants," don't ***ever*** call them secretaries; they hate it.

Loyola's Pam Occhipinti tells you, "Never forget Secretaries' Day. It's ***so*** important to them!" Similarly, remember your secretary's birthday. If (s)he has a personal tragedy, send a condolence card and flowers.

Make a point of getting to know all of the support staffers, not just the secretaries. As Hamline's Vince Thomas says, "At my firm, our word processing department produced really long documents. Once in a while, instead of leaving things in the pick-up box, I'd walk my work down to them and spend a few minutes chatting. They obviously appreciated it. They were so used to having their contact with attorneys consist of people storming down to them and screaming 'You screwed this up!'"

When your secretary—or any other support staffer—does something for you, don't forget to say "thank you."

And finally, be appreciative of their time and sensitive to their workload. Be willing to pitch in and help them out when the situation calls for it. As Bart Schorsch writes in *The Student Lawyer,* "A few minutes helping to arrange a file or sift through documents might pay off for you later, either in experience or familiarity with a case or problem."

SMART HUMAN TRICK . . .

Junior associate at a large firm with several offices. After a year at one of the firm's offices, he gets transferred to a different office. On his last day, he buys flowers for his secretary. As he says, "I'd never had a secretary before, and I'd been very happy with her work. So I put a note on the flowers that said 'Thanks for being so kind to me.' Later that week, we had a firm-wide event with all of the lawyers and support staff. All of the female lawyers from my old office ran up to me and said, 'Wow! What a nice guy! You made her day!' This secretary told **everybody** about those flowers. I've never had any problem working with a secretary since. I honestly did it just because she was nice to me, but to tell you the truth, that was sixty bucks well spent—the goodwill it generated was priceless!"

CAREER LIMITING MOVE . . .

First year associate at a very large Midwestern firm. The firm handles enormous deals which involve tons of paperwork. One night, the paralegals and lawyers are there all night working on 200 document sets for a deal. A page in every set has to be replaced, and the first year associate decides that even though it's crunch time, it's beneath him to help take staples out of the document sets to make the replacement. Half an hour later, a mid-level associate walks into the room, and asks, 'What's going on here?' When the paralegals tell him about the mistake, he rolls up his sleeves to help. As one of the paralegals points out, "With that one simple act the mid-level associate got known as a person to work for. A simple act like that gets you further than all of the black letter law you know. The first year? He was black-balled."

7. **When you're new, be friendly with support staffers, but be careful about having the shoulder your secretary cries on.**

I've already stressed the importance of being friendly with support staffers, but as Hofstra's Rebecca Katz-White points out, "Be careful about being the one your assistant comes to to talk about personal issues. You can't afford to be in that role."

The fact is, if your secretary comes to you and leans on you for advice about his/her personal life, it's a minefield. Number one, it'll take up your valuable office time. Number two, your attitude about your secretary will change. But because you're human, you're flattered when someone wants your advice. Watch out! You need to be humane but wary. Give your assistant the time to get help, saying something like, "I'd love to help out but I'm not a professional," and refer them to a therapist. You can be understanding, but you can't be a psychologist.

This sounds cold, but remember that I'm only talking about the situation where you're a brand-new lawyer. After a while you'll have a track record with your secretary such that you're in a position to know that they'll be professional when they get their professional life together, and you can be much more flexible. But when you're starting out, you don't know that, so you can't take the chance. Think of trying to explain to your supervising attorney, "I'm sorry I'm going to miss your deadline, but my secretary has been crying on my shoulder about her divorce, so I didn't get a chance to write the memo and she didn't get a chance to type it."

8. Figuring out exactly what the heck it is that secretaries *do*, when you've never had a secretary before

As Carlton Fields' Eric Adams points out, "It's hard to learn delegation. When you get out of law school, you're used to being the delegatee."

What secretaries actually do varies from employer to employer, and their duties have evolved over time. As Akin Gump's J.D. Neary says, "They do different things now than typing!" For instance, they'll typically help you with your time sheets. They revise documents (although if you've only made small mistakes, it's probably faster to jump onto the computer and make the changes yourself. As St. Thomas' Michelle Fongyee points out, "Your secretary isn't sitting there waiting for you to come up with work. Sometimes it's easier to do it yourself."). You can expect them to help out with distributions, putting one of each document into each packet. They can help draft, or edit if you dictate your documents. Eric Adams points out that "They're great proofreaders because they aren't lawyers. They'll catch stuff that you'll miss because you're too familiar with your own work." They also act as liaison with opposing counsel and they'll help out with scheduling.

You should also remember that your secretary is your only line of defense when people are looking for you. ***Always*** tell your secretary where you are, whether it's the library, a training session, the bathroom, ***anywhere***.

Hofstra's Rebecca Katz-White suggests that you "be prepared to do your own word processing to avoid relying on a secretary. Ask your secretary to teach you shortcuts and function keys to limit the amount of time your secretary will have to spend on your work. Your secretary will appreciate it."

As a new lawyer you're likely to be sharing a secretary (if you get one at all). The person (or people) you're sharing with will be more senior than you. You have to be mindful of this for two reasons. Number one, as Rebecca Katz-White points out, "You need to be cautious not to step on the toes of the more senior person." Be conscious of when, and how, the other lawyers use the secretary. Also remember that the secretary will have influence with the lawyers with whom you share him or her. As one lawyer points out, "When I was a new associate, I shared a secretary with a powerful partner. I gave her a Christmas present and made absolutely sure that she liked me, because she had the partner's ear."

Finally, don't overlook perhaps the most valuable contribution your secretary can make: (S)he'll probably be plugged into the employer's grapevine, and can pass along to you valuable inside skinny. ***Especially*** if the news is bad—it concerns somebody's negative opinion of you, for instance—be sure to say thank you and not betray any emotion. You need to know what's being said, and if you punish your secretary for telling you, you'll discourage her from telling you anything else.

9. **Learn how long administrative functions take, and act accordingly.**

In order to make your deadlines, you need to know how long it takes to do everything that you don't do. Photocopying, faxing, word processing, envelope stuffing—they all take time. Ask people who regularly do these tasks for rules of thumb about how long they take. Once you know, you can build this information into your schedule so that you're not constantly racing to support staffers with a frantic last-minute rush project. Most people ***don't*** bother with this, and if you do, the support staff will notice and appreciate it.

If you're going to be giving support staffers work late at night, Denver's Jennifer Loud Ungar suggests that you "Let staff people know about it as soon as you can. Copy room people, word processors—they appreciate being warned. If you don't give them notice up front, you risk the possibility that nobody will be available to help you out." Furthermore, if you're going to need help after hours—typically after 5 p.m. or so—be ***very*** careful. Overtime work costs employers a lot of money, and it won't reflect well on your competence if you're routinely incurring overtime expenses.

10. Learn how to use office equipment, *especially* if you work for the government.

I know, I know—you're thinking, when am I going to get to the point where ***I'm*** the one who doesn't have to know how office machines work? The answer is: Not yet. When you're new, Michelle Fongyee suggests that you "Learn the fax and the copy machine, and expect to pick up the phone. Your secretary can't pick up every call, especially if (s)he works for other lawyers as well. Try to help out. Your secretary will appreciate it and your work will get done."

If you work for the government, your secretarial help is likely to be scant indeed. One government lawyer said that "I always do my own typing, copying, faxes, envelopes. Everybody here does. We have a secretary, but she works for us according to seniority, so when you're new you can't count on anything being done for you. But because everybody's in the same boat, you don't feel like a martyr."

11. How to handle mistakes your secretary makes

You're probably thinking that you're worried enough about your own competence; you don't want to contemplate whether or not your secretary can do a good job! But the fact is, your secretary is human, too. (S)he'll make mistakes. As Lewis and Clark's Lisa Lesage says, "Don't flame out over mistakes. Be constructive!" If you find that your secretary is routinely making mistakes, be careful how you handle it. Don't point fingers. Instead, ***calmly*** say something like, "The last two briefs I wrote went out without the right attachments. Partner X really chewed me out. How can we make sure that it doesn't happen again? Any suggestions for how we can change things?" Be careful about the changes you institute—if you're too anal you'll drive your secretary crazy. One attorney talked about a colleague at his firm who had been burned when his secretary put the wrong letters in envelopes and sent them out. After that, with every subsequent secretary he had, he made sure that before the secretary sealed any envelope, she'd have to bring it to him to see that she'd stuffed them correctly. His secretaries went ***nuts*** doing this. As the attorney pointed out, "You can be picky, but you have to be mindful of human nature."

If the mistakes keep happening—in other words, your secretary is an idiot—again, don't be blunt. As Chicago-Kent's Stephanie Rever Chu says, "Think hard before you complain—you don't want to get a reputation as being difficult to work with, otherwise you'll get bounced from secretary to secretary." Go to the office manager (if there is one) or a supervising attorney and say something along the lines of, "I'm having trouble getting my secretary to do X. Can you give me some advice about how I ought to handle it?" The facts themselves will tell anybody exactly where the problem lies; you don't need to editorialize. If you take this approach, you'll solve the problem without seeming like a jerk yourself.

Incidentally, remember that when it comes to work that goes through your secretary, ***you're*** responsible. It's effectively your mistake. As Venable, Baetjer's Stefan Tucker says, "If you send a letter to 'Dear David' and Richard Smith is the addressee, the rest of what you say is irrelevant. It's easy to blame your secretary. But the buck doesn't even stop with ***you***—it stops with ***your*** boss." One lawyer talked about an incident where her secretary accidentally sent a draft document to opposing counsel. "I looked stupid. I shouldn't have allowed it to be sent, even though it was technically my secretary who did it."

12. You're a woman, your secretary's a woman—you've got some special issues to confront.

When you're the same gender as your secretary, you've got a whole added dynamic going on. Especially if you're younger than your secretary, you're likely to be faced with a real authority problem. I talked with many young female attorneys who bemoaned the fact that their secretaries just wouldn't do their work. Unanswered phones. Messages not taken. Work put on the bottom of the pile.

How to handle it? You've got a fine line to walk. On the one hand, you can't be too buddy-buddy. You can't let them think that because you're friends, they can walk all over you. As one female lawyer pointed out, "After the secretary throws you a baby shower, it's hard to say, 'I need this by 10 a.m.'" If you've shared the details of your personal life, your dating fiascos, your family problems with your secretary, it's hard to assert authority. So you want to be friendly, but not friends.

On the other hand, you don't want to be the queen bee. Be sensitive to the possibility that your secretary doesn't view you as a "real boss." She might balk at being asked or told to do things by you. If you detect this, the best advice I heard was to be calm and straightforward about it. Humour helps. One young woman associate told of arriving for her first day of work, and having her secretary boldly say: "I don't like working with women attorneys." The associate laughingly replied, "Well, I don't really like working with women secretaries, but why don't we just take this one day at a time and see how it goes?" They got along great after that!

Georgetown's Abbie Willard recommends that you "Non-threateningly, and without anger, say, 'It won't serve either one of us if you don't do my work. It'll reflect on you. I know you're used to male bosses. But my work needs to get done. I understand it, I've had these issues myself.' Put it on the table!" Georgetown's Beth Sherman suggests, "Tell your secretary, 'I know you're really busy doing work for X, but I need my phone answered. How can we do that?'"

Hofstra's Caroline Levy tells you to "Recognize that what your secretary does is an area of expertise. You're working with them as a team. Show deference to what you can learn from her. Ask, 'Can you tell me how this is done?' or 'Do they send a courtesy copy of this to the judge?' Instead of saying 'Get this motion typed!' try, 'How does X like to start his motions?' If you inconvenience them, apologize! Say, 'I'm sorry, it took me too long to write this affidavit, can you handle it for me this afternoon? Are you working on anything else? I'll talk to the attorney you're doing work for right now . . . ' It's really a matter of being polite and tactful.'"

It may be that despite your best efforts, your secretary is dead set against working for a woman and there's nothing you can do to change that. One female associate talked about being assigned a secretary who wouldn't even acknowledge her existence. She tried being friendly, pleading, begging, cajoling—nothing. When the associate subtly brought up the matter to other associates, they breezily responded, "Oh, Diana hates working for women. She does that to every woman she's assigned to." The associate went straight to the secretarial supervisor and described the problem—it wasn't a surprise. The associate pointed out, "I wanted to work with her, but she just wasn't having it. Ultimately, the work's got to get done, and if she wouldn't do it—I needed somebody who ***would.***"

F. Birds Do It, Bees Do It . . . The Ins And Outs Of Office Romances

It's too easy to say "Holster your libido" when it comes to office romances, although it's true that abstinence is the only way to guarantee you'll never get into romantic trouble at the office. "Don't get your honey where you get your money" is certainly the standard to which you should aspire. As one lawyer put it, "Leave the office and take a cold shower!" I've heard story after story about romances gone bad, and sometimes they involve spectacular bad judgment. The partner married to a fellow partner who's pregnant, while he's having a romance with a female associate in another department at the same firm. People bragging about how many summer clerks they've "nailed." As author

Ronna Lichtenberg says, "Texas football coach Darrell Royal once said that when you throw a forward pass there are three things that can happen, and two of them are bad. It's even worse with office sex—there are many, many more bad endings than happy ones!"

Bad idea or not, office romances are rampant. Studies show that 80% of people have either had an office romance or know of one (and my hunch is that the other 20% aren't watching too carefully). And a third of ***all*** dating relationships start at work. So any large organization that tells you, "Oh, everybody here is just friends" is probably ignoring a bit of hooky-dooky at least once in a while. So it's kind of like saying, "Make sure you always get eight hours of sleep." It's a good idea but most of us have quite a time trying to live up to it. If you and/or the person you've got the hots for is married, there's absolutely no question that an office romance can be nothing but disastrous, not only on a personal level but also to your reputation. But if you're single . . . it's tough to overcome temptation at least sometime in your working life.

For one thing, who's your applicant pool? People climb Mount Everest "because it's there." People wind up dating people at work "because they're there." After all, you're at work for most of the day. You see the people you work with more than you see your family and anybody else outside the office. And you know some valuable things about them. Number one, you see them in their "natural habitat"; that is, not under the pressure of a dating situation. And number two, you know they're gainfully employed and you know "each other's schedules, and you know ***what*** they do and you understand it," as one recruiting coordinator pointed out.

Other than presence, pressure at work often makes for sexual tension. As Ronna Lichtenberg says, "Sexual energy in the office is inevitable." That doesn't mean you have to act on it—and the wiser course is ***not*** to do so—but there's no denying that it's ***there***. I've heard story after story about junior associates working around the clock on a deal or a case, and suddenly, that person they wouldn't have dated on a bet is the most enticing thing since . . . well, since Elmer Fudd sat in the life raft with Daffy Duck and hallucinated that Daffy was a roast turkey.

On top of that, it turns out that studies have shown that half of all workplace romances result in either marriage or a long-term relationship. Those aren't terrible odds.

The reason people tell you to avoid office romances is because they're fraught with peril. I once saw a cartoon in the *New Yorker*. It showed a bunch of guys at a board meeting. The chairman of the board is pointing to a chart, and saying, "Gentlemen, the upside potential is tremendous. The downside risk is jail." The downside risk of office romances is that if it turns sour you could lose your job and/or your reputation, and/or you could cost your employer millions in a sexual harassment suit. Let's face it, there are only two things that can happen when you date somebody: either you get married or you break up. Most of the time you break up. And workplace breakups are the ***worst.***

What I'm going to do in this section is talk about what to be aware of ***before*** you take the plunge into an office romance, and if your assessment after that is "Damn the torpedoes! Full speed ahead!" I'll talk about the way you should conduct an office romance. And then we'll wind up talking about a couple of other little romance-y things. Let's go!

1. **What to be aware of before you "take the plunge" into an office romance**

   a. **If your office has an anti-fraternization policy, it doesn't have teeth—but it does tell you how they feel about such things.**

   Many lawyers pointed out to me that different offices have different cultures when it comes to dating. I've heard about places where coworkers marry, divorce, and marry someone else in the firm, and the general attitude is "It's nobody's business." But if your office has an anti-fraternization policy—and your perception of the culture is that interoffice dating is frowned upon—it's not going to do your reputation and career prospects any good to be seen dating somebody at work.

   b. **Think about this: What happens if it blows up? Will you have a "boiled bunny" situation on your hands? Will you be out of a job?**

   The sad and sometimes vicious aftermath of a failed romance is difficult enough to deal with in your ***personal*** life. At work, it's ten times worse. The reality is this: If things go bad, you should expect that one of you will have to leave the office. (If you're at different levels in the hierarchy, things could be even worse, as I'll talk about in a minute.)

Apart from the threat to your career, consider the toll it can take on you personally. Close your eyes for a moment, and visualize any romance you've had in the past that resulted in a break-up. (Happy thought, eh?) Now think about how things would have been if, after the break-up—whether you were the breaker or the breakee—you had to see that person ***every day***. Yikes!

Now it might be that you are both sensible grown-ups and you both accept that when it's over, you let it go, and you don't mope around the office. That's the best-case scenario. The problem is, you can't guarantee it. *Fatal Attraction* is the worst-case scenario, where Michael Douglas tried to call things off with psycho Glenn Close and she boiled his kid's bunny. That was actually the ***nicest*** thing she did. So the fact is, even the best-laid plans—and people—can go wrong, and you've got to be prepared for that.

If a romance ends badly, and you're walking around openly heartbroken, your reputation will suffer because people will perceive that you're out of control. If you're right as rain but your former inamorata is walking around weeping, you'll be perceived as a heel. Either way, it doesn't do your image any good.

The watchword here is "look before you leap." Don't jump into an office romance without acknowledging what might happen down the road!

c. An affair with someone married *can't* end happily.

This was the only hard and fast rule that I heard from everybody I interviewed. "If you're married, keep your pecker (or feminine equivalent) in your pants," advised one lawyer. Enough said.

2. If you *do* conduct an office romance, here's how to do it.

Nothing destroys a career faster than a badly-handled romance. The key words in that sentence are "badly-handled." If you're single, your romantic target is single, and you decide to leap into the arms of Eros, here's how to conduct yourselves to minimize the fall-out:

a. To tell or not to tell? It's not as big a deal as you think.

When people get together at the office, one of the issues that comes up is: should we tell anybody? I heard opinions both ways. Some people say, "Don't tell. It's your own business." Other people say, "Tell. They'll find out anyway." Most people say, "It doesn't matter whether you tell or not. Everybody will know anyway." It's what people call "water-cooler osmosis." There's something in the air, and eventually people will put the pieces together and figure out what's going on.

If you work in an office with an anti-fraternization policy or a culture that is firmly anti-dating, you should absolutely not tell anybody at work. Not even one person (because once you've told one person, you've told everybody. You can't expect ***anybody*** to keep that secret). In any other kind of office, you want to be discreet. I'll discuss the elements of discretion in just a second. But the way to be discreet in terms of telling people is that on the one hand you don't want to send out engraved invitations, or a "send all" e-mail announcing your relationship. On the other hand, don't lie when people ask whether you're seeing each other. Admit it but then stay low-key about it.

b. Be *discreet.*

What gets a lot of people in trouble with office romances isn't the ***fact*** of the romance, but the way it's conducted. The watchword here is discretion. What does that mean?

1) Do *not* conduct a romance with somebody outside of your rung on the ladder at work.

Many people told me that some of the biggest problems with office romances come about when one of the romancers is more powerful than the other. I'm not saying such romances never work out; on rare occasions they do. But the downside risks are significant, as we're about to discuss. So the rule of thumb is this: if you're an associate, confine your romantic applicant pool to other associates. Stay away from partners, support staffers, and summer clerks. If you're a summer clerk, stick with other summer clerks. Why?

a) If you date "above" your station, you'll be the target of gossip and political controversy.

   You don't want to get the reputation of trading sex for advantages at the office, because it will stick with you forever.

b) Keep your mitts—and everything else!—off the clerkship meat. If you date "below" your station, you're risking a sexual harassment suit for your employer. And you're engaging in conduct that most people view with extreme disdain.

   When the "power thing" comes into play in a romantic relationship, there's plenty of opportunity for trouble, particularly in the supervisor/supervisee realm. Virtually every employer has rules forbidding that kind of relationship, and they take them very seriously, unlike rules against dating between coworkers of equal station. If you are a summer clerk, be aware that if you get into a fling with a secretary at work, your employer will back the secretary and ***not*** you if the romance ends badly. While romances out of your station can occasionally end well, the risk just isn't worth it!

CAREER LIMITING MOVE . . .

Recruiting coordinator, large firm: "The junior associates at our firm are all over the summer clerks. We tell them not to. We tell them they're endangering their careers, and that if the summer clerks they fool around with don't get hired back, the firm could be looking at a sexual harassment suit, a 'woman

> scorned' problem. But they ignore it. They view summer clerks as a notch on their belt. We ask our incoming summer clerks to send in a picture and a short bio. When the photos start coming in, the junior associates will come into my office to flip through the pictures, and they'll ask, 'Does she **really** look like this?' or 'Why didn't we hire anybody hot?' It's hard to take somebody seriously as a professional after you hear them talk like that. And picking up the pieces for broken hearts can be tricky. It's hard enough to move up the ranks here, without having a black mark against your name because you can't control your libido."

2) Don't have more contact with your honey at work than the work itself demands.

   If you are constantly stopping by your sweetheart's desk, e-mailing him or her, or you spend a lot of time on conversation behind closed doors, people will know something's up. If the two of you are in different departments at the same firm, people will notice if one of you pops up in the other department when you've got no business reason to be there. As Georgetown's Anna Davis recommends, "Don't rub your romance in people's faces. Don't spend more time together at work than you would if you weren't seeing each other."

3) No PDA's even if you think no one's looking. And watch for subtle cues!

   If you engage in a quick smooch at the copy machine when you think no one's looking, if you give them a quick little smile or a wink, ***somebody's*** going to smoke you out. It takes tremendous self-esteem to conduct an office romance well, because you shouldn't get—or offer—any little reassurances at work.

   Even if you were only friends—which you're not—you might engage in conduct that people will misinterpret as romantic involvement. Make a point of avoiding that, too. For instance, if you help your girlfriend on with her coat, you're just being chivalrous—but people will assume you're dating. If you go to a firm function and get into your boyfriend's car to leave, people will think you've got a thing going on.

4) Don't use your secretary or a colleague as a confidant.

   Maybe it's a chick thing, but I know that I spend a lot of time with my close girlfriends sifting through our romantic relationships. "Gee, should I say this to him?" "Here's what he did, what do you think?" that kind of stuff. If you do the same thing, make sure that your confidant is ***not*** somebody that you work with. You don't need the details of your romance traveling the jungle drums at the office. It will impact people's perception of you in ways that are unfair, so don't let it happen!

5) Don't disclose sensitive information to each other.

   It's kind of unfair. The thing that brings you together in the first place is everything that you have in common at work. Now I'm telling you that once you've hooked up, you should keep your work under your hat. Well, that's not entirely true, but you still have to be sensitive to confidential information. Don't let your romantic feelings cloud your professionalism.

CAREER LIMITING MOVE . . .

Female summer clerk at a large firm. She gets into a hot and heavy romance with a senior associate who happens to be on the hiring committee. She leans on him for information about what goes on in the hiring committee meetings. She turns around and blabs what he tells her to other summer clerks, and people quickly put together where she got her information—and why. The managing partner calls him into his office, and says, "What were you **thinking** about? What goes on in hiring committee meetings is confidential!" He sheepishly responds, "But I told her not to tell."

The summer clerk is not given an offer, and things get so uncomfortable for the associate that he leaves, as well.

6) Don't let your romance interfere with your work.

   If you've got love (or lust) on your mind, it can be hard to focus on your work. But you ***have*** to. You've got hours to put in and billables to produce. I know it's really, really, really hard to accomplish, but don't let your romance dominate your time at the office. And when you're at employer social events, I've stressed to you the importance of taking advantage of getting to know other people at work. You can't spend that time gazing into each other's eyes and sharing private jokes. Think of employer social events as work, and save the canoodling for later on!

7) Realize that no matter how carefully you try and disguise an office romance, sometimes it'll come out anyway.

   One lawyer told me about "Two associates who are dating but who go to extremes to keep it from everybody else at work. They never go out together at places where there are lots of people, they don't tell anyone at the firm, and they avoid each other at the office. One day they go for a hike in a mountain range near the city where they live and work. The trails are pretty extensive, and they go way out and find themselves in the middle of nowhere when it starts getting dark. They can't get back in time, and they are forced to call for help. The authorities wind up sending a helicopter to pick them up, and the press picks up on this. The press sends its own helicopters, films the rescue and then has a camera crew at the place where they drop the two law firm lovers. Their secret was out in a big way!"

3. If you find out that other colleagues have a thing going on, keep it to yourself.

Maybe it's not your romance that's the issue—it's something you stumble upon at work, sometimes literally! Whether you hear about an office romance or see evidence of it yourself, don't say anything. Don't answer questions from others about the romance. Just say, "I don't really know," and change the subject. Passing along personal information about people, even in response to questions, is really bad. It makes you look like a gossip, and that hurts your reputation. Even if you know about romances, even if the participants ***tell*** you about it, it's still none of your business. Keep the secret!

CAREER LIMITING MOVE . . .

New associate, large firm, office Christmas party. Somebody says, 'Hey, have you seen Partner Fred?' and the associate says, 'I thought he was here.' The associate goes to the partner's office looking for him. He knocks on the partner's door, opens it—and sees the partner and the partner's secretary getting after it on the desk. The new associate promptly closes the door and goes back to the party. When the fellow partygoer asks, 'Did you find him?' the new associate shakes his head. The look on his face suggests something's up, and a close buddy says, 'What's going on?' The new associate says, 'You can't tell anybody . . . ' and tells him what he saw. Within a day, the item is all over the office. It winds up being political suicide. The new associate leaves the firm.

4. Stopping an unwanted romance in its tracks—how to handle people hitting on you at work

If you're an attractive woman, remember that the men at work aren't monks. You'll be likely to get as much male attention as you do in every other part of your life. If you want to avoid office romances—bravo for you!—you use the same strategies you've used all of your life.

a. When you're new at work, introduce your spouse or boyfriend/girlfriend to people at the office and talk about him/her frequently. This is the social equivalent of tomcats marking the furniture. You're indicating "I'm not interested in romance," and in doing so, you're actually making men more comfortable around you because there won't be any potential dating tension.

b. Don't send conflicting signals by commenting on the pathetic state of your love life or by flirting. If you routinely find people coming on to you even though you're not interested, go to your law school career services director and sit down and talk about it—and see if there's something about your communicating style that you need to change, for your own good!

c. Turn down opportunities that smell of a come-on. Don't go out for drinks with just one man. If he suggests a casual after-work drink, say, "Let's see who else is available too!"

d. If somebody from work asks you out, come straight out and tell them, "I'd love to go out but I have a rule that I don't date anyone I work with." Then—make sure that you don't!

G. Paying Attention To Things You've Never Paid Attention To Before: E-Mail, The Phone, And The Internet

1. E-mail—It can save your bacon, and cook your goose.

I think e-mail is the greatest thing since sliced bread. (I wonder what the greatest thing was ***before*** sliced bread?) It can save you a ton of time, but it can also get you into a lot of trouble. Here, we'll talk about a bunch of good ways to use e-mail, and the traps to avoid.

a. How e-mail can save your bacon

There are two basic uses of e-mail at work: to gather information and to cover your butt.

When you have a quick question for somebody, e-mail is a great way to ask it. If you have a supervisor who is either very busy or just doesn't like face-to-face communication, e-mail can be a lifesaver. And if you're asking a general question: "Has anybody done any Statute of Limitations work?" "Does anybody have any advice about Judge so-and-so?" e-mail saves you the trouble of asking around individually.

The "cover your butt" function is an often-overlooked—and underutilized—use of e-mail. Whether it's protecting your ideas or clarifying issues with clients or distancing yourself from a colleague's questionably ethical conduct, you can use e-mails just as you would a memo. For instance, e-mail is a great way to mark ideas as your own. You can send an e-mail to a colleague saying, "I'm glad you like my idea for X and I appreciate your feedback on it. I've thought of other ways to improve it. Can we chat?" You could accomplish this face-to-face or on the phone, but in an e-mail you've got a record of it—and exactly whose idea is being discussed. Print it and keep it!

b. Minimize (or eliminate) personal e-mails at work.

If they want to, your employer can ban personal use of e-mail entirely. Even if they don't—be careful. In general, employers frown on personal e-mail. And if you're the one who receives an e-mail from a friend that has a virus attached—or the large attachment on a personal e-mail you receive at the office crashes the employer's computer (yes, it's happened)—it's a black mark against your record that you just don't need. As a rule of thumb, have your friends e-mail you at home!

c. Anybody can potentially read your office e-mail. Think about that before you e-mail (or receive) *anything*.

The thought probably creeps you out. I think it's a natural instinct to treat e-mail like a private chat. But you can't count on that, unfortunately. More and more employers are scouring their employees' e-mails. Furthermore, once you hit the send button, you have no idea where your e-mail might wind up. When you send anything, ***assume*** that it could appear on the front page (like Monica Lewinsky's) or in court (like Bill Gates'). And even if the e-mail itself isn't forwarded, if the recipient prints it out, the whole world can see it!

CAREER LIMITING MOVE . . .

A judge sent sexually harassing e-mails to other judges and their secretaries. The e-mails were published "as is" in the local paper.

CAREER LIMITING MOVE . . .

Large firm in New York, married associate having an affair with his secretary. They e-mail racy stuff back and forth to each other. He's so tickled by one of her e-mails that he hits the "print" button, walks out of his office to the printer—and sees a colleague waiting at the printer for another document to print. The colleague sees the e-mail from the secretary. The secret is out.

CAREER LIMITING MOVE . . .

Married associate, conducting an affair with another married associate. People are suspicious, but nobody knows for sure what's going on. The guy writes a very personal e-mail to the woman. He goes to send it to her, inadvertently highlighting the "Everyone" button instead of her name, which begins with an "E."

d. One man's meat is another man's poison pen: Be careful with jokes and joke lists.

You probably get as many jokes e-mailed to you as I do. Maybe more. Some of the stuff is a howl. Some of it's goofy. And some of it is actively offensive. The fact is, it doesn't matter for me—I don't get my e-mail at, or send e-mail from, an office with other people in it. If you receive jokes and want to pass them on to people at work, be ***very*** careful to edit for content before you do so. Don't send e-mails to colleagues, or from your office, that contain anything profane, political, or otherwise in very bad taste, no matter how hilarious you think they are. When you're relatively new at work, and you're talking about colleagues as opposed to friends, you don't know whom you might offend. It's not worth the risk. Save jokes for your friends outside of work if you have ***any*** doubt about their appropriateness.

Incidentally, if you ***do*** send out jokes on a routine basis, do it from your home computer. St. Thomas' Michelle Fongyee points out that "If you're constantly sending out joke lists during the day, people will start asking: 'When are you getting your work done?'"

e. If you've got nothing nice to say—don't e-mail it.

When someone really burns your biscuits, it's tempting to say to yourself, "I'll give them a piece of ***my*** mind!" and fire off a screaming e-mail. As is true with memos and letters, once you put something negative in an e-mail, it's memorialized ***forever***. You don't need that particular albatross hanging around your neck for life.

Take a leaf from Abe Lincoln's book when it comes to handling anger in writing. Whenever anyone did anything that made Lincoln angry, he would fire off a nasty letter to the offender, outlining exactly what he thought of him. Then he'd put the letter in a drawer. He never sent any of those letters.

That's a great idea. If you're angry with somebody, pour your feelings out on paper (or computer)—and leave it at that. Throw away the paper, delete the file. In the section "Dealing With Jerks, Screamers, And Other Dwellers Of The Nether Anatomy," I talk about dealing with people when you're mad. Firing off a negative e-mail to them is ***never*** a good idea.

f. Don't use office e-mail to discuss professional colleagues with your friends.

Don't make any negative comments in e-mails to friends about people at the office or in the profession. If you want to blow off steam, talk to friends in person or over the phone, from home. You never know where a negative e-mail might wind up.

CAREER LIMITING MOVE . . .

A lawyer sent an e-mail to a friend, saying, "Based on my experiences with black judges, this guy's not as dumb as most of them." The friend took the e-mail to a reporter, and it wound up on the front page of the paper.

CAREER LIMITING MOVE . . .

A lawyer whom we'll call Porky gets an e-mail from a colleague reading, "Have you ever argued a case in Judge X's court? Any tips?" Porky e-mails back, "He is a very nasty person. He will make your life hell. When he was a kid I bet they had to tie a pork chop around his neck to get a dog to play with him." The recipient liked the "pork chop" line so much he forwarded it to another friend. The e-mail wound up getting forwarded to the judge himself. As a colleague of Porky's noted,"How do you suppose our firm does in front of that judge **now**?"

CAREER LIMITING MOVE . . .

New lawyer, works for the general counsel's office at a state college in the Midwest. She uses her office e-mail for personal exchanges and gossip, with catty messages about coworkers and supervisors. She is horrified to find her e-mails in a newspaper exposé about state employee misuse of e-mail.

g. Don't discount the value of face-to-face communication.

E-mail is ***so*** easy to use that it's easy to let it take over, kind of like communicative kudzu. That's a mistake. As lawyers at Arnold & Porter point out, "It's easy to misinterpret the tone and intent of e-mail." Georgetown's Abbie Willard adds that "In e-mail, if you're trying to be funny, there's no inflection. What you say can seem stupid or offensive."

In addition, much of what you learn when you listen to people involves the ***way*** they say something, rather than ***what*** they say. Body language counts for a ***lot***, and it's lost in e-mail. So don't surrender your human contact to e-mail.

h. Remember that e-mails between you and your clients (and *anything* else confidential) deserve special attention.

As Carlton Fields' Kevin Napper advises, "E-mail you send is ***not*** confidential. If you want it to be confidential, make a point of marking it 'confidential.' And if it's really secret, don't use e-mail at all. Send it by regular mail."

Lisa Lesage points out that "When it comes to privileged communications, you're better off with a phone call. ***Nobody*** can get at those." If you ***do*** exchange any e-mails with clients, be sure to print out and file all such communications, and always include attorney-client and/or work product disclaimers on the e-mail. Your employer will have standard wording for these. Use it!

i. Proofread your e-mails for typos.

E-mail is casual, but it's not ***that*** casual. You don't want your e-mails to suggest that you're semi-literate, even if you're just in a hurry. Write e-mail as carefully as you'd write anything else your employer sees. As NYU's Gail Cutter says, "Proofread your e-mails—you're always being judged for your attention to detail."

2. The telephone—talking (and shutting up) and leaving messages

a. Personal phone calls at the office

Employers don't listen in on your phone calls. (At least, ***most*** of them don't. I talked with one lawyer who'd clerked at a firm that bugged the phones and monitored the conversations at the office, "just so they knew what was going on." Ugh. Thankfully ***that's*** rare.) But just the same, be careful with the personal calls you make from work. Why? It's got to do with the amount of ***time*** you spend on personal calls. Employers ***do*** track phone calls that are made from every phone at the office. You'll be charged for calls you make that aren't on employer business. And if you routinely receive personal calls at the office, your secretary or the receptionist will know. ***Everybody*** gets personal calls, but you should minimize them to the extent you can. Also, remember that people can overhear you. If you ***have*** to speak about something personal and sensitive at work, close your door—or go outside and use your cell phone or a public phone.

CAREER LIMITING MOVE . . .

New associate at a large D.C. firm. After his first month there, a partner was looking over the phone call list, and found that the associate was spending two hours on the phone every day—talking to his mother, who lived on the other side of the country.

CAREER LIMITING MOVE . . .

New associate at a Southern firm, heavily involved in the Junior League. The associate goes to the office manager and complains, 'My secretary spends too much time on the phone. Can you go talk to her?' When the office manager confronts the secretary, the secretary harrumphs, '**She** should talk. She spends **twice** as much time talking about personal stuff than **I** do!' As the office manager comments, "Lead by example. Do your personal business behind closed doors!"

CAREER LIMITING MOVE . . .

New associate, West Coast firm. Her family is in the Midwest. She tells herself, 'I work long hours. I'm entitled to make a few phone calls on the firm's dime.' She calls her family. At the end of the first two months, she gets a phone log. To her horror, it shows every single phone call she'd made—including the ones to her family. The firm makes her pay for her calls. As she comments, "All calls are accounted for at work. **Somebody's** paying for them. When you make calls from the office, they're not a secret. Everybody knows!"

b. Remember, you have no "reasonable expectation of privacy" on the phone. Ask Monica Lewinsky. Or Prince Charles.

Maybe you remember a few years back, the intercepted phone call, allegedly between Prince Charles and his lady friend Camilla Parker Bowles, which had him wishing to be reincarnated as—ahem—an item of personal hygiene associated with her. While I'm not worried about that happening to you, remember that phone calls do not come with guaranteed privacy. Watch out especially if the person you're talking to has you on speakerphone. You have no idea who else might be in the room with them. You can just say something like, "I'm getting an echo here—can you pick up the receiver'" Problem solved.

Also, be aware that anybody could be walking by your office door and pick up a snippet of your conversation at work. So when you talk on the phone at the office, be discreet!

c. When you talk . . .

1) If you're angry, don't yell.

Fighting on the phone with ***anyone*** doesn't make you sound professional. Keep your temper. Squeeze one of those frustration toys if you have to. Take a deep breath. Just keep your voice in check!

2) Speak clearly, politely—and smile.

It may sound silly to smile while you're on the phone. Who can see it? But you should try it anyway. People can hear it in your voice, and if you're looking for information from a supervisor, client, government agency or anyone else, you'll get what you want a lot more easily if you sound friendly. As Bart Schorsch writes in *The Student Lawyer*, "The person you are talking to can't see your new suit, smell your delightful cologne, or know your GPA or class rank. All they have is a voice and the word 'lawyer.' A few polite words and a professional demeanor will take you a long way."

d. The art of leaving messages

1) Don't eat or—belch!—drink while you talk.

Munch munch—oh, sorry, I was just trying to squeeze in a bite. Don't combine your fueling and message-leaving functions. It sounds ***really*** bad.

2) Leave fuller information than you think you have to.

As Greenberg Traurig's Sharon Abrahams says, "The biggest complaint people have with voice mail is that callers make assumptions and don't leave enough information. They may know several people with your first name. Also, they might not have your number memorized, or be near their phone book when they retrieve your message. So identify yourself completely, give your phone number, why you called, and when's a good time to call back. 'It's Dorothy Dale, extension 666, I'm looking for the Toto file. Call me back as soon as you can.' Good. Done."

3) Don't leave a message containing anything you don't want anybody else to hear.

You leave a message for your colleague Julius Caesar, saying, "Caesar, I just can't deal with that backstabber Brutus any more. Call me." Caesar walks into his office to check his message accompanied by Brutus. Oops! The moral: don't leave a message containing "for your ears only" information.

e. Handling your own voice-mail

1) Change your voice-mail message when you're away from the office. And always be *reachable* (at least, during the week).

At Sharon Abrahams advises, "Change your message when you're not in, to reflect where you are, when you'll be back, and how to reach you. If you're not reachable, say so, and say who the caller might contact instead, like your assistant."

2) Check your messages on weekends if there's *any chance whatsoever* that somebody at work (or a client) might try to reach you.

   That chomps, huh? As though tethering yourself to the office all week wasn't enough! But the fact is, it's a good idea to check your office messages at least once over the weekend, in case there's an emergency. If you ***know*** there are partners who ***expect*** you to check your messages, you ***absolutely*** should do it. One junior associate said that "At my firm, there's a partner who calls you at work on Saturday or Sunday, leaving a project to be completed by Monday morning. If you don't check and he happens to leave you a message, you miss the Monday deadline." Nice guy, huh? But you get the point. Check your messages.

3) Return calls promptly.

   Whether the caller is your supervisor or a colleague or a client, you've got to get back on the horn with them ASAP. Try and do it within an hour; or at least, that same day. And if ***that's*** not possible—geez, do it as soon as you can. Believe it or not, one of the prime motivators of malpractice suits against lawyers is unreturned phone calls! You need to call at least to acknowledge that you got the call, whether or not you have the information the caller requested. And if your supervisor calls and asks you to do something, don't just do it—also let them know you're on it.

3. The Internet.

I don't have to tell you that the Internet is a phenomenal research tool. In Appendix A, you'll find a whole flock of useful web sites. But that's not our focus here. When you use the Internet at work, remember that your employer can easily track your web usage. If you have to visit dirtypanties.com (I heard that there actually ***was*** such a web site), do it from home. And get professional help while you're at it. At work, "'Extracurricular' web surfing constitutes a misuse of employer time and property," says Gail Cutter. Nobody cares if you scan the web for headlines or sports scores or stock quotes a few times a day, but other than that, save it for home.

It may be that you visit chat rooms for lawyers; some local bar associations have them, and I gather they can be pretty lively places to visit (not as lively as dirtypanties.com, but everything's relative). As Lewis & Clark's Lisa Lesage points out, "If you comment about facts of a case in lawyer chat rooms on-line, be careful that you don't reveal privileged information. There's no expectation of privacy in an Internet chat room."

H. Social Graces, Or—How *Not* To Be Seen As A Pig, And How To Make Conversation With *Anybody* In Any Social Situation

1. Social Functions. As Woody Allen Says Of Life: "80% of it is showing up." Here's how to handle the other 20%!

If you don't feel entirely comfortable in employer-related social situations, you're far from alone. Dr. Joy Browne, my favourite radio psychologist, reports that 83% of people think of themselves as shy. Boston University's Betsy Armour says that "Lawyers as a group are not comfortable with cocktail parties. It's a necessary evil." Georgia State's Vickie Brown adds, "If you're new, you're intimidated. Everybody is." Sharon Abrahams, who runs business etiquette seminars around the country, says that the most common question she gets from summer clerks and new lawyers is: What do I talk about?

I'll tell you how to feel more comfortable, and what to say when you ***do*** talk to people. Here are a few ideas for you:

a. It's not the Bataan Death March. It's a *party.*

Socializing is really a lot of fun if you approach it as a learning experience. Will Rogers used to say that a stranger is just a friend he hadn't met yet. For all you know, somebody you meet at an employer event could turn into a lifelong friend. And no matter how much you dread it, remember that "You've got to achieve a level of comfort with professional social situations at some point," says Betsy Armour. "You've got to start sooner or later. So you might as well start now."

b. Don't walk in alone.

Betsy Armour suggests that you buddy up with someone, and walk in together with another summer clerk or associate so that you don't feel so intimidated. (However, once you're at the event, don't cling to your buddy. The reason you're there is to meet, and talk with, other people. So split up as soon as you arrive!)

c. Talk about what's in the news.

Sharon Abrahams recommends that you talk about what's in the news. "I give people a list," she says. "Listen to the news, read the newspaper, scan *Time* and *Newsweek* and *Business Week*. If you don't have time to watch the news, listen to National Public Radio's *All Things Considered* and *Morning Edition*, at least at the top of the hour and at the half hour for the headlines." What she's saying is, make yourself an interesting conversational partner! The easiest way to talk with people is to mention something that you heard in the news, or an interesting story you heard or read. "Can you believe they found water on Mars? I heard that they think . . . " One thing you should avoid discussing is what you're working on. As Kentucky's Drusilla Bakert advises, "Try to find something to talk about other than the fascinating memo you're working on." While an interest in your work is something that every employer looks for, sometimes you've got to turn it off. Lawyers work hard. They ***like*** to get away just as much as you do!

Prepare to have clients present at some social functions by "keeping up with what's going on in your clients' industries," says

Sharon Abrahams. If they're in biotech, read up on the human genome. If they're car dealers, keep up with gas-electric cars, ethanol—whatever issues face them. This way, when you talk with them, they'll see that you're taking an interest in their business, and that makes you an ***excellent*** potential rainmaker (and a charming conversationalist, to boot!).

d. **Don't say anything that will embarrass people.**

When you're new, it's not the time to test your skills as a provocateur. There are ***tons*** of interesting things to talk about without stretching the bounds of good taste. ***Tons.*** Virtually anything in the newspaper is fair game. Don't say anything that will make people question your judgment—and wonder whether you can act decorously around clients.

Out at a bar with partners and summer clerks, one summer clerk is sitting next to a partner. She points to a bowl of peanuts on the bar and casually says, "Did you know they did a study that showed that ninety percent of peanuts on bars have urine on them?" She goes on to explain it's because men go to the john, don't wash their hands, and come back to the bar where they grab at the peanuts. "I thought I was going to choke," comments the partner.

e. **Only discuss politics if you and the colleagues with whom you are speaking have the same views.**

Save political debates for your friends ***outside*** of work. As Sharon Abrahams advises, "When it comes to talking politics, know the politics of the firm you're going to. If you disagree, don't discuss politics at all." The fact is, they're not going to convince you, and you're not going to convince them. And ***you*** may like a good political throw-down, but they might not—and you can't risk it. So if you see a photo on your boss's office wall of him shaking hands with President Reagan, don't spout off about how you think George Bush is an empty suit.

Staunch Republican new associate, very liberal firm. He takes every opportunity to make what he believes are provocative, joking comments about Democratic politicians. Within six months, he's asked to leave the firm.

f. If you're shy, talk one-on-one.

Denver's Pat Powell suggests that you socialize in your "comfort zone." "You don't have to be the life of the party, dancing in the middle of the floor. You can sit and talk to people one-on-one, if you prefer it."

g. Take advantage of social events to cultivate powerful people and especially people you want to work for.

In the chapter on being your own career counselor, I talk about the fact that the best way to get the work you want is to go to people you want to work for, and ***ask*** for it. At a social event, you won't ask for work—but you ***can*** get to know the people you want to work for so that they know you and feel comfortable with you. As Georgia State's Vickie Brown suggests, "Just extend a hand and say, 'I haven't met you, and I wanted to say hello.' Say what you've liked so far about your summer clerkship (or new job) to muckety-mucks, and be honest about it. Nobody likes a phony suck-up, but everybody loves hearing honest compliments. And don't feel funny about it. They never get sick of hearing positive comments; nobody does!"

h. Ask questions!

As communications guru Dale Carnegie always said, if you get people to talk about themselves, they'll love you. Ask clients, "'How did you get into this business?' 'What do you like about it?' 'Where will it be in five years?' Then shut up and listen!" says

Sharon Abrahams. Ask lawyers, "What's your most interesting case?" "What are you working on?" "Where did you grow up?" If you know something interesting they've done, bring it up! Often when you meet a group of people, you'll learn interesting things about other people in the group. You might be talking to one associate who says, "Hey, did you know that Sean climbed Mount Rainier?" or "Did you know that Eleanor once met President Kennedy?" When you meet Sean or Eleanor, ***ask*** them about the incident you already know about. Don't worry about asking them about an incident they've probably discussed a lot of times with other people. Don Larsen, the New York Yankee pitcher who pitched a perfect game in the 1956 World Series, was once asked, "Don't you ever get tired of people asking you about your perfect game?" He answered: "Why ***would*** I?"

i. Use "personal disclosure" to break the ice.

Sharon Abrahams recommends that you break the ice with personal disclosure, "something inoffensive about yourself." "I've never been to this event before—have you?" "I never know how to make a choice at a salad bar like this." She suggests that you ***practice*** talking to people in all kinds of settings—at the cleaners, the drugstore, all over the place. "Nobody cares if you look foolish there—and you'll polish your conversational skills," she says.

j. Don't expect everyone you meet to be a sparkling conversationalist in return!

Virtually everybody is interesting if you get them talking about something that fires them up. But some people . . . well, not everybody's going to be your cup of tea. Sometimes people are preoccupied, or wanting to be somewhere else, or obnoxious. I was at a party a little while ago, and the person I was talking to asked, "So what do you do?" I answered, "I'm a writer," and he went on, "No—I mean, what do you do for a ***living***?" Oh, well then—I'm a prostitute. Duh. See ya. If for whatever reason the conversation isn't catching fire, stay for a minute or two so you don't seem rude, and then excuse yourself with a smile—and don't come back.

2. Now that you're a "real lawyer," you *still* can't get tanked at employer social events . . . even though they can't withdraw your offer!

When we talked about summer clerkships, in the "1,640-Hour Interview" chapter, I talked about how you can't drink heavily at summer social events because your employer is judging you even at parties. When you start to work after you graduate, it's tempting to think, "Hey! I'm in! Party down!" It's true that you're no longer being sniffed over as offer material, but these are ***still*** your professional colleagues, and you have to show ***some*** decorum. Getting drunk obliterates your good judgment. Before you know it, you're hitting on a colleague (bad news) or exposing client secrets in a crowded bar (***really*** bad news).

So you should reread "Employer Social Events Aren't The Place To prove Your Beer-Drinking Capacity And Your Ability To Belch The Alphabet . . . And Other Alcohol-Related Advice." It's in the "1,640-Hour Interview" chapter. There you'll find everything you need to know about nursing drinks without seeming like a dweeb.

CAREER LIMITING MOVE . . .

Two junior associates go to interview students at a law school in New York. The two go to lunch and get hammered. They stumble back to school for the afternoon interviews. The next interviewee they talk to says, "I'm sorry, I didn't get your names." They write their names on Post-It Notes and stick them to their foreheads, shrieking with laughter.

CAREER LIMITING MOVE . . .

A number of lawyers from a small firm attend a testimonial dinner for a local judge. One of the senior partners sits on the dais with a number of other luminaries. His colleagues sit at a table in the audience. As the evening progresses and the speeches drone on and on, the partner's colleagues notice he is getting increasingly drunk. After an hour or two, the partner looks around, as though uncomfortable, during a particularly long speech. He picks up a smoked glass water pitcher in front of him. It disappears under the table. A minute later, he puts the water pitcher back on the table. It's full. And he's smiling a relieved smile.

3. **Don't drink the contents of the finger bowl, and other hazards of dining with your colleagues**

   If you eat as though you learned your manners at a hot dog eating contest, nobody's going to want to socialize with you—and they won't turn you loose in front of clients. Nobody expects you to be able to negotiate a 24-piece place setting of Queen Anne cutlery, or to wield an escargot utensil like a pro (remember Julia Roberts in "Pretty Woman"?). But you ***do*** have to have some modicum of good manners!

   What I'll do here is to give you a very brief primer on common dining faux pas. My source for much of this advice is the wonderful Sharon Abrahams of Greenberg Traurig. She is an etiquette guru and runs seminars about business etiquette (her contact information is in Appendix C, at the back of the book).

   Let's see what you need to know!

   a. **The cardinal rule: If you can't identify it, don't eat it or touch it until you've see somebody *else* try it first.**

      Once you've been working for a little while, you can be an adventurous diner (as long as there aren't any clients present). But as a summer clerk or brand-new associate, people's opinions of you are still being formed. Stick with what you know! If you see a bowl with lemon floating in it sitting near your salad, it's not salad dressing. Don't drink it. It's a "finger bowl," designed to rinse your fingers before the next course. If you sit down and see a little plate with what looks like a quarter-sized embossed dinner mint on it, don't pick it up and pop it in your mouth. It's formed butter, and it's meant for your bread roll. Look around and see what other people do with something unfamiliar before you try it yourself!

EMBARRASSING (BUT KIND OF ENDEARING) MOMENT . . .

Interview lunch. New York law firm, student from a small town in the Midwest. One partner and two associates take the student to an exquisite Chinese restaurant. The partner orders for the table. One of the dishes he orders is Mu Shu Chicken, a dish which is served with thin pancakes that look something like flour tortillas. When the dishes arrive, the waiter puts the Mu Shu pancakes next to the student. Mistaking them for face towels, she picks one up and dabs her face with it. The lawyers, not wanting to embarrass her, do the same.

b. Throughout the meal: How to show people you were raised in a house with a table, not a trough.

1) For every course, wait until everyone is served before you dig in.

If the dishes come out at different times, that's not your signal to strap on the feed bag. Sit tight. It's up to the person (or people) who is still waiting to fire the starter's pistol and give you permission to start. Don't dig in until you get the green light from them.

2) No "boarding house reaches"—if you want something that's not in front of you, ask that it be passed to you.

A lawyer at one firm talked about being at lunch with a colleague who "reached across my place for the butter. I could have bitten him, his arm was so close to my face. Even worse, he dropped his sleeve in my dish!"

3) It's not a bib, it's a napkin. It goes on your lap.

4) Silverware—You work your way from the outside in.

No matter how many forks, knives, and spoons are placed in front of you, the rule is always the same: The cutlery at the outside goes first, and you work your way inward, toward the plate, with every course. If you have any questions about which fork goes with what, discreetly ask the waiter.

SMART HUMAN TRICK . . .

Associate at a large firm in Washington, D.C. She is at dinner at a very fancy restaurant with partners and clients. She has eighteen pieces of cutlery in her place setting. She surreptitiously calls over the waiter, and says, "What the heck do I do with this?" as she gestures toward the cutlery. The waiter smiles, and says, "Barbara Bush asks the same thing."

5) No "wandering forks."

   One lawyer told me about a lunch she'd had with the managing partner of the firm and a few other associates. "We all get our meals, and the next thing you know, the managing partner says, 'Hey, yours looks good!' And stabs a piece of chicken on my plate. I had ***no*** idea how to react."

6) No "train wreck in a tunnel." If there's food in your mouth, your lips should be closed.

   As Sharon Abrahams says, "Chewing with your mouth open is OK if you're three years old and you have a stuffed nose. Otherwise, it's not OK." She adds that like much of good manners, "It's just common sense. If you talk with your mouth full, you can choke."

CAREER LIMITING MOVE AND A SMART HUMAN TRICK . . .

Summer clerk at a large firm. He's brilliant, #1 in his law school class. At firm cocktail parties, he chews with his mouth open and spits partially-masticated bits of food at people. The managing partner calls in the recruiting coordinator and says, "We can't hire this guy. He's socially unacceptable." The recruiting coordinator gently breaks the issue to the clerk, who takes it well. He goes out to "practice" dinners with friends, asking them to critique his manners. He cleans up his act, and winds up with an offer.

7) If you've used a fork or knife, it never goes back on the table—only onto the plate.

   Sometimes you'll only be given one knife, and you use it for your salad. You'll need a knife for your main dish. What do you do? Don't put it back on the table, and for gosh sakes don't wipe it off with your napkin. Instead, just ask the waiter for another one.

8) When you're done, put your silverware side by side on your plate to indicate you're finished. Don't crisscross it on the plate.

EMBARRASSING MOMENT . . .

Junior associate, on a business trip to London. She dines alone at a fine restaurant. Shortly after she begins to eat her entrée, she gets up to go to the restroom, leaving her knife and fork side by side on her nearly-full plate. She comes back to find her dinner cleared away. The waiter thought she was finished. [This is Kimm talking. I grew up in England. They take this cutlery stuff ***very*** seriously!]

9) No elbows on the table.

10) Cell phones and beepers off! (Or set them on vibrate, which is more fun anyway.)

    Do you remember the TV ad where the guy's cell phone rings during a grand pause in an opera, and he answers it, and the diva on stage throws a flaming spear through the phone to the wild applause of everyone in the audience? ***Everybody*** feels that way about cell phones. Unless you're anticipating an urgent client call, your wife's about to give birth, or the President is going to consult you any minute about pushing the button, turn ***off*** your cell phone when you sit down to eat.

If you set your beeper or cell phone on vibrate, "Get up and excuse yourself," advises Sharon Abrahams. "Don't look at the beeper at the table, or—God forbid!—talk on the cell phone."

11) Don't throw your weight around with the help. It'll make you look bad.

 CAREER LIMITING MOVE . . .

Summer associate sits in a restaurant with other summer clerks, attorneys and members of the Recruiting Department. He is extremely rude and demanding to the waiter. The incident is discussed extensively at the Employment Committee meeting when offer decisions are being made.

 CAREER LIMITING MOVE . . .

Summer clerk, dining with other summer clerks and two partners at a fancy restaurant. One of the partners, the managing partner of the firm, is getting flustered trying to attract the waiter's attention. The waiter is standing at a wait station some distance away. The summer clerk stands up, and throws his fork at the waiter to attract his attention.

12) Discussion taboos.

You've heard the old saw about avoiding sex, politics, and religion. Current affairs is a safe conversation topic, although as Sharon Abrahams points out, "During the Monica Lewinsky scandal, current affairs were all about sex and politics. So sometimes you can't avoid it!"

One other topic is off-limits, and it's anything gross. This isn't the time to discuss that surgery special you saw on the *Discovery Channel*, or the *Road Kill Cookbook* you just heard about—or anything disgusting you've ever eaten. When you're eating with your friends, heck, anything's fair game. But these are ***business*** meals we're talking about, and you have to be a bit more careful.

CAREER LIMITING MOVE . . .

Summer clerk at a large New York firm, eating dinner with two other clerks and two associates. "One of the other clerks starts talking about something called 'Wiggle fish' while we're looking at the menus. Someone asks him what it is, and he says, 'It's these little fish, and they're alive when you put them in your mouth. That's why they call them 'wiggle fish.' They don't die until you bite down on them.' I could see from the looks on the faces of the associates that they were grossed out. But the other clerk didn't notice. He goes on, 'That's **nothing**. I saw this movie 'Faces of Death,' where people are eating live monkey brains. They clamp this monkey's head through a hole in the middle of the table . . . ' I looked over at the two associates. They're looking at this guy as though they're thinking, 'Have you lost your **mind**?'"

13) If you have to use the rest room, just excuse yourself—you don't need to add, "I've got to drain the lizard."

Trust me. If you get up from the table in the middle of a meal and say, "Excuse me," nobody's going to think you suddenly got called to appear on "Who Wants To Be A Millionaire?" You don't have to announce where you're going any more than you have to be specific about what you're going to do in there. And especially if you don't know your fellow diners really well, avoid cute euphemisms. Remember Robert Wagner in *Austin Powers*, where he plays Dr. Evil's underling, and he's sitting in a casino at a blackjack table. He gets up and says, "Excuse me, I've got to go to the little boys' room." That was ***supposed*** to be funny. You don't want that image with your professional colleagues!

Sharon Abrahams points out that it's much more polite if you hit the john before you sit down. If you do have to excuse yourself during the meal, "Leave your napkin on your chair if you're coming back, and on the table if it's at the end of the meal and you won't be returning to the table."

14) Relax your formal manners in a casual setting, like a firm picnic.

Plastic cutlery doesn't come with four kinds of forks. If you're at a casual do, don't cut the meat off the ribs with a knife and fork while you're balancing a plate on your lap. If everybody's eating ribs and corn on the cob, then use your fingers—but be as tidy as possible! A picnic is not a license to let your face look like a Jackson Pollack painted in barbecue sauce.

c. Ordering the food. It's a minefield!

1) Don't order anything you've never eaten before just because it sounds exotic.

A lunch or dinner with new colleagues is not the time to explore brave new culinary worlds. It might turn out to be something you hate—or can't figure out.

EMBARRASSING MOMENT . . .

Summer clerk at a large Los Angeles firm. The clerk had never tried artichokes before, and ordered one. "It came out on a plate and it was arranged like a beautiful flower. I didn't know how to eat it. I didn't know you're supposed to eat the edible part off the leaf. Instead, I put a leaf in my mouth and chewed and chewed and chewed. I was dying. It was like a huge tumbleweed in my mouth. Finally, in desperation, I spit it into my napkin, dropped the napkin on the floor, and kicked it away from the table!"

2) While you're still a summer clerk, don't order the most expensive thing on the menu.

As Sharon Abrahams points out, "For an interview or summer clerkship dinner, you use the same rule you'd use on a date when it comes to the price of your entrée: don't read from right to left and order something because it's the most expensive thing on the menu!"

There's only one exception to this. If your host says, "Oh, you really should try the chateaubriand stuffed with foie gras in truffled 24-karat-gold sauce. It's delightful"—then you've got a free pass. Go ahead and order it!

3) Don't order *any* food that can sabotage you.

There are only a few foods that are on the banned list when you're dining with colleagues, and they're pretty obvious. Sharon Abrahams calls these the foods that can "sabotage" you, like "French onion soup (the cheese strings are simply uncuttable), and anything you eat with your hands—corn on the cob, ribs, fried chicken, lobster, crab legs. And don't order a burger. As soon as you put a burger together and take a bite, whoosh! The burger flies out the other side. It's messy and greasy. Order your burger without a bun and tell them you're on the Zone diet. Then eat it with a knife and fork."

You ***can*** order chicken on the bone, but when you get it you have to cut the chicken off the bone and eat it with a fork. "You can't pick up the chicken bones and eat the last gobbet of meat from them," says Sharon Abrahams.

CAREER LIMITING MOVE . . .

Medium-sized firm, buys a table's worth of tickets for a dinner honoring a retiring judge. Several of the lawyers take along the three summer clerks. The food is Chinese, and it's served from a buffet. One of the summer clerks picks up a plate of Chinese ribs from the buffet and brings it back to the table. She eats the meat off the bone, and then—to the slack-jawed astonishment of her colleagues—she proceeds to eat the bones themselves, with a loud Crrunch! Crrrunch! as she snaps off every bite.

4) If you follow a special diet, handle it *discreetly*.

As Sharon Abrahams recommends, "If you follow a diet that is kosher or vegetarian or you only eat plants that don't kill the plant they come from or you have allergies, call over the waiter and tell them ***quietly*** what your diet restrictions are. I'm allergic to wheat, so I can't have soy sauce, and I often have to mention that to the waiter. You ***have*** to take responsibility for your own food."

If you're ordering from a menu, it's simple enough to have your meal prepared specially. If the meal is catered, Sharon Abrahams suggests that you "Call ahead and ask for the menu. If you can't eat it, ask for 'just a salad' or whatever you ***can*** eat. They'll accommodate you."

5) Ordering drinks and wine.

When it comes to drinks with meals, "The days of the three-martini lunches are over," says Sharon Abrahams. "Getting drunk doesn't impress people. At lunch, don't drink at all. At dinner, if someone else wants to order wine, fine. You can have one glass, no more."

What if a superior asks if you want a drink at dinner, and they haven't ordered yet? As Georgetown's Beth Sherman advises, "Be careful. You can say, 'I haven't decided yet. Why don't you start?' If they order a drink, then you can, too—but remember to stop at one drink."

If they ask you to order the wine and you've never done that before, it can be embarrassing. Beth Sherman suggests that you say, "Thanks, I appreciate the compliment," and then ask the waiter for a wine recommendation, and then you can get a consensus from the table about the wine everybody would like to drink.

d. Time to chow!

1) Which is my bread plate? Which is my water glass?

This used to trip me up all the time. I'd sit down with people, we'd all grab the bread plate we thought was ours—and someone would wind up without a plate while somebody on the other side of the table had two.

Here's the rule, per Sharon Abrahams: "Your bread plate is on your left, and your water glass is on your right."

2) Much ado about bread . . .

OK. I said you couldn't eat with your hands. But you'd look like a major dork if you used a knife and fork to eat a dinner roll!

Instead, Sharon Abrahams says that "You ***can*** eat the bread with your hands. They did it in the Bible, so it's OK for you, too. You take one roll, put it on your plate, take one pat of butter and put it on your plate. Break the roll up into two pieces, then each half into two. Butter the piece you're going to eat. You can bite it and put it back down; you don't have to break the roll into bite-sized pieces."

What if the bread arrives in a loaf, instead of individual rolls? You can't tear the loaf apart with your hands. You're not Piltdown Man. You're ***civilized***. Instead, "Use the napkin that comes with the loaf to hold the loaf down with one hand," says Sharon Abrahams, "and cut off your slice."

3) Cutting up your meat. Don't mince the whole meal before you take a bite.

Sharon Abrahams tells you that "If you eat the American way, with your fork in your right and the knife in your left (as opposed to the European way, which is the reverse), you don't cut up a whole steak with your fork in your left hand before you transfer the fork to your right hand to eat. Cut off three or four bites, eat those bites, and then cut up some more."

4) If my dessert comes in a chocolate cup, can I eat the cup?

   Of course! That's the best part. Otherwise they might as well serve your chocolate mousse in a baggie. Sharon Abrahams says that you should "Hold down the cup with one utensil and break it with another. If you don't hold it down, it'll fly! Then you stick the bits of cup to your spoon with a bit of the mousse."

5) At a catered sit-down event, signal that you don't want coffee by turning your cup over.

e. "Can I have a doggy bag?" What To Do When You're Done Eating.

1) No doggy bags. Darn!

   Especially if you're a summer clerk and you're spending your summer at a large firm, you'll probably go out to lunch several times a week. No matter how often you dine out with colleagues (unless it's a group of friends), you can't take a doggy bag. If you're a new associate and you're taking summer clerks or interviewees to lunch, a doggy bag is also verboten. I'm not suggesting that you clean your plate. At a lot of restaurants, the portions look more like something Fred Flintstone would eat. But like the saying goes, you can't take it with you. It doesn't look professional.

CAREER LIMITING MOVE . . .

Summer associate, large Midwest law firm. At lunch, she would finish the food off everyone else's plates at the table, and if she was too full, she'd ask for a doggy bag—not just for her own plate, but everyone else's as well.

2) "How much do I tip?"

Sharon Abrahams advises that "At upscale restaurants, 18 to 20% is de rigeur. At a regular restaurant, 15% is OK."

f. Disaster strikes! What to do when something goes wrong at a meal.

1) "Ewww! I took a bite, and it's *disgusting.*"

You take a bite and it's gross. What do you do? Sharon Abrahams says that "There are two rules. If it's something inedible, like bone, gristle, or a hunk of fat—you discreetly spit it into your napkin, and ask the waiter for a new napkin. If you don't like it, tough noogies." Swallow it quickly and chase it down with some water or a bite of bread to get rid of the taste. You can't pull a Tom Hanks in the movie "Big," where he tries caviar for the first time, hates it, and tries to hoover it off his tongue with a napkin.

2) "I dropped my fork!"

Easy. If you drop a piece of cutlery, just ask for another one. You never pick it up. And you never ever ***ever*** pick it up, wipe it off, and continue using it. It's a lot quicker, but it's simply not done!

Not as though any of us have ever eaten anything off the floor. Heaven forbid. You're at home, the apple slips out of your hand, you pick it up, wipe it on your shirt, and eat it. Right? I remember once when my little niece Emily was three years old. My brother Keir, sister-in-law Ellie, and Emmy and I went to the zoo. We were there all day and towards the end of the afternoon, Emmy was at the end of her little string. She was whining for ice cream. Keir bought her a cone, just as the vendor was closing up shop. As he's wheeling her away from the ice cream stand, she takes one lick of the cone, and the scoop of ice cream goes splat on the ground next to her stroller. She starts to scream. Keir looks around to make sure no one's looking, and makes a snap judgment: he quickly reaches down and scoops up the ice cream in his hand and plops it back on the cone in Emmy's hand. She's happy.

Hey. Come on. If you've got kids, you've done stuff like that, too. But when you're at a business meal, if it hits the turf—don't touch it!

3) "Oops! I spilled it!"

Sharon Abrahams advises that if you spill something on yourself, you hail the water, ask for club soda, and excuse yourself to go to the restroom and wipe off your clothes.

If you spill something on someone else, apologize profusely, hail the waiter for the club soda, and offer to pay the dry cleaning bill—in fact, insist on it. ***Don't***, however, try to dab the spill off their clothes yourself. The stories are legion about embarrassed summer clerks trying to dab the spilled Coke from a female associate's chest or a male associate's lap. In those cases, the cure is worse than the disease!

4. Cocktail parties, or—How do I shake hands when I'm holding chicken wings and a beer?

a. When to show up.

What do you do if there's a cocktail party at 7, followed by dinner at 8? Sharon Abrahams suggests that "If you're a summer clerk or you're new at work, there are definitely people there you want to or should see. You should arrive at the cocktail party on time and look around for the person you most want to sit with at dinner. Make a beeline for that person, introduce yourself, ask where they're sitting, and ask 'Mind if I sit with you?' Go away for the rest of the cocktail hour and then come back to them at dinner. Arrange your dinner partners at the start of the cocktail party, because once you're sitting down at dinner, you're stuck with the people you're sitting with."

b. Recognize that the point of the function is the people—not the food.

If you're going to a work-oriented cocktail party, you're there for the people. As Sharon Abrahams says, "Don't go hungry to a cocktail party! You don't want to stand at the buffet table stuffing yourself or spend the evening following around the trays of hors d'oeuvres. Apart from anything else, it's always fattening food that's bad for you. Instead, go to the cocktail party full. Eat your burger in the car if you have to. If you don't have time to eat first, go and eat in a corner, do a tooth check to make sure there's no spinach stuck between your front teeth, and then socialize. You can't eat and talk. Especially with those little skewers of food. If you're holding one, and a plate, and a drink, you can't shake hands."

c. *Never* pick up buffet food with your hands.

Summer associate at a large firm. The firm has arranged a Friday morning training session, complete with a breakfast buffet. The summer associate goes to the buffet table, picks up some french toast sticks with her fingers—and stands at the buffet table eating them, one after the other, from the serving tray.

5. When a superior invites you to dinner at their home . . .

a. What if you have dietary restrictions?

Maybe you're a vegetarian or you're allergic to nuts. The socially correct thing to do is to go to the dinner party and eat whatever you can. At a large dinner party that's exactly right. Having said that, when I throw dinner parties I always ask my guests if they have any allergies or dislikes that I should know about. I ***want*** them to be happy, and if that means preparing an extra dish, I don't mind that!

If it's an intimate dinner—perhaps just you, your date or spouse, and your hosts—your skipping a course or a dish would be more obvious. What you could do in that situation is to be ***very*** gentle about it, and say something like, "Thanks for the invitation. I'm delighted to come. I'm a vegetarian but I'll be happy eating any salad or bread or vegetables that you serve; please don't make special arrangements for me." Of course they ***will*** do something special for you but you haven't been rude! Otherwise you could say something like, "I love to cook, myself—but I drive my guests nuts because I'm a vegetarian and I don't cook meat." That way you're letting them know without being demanding.

The thing to avoid in any social setting is shrieking, "Do you realize you're eating dead animals?" Don't skewer people for ***their*** choices any more than you'd want to be vilified for yours!

b. Don't show up empty-handed.

As Sharon Abrahams advises, "If you are invited to your supervisor's house for dinner, bring a gift. A box of Godivas, a bottle of wine, flowers with no strong scent. If you bring wine, remember that the hostess is ***not*** obligated to serve what you bring—don't get your nose out of joint!" If they cellar your bottle of white burgundy and pull out the cranberry wine with the screw top, that's the way it goes.

c. Be on time.

Duh. For a dinner party, don't show up late. Your hosts won't appreciate it, and neither will the soufflé.

d. Before you leave, seek out the hosts and thank them.

If the dinner party is a little larger so that your hosts could be absorbed with other people when you leave, don't slink away into the night. Always say your thank-you's first.

e. Follow up with a thank-you note.

Thank-you notes make an ***incredible*** impression. As Sharon Abrahams says, "They differentiate you." She adds, "Don't e-mail your thank-you's or fax them. Send a personal note." I keep a stack of note cards for just such purposes. You can get any kind—with your initials or some neutral picture. (Mine have Tiffany windows on them. They're beautiful, and always suitable. I get them from Papyrus in New York City.) Keep them handy and use them frequently. People will notice!

SMART HUMAN TRICK . . .

Large Florida law firm throws a cocktail party at a law school where it's interviewing. It invites the hundred or so law students it will be interviewing the following day. Of the hundred students who attend the cocktail party, only one of them writes a note afterwards to the managing partner, thanking him for inviting him to the cocktail party. Even though his grades are mediocre, he winds up with a job offer over better students "because he had the decency to write," says the partner. "If you want to stand out from the crowd, do the ten-minute thing that makes you shine!"

SMART HUMAN TRICK . . .

Recruiting Coordinator, large New York firm, tells the following story: "We routinely take our summer clerks out to the movies. One summer clerk had guests in from out of town the day of one of our movie 'field trips.' I told him, 'Bring them along.' The summer clerk sent me a thank you, and his guests did the same. It's a little thing that makes a big impression. It creates a happy feeling."

I. Work Is Work, Your Personal Life Is Your Personal Life . . . And People At Work Are Colleagues First And Friends Second.

That sounds awfully cold, doesn't it? But it's the truth. It's important to like your work and the people you work with. You spend more of your waking hours working than playing. But it's dangerously seductive to get your work and private lives muddled. At work, you've got to have your emotions under control and your private life out of sight.

There are going to be times when you want to tear your hair out or scream or cry. Fine. Get out of the office or do it behind closed doors. Screaming at a coworker will make people think you can't control yourself, and they'll be reluctant to give you responsibility where you'll have contact with clients. Tears of frustration will make people think you can't handle the pressure of being a lawyer, and you don't want that.

If you go through a personal tragedy—God forbid—nobody expects you to be a tower of strength. Cry, but do it discreetly. Who you tell and what you do about it depends on the nature of the tragedy. If it's a break-up with a boyfriend or girlfriend or the loss of a pet, you're better off not telling anybody at work at all. While these kinds of events can be devastating—gosh, I've seen people cry more over the death of their dog than when they lost their grandparents—on the tragedy scale they don't rank very high. One lawyer suggests that with troubles like these, "Leave at 5 p.m. if you must for a few nights and cry for the evening, then go to bed and get up and go to the office and put it out of your mind for the next eight or nine hours. That's what a professional does. An amateur cries at her desk and tells all her coworkers her troubles. The problem will still be there at 5 p.m. Cry about it then if you must. If it's too much and too serious, it's a good time to take some vacation time."

If the personal trouble is one that anyone would recognize as more serious—a death or serious illness of a spouse or family member, for instance—gather your wits about you and explain briefly what's going on to your supervisor and perhaps a very close colleague. You'll probably find them tremendously supportive. But don't make your private business general news. Save your tears for when you're with your family and outside friends, and get with them as soon as possible. Do whatever you need to do to make yourself feel better, but do it away from the view of your colleagues in general. You're no help to anyone, including yourself, if you're so torn up inside that you can't pay attention to the work you're supposed to be doing. Take time off, talk to a therapist—your emotional health is ultimately more important than anything else—but when you're at the office, people need to see you focusing on your work. It ***is*** cold, but it's the truth.

One hiring partner told me about a young associate at his firm who was going through a double whammy—a divorce ***and*** a bankruptcy. He said, "We all felt terrible for her, but it was ***way*** too common knowledge. She stayed at work, but couldn't do anything. Her supervisor gave her work that just sat there. She really needed to take a leave of absence, but she just wouldn't do it."

Incidentally, I'm not trying to suggest that your coworkers won't be sympathetic. They may be incredibly sympathetic. They might startle you with the depth of their caring; I've heard many, many wonderful stories about coworkers coming through in a crisis. What I ***am*** saying is that you can't ***count*** on that, and you've got to soldier on as best you can in the circumstances.

Don't ever, ever share with colleagues any information about your private life that reflects adversely on your professionalism. The partner at one firm in New England told me about a summer clerk she'd hired. "He was giving me a ride to a client meeting, and the whole time he's whining about how he's so bad with his finances, he's overdrawn, he's going to be lucky if he's not evicted. The whole time I was thinking to myself, 'And I'd trust *you* with client matters?'"

When it comes to friendships at work, as Ronna Lichtenberg says in her book *Work Would Be Great If It Weren't For The People*, "Friends are what you have outside the office. Inside you can have cordial relations, nice lunches, long conversations, and good buddies, but that's it . . . It's not until you leave your office that you discover who your friends are." Amen to that. Many, many people echoed that advice. NYU's Gail Cutter points out that "People at work are your professional colleagues more than they are your friends, and their primary concern is the work of the firm." A public interest lawyer said that "I socialize with supervisors, but I know that if I screw up they're my boss first and my friend second." Remember that your first loyalty, and that of everyone you work with, is to the employer, not each other. That leaves a lot of wiggle room for wonderful friendships—but they're not without their limits. Most of the things you'd share—plays or movies you've seen, books or magazine articles you've read, TV shows you've watched, sports activities, cute things your kid said—those are safe. But keep in mind that every time you share anything about yourself, you should act judiciously. That's why it's important to maintain a life, and friends, ***outside*** of work. As

Quinnipiac's Diane Ballou recommends, "The less people know about you, the better. Don't talk about your dates. Listen more than you talk. Then less can be said about you!"

CAREER LIMITING MOVE . . .

In-house patent lawyer. He's friends with many people at the company, including an older man in manufacturing. The company has a big layoff, and the older friend is one of the people laid off. He's furious, and becomes part of a lawsuit against the company alleging age discrimination. The case is handled by outside counsel. The guy who gets laid off calls the in-house patent lawyer, saying, "Let's have lunch." The in-house lawyer is uncomfortable, but likes the guy, and so he accepts the invitation. He says, "At lunch, all this guy wanted to do was pump me for information about what was going on at work. It was extremely uncomfortable. I dodged his questions. I couldn't believe he'd actually think I'd say something negative about the company—especially with him suing us! And I really didn't like hearing all kinds of bile about the company, because after all, I still had to work there. When I got back to my office, my secretary had mentioned to my boss that I was having lunch with this guy. My boss chewed my head off, questioned my loyalty—and my intelligence. I realized that until this whole thing blew over, I really couldn't be friends with this guy."

CHAPTER FIVE

How To Crush Research And Writing Assignments

In this section, I'm going to make sure that you start your career convincing your employer that you've got excellent research and writing skills. At most legal employers, your research and writing will set the table for everything else you do. You'll develop a great reputation, you'll get increasing levels of responsibility, and you'll be on your way to the top. Having talked with many, many people about handling research and writing assignments, I am absolutely convinced that virtually every mistake that summer clerks and new associates make is easily avoidable. Once you've read this section, ***you*** won't make ***any*** of those mistakes!

At many different kinds of legal employers, you'll start out doing a lot of legal research and writing. It's ***crucial*** that you get it right from the start. As the associate at one California firm commented, "As a new associate, you have nothing but your smarts and your reputation. It's critical that your first assignments are outstanding, since those assignments will establish your reputation." Syracuse's Alex Epsilanty adds, "If you have a couple of bad projects from vocal partners, it's hard to rehabilitate your reputation." Hamline's Vince Thomas points out that "You can't say, 'Well, I wrote the best memo I could, but you didn't give me all the facts' or 'I didn't go to school in this state so I didn't know about X treatise on state law' or 'You wouldn't let me see the case file.'"

In a nutshell, let's see what you have to do to excel on research and writing assignments. You need to:

1. Get the assignment perfectly clear;
2. Accept the assignment with enthusiasm;
3. Do thorough, accurate, and efficient research;
4. Hand in the work on time, and keep the lines of communication open with your assigning attorney for any deadline problems;
5. Solve the client's problem, offering alternative solutions where appropriate;
6. Give the answer in the format the assigning attorney asked for;
7. Hand in work that is neat, grammatically flawless, well-organized, and typographically perfect.

In this section, we'll go over all of these things, in detail. If you follow the advice here, there's no significant way in which you could possibly drop the ball on an assignment.

A. Recognize The Importance Of What You're Doing. You're Not Really Performing Research Assignments. You're Solving Client Problems.

There's a big difference between practicing law and being a law student. As a lawyer, people—your employer's clients—are basing their actions on ***your*** advice. If you are at a small firm, with lots of immediate client contact, you'll recognize immediately what an awesome responsibility that is. If you're at a larger employer, where there are more senior attorneys as a "buffer" between you and the client, it's easier to forget.

No matter ***where*** you work, you are client-driven, whether you work for a private firm, for a company, or for the government. You are there to solve problems. That means you can't take your work casually! It's got to be accurate, because people are depending on it. It's got to be performed efficiently, because somebody's paying for it. And most importantly, it has to provide an ***answer***. As Georgetown's Beth Sherman points out, "The difference between school and work is that you need to have an ***answer***. In law school, you only need to identify the issues. In the real world, lawyers and clients need to know, 'What do I do?'"

B. Receiving The Assignment: Getting It All, And Getting It *Right*

Here's what you want to do.

1. **When an attorney calls you to his/her office, they're probably not checking to see if you saw the game last night. Come prepared.**

   Always carry a pad and pen with you when you're summoned to an attorney's office. If they nab you in the hallway, "Grab a pad and a pen from the nearest secretary," advises Dickinson's Elaine Bourne.

2. **Exhibit enthusiasm for the project—take notes, look attentive, ask questions, and say "Thank you."**

   I've mentioned to you elsewhere that nobody owns your thoughts but you. It's OK if you think the assignment you're getting is a barking dog with fleas. But you won't do yourself a favour if you let the assigning attorney ***see*** that. As lawyers at Waller Lansden recommend, "Associates who stand out are ones who, when they're asked if they'd like to work on a particular project, show enthusiasm and not just a deadpan 'I can do it.'"

   If you disdain a project from the start, you're not likely to perform well on it. And if you ***don't*** do the tedious things well, you can't expect to be rewarded with more exciting projects. As Georgetown's Marilyn Tucker says, "They expect the same performance on ***all*** assignments, whether cutting edge or routine."

   Incidentally, more than one lawyer told me about the popular habit some associates have of cherry-picking pro bono projects and hanging on to them so that any time someone tries to assign them a project they don't want to do, they can pull out the pro bono project and say, "I'm sorry, I can't do it." The firms know it goes on—nobody's getting away with it! It's easier just to bite the bullet and get the distasteful project over with! (If you keep getting a bunch of chimp work, I've addressed that in another section, called "How to Handle Chimp Work Without Going Bananas.")

So the spirit you want to exhibit is that you're grateful for the project and eager to get started on it. A partner at Davis Wright Tremaine described giving an assignment to an associate and then having to "step aside because she'd charge through and take the initiative to see it through." Assigning attorneys just eat that stuff up with a spoon. Let them see it from ***you.***

3. *Always* write down assignments. *Always.*

I remember reading a really interesting book, a biography called *The Mind of Somebody or Other*—I forget. Which is ironic because it was about a man with a perfect, endless memory. He could literally remember ***anything***. He was working at a newspaper in Leipzig, or someplace like that. He was a reporter. And every morning when the editor would get all of the reporters together to give them their assignments, everybody would scribble furiously to get down the details of who they were supposed to see and the stories they were to research. All except for this guy. At first the editor thought he was being disrespectful and blowing off his work, but it turns out he was memorizing every word, not just of his own assignments but those of all of the other reporters as well. He starts getting famous for his memory, and winds up having a big stage show where he could recount anything people asked him—like a list of 500 numbers. (I didn't say it was an ***interesting*** show.) All kinds of psychologists check him out, and find out that the reason he can remember an endless number of things is that words aren't just words to him; they've got colour and texture and flavour, so they're unforgettable. But as he gets older his mind gets so crowded with colours and textures and flavours, even for stupid things like phone numbers, that he cracks up and dies. It was really kind of a sad story.

Hey! But I ***do*** have a point in telling you about him. Namely: You're not him. You can't remember everything. So when you get an assignment, write it down! Why? It's mostly a CYA thing. If you go off in the wrong direction, you want to be able to point to what the attorney told you—not your own misinterpretation or foggy memory. Also, if you get pulled away by another project and have to come ***back*** to this one, you'll ***never*** remember it without having notes to refer to.

4. Don't assume that your assigning attorney is a good delegator. *Expect* to have questions to ask.

According to Kentucky's Drusilla Bakert, "Lawyers aren't trained to delegate work, and often do a poor job of it. The lawyer may assume that you know more than you do, or forget that he or she has left out something important. Don't hesitate to ask for fear of looking stupid for all the information you need. The usual response will be, 'I forgot you don't learn that in law school.'"

5. Make sure you learn the *nature* of the final product the assigning attorney wants.

It's ***vital*** to give your assigning attorney what (s)he wants. You can't do that if you don't get it straight, up front. As Brooklyn's Joan King says, "Stories are legion about associates who get pilloried for not clarifying assignments: 'I didn't want a ten-page memo. I wanted you to ***tell*** me the answer!'" Dennis Kennedy adds, "Nothing gets lawyers into more trouble than writing for the wrong audience. An attorney who wants a three-page memo ***never*** wants a Law Review article, no matter how good it may be."

So, what do you need to know? Listen for the following elements in your assignment, and if the assigning attorney doesn't mention them, ***ask*** for clarification.

a. Who's the audience?

Is it an internal memo for the assigning attorney or other lawyer(s) at the office? Or is it a complaint, a motion, a brief, or another court document? Or is it an opinion letter? Different types of documents have to be approached very differently. As Cardozo's Judy Mender says, "You can't just state the pros and cons of each side's arguments in an opinion letter. It's not like a law school writing assignment. As the name suggests, it ***has*** to include an opinion."

If the nature of the audience you're writing for doesn't give it away, ask whether your work should be persuasive or explanatory. For instance, the slant you take in your finished product is going to be different if the assigning attorney asks you, "Tell me where things stand on this issue" as opposed to "Find out if we can file suit."

b. How long should the finished product be?

View the page guideline you receive as a guillotine. Your assigning attorney no doubt believes that you could thoroughly explore ***any*** issue in a Law Review article. Pay attention to the page length the assigning attorney suggests to you as a way of gauging the depth of your research. For one thing, ***somebody's*** paying for the time you spend researching, and the project might not merit a monumental effort. And second, your assigning attorney's time is valuable, and (s)he won't want to spend more time digesting your work product than is absolutely necessary.

c. How do they want the material presented—in writing, in person, or by phone or e-mail?

Listen carefully to ***how*** your assigning attorney wants to get your results. Golden Gate's Susanne Aronowitz points out that if your assigning attorney says, "Just tell me what you find," all they expect is a quick oral report. Don't do any more than that! As William & Mary's Fred Thrasher says, "If they want a two-minute oral report at the end of the day, don't wait three days and give them a brief!"

6. Get all of the "administrative details."

You need to ascertain the client or matter name and number, and any other tracking information that's relevant. Without it, you'll make it more difficult to bill your work to the appropriate client and/or account. Impress your assigning attorney by showing your appreciation of the business aspect of your work.

7. **Get all of the facts (we'll talk later about what to do when you find you don't have them all!)**

One of the things that will strike you first about being a "real lawyer" instead of a student is that the facts are never as clear as they were on law school exams. Getting the facts is a real bane to any new associate.

What you want to do is to ask all the questions you need to ask, ***when you get the assignment***, to make sure you understand who the players are, exactly what happened, and what you're being asked. Marilyn Tucker advises that it's a mistake to go on the assumption that the assigning attorney is giving you all the facts and everything you need to know to proceed. "The reality is, you probably only have partial information." As Texas Tech's Kay Fletcher says, "Your first question has to be, 'What's the issue here?' You need to know! A partner might ask you, 'I've got a statement made at the accident by the other victim in the accident. Is it admissible?' You do your research and come back, and the partner mentions, 'Oh, she was being handcuffed and led away at the time.' It totally throws you off if you don't have the facts straight!"

Harvard's Mark Weber points out that "It's easy to just scribble down the facts without understanding the situation. Nobody wants to look stupid by asking questions. But you can't give people what they want without being crystal clear on the facts." Elaine Bourne adds that "All you have to say is, 'Am I understanding this correctly? Do I have the facts right?' Even if the assigning attorney seems impatient, that two minutes saves a ton of time down the road!"

Florida's Ann Skalaski recommends that you treat your assigning attorney like you'd treat a client. "If a client stated a problem, you'd have no problem asking for more facts," she says. "You have to treat the person giving you an assignment just the same way."

8. **Clarify the issue.**

If it's not clear to you what the issue you're being asked to research is, ***ask questions*** to get it straight in your mind before you leave the assigning attorney's office. If you're intimidated or you know that the assigning attorney by reputation won't answer any questions, then ask more junior associates who may have worked on the same matter, or the attorney's secretary (who often will know a great deal about the attorney's work).

As lawyers at Gardner Carton point out, "Not asking enough questions and charging off in the wrong direction is a big mistake that junior associates often make. They can miss the connection that their time is money, and the client doesn't appreciate paying—or the partner doesn't appreciate writing off—hours of unnecessary research when a few well-timed questions could have clarified an issue."

Suffolk's Mary Karen Rogers makes the point even more emphatically: "If you don't have a clear understanding of the issue, it's like a disease—it gets worse and worse if you don't correct it. Your research gets further and further off-base."

CAREER LIMITING MOVE . . .

New associate at a large West Coast firm. Partner called him to his office and said, "Just give me a general outline memo on the law of anti-dumping." The associate was concerned that it would show his ignorance if he asked any questions. He spent the weekend reading up on toxic waste and the rules on illegally dumping garbage in the state. He was very proud of his work . . . until he turned it in. It turned out that "anti-dumping" in the way the partner meant it had to do with illegal dumping of foreign goods in the U.S. market.

9. Understand the client and the client's goal.

As lawyers at Winston & Strawn point out, "Law is not practiced in a vacuum." In order to be able to give clients what they want, you have to understand them and what they're after. The reason this is so crucial is that it gives you the framework for your assignment, and just as importantly, it gives you an avenue for coming up with alternative solutions—a ***great*** way to make yourself shine, as we'll talk about in more detail a little later on.

If the assigning attorney doesn't give you the client background, ask if you can see the case file. If you don't feel comfortable asking for anything at all, ask your mentor (if you have one) or find other, more junior attorneys who can fill you in on the client and the nature of the problem without taking up a senior attorney's valuable time.

10. Ask for time estimates, and with those, you've got maybe a starting point for figuring out how long the project will *really* take you.

Ask the assigning attorney how long the project ought to take you. But don't be too alarmed by what you hear. As Marilyn Tucker points out, experienced associates often say that it actually takes three to five times longer for a new associate to do a project than senior attorneys realize. There are several reasons for this. One is that people who've been practicing a while have a lot of relevant material stuffed into their heads. You don't have that cranial treasure trove yet. You've got to ***look*** for stuff, and that takes a lot longer. Also, it might have been years since your assigning attorney had to do research, and they'll underestimate because of that.

There's one thing a time estimate ***does*** tell you, and it's the "billability" of the matter—that is, how much the assigning attorney thinks your research is worth to the client. It may be that the client won't or can't pay for extensive research. You've of course still got to do competent work, but you can't be as creative with a choke-hold on your time budget. That's probably only likely to happen at a small firm or ***any*** situation where you have cash-strapped clients.

As we'll discuss in just a minute, regardless of the time estimate you get, check back with the assigning attorney once you've done a bit of research to ensure that you're on the right track. That way the assigning attorney can monitor your progress and make sure you're meeting his/her expectations, regardless of any preliminary time estimates (s)he gave you.

11. Ask for a deadline, if the assigning attorney doesn't give you one.

Getting work done ***on time*** is one of the most valuable skills you can exhibit. Don't leave the assigning attorney's office without knowing when the project is due. (We'll talk a ***lot*** about handling deadlines in a few minutes.)

12. Unless the assigning attorney is very senior or otherwise busy or seems unwilling, ask for leads on starting the assignment.

This can be a little tricky. If the assigning attorney is very brusque and matter of fact, it may not be a good idea to say, "Gee, can you give me some pointers on where I oughtta start?" Ditto if (s)he is a very senior muckety-muck. You'll have to judge the situation and interpret the attorney's attitude. NYU's Gail Cutter suggests that if the assigning attorney is a partner or senior associate, you should ask for a junior attorney to whom you might refer your questions. "It's often not cost-effective or even possible for a busy partner or senior associate to guide you through the assignment," she says.

If the attorney seems more relaxed, friendly, or less hurried, go ahead and ask for ideas about where to start your research, "like another case file or a book or a person," says Dickinson's Elaine Bourne. "Don't ask in a way that suggests you expect them to do the work—explain that you're only looking for a starting point." If there's any possibility that the assigning attorney will be forthcoming, it doesn't hurt to ask. You'll show your eagerness to do a good job—and you'll save yourself time and frustration, too!

13. Repeat the assignment—in its bare essentials—back to the assigning attorney before you leave his/her office.

Everybody agrees that you should echo the assignment back to the assigning attorney before you leave. That way if there's any confusion, you can clear it up before you waste even one moment of research time. Referring to your notes, Denver's Jennifer Loud Ungar advises that "You should say the assignment back to the attorney before you walk out the door. Make it brief. Say, 'I hear that you want a memo/letter/whatever on X issue by Z date.'"

To be extra sure, show the attorney your notes so they can see for themselves the basis on which you'll proceed. Keep your notes in a readily-retrievable file and date them. This is the ultimate CYA move. An attorney who looks at your notes can't fail to see whether you've got all the facts that (s)he transmitted to you. If the attorneys you work for know that you make a practice of showing them your notes before you start to work, they'll never be able to argue that a missed issue was your fault. Furthermore, seeing your notes may jog their memory for facts they might have missed.

You can also send the attorney a confirming e-mail or memo. As Golden Gate's Susanne Aronowitz says, "Make it simple, something like, 'Just confirming that by Friday you want a memo relating to these facts and covering these issues.'" That way, if the attorney doesn't respond, you can assume that you've got everything straight.

SMART HUMAN TRICK . . .

New associate, doing a research assignment for a senior partner. She works on it for twenty-five hours and then turns it in. Within an hour, he tears into her office. "You missed the most important point!" He tells her a fact. She responds calmly, "You didn't tell me that fact." "Yes, I did!" he fumes. She always makes a point of showing assigning attorneys her notes before she leaves their office. She reaches over and pulls out her notes on the assignment he gave her. She holds it out to him. "I asked you if this was right and you said it was." He storms out of her office. The next day, he comes back in, looking sheepish, and apologizes. "That fact I told you about yesterday? I remembered that it came to me when I was playing golf after I talked to you, and I forgot to tell you about it." As the new associate comments later on, "Showing him my notes saved me. Otherwise it would have been all over the firm that I'm incompetent."

CAREER LIMITING MOVE . . .

Summer clerk. Senior associate gives him an assignment to do for a partner, with whom the summer clerk has been working closely. The summer clerk doesn't jot down any notes, figuring that the assignment is pretty simple. When the summer clerk turns in his work, the partner tells him that he's missed an issue. The clerk points to the senior associate—who is sitting in the room—and says, "**You** made me miss that issue. You didn't tell me about it!" The senior associate denies it, and both the partner and senior associate are embarrassed. The summer clerk has no way to back up his claim, since he didn't write anything down.

C. FINDING WHAT YOU'RE SUPPOSED TO FIND: HOW TO DO THE RESEARCH

1. Do all of your research with your goal in mind: finding an answer for the client.

It's easy to become distracted when you're researching. If you're going from Boston to New York, don't dawdle in Montreal. Duke's Jill Miller says, "Partners don't want you to present all sides of an argument ***without*** drawing your own conclusion." Akin Gump's J.D. Neary agrees. "Remember, the attorney who assigned you the project wants you to tell them: What should I tell the client? And what will I have to know that the ***other*** side will have?"

I've written screenplays for years. (If you've seen me give my *Guerrilla Tactics* seminar, you know that my dream is to win an Oscar for Best Original Screenplay.) My teacher and mentor, Stewart Bronfeld, handed me a little piece of paper with a rectangle drawn on it the very first day we met. "Tape this to the wall in front of your desk," he said. "It represents the screen. It will remind you that for everything you write, think about how it will come across to the audience." When ***you*** work on a research project, ***always*** keep your goal in mind: providing an answer. If you do that, you'll keep your research focused and efficient.

CAREER LIMITING MOVE . . .

New associate is assigned a project for a client that organizes summer concerts for municipalities. The concerts often involve platforms and stages. The client wants to know whether or not it has to make its temporary structures compatible with the Americans With Disabilities Act. The new associate goes away and does some research. She comes back to the assigning attorney and says, "I researched it as much as I could, but all of the cases are contradictory. I guess my answer would have to be, 'I don't know.'" The assigning attorney looks at her evenly, and says: "But—do they build the ramps, or not?"

2. **Think about the problem before you plunge into your research.**

Time you spend planning your research is ***not*** wasted time. You can save a lot of time on research—which translates into a lot of money for your client—if you do a little advance planning. As Harvard's Mark Weber says, "It's very easy to slip into the mode of 'get an assignment and get it done.' When I was a new associate, one of my supervising lawyers said, 'You can look out the window and ***think*** about something. ***Understand*** the problem. Get an idea of the big picture before you run to the library or jump on-line.'"

3. **How to start your research. Don't reinvent the wheel—or otherwise have a Homer Simpson moment!**

   a. If the format you've been asked to work in is new to you at this employer—a letter to a client, a memo, a court document, whatever—ask for samples either from the attorney, the attorney's secretary, or any other lawyer in the firm. Firms have different preferred styles for everything they do, and what flies as an internal memo style at one firm won't necessarily suit the lawyer at another firm. Ask for forms and templates, look at the firm's brief bank (a collection of all of the briefs the attorneys have written), and see if the firm has a "form book." As Dickinson's Elaine Bourne explains, "The form book is a kind of reference book particular to the firm. It will show things like cases that the firm handles on a regular basis, perhaps standard complaints for different kinds of cases, standard contracts, things that come up all the time." Other firms call these kinds of samples "Go-bys." If you can save time for your client by relying on work your firm has done before, you'll be a hero to that client. For instance, last year, before I got married, my husband suggested that we get a prenuptial agreement (not very romantic, I know). I called our lawyer, and he said, "No problem. I had to do one for another client just a couple of months ago. I'll use that and tailor it to you. It should be pretty cheap." You can imagine how I loved hearing that!

CAREER LIMITING MOVE . . .

New associate at a small firm. He is asked to draft a complaint, and gathers samples from some of the attorneys to get an idea of the style the firm likes. He then turns around and gives the attorney who assigned him the project something that doesn't even resemble a simple complaint. When the assigning attorney asks him, "Didn't you read all of those complaints you gathered up?" the new associate responds, "I did, but I thought that complaint format was boring. I wanted to be creative." (When firms talk about creativity, they're talking about thinking outside the box in solving problems—not drafting complaints!)

b. If your assignment deals with a statute—read the statute ***first***! (It seems obvious, but some new associates skip this most vital step!)

c. If you're doing transactional work, and you're not familiar with the overall structure of a deal you've been assigned to help with, NYU's Gail Cutter advises you to ask a junior associate in the department for general materials used in the firm's in-house training courses. "If you rely on these materials, ask whether the time you spend reading should be chargeable to a training account or billable to the client," she adds.

d. Ask the attorney if you can see the case file to give yourself context for the issue you're researching.

e. If the topic you've been assigned is totally unfamiliar to you, "start your research with hornbooks and treatises to get a general grasp of the area," says NYU's Gail Cutter.

f. If your firm has a law librarian (or more than one), go to that person for advice on how to start. Law librarians are a frequently-overlooked source of tremendous information.

g. Don't set yourself up for a Homer Simpson moment—"doh!"—doing a whole bunch of work before realizing that somebody else in the office has done the whole thing before, and would have shared his/her knowledge with you if only you'd asked. As I mentioned earlier, find out if your firm has a brief bank, and if so check it to see if anyone has written about this topic before. (If it doesn't have a brief bank, start one. You'll be a hero.) Ask around to see if anyone in the firm has worked on this kind of project before, either on this topic or in this format (*e.g.*, a motion). If your firm's e-mail system is used for queries like this, go ahead and use it—it's more efficient than asking people individually. ***However***, be ***very*** careful about doing this if you are a summer clerk. Remember, "They want to see ***your*** thought process, ***your*** research," says Jim Lovelace. "It's possible to ask for too much information!" But as a new associate, you'll be rewarded for being efficient. One lawyer recounted that when she was a new associate, she worked hard on a memo for a partner. When she gave it to her secretary to type it up, the secretary responded, "Gee, we had a case similar to this last year." The new associate realized that she could have saved herself tons of time if she'd asked around before performing her research from scratch. An associate at another firm talked about turning in a project to his supervising partner, who said, "This is fine, it just needs a Certificate of Service." The associate had no idea what that was, and he researched it for two hours. "I was tearing my hair out. It didn't seem to be written down ***anywhere***. Finally I asked another associate. It turns out a 'Certificate of Service' is just a statement that says 'I certify this was served on Joe Schmo,' and a freakin' stamp."

h. As Nova Southeastern's Pat Jason recommends, ask the assigning attorney's secretary if there is any correspondence with the client dealing with your issue. "It's hard to admit you don't know something, but it can really help you out to ask the secretary something like, 'Is there correspondence on land use with this client before?'"

i. Consider sources outside of your office. As Hofstra's Caroline Levy points out, "Most bar associations have a mentoring directory for guidance. The directory will include the names of lawyers who have volunteered to help with general advice on handling all different kinds of matters. They're listed by subject matter, so they're easy to track down."

4. Keep accurate notes as you proceed.

As you move through your research, paper the world. Keep track of every source you look at and take notes on the cases you read. Here's why: you never know when you're going to be pulled away from your research to work on an emergency project. If you have to put down what you're doing and come back to it later, thorough notes will save you a ton of time.

5. Don't expect an easy answer.

Sometimes you'll get a research assignment, look at it and think, "Geez, this is ***easy.***" That's a dangerous rush to judgment. As a rule of thumb, as Dennis Kennedy says, assume that nobody will give you an assignment that would have taken them just a few minutes to do themselves. As a lawyer at Wyatt Tarrant points out, "I've often seen new associates who think the answer to an issue is obvious. My experience is that when an attorney with years of experience requests research, the answer isn't so obvious!" Lawyers at Lord Bissell add: "Questions from clients don't always offer clear, easy-to-find answers. Don't just react! ***Think.***"

6. How to handle very complex facts and difficult issues

First of all, tell yourself—over and over again—that you ***will*** come up with a solution, no matter how difficult the project seems at the outset.

Don't "horribilize" the situation and tell yourself, "I'll ***never*** get this." As Brooklyn's Joan King advises, "With tough assignments, if you start positively, you're likely to turn up alternatives."

If the situation is complex—you know, like a law school exam—Gail Cutter recommends that you "diagram the parties so that you can be clear about the facts." If the project seems overwhelming, you should start by making a list of all that you're going to do. Break the project into small pieces and write them down, listing every task. You'll find that even the most difficult tasks can be broken down into do-able chunks, and when you focus on ***those*** instead of the big picture, you'll find that it's manageable after all.

7. "Lassie was a dog, right?" There *is* such a thing as a stupid question. But asking *smart* questions is something you've got to learn to do.

Nobody expects you to know anything practical when you graduate from law school. They ***know*** there's a huge difference between what you learn in school and what you have to do in the real world, and they expect you to have to ask questions. You've undoubtedly heard the old saw, "There's no such thing as a stupid question." Wellll . . . based on what I heard from people, there ***are*** stupid questions, and it's important to avoid asking them—while the flipside of that is that you shouldn't be scared into asking no questions at all. As Suffolk's Jim Whitters says, "You can't barge ahead without being willing to ask for advice. But you can't get the reputation, 'He's always asking questions.'" Hofstra's Rebecca Katz-White adds that "One of your tasks as a new attorney is to ***learn*** how to gauge questions that you've got to ask vs. the ones that you have to research first yourself."

Here's how you ought to handle asking questions:

a. Set your "ask-o-meter" on medium-low.

Most people are afraid to ask any questions ***at all*** for fear of looking stupid. While some questions (and questioning techniques) should be avoided, lots of questions just have to be asked, and you shouldn't avoid asking them. If you hate the idea of asking questions, err on the side of asking rather than staying quiet. It's easy to think, as John Marshall's Bill Chamberlain points out, "Gee, they're paying me all this money, I should know this." Not necessarily! As lawyers at the United Mine Workers of America point out, "When in doubt, ask. At best, your questions can flatter the 'askee'; at worst, they can save you from making a fool of yourself by making it appear that you know what you're doing when you really don't."

Two kinds of questions that you can't avoid asking are those that deal with facts and the nature of the issue. You can't research your way around those. If you waste hours or days making a wrong assumption about the facts or misframing an issue, you can ***only*** make your assigning attorney angry.

b. Make sure you do whatever research you *can* before you ask a question.

As Syracuse's Alex Epsilanty comments, "Lawyers always say, 'Don't think on my time.' What they mean is—think ***before*** you ask them questions!" Here's what they mean when they say that:

1) Don't constantly come back to your assigning attorney with question after question. A partner at one firm said that "I'll sometimes have an associate working on an assignment who will bounce into my office half an hour after they get the project and say, 'I found this case, what do you think?' then twenty minutes later they're back, 'I found this statute.' It would be so much more efficient if they asked, 'Can I schedule a half hour with you tomorrow morning to discuss the seven cases and statutes with you that may help or hurt our case?'" Drusilla Bakert suggests that you do whatever research you can and then contact the attorney, saying, "I have a couple of questions. When would be a good time to talk about them?" That way you're walking the "fine line between checking with people and bugging them," she adds.

CAREER LIMITING MOVE . . .

New associate is unsure of her research skills. She checks in with her mentor constantly for advice about how to proceed. He turns to her one day, exasperated, and says, "Let me introduce you to the library."

2) "Think through the issue step by step and be sure your questions are coherent and make sense," advises Gail Cutter. "And make sure you write down your questions and take them in with you when you talk to the assigning attorney, so you stay on track." And when you actually ask your questions, Alex Epsilanty advises that you "get over your oratory skills and get to the ***point.***" Lawyers are busy. Ask them what you want to know as quickly as you can, and get back to work.

c. If you're in doubt about asking the assigning attorney a question, use e-mail—or ask somebody else *first.*

Different attorneys need to be approached differently. If you're new, it may be difficult to differentiate between attorneys who will readily accept questions, and those who have to be approached more carefully. As Dennis Kennedy suggests, "If you're working for somebody who's hard to question—maybe it seems as though his phone is always glued to his ear, for instance—you've got to come up with other strategies. It might be e-mail. It might be a phone call or voice mail. It might be hanging around outside his door like a lost dog until he is off the phone, and then charging in. Generally, an attorney's secretary is the best resource for figuring out how to approach him. You can also talk to others who've worked for the attorney before. ***Somebody*** knows how to approach him, and you need to be one of those in the know."

SMART HUMAN TRICK . . .

The most influential partner in the office approaches a new associate on the associate's fourth day with the firm. The partner has a reputation for spending twenty seconds or less in detailing the facts of projects he needs completed, and demanding thorough and quick turnaround. He dumps a project on the new associate in his customary way. When he leaves the associate's office, the associate is dumbfounded. He has a few scribbled notes and beyond that, no idea what to do. He asks a more senior associate about the best way to approach the partner with questions, and the senior associate responds, "You can't. Questions are one of his pet peeves. Talk to his secretary." The new associate goes to the partner's secretary with his problem and asks for her help. It turns out that she knows more facts about the case and the client than the partner ever did. With her help "filling in the blanks," the associate gets the project done perfectly and on time. After that, the partner tells others in the firm that the new associate is "a quick study, brilliant."

8. Everything you need to know *before* you use on-line research tools—you know, Lexis and Westlaw

When my niece Emily was very little, we took her Halloweening in her neighborhood. (I know what you're thinking. OK, I'll tell you. She was dressed like a pumpkin.) She had never really been to other people's houses before. At the first few houses we visited, she would hold out her little Halloween basket only with a great deal of urging. But then when she got into the swing of things, at each house she'd thrust out the bag and say, "Fill it up." After that, she kept wanting to visit the neighbors, believing that every time you knocked on somebody's door, they'd give you candy.

When you're in law school, it's very easy to mistake Lexis and Westlaw for Halloween candy. But the catch is this: unlike Halloween candy, on-line research isn't free. In fact, it's ***very*** expensive. Law school just seduces you into thinking otherwise. When you get out into the real world, you'll find that there are some times when Lexis and Westlaw are just unbeatable, and you ***have*** to use them. There are other times when it's not the most cost-effective thing to do (and even if you figure that's not ***your*** concern, your firm's clients will care—and that means your assigning attorney will care, too).

Here's what you need to do when it comes to using on-line research tools:

a. **Don't overlook Internet-based research tools that you can use for free.**

I've got a long list of them, courtesy of Lisa Smith Butler, who teaches a class at Nova Southeastern on this very topic. You'll find that list in Appendix A.

b. **Do your strategizing and basic "book research" first.**

The temptation to jump straight into Lexis or Westlaw is dangerous. For one thing, a lot of lawyers say that you should come up with your research strategy and do your initial research off-line. As St. Thomas' Michelle Fongyee explains, "Lexis and Westlaw don't teach you how to analyze. It's easy to throw out a word and get off-track. You can wind up wasting a lot of time." Not only that, but a lot of older lawyers are very suspicious of computer research. If you're working at a firm of older attorneys who aren't technically savvy, they'll be very suspicious of you if you come across as unable to crack a book to find what you want. As Marilyn Tucker advises, "Think of Lexis and Westlaw as means of complementing your research. Fit them in where they are most time and cost efficient. Think about the issue. Is it a property problem? Start with the digests or hornbooks. Is it a tax problem? Looseleafs. Is it administrative? Go to the Federal Register or Code of Federal Regulations."

c. **Check with your employer *before* you use Lexis or Westlaw.**

It's ***very*** expensive. As Kentucky's Drusilla Bakert points out, "Students are so used to it being free through law school that they tend to use it even for the simplest research. It's incredibly easy to rack up huge bills." Florida State's Stephanie Redfearn adds that "Don't assume clients will pay a $500 Lexis bill. Before you do substantial on-line research, ask the assigning attorney if the client will pay for it!" Even if it turns out that using on-line research is perfectly appropriate in the circumstances, they'll appreciate that you had the good—here's that word again!—judgment to ask first.

New associate at large firm. She feels very unsure of her research skills and spends a lot of time on-line. The client in question is huge, and so she doesn't think to ask about the propriety of getting on-line. At the end of the month, she has racked up $10,000—which the client won't pay and her supervising partner has to write off. Her reputation never recovers, and she leaves the firm shortly thereafter.

New associate working with a very prestigious partner. The partner has the new associate doing research on the largest personal injury verdict in the history of the firm. The firm is representing the defendant. The new associate is programmed to ask "Can I use the computer to do research?" The partner strokes his chin for a moment, and then responds sarcastically, "Hmm. Let's see. Interest is running at $45,000 a day on this verdict. Well, OK. Go ahead and use it." The new associate reddens, and the partner adds, smiling: "In this case you didn't have to ask. But I'm glad you did. That's a good policy."

d. Make the most of whatever on-line research you *do* perform.

When you ***do*** use on-line resources, use them efficiently. There are a bunch of ways to do this. Valparaiso's Gail Peshel urges you to "take advantage of advance training, in March and April at school before you graduate. They always give a bunch of great advice at those training sessions."

Once you start work, recognize that just because you ***find*** cases on-line, you don't have to ***read*** them on-line. As Cardozo's Judy Mender suggests, "Perhaps the most efficient use of on-line research is to generate a list of citations, shepardize them, and then get off-line and read the cases in books. Reading on-line isn't only wasteful—it's hard on the eyes, as well!"

Lawyers at Goulston Storrs suggest that you take advantage of the Lexis and Westlaw customer support to figure out the search strategy best suited for your particular project. As Miami's Marcy Cox points out, Lexis and Westlaw have toll-free numbers that you can call to "lay out your issue and find out if you've missed anything." As Cardozo's Judy Mender points out, this helps you avoid the kind of on-line "trial and error" process that most of us got used to using in law school!

If you're at a large firm, Georgetown's Anna Davis advises you to "go to your research librarians. They'll train you on searches. They'll show you shortcuts that will help minimize the cost of the research."

e. Recognize the situations where on-line research absolutely, positively can't be beat.

There are some things that just can't be accomplished as well off-line as they can be on Lexis and Westlaw. One of these is large multi-state searches. As Denver's Jennifer Loud Ungar points out, "You just can't do that huge fifty-state search efficiently any other way."

You can also do a quick search once you've done your book research to make sure that you haven't missed a major case. Nothing can make you look as goofy as overlooking a case central to your project.

Finally, and most importantly, shepardize on-line. If your employer will let you use on-line resources at all, this is the thing they'll let you do. Lexis and Westlaw are absolutely up-to-the-minute when it comes to the state of the law. They'll know if something changed—well, since you started reading this sentence. Your clients will demand "good law," and shepardizing on-line is the one sure way to provide it to them.

f. **Don't forget the value of the world's most powerful computer.**

Namely: the human brain. It never hurts to ask a colleague who does the kind of work you're researching, "Got any good advice where I ought to start?" A person who handles an area all the time is a better and faster resource than any book or computer.

9. **Don't vanish for the duration. Check in with progress reports.**

When you get a research assignment, you might be tempted to go away and hide until you get it done. You might be concerned about seeming inefficient. You might worry that you're taking too long. You might perceive that your assigning attorney is busy and doesn't want to be bugged by you.

The fact is, it's a good idea to check in periodically with your assigning attorney as your work progresses. Here's why: It will stop you from going on a wild goose chase. If you check back after a few hours and say, "Here's what I've found. This is how long it's taking me. Is that OK?" you won't miss any issues and you'll be letting the assigning attorney know how you're doing time-wise. Nothing makes lawyers angrier than the common non-responsiveness of new lawyers. If you keep them in the loop, you'll make them happy. As Oregon's Merv Loya points out, "If you give them a mini-report on your research early on, they can correct anything that needs to be corrected. If you spend fifty hours researching on a twenty-hour question before you get back to your assigning attorney, that attorney will hit the roof."

If you get the impression that the assigning attorney is busy, or (s)he's often away from the office so you can't check with him/her personally, or for any other reason a person-to-person drop-in doesn't make sense, consider using voice-mail or e-mail for your updates. One new associate told of how she would avoid bugging lawyers about their projects during the day; instead, she'd regularly leave voice mail messages late in the afternoon or at night letting them know about her progress on their project, and asking them any non-urgent questions she had. If you do this, you're doing your attorney a favour by saving them time and letting them get back to you when it's convenient.

What if the assigning attorney asks ***you*** for a progress report while you're still doing your research? Of course you shouldn't hide from them. Be available for an honest assessment on how you're doing. But as Golden Gate's Susanne Aronowitz points out, "How's your research going?" is a ***very*** dangerous question. As she advises, "***Never*** answer it definitively. Say 'Every case is interesting, I'm still researching.' ***Don't*** speculate about what you're going to wind up with. The next case you find may disagree, and the assigning attorney will be left questioning your skills."

10. *Immediately* notify your assigning attorney if you turn up something unexpected in your research.

You might find as you research that you find something out-of-the-ordinary. For instance, it might be that when you got the assignment, the assigning attorney said, "The leading case in this area is *Hatfield v. McCoy*. Start there." As you research, you find that *Hatfield v. McCoy* has just been overturned. Tell the attorney!

Similarly, you may find that other issues crop up, ones that your assigning attorney might not have thought about. Again, let the attorney know what you're finding. As Willcox & Savage's Joni Coleman Fitzgerald advises, "Your research on a litigation issue may result in a case that could change the entire scope of the project. When you come across an unexpected development, let your attorney know about it."

11. Deadlines, and how you handle deadlines you're going to miss—or—You don't have a typewriter. You aren't a monkey. And they don't want you to write *Hamlet*.

You've probably heard that old saw about how if you give a million monkeys a million typewriters, eventually one of them will write *Hamlet*. Well, you don't live in the world of old saws. You're in the business of law, and the business of law means that things have to get done on time.

One of the biggest complaints I heard from lawyers all over the country was the lamentation that summer clerks and new associates ignore deadlines. It doesn't matter how good your work ***could*** theoretically be if you had extra time to polish it up. Lawyers only care about what you can get done ***on time***. If you're working for a litigator, the court won't want to hear that you needed extra time to finish your research. And clients will only pay so much for research, no matter how perfect it could be if you had an endless time budget for it. No matter what setting you work in, you've got to pay attention to the calendar! As Harvard's Mark Weber says, "In school, you're rewarded for what punishes you at work. In law school, you're rewarded for spending gobs of time. At work, you're considered inefficient. You've got to make your deadlines."

Here's what you need to know about handling deadlines.

a. Always assume that your deadline is "real."

You hear all kinds of nasty stories about lawyers who give clerks or associates deadlines, and then don't even look at the work that the clerk/associate busted his hump to complete until three weeks later. That bites, and maybe the lawyer who did that is just a jerk. But nonetheless, as lawyers at Sidley & Austin point out, as a new associate you are not in a position to judge the "reality" of the deadlines you're given. It might be that the lawyer intended to use your work, but something else intervened. Or maybe the case was postponed. Or ***whatever***. Bite the bullet on it and treat every deadline as though it's real.

b. Budget in time for editing and word processing.

As Vermont's Pavel Wonsowicz says, "You don't know how to spin doctor as a new associate. It will take you a ***lot*** of time to edit your own work. The best advice I ever got was to spend as much time editing as writing. The fact is, it's time well spent. If you are perceived as a good writer, it helps you as a lawyer."

When it comes to getting the project into presentable form, Marilyn Tucker advises that you "learn to set interim deadlines, to work backwards and plan for the unexpected. If you are relying on the word processing department, you'll need to have your draft in early in order to get it back with enough time to rework it. Waiting until the last minute not only puts pressure on the staff but, if a rush comes in from someone else, you are the one to get bumped."

c. What to do if you're going to miss a deadline . . .

1) Don't ever, ever, ever, ever avoid the assigning attorney until after the deadline has passed.

Stories are legion about associates who don't say anything until their deadline is long gone. The partner at one firm recounted how "The number one complaint of partners here is that the associates are not responsive. We give them assignments, they ask for deadlines, we'll say a week from tomorrow. They don't come to see us. They avoid us. Then when we track them down, it's 'Oh, I haven't gotten around to it yet.'" As Miami's Marcy Cox says, "You get an assignment and you don't make the deadline, and all of a sudden you're avoiding the attorney who assigned it to you as though you owe him money." No matter how angry the attorney will be if you tell them up front, that's ***nothing*** compared to the chunk they'll tear out of your hide if you wait until later on.

2) Recognize that having to work late doesn't mean that you're going to miss the deadline.

It means you're going to work late. Ha ha! That's why you didn't want to tell them in the first place, right? That's certainly why ***I*** wouldn't want to say anything. "You want me to come in on ***what*** day and finish it? You want me to stay ***how*** late?" It kind of chomps, but let's face it. The work comes first. Finishing work on time is a great reputation to cultivate, and if worse comes to worst, you can always work at home and e-mail yourself a draft at work to complete there. As Carlton Fields' Elizabeth Zabak says, "If meeting a deadline means working late, do it. Skip the social event. After all, the attorney and the client are relying on you." Emory's Carolyn Bregman adds, "You're not going to score any points if you show up on Friday for a Monday deadline and say, 'I won't be done. And I'm going away for the weekend.'"

3) Say something as soon as you realize you're not going to make the deadline.

   The sooner the better. As Carlton Fields' Kevin Napper says, "When associates are going to miss a deadline, there are almost always other options as long as they let me know early enough. You can't say it at the last moment!" Maybe the research is taking longer than you thought. It may be that you came up with so many alternatives that the project is much bigger than the attorney thought it was (or you're just a freakin' great researcher). Or maybe other lawyers have dumped stuff in your lap which they claim is urgent, and you've had to put this particular project aside. Or perhaps you're waiting to hear from the other side (the court, or opposing counsel, or whoever), and you haven't received an answer that the assigning attorney is waiting for.

   It doesn't matter what the reason is. As soon as you know you're not going to make a deadline, you've got to say something. As Carolyn Bregman suggests, say something like, "I don't think I'm going to make the deadline because of these other things. How should I handle it?" If you don't feel comfortable going directly to the assigning attorney, try going to your mentor or recruiting coordinator (if you're a summer clerk) or a trusted associate first for advice about what to say. But you've got to say something. For one thing, if you give an attorney enough lead time, (s)he will be able to make other arrangements. It may be that the deadline was not as firm as you thought it was.

12. How to dazzle attorneys by going above and beyond what they ask you for—but be *judicious* about it, because sometimes a cigar is just a cigar!

Remember that whenever you're given an assignment to do, it's ultimately designed to help a client solve a problem. If you demonstrate an awareness of that in the work you do, you're "thinking like a partner"—and you will rocket ahead in terms of the responsibility you'll be given and the trust and confidence your superiors will show in you.

That's what lawyers are talking about when they talk about taking "ownership" of a project. What they want you to do is to be able to think beyond what your particular assignment is and probe what the client is trying to accomplish. I'm going to give you an example from my own experience to show you what I'm talking about.

If you graduated from law school within the last few years, you're probably familiar with a study aid I created: *Law In A Flash*. It's those funny flash cards in the yellow boxes. When my partners and I were running that company, there were only four or five of us in the office, and we got a ton of phone calls, usually from law school bookstores and students who were ordering *Law In A Flash*. We had a toll-free number for them to call in on. Once, we started getting a lot of wrong numbers. People were calling us and saying things like, "I can't pay my bills, I need your service . . . " We would tell them they had the wrong number but they'd ***insist*** they got it right. We were puzzled and we were also annoyed. These phone calls were taking up a lot of time, and they were running up our phone bill dramatically, since the phone calls were only free for the people calling us. They were costing us a ***bundle***.

Finally, we figured out that there was a lawyer someplace out west who was running ads on late-night TV, saying that for a fee he'd handle all of people's creditors for them, get them to stop calling, that kind of thing. The thing was, his phone number was ***exactly*** like our phone number, but instead of "800" as a prefix it had the local area code. These poor folks who were watching his infomercials, bleary-eyed at two in the morning, were overlooking the area code and just assuming his number was toll-free.

After a bit of searching we tracked down this lawyer and I called him, explained the situation to him, and asked for his help. He was pretty chesty about it, and told me it wasn't his problem. So we kept on answering these calls, and they were getting more and more numerous. I called him a few more times—no luck. He wasn't even ***taking*** my calls after a while. I started getting mad. And then I passed a brain stone. I called the consumer affairs division of the city where this guy was conducting his business, and asked them if they had a free consumer debt consolidation service. They did. And beyond that, they knew this guy and said that they could do for free what this guy was charging money for. I got the phone number for that service, and I called this lawyer back. As usual, he wouldn't talk to me. So I told his office manager, "Look. It dawned on me that these phone calls we're getting, they're not yours at all. They're ***ours***. And this is what I'm going to do. Every time we get a call about debt consolidation, we're going to refer the caller to the free debt consolidation service ***unless*** you send us a thousand dollars a month to take names and phone numbers for you." As I expected, the lawyer himself got on the phone, sputtering, "You can't do that! That's not fair!" I told him in my most businesslike voice (I don't have much of one, mind you)—that's my deal. Take it or leave it.

We never got one of those phone calls again.

I don't mean to pat myself on the back, but when people talk about creative solutions, that's the kind of thinking they're talking about. When attorney Greg Craig was representing Manuel Gonzalez in the Elian Gonzalez case, he was clever enough to bring along a disposable camera when father and son were reunited, knowing how valuable the images of that reunion would be. Now ***that's*** thinking outside the box! How does this translate into ***your*** work?

a. "Don't take a narrow view of your 'assignment,'" per lawyers at Arnold and Porter. Marilyn Tucker recommends that you "Start training yourself to expect contingencies and problems and to think beyond the research question." "For example, if the result of a research memo is a suggestion that a motion be filed, you should at least sketch out what would be involved in the motion and volunteer to prepare a draft," as lawyers at Perkins Coie advise. Georgetown's Beth Sherman adds that "Being willing to follow through makes a huge impact, saying something like, 'Here's my research, in doing it it occurred to me it has this effect on these papers we'll have to file.'" Harvard's Mark Weber offers the following example: "You're asked to draft a complaint with tortious claims. You come back and say, 'There might be another theory we could pursue, another claim to make.' That's creativity. That's what they want. They don't want you to parrot back the casebook."

Many times this requires you to do a kind of trans-subject thinking that law school expressly ***didn't*** prepare you to do. Remember the Palsgraf case? The lady who was hit on the head with the scales that fell on her when the package exploded at the train station? Yeah, you remember it. You've tried to forget it, but you remember it. Well, the tort claim in that case was the central issue, and the foreseeability of the result. If you had a fact pattern like that on your law school Torts exam and you mentioned the possibility of a contract claim by Mrs. Palsgraf against the railroad—based on a contract for them to deliver her safely to her destination without getting hit in the head by scales—you wouldn't have gotten any points for it from your Torts professor. But if your firm represented Mrs. Palsgraf in her claim against the railroad, bringing up the possibility of a contract claim when you were told to research the negligence claim would make you a superstar.

b. Don't be too quick to assume that your research is at a dead end. As Brooklyn's Joan King puts it, "You need the right attitude about your research. You can't just tell yourself, 'Boy, is this a ***loser***.' You need to take the view that 'we ***can*** do something for this client.' It doesn't mean you will distort your research. But if a corporate client wants to do something, it's your job to find out ***how***, not ***whether***, they can. It opens up your horizons to think that way." Drusilla Bakert says that "If you're asked the question, 'See if I can file this motion,' don't go back and say 'no.' Great people go beyond that and say, 'No, but you can accomplish the same goal this other way." As lawyers at Sidley & Austin put it, "Recognize that there might be more than one way to approach an issue."

c. A way to incorporate "thinking outside the box" into research memos is to do as Marilyn Tucker suggests, and "include a section that notes new issues raised by your research which were not assigned in the original problem. Doing so alerts the assigning attorney to problems (s)he may not have known existed."

d. Now that I've got you all excited about this whole "value-added" concept, here's a ***great big*** word of warning: ***Being creative isn't always a good thing.*** As Sigmund Freud said, "Sometimes a cigar is just a cigar." ***Only*** use the "value added" strategy when three criteria are met: one, other projects you're working on won't suffer; two, you can meet your deadline; and three, what you're proposing is clearly relevant. As Willcox & Savage's Joni Coleman Fitzgerald warns, "It's counterproductive to spend a lot of time searching for ways to be creative when the project may require a simple, straightforward answer. You need to use good judgment and take the opportunities when they're available."

New associate at a New York firm. He immediately impresses everybody he works for. He's cocky, but he does assignments quickly and well, so "if anybody could get away with being cocky, he could," commented a lawyer at the firm. A partner who is particularly impressed with this new associate goes to the managing partner and says, "You've got to use this guy and see how good he is." The managing partner grudgingly gives him an assignment. He makes it a very narrow one, because he doesn't trust new lawyers very much. On Tuesday morning, he calls in the new associate, and says, "I want you to find the Statute of Limitations for this issue. I'm meeting the client Friday morning so I need an answer by then. We need to find out if we need to file a complaint right away or if we have breathing room. It shouldn't take you any time. Just look at the New York Statute of Limitations and write down what the statute of limitations is for this issue, and give it to me. Then you can sit in on the meeting with the client."

The new associate asks the managing partner's secretary for the file on the case, so that he can read the facts. That's usually an excellent idea, but it isn't necessary in this case; the assignment is very narrow. But in reading the file he sees that the corporate client is a Delaware corporation, and figures that what he really needs is the relevant ***Delaware*** statute, not the New York one. So he researches the Delaware statute of limitations.

Five minutes before the managing partner is due to meet with the client on Friday, he calls in the new associate, and asks, "What did you find out?"

The new associate responds, "We're OK. We've got lots of time. Incidentally, I researched Delaware because the client is a Delaware corporation."

The managing partner sputters, "What? I told you ***New York***. It's the ***parent*** company that's a Delaware corporation. Our client is the ***subsidiary***, and it's a ***New York*** corporation."

While this conversation is going on, the client is waiting in the conference room. The partner who'd recommended the new associate to the managing partner happens to walk by the managing partner's office as the managing partner is confronting the new associate. The managing partner calls in the other partner, and says, "Go research this issue right now. Put the answer on a slip of paper and slide it under the door to the conference room." The managing partner turns to the new associate and says, "You don't need to be at this meeting." The new associate's stellar reputation is gone.

13. What to do if you just get stuck

You might get to the point in a research project where you're just beating your head against the wall. You've looked and looked and looked and there's just ***nothing there***. What should you do?

First of all, don't be too quick to ring down the curtain. Tell yourself that there ***is*** a solution, somewhere. It may be that the most promising sources didn't pan out, but ***something*** will. One partner told me about an associate of his who tended to be negative, and didn't seek out alternatives. "She'd come into my office, saying 'There isn't anything.' I'd ask, 'Well, what about . . . ' and then send her out to research some more. She was a smart girl, but she didn't seem to realize that sometimes reasonable research isn't enough!" Harvard's Mark Weber recalls that when he was a new associate, "I had to research an issue that apparently had no case law on it whatsoever. I went back to the partner who gave me the assignment and said, 'There's nothing out there.' He responded, 'We know that. That's why we gave you the assignment.' I learned then and there," he adds, "that sometimes you've got to think outside the box."

14. If you're hitting a brick wall, here are three things to try:

a. Squeeze the cases you've found a little harder. It may be that their central points don't help you, but ***something*** in there is a lead. As Brooklyn's Joan King advises, "Leave pathways open to catch even the most subtle dictum. Ask where the dictum can lead you."

b. If the cases you've found aren't on point, be sure to go back to secondary sources (you know—hornbooks) to see if the law really is unclear, then "use analogies to similar factual or legal situations," says Gail Cutter.

c. If neither (a) nor (b) work, go to the assigning attorney and explain the dilemma, advises Brooklyn's Joan King. "Say to them, 'I know I need an answer to this. I've done X and Y and Z amount of research, and this is what I've found. What the heck do I do?' Sometimes you ***need*** to rely on people."

15. Remember, if it's not shepardized, it's not good law.

Boy, do people tell tons of stories about ***this***. Giving a client out-of-date law is just about the worst thing you can do. As Loyola's Pam Occhipinti says, "If your work is out of date, it's no good—and it'll never be forgotten."

So make sure your research is thorough. As Syracuse's Alex Epsilanty says, "If there are holes in your research, no one will want to work with you. They won't be able to trust you." Also, be sure that you don't overlook cases directly contrary to the cases that support your client. As McDonnell Boehnen's Brad Hulbert points out, "You can't go back to the partner and say, 'But you didn't say that you wanted to know about all the major cases that make our position look ridiculous.'" They might not tell you directly, but they ***assume*** you'll point out those cases. I'm not going to beat this point to death because you've just spent three years in school, and you've done a bunch of research. You ***know*** how to do it right. Make sure you bring your best research skills to bear at work!

As I mentioned earlier, one of the very best uses of Lexis and Westlaw is to make sure the cases you're relying on are up-to-date. If you don't have access to Lexis or Westlaw, then check the pocket parts on the books you're using. If you ***do*** have Lexis or Westlaw, make sure that you use the full cite-checking function.

 CAREER LIMITING MOVE . . .

Summer clerk at a large Midwest firm. He's got a **ton** of work to do. He gets a research assignment from a partner, and it turns out that he had researched that very issue for a law school class, just last Fall. He submits the paper that he'd written for law school.

It turns out that there's a new case, and because the clerk didn't do any research, he didn't find it. The partner, relying on the clerk's paper, calls the client and says, "Go ahead and do what you wanted to do. It's fine." The client consults with his accountant, who says, horrified, "You **can't** do that! You'll go to jail!" When word gets back to the firm, the clerk is mortified.

 CAREER LIMITING MOVE . . .

Summer associate, large firm, first assignment of the summer. A partner told him to cite check a brief being submitted to the circuit court. The clerk came back and said that all of the case law was valid. In fact, some of the law in the brief was out of date. The partner was furious.

It turns out that the clerk had used a shortcut that only told whether a case was **totally** overturned, not **partially** overturned. The particular points on which the partner had relied had been overturned even though the cases themselves hadn't been. Needless to say, the clerk didn't get an offer.

CAREER LIMITING MOVE . . .

New associate at a medium-sized firm. He turns in a research assignment, commenting, "By the way, I didn't get a chance to shepardize any of the cases I cited. I didn't have time." The partner he gives the work to comments later on, "It was the last time I trusted him."

D. TIME TO PUT PEN TO PAPER (OR FINGERS TO KEYBOARD): HOW TO WRITE WHAT THEY WANT TO READ

Now you've got to take all of that brilliant research and turn it into a flawless written product. As lawyers at Wyatt Tarrant recommend, "The most obvious way to stand out is to produce outstanding legal work that reflects careful thought, thorough research, creative analysis, clear writing that reflects superior style and readability, and real potential for handling yourself well in court and with clients." You've got a stack of research materials in front of you. How do you get from here to there?

1. If you've never worked for this assigning attorney before, do an "audience analysis."

You'll quickly find that there is no such thing as one perfect writing style. You need to be what Marilyn Tucker describes as a "legal chameleon"—adapt your style to suit each attorney you work for.

How do you do this? Ask the attorney, or the attorney's secretary, or another more senior attorney who's worked for this attorney before, for examples of writings in the format you've been assigned (letter, memo, pleadings, briefs, whatever) that the attorney has written and/or has particularly admired. You're looking for "style, approach, and formality," says Marilyn Tucker. As Carlton Fields' Eric Adams points out, "Some attorneys write like Hemingway, in short sentences. Others write like James Joyce, with interlaced footnotes and complex sentences. Tailor your style." Still others "obsess about punctuation, while somebody else might just want the work done, even in an outline form, with no excess time beyond getting to the ***answer***," says George Washington's Jim Lovelace. "No matter who you work for, you've got to figure out what (s)he ***likes***. What's (s)he written? Who's had success working for this attorney? Don't be afraid to ask questions!"

SMART HUMAN TRICK . . .

New litigation associate. He's assigned to a partner. He checks around and learns that this particular partner is a real pit bull, very aggressive, that he likes to "take no prisoners" when it comes to dealing with the opposition.

The partner has a case in federal court, and tells the new associate, "I want you to handle this issue. I want to see how you do." The judge chastises the new associate for not having a document. The new associate blames it on opposing counsel, and instead of resolving things quietly, the new associate starts talking loudly, berating the opposing counsel. The judge holds the new associate in contempt and fines him $100. On the way out of the courtroom, the partner offers to pay the new associate's fine. He's thrilled with the new associate's performance. "They're scared of us now! They'll settle. You watch." The new associate comments later on, "I never would have done that if I'd been working for someone who was more thoughtful and cerebral and didn't like a fight. But I knew this guy would love it, so I gave him what he wanted."

2. Write from an outline.

As Syracuse's Alex Epsilanty says, one of the biggest flaws you can make in a piece of writing is not to organize it well. If you write from an outline, that can't happen.

3. If the lawyer mentioned a certain case when (s)he gave you the assignment or anytime during your research, be sure to mention it in your final product.

It may be that during your research, you find that the case the attorney cited to you is actually bad law. Or maybe you've found cases that are more on point. Regardless, Drusilla Bakert advises that if the assigning attorney mentioned the name of a case to you, they'll be looking for it in the work you turn in. Make sure it's there!

CAREER LIMITING MOVE . . .

Summer clerk at a large firm. Partner asks her to research an issue. She has difficulty finding anything applicable, and goes back to him looking for guidance. He mentions the name of a case. It turns out that the case he mentions has been overruled. She does the best she can, looking for rules in secondary sources. When she turns in the assignment, he calls her back to his office half an hour later, and, beet-red, asks, "Where's that goddamn case I gave you? This is a piece of s***!" She explains that it had been overruled. She is right, but he is embarrassed, and mumbles, "Well, you should have mentioned that."

4. Don't forget the "A" in "IRAC."

Arrgh! I know what you're thinking. Are you ***ever*** going to get away from IRAC? Well—no. The reason I mention it here is that when you've done a whole ton of research, the temptation is to just disgorge everything you've found. As Georgetown's Marilyn Tucker says, "It's not enough to write a good reiteration of the law on a specific topic but fail to analyze the law and how it relates to the pattern of your case." Willcox & Savage's Joni Coleman Fitzgerald adds, "Most attorneys are not looking for a summary of cases when they assign projects to associates. Attorneys want to see that you can apply your research to the facts of their particular case or issue."

5. Be clear, be brief, and be seated.

Have you heard that saying before, about wedding toasts, "Be funny, be brief, and be seated"? I hadn't either until my new brother-in-law said it at my wedding, as an introduction to his own toast.

Whether you've heard the saying or not, when you're writing something for an attorney, brevity is really important. As one lawyer put it, "A B- student who figures it out in a page is more valuable than a Law Review student who goes on for seventeen pages. So many people get quality and quantity confused." Kentucky's Drusilla Bakert points out that "When a lawyer asks for an answer to a particular question, that's ***all*** (s)he's looking for. Don't respond to a narrow securities question with a ten-page treatise on the history of 10b-6 motions. When a lawyer asks for 'X,' (s)he'll be annoyed, not impressed, if you respond with the entire alphabet." Dennis Kennedy recounts that "When I was the director of a summer program, I used to give my own evaluation of summer interns' written work by taking it home the night before the review and reading it all at once with the TV on before I went to bed. I figured that that approach gave me the perspective of a typical harried, tired, and distracted attorney who only wants to get to the point. If I could easily find the main points and conclusions, I knew that the intern had done a great job."

Syracuse's Alex Epsilanty recommends that after you finish writing, go back over each line and ask yourself: Is it necessary? Why did I say it? Does it relate back to the topic? She also suggests you try reading it out loud, or try explaining what you're writing to someone else. "It'll be more concise that way," she says. Vermont's Pavel Wonsowicz suggests putting your writing to the "Mom" test. "Pretend you're explaining it to your mom, and not your boss."

Paul Bran of Dickstein, Shapiro also suggests that when you read back over what you've done, "Take at least a few seconds to reflect on the audience. Judge? Partner? Client? No matter who it is, if you want to persuade, think of who you're trying to persuade. For a judge—will (s)he buy this argument? If it's a memo to a partner, is the issue so complex that it'll put him/her to sleep and draw away from the strength of the first two arguments? If that's the case, drop some things to footnotes! Make strategic decisions about what will sell. You can still show how creative you are in a footnote, or mention issues that you found but didn't include for the following reasons. A good lawyer knows when to shut up and stop."

Finally—as I mentioned when we talked about clarifying the assignment, earlier in this section—if the attorney gave you a page limit, make sure you obey that limit! One lawyer talked about his first writing assignment, where he was asked to write a synopsis for the CEO of a corporate client about the next big issue in litigation. "The partner told me, 'keep it short. Give me two pages.' I wrote five pages, which I considered short. I took it to the partner, and she said, 'This is great. Now make it two pages long.' The CEO didn't have the time or impetus to read five pages, and the partner knew it."

6. There's no such thing as "just a draft."

As Harvard's Laura Share Kalin points out, "Sometimes they'll say, 'Oh, just give me a draft.' Don't fall for it." Lewis & Clark's Lisa Lesage says that "Even if they say they only want a draft, ***everything*** you write must be ready for the eyes of a client or a partner. It should be complete, accurate, thorough, and formatted correctly." Alex Epsilanty adds that "When lawyers ask new associates and summer clerks for a draft, they sometimes get a pile of notes. It drives them over the wall!"

If what they want is a final product and not a draft, then why don't they just ***say*** that, you're wondering. Well, it's not entirely deliberate. Sometimes, as Marilyn Tucker points out, they're thinking about the work they get from mid-level associates. Once you've got a few years of practice under your belt, then your "drafts" will look a lot more like final products.

Here are the reasons why you want a "draft" to be picture-perfect:

a. "They're forming an opinion of you, even if they say, 'Oh, nothing fancy, just pull something together,'" says Golden Gate's Susanne Aronowitz.

b. Once you turn in your work, as Marilyn Tucker points out, the assigning attorney will often forget that what you were asked to produce was a first draft. (S)he may look at what you've given him/her—handwritten notes, a typo-filled or gramatically incorrect document—and think you've lost your mind. As Hamline's Vince Thomas says, "People won't think, 'Oh, he was hurrying,' they'll think, 'He's an idiot.' Write everything as if your career depends on it, because it ***does***, even if you're just writing to the other associates in the firm."

If the attorney you're working for really is in such a time crunch that they mean it when they say "draft," then CYA. Send an e-mail or memo confirming that the work you're doing is "just a draft" as per their request, and parrot back any comments that they made to you about whether a stack of highlighted cases or handwritten sheets will suffice. And when you turn in the work, make sure that it is as standard as you have time to make it, and clearly write "DRAFT" across the top of every page.

CAREER LIMITING MOVE . . .

Law clerk, working at a firm during his third year in law school. Three days before Christmas, an attorney asks him to do a rush project that he has to deal with the very next day. The clerk explains that he has a plane ticket booked for the following day to go home and see his family, and the attorney responds, "That's fine. Give me whatever you find, your handwritten notes, anything. I don't care if it's typed. I'd rather that I just get your research." On the clerk's return from Christmas vacation two weeks later, he finds that the attorney hasn't looked at the materials the clerk handed in before Christmas. When the attorney **does** get around to it, he complains to everybody about the clerk's unprofessionalism and his disbelief that the clerk would hand in something that was handwritten.

7. "The anals of criminal law," or—Make sure your written product is *perfect*.

You want to hand in written work that's as perfect as you can make it. I've already addressed the quality of your research and the way your written work is organized. What we're talking about here is the "polishing" step. You've got to make sure that your grammar is perfect, your work is neat, your spelling is flawless, your blue book form is—well—by the book. The fact is, it doesn't matter if your substantive work is great. As lawyers at Latham and Watkins point out, "If you don't attend to the details—organization, grammar, typos—people will assume that you failed to attend to the substantive points as well."

a. Make sure your grammar is well.

Sitting and reading over a writing assignment isn't the ideal time for polishing your writing skills. If you're not sure your grammar is as good as it should be, do yourself a few favours. Number one, get yourself a good grammar book and keep it handy. I particularly like two grammar books, mostly because they're funny: *Woe is I* and *The Transitive Vampire*. You probably have the Strunk and White book *The Elements of Style* from law school, and if you're happy with that, great—rely on that instead.

Number two, have somebody you trust read over your work before you hand it in. People at work are going to get fed up with you in a hurry if you continue to make the same grammar mistakes, so don't press your luck there. If you get any feedback at all that your grammar needs work, hire yourself a tutor from the local high school or college.

Number three, xerox this list and keep it handy. Somebody sent it to me over the Internet, and I think it's not just funny but useful as well.

"Rules for Writers"

1. Verbs has to agree with their subjects.
2. And don't start a sentence with a conjunction.
3. It is wrong to ever split an infinitive.
4. Avoid cliches like the plague. They're old hat.
5. Be more or less specific.

6. Parenthetical remarks (however relevant) are (usually) unnecessary.
7. Also, too, never, ever use repetitive redundancies.
8. No sentence fragments.
9. Don't use no double negatives.
10. Proofread carefully to see if you any words out.

CAREER LIMITING MOVE . . .

Recruiting coordinator is called into the office of a senior partner at a large firm. "I think I just made one of our summer clerks cry," he says. It turns out that a summer clerk had handed him a memo he'd requested. He glanced at it. On the first line, it said, "As you requested, the client and me talked . . . " He'd thrown it at her and told her he wasn't going to read it until it was correct. She took it and returned half an hour later. She handed him a document that started with the words, "As you requested, the client and me talked . . . " He exploded at her, "Is this a **joke**?" and she left, crying.

b. Proofread. Spell checking is a great first step, but it's *only* a first step.

In its "No Comment" section, *Consumer Reports Magazine* reprinted a business mailer that had been sent out by a very prominent business seminar provider. The mailer featured different kinds of classes the seminar provider offered, including one called "Mistake-Free Grammar & Proofreading." Next to that offering was a seminar titled "How to Handle People with Tack & Skill." *Consumer Reports* pointed out in essence that the people who offer the "tack and skill" seminar ought to take the "proofreading" seminar themselves!

Now, I have a question for you. How much stock would you put in the "Tack & Skill" seminar? Probably not much. And it's because that typo would make you question the content of the course.

When you hand in work to an attorney, you've got very much the same problem. If your work has typos, the attorney who reads it won't know whether what you've said is reliable. As Gail Cutter says, "If you don't demonstrate your care and diligence on simple tasks like proofreading, you'll never be entrusted with complex matters."

On top of that, typos in legal documents can have ***very*** serious consequences. If your work goes out with a mistake, it could be worth a lot of money. As Denver's Jennifer Loud Ungar points out by way of example, "The difference between LLC and L.L.C. can be costly. Even though there's no difference between LLC and L.L.C. in the abstract, if the opposing client's name is ABC, LLC you write ABC, L.L.C. on the signature line of the contract, you might not have obliged the correct entity."

While spell-checking takes you part of the way there, as that example shows, you've got to proofread as well. That's because some words are easily misspelled as other words, so spell-check won't pick them up. Most of the funnier examples I've seen have to do with resumes and cover letters. One young woman's cover letter talked about her "precious lobs," where what she meant to say was "previous jobs." Another student had a letter that lauded his summer experience, saying that "I've seen things that will go down in the anals of criminal law." In my *Guerrilla Tactics* book I talk about the young woman who sent out a three-hundred-piece mass mailer in search of a job, only to realize the next day that in the objective line of her resume, "Seeking a position in public interest," she'd mistakenly left the "l" out of "public." Loyola's Pam Occhipinti recounts how, as a lawyer herself, she waited at the fax machine for a fax from opposing counsel. As it came through, the word "transmission" at the top of the page was missing an "s."

I know proofreading is boring. But you've got to do it. It's very dangerous to assume that your secretary will catch your mistakes, or the partner will review your work before it goes to the client or the court. As lawyers at Akin Gump point out, "It wastes client money to have a senior attorney do your editing!" And you can't assume that a partner won't mind a few rough edges in your work. As lawyers at Perkins Coie point out, "They ***do*** mind. And they ***will*** remember."

To make sure that you've proofread perfectly, Carlton Fields' Hardy Roberts suggests that you "Read your document backwards, starting with page 10, then 9, then 8—take it out of context so that you'll catch things that would have escaped your notice normally." Chicago-Kent's Stephanie Rever Chu adds that you should hand-count pages and hand-count exhibits.

All of this fine-toothed-combing is worth it in the long run. As Hardy Roberts says, "Over time, your typos disappear. Your work gets more perfect." So you've got ***that*** to look forward to. And it's just a lot easier to develop a reputation up front for perfection, so that people will cut you a break later on. As Marilyn Tucker advises, "Your written work lives on. Long after you've forgotten about it, it's still there. It doesn't disappear. Make it perfect."

c. Make sure your work is "complete."

Before you hand anything in, check samples of work in the format you've been requested to produce—remember, I told you about this in the beginning of the research section—just to be sure that you haven't left anything out that could come back and embarrass you.

As lawyers at Barnes & Thornburg advise, "Don't hand in incomplete work product. For instance, drafting a pleading and submitting it without a signature line gives the impression that you're not confident the pleading is worthy of a signature. If that's the case, go back and rework it until it ***is*** ready for a signature. Otherwise, it gives the impression that you don't appreciate the partner's time, in that the partner can prepare the signature line just as easily as you can."

d. Appearance counts!

You work hard on your projects. You don't want them to look like the written equivalent of Pig Pen in the Charlie Brown cartoons. One partner lamented work he'd received from a new associate:

"He handed me a bunch of xeroxed cases that I'd asked for, but they looked terrible. The pages were wrinkled and catercornered. And he had highlighted great big sections he wanted me to read with a "Z"—he didn't even bother to highlight the lines individually! His work was good, but it just didn't ***look*** that way. I showed him something I'd received from another clerk. It was a neat, unwrinkled stack of cases with tabs on some of the pages and a summary on each tab. It looked perfect. As I explained to him, the presentation creates an impression of the work. If you're going to take the time to do it, make it look professional!"

8. Remember that at some point, you've just got to let it go.

As a lawyer at Goulston Storrs observes, "You can always edit a written assignment again. You will always find some word that you want to change or some concept that you need to tweak. However, at some point the edits become counterproductive. It can be a very scary thing to turn in a written assignment. But I've found that the memos I've been the most nervous about turning in have come back with the least edits and revisions!"

9. Just before you hand in your work, shepardize it one more time.

Florida State's Stephanie Redfearn reflects on a case she handled as a new lawyer. "The day before we filed our brief in a case—the ***day*** before—a higher court reversed a case that we'd relied on. The only way we knew it was to do an instant-cite search on Lexis. That saved us. It's ***imperative*** that you know that your cases are still good when you file documents with a court!"

10. Anticipate that you'll have to defend your work.

When you hand in a written assignment, anticipate that the attorney will ask you, "Are you comfortable with your answer? Did you cover your bases?" As Alex Epsilanty says, "Look them in the eye and say, 'Yes, I am' and 'Yes, I did.' Be confident! When they ask you about your work, don't back down and say, 'I think it's OK' or 'I did the best I could.' They want to hear that you're confident with your work and that they can rely on it as a result."

CHAPTER SIX

Handling Everybody Outside The Office—Clients, Opposing Counsel, Judges, Court Personnel . . . and the Media

Depending on where you start your career, you may spend most of your time with people other than your colleagues. If you work at a small firm, you're a prosecutor, or you represent low-income clients, you're not going to spend much time (if any) on research and writing assignments. What you say and how you behave with clients, opposing counsel, judges, and court personnel, has a ***huge*** impact on your success. And when it comes to dealing with the media, you've got to be ***very*** careful about what you say! It's those topics that we'll address in this chapter.

Incidentally, things like handling court cases—everything from discovery to arguments in court to questioning witnesses to jury issues—is, to borrow a phrase you see so often in books, "outside the scope of this book." There are lots of CLEs on those topics, and if you're a prosecutor you'll go through formal training sessions to whip you into shape on those matters. Our focus here is on the kinds of things you don't learn in training and CLEs. Let's get started!

A. Handling Clients

If you work for any private employer, clients are the lifeblood of your business. Whether you deal with clients directly from the start or you grow into the "front person" under someone else's supervision, you need excellent client relations skills from the start. Here's what you need to know about clients!

1. The golden rules of client relations

a. The premier golden rule of client relations is—well—the golden rule.

As Harvard's Mark Weber points out, "Whenever you do ***anything*** for a client, remember the golden rule. Think of how you'd want to be treated if it was ***your*** case, if ***you*** were paying the bills. When I was practicing law, I once repped my family in litigation. Until then, I had no idea what it was like to be a client. Your client waits all day to hear from you! Your client's dog bite, their business deal, it consumes them. Be sensitive to them."

b. Remember that whether you agree or disagree with clients, like them or don't care for them—they pay the bills.

Lawyers at Sidley and Austin point out that "Sometimes clients are wrong, and sometimes they need to be told that. But summer clerks and new associates need to remember that law is a service business. Clients pay the bills!" One lawyer tells of how "When I was a new associate, I was talking to my supervisor about a client of ours, and I said, 'I can't believe how ***stupid*** this guy is. How does he get himself into problems like this?' My supervisor shot back, 'Watch it! His problems pay your salary. You need an attitude adjustment. "Thank God I'm here to help him" is what you have to think.'"

c. Keep clients in the loop on the progress of their case or deal.

You may be very conscious of what's going on with your client's case. Your client isn't—unless you keep them posted. As Lewis & Clark's Lisa Lesage recommends:

1. Copy clients on any correspondence and pleadings that you send out for them; and
2. If the case drags on for months, contact them by letter once a month, even if you've only got two or three lines to tell them: "The status hasn't changed, I'm waiting for X, I'll keep you posted."

d. Avoid a major source of malpractice claims: Return client calls *promptly* (and psst—how to make your supervisor look good).

Not hearing back from their lawyers makes clients ***nuts***. No matter how busy you are, make a point of responding to clients within 24 hours at the outside. Even better, try to respond the same day. Lisa Lesage suggests returning client calls twice a day, once before lunch and once right before the end of the day. As Nova Southeastern's Jennifer Silverman adds, "Even if you haven't been able to do what you thought you could do since the last time you spoke with your client, return the call and tell them anyway. The ***worst*** thing for a client is just being left out in the cold."

This ***doesn't*** mean that you need to be a slave to the telephone. As Lisa Lesage says, "You don't need to answer the phone constantly. Put in blocks of time when you'll return calls, and let your secretary know when that is so (s)he can tell clients."

If you work for a supervisor who has primary responsibility for a client, you don't want it getting back to that supervisor that you ignored a client. As a lawyer at Waller Lansden says, "If a member of the firm has a client who says that (s)he left a message for an associate several hours ago and the associate hasn't returned the call, the member's first thought is going to be, 'If ***I*** have the time to return this call, then the associate sure should.'"

Incidentally, if your supervisor is out of town or otherwise tied up when a client calls, Marilyn Tucker points out that you can "Help your supervisor out, make him/her look good, and at the same time appease the client. Even though you are the new kid on the block and may not have an answer to the client's question, return the call. Hearing from you is better than no communication at all. Then write a short note to the senior attorney and to the file recording the contact with the client."

e. Don't *ever* forget your duty of confidentiality to the client. Keep secrets!

Everything your client tells you or your firm, every element of their business and their case, is a ***secret***. If you're working on something interesting, it's a ***huge*** temptation to talk about it with your friends and family. Do whatever you need to do to resist the temptation! As South Carolina's Phyllis Burkhard says, "Even if you don't reveal names, you'll be in big trouble if someone passes on an 'amusing' story about a client, and the client or someone he knows recognizes who the story is about." So when you're out swapping war stories with friends from school, you're going to have to be very careful about what you offer. And at family picnics, when your mom says, "Oh, tell Uncle Frank about all the interesting things you're doing," you're going to have to be circumspect. As Dewey Ballantine's John Ragosta comments, "I suspect many a career has suffered from a partner's overhearing a casual business conversation unwisely held in a crowded elevator."

Also keep in mind that if you talk about another client's case with your client, they'll assume that you are, in turn, blabbing *their* case to others. If you must discuss analogies, use fact patterns sweeping enough that they aren't traceable to a particular client.

You should be similarly cautious when you prepare documents. As John Ragosta suggests, "In preparing any privileged document, always note PRIVILEGED AND CONFIDENTIAL across the top. This demonstrates professional awareness and is invaluable should your documents ever be subject to a discovery request."

CAREER LIMITING MOVE . . .

A junior associate is indiscreetly and loudly discussing his law firm, firm politics, and confidential client information with his wife at a restaurant. What he doesn't know is that a partner whom he doesn't recognize is sitting at a nearby table—listening to every word.

CAREER LIMITING MOVE . . .

From John Ragosta: "Early in my career I showed up unexpectedly for dinner one night, after I'd been working all my waking hours on one project for quite a while—and explained to my wife that the principals in a well-publicized antitrust suit had agreed to settle. The next evening my wife told me that a neighbor had been very interested to hear the case was settling. I lived in dread, until the news was publicly announced, that a leak might be traced back to my dinner table. My lesson was learned, however: Confidences—even small ones—must be protected."

2. Before you meet with clients for the first time—prepare yourself!

Whenever you start in a new practice area, ask your colleagues for the characteristics of problem clients in the practice area, and what you should be on the alert for. Also, look for tips from lawyers you meet at bar functions, CLEs, and even in chat rooms on the Web (some local bar associations have their own). As Hutton & Simpson's Mary-Lynne Fisher says, "80% of your problems come from 20% of your clients. The sooner you can identify the characteristics those clients share, the better off you are."

For instance, if you're a man and you do domestic relations work, anticipate that your female clients may fall in love with you. It's a matter of what Sigmund Freud described as "transference." Essentially, when a marriage is broken, the spouses typically haven't had a close confidant of the opposite sex for some time. When they can confide in ***you***, they tend to transfer their affections to you. You may be thinking, 'Hey—you consider that a ***problem***?' Well, it ***can*** be. And it's certainly a professional hazard. The point is, learn at the beginning what to expect from your clients, and proceed accordingly.

3. The business aspects of dealing with clients: retainers and billing

a. Preparing your clients for what their case will cost

Wake Forest's Bill Barrett points out that "Clients have no idea how much things cost." You have to ***prepare*** them for it. The most obvious way to do that is with a well-thought-out retainer.

As a new lawyer, unless you're a sole practitioner, you'll have other people to lean on when it comes to calculating an appropriate retainer in any given case. In essence, a retainer reflects how much time a matter is likely to take. If you are on the front lines when it comes to asking for a retainer, Jennifer Silverman points out that "You need to be firm about getting the retainer." As a new lawyer, you may feel funny about asking clients for money when you haven't done any work for them yet. But you ***have*** to. If a client balks at paying a retainer, maybe they won't pay at all. Would you be willing to do the work on a pro bono basis—or perhaps more importantly, would your boss want you to do that?

Ironically, insisting on a retainer lets your client know that you're savvy enough to help them solve their problems. After all, if you can't be firm with your client on a retainer, how will you stand up to people on the ***other*** side?

 SMART HUMAN TRICK . . .

Junior associate, bankruptcy firm: "I sat in with a partner on an initial meeting with a client. The partner asked the client for a $100,000 payment up front. The client responded, 'Wow, that's a lot of money. Can you cut the retainer? Can't we pay as we go?' The partner looked the client in the eye and responded, 'You wouldn't want a bankruptcy attorney representing you who was stupid enough to extend you credit, would you?' The client paid the full retainer without another word of protest."

SMART HUMAN TRICK . . .

As Joseph Cammarata, one-time attorney for Paula Corbin Jones, says: "If a client comes to you and says, 'It's not about money, it's about principle, remember this: Principle gets expensive.'"

b. Bill often—and in detail.

Jennifer Silverman advises you to "bill clients at least once a month. Get a billing program that generates bills frequently, so that clients aren't blindsided. It's a pain to send out frequent bills, but don't let it fall behind. That's where most lawyers at small firms make mistakes." Bill Barrett adds that you should "Make the bills detailed. Bill by tenths of hours. And include phone calls. Let clients know ***everything*** that's being billed." (For lots of details on billables, see the chapter called "Econ 101," on page 148.)

If clients are reluctant to pay, Golden Gate's Susanne Aronowitz advises that "You can only send reminders, or offer a payment plan. Have the senior person who negotiated the price call and ask the client for payment. Remember, you can't withhold further services just because a client doesn't pay. It's unethical. And sometimes there's a legitimate reason, like the client lost their job."

4. Communicating with clients

a. In the initial interview, rely on "intake sheets."

Lisa Lesage recommends that you "Have intake forms where you can record all pertinent information on the client's first visit. Don't annoy them with calls to follow up. Intake sheets are basically check-off sheets. You find them in CLE books and how-to books, or you can call an experienced attorney in the local bar for advice about intake sheets. Another place to start for certain kinds of issues is the law itself. For instance, if you're doing a fair housing law case, think about what facts you need, or ask a law librarian, or ask people at the young lawyers' section or appropriate specialty section of the local bar. If you ask your client the right questions right from the start, you'll look like you know what you're doing!"

b. Be on time!

No client wants to feel as though they're not your first priority. When you arrange a meeting with clients, be on time. If they're coming to your office to see you, come out to the reception area to greet them. If you just can't avoid being late meeting them, be certain that somebody else in your office (like your secretary) greets them promptly and makes sure they're comfortable. If you have to reschedule the meeting, have your secretary contact them, explain the delay, apologize for the inconvenience to them, and reschedule the meeting. Remember—treat clients as you'd want to be treated!

c. Give the client your full attention.

Lisa Lesage recommends that you "Develop a sense of rapport and respect from the start. Give clients your full attention. Don't let phone calls or visits interrupt."

d. Remember that people don't have legal problems. They have problems with legal aspects.

The 19th-century physician Sir William Ostler said, "The good physician treats the disease, but the great physician treats the patient." Similarly, a good lawyer understands the problem, but the great lawyer understands the client. You can't be an excellent lawyer without taking a holistic approach to client service. It's not spotting issues and applying the law. It's part psychology, as well. As Florida State's Stephanie Redfearn says, "Being a counselor means ***counseling***!"

So what should you do? The client of one large firm said, "Be a friend first; establish trust." Another said, "When I talk to my lawyers I want to sense from them, 'I understand you and I like you.'" Kentucky Public Defender Sarah Madden says "You've got to make clients feel better when they walk out than when they came in. It's not all about winning. It's about showing that you care." That counts for corporate clients, as well. Learn something about their business. You can't give a corporate client the service it deserves unless you understand the context of the questions they ask you and their business goals.

Finally, give clients the level of service they want. As Stephanie Redfearn says, "If clients want their hand held through the process, then do it!"

e. Focus on your client's goal. *Listen* to them!

"At the initial interview, find out what's ***really*** bothering the client," advises Mary-Lynne Fisher. For instance, Bill Barrett says that "When you get absurd disputes about absurd things, you've got to cut through what's said to what they ***mean***. When people spend thousands fighting over a dog, is it really about the dog? No. It's about hurting each other."

The key to figuring out your client's goal? Asking good questions, and ***listening***, really listening, to the answers. If you get a sense that what's on your client's mind isn't what they say it is, ask questions to hone in on what's really going on. Elaine Bourne says that "When you ask a question, ***wait*** for an answer. Don't make assumptions. As a lawyer, you don't need to be the one talking. Listen to what's said and what's not said. Don't jump in and fill silences. Silences are ***useful***." In the "The 'People Part Of Work" chapter, I talk about the benefit of being a dynamic listener in getting the full story. Develop that skill. (you'll find that on page XX).

When you ***do*** get the full story, recognize that sometimes it's a problem neither you nor the legal system can solve. As Bill Barrett says, "You need to pull the ripcord when your client's problems are legal. Be sensitive to when you should make referrals to other people, like therapists and social workers. Build up a network of people in social services."

One lawyer talked about getting a divorce case as a new lawyer. "The wife, our client, would call and say, 'Can you believe he did this?' I would respond, 'We can do this and this and this . . . ' I wasn't listening! What she was really communicating was that she was hurt and she wanted to get back at him. She wanted revenge.

It would have been better to address the hurt than list her legal options."

Focus on what you ***can*** do for your client, what their legal options are, and recognize that as a lawyer, that's ***all*** you can do. If your client comes to you with a claim for which the Statute of Limitations has run out, game, set, match. You can't do ***anything***.

When a client ***does*** have a problem you can solve, focus on the client's ***goal***. As one client complained to their law firm, "Sometimes we ask what time it is and you tell us how to build a clock." Stories are legion about deals that got away because the lawyers got lost in the details. One corporate president talked about a time when "We wanted to buy this little company, we loved the products they made, we liked the people. I turned it over to the legal department to iron out the details and draw up an agreement. The lawyers started focusing on all kinds of remote contingencies and contingencies on contingencies. The people at the little company were getting angry and put off. While our legal department futzed around, another company swooped in and did the deal. I was ***furious***."

CAREER LIMITING MOVE . . .

Junior associate: "My first week with the firm, I worked on a matter for a huge client. This client wanted to lease a property, and I was assigned to review the lease. I met with the client, and the client asked, 'Did you review the lease?' I said, 'Yes, there are 45 problems with it.' The client said, 'The question is, is it a property I want? Is it the rent I want to pay? Is it a 99-year lease? Can I combine it with other properties? If so, then I don't care about those 45 problems. Don't screw up this deal!'"

f. Keep your clients' expectations reasonable. Law is the art of the *real*.

People hear things much the way the dog Sandy does in the famous "Far Side" cartoon. Remember, it's the one where

Sandy's master is saying something like, "Bad dog, Sandy! You shouldn't drink out of the toilet, Sandy! If I have to tell you one more time . . . " and the whole time what Sandy is hearing is "Blah blah blah Sandy, Blah blah blah Sandy . . . "

Similarly, if you tell a client "We could recover as much as half a million dollars," "The court should rule within three weeks," "You might be able to do the deal for as little as a hundred thousand," your client hears: I'll win half a million dollars. I'll hear in three weeks. I'll get the deal for a hundred thou." People gloss over tempering language like "might," "should," and "could."

Remember that when you give clients expectations. Be conservative in your wording, and ***write things down***, either in an e-mail or in a follow-up letter. And build in cushions when you give time estimates. As Hofstra's Caroline Levy says, "Always build in extra time. For decisions on motions, maybe it ordinarily takes four weeks. Tell the client you expect an answer in six weeks—so the client is happy rather than mad when the answer is two weeks late!"

A lawyer at a small firm said that "We were representing a client who'd been in a car accident. This guy had it in his mind that he wasn't going to accept anything less than half a million bucks as a settlement, and we hadn't really addressed that with him. We got what we perceived as a good offer—80% of the policy limit, which was a hundred thousand dollars. We told the client about the offer, and he wouldn't hear anything of it. We didn't know what to do. We should have told him what he could realistically expect. He was never going to get an extra four hundred thousand dollars over the policy limit. Never."

You need to rein in your clients for their own good. If your client demands so much that their opponent declares bankruptcy, that's not a positive for your client—or you. If you routinely overreach, pushing just because you can, you'll develop a reputation that will hurt your clients.

g. List problems for your client and immediately follow up with possible solutions. Inform them of consequences!

As lawyers at Goulston Storrs advise, "If you are aware of consequences to your clients' actions, it's your duty to inform the client of those consequences and let the client decide on the course of action. For instance, if the client is thinking about rejecting a settlement offer, you have to tell him/her that (s)he's likely to incur a substantial amount of legal fees preparing for trial in the next few months, and let him/her decide whether to proceed. Don't be afraid to counsel the client, rather than just take orders!"

h. Answering questions from clients—and how to say artfully "I don't know"!

Have you ever noticed that you just kind of assume that any doctor can answer any medical question, no matter what specialty they practice? You meet a podiatrist at a party, and it's "Doc, I have this tickle in my throat . . . "

Clients feel the same way about ***you***. Once you've graduated from law school (or even while you're still ***in*** school), people think you know every single minute rule of law off the top of your head. They'll put you on the spot. "I just need a quick answer . . . " "Off the top of your head, do you think it's OK to . . . " "Listen, I don't want you to spend any time on this. I just need to know . . . "

Watch out! Until you've got some experience under your belt, you're treading on ***very*** thin ice. Here's why. Maybe you really ***do*** know the answer to their question, and you'll look like a genius. But when you're new to the practice, you can't be sure that you're right. Maybe you studied the exact issue the client's asking about just last semester. Well, maybe the law's changed since then. Or maybe the rule in this particular jurisdiction doesn't match the general rule you learned in school. Until you've handled a certain practice area for a while so that the issues repeat themselves and you ***do*** have the relevant rules in your head, ***don't*** give snap answers to legal questions from clients!

The downside risk of giving the wrong answer to a client is huge. As Cardozo's Judy Mender points out, "If you provide the wrong information, intentionally or not, you could set up a difficult situation. If the client relies on your answer, you may have committed malpractice. Or if you answer and then do your research and return with a different opinion, then you've called into question your initial judgment and legal instincts, and you've set up expectations which may not be realistic. Either way, you can only irritate a client and weaken your relationship."

So you can't give an answer "right now." You also can't say, "Here's what I think the answer is, but I'm not sure." The client will immediately forget the "I'm not sure" and assume they have their answer.

You also want to avoid using the words "I don't know." Don't hit them over the head with your lack of knowledge! Instead, be subtle about it. Assure the client matter-of-factly that you'll get back to them quickly with an answer. Tell them ***when*** you'll call them back—and then do it! Ask someone else at the office who ***is*** familiar with what the client asked about—they ***will*** be able to give you an answer off the top of their head!—and if you can't get the answer quickly that way, research it. As Carlton Fields' Hardy Roberts points out, "Every lawyer gets questions every day that they can't answer. Look at the talking heads you see on TV. They talk without answering the question if they don't know the answer. They'll say 'It depends' and then talk about what they ***do*** know. With clients, say, 'I can find it out for you.'" Stephanie Redfearn adds "You can say, 'There are issues involved with it. We'll research it and get back to you quickly.'"

If a client leaves a question for you on voice mail, NYU's Gail Cutter advises that if you don't know the answer, "Don't dodge the call. Call them back and tell them you're working on their question, or that you're researching it or conferring with partners or associates, whichever is appropriate."

Sooner than you think, you'll develop expertise such that you really will be able to answer some questions without verifying your answer first. And even when you ***are*** a senior attorney, lawyers at Goulston Storrs point out that "Even the most experienced practitioners have to look up some things to answer clients' questions. It's not just you!"

In the meantime, as John Marshall's Bill Chamberlain says, "It's tempting to feel as though you have to give brilliant advice every time a client asks you a question. It's hard on you as a new lawyer to set limits and keep a sense of yourself—but you ***can*** do it!"

i. Ask your supervisor about what's OK to reveal to the client.

Don't assume that because you're working on the client's case, it's "open season" with anything having to do with the case. As Susanne Aronowitz says, "Getting interrogatories doesn't mean you can share strategy with the client. Clarify with superiors what's in-bounds to discuss before you say anything."

j. If your supervisor is the client's main contact, tell your supervisor when the client says *anything* relevant to you.

Susanne Aronowitz says that "If a client tells you something material, ***immediately*** tell a superior. The client assumes if you know, the firm knows. They may not bother to repeat what they told you to somebody else."

k. Don't ask your supervisor questions in front of the client.

When you're new, there's a ***lot*** you're curious about. If you see something go on when a client is around and you want to understand it better, wait until the client's gone before you ask. Write it down if you have to. Why? Because even though you feel as though you don't know much, the client views you as a fully-fledged attorney. They won't have much faith in you if they hear you asking your supervisor questions.

CAREER LIMITING MOVE . . .

Summer clerk at a medium-sized firm. He attends a trial with his supervising partner and the client. During a break in the trial, while the clerk, client and partner are sitting together, the clerk asks, "Why did their lawyer call that doctor back to the stand?" The partner quickly changes the subject. Subsequently, out of the client's hearing, the attorney said to the clerk, "Don't ask questions in front of clients! The client hears a question and assumes, 'This person doesn't know anything.'"

1. Be friendly but guarded with clients.

Lawyers at Hillis Clark point out that "Clients want to feel that their lawyer is a ***real person***. Don't be shy about sharing appropriate information about yourself. Inevitably, the response is positive, and it is essential for good and lasting relationships with clients." Your hobbies, books you've read, movies you've seen, cute stories about your kids—that's all safe.

By the same token, as Harvard's Mark Weber warns, "Lawyers have a common phrase: your client can become your worst enemy. They can turn on you. If something doesn't go as they anticipated, they'll turn. No matter what, be a good communicator, but don't let your guard down. You can become friendly but you're still their attorney. When you're corresponding or communicating, that letter to the client or to opposing counsel can become Exhibit A against you."

When it comes to kidding around with a client, be careful. Even if your supervisor has a joky, friendly relationship with a client, that doesn't necessarily mean you can follow suit. The joshing they'll take from your boss doesn't open the door to ***your*** teasing. Err on the side of caution. As lawyers at Cowles & Thompson say, "It's a big mistake not to know where to draw the line in 'kidding' with friendly clients." Just as your colleagues are colleagues first and friends second, the same is true for clients—at least when you're the new kid on the block!

On the other hand, when you're socializing with clients, don't throw your work in their face. Let ***them*** set the tone.

CAREER LIMITING MOVE . . .

New associate at a large New England law firm. He's brilliant and a workaholic, and his superiors take advantage of this, shoveling work at him. His supervising partner comes to his office and says, "I'm going out to dinner with client X tonight. You're doing some of their work. Why don't you come along, get to know them?" The associate balks, citing his workload. The partner reassures him, "Don't worry about it. Come on." The associate reluctantly goes, but he's very nervous—he has **lots** of work to do. While the others are having fun and drinking, he's getting more and more tightly wound. They have an 8 p.m. reservation, and at 8:45—when they're still not seated—he yells at the hostess, "Where's our table? We were supposed to have a table at 8 o'clock!" At 10:30, he excuses himself to go back to work.

The following day, his supervising partner walks into his office and **cremates** him. "Even if you've got work to do, don't make clients feel uncomfortable! I don't care if you have to come back here and work after dinner to meet your deadline. You made them feel as though you were shaky with your work, as though you don't have any confidence."

Finally, be ***very*** tactful about bragging to clients about perks when you're on their nickel. As George Washington's Jim Lovelace advises, "If a partner tells you to stay at the Four Seasons, be mindful of bragging to the client about the great accommodations or great meal you had last night. Their existence may be different than yours. If the client is very wealthy, there wouldn't be a problem. But if it's somebody who's middle management at a large corporate client, you've got to be more careful."

2. If you're starting your career at a large firm, here are some additional tips for you.

If you start your career with a large firm, you've got some client issues that are different from new lawyers in other settings. When you're not the lawyer on the "front line"—when it's a lawyer one or two or three layers above you who's dealing with the client—here's what you need to know:

a. ***Ask* for opportunities to see clients.**

One lawyer recommends that "The best way to learn how to interact with clients is to ***ask*** to sit in when the lawyers you work for meet with clients. Watch the relationship they have. See what's important to clients." One of the things that you'll find is that there's no such thing as an "institutional" client. Even if the client is a huge corporation, there's still a person who cares a lot. Don't forget that when you interact with them!

b. **How to handle meetings with clients**

As a new associate at a large firm, you won't be conducting your own meetings with clients. You'll be sitting in on meetings with other, more senior lawyers. What do you do? As Dennis Kennedy says, "I've seen more young attorneys go up in flames in this situation than any other. Understand that the client sees you as expensive surplusage, and you don't want to remind the client of that! Here are a few good rules:

1) Speak only when spoken to. I always believed that you went into a meeting with the client seeing you as the bright, young attorney. It's easier than you think to change that opinion!

2) There is no joke that you can tell that will be a guaranteed winner. Ever. Don't take the risk.

3) Never correct the lead attorney no matter how wrong you think (s)he is. It's more likely that you are wrong. Mention it after the meeting—the attorney will make the call to the client if the correction is necessary.

4) Most of the time you are in a meeting you are there to take notes and to observe and learn how to conduct a meeting. Do that. The fact that you won the client counseling competition in law school does not give you a license to think you've learned it all.

5) If you are asked to summarize your research for a client, try to hit the main points and finish within a minute. If the client

has further questions, (s)he'll ask. Almost no client will want to hear about the fascinating distinction you've found between two obscure cases on a tangential point. The client is thinking ***action***.

6) The bottom line: talk with the lead attorney about what (s)he wants you to do in the meeting!"

As Dewey Ballantine's John Ragosta points out, "The note-taking function can be vital. Take ***detailed*** notes. Who said what? Who responded? Get quotes when possible. As an associate, I frequently found that my notes provided a detailed summary of a meeting that was often relevant even several years later. The notes might enable us to tell a government official or industry representative that 'At a meeting on X date, attended by Messrs. Jones, Smith and Ms. Wilcox, Mr. Jones indicated that there was no need to seek additional commitments, as recourse to sanctions is clearly provided.' This kind of attention to detail is a powerful tool for any lawyer, but it can quickly make a junior lawyer indispensable."

c. Watch what you say to clients. Don't overstep your bounds!

As a new associate at a large firm, you're in an interesting position. As I've mentioned in other chapters, like the "How To Crush Research Assignments" chapter, your superiors ***want*** to see you take the initiative. But what they mean is ***intellectual*** initiative in solving client problems, not taking client problems into your own hands directly.

As lawyers at Latham & Watkins point out, "When you interact directly with a client, the key is keeping the client happy while not overstepping the bounds of your experience. Always check back with supervisors! Taking 'ownership' of a project is good, but taking ownership too far and getting out ahead of supervisors in talking with clients and/or third parties can create awkward situations." Lawyers at Lord Bissell agree, saying, "Use your common sense. Don't take a position on behalf of a client or the firm without checking with superiors first. We want people to show initiative and independence, but you can show that without being a 'cowboy.'"

Although you never want to be dishonest with a client, remember that you're not the one with primary client responsibility. It's up to more senior lawyers to have "tough" conversations with clients, like explaining the weakness of their case or talking them out of a certain strategy.

d. **Your cases are unlikely to be very emotional. The issue often is: Who gets the money? That's what your clients are interested in.**

A lot of what's going on with clients of big firms is wealth distribution, according to a senior partner at one large firm. You won't get a lot of gut-wrenching issues. A partner at another firm, who handles bankruptcies, says, "There's no emotion in this work. It's creative lawyering. With large bankruptcies like the ones I handle, it's just money that's involved. Who's going to get the money? My client, or the other guy? With these big bankruptcies, you've got a situation where a bunch of wealthy guys put in money on a mortgage twenty years ago and they've all got their write-offs, you're just gladiators doing battle over a hunk of meat. It's a chess game against some vulture fund. Nobody's losing their house over it, nobody's losing custody of their children. It's just money. When I do a mass bankruptcy where there are hundreds of millions or billions of dollars at stake, I can get into some really creative lawyering because the amount in controversy is so large we have the luxury of lots of research and creativity. So does the other side, so it's law 'out on the edge.' Smaller bankruptcies are ***much*** more personal, more difficult, more meaningful. But for those, for consumer bankruptcy, lawyers run it more like a mill. They have lots of paralegals handling things, otherwise it's not profitable. In those situations you can't justify the time necessary to make it creative."

3. **You're representing low-income clients. Here are some tips to keep in mind.**

In many ways, the issues around serving low-income clients are the same as they would be for any client, no matter how wealthy. Treat them with respect. Return their phone calls promptly. Research answers to their questions; don't give them snap judgments. But there ***are*** some differences. Here's what you need to know:

a. "I'm not paying you. How good can you be?"

You may find that some clients will be disrespectful to you, figuring they "get what they pay for," and if they're not paying, you're no good. If you get that impression, stay calm and say, "If you want legal representation, I'm the one available. If not, you can walk out."

Especially if you are fresh out of school, you have to be aware of the fact that your context might not be helping you out. As American's Jill Barr, a former public interest lawyer herself, advises, "If you go to a law firm fresh out of school, clients see you with five other attorneys around. They ***know*** you're a lawyer. In legal services, they're only seeing ***you***. They'll ask, 'Are you really an attorney?' Get that diploma framed and hanging behind your head!"

Also recognize that if the first time they see you you're talking to the judge and prosecutor, "They'll assume you're in cahoots," says former public defender Rebecca Katz-White. "You have to show them and say to them, 'I'm here and paid to represent you. The fact that I know the judge and prosecutor will help you because they trust me.' And sometimes it works to bluster in court for the benefit of your clients."

b. Expect that sometimes clients will be *very* grateful—and sometimes they won't be grateful at all.

Sometimes your clients will feel guilty that they're not paying you. You'll find that they want to make dinner for you, or give you a gift, or pay you what money they can afford. Your employer will undoubtedly tell you that you can't accept anything from clients that smacks of payment for services, because that calls into question whether or not your office will structure its services around who pays and who doesn't. It doesn't mean you can't accept ***anything***, but you've got to be ***very*** careful. Some people make a rule of not accepting anything at all. As one public interest lawyer said, "I always make an excuse. If they want to make me dinner, I decline saying 'I have to be back at the office.' I don't want to offend them, but I want to keep it professional!"

On the flipside of that, there are some clients who won't be grateful at all, and you have to prepare yourself for that, as well. "Sometimes you'll get somebody their Social Security benefits, you turn to say 'congratulations,' and they're out the door. It happens," comments one public interest lawyer.

c. Fight the temptation to offer snap judgments.

Sometimes you'll have clients who've been mistreated, and you just ***know*** that what happened to them ***has*** to be illegal. As one public interest lawyer points out, "If you have a person who's been harassed by a collection agency, it's tempting to say, 'I'm sure that's not legal,' when it really is legal for the collection agency to say what they did." Instead, "Don't promise anything!" she adds. "Say something like, 'That sounds like a case we can take. We'll have to do more research.' You're thinking to yourself, 'Oh my God, I don't know a darn thing. I've got to prove that I do.' But you shouldn't. Don't make any commitments. You don't want an angry client!"

d. Don't judge your clients based on their living conditions.

One public interest lawyer points out that "Sometimes you have to go to the client's home. Maybe the bus isn't running and they can't come to you. You have to be prepared not to judge people based on their living conditions or how they treat their kids. Maybe the kitchen hasn't been cleaned in two years, maybe the kids are filthy dirty, and you're there to help them with a utility shut-off case. You have to keep your focus, 'I'm her lawyer,' and do what you can to help with the problem you're there to handle."

e. Handling the emotional aspects of the work. Have a support network ready!

There's no question that representing poor people is emotionally wrenching. The situations you'll see can be heartbreaking. As one public defender pointed out, "It's very intense. People's lives are involved. Even for a misdemeanor, they can go to jail for three weeks and lose their job." Even for civil cases, "They'll pull your heartstrings," says one Legal Aid lawyer.

Every public interest lawyer I talked to agreed that "You have to keep yourself at arm's length." While some said that "You can't do this work without some emotion—if you don't care you can't do it well," others said that "You can have emotion about the issue without getting wrapped up in the facts." One summed it up by saying, "You can't let it control your life." The temptation is to step in and start calling building inspectors, helping to get the house repaired, calling the employer to give the client time off, driving the kids to school. But you can't do it and maintain your sanity—and ability to help other clients. Instead, "You have to ***focus*** on the legal issue, because that's where you ***can*** help them," says Jill Barr. "Don't be unsympathetic, but focus on what you can ***do***. When the client tells a long story, you can say, 'I'm really sorry that happened to you, but we're here today to focus on X.'"

Remember that even if you can't help with non-legal issues, you can refer clients to people who ***can***. Jill Barr says that "It's important to get involved in the community to have a circle of referrals you can trust, like someone in the social security administration, or Low Income Housing Development organizations, or people on the boards of directors of developers and banks. Get to know local social workers." That way, when you talk with a client in a particularly harsh situation, you can "Acknowledge the difficulty of the situation, and say, 'That's not something we can help you with here—at the end of today I'll give you a couple of referrals.'"

EMOTIONALLY DRAINING MOVE . . .

Legal Aid lawyer, West Coast: "I had a client whose boyfriend had stolen her credit cards and used them. That was the issue.

But the rest of the story was heartbreaking. She and the boyfriend had been building a house together. They moved into it with her four kids before it was finished, living in one room while they worked on the rest of it. Once he maxed out her credit cards, he disappeared. She's stuck in this house that wasn't even finished—there wasn't a roof on some of the rooms! She was such a sweet woman and she was in such a fix, I stepped in and started helping her out. I cajoled local builders to help her, I helped with the kids, I ran interference with her employer. I finally went to my supervisor and said, 'I've gotten myself into this situation, and I don't know how to extract myself.' The fact was, the only issue I could really handle for her was the credit card problem. When I bailed out of everything else, I really let her down. In her eyes, I was her boyfriend all over again—I'd abandoned her. I learned an important lesson from that. You've got to **focus** on the legal issue. It's a matter of survival."

4. Handling sticky situations

a. Your client's case stinks. What do you do?

As a lawyer, you've got the obligation to act in the best interests of your client. But as Bill Barrett points out, "Sometimes what your professional discretion tells you is in your client's best interests isn't necessarily what the client ***wants*** you to do."

You don't want to blurt out, "What? Are you ***crazy***? You've got no case!" Instead, you need to stress to the client that their odds of prevailing are very slim, and/or make plain to them how much their desired course of action is going to cost them. Obviously, if they want you to do something unethical, you just can't. Whenever you rein in your client, be sure to ***write down*** the points your client and you both made, either in a "memo to file" or in a confirming e-mail or letter to the client. Paper the world! When you've got a client who disagrees with you, you've got a potential malpractice suit, and you need all your ducks in a row.

If your supervisor is the "point person" with the client whose case is a stink-er-oo, "Don't single-handedly destroy the relationship with that client," says Judy Mender. "For all you know, the client may be a great source of business, a family friend of the partner, whoever." You can always say to a client, "I want to do more research" to give yourself time to regroup and/or talk with others.

Finally, remember that it's important not to alienate a client no matter ***how*** terrible their case is. As Kentucky Public Defender Sarah Madden points out, "Maybe the case they're walking in with isn't any good—but maybe their next case ***will*** be. It doesn't do you any good to alienate them. Be gentle."

SMART HUMAN TRICK . . .

As reported in The New Yorker: A new lawyer is accused of insider trading. Authorities had videotaped her accepting marked hundred-dollar bills, twenty-three of which were later found in her apartment. When her lawyer sees the tape, he tells her: "There are two phases of a criminal case—the guilt-determining phase and the sentencing phase. I think we should focus on the sentencing phase."

SMART HUMAN TRICK . . .

New associate at a small firm. The president of a big client wants to sue his neighbor because of a noisy sprinkler. The sprinkler would go on at 6 a.m. and wake him up every day. A partner asks the associate to handle the case. The client barrages her with phone calls every day. He yanks her out of meetings constantly to rant about the case. He expects to win a huge settlement. Whenever she approaches her partner to talk about the case, he says, "Just handle it." She eventually goes to another partner in the firm in desperation, and the other partner says, "That guy is a personal friend of X's. He kisses his butt. So you have to, as well. Tell him that the odds of prevailing are slim, but otherwise, put up with it." After that, every time she gets a call from the client, she says, "Oh, it's good to talk to you . . . " and listens calmly as he goes on and on.

b. Your client's situation is emotionally heart-wrenching.

Some kinds of practice are exceptionally emotional. Domestic relations, for instance, can be draining. You might have a spouse violating a restraining order, pulling up to your client's house at three in the morning to empty the house of furniture. If your client needs you to handle that problem at three in the morning, then you've got to do it. But as Hofstra's Caroline Levy says, "Yes, you want to advocate. But you don't want to adopt your clients' problems as your own." Bill Barrett agrees, saying, "You have to remove yourself emotionally. It's easier said than done, but it's necessary."

If you don't keep the emotional aspect of your work under control, you'll have a hard time being a good advocate. As Caroline Levy says, "You need objectivity to represent your client. You want to be sensitive to problems, but don't adopt their anger at the other side. Clients do sometimes need hand-holding. But keep your emotions at bay. When they tell you a heart-wrenching story, you can say, 'This is not a great situation,' and then point out what you can do for the client, talk to him/her about what the other lawyer is like, what the judge is like."

c. You think your client is lying to you.

Sometimes you might have clients who lie. If you do criminal defense work, every criminal defense attorney I spoke with basically agreed with what one of them said: "Never trust your client. Always assume they're lying." Another commented, "I heard a criminal lawyer being interviewed on TV, and he said, 'My job is to liberate the innocent.' I thought, that's swell, but what do you do the other ninety percent of the time?" One lawyer talked about a client he represented who was accused of arson. The client swore to him, "I ***couldn't*** have done it. I was in jail that night." The lawyer checked into the alibi, and sure enough, the guy ***was*** in prison—the week before!

What do you do? Reread the Code of Ethics and ***memorize*** the sections on the kind of evidence you can put on. And whatever you do, "***Never*** ask your client whether they did it! It's a question whose answer you don't want. When you see attorneys who withdraw from representing criminal clients and you can't figure out why, I'll bet you dollars to doughnuts that the client blurted out, 'I did it. I didn't mean to, but . . . ' After that, you can't put on a case arguing that they're innocent," says one criminal defense lawyer.

Incidentally, if you want to spot liars in ***any*** context, their body language often gives them away. Here are the signs you want to watch for:

1. Their pupils dilate. Pupils enlarge due to emotional response or excitation.
2. Coughing or a cracking voice. A dry throat is the psychological response to being uncomfortable.
3. Speaking more quickly or slowly all of a sudden. If a person is trying to talk and form a lie at the same time, their speech will slow down. If they suddenly speak too quickly, they're likely blurting out a lie they've already formulated, and they're anxious to get it out.
4. Too much or too little eye contact. If someone stares you down, they're trying too hard to be sincere. Looking away is a classic indication of a feeling of guilt.
5. Answers that are vague and evasive. If a person is asked, "What were you doing Saturday afternoon?" and they respond "We were just hanging out," and to the follow-up question "Hanging out doing what?" there's a shrug and a "Just hanging out," they're likely uncomfortable with the line of questions.

d. Your client wants you to do something inadvisable.

If a client wants you to do something against your best judgment, Valparaiso's Gail Peshel recommends that you "Put things in writing, pros and cons. In the heat of the moment a client can be upset, but will cool down later and be more rational."

e. Your client is buggin' or pitching a fit.

You're in a service business, and sometimes the people you serve will be openly angry. How should you handle it?

A little bit of background spadework can save you a lot of trouble. As we talked about earlier in this chapter, you should always keep your clients' expectations reasonable and avoid making promises you can't keep. That can minimize client outbursts, because a common source of them is frustrated expectations.

But sometimes it's unavoidable. Somebody's going to call you and pitch a fit. How should you handle it?

1) Set your personal react-o-meter on "0."

You've ***got*** to keep your cool even if the client is irate. As Georgetown's Abbie Willard says, "No anger, fear, crying—keep your professional composure!" If you haven't worked in a service business before, this may be tough. ***Really*** tough, especially if they're spewing abuse directed at you or your firm. But what you have to remember is that nobody's yelling at you ***personally***. They're yelling at a person in your position who just ***happens*** to be you. Don't pour gas on the flame by screaming, "Oh, yeah! Your Mutha!" Take deep breaths and stay calm!

2) Don't interrupt.

Listen carefully and sympathetically to what the client is saying. Don't cut in until you understand why the client is irate. Gail Peshel advises that you "Look at the issue and not the emotion." Use words like "I hear that you're upset because . . . " and thank them for calling.

3) Take action depending on the nature of the client's distress.

Sometimes clients just have to vent. That's fine. You're a counselor. It happens. If you perceive that they need other kinds of help—like therapy—that's a referral you or your superior may want to make (if you're working on a case with a more senior person, discuss the referral with them first).

If the client's anger has something to do with the matter your firm is handling ***or*** something you or anyone in your firm did, take ***excellent*** notes of the conversation. When the client is done screaming, repeat back your understanding of the problem. If it's something you or your firm did, apologize. And apologizing means not adding the word "but . . . " "I'm sorry, but . . . " No! Just apologize and don't offer an excuse. When someone is angry they don't want to hear excuses. They'll resent it. Tell them that you will pursue it immediately and get back to them yourself. Don't make any promises about the resolution unless it's a matter that you know for a fact you or someone you work for can resolve. And don't agree that somebody else's actions were incorrect! You have no idea at this point what happened; all you know is that the client is upset and they're giving you their version of the facts. You don't want to validate something that may, in fact, be incorrect.

4) Talk to lawyers who have been around the block.

"Bring the problem to someone more senior than you who has worked on the matter and talk to them about how the problem should be handled," recommends a lawyer at Goulston Storrs. Abbie Willard recommends that you "***Never*** let a partner be surprised by an unhappy client! Let the partner know why the client is upset, and what, if anything, ***you*** can do about it."

5) Know when enough's enough.

While your prime directive is serving the client, you ***don't*** have to listen to someone berate you on and on and on. As lawyers at Goulston Storrs point out, "This ***is*** a service business, but that doesn't mean you have to fall on your sword. You don't have to take excessive verbal abuse from clients. As soon as you've got the point, you don't need to hear more.

Take the matter to someone more senior and ask them how to handle it."

B. Advice For Everybody Who Spends Time In Court, Whether You Represent The United States, "The People," The State, Or Clients

1. Handling judges. Get out your kid gloves!

a. Get to know judges' styles.

All judges are different! Ask other lawyers in the firm (or other prosecutors in the office) for their impression ***before*** you argue a case before a judge with whom you're not familiar. As Jones Vargas' Karl Nielson says, "Knowing the judge's likes and dislikes, his or her requirements, pet peeves, and the like, is so much more critical than you can imagine just coming out of law school. Knowing the judge will help you avoid the many pitfalls involved in learning the ropes of practice before the courts."

It may be that some judges require you to call and conference a case before you make a motion. Perhaps the judge insists that you use his middle name when you speak with him. One lawyer talked about a judge who always, in matrimonial cases, had a policy of interviewing the family and then taking the lawyers to lunch at his house to discuss the family. Whatever a judge wants to do in his or her court, that's the way it is! Adapt your style and strategy accordingly. It's like that line from *To Kill A Mockingbird* about guests: "If he wants to pour syrup on the tablecloth and eat it, he can."

It also makes sense to get friendly with court reporters. Because they see judges all the time, they can clue you in to the judge's mood and anything that seems to be impressing or riling him/her on any given day.

b. Handle judges with kid gloves!

Always treat judges with respect, no matter ***how*** you feel about them or how they treat you. What does that mean?

Always speak deferentially to them. Regardless of how you feel about them personally, they're judges, for chrissakes. Don't question their judgment, their intelligence, their perception—***nothing***. One lawyer told me about a case where the judge asked opposing counsel a question, and the guy responded, "Judge, I think you're a little off-focus." The lawyer laughs, "The court went dead quiet—and in that moment, he lost the case."

Be respectful of their time. As Hofstra's Caroline Levy recommends, "You're sometimes expected to be in three courtrooms at once to hear their calendars. If so, let them know where you'll be so they can find you." And if you're going to be late for court due to something out of your control, ***call*** both your judge and the adversary and let them know! People are more understanding than you think they'll be.

Finally, if a judge upsets you, don't let it show. Take deep breaths. Count to ten. Maintain a professional composure ***all*** the time. Blow off steam once you're out of the courthouse!

2. *Always* be civil and professional, no matter how much of a buttmunch you're dealing with.

One lawyer recommends that "You need to maintain the highest level of civility and professionalism because (1) no matter the arena, you're always an attorney in terms of your ethical and professional responsibilities, and (2) all you have in the end is your name and reputation, so keep both clean!" Golden Gate's Susanne Aronowitz adds, "Don't assume people are out to get you. Be collegial. Be accommodating, grant extensions in discovery, as long as they won't impact your case. You'll need favors down the road and won't get them if you're a jerk when ***other*** people need favors from you."

3. Remember *everybody* is a potential juror.

As Arkansas' Claudia Driver says, "You might want to shout an obscenity at that jerk forcing you onto the shoulder of the road, but next week you could be asking voir dire questions of that same person! For all you know, they were trying to remove the dog from the baby at 45 miles an hour in four lanes of traffic on a bad day when you decided to hurl colourful language at them. They'll have a very bad feeling about you. The odds are against you even more in a small town!" If you flip the bird at somebody when they beat you out for a parking space, you don't know where that person will pop up again. The watchword here? Be civil. It's good advice for ***everybody.*** If you spend time in the courtroom, it can save your bacon!

4. Act more confidently than you feel!

If you're new, being in a courtroom can make you feel the way Dorothy felt when she first approached the Wizard of Oz. ***Everybody*** feels the same way! That feeling is exacerbated by the fact that law school doesn't really leave you prepared for court. As a lawyer for the United Mine Workers of America points out, "Even with three grueling years of law school under your belt, you don't know how to be a lawyer yet, even if you've participated in clinical programs, competed in moot court competitions, and taken trial practice courses." Relax! As the old saying goes, "This too shall pass." Hofstra's Caroline Levy points out that "It can be tough and tiring, but pretty quickly you find that cases repeat themselves." Lawyers at the Federal Defender's Office in Chicago say, "You'll ***never*** know as much as you wish you did, but with time, it all gets easier and less nerve-wracking!"

In the meantime, ***fake*** it. ***Nobody*** knows how nervous you really are. If your voice is steady, you're prepared, and you speak with confidence while looking people in the eye, they'll never realize you're quaking on the inside. As Minnesota's Nora Klaphake says, "Remember confidence before competence! If you look professional, your clients and opposing counsel will treat you as competent, even if you don't feel that way. Never let them see you sweat!"

SMART HUMAN TRICK . . .

Litigator, small firm: "I arrived at my first court trial to find that the arresting officer who was my key witness had never testified in court before. Needless to say, I didn't tell him that I had never tried a case before! I acted as if I had done this a million times. He gained confidence from my attitude, I put him on the stand, and we won."

5. Be nice to court personnel.

Being a nice person is good advice in every aspect of your life. It's just a much happier life if you smile at people and they smile back to you. When it comes to dealing with court personnel, it's crucial to be pleasant. Because, let's face it—OK, you've got a law degree. Congratulations. But when you're dealing with court personnel, they may not have your education, but they've got a ***lot*** of power, and if you don't treat them with respect, you'll discover that in a ***hurry***. One litigator points out that "People at the courthouse won't do what you want them to do just because you're a lawyer. They can make your life a living hell."

If you're at the courthouse for the first time, don't be afraid to say to court personnel, "This is my first time here. Can you help me out?" As one lawyer points out, "If you're deferential to them, they'll help you. They help get your case through the system!" Another lawyer points out that "If you're at the courthouse frequently, you get a reputation fast. You don't get a second chance to make a first impression on court clerks, docket clerks, court reporters. You can get a lot of breaks from them if you're nice!" One litigator said that "I always make a point of being nice to folks at court. It really does pay you back. I got stuck in traffic, and I was racing to court because I wanted a motion heard the following week. I missed the deadline. I explained the traffic situation to the clerk, and she put it on the calendar for me anyway. She didn't ***have*** to. If you're nasty to clerks, things can easily go the other way. If you file your document on time, you find out that oops, it got dropped, and it didn't get filed until two days later and you missed your Statute of Limitations."

6. Preparation beats skill. Do your homework!

As Loyola's Pam Occhipinti points out, "Remember that when you go to court, preparation beats skill 90 out of 100 times. You can't get ***too*** confident. Be conscious of trying to give your best!" Cover ***all*** your bases.

As Jolley Urga's Brian Tanko says, "The quickest way to earn respect is reading the Rules of Civil Procedure."

You may not be the most experienced lawyer on the planet, but good preparation can make up for that. Lawyers at Wyatt Tarrant point out that "Preparation will put a new attorney on the same playing field as a seasoned attorney. Furthermore, it'll go a long way toward alleviating the butterflies you get appearing in court!" Being prepared also impresses judges. As one prosecutor comments, "If you're right on the law and the judge sees that you know what you're doing, they won't question you as much. It makes your life easier."

If you're conscious of being well-prepared, you'll think of contingencies that other people might overlook. One new litigator talked about preparing for court the way she'd prepped for interviews and final exams. "When I came to my firm, a partner gave me a case to handle and said, 'It's very unlikely you'll win this, but it's a good way for you to get experience.' I thought back on how I'd worked on preparing for interviews, trying to think of every question an interviewer could ask me. I thought about final exams, where I thought about every issue the professor could ask about. I really busted my butt to cover my bases. And we won!"

7. Be alert to times when it's best to shut up!

Many litigators pointed out to me that it's easy to get into court and have your common sense jump right out of your head. No matter how preoccupied you are with the points you want to make, be alert to what's going on. Remember your goal is to put on your best case, and sometimes that means shutting up. As Dickstein Shapiro's Paul Bran points out, "If a judge says to you, 'I'm inclined to rule in your favour. Do you want to add anything?' the answer is '***No***!' Don't mess it up!"

8. You'll stumble. It's your recovery that counts.

As Dickinson's Elaine Bourne points out, "Learn to laugh at yourself. You'll stumble over a question. It happens. The recovery is important." Maintain your composure and get over it!

I remember watching ESPN late one night. The announcer was giving an injury report on college football players. He's running down this list, and he gets to this one quarterback. He ***means*** to say that this guy had been unable to play because of a slipped disk in his neck. But instead of saying "disk," he leaves out the "s." He immediately realizes his mistake, and says, "That is to say, slipped ***disk***." You could hear the crew in the background just collapsing with laughter, and the look on the announcer's face suggested that he just wanted to explode. But he didn't. He calmly gave the rest of the injury report. I don't know ***how***, mind you, but he did it.

Similarly, when I dance in shows, it's very easy to make a mistake and grimace. My teacher, Jody Foster, always says, "Nobody in the audience knows you made a mistake. ***You're*** the only one who knows. But if you make a face, ***everybody*** will know something's wrong." He's absolutely right. And the same goes when you're in court. If you make a mistake, laugh briefly if it's funny, and then move on. People will take their cue from you. Nobody else will make a big deal out of it if you don't!

9. You can't control what you can't control. Remember that the law is unpredictable.

No matter how well you prepare, no matter how good your case is, sometimes you won't win. As Lisa Lesage says, "You never know how cases will come out." Juries, witnesses, and judges are unpredictable. As one prosecutor points out, "Some judges are pro state, some are pro defense, some are clueless. You just have to make your best case." So do your best, and remember the serenity prayer: have the serenity to accept the things you can't change.

Similarly, when you win, be gracious. Save your victory dance for later. As Bart Schorsch writes in *The Student Lawyer,* "In every single lawsuit, somebody eats it and somebody feeds it. If you are feeding it today, you might be eating it tomorrow. Be gracious in victory as well as defeat."

10. More tips for you if you're a prosecutor

If you're starting your career as a prosecutor, you're in a unique position. Unlike lawyers for law firms, you don't have to worry about billable hours or soliciting business. And unlike new associates at large firms, you don't have to do any writing. As one prosecutor points out, "In advocacy competitions in school, you have to do a brief. You don't have to memorialize anything in prosecutors' offices. Appellate teams do that. You don't have to do any long briefs the way you do in moot court." But there are other issues you face, like handling defense lawyers and victims, knowing how to charge a case. Let's see what you need to know . . .

a. Learn by observation!

When you become a prosecutor, be a sponge and soak up as much expertise as you can from your colleagues. Go to the courthouse before you even start work, if you have the chance, and watch your soon-to-be-colleagues presenting cases. See how they deal with the judge, with juries, with defendants. There's no better way to get your feet wet!

When you start work, you will get some training. You'll go to "baby prosecutor school," and you'll have seminars on different kinds of crimes and different elements of your job. And there are books you can turn to, including the "prosecutor's book," which gives you, among other things, elements of crimes. Also, depending on where you work, you have access to databases; for instance, U.S. Attorneys have their own database where they swap information. And when you start to work, they won't throw you to the wolves. As Assistant State's Attorney Rich Colangelo says, "They look over your shoulder. They want you to get your dispositions in line with everybody else in the office. They don't want you to be the 'weak link'—the one defense attorneys perceive as 'softer' than everybody else.'"

But the fact remains, much of what you learn is through observation. Rich Colangelo points out that "It's ***all*** about dealing with people. ***Watch***. See what a case is worth. Law school doesn't tell you the elements you need to prove. You don't come out knowing the possible disposition of cases. You only learn that by watching."

b. Ask *lots* of questions. You're not alone!

As one prosecutor says, "Never let yourself feel isolated. You don't know everything." Another prosecutor points out that since you don't have any billing pressure as a prosecutor, you've got more leeway to bat around questions with your colleagues. Rich Colangelo says that "You need to ask more experienced attorneys to understand many things you don't learn in school. For instance, in a drug case, you've got a guy with a prior conviction, he sells drugs to an undercover cop—what's it worth?" Keep in mind that when you ask questions, "Be sure to have a strategy in mind before you ask," he adds. "If you ask a prosecutor, 'I'm not too familiar with this. What would you do?' they're likely to say, 'Well, what do ***you*** think?' Don't be caught off-guard. They're testing you! Have a strategy ready."

c. Speak with confidence!

When you start out in ***any*** new job, you're unlikely to feel very confident. As you should in any other job—***fake*** it. Nobody sees how you feel. They only hear how you sound, see how you look. You'll develop ***real*** confidence soon enough, but in the meantime, don't let people see your nerves! As one prosecutor points out, "It gets a lot easier pretty quickly. But the first time you stand up in court, asking for even something as simple as a continuance is intimidating!"

Don't let your voice quaver. Speak calmly and firmly. Stand up straight. Look people in the eye. As Rich Colangelo says, "You're on center stage! You have to speak with confidence. You don't want to be the small fish. You don't want people to push you around." Another prosecutor points out that "If you feel anxious when you're in court, ***tell*** yourself 'I'm smart, I can think and talk my way out of anything.' Because you ***can***."

d. Keep up with new cases. It's easy! You've only got one subject: Criminal Law.

As is true for every other lawyer, you've got to keep up with developments in the law. In almost every prosecutor's office, when there are big new cases that come down, they'll be circulated around. You'll see them. As one prosecutor explains, "If something huge came out, like a change in the standard for probable cause, someone in the office will research it and present it to everybody else." On top of that, every state has a legal publication that outlines new cases. Rich Colangelo recommends that you "Scan that, and look for criminal cases pertaining to what you're doing. Flag the case. Search for issues. For instance, if you're handling sexual assault cases, you might find one that involves proving the risk of injury. Then keep a small notebook in which you cite the case and why it's important to you. It's a trick that I learned from my boss, and it creates a great reference tool."

e. **Be aware that in some very political offices, there can be a lot of pressure on you to win your cases.**

I didn't talk to any prosecutors who felt that they were under serious pressure to win, although some of them said that they'd heard from other prosecutors about that kind of pressure. No matter ***where*** you are, resolve to put on the best case you can, and ignore any other pressure. As one prosecutor points out, "Frankly, once a case makes it through the grand jury process, it's a pretty good case for the prosecution. There's no pressure to 'win at all costs,' but you know that you've got a good case." Another adds that "Trials are competitive, it's just the way they are. But you create your own pressure!"

f. **When you make arguments in a case, have a list of cases written up in advance to hand to the judge in support of your arguments.**

g. **Get familiar with the styles of different judges, and change your strategy accordingly.**

Before you argue a case before a judge, get with your colleagues to learn the judge's style. As one prosecutor explains it, "All judges are different. Some of them want to 'split the baby.' So you offer a longer sentence, knowing that the judge will knock it down to what you originally wanted. Other judges come up with their own left-field guess about what the penalty should be, and for those judges, you manipulate the charges with a mandatory sentence so that their discretion is removed. Sometimes you'll find judges who hate mandatory sentences, they hate having their hands tied. For them, you ***never*** talk about mandatory sentences; they don't want to hear it."

h. Don't overcharge the case just because the defendant is a real creep.

One prosecutor warns you against "overcharging the case. Maybe the guy is a scumbag, and maybe he should go away for thirty years even though the crime he committed was a five-year crime. Don't succumb to the temptation to overcharge it. You'll just piss off the jury—which is getting a few bucks a day, so they're ***already*** not very happy."

i. When you start out, remember that your DMV violator today might be in your jury pool tomorrow.

As one prosecutor explains it, "When you start out as a prosecutor, you handle small things, DMV-type work. You get two minutes per person. Some of them cop an attitude, and you're tempted to cop one right back. I did. Then one day I realized, 'Wait a minute. These people, they're just ***speeders***. They're just like my friends and me. Jurors come from the DMV docket.' So I dropped the attitude. It's possible to smile and still do the job. Treat people nicely, and they'll like you, even if you're technically on the other side."

j. Dealing with defense attorneys.

One prosecutor points out that "It's easy to develop an 'us' and 'them' mentality," but "You always have to remember: the defense attorney you hate today might represent your wife's divorce tomorrow. And if you're in a small town, you might have kids on the same soccer teams. Just deal with them professionally." Just as you do with judges, learn the different styles of defense attorneys. You'll see them over and over again. One prosecutor says that "Some defense attorney are trustworthy. If they tell you 'There's a problem with this case,' you believe them. Others, if they said, 'It's daylight outside,' you'd look anyway. You can't trust them. But you learn that, and you ask other prosecutors about local personalities. They develop reputations. We have one guy we call the drip. Working with him is like watching water drip onto a stone. Drip, drip, drip. He tries to wear you down. You're prepared for it, so it doesn't affect you. Others, they'll do a little dance, 'My guy's not a bad guy,' you've heard him say the same thing about his last fifty clients. So you can put it in perspective. You learn their tactics and you handle them accordingly."

Always be prepared when you deal with defense attorneys. Read the file! As one prosecutor points out, "Defense attorneys will challenge you. They won't even know what the person is charged with, but they'll challenge you, figuring you aren't familiar with the file. Know the potential penalty, the elements, be a step ahead! A lawyer will say to you, 'I'm representing Joe Gazatz. You can't prove the case.' You need to be able to say, 'Oh, really?'"

k. Dealing with witnesses.

One prosecutor advises that "When you deal with witnesses, be ***very*** businesslike. It's difficult, at best. You need to go over every detail they're going to say. Something can happen, you can have two witnesses three feet away from each other who see it, and they tell totally different stories—but they both believe they're telling the truth! People filter things so differently. What you have to do is to ask ***exactly*** the same question to every witness. Have the questions written down, and repeat them word for word to each witness. If you say to one, 'How fast was the car going when it hit the tree?' then that's what you've got to say to the other witness, as well. If you say, 'How fast was it going when it ***smashed into*** the tree?' you'll get a speed that's a lot faster, because of those words 'smashed into.' If you ask the same questions and the witnesses come up with different answers, and they're both saying the defendant didn't do it, you can say, "They couldn't both have seen it. They're telling two different stories.'"

l. Handling victims.

One prosecutor points out that "even though you really don't have clients when you're a prosecutor, victims are ***kind*** of your clients." Most prosecutors' offices have a "victim and witness coordinator" who tells the victim where the case stands, for instance, "We've submitted this and we're asking for a court date." In other offices, you have more contact with victims. When you do deal with them, be sure that you speak calmly and with deliberation, so that they perceive you're in control. One female prosecutor says that "Many women say 'mm-hmm' when people talk. You don't want to do that with victims or even witnesses, for that matter. It makes them think you're agreeing with them when what you're really saying is, 'I'm listening. Go on.' You want to get ***all*** the facts. Victims sometimes try to leave out relevant facts, worrying that if they tell you everything, there won't be a conviction." Be aware that if the case doesn't get resolved to their satisfaction, "Victims will complain, but you understand it. They need to vent," says one prosecutor.

Depending on the crime, dealing with witnesses can be a terribly gut-wrenching process. As one prosecutor says, "When you deal with victims of child abuse, you learn about things you shouldn't have to know. You learn how to distinguish a splash scald from an immersion scald, and the difference between a twisting fracture and a clean snap. You learn the telltale signs of abuse. You have an immersion scald, a twisting fracture—no kid gets those from an accident. You don't want to know this stuff. But if you believe in what you're doing, you can deal with it. Just focus on what you're doing: you're building a case."

m. Outside of work, remember your job!

One prosecutor laughingly said that "When you're out on the freeway, you're speeding, it's easy to think, 'Hey! I've got a free pass! I'm a prosecutor!' You have to fight that attitude! A prosecutor ***does*** represent the public. You want to represent the ***best*** of it." Another prosecutor added that "Whether you're a prosecutor or not, there are some nightclubs, you'd just be stupid to go there. You don't have to change your life outside of work just because of your job. But when you see people in a store, and you know that they were in on a speeding ticket last week, and they look at you and say, 'Hmm—where do I know you from?' don't take the bait. Tell them about something else in your life, 'Oh, maybe the YMCA,' or 'I teach at so-and-so college.'"

n. Lights! Camera! Handling the media.

As one prosecutor explains, "Some reporters are good, some aren't. When a case is pending, you can't say anything about it. Once you get into court, you need to know that everything you say in court is fair game. If you go into the facts on the record, you're giving them what they want to know. But if the reporter is a jerk, if you've had trouble with them before, you can just stipulate to the facts and reporters can't get anything. And don't buy that 'off the record' line. I've been burned a few times with that. If you don't want them to print it, don't say it."

11. More tips for you if you represent clients

a. Rely on other people in learning the ropes. You're *never* alone!

When you start out as a litigator, there's a ***lot*** to learn. As Susanne Aronowitz says, "You don't know how things get filed with the court. You don't know what pleadings look like. 'Meet and confer with opposing counsel'—what does that ***mean***? Clinics in school help, but if you didn't do that, maybe you won't know what local rules are on stapling documents for court. What's a proof of service? Which deadlines are 'hard' and which are 'soft'? How do you count time on deadlines? The Federal Rules of Civil Procedure aren't the only rules you need to know!" It can be overwhelming!

Make things easier on yourself by relying on others. Start with people in your own office, who are just as vested in your clients' success as you are. As Oregon's Jane Steckbeck says, "You'll be asked to do a bunch of things you've never done before. Maybe you haven't, but somebody else ***has***." One lawyer talked about how when he first started with his firm, his partner said, "You've got to do expert witness depositions in two days." He said, "I had ***never*** done it before and I had ***no idea*** where to start. I asked around the office. Another associate gave me a book called the *Depositions Handbook*, and there was a chapter in there on expert depositions. Thank God! The fact is, you can't be cowed. I had a colleague who had to take on a lot of responsibility fast, and she sat in her office, crying. She didn't want to do it. I know how she felt, but it's like the old saying, 'Feel the fear and do it anyway.' Turn to other people who have expertise that you ***don't*** have. They'll help you through!"

Other than your colleagues, there are ***lots*** of resources at your disposal. Lisa Lesage recommends that you go to the local bar association and find lawyers who handle the kind of cases you just got. She says, "Lawyers ***love*** to talk about themselves and what they know, and they love to give advice about cases! The magic words are, 'I've got this case. Can I take you out to lunch to learn about criminal law?' You'll be amazed. They'll tell you what to do, they'll send pleadings. People are really helpful."

Susanne Aronowitz suggests contacting your clinical professor at law school, or the alumni association, or any other professor who might be helpful. "Graduation isn't divorce! Stay in touch with your professors. Always come back to ask for things. You paid a lot of money for school. Stay in touch!"

b. Be nice to sheriffs.

I've told you before, be nice to everybody. It's as true for sheriffs as it is for anybody else. As one litigator suggests, "If you want summonses served on time, be nice to sheriffs! It doesn't matter if you like them or not. My boss was appalled. He said to me, 'But he's ***disgusting***! He has tobacco dripping from his chin, he calls you Sweetie. How can you be nice to him?' I said, 'That's as may be, but my summonses get delivered on time. It doesn't take ***anything*** to be nice to people.'"

c. When it comes to dealing with opposing counsel, be cordial—but guarded. Being an advocate doesn't mean being a jerk!

As St. Louis University's Wendy Werner says, "Understand when you're being an advocate and when you're being a jerk. You may get a much better deal for your client if you treat the other lawyer with courtesy and respect. You'll get a better outcome." What should you do?

1) Remember that you can accomplish more quietly than you can yelling.

   As Georgetown's Anna Davis says, "In deposition training, you learn that you can be really friendly but ask some really deadly questions." Perhaps you saw the deposition in the Microsoft case, where David Boies, by most estimations, took apart Bill Gates. He didn't do it with bluster. If you read anything about Boies—and you should, he's an amazing lawyer—he prepares better than anybody, working phenomenal hours. He patiently draws out responses from witnesses on cross-examination or in depositions, allowing them to paint themselves into their own corner. He is charming, polite and respectful. His opponents have only good things to say about him.

2) Remember that no matter how big a city you work in, the world really is small. You *need* a good reputation, because you'll always need professional courtesies.

   As Carlton Fields' Kevin Napper says, "Your reputation will precede you. If you're professional and your word is your bond, if you do what you say you're going to do or explain why you can't, you'll get professional courtesies. ***Everyone*** knows who's dishonest and a jerk and who practices close to the edge. They get treated accordingly." Another lawyer adds, "Some people are a pain in every case. They throw discovery at you. They're just jerks for the sake of being jerks. You just wait, knowing that sometime, you'll have an opportunity to get them back."

   When it comes to professional courtesies, remember that there are lots of rules that aren't engraved in stone. When you're involved in a case, for instance, there are many times when deadlines can be stretched with the consent of the opposition, where you can get more time for discovery or an adjournment if the other side agrees.

There will certainly be times when it's not in the best interest of your client to grant courtesies. If that's the case, ***explain*** to the opposing counsel why you can't do what they asked you to do. If you tell them why you can't comply, you won't look like a jerk.

If you're tough as nails and you ***don't*** grant those courtesies when you easily could, it'll come back to bite you—and your clients. Some time ***you'll*** be the one needing an extension, and if you have the reputation for not granting them yourself, nobody will give you the time of day. You'll find people filing motions against your client on the Wednesday before Thanksgiving, requiring that you respond within five days. That doesn't help ***anybody***. There are plenty of ways to serve your clients without being a turd!

3) Have respect for your opponent's position, no matter how hare-brained it seems.

   As lawyers at Morrison & Foerster suggest, "You need to understand and respect your opponent's position, no matter how hare-brained it seems at first. It makes resolution of the dispute more likely, and helps win the fight if one is necessary."

4) Keep in mind what your client's goal is. It might not be being the "winner."

   As a lawyer at Morrison & Foerster points out, "If you can get what you need, then you don't have to be declared the 'winner.'" It's very easy to lose sight of that when you're locking horns with opposing counsel.

   One matrimonial attorney told me this story: "I was representing a woman in a divorce case, and the husband and his lawyer were being real jerks. The guy had his own business, and he was clearly hiding assets somehow, although the wife didn't think he had much money. The wife had a very responsible full-time job. The husband's lawyer kept calling me, demanding a ten-thousand-dollar cash settlement for his client. This guy really pissed me off, and I really wanted to fight him. The wife was spitting mad, as well. What they were asking for clearly wasn't fair. I was preparing the wife for a trial. But then I took a step back, and thought, wait a minute: if we go to trial, the fees are going to be a lot more than ten thousand dollars. It's going to eat up her entire nest egg. One of the toughest conversations I ever had with her was to point out that if she ***didn't*** challenge the ten thousand dollars, if she just paid it, she was really going to win. She was going to get this ugly divorce behind her and come out with more money, to boot. Neither one of us was happy about it but it was clearly the right thing to do. So, fine, technically the husband 'won.' He got my client to pay up. But my client and I both knew who was really the winner. He and his lawyer were both idiots."

d. Consider taking an 'Acting for Lawyers' class.

Elaine Bourne says that "Taking an 'Acting for Lawyers' class gives you greater confidence when you go into court. You'll find courses like it taught through adult ed most everywhere. It's a fun class! You'll learn things like getting your point across with more than words, mock openings and closings. It's kind of like mock interviews for lawyers."

C. *Never* Air Your Dirty Laundry In The Media!

Quick! If you had to choose between your boss liking you, and a reporter you don't know and whom you'll never talk to again liking you, which would you choose? Hmm, let me guess. I don't know about you, but I think the idea of a paycheck is rather enticing. If you do, too, then ***never ever ever*** say anything unflattering about your employer to any reporter.

A *Wall Street Journal* article, detailing the grueling life of new associates at some law firms, included the following passage (I've changed the name of the firm and the associate named in the article):

> "For most young lawyers, working at a law firm is still a grind. Bart Simpson, a first-year associate at Onnest & Fortrue, says he recently spent a week looking through boxes of papers in a 'dark, dank, dirty warehouse in Vernon, California.' When he isn't sifting through dusty crates, he can usually be found in his office . . . where he typically works from 8 a.m. to 8 p.m. Weekends? Still working. Mr. Simpson says he clocks in from noon to 6 p.m. two or three Saturdays a month, although he adds that he believes his work is valued, and 'it could be a lot worse.'"

Now, I ask you—how are this guy's partners going to respond to ***this***? In the *Wall Street Journal?* Even though he did acquit himself a bit toward the end, for chrissakes, ***nobody's*** going to be happy to see ***this*** in the paper! Don't ***ever*** skewer your employer in print or on web sites. ***Ever***. The partner at one large firm said, "I read an interview in a paper with first year associates, 'Oh, how hard we worked to get here.' I'm looking at how much we pay them, and I'm thinking, 'I'm not feeling sorry for you.'" Texas Tech's Kay Fletcher adds, "If you complain to the media about your work, think about the effect it'll have on your clients. They'll be thinking, 'Thanks a lot! It's ***my*** work!'"

If you work for a law firm and a reporter calls you, refer them to the firm's marketing person or hiring partner or a senior attorney, depending on what they're calling about. If you do any interviews, keep everything positive. Miami's Karen Scully-Clemmons advises that you use the same "Bull Durham" speech that you use when partners ask how you're doing: "I'm just happy to be here, all I want is to help the team . . . ." Miami's Marcy Cox recommends that you "***never*** give quotes about salaries. Always refer them to somebody else in the firm."

It may be that you figure, 'it would be good for my employer to see this. Things around here have to change. Maybe publicity will do that.' That's a risky strategy, and here's why: the media isn't your friend. Even if you think you're the good guy, they're after a good story, even if that means making you look bad. ***Everybody*** who's ever been interviewed by the press (me included) has found themselves flattered by being fawned over by a reporter, only to have their words appear either twisted or out-of-context in print. Giving savvy interviews is a very precise art, and as a new lawyer, it's very hard to parse your words so surgically that what comes out is exactly what you wanted to say. Once the media genie is out of the bottle, there's no putting it back in. Your words are there, memorialized, for everyone—including your boss—to see.

Incidentally, as Georgetown's Abbie Willard recommends, "If you're not going to talk to the press, don't say 'No comment.' That's even worse than not saying anything. When you see 'no comment' in the newspaper, you think, 'Ah Hah. So it's ***true***.' Just don't say ***anything***. Refer them to somebody else. You're not a press contact—you're a lawyer."

CAREER LIMITING MOVE . . .

Lawyer at a large Midwestern firm. He's a specialist on franchise law. He's at the courthouse one day, and a reporter walks up to him, and says, "You do a lot of work with franchises. What about where gas stations have underground tanks that are leaking gasoline? Is the oil company they got the franchise from liable for those leaks?" The lawyer responds, "Yes, absolutely." He shows up on TV, in a report about a big oil company that happens to be represented by a partner at his own firm! As a fellow partner commented, "It hurt him **big** time."

CAREER LIMITING MOVE . . .

Junior associate at a large firm, goes to a local bar association meeting. A reporter is standing outside, and asking people, "Do you think paralegals should need to have paralegal certificates, or is a bachelor's degree enough?" The junior associate stops and offers his opinion, "A bachelor's degree by itself isn't enough. They're not qualified." The resulting article slams paralegals, and quotes the junior associate. It turns out that the managing partner's daughter is a paralegal at the firm—and she doesn't have a certificate. The firm's paralegals all have their daggers out for the junior associate, and the managing partner is none to happy with him, either.

CHAPTER SEVEN

When Your Boss Is A Judge: Handling Judicial Clerkships

If you are starting your legal career with a judicial clerkship, you've made an excellent move! Most lawyers who did the same thing look back on their clerkships as the happiest years of their professional lives. You'll have a phenomenal opportunity to get "behind the scenes" of the legal system. You'll have an amazing opportunity to make an impact through your judge's opinions. You'll ideally create a lifelong mentor in the person of your judge. And you'll come out at the other end with a credential that has a considerable amount of cachet. Bravo for you!

What we'll do in this chapter is to talk about what you need to know to handle your clerkship as well as you possibly can. My principal source for this chapter is the wonderful Debra Strauss, who is without question America's judicial clerkship maven. She has a new book coming out on judicial clerkships, called *Behind the Bench: a Guide to Judicial Clerkships*, and if you're going to be doing a clerkship (or you're thinking about looking for one!) I strongly urge you to read it. Debra not only conducts seminars around the country about judicial clerkships, but she's a former federal judicial clerk herself. If there's anything to know about judicial clerkships, she knows it! (I've included contact information for her in Appendix C at the back of this book.)

OK. Let's see what you need to know about being a judicial clerk.

A. THE JUDGE'S WORLD, AND HOW YOU FIT INTO IT.

Unless your judge is newly appointed, you're walking into a well-oiled machine. You need to be particularly mindful of a few things:

1. **You're likely to have a tremendous amount of influence over your judge's opinions.**

   As Debra Strauss says, "Your impact can be so great that it's downright scary or overwhelming." Former judicial clerk Jason Murray says "The thing I found most shocking about my clerkship was how much input clerks have. I always thought that judges sit and write grand opinions, based on summaries of cases from their clerks. That's not the way it is! The judge gives you parameters, and you write the first cut yourself. The judge might say, 'We'll affirm for these reasons and you just find the cases/law to support it.' The judge will mark it up, make it bleed, you revise it until (s)he's ready to sign off on it. Sometimes judges will just add a comma here and there and it's ready to go. Some judges write all of their opinions, but most are too busy for that. They only have time to edit, to offer guidance. It's their opinion, but you have a lot more input than you thought you would." Former judicial clerk Donna Gerson had the same experience. "My judge would sometimes just hand me a file and say, 'I'm denying summary judgement. You draft the opinion and I'll review it with you.' Other times, he would simply hand me a file and ask me to form my own decision that he'd review with me, and either agree or disagree. It was incredible."

2. **You're unlikely to get much by way of support.**

   As Debra Strauss points out, "You'll probably be typing up your own memos and opinions on the computer. You won't have much library help.

It probably won't be hard for you to get used to, because you're used to law school, not a large law firm where you've got a vast support staff!"

3. **Avoid the professional 'Scarlet Letter': "A" for "Arrogance."**

If you got a judicial clerkship in the first place, you probably have sterling paper credentials. And that's a wonderful thing. But as I've pointed out elsewhere in this book, park your ego at the door. It's particularly important in a judicial clerkship. While you don't have to be told to treat the judge with respect (well, at least I ***hope*** not), you've got to be just as careful with co-clerks and the judge's secretary. Former judicial clerk Stefan Tucker remembers that when he walked into his judge's chambers the first day of his clerkship, the judge said, "Meet my secretary. Mr. Tucker, Mrs. P has been here for twenty-five years. She will be here until I retire. If you ever disagree with her, she stays, and you go." Debra Strauss adds that, "Your judge's secretary is a great conduit between you and the judge, if you want to check with her about the judge's practices and preferences first rather than bother the judge with minor matters or if you're worried about looking foolish. She can also be a great ally if you ever want to lobby for some change in an age-old practice—although you never want to be the one trying to 'rock the boat'!"

4. **You work the hours your judge wants you to work.**

Maybe you'll work reasonable hours, but you can't count on that. There's a huge range of hours; even judicial clerks for the United States Supreme Court work different hours depending on the justice for whom they clerk. The bottom line is, you take what you get. If your judge wants you there late, you stay late. As Jason Murray says, "If your judge wants you in by seven a.m., that's when you show up. It's their game and their rules."

5. **Dress respectfully.**

It's easy to think that if you're working for a judge, you can let your appearance slip. After all, everything you're doing is behind the scenes—right? Not quite. Dress conservatively, at least until you get a firm idea that it's all right to dress more casually.

CAREER LIMITING MOVE . . .

Male law school graduate, about to start a judicial clerkship. He decides to get a 'Trainspotting' haircut, bleached blond with black roots. The first day he goes to work, he has lunch with a friend. "How did the judge like your haircut?" the friend asks. The clerk answers, glumly, "It wasn't such a hot idea. He sent me home and said I can't come back until I dye my hair."

B. THE LAW CLERK'S BIBLE—THE ONE BOOK YOU *HAVE* TO HAVE!

Debra Strauss strongly recommends that you pick up a copy of the *Chambers Handbook.* "It contains very accurate information and it's very condensed." However, she cautions that "The *Handbook* was published by West in 1994, and some of the rules in it might have changed by the time you enter your clerkship. Even if you use the *Handbook*, you should always check with your judge and the Clerk's Office of your court, which often publish local rules and practices. Most judges will also have some sort of written instructions for incoming law clerks, as well as special rules for attorneys for trials, conferences and other pretrial matters, and you need to be familiar with all of those, as well."

C. RESEARCH AND WRITING TIPS

1. It's time to brush the dust off of all those books you figured you'd put behind you—the Federal Rules of Civil Procedure, for instance.

Debra Strauss says that, "The *Chambers Handbook* includes a section on research and writing for judicial clerkships, and that's very useful." In addition to that, there are some key reference materials for law clerks:

a. The Federal Rules of Evidence,
b. The Federal Rules of Civil Procedure,

c. The Federal Rules Of Criminal Procedure,
d. The Federal Rules of Appellate Procedure,
e. The U.S. Bankruptcy Code,
f. State substantive law and procedural rules, and
g. The Blue Book (although judges don't follow it as religiously as do law students).

2. Remember, you *have* to draw a conclusion!

This isn't like law school. You don't get most of your points for spotting the issues. As Debra Strauss advises, "Be practical, concise, and reach a definite conclusion. Remember, these are real people with real factual disputes that need to be resolved on a case by case basis."

3. Deadlines count!

"Unlike in law school, deadlines are critically important to judges," says Debra Strauss. "You simply can't tell the litigants in court that you aren't ready or you need an extension. Remember, in some form, you are the judge, and you need to preserve the dignity of the Court."

4. Be ready to juggle multiple cases and think on your feet.

When you leave your clerkship and go into private practice, you'll have to juggle multiple projects. You get some experience doing that for a judge, in the sense that "You have to be prepared to juggle many cases and make a lot of on-the-spot decision making," advises Debra Strauss.

5. Take advantage of Lexis and Westlaw training—but don't count on being able to use a computer at work!

Debra Strauss recommends taking advantage of Lexis and Westlaw training classes for judicial clerks, if they're available to you, to learn how to research legal issues and check case and statutory citations. "As a caveat on computer research versus books—and I believe this is good advice for your general law practice as well—be sure you are comfortable using both forms of research. Some judges are old-timers and trust the books more; they may want you to run in to chambers during a trial, pull out a couple of pertinent cases, and run back into the courtroom to hand the books up to the judge on the bench. Believe me, I had dreams about the adrenalin rush from this for years after my own clerkship experiences! If your judge says 'Go back and find me cases on this issue' you've ***got*** to be comfortable with book research." Debra adds, "Apart from that, you might have a situation where one of the other sources is unavailable to you; if you're in a satellite courthouse, you either may not have Lexis/Westlaw access. Or your book library may be incomplete due to expense and space constraints. So you've got to be comfortable with both forms of research."

D. You've Got A Special Job—With Special Responsibilities.

Debra Strauss points out that "Most people are unaware that there is a special code of ethics for law clerks. It is presented in some detail in the *Chambers Handbook*. You should read it on your own and become familiar with it, but just so you know, it includes restrictions on political activity as well as strict guidelines regarding the confidentiality of cases." In terms of confidentiality, Debra cautions you to "Always be careful in elevators, hallways, and in your outside life as well—you never know who may be listening. A litigant, attorney, juror, witness, and even family members or friends of the parties involved may be sitting in the next booth or standing behind your back, out of view. The same is true of your conversations with the law clerks, judges, and staff of other chambers—remember not to divulge any confidential information about the practices of, or the cases in, your judge's chambers."

The bottom line is this. When you clerk for a judge, you're likely developing a mentor that you'll have for the rest of your life. Treat the judge—and the experience—with respect!

CHAPTER EIGHT

Dealing With Jerks, Screamers, And Other Dwellers Of The Nether Anatomy

Jerks. Idiots. Tyrants. You won't get all the way through your professional life without working for someone you don't see eye-to-eye with, any more than you got through school without having a teacher here and there that you couldn't stand. What do you do when you work for somebody who drives you ape-dung? That's what we'll be talking about in this chapter.

If there's only one thing you take away from this chapter, it's this: There's only one person whose behavior you can control, and it's you. That bit of wisdom comes from my favourite radio shrink, Dr. Joy Browne. And boy, it's really useful in any situation where you're dealing with someone who makes you want to scream. You can't do a single thing about anybody else's behavior. Whether they're rude or boorish or in any way unreasonable, you've got to focus on your reaction to that behavior. That's not to say that there aren't some measures you can take to try and make your working relationship more harmonious, but it ***does*** focus your attentions on the area where they can do the most good.

With that in mind, let's take a look at what we'll talk about here. We'll start out by talking about some things you have to keep in mind when you go to work, and the kind of people you'll work with. We'll talk about sizing people up. And we'll wind up discussing how you have to deal with people who make you nuts, both in the moment and thereafter. Let's get started!

A. Prepare Yourself For The "Real World Of Jerks."

I don't believe that the world is full of jerks and idiots. But there are certainly a few of them wandering around, and the larger an organization you work for, the more likely it is you'll work with one (or more) of them. I love the Dilbert comic strip, and the pointy-headed boss. In one of the strips, the boss is in a meeting with Dilbert, and in front of their colleagues, the boss responds to an idea of Dilbert's by sneering: "Whose shoe did you scrape this off of?"

In talking to lawyers all over the country for this book, I heard tons of stories about supervisors who are just unbelievable. At one firm, a partner called one of his associates from a plane, screaming into the phone, "Get my meal ***changed***!" At another firm, a partner in a fit of pique threw his office furniture through an upper-story window. At yet another firm, a female associate went to the ladies room, only to hear an irate voice in the hallway screaming: "Get out here! I need you ***right now***!" It was her supervisor. At one large firm, an associate was going away with his wife for a much-needed weekend in the country. At 5 p.m. on Friday afternoon, a partner known for pulling this same schmuck routine on every associate, tells this particular associate, "I have to speak on Monday about the impact of this new statute on the telecommunications industry. I'll need about sixty pages. Have it on my desk by Monday morning." The associate fumed, knowing that the partner wouldn't read it, he'd be drunk on the plane, and he'd wind up improvising. He also knew that the ***partner*** knew he was going away for the weekend, that the speaking engagement had been planned weeks before, and it was a false emergency just to pull his chain. So the associate wrote twenty pages Friday night, and then he wrote, "Improvise, motherf*****r," and after that wrote forty pages of random words over and over again. The partner never noticed.

Ideally you'll never work for any of these charm school graduates. But the fact is, you'll find people in ***any*** organization who are varying degrees of "hard to work for." As Boston University's Betsy Armour says, "You need to be a grown-up! Not everybody will be warm and fuzzy. There will be yellers and screamers." One of the most difficult things about being a new lawyer is that you're expected to bend, to be flexible. You should never tolerate behavior that is unethical, harassing or discriminatory. But when it comes to work styles—people who are yellers or screamers or hyper-critical or ***whatever***—you've got to expect it. It'll happen. We'll talk about how to deal with it, but realize that it's ***out there***. Here's what you have to realize about dealing with difficult supervisors:

1. **Don't rely on other people's views in forming your own opinion about your supervisor.**

   One partner advises, "You'll find people who are labeled as screamers or unpleasable or unreachable. Take those comments with a grain of salt. Make up your ***own*** mind." Remember that everybody filters the world through their own particular prism. Maybe the person somebody else finds prickly you find intellectually stimulating. Maybe there's something in the chemistry between them that isn't true for you. We all know people who rub us the wrong way but leave other people unmoved. Don't pick up other people's prejudices. As Golden Gate's Susanne Aronowitz says, "Don't be afraid of the partner with the loudest bark! That person may be the first one to recognize good work and stick by you. Just because they yell a lot doesn't make them mean-spirited." File what people say about other people, anticipate that you ***might*** find what they say is true, but don't tell yourself that you've got an accurate snapshot of ***anybody*** based on comments from other people.

2. **Their behavior isn't directed at you.**

   If someone's yelling "You idiot!" at you, it's hard to tell yourself that it's not personal! But the fact is, people's behavior has everything to do with their own background, what's going on in their own life, and very little to do with you. You'll find people who will disappoint you, make you angry, make you want to cry, but most of the time, they don't mean to—it's just the way they are. As lawyers at Wyatt Tarrant point out, "Don't take it personally if you don't get along with a partner! Realize that partners' personality flaws are basically their own problem. If a partner is an unreasonable tyrant, you won't be the first to discover it. The world is full of unreasonable tyrants, however, and a law firm is not exempt—partners and clients alike!"

So when somebody yells at you or treats you badly, don't immediately assume that there's something wrong with you. Their attitude likely has nothing whatsoever to do with you.

3. Recognize the personality flaws that make them the way they are.

If somebody is a jerk, take a step back and think about how awful it must be to go through life having people hate you and say nasty things about you behind your back. Instead of inspiring anger in you, they should really inspire pity because somebody who's a jerk is truly pathetic. And there's ***always*** something driving their jerk-ism. For instance, people who are hypercritical like to demean other people because it makes them feel superior. Well-adjusted people don't have to be critics or bullies. We'll talk in a minute about how to deal with certain personality types, but for now, just remember: it's a flaw of theirs that makes them intolerable. And that's kind of sad.

4. Recognize that being a good supervisor requires a unique blend of skills—which most people don't have.

Perhaps you've heard the old saying, "Never attribute to malice what can be explained by incompetence." Being a really good boss requires a magic blend of skill, personality, and knowledge that a lot of people don't possess. Giving clear instructions, providing excellent feedback, mentoring—that doesn't describe everybody in the Universe. Apart from anything else, lawyers aren't ***trained*** to be managers. You went to law school. You ***know*** that. Lawyers aren't trained to be managers any more than law school professors are trained to teach. (I am ***not*** going there!) So cut your boss a bit of slack. What you attribute to malevolence could at least in part be bad managing.

5. Rest assured that if somebody is truly a jerk, everybody in the office knows it.

You may feel as though the jerkiness of your boss is a secret, but it's not. Everybody in every organization knows who the jerks are. As one lawyer explained it, "I love my firm, but there are people here that I don't care for. Some people don't fit in but they have a big book of business. They're jerks, people have run-ins with them. On the hiring committee their reviews of their associates are totally ignored, because everybody knows that they're impossible. It's obvious that when they have a problem with associates, it's ***their*** problem, and not the associates'. But they're not going anywhere—not as long as they continue to harpoon big clients."

B. What You Can Do About Working For A Jerk, And Why "Yeah, Well, *You* Can Kiss My Ass" Is *Not* A Wise Strategy

What we'll go over in this section are coping mechanisms that will help you work for anybody you can't stand. We'll talk about what you should do "in the moment" (and what you should ***avoid*** doing), and what you can do in the longer term. And yes, we'll even talk about the possibility of quitting your job. Sometimes it comes to that. But let's talk about everything else you should do before you pull the ripcord on your job!

1. Ask yourself the $64,000 question: "Could it be *me*?"

When you work for somebody you can't stand, the most understandable thing in the world is to point the finger and say, "It's ***them***! It's ***them***!" And maybe it is. But the most vital step you can take, before you start offloading blame, is to look and see if there's ***any*** truth in what they say to you or about you, and see if there's anything in the way ***you*** behave or in ***your*** perceptions that contribute to the situation. The fact is, when people push your buttons, you need to remember that they're ***your*** buttons. ***Nobody*** else can make you feel stupid or guilty or incompetent. They can ***try***, but they require you as a co-conspirator to succeed. As Harvard's Mark Weber says, "Whenever you have an intense reaction to someone, you need to ask, 'What does it bring up in ***me***? Why am ***I*** reacting this way?'"

I'm not going to get Freudian on you—I don't care if you have dreams about hot dogs chasing donuts through tunnels—but I do want to point out what's going on when you interact with your boss. Simply put, your mind isn't a camera. It's a filter. It filters the world through the lens of your own experience. When you react to your boss, you're reacting to other authority figures in your life—that is, your parents. You come to your job with messages from your entire life. Some of those messages are positive, and some aren't. The first thing you need to be conscious of is that you ***had*** this "training" and you need to figure out how constructive or destructive that training was. Once you're aware of why you react the way you react to your boss, you can change everything.

I'll give you an example. I have a friend who grew up the youngest in a large family, with really critical older siblings. Every time she piped up with an observation or idea when she was a kid, she'd be laughed at. Now, at work, any criticism at all makes her ***crazy***, no matter how small it is. But it's not the person who's criticizing her that she's responding to. It's her family. Think about the things that make ***you*** nuts, and look at that baggage you bring to work to see if you're responding to something you brought in, not what's there. In every relationship you have for the rest of your life, you'll ***always*** be happier if you go through this exercise. At work, it can make an intolerable relationship with your boss ***so*** much easier to handle!

2. How to handle yourself "in the moment." Count to ten. Remain calm!

When someone's baggin' on you, the ***worst*** thing you can do is to respond in kind. As Hendrie Weisinger writes in *Emotional Intelligence At Work*, "If someone berates you, your gut will tell you to strike back, stoking the fire and making the person even ***more*** angry with you. Does that help you? No!" William & Mary's Rob Kaplan adds, "You won't win a battle with that person! Having to deal with jerks is why God invented Prozac."

You've ***got*** to restrain yourself. Imagine one of those zippers that Michael Keaton used to zip Geena Davis' lips closed in *Beetlejuice*. No matter how you feel, do ***not*** say what's on your mind. Bite your tongue.

Count to ten. If you're around other people when your supervisor tears you a new one, ***never*** show anything but respect for him/her, even though (s)he's clearly not acting in a way that deserves it. If you shout back, you'll lose the empathy of your colleagues even if they agree with you. If you take it like a (wo)man, they'll be on your side. Speak calmly. Take deep breaths. As soon as you can, go to the john and dab water on your face and wrists. Close your office door and cry. But never, ever, ever let them see you sweat.

SMART HUMAN TRICK . . .

Junior associate, large firm: "I worked for a partner who was just a maniac. I had heard before I worked for him that he once threw a stapler at one of his associates, and when it missed, he chased him down the hall. I was prepared for the worst. And I got it. I handed him an assignment, with a Post-It attached to it that said 'Please review.' He looked at the Post-It and proceeded to whale on me for half an hour. 'What the hell does this mean? Do I sign it? Or do I read it? Or do I cite check it? Huh?' Half an hour of that crap! I just swallowed hard, grimaced, and said, 'OK, I understand.' There was no way I was going to give this jerk the pleasure of seeing me squirm."

SMART HUMAN TRICK . . .

New associate at a large firm. After receiving a verbal lashing from a particularly hostile partner, he resists the urge to defend himself or fight back or even interrupt. Instead, after allowing this notoriously abusive man to rant and rave until he is red in the face, the young associate simply looks up casually from his desk and responds, "Duly noted." The partner is speechless. He turns and leaves. There's nothing else to say!

If you are alone with the person who's having a hissy fit, Minnesota's Susan Gainen recommends that you "Try the techniques that your parents used on you when ***you*** were having a tantrum. Either leave the room, saying 'I'll be back when you calm down,' or ask, 'Are you feeling all right?' or 'Can I get you a drink of water?'"

The bottom line is that in the moment you're being yelled at, you don't want to respond in kind. If it turns out that there's a pattern of behavior that marks your boss as a bully, we'll talk about how you deal with that. But when the tongue-lashing is going on, ***don't*** react.

3. Handling a jerk-y boss when the storm has passed

Nobody, no matter how much of a jerk, is a complete tool ***all*** the time. How do you handle a relationship of ***any*** length with a really difficult supervisor?

a. Don't hyperbolize the problem. You'll make it insoluble!

As Dr. Joy Browne says, "Don't hyperbolize situations. Don't tell yourself, 'He's the worst boss,' 'She's the biggest jerk,' 'This will ***never*** work.' When you do that, you turn problems into obstacles. Don't do it! You ***can*** solve problems." There's always a way to resolve a situation, whether it's with the person directly, recruiting other people's help, or making a change elsewhere in the office or even outside of it. But don't jump to step "Z" without couching the problem in your mind to make it as easy to handle as possible!

b. Address them directly. Don't badmouth them behind their back at work.

When you've got a problem with a superior, don't fall into the trap of lacing them up and down behind your superior's back—not at the office, anyway. (You can rant all you want to your family and friends ***outside*** of work.) Griping at the office will inevitably get back to them, and just fan the flames. Even if it doesn't, you don't know who's friends with whom. As Hofstra's Rebecca Katz-White points out, "You may think your boss is a jerk, but if you badmouth them behind their back, you have to assume that the person you can't stand is the best friend of the next person you'll work for." On top of that, when you talk to other people, you start applying labels. As soon as you've said "He's a jerk" or "She's an idiot," you won't move past those characterizations. Labeling effectively stops you from coming up with a solution to the problem.

Instead, give them a chance to solve the problem with you. It doesn't matter that you're not the cause of the problem; you've got more to gain by fixing it. You'll often find that just taking them on will elevate their respect for you! Sit down face to face, rid your voice of anger or criticism, and speak matter-of-factly. Don't raise your voice, even if the superior raises his/hers. Speak clearly about what's bothering you, and be specific—cite comments and behavior, and if you have proposals for what you'd like to see change, bring them up. Be sure to couch your comments respectfully; if possible, cite things you like about working for them as well as things you don't like (I realize it might take an effort!).

SMART HUMAN TRICK . . .

New lawyer at a government agency. His boss had been out of the office when he started. The first day the boss came back to the office, instead of introducing himself, he walked over to the new lawyer, and said, "What the hell has been going on here? Take care of this fax!" No introduction, no nothing. He was apparently angry about something that hadn't been done in his absence, and took it out on the new guy. The new lawyer took care of the fax, and went to his boss's office to tell him. He walked in and closed the door behind him, and said calmly, "I took care of this, as you requested. But we need to find a way to work together that treats me with respect." The lawyer reported, "After that, we became good friends. He was testing me, that's all."

SMART HUMAN TRICK . . .

New associate, large West Coast firm: "My supervisor was a real bastard. He made a point of giving me work every Friday afternoon at 5 o'clock. It wouldn't be a big project, and it wouldn't be time-sensitive, but he always wanted it done on Friday because he was always in the office first thing Saturday morning. And that would mean I'd have to stay every Friday until midnight. I got to the point I was just shaking with anger. Finally, I calmed myself down and went to his office and said, 'Would it be all right if I checked with you on Fridays at lunchtime to see if you have any work that needs to be completed before the end of the day? I'm staying until midnight on Fridays trying to complete your Friday assignments.' I was completely unprepared for his reaction. He was completely uncomprehending about what he was doing. I don't think it ever dawned on him what his Friday afternoon assignments were doing to me! He had no problem with the change. Telling him about it was all I had to do. I can't believe now that I almost quit my job over that."

SMART HUMAN TRICK . . .

New associate at a large firm. He's working with a tough corporate partner, and the partner keeps berating him, "You idiot! Don't you know anything?" It's getting to him. He sits down with the partner and says, "I know I'm disappointing you, but I need some guidance from you about what I can do better. I want to learn from you. But I can't do that if all you ever tell me is that I don't know anything." As the associate reports, "It turns out that this guy assumed I knew how corporate deals worked. I didn't know **anything** about it. Once I explained that to him, he explained it all to me. 'This is how you lay out papers, this is how the signatures work . . . .' It was great. It wasn't easy to face him down, but it made me realize he wasn't such a tough supervisor after all."

c. Admit straight out to your supervisor what your "buttons" are.

If your boss harshly criticizes you over something that's a particularly sore point with you, ***tell*** them about it. For instance, maybe you're painfully shy, but you really want to be a great litigator. It takes all of the confidence you can muster to stand up in court and speak, even if all you're doing is asking for a continuance. If your boss criticizes you about it, say, "I know you couldn't possibly know this, but I'm naturally a very shy person. I'm doing what I can to overcome it, and I'd really like your advice about speaking with more confidence. But when you criticize me without offering suggestions, it really makes me feel bad." As author Ronna Lichtenberg points out, "When somebody pushes your buttons, one of the best ways to go is to admit vulnerability. They can't push your buttons if you get there first."

d. Change your communication style to suit your boss.

It may be that you and your boss lock horns because you communicate differently. Modify what you do to make it easier on both of you! If they're terse and matter-of-fact and you like to talk things out, learn to get to the point more quickly so that you can be in and out of their office in a hurry. As Chicago's Suzanne Mitchell says, "You need to acknowledge different skills! People have different communication styles. It doesn't mean your boss hates you because (s)he communicates differently than you do!"

Maybe someone is sarcastic and rude in person, so you e-mail them to minimize your contact with them. One lawyer says that, "The first partner I worked for was totally lacking in tact and diplomacy. I ***hated*** working with him. Then somebody recommended to me, 'Don't ask him questions in person. Send him memos so that he can respond in writing 'yes' or 'no.'"

e. Look "past the drink." That is, see if you can find the valuable advisor behind the horrible façade.

One lawyer talked about having a difficult boss, saying that, "Even though this guy was really tough, I knew that he was really smart and I could learn a lot from him. He was just a loose cannon. I used to cringe when my phone would ring and I'd see that the call was coming from his extension. But I came to realize that what made him so prickly was the fact that he was so smart he was always seventeen steps ahead of everybody else, and it frustrated him. He lacked tact and diplomacy but he was always right. I told myself, 'You might not like the way he says it, but look past it to the substance of what he says.' I wound up learning a tremendous amount from him."

f. *Don't* avoid your boss just because you can't stand him/her.

It's human nature to avoid painful situations. But you're making a mistake if you avoid your boss just because (s)he's a jerk. As long as (s)he's your supervisor—and we'll talk in a minute about how to get out of ***that*** situation!—(s)he's got a considerable amount of control over you. As Georgetown's Marilyn Tucker says, "New associates often brag about their success in 'avoiding' partners with whom communication is difficult. While it's true that you need to work harder to communicate with attorneys who are shy or easily bothered, don't take the path of least resistance. Find a way to stay in constant touch." That's where e-mails and memos can be useful. If you don't like face-to-face contact with them, you don't have to do ***that***. But you have to do ***something***.

g. Find a quality that you like about the person you can't stand.

You might be thinking, "Find a quality I ***like***? About ***him***? I can't stand ***anything*** about him!" Aw, come on. There must be ***something***. I don't care if your supervisor is proud of her bowling or he's a great fly fisherman or she knows all about local judges. Compliment them about something that they're proud of, and ask for their help regarding that quality. If you're also a fisherman, ask about using a certain kind of lure. When you're working on a case, ask for advice about dealing with a particular judge. You get the point. Many times you can defang a man-eating lawyer by looking for a point of particular pride, and acknowledging it.

h. If the problem with your boss is that (s)he's a control freak, play into it.

If your boss wants to know every jot and tittle of what you do, then play it that way. This is just a matter of flexibility on your part.

It might drive you crazy, but copy your boss on everything, give him/her a complete log of your time on a daily basis—whatever it takes. If you do as I suggest in the "Getting Organized" section of "Getting Off On The Right Foot," you're papering the world anyway. It's not that big a deal to add another copy for your boss!

i. **Solicit other people's help in dealing with your boss—but do it *tactfully*!**

You can't just go to other people in the office and say, "How the hell am I supposed to put up with that jag-off?" As UCLA's Amy Berenson Mallow says, "Be tactful! Don't do anything to smear your own name. Be diplomatic. Your reputation is more on the line than theirs!" Instead, say to people, "Maybe it's just me, but I could really use some advice on working with . . . " or "I really want to do a good job for X. Could you help me out with some tips about giving him the kind of work he wants?" As I've mentioned before, if somebody is a pain in the butt, everybody in the office knows it. Ask other associates for advice about dealing with him or her. If you have a mentor, that's another good resource. And you might even consider asking the person's secretary for tips. As Harvard's Mark Weber says, "A difficult person's secretary can tell you if he's having a bad day, or the best time of day to contact him."

j. **If tact and diplomacy and tips you get from other people don't soften your supervisor's stance, (s)he's just a bully. If you're told, 'Just deal with it any way you can, (s)he's just a jerk,' then throw caution to the wind. *As long as (s)he's not in a position to fire you*, take him/her on. (S)he'll never respect you otherwise.**

Most people respond if you approach them tactfully. If you sit down and talk directly with them, behaving calmly and rationally, they'll typically stop treating you badly. But if they don't, what you're dealing with is a bully. They're pretty easy to spot. If you ask them for specific examples of what it is that they don't like about your work and they can't give you sensible answers, then what you're talking about is someone who intentionally crushes people and can't take personal responsibility for their problems. If you are silent to a bully, you'll only get bullied more. Bullies won't back down unless you stand up to them. And ***everybody*** agrees that even though you need to be flexible, you do ***not*** have to tolerate an abusive situation. And that's what bullies put you into.

What should you do? If the person in question is sufficiently powerful to fire you—it's a partner, for instance—then you should move on to talking to other people about being transferred to another supervisor or office. But if it's not—if it's a senior associate, for example, or you really like the work and don't want to make a move, and everybody has said, 'You've got to put up with it. Everybody knows he's a jerk. Do whatever you have to do'—then you should take action.

The next time the bully berates you, stand up to them. Stand up—literally. It's harder to intimidate a person who's standing up. Then calmly, slowly, and firmly, use "you" statements. "You need to show me respect when you speak with me . . . " "You need to calm down . . . " "You might get away with this with other people, but you won't with me . . . " "Your behavior is out of line." The "I" statements that you use with anyone other than a bully won't work. "I feel let down when you . . . " "I'm hurt when you . . . " That doesn't work. Bullies don't care about your feelings. That's what makes them bullies. If you use "you" statements, bullies back off.

Taking on a bully is a high-risk strategy. It may be your exit strategy. But if you otherwise like your job and don't want to leave, it may be the only thing you can do to restore some semblance of sanity in your work life!

k. If things don't get better, ask for a reassignment (if the organization is large enough) or consider quitting (if it's not). But don't make quitting the first option you try!

As the partner at one large firm points out, "With a firm like ours, we can reassign personalities. There's somebody to get along with everybody. There are different 'partner flavors.'" Furthermore, employers really don't want you to leave. They make a big investment in training you, and they'd rather know that you're miserable and want a change than to hear you say, "I'm handing in my resignation."

If you've gone through every possibility of working with your supervisor—you've checked your own baggage, you've tried talking to them directly, you've asked other people for advice—and nothing works, then there's no shame in requesting a transfer. People can't possibly look at ***you*** as the source of a personality problem if you've behaved professionally in trying to resolve the situation. But if all of your efforts have failed, then you're left with no choice. Don't let a bad relationship with a supervisor taint your work so badly that you feel compelled to leave.

If your employer is small and you don't have any other options, then you may have to quit if the relationship is bad enough. If your boss makes you miserable, you're probably not learning a lot from him or her. Get your ducks in a row, and follow the advice in the chapter called "Being Your Own Career Coach," so that you can move on to something that you really do enjoy!

CHAPTER NINE

Handling Things You Don't Want To Handle: Mistakes, Too Much Work, Chimp Work, Ethical Issues, and Sexual Harassment.

A. Mistakes! It's Not Whether You'll Make Them. (You Will.) It's What You Do *Next* That Counts.

The good news is that your career can recover from mistakes. There's no such thing as a fatal mistake. There ***are*** massive, spectacular failures of judgment that can tank your job with this particular employer, no doubt about that. If you avoid getting drunk you can forestall many of those. They did a study several years ago in Miami, showing that if you didn't deal drugs and you stayed out of bars you had virtually no chance of being murdered. Not getting drunk around your colleagues is a similarly good idea.

I'm not going to deal with massive vapour locks here. If you call an opposing party directly instead of their lawyer, or you make a pass at the managing partner's wife, or you grope your secretary, or you lose an irreplaceable file, or you blow a deadline and the Statute of Limitations runs out so your client can't file their claim, you're on your own. Grovel in mortification and beg for another chance, and check with your malpractice insurance carrier. What we'll deal with here are the work-oriented mistakes that I heard about more often:

screwing up facts, missing (non-fatal) deadlines, using out-of-date law for lack of shepardizing, serious typos, handing in court documents that are faulty. That kind of stuff. No matter how careful you are, ***sometime*** you'll make a mistake. And as we'll see, when it comes to mistakes, it's not so much what you ***do***—it's what you do ***afterwards***.

Here's what you need to know.

1. You blew it, and you know it. Take a deep breath.

As Arizona's Mary Birmingham says, "When you start your job, you want to please everyone, go faster, do better. But you'll make mistakes. ***Everybody*** does." Lawyers at Snell & Wilmer add that "You'll make mistakes, but you'll get over it!" That's hard to believe when ***you're*** the one on the hot seat. You look at your superiors and think, "***They*** never did something as stupid as this!" Sure they did. You just don't know about their mistakes. People don't go around bragging about them, you know.

When you make a mistake, you need to know this: Your worth as a lawyer and as a human being is not at stake over one miscalculation. And no matter how big it seems right now, this too shall pass. It seems like a big deal because it's you, and it's right now. Nobody focuses on you as much as you think they do. They've got their own thing goin' on. ***Especially*** if you pick up the pieces well, it will blow over before you know it.

2. "My Bad." Admit your mistake to the assigning attorney. Mistakes that aren't corrected have a name: Malpractice.

When you are working on something, you have the obligation to make it as perfect as you can. The moment it leaves your hands, you have the duty to the case, the client, and your employer to correct ***any*** mistake you made and lessen any potential ill effects. John Marshall's Bill Chamberlain recalls a piece of advice a senior associate gave him when he was practicing law: "'I can't do anything to fix it if I don't know it's broken.' Don't cover it up and expect it to go away. Don't hope that nobody will find out. Don't say to yourself, 'Oh, everybody makes mistakes. It's no big deal.' ***Tell*** them!" As a lawyer at Goulston Storrs says, "No matter how embarrassing and awkward it can be to admit to a mistake, especially to someone you're trying to impress, it's a thousand times worse to be caught in a mistake you've ignored or tried to cover up." Carlton Fields' Kevin Napper agrees. "It's not what you do, it's what you do next. The cover-up is worse than the crime." Dickinson's Elaine Bourne points out that "Even if the mistake is just transposing a couple of numbers, you've got to let the assigning attorney know about it. It's embarrassing, but a mistake ***always*** comes out."

Confessing to a mistake has the added benefit that "Next time you say 'I didn't do it,' they'll believe you," observes Georgetown's Anna Davis.

CAREER LIMITING MOVE . . .

Female associate at a large East Coast firm. She fails to file a notice of appeal on time. Senior partner at the firm comments, "Absent an act of Congress, this means that the right to appeal is waived. During a meeting with the client to explain why the failure to file the notice was not really so bad, the associate announces that it's time for aerobics and leaves the meeting. Bad news."

CAREER LIMITING MOVE . . .

Summer clerk at a New York firm. He turns in an assignment. The attorney checking it realizes that there is a serious error in the research. He says to the clerk, "There's an error here. It's critical." The clerk responds, "I knew I'd made a mistake, but I'd already turned it in." As the attorney comments, "It's not a school paper! It has ramifications!"

SMART HUMAN TRICK . . .

Junior associate at a small firm. "We do a lot of real estate work. I blew a description in a deed, and realized it the week after I drew up the deed. It was pretty small—I had the property line a foot and a half from where it was supposed to be. It was a pain to get it corrected, but if I'd waited more than sixty days to fix it, it would have been even worse. As it turns out, the people really weren't mad at all. They thanked me for changing it! A few months later, it came home to me how smart it was to make that change. It turns out that one of my colleagues had made a mistake in a description in a deed a couple of years before, and he figured, nobody will ever know, it's only ten inches off. We came to find out that the client had built a garage right on the edge of the property, and because of the mistake in the deed, the eave on the garage was hanging ten inches onto his neighbor's property! They wound up in court arguing over whether the guy had to take the garage down because of the overhanging eave. It was a **nightmare**."

a. **Be *careful* and *gentle* in confessing. If it's not a 'pants on fire' emergency, think of solutions *first.* If it *is* a 'pants on fire' emergency, confess *right now.***

Be careful as to how you go about breaking the news of your mistake. As Emory's Carolyn Bregman says, "Not everything is a 'pants on fire' emergency. Don't give your superiors a heart attack if you don't have to. Don't run in there saying 'Oh my God, I've made a bad mistake, I don't know what to do.' Instead, break it gently. Remember the old joke about the two brothers. One of them goes out of town, asks the other one to look after his cat. The vacationing brother calls home every day to check up on his cat. Four days into his vacation, he calls and asks, "How's my cat?" and the other brother responds, "It died." The vacationing brother is devastated, and berates the other brother. "Geez, it's bad enough my cat died! Why did you have to blurt it out like that? Couldn't you have broken it to me gently?" The other brother doesn't get it. "What do you mean?" The vacationing brother explains, "Well, when I called today, you could have said, 'The cat's up on the roof,' and then tomorrow when I call, you could have said, 'Everybody in the neighborhood is trying to get the cat to come down, but she won't move,' and then the third day you could say, 'The cat got scared and jumped off the roof. I took her to the vet and she's there now,' and the fourth day you could say, 'We did everything we could, but the cat died.' The other brother feels chastened and apologizes for being insensitive. They go on talking. The vacationing brother asks, "By the way—how's Mom?" The other brother pauses, and says, "She's up on the roof."

So before you make your supervisor's heart jump through the roof of his/her mouth, ***think*** about the urgency of the mistake. If you handed in a document with mistakes in it, and it's not imminently going to leave the office, Carlton Fields' Hardy Roberts advises you to "Talk to a mentor or another lawyer if you're not sure if it's a big deal or not." If it's typos and the document hasn't yet left the office, correct them and hand in a corrected document when you admit to the mistake. If you didn't shepardize (Bad! Bad! Bad!), and you cite a case for the proposition, say, that the movant bears the burden of proof on an issue, and after you turn in the memo you find that the case supporting that proposition was overruled by ***another*** case, check and see what the other case says. Maybe the law is still good. If the case was overruled on another issue, your rule is still valid. You were wrong not to say that in your memo, but by the same token, you don't need to run into the assigning attorney's office screaming "The sky is falling! The sky is falling!" Think about whether or not the document can be supplemented or replaced, and if so, supplement it or replace it. "If you alarm lawyers unnecessarily, they'll never trust you again," says Carolyn Bregman.

CAREER LIMITING MOVE (BUT NOT MUCH OF ONE) . . .

Female associate at a small firm. She sends a proposed order to a court to sign. She intends to write "public employee" on the order, but she accidentally leaves the "l" out of "public." The court sends it back, saying "We can't sign this." The associate reflects, "Fortunately, there wasn't much on the line. Everybody laughed!"

If the document on which you made a mistake is about to leave the office, you don't have time for corrective measures before you 'fess up. Just admit what you did, and immediately become part of the solution.

SMART HUMAN TRICK (BUT IT DOESN'T START OUT THAT WAY) . . .

Mid-level tax associate: "I wrote a memo and turned it in, and in the middle of the night, I woke up in a cold sweat, realizing that I hadn't checked the pocket part when I shepardized. I got up out of bed and left a message on my supervisor's voice mail at the office, saying, 'I didn't check the pocket part. Wait before you do anything with the memo.' I raced to the office first thing in the morning, checked, and sure enough, my case had been overruled. I got in early enough that I could change the memo and hand it to my supervisor when he walked in.

If the document has already left the office, Chicago Kent's Stephanie Rever Chu advises you to "Update your research, draft a letter to the client from the partner, blaming you for the mistake, and be there when the partner walks in!" One junior associate talked about a mistake he made within six months of starting a new job. He forgot to shepardize (does this sound like a recurring theme?), and the research he did went to a partner, who based a motion on that research—and filed it. When the junior associate realized what had happened, he was mortified. He rewrote the motion and filing papers. Then he wrote a letter to the client on the partner's behalf, assigning himself full responsibility for the mistake. And he was standing in the partner's office when he arrived. The associate says, "Those minutes standing in his office were the longest minutes of my life. Fortunately, the partner was so impressed with the way I'd handled it that he wasn't too upset. But if I hadn't done what I did—it could have been ***awful.***"

b. Don't blame anybody else, even if someone else contributed to the mistake. Take personal responsibility for your mistakes. Your reputation as a stand-up person is on the line!

Admitting to a mistake means taking ***personal responsibility*** for it. As Pepperdine's Carol Allemeier advises, "Don't try to make excuses. Just apologize and try to fix it. Especially with somebody who tends to be a screamer in the first place, the more you try to 'explain,' the more gas you're throwing on their fire. When my husband was at West Point, first year cadets were only allowed to answer an upper classperson with 'Yes, Sir,' 'No, Sir,' or 'No excuse, Sir.' It's surprising how much discipline it takes to do that. We all want to explain!"

Ronna Lichtenberg writes in *Work Would Be Great If It Weren't For The People*, "When you've done something wrong, groveling in mortification is the only proper response. Making excuses for your errors is unseemly, pathetic, and makes the offended party even angrier. Take the blame; it's the only attractive response."

Don't blame the assigning attorney because they didn't give you the complete facts. And don't blame your secretary. As Denver's Jennifer Loud Ungar says, "Even if it's your secretary's fault, it is common professionalism among lawyers to take the heat for their secretary. This means you have to allow extra time to review something you gave your secretary before it's due! You can't assume their work will be perfect every time. They make mistakes, too!"

c. Show that you rue the mistake.

No, screaming and crying and threatening to kill yourself is not what I'm talking about. But if you say things like "I'm horrified that I made this mistake" or "I apologize for putting you in this position" or "I'm sorry I let you down," those are positives. They show that you take your work seriously. As Baker Botts' Bart Showalter says, "Ruefulness is a great attribute. It shows personal responsibility. Everybody screws up sometime, everybody misses a deadline. The difference between those who make it and those who don't is the way they react afterwards, taking responsibility and helping to cure the problem."

3. **Don't broadcast your mistake to colleagues. Keep it low-key.**

As Hardy Roberts advises, "When you screw up, don't broadcast it. Tell who you have to, fix it, and move on with your life. Things grow on the grapevine, and you don't want that. 'So-and-so forgot affirmative defenses,' turns into 'We lost the case.'"

4. **Look at how you can avoid making the same mistake again.**

Nobody really cares about it if you make one, correctable mistake. The senior partner at one law firm said, "The only way you don't make mistakes is if you're not working. However, if you make the ***same*** mistakes again, you won't be working here." Lawyers at Proskauer Rose agree, saying "A junior associate's career won't be measured on one error, minor or major. You measure careers over time. Continued sloppiness is never good." The only way to avoid making the same mistakes over and over again is to take a look at the situation and see what you did wrong. If you didn't shepardize or proofread, that's easy enough to fix. If you got sloppy drunk at a party and said inappropriate things, you'll be ordering seltzer from now on. As Hendrie Weisinger writes in *Emotional Intelligence At Work*, "Don't focus on the problem. Focus on solving the situation that ***caused*** the problem. If you lost a file, the lost file isn't the problem. Your disorganization ***is***."

5. **Forget about it!**

As Gunster Yoakley's Kelly Toole says, "With a mistake, report it, fix it, move on and forget it." Georgetown's Marilyn Tucker agrees. "Don't lose time ruminating over mistakes! It's part of growing. Make the necessary corrections, learn from the mistake and then put it to rest. Don't flagellate yourself over and over again."

Golden Gate's Susanne Aronowitz adds that "Afterwards, never talk or joke about mistakes you've made. Don't remind people that you made the mistake!" If you don't bring it to people's attention, they'll forget about it. And that's exactly what you want them to do!

B. Handling Chimp Work Without Going Bananas!

If you come out of school expecting that you'll always work on the kinds of cases you studied in school, you're setting yourself up for some major disappointment. Unless you break out on your own and stumble onto the next *Miranda*, or you go to a firm that happens to harpoon a big one and you're positioned to do a big piece of it, you're not going to be working on big cutting-edge landmark cases as a new lawyer. And at prosecutor's offices, it's not the new guy who gets the biggest cases—you get your feet wet on smaller stuff first.

When you start your job, your chimp work factor depends on where you go and what you do. If you're in public interest or a prosecutor's office, there's just no such thing as chimp work. If you're at a law firm, as a general rule, the bigger the firm, the more chimp work you'll face (although every new lawyer has to handle some drudgework. At a small firm, you'll spend more time doing tasks that are delegated to support staffers at large firms). Even at large firms, the amount of chimp work dropped in your lap depends on how thickly staffed your specialty is, how many staff attorneys and paralegals your firm has, and ***what*** your specialty is. If you start your career in antitrust or mass torts or complex litigation . . . pass me a banana.

If you're faced with the prospect of substantial chimp work, here's what you need to know:

1. "Why me, Lord?" Understand why you're getting it.

Every practicing lawyer has war stories about the chimp work they had to do when ***they*** were starting out. The partner at one large firm laughs when he talks about his first six months at his firm: "I started on a big antitrust case, traveling around the country looking for documents that might be responsive to a civil demand letter regarding price fixing. I had little sticky notes, and I'd write, 'This may impact Item #4 on their list.' I spent six months doing that and only that—putting little stickies on documents." A lawyer at another firm talked about a room at his firm called the 'Insurance Box' room. "It doesn't have any windows. It's full of box after box of insurance class action documents. They rotate people in and out of it because it drives people insane." An associate at a small real estate firm said "When I started out, if I spent one more day at town hall combing through land records I thought I was going to shoot somebody." A prosecutor reports that "I started out doing hundreds and hundreds of DMV cases. I must have heard every excuse there was for 'why I was speeding.' I thought I'd go crazy."

If chimp work sounds like it bites—it does. Nobody denies it. But whether you call it "paying your dues" or "hazing" or "a rite of passage," it's ***there***. And it's important to understand ***why*** it's there. Lawyers offer a few explanations:

a. It's gotta be done by ***somebody***, and if it requires an attorney, a senior partner or prosecutor sure isn't going to do it. Some lawyers put it much more elegantly: "A watch needs every gear to work." The fact is, "If there was a more efficient way to do it, we would do ***that***," says one senior lawyer. "We've all done it ourselves."

b. If you're going to be a supervising attorney at some point, "Then you have to understand the nuts and bolts of everything your office does," says one lawyer.

c. Sometimes it's the nature of the work. Big clients plus big matters equals chimp work. While every large firm has sexy projects as well, the big clients that pay the big bucks entail some menial work. And if you want the big paycheck, you've got to respect the source of the green.

CAREER LIMITING MOVE . . .

New associate at a large firm. He's particularly interested in small clients because he wants lots of client contact (a reasonable goal!). A partner asks him to help out on a project for a big, new institutional client. The associate responds, "I don't want to do it. I only want to work with small clients." The partner responds, "Listen. I'm not crazy about it either, but we all have to do what's in the best interest of the firm. This client will pay big bills. You'll get some work on small clients as well. But you need to do the blocking and tackling work. We're **all** cogs in wheels."

[This is Kimm talking. There are right ways and wrong ways to seek out great work. I talk about the right ways to do it in the chapter "Being Your Own Career Coach."]

d. Look at it from the client's perspective. As St. Louis University's Wendy Werner points out, "If you were up for a capital offense, would you want a lawyer six months out of school handling your appeal? Or defending a multi-million dollar med-mal case?" "You ***need*** to work your way up so you earn respect from colleagues ***and*** clients," says Loyola's Pam Occhipinti.

e. It's in the nature of being new at ***anything***. A lawyer at one firm points out, "The practice of law at first is 10% pure exhilaration, 10% depression, and 80% tedium. As you progress, the tedium ratio lessens significantly."

So—chimp work is there. That's the way it is. How do you deal with it—and minimize it? Let's talk about that now.

2. The attitude that'll stick you with crappy work *forever*. It's an easy trap to fall into!

I'm not suggesting that you should be ***happy*** about doing menial work. You don't need to view it the way the Omega pledges viewed the spanking ritual in *Animal House*—"Please Sir, can I have another?" But the fact is a lot of new lawyers have the wrong idea about how to get out of chimp work. As Emory's Carolyn Bregman says, "It's easy to fall into the trap of thinking, 'If I show happiness doing this, it's all I'll get.'" No! Instead, if you show that you handle menial stuff well, you're more likely to get better work (as long as you do what I suggest in #3, below). As Carlton Fields' Elizabeth Zabak says, "When partners see that you are positive and hard-working on every assignment, they'll want to work with you on more responsible matters." Florida State's Stephanie Redfearn agrees, saying, "If you do menial tasks with panache, that makes attorneys want to assign you more responsibility. They'll think, 'If he did this well, he can handle ***more*** responsibility.'"

So what attitude ***should*** you have? Acknowledge to yourself and everyone else that you know menial work is part of your job. Get out of it what you can. Learn what you can. As one lawyer said, "If you're in a warehouse for a few months on document production, look at it as learning all aspects of a case. 'I can recognize attorney/client privileged documents at fifty paces!'" If you have to file documents at the courthouse, make friends at court. It'll help you when you have to argue cases. View those DMV defendants as potential jurors. If nothing else, menial work—document reviews, proofreading, copying, insignificant cases—it all makes you appreciate everything else you'll do in future even ***more***. As Yankees' manager Joe Torre says, "Nothing is good or bad except by comparison."

3. Getting the chimp work phase of your career behind you—*fast.*

You may have to put up with chimp work, but if you do the right things you won't have to put up with it for ***long***. Basically, what you want to do is "Actively seek out additional projects without badmouthing what you're doing now," says Minnesota's Sue Gainen. For instance, Vermont's Pavel Wonsowicz suggests that you "Help partners with articles that they're writing for professional journals. They ***all*** want to publish. It makes them look good to people higher up on the food chain ***and*** it sometimes brings in clients. If you help out a partner with an article, they'll say, 'I really owe that kid. He helped me out with that boring article.'"

Cardozo's Judy Mender suggests that you "Actively seek out more challenging projects. It may lead to you being stretched fairly thin—at least temporarily—but in time, if you make yourself invaluable on more important projects, your employer will probably not want to waste you on smaller things." Pavel Wonsowicz agrees, saying, "Excel on any meaty issues you get. Eat time if you have to. They'll perceive that you're ready for the 'next step.' That's more important than paying dues!"

Carlton Fields' Eric Adams suggests that you "Let superiors know CLE's you want to take, articles you want to write." In addition, he advises you to "Sit down and talk with partners about cases you find interesting, just because you're interested! You might find yourself working for that partner."

Another way to avoid a ton of scut work is to declare an interest, if you're at a large firm and you're unassigned. As one mid-level associate pointed out, "If you don't declare an interest, you'll get drudge work. If you say 'I really want corporate,' they'll cut you in on deals right away. If you decide that you hate it, you can tactfully seek out projects from another department that interests you. You've got to be careful about stating a lack of affection with anything you're doing, but there's ***always*** a way to make a change."

If you've got a mentor at work, chimp work is a good problem to discuss with them. Sit down with them and ask about goals you should set, strategies you should implement, to move your career ahead.

What happens if nothing works? As one partner said, "Some firms will rotate you out of big document reviews, give everyone a share of the load. But don't count on ***that***. Clients don't want to spend money on start-up costs, transition costs—firms have to eat it. And some of them won't." And sometimes you get mired in a certain kind of role no matter how hard you struggle out of it. Although lawyers disagree about when to pull the ripcord—I heard anywhere from nine months to a year and a half—they agree that at some point, you've got to vote with your feet, and quit. A partner at one large firm said bluntly, "If I were stuck coding documents for eighteen months, I'd quit. If you want to move ahead you need to get experiences you can build on to different levels. You can't get bogged down. Getting good work in your first couple of years is critical." A partner at another large firm agrees, adding, "Some lawyers get stuck for three to four years on one case with one client, and it's still in the discovery phase. That's ***very*** dangerous. There's a lot you're not learning. You're not in the courtroom, you're not conducting depositions, you're not drafting briefs or memos or motions. After a while you can't be put off any more. If you've communicated you want something else and they keep telling you 'hang in there,' after a while, you've got to leave. You aren't helping your career."

C. HELP! I'M DROWNING! WHAT TO DO WHEN YOU'VE GOT TOO MUCH WORK (OR TOO LITTLE . . .)

1. Why does overload happen? It's usually a compliment!

It's important to avoid assuming that they're out to get you if they're loading you down with work! The "too-much-work" syndrome has several sources.

a. If your work product is perceived as great, they'll ladle on more.

As American's Matt Pascocello explains, "If you are cursed with the ability to work well and hard, that's like waving a red cape in front of a bull. They'll charge forward and give you more. Anyone who does well and keeps saying 'Yes' to more work is a person partners will keep going back to." The solution isn't to tank your work quality or snap 'no' at new projects (we'll discuss what you ***should*** do in a minute). But the fact is, being overloaded tells you that superiors ***want*** to work with you, and that's a compliment!

b. It's an occupational hazard. Everybody belongs to the circus. Everybody has to juggle.

In this one respect, work is something like law school. In school, you don't take one class at a time and concentrate on it exclusively (instead, as a third year, you take five classes, blow them all off and go to Happy Hour). At work, whether you're a public interest lawyer or a private lawyer, you'll have lots of plates in the air, and, as Georgetown's Marilyn Tucker points out, it can be ***very*** frustrating. "It's important to accept the fact that you'll always have a lot of work to do, and be comfortable with that feeling," say lawyers at Goulston Storrs. "Just as you learn substantive legal skills, developing the ability to juggle a large volume of work is part of your professional development. It ***does*** get easier!"

c. You're not the focus of your superiors' world. They often honestly don't know how much work you have on your plate.

It's true that some law firms, corporations and government employers have people who control the flow of assignments to new lawyers. Even in those situations, lawyers will often skirt the system and assign work to new lawyers, particularly ones they like. No matter whether your employer has a formal assignment system or not, remember that "Senior lawyers usually don't know what others have given you," says UCLA's Amy Berenson Mallow. "They don't know what the demands of your other projects are," adds a lawyer at Goulston Storrs. Your superiors are typically very busy and won't know without hearing it from you that you're overloaded. So don't feel incompetent because you're loaded to the gills when new work is offered to you. It's often a misunderstanding about exactly how much work you already have on your plate!

d. Senior attorneys often forget how long it takes to complete projects when you're at the front end of the learning curve.

Sometimes it's been a while—occasionally a ***long*** while—since the people who give you work were beginners themselves. As lawyers at Goulston Storrs point out, "In most cases, it takes new associates ***much*** longer to complete a project than a more senior lawyer would require." If an assigner isn't thinking about it, they won't remember that what would take them one hour will take ***you*** four. That quickly leads to overloads.

e. If you're making huge green, it'll come out in the workload.

To put it bluntly, if they pay you more, they'll work you harder. The more money you make the more of an overload you need to expect. You ***still*** shouldn't kill yourself, and you ***still*** need to turn down work when you're truly overloaded (and we'll talk about how to do that in just a minute). But as the senior partner at one firm bluntly points out, "With these salaries, all I want to hear when I assign work to a new associate is overjoyed gratefulness." Turning down work when you're hauling in megabucks is a true exercise in diplomacy. But as a baseline, you've got to expect to be busier if you're making lots o' dough as a newcomer.

2. Don't kill yourself! A dead associate is not a source of revenue . . . and other reasons to avoid taking on too much work.

When you're new, you ***want*** to be seen as super-competent, and you figure if they're giving you work, they must think you have time for it. As I've already explained, that's not true. And it's also dangerous. Here's why:

a. You get evaluated on the basis of the work you complete, not what you *don't* do.

Taking on more work than you can handle and screwing it up as a result will trash your reputation. ***Everybody*** agrees on this. Florida State's Stephanie Redfearn says, "The ***most*** important thing is being able to turn in quality work!" Lawyers at Sidley & Austin point out that "It's better to have one great review and one slightly disappointed lawyer who ***doesn't*** fill out a review form than to have two bad reviews." Lawyers at Winston & Strawn add that "No one will ever remember that you said you were too busy to take on a new assignment . . . they'll always remember that you said you could take it on and then were too busy to do a good job." And Georgetown's Marilyn Tucker points out that "Written work lives on!"

We'll talk in a minute about how to say "no" without torquing anybody off. The point here is: Don't take on more than you can handle. Your enthusiasm won't compensate for half-assed work.

b. Missed deadlines will make you look bad.

When you've got too much to do, something's got to give. If it's not quality, it's timeliness. It's easy to think, "I'll hand it in a little late. At least I'm getting it done." When I talked about deadlines in the "How To Crush Research And Writing Assignments" chapter, I talked about the importance of making deadlines (and warning ***ahead*** of time if you think you can't). Often there are "outside" time pressures, from clients and courts, that make deadlines real. If you take on too much and can't finish in time, as lawyers at Stites & Harbison point out, "While you may be trying to make a good impression, it's detrimental to your reputation if you can't deliver work product in a timely manner."

c. **Nobody's interested in the quality of your life as much as *you* are.**

As Matt Pascocello points out, "They expect ***you*** to respect your time, your life, your balance!" You're ultimately the one who benefits the most if you keep your workload sane.

3. **How to avoid getting overloaded—*before* you get the assignment that breaks the camel's back!**

Before you get too much work in the first place, there are a few things you can do to stave off an overload. They include:

a. **Give your supervisor a weekly memo outlining what you're doing.**

If you keep your supervisor informed of your workload, you'll go a long way to preventing a deluge. Even without your saying a word, your supervisor can pass along to others at the office the fact that you've got all you can handle right now. That way, you can avoid being in the awkward position of having to turn down work.

b. **Keep an updated list of everything you're working on.**

Make a point of having an updated list, ***every day***, of the projects you're working on, who they're for, and when they're due (also include a ***realistic*** time estimate, if you have one). Not only does it help ***you*** if you can visualize what you've got to do, but if an attorney stops by your office (or calls you to theirs) to give you an assignment, you can say, "I'd love to do it. Here's what I'm working on now"—and hand over your list. "Can you tell me how to prioritize your work?" If you're loaded down, you're showing them rather than telling them! Lawyers prefer to draw their own conclusions. You'll avoid overloads without having to say "No" to work.

c. **Get organized!**

I talk in the "Getting Off On The Right Foot" chapter about how to get organized. Once you ***are*** organized, you'll find you can get stuff done more quickly because you waste less time hunting around for what you need. It'll help you avoid being overloaded, because you'll be able to get more done in less time.

d. Find out who the six-hundred pound gorillas are: Lawyers whose work you can't turn down.

In a minute, I'll talk about how to turn down work artfully. But at ***every*** office, there are some powerful lawyers whose work you ***cannot*** turn down ***no matter what.*** You need to know up front who they are! Ask your mentor (if you have one in-house), the recruiting coordinator, or associates more senior than you. As a rule of thumb, "The biggest partner gets their work done first," advises Georgetown's Beth Sherman. If the head of your department comes to you with an assignment, you probably can't turn it down.

One partner talked about an experience where, as a junior associate, he turned down an assignment from the head of his department, a guy named Mike, because he was too busy to handle it. Right after that, he was talking to a junior associate in the department, who told him: "Here's something you need to know: Don't say no to Mike. Don't ***ever*** say no to Mike." The partner says, "I immediately went back to Mike, and said, 'I've reshuffled things. I can do whatever you need me to do.'" The partner comments, "There are people you need to put on a pedestal. If they need it, you do it. That's it."

On the other hand, there are people you can afford to push back, and you have to be subtle about finding out who they are. One associate talked about being loaded down with work, back-to-back hearings and traveling. A partner came in and assigned him something on Friday that he needed completed by the following Wednesday. The associate tried to explain about his busy schedule instead of saying an out-and-out "no." The partner got exasperated and said, "Can you do it by Wednesday or not?" The associate said, "No." The partner stormed out and the associate was worried about honking him off. The associate mentioned it to a colleague, asking "What should I have done?" The colleague shrugged and said, "Don't worry. Nobody cares about that guy. He's a jerk. Some people you can piss of and nobody cares."

CAREER LIMITING MOVE . . .

New associate at a large firm. He's so busy he "can't see daylight." The managing partner of the firm walks into his office and says, "Can you do a project for me?" The associate, at the end of his rope, responds, "Honestly? No." The managing partner turns on his heel and walks out.

Several hours later, the managing partner summons the associate to his office. When the associate walks in, the managing partner is shaking with anger. He's bright red. He says, "Young man, let me give you a piece of advice. Don't you **ever** say no to me. **Ever**."

e. Ask your colleagues about the best way to turn down work from individual lawyers.

Although I'm going to give you general strategies for turning down work, it always pays to learn the quirks of people who assign work to ***you***. Missouri's Gerald Beechum advises you to "Ask about people's styles, how to approach them." Do some people prefer you to be blunt and say, "No, I can't do it right now . . . "? Or do you have to be more subtle? Determining people's styles ahead of time can save you from making a misstep. And figuring out where you're likely to be tagged with more projects when you're loaded down can help you avoid those situations.

SMART HUMAN TRICK . . .

Mid-level associate, large firm: "At my firm, we used to have a 'First Friday of the Month' party at work, in the late afternoon. They had to change it to Wednesday, because partners knew that if associates went to that party, they had time and the partners would jump on the associates to do work for them over the weekend. So associates started not showing up!"

f. Find out if your organization has a 'gatekeeper' to keep an eye on your workload.

Depending on where you work, you may have a work allocator or mentor to help control your workload. If so, ***always*** keep that person informed of what you're doing, especially if someone outside your "chain of command" gives you work to do. There's no point in stressing yourself out if someone's built into the system to help you sort out your workload.

g. Fine-tune your own time estimates.

One of the most difficult things you need to do as a new lawyer is to figure out how long projects will really take you to complete. Senior attorneys don't remember what it's like to be you, and their estimates can be ***way*** off. The reason it's important to learn how to estimate more accurately is that without that skill, you don't really know whether you're overloaded or not. One clue you have is your pre-work pace. As Brooklyn's Joan King says, "You may not have done work assignments before, but you ***have*** done research assignments in school, and you know your work pace from those. Are you fast, or slow and meticulous, or somewhere in between? Whatever your pace is, it's OK. It's ***you***. But it helps you plan accordingly."

Once you have a few assignments under your belt, you'll quickly learn how to gauge how long projects will take you—and have a better grasp of your workload as a result!

4. It's not *whether* you turn down work—it's *how* you do it: How to turn down work without saying the dreaded "no."

Here's the thing. You can't take on assignments you're too busy to handle. But at the same time, you don't want to develop a reputation for turning down work. How do you negotiate between the Scylla and Charybdis? It has everything to do with ***what you say*** to the attorney who's trying to assign you work. As American's Matt Pascocello says, "Saying no isn't the kiss of death—if it's done responsibly!" Here are some successful strategies to try:

a. Come to bury Caesar, not to praise him.

That is, profess a willingness to do the work at the outset, and move on from there. Say, "Yes, when do you need it?" It may be that the deadline is far enough away that you really can squeeze it in. If not, say "I'd love to help out. Here's what I'm working on now." As I mentioned before, if you hand over a list of your current assignments, the assigning attorney may figure out from that alone that you can't do the new assignment. Or you can say, "I'm happy to take your assignment, but I have assignments for X, Y and Z, and I don't know if I can make your deadline." You may find that the attorney will talk to X, Y and Z to rearrange your schedule, and that by itself gets you off the hook. "Let them duke it out between themselves," as Milbank Tweed's Kathleen Brady advises.

b. Suggest that the assigning attorney talk directly with the person you're doing work for now.

For instance, you can say, "I'd love to help you out, but I'm working on this project for Partner Porky. If you need me to help out, perhaps you could talk to Porky and see if he'd be willing to switch."

c. Have the assigning attorney help organize your priorities.

As Brooklyn's Joan King says, "It's hard at first to judge how much time projects take." If an attorney approaches you with new work and you just don't have the experience to tell you how long it will take to finish off what's already on your plate, ***tell*** them what you're doing. Say, "Yes, I'd love to do the work for you. Right now I have these four assignments with these deadlines. You know more about how long these things take than I do. Can I fit in your work? They'll probably decide for you." As Georgetown's Abbie Willard says, "Asking for advice about organizing your priorities shows sensitivity, not a lack of competence."

d. Don't prioritize your own assignments. Defer to people who assign your work.

As one hiring partner advises, "There will always be many demands on your time from lots of different people, all of whom think their project is the most important." Whatever you do, ***don't*** take it on yourself to decide whose work takes priority. As one lawyer told me, "There are likely to be politics you don't know about. If ***you*** go to the partner whose work you're doing and say, 'X just asked me to do this project for him right now. Can I switch?' You might hear, 'What do you ***mean***? You're doing ***my*** work!' You're dealing with busy lawyers. It's dangerous to throw them off schedule. Let ***others*** prioritize your work." Don't take the heat if you don't have to!

e. Don't be a sap. Always say "yes" when you're asked if you're busy.

You don't want to cultivate the image that you're not busy. It will make people wonder, "Why doesn't (s)he have a lot to do? Maybe (s)he's not competent, and everybody knows it but me." Obviously, if an assigning attorney walks up to you while you're photocopying your body parts, it's hard to say you're busy—at least, not with a straight face. But if they come to your office or call you to theirs, and say, "Are you busy?" ***always*** say, "Yes, but I'd love to help you out."

f. If your projects *do* get shuffled, apprise all your assigning attorneys of the shift.

Valparaiso's Gail Peshel advises that "If someone gets shoved to the back burner, give them a status report so they know where you are. That way they won't be mad at you."

g. If you do have to turn down work, state your enthusiasm for working with the assigning attorney imminently.

Chicago-Kent's Stephanie Rever Chu advises that "If you have to turn down work, say 'I'm sorry I can't work with you right now, but I'd really like the chance to work with you. I'm hoping that by next week I'll be free, and I'll come back to you." And follow up—as soon as you're free, go visit to see if they have projects for you. Brooklyn's John King agrees, suggesting that you say "you're working on a memo for John Doe which is due next week, and that you'd be pleased to work on the new project then." Another way to accomplish this is with a reference to the client's needs, saying "I can get my current work out of the way by Friday, and do this for you then. Would that meet with the client's needs?"

5. **If you've already taken on too much work—don't be a martyr!**

   Sometimes, despite your best efforts, you just get bogged down. As Boston University's Betsy Armour points out, "It's ***hard*** for new lawyers to balance their workload. Maybe you're facing conflicting or constricting deadlines. You can't be a martyr! Don't tell yourself 'I can figure this out.' You need to communicate what's going on." "Go to a recruiting coordinator, practice group head, your mentor, or the assigning attorneys for help in prioritizing or redistributing your work," advises Carlton Fields' Elizabeth Zabak. Other people can help you figure out what really does need to be done right away, what can be offloaded, and which projects have more "wiggle room." Don't suffer in silence!

6. **What if your problem isn't too *much* work, but too little? It's not the time to polish up your computer Solitaire skills!**

   As I discuss in the "Being Your Own Career Coach" chapter, taking the initiative in getting the work you want is the biggest favour you can do for your career. Whether you're underloaded because people are suspicious of your competence (Yikes! I hope not!) or they just don't know that you're not busy, the solution is the same. Be proactive! As Kentucky's Drusilla Bakert advises, "No matter where you work, there may be occasions when you're not busy. If this happens, whatever you do, don't stretch out the work you ***do*** have. Don't take two weeks to perfect a two-page memo! Don't spend your time on personal matters or on the phone complaining loudly to friends working elsewhere. And don't hang out in the office library reading newspapers! Whether the lack of work is your fault or not, your employer won't reward what they see as laziness or a lack of initiative. Drum up the work yourself. If there is someone in charge of your assignments, go to them and volunteer your time. If nobody is in charge of the work you get, go around and ask other lawyers if there's something you can work on for them. If there's a particular practice area that interests you, be sure to get to know the attorneys who work in that area and ask if you can help them. You may shake loose not just a memo or two but some work that really excites you! If you aren't able at first to find any more work, hide that as best you can by boning up on your legal reading. Don't let yourself be seen twiddling your thumbs!"

D. Ethical Issues: How To Avoid Being Led Away In Handcuffs And At The Same Time Avoid Torquing Off Your Boss

I don't have to tell you that if you do something unethical, you risk losing your license to practice law. But in practical terms, things are often not quite so cut and dried. If they ***were***, nobody would ever do anything unethical. You can be under ***lots*** of pressure as a lawyer, and that's what causes ethical problems. Your boss may press you to do something that makes you uncomfortable, and you worry that if you speak up you may lose your job. A major client wants you to bend the rules a little, implying that if you don't, you'll lose their business. You're at a prosecutor's office, and your boss pressures you to "get a conviction," and you interpret that to mean, "Do ***whatever*** it takes, ethical or not." You're still in school, and the employer you'll be working for when you graduate asks you to use your Lexis or Westlaw student ID to do research for them. You worry that if you don't, you'll jeopardize your job before you even ***start***.

In this section, we'll talk about how to handle ethical dilemmas, and how to resolve ethical issues without destroying yourself politically at the office. We'll also discuss what to do if you determine that the behavior being pressed on you is truly unethical. (As we'll see, it's pretty straightforward. Refuse to do it. If they insist—leave.)

1. Protect yourself up front from ethical problems.

Ideally you never want to be in the situation where your boss comes to you and says "Hey—bury this gun for me, will you?" There are a couple of prophylactic measures you can take to protect yourself from ever having that happen. One is to "establish yourself from the start as a rule-following, I-dotting, T-crossing person," says DePanfilis & Vallerie's Carrie Colangelo. Don't brag about how you've gotten away with things in the past, and don't make approving noises when other people tell you about what ***they've*** done. "The kid at the checkout missed the case of soda under my cart," "I wrote off more miles on my car than I ***drove*** last year"—don't respond, "Wow!" When you turn in your time sheets, make them precise, and let your supervisors ***know*** that. Don't pad expense reports. Don't suggest in any way that you've got lax standards. That may well encourage an unscrupulous supervisor to ask you to do something unethical at work.

Secondly, make sure that you keep accurate records. I talk all about that in the "Getting Off On the Right Foot" Chapter in the section called "Getting Organized." If you keep accurate records of what you do, communications with clients, and you have memos to file and backup e-mails, you'll help protect yourself if you're ever charged with an ethical breach.

2. When you're faced with an ethical issue, don't jump to the conclusion that what you're being asked to do is unethical. There are a *lot* more 'gray areas' than you think.

Some things are obvious. Destroying evidence. Paying bar dues out of trust accounts. Padding bills. But many lawyers told me that new lawyers tend to think that a lot of behavior is unethical when it really isn't. It's important to figure out if something is really an ethics problem—or you've got something on your mind making you ***think*** it is. It could be that you don't approve of the client or what they want to do. Perhaps you're ***sure*** that the client is lying but you have nothing to prove it. Or maybe you think you heard someplace that something's unethical, but when you look it up you find that the rule you thought you heard wasn't accurate.

Incidentally, "If you turn in your billables and your supervisor cuts your hours, it's not an ethical issue," says Nova Southeastern's Pat Jason. "That's looking out for the client. It's perfectly ethical."

So—how do you figure out if something is ethical or not? That's what we'll tackle next.

3. Finding out whether something is truly unethical *without* upsetting the apple cart.

It depends on the source of the questionable behavior and the nature of your employer. If it's the client, buy time so that you can find out whether the behavior is ethical or not. If you're a junior person, say, "I hear what you want, let me talk to X [your superior] about it and get back to you." If it's your client, say, "I hear what you're saying. Let me think about this strategy. I'll call you back at X time."

The situation is different if it's your superior who's requesting what you believe might be unethical behavior. The problem is this: especially if you're new, you don't know how your boss will react to having his/her ethics questioned. Some lawyers will take it in stride. Some won't, and they'll be hacked that you'd even question their ethics. You're better off ***not*** asking them directly unless you're ***sure*** of how they'll react. If you're ***not*** sure, what you should do depends on the nature of your employer. If the person who's asking you to do something unethical is not at the most senior level in the office—for instance, it's a senior associate—go to someone ***more*** senior to ask for advice. If you're at a large firm or in a large office of any kind, go to someone else you trust—be it a mentor, a risk management partner, or anyone else at work whom you trust—and say, "I'm not really sure about this one—what do you think?" and lay out the problem. Or you could say, "I'm new, but last semester in school we studied this, and it seems to me it's against the code of professional ethics." Pitch the question as though you want to be educated, not as though you're pointing an accusatory finger. They'll do one of two things: They'll assure you that what you've been asked to do is ethical (and that's what'll happen the vast majority of the time). Or they'll tell you that it's ***not*** ethical, and if that's the case, you need to ask them how best to handle it. Maybe they'll talk to your supervisor directly. Or they'll brainstorm with you about alternative strategies. Either way, you've taken a great burden from your shoulders by going to someone who knows your supervisor better than ***you*** do.

If you work in a smaller office—or you work in a large organization and don't feel comfortable going to someone in-house—there's a whole raft of possibilities for you in determining whether or not something is unethical. If you have other close friends in the legal community, you can bounce the situation—in very general terms—off them. You can say, "Am I nuts, or is this a problem?" You can call your ethics professor from law school and use them as a sounding board. Or you can call your state bar association's hotline. Florida, for instance has an ethics hotline that gets 20,000 calls a year and they give opinions over the phone. You could also contact the ABA's ethics hotline. It's called ETHICSearch, and you can reach them by phone at 312-988-5323, or fax at 312-988-5491, or e-mail at ***ethicsearch@staff.abanet.org*** (needless to say, if you call, call from your cell phone or a public phone; if you e-mail, e-mail from home; and if you fax, fax from Kinko's. You don't need to have your employer see a record of your contact on the phone bill!) ETHICSearch lawyers can often give you an authority on point immediately and/or e-mail or fax you the authorities you need to understand the issue and resolve the problem (like relevant ethics opinions and rules). The initial consultation is free, and if you want additional research, it costs $45/hour for ABA members and $60/hour for non-members. You could even contact a legal ethics lawyer—there are lawyers who devote some or all of their practice to handling ethical questions for other lawyers—and ask ***them.*** If you're sufficiently concerned or flummoxed, that's a possibility. And that has the benefit of proving, should the issue ever arise, that you took steps to ensure that you were doing the right thing. The bottom line is, there are a bunch of resources available to you for resolving ethical issues.Take advantage of them!

Now, it ***may*** be that after asking around a bit, you don't have a definitive answer on whether or not the behavior is unethical. There's a ***lot*** of gray area in ethics! In that case, the rule is that if you're acting under the direction of another lawyer, you can rely on their interpretation of an ethics rule as long as it's ***reasonable.*** There's a bit of judgment there—

you couldn't, for instance, follow the advice of a superior saying, "Oh, go ahead and hide the body. It's ethical. Trust me." But for an issue that is truly questionable, the rules suggest that you're protected.

4. Handling the situation once you know something is unethical.

Again, it depends on the source: whether it's a client or a superior who requested the unethical behavior.

If it's a client, it depends whether you're their attorney or if it's your supervisor who's the point person. If your boss is the one with the principal responsibility for the client, then your boss will handle the matter. If instead you are the front person with the client, you can always point out other alternatives that ***are*** ethical. "Why don't we think of other alternatives . . . " You can also point out that what they're trying to do ultimately won't work. Pass the ball! For instance, you can say, "A jury will not believe this."

If they back you into a corner, you've basically got to say, "What you're asking me to do will put my license to practice at risk. I wouldn't do it for anybody ***against*** you, and I can't do it ***for*** you. And neither can any other lawyer." I know that's easy to say when I'm sitting here writing a book instead of staring down a big client. But apart from any other ramification of unethical behavior, think about this: Once a client convinces you to do something unethical, they've got you by the short hairs. They can blackmail you professionally. You can't ever again say "I won't do that" because they know you already ***did*** something unethical. It's just not worth it!

SMART HUMAN TRICK . . .

Mid-level associate, New England firm: "We represented a chain of stores who leased space from larger stores. The deal was that they were supposed to pay rent based on how much they sold, and it was pretty clear that they were hiding some of their sales. In order to get out of paying the larger stores, they were contemplating filing bankruptcy. Finally one day the CEO asked me to do something that was clearly outside the scope of my duties as a lawyer. He wanted me to use a document where he had whited out some of the words; I'd seen it before, so I knew something was different. I told my supervisor, and the supervisor immediately responded, 'Get rid of the client. It takes years to develop a professional reputation. You can lose it in an instant. Don't let a client put you in that position.'"

If it's your boss, again, break it gently. Look past their specific request to the goal they are trying to reach, and see if there isn't an ethical way to accomplish that goal. Perhaps there's a client who's insisting on a particular answer, and your supervisor is feeling that pressure. Instead of saying, "This is wrong!" or "This is unethical!" say, "Can we take a look from this perspective?" or "This troubles me. I hear what you're asking me. But can we talk about other strategies?" Maybe they interpret the rules differently than you did, and if they can support their argument, as I mentioned just a minute ago, the ethics rules say you're covered (mind you that's only true for areas that are ***truly*** gray, ***not*** for things that are more straightforward). As Dickinson's Elaine Bourne suggests, "Do a memo to file, cc: somebody else if that's feasible"—cover yourself!

If your boss doesn't take the bait and insists that you do something that you're fairly sure is unethical, you just can't do it. As Venable, Baetjer's Stefan Tucker advises, "Once you ascertain for sure that it's unethical, say to them, 'I'm sorry. I can't do it.'" If it costs you your job, you're well rid of it. As Loyola's Pam Occhipinti says, "My father always told me, 'You can always make all the money in the world, but you can't make your name back.' Don't compromise your reputation!" Flaherty, Sensabaugh's Scott Kaminski agrees: "In the practice of law, your reputation is everything. Never do anything that would compromise your reputation, no matter the reason." ***No*** job is worth committing an ethical breach, no matter how it looks when you're sitting in the hot seat. If your boss is a sleazeball, other lawyers know it, and you don't want to be tarred with that same brush. As Pam Occhipinti says, "One associate I know worked for three partners in a plaintiff's personal injury firm. One day all three partners were arrested for stealing from clients. Realize that if your boss is disbarred, you'll be investigated, too." As soon as you know the real story—get out.

SMART HUMAN TRICK . . .

Junior associate, Midwestern firm: "Our firm had a 'partner from hell,' who always waited until the last minute to do tremendously important work. Then he'd make a frantic pass through the hallways, grabbing whatever hapless associate(s) he could find. When the last minute work was done, he'd inevitably blame the associate for whatever went wrong, missed issues, bad cites. Fortunately, nobody at the office was ever fooled.

Once he strode into my office at 4:30 in the afternoon, half an hour before the courthouse closed, and plopped a one-inch thick complaint on my desk. He told me to sign it and get it filed. A firm in another state had sent it over by federal express and he had promised them he'd have it filed that day. The partner left my office and I sat there staring at this behemoth of a complaint, just stunned. After about five minutes, I collected my wits. I knew that under FRCP Rule 11, there was no way I could sign and file the complaint by five o'clock, and comply with the rule. There was no way I could verify the items in the complaint in any way, shape or form in less than half an hour!

I walked to the partner's office, looked him in the eye, and said, 'Under Rule 11, I cannot, and will not, sign this complaint today.' He looked at me, absolutely flabbergasted that I had the nerve to stand up to him. Then he said in distress, 'But I can't do it, either!' essentially admitting that he tried to bamboozle me into doing something he knew was unethical!

Fortunately for him, the Statute of Limitations was not an issue, so he called the out-of-state firm and asked if they minded whether he took another day to review the complaint and comply with Rule 11. No problem. I read and checked out the complaint and the next day had it filed.

> After that incident, that partner never asked me to do his dirty work for him again."

Incidentally, if it comes to that—and you have to look for another job—be careful how you bring up the topic with future employers. If there are other reasons you wanted to leave the employer—like you wanted to change practice areas or settings or move to another city—focus on those. When it comes to the ethics problems, as Hofstra's Caroline Levy says, "Couch it in diplomatic terms, like 'I had some reservations about the practice' or 'I was uncomfortable' or 'Our styles weren't compatible.' The fact is, if somebody is sleazy, everybody in the legal community already knows it!" If you're pressed on the issue, Elaine Bourne says, "Then tell them. Dance around it until you're cornered, and then say, 'They asked me to do some things that I researched and found to be outside the rules of ethics. Frankly, if you asked me to do those things for you, I wouldn't do them for you, either.'" Face it. If a prospective employer wanted you to do something unethical for them, you don't want ***that*** job, either!

5. What to do if you find out that the behavior is ethical—but you're *still* not happy with it

If you ascertain that what you're being asked to do is ethical, and you're disappointed with that—there's something else going on. It's entirely possible that something could be ethical but still make your hair stand on end. Maybe you just can't bring yourself to represent people you consider sleazoids. Or maybe you've got moral problems with the kinds of businesses your firm represents. Or maybe you think your bosses are sleazy, even though what they're doing is technically on the right side of the ethics code. You know what? It's not the right job for you. As Nova Southeastern's Pat Jason says, "If you're uncomfortable, it's not a good fit for you. It's a sign." John Marshall's Bill Chamberlain adds, "They may be paying your salary, but it's still ***your*** life." To figure out what to do, look at the chapter called "Being Your Own Career Coach," where we talk all about those kinds of issues. That's not an ethical problem—that's a career issue!

E. SEXUAL HARASSMENT: STOPPING A PROBLEM BEFORE IT *IS* A PROBLEM

What I'm going to do in this section is to focus on the kind of behavior that can help stop sexual harassment in its tracks. I'm going to open your eyes about what can constitute sexual harassment if you're a man, and I'll explain actions you can undertake as a woman to stop matters from escalating to the point where you're truly uncomfortable. I'm ***not*** going to give you a primer on sexual harassment law. If things get that far, you need to talk to someone at your employer, or your career services director at your law school, or someone in Washington, either at the EEOC, or the National Organization of Women, or the Women's Legal Defense Fund. A sexual harassment lawsuit is a big deal and it's ***well*** beyond the scope of this book.

I got the definite impression talking to people all over the country that a lot of sexually harassing behavior can be stopped at the source if men know what kinds of behavior and language can be offensive, and if women know how to address it. And ***that's*** what we'll try to accomplish here.

1. A few facts about sexual harassment

a. Understand what it is!

I'm no lawyer—you are!—but I can describe for you the two basic kinds of sexual harassment claims. There's the type we typically think of when we think about sexual harassment: a supervisor predicates an underling's continued employment or advancement on succumbing to sexual demands. Then there's what's called "hostile environment" sexual harassment, which basically involves words or conduct that interfere with someone's work or make the office environment uncomfortable, including flirting, touching, inappropriate e-mails, nude pin-ups, inappropriate comments, foul language, lewd gestures, and/or comments about someone's dress or appearance. You can see that "hostile environment" is kind of a "catch-all" sexual harassment claim, and it's where a lot of men get into trouble sometimes without even realizing it.

b. Understand that legal employers are absolutely *paranoid* about it.

The perception that every law firm is a "good old boys club" where people say, "Oh, boys will be boys" is just wrong. Legal employers are very aware of how big a deal sexual harassment is. If you are a new associate and you are accused of sexual harassment, your career with that employer is basically toast. When firms have men in a position of power who are known letchers, they will take active steps to ensure that that partner is ***never*** alone in the company of a female associate. Having said that, it's important not to be naive about what happens in the event that you are sexually harassed. If you are in a small firm, you're probably going to have to vote with your feet and leave the firm. As one female associate at a small firm commented, "You can say to them, 'I don't need to remind you that XYZ,' but the bottom line is, it's hard to work for somebody you don't respect." If you've documented the behavior well, you can probably negotiate a great reference. But you are unlikely to be able to change the behavior. If you are at a large firm and the harasser is a powerful partner, they're not going anywhere. You can negotiate a move to another department or your own exit strategy from the firm, but as the recruiting coordinator at one large firm noted, "We don't want the lawsuit, but we can't lose all that business, either."

c. Realize that most people aren't, and will never be, sexual harassers.

That's the assessment of Drs. Wanda Dobrich and Steven Dranoff, authors of an excellent book on the subject, *The First Line of Defense—A Guide To Protecting Yourself Against Sexual Harassment.* Men and women by and large work together very harmoniously. Most people, men ***and*** women, are horrified and appalled by sexual harassment. When we're talking about sexual harassment, we're talking about an ***abnormal*** situation.

2. What you need to know if you're a man

I saw a great t-shirt that said, "When I talk dirty to a woman it's sexual harassment. When a woman talks dirty to me, it's $3.95 a minute." While in theory women can harass men, it's usually the other way around. You're behavior is under the microscope. Now, with all of the advice I'm going to give you, I'm going to sound like a terrible scold. Often, you could probably get away with a lot of the behavior I'm going to describe. Maybe the person you're joking with shares your sense of humour. But the problem is, as a new lawyer you can't afford the downside risk—which is losing your job. So what I'm going to tell you will save you from what could be truly monstrous consequences. Let's see what you need to know:

a. No, you can't "just be yourself"—not around women at work, anyway.

A lot of times, men will say, "But do I have to watch ***everything*** I say? Can't I ever ***relax***?" Nope. But then, you can't relax at work, anyway. You can't engage in behavior that could be construed as sexually harassing any more than you could strip down to your underwear, put your feet up on the desk, and drink beer all day. Outside of work, you can do anything you want. If you joke around inappropriately with women who are your friends and not your colleagues, they can't sue you. They can't get you fired. They can splash a beer in your face and terminate the friendship, but that's about it. But at work, "being yourself" just isn't possible. Next question?

b. Don't say anything about women's bodies, even if you mean it as a compliment.

Trust me, if you've got a female colleague who's a hottie, she's got a mirror. She knows it. She doesn't need you to verify it—and she might be offended if you do. Even if you think she'd be thrilled to hear you say, "Gee, have you ever modeled?" don't say it!

CAREER LIMITING MOVE . . .

Male summer clerk at a large firm in the Midwest. He is working in the library. A female summer clerk sits at the same table. He looks up from his work, and they start chatting about the firm picnic at a local resort that's coming up next weekend. He says, 'Boy, would I like to see you in a wet T-shirt,' and he elaborates on it. Unbeknownst to him, there are two senior associates in the library, standing nearby. They overhear him. They immediately escort him out of the library and talk to him. He comes back and apologizes to her. And even though he has excellent paper credentials and his work product is good, he doesn't get an offer.

c. **Don't *ever* say *anything* that implies or refers to a woman's sexual performance.**

A junior associate at one law firm was asked to leave when he went to the office of a female colleague and said, "You must be the oldest living virgin in America." At another firm, a lawyer was asked to leave when he took a new female associate out to lunch, and said to her, "You're Japanese. I understand that Japanese women will do ***anything*** to please their men. Is that true?"

It doesn't matter if you're just saying something to be provocative. Provocative is fine when you're outside of work and all you're risking is a slap. It's not OK with female colleagues.

d. **No touching. Not even a friendly arm around the shoulder.**

Whether it's a playful pat on the butt, a shoulder massage, anything—don't risk it. Pretend your female colleagues are surrounded by a force field. Hands off!

e. **No joking about sexual favours. Have you lost your *mind*?**

CAREER LIMITING MOVE . . .

First day of the summer program, large firm. A female summer clerk gets to her office, and finds that she's going to be sharing it with a guy. Immediately after they meet, she says, "I'm starving." He grabs his crotch and says, "Why don't you try this?" She is stunned. She responds, "What's **wrong** with you? You don't even **know** me!" He introduces himself, and says, laughingly, "I knew you were cool. I knew I could joke with you!" The female clerk responds, "It's not a goddamned frat party. It's a **job**!"

f. **No long looks or gazes.**

Pretend you're a horse in Central Park, and put your blinders on. Your admiring look could be misinterpreted as a leer. Don't risk it.

g. **No 'subtle comments' about someone's shampoo or perfume or clothes. There's no such thing as subtlety when it comes to sexual harassment.**

You may think that you're just being complimentary when you say to a woman, "Your hair smells great. Are you using a new shampoo?" You might think you're gently teasing when you say, "What's the matter? PMS?" As Wanda Dobrich and Steven Dranoff say in *The First Line Of Defense—A Guide To Protecting Yourself Against Sexual Harassment*, "subtle sexual harassment is only subtle to the harasser." Just assume that ***any*** comments about the way someone looks or seems or smells is off limits, no matter how kindly you mean it.

h. **Don't put your female colleagues on your e-mail joke list.**

E-mailed jokes that are offensive can easily be characterized as sexual harassment. I know, I know—a lot of times you're just forwarding a joke that you got from somebody else, maybe somebody else who is a woman. Don't pass it on if you wouldn't tell it to your grandmother.

i. **Even if the person you're joking with seems to be playing along, you can't be sure that they're comfortable with it.**

As Emory's Carolyn Bregman says, "You have no idea when someone's capacity for joking has been reached. There's no way to tell in context what will push somebody over the edge. Assume zero tolerance. Remember that work's work and not work is not work, and you have to be careful with joking and playing."

j. **As a rule of thumb, if you wouldn't say it around your mom, don't say it around your female colleagues.**

You may not be sensitive to the sensibilities of women your age, but you're undoubtedly a lot better about watching what you say in front of your mom. You wouldn't make offhand comments about sex or degrading things about women in front of ***her***. Don't do it in front of your female colleagues, either.

k. **Don't assume that if you didn't mean offense, they won't take offense.**

As Georgia State's Vickie Brown points out, "There are gender differences in conversation. You need to be aware of your audience. Even if you think it's OK to say it, it might not be. It doesn't matter what you ***meant***. It matters how they ***take*** it."

3. **What you need to know if you're a woman**

If you're a woman, the first time anybody makes an inappropriate comment to you at work is probably not the first time it's ever happened to you in your life. Work is just a macrocosm of the real world. There are a bunch of great people and . . . a few not-so-great people. There are a lot of great guys who'll help you on with your coat and hold the door open for you, and they're just being courtly. They're not coming on to you. But there are creepy guys as well. If you want to make your life as comfortable as it can be, every female attorney and career counselor I spoke with would encourage you to take steps to minimize sexual harassment problems. There ***are*** things you can do to avoid being a victim, and you should do them!

a. **Distinguish between men who are real creeps, and the "testosterone pit"—that is, men who should know better, but don't.**

If someone is a real creep, Drs. Wanda Dobrich and Steven Dranoff say that "You have to be assertive from the start, or your aggressor will believe you're playing a game of cat and mouse." If someone asks you out for drinks after work—just the two of you—

or otherwise makes you feel as though they're coming on to you, you ***have*** to tell them in no uncertain terms that you're not interested. Don't leave that door open! But as I said earlier in this section, most men are not sexual harassers. They're talking the way they've always talked with their buddies, and they go on doing the same thing in a professional setting. Although it's possible to characterize a lot of kidding, joking behavior as creating a "hostile environment," every female attorney with whom I spoke agreed that you'd be exercising questionable judgment in doing so. One lawyer who represents a lot of sexual harassment victims says, "I get so many calls from people talking about what so-and-so said at the office, and I just laugh at them. They think, hey, one half-assed comment and I'm a millionaire! A sexual harassment suit is a serious matter with serious consequences. Your colleagues will steer clear of you. Your next employer may look askance at you thinking that you're the type who rocks the boat, even if you were totally in the right. It's a ***big thing*** and you shouldn't take it lightly." Finding sexual harassment in every comment won't help anybody, including you. As one recruiting coordinator points out, "If it's said in a lighthearted way, take it the way it was intended. Blow it off."

b. If somebody asks you "Hey, how about it," reject him/her gently— but firmly.

Sometimes men subscribe to the belief "There's no harm in asking." In most cases, if a man hears a definite "no," he accepts it. Don't make the mistake a lot of women make without realizing it—***thinking*** you've said no when you really haven't. If someone massages your shoulders and you sit stock still and say nothing, thinking they'll get the message, they might not. If someone invites you out for a drink after work and you say, "Not tonight, I'm busy," that's not really closing the door to further invitations. Using the wording that Georgetown's Abbie Willard recommends—"I'm really uncomfortable having a drink after work, so no, thank you"—***does*** make it plain what you're saying. As

Kentucky's Drusilla Bakert recommends, "a firm 'thanks but no thanks' is what you need. 'I make a policy of not dating people I work with' works fine." If the behavior continues, then you're talking about facing the possibility of taking further steps, like telling someone else at work (or outside of it). But at the very least, say a firm "no" first. As one lawyer put it, "If you don't say 'no' at least once before you report the guy, a lot of people will think, 'Well, she should have just said 'no.' It's not fair, but that's the way it is. If you say 'no' and that doesn't work, that's a different matter."

c. When people make lewd remarks in your presence, write down their remarks and give them back to the people who said them.

When you're talking about frat boy talk, it's important to realize that a lot of men don't realize how offensive it can be. Susan Estes, a very successful bond trader on Wall Street who was profiled in the *Wall Street Journal,* came up with a very creative way of dealing with crude behavior. Whenever her fellow bond traders made lewd remarks, she would jot down the comments on a card and read them back. The men who'd made the comments would laugh nervously, but as one of them commented, when they heard their comments read back to them, "We became aware that the vulgarities sounded silly and were inappropriate. She really changed me." As Estes herself remarked: "Sometimes it pays to be confrontational—but often it doesn't."

d. Don't encourage jokes that make you uncomfortable by laughing at them.

As Valparaiso's Gail Peshel advises, "If you don't like inappropriate jokes, you can't promote them! You need to stop the joke telling in a way that won't jeopardize you. Don't laugh. Or try to appear as though you didn't hear the joke. Or change the subject. If the joke teller doesn't get the reaction they want, they'll stop telling that kind of joke."

e. Let people know that you're uncomfortable with their joking—*gently.*

There's nothing that stops you from stomping your foot and saying, "I find that offensive!" You'll make the person you say that to feel bad, but it's certainly your prerogative to do so. However, many female lawyers and career counselors with whom I spoke suggested that you be gentle in conveying that you've reached your limits. For instance, if the talk starts getting out of control at a firm event, you can say, "Oops! I think that's my exit line," and walk away from the group to speak with other people. Texas Tech's Kay Fletcher suggests that you might smile and say, "You know, this could be toned down a bit and I'd feel a whole lot more comfortable."

f. Don't assume that everybody thinks it's funny except for you.

As Vickie Brown points out, "Watch the crowd when someone's saying something sexually inappropriate. Watch the reaction. You'll find other people who don't feel uncomfortable. Leave the group with them. Don't hang around if you're not enjoying yourself."

g. Dress as though you're going to church or temple.

You wouldn't wear something sexy to church or to temple (at least, I hope not). Don't wear sexy stuff to work, either. I know this sounds terrible, and smacks of, "Well, she asked for it" thinking. But I heard from too many people in all kinds of work situations that if you take your wardrobe cues from Ally McBeal, people are going to question your judgment for a whole variety of reasons—including setting yourself up to be hit on by men at work. Save your sexy wardrobe for nightclubs. Dress conservatively for work, if for no other reason than to be taken seriously as a professional!

h. Try to use humour to combat offensive behavior.

Humour doesn't work in ***every*** situation. If somebody's truly a harasser, they won't be dissuaded by your rapier-like wit. But for casual frat-boy inappropriateness, it's great—as long as you're comfortable with it. As Arizona's Mary Birmingham advises, "Humour is one of the most disarming things anybody can use." One associate talked about working for two male partners. When she knocked on their doors, they'd respond, "Take off your clothes and come in," and she'd answer, "Only if yours are off already." When told "You must be the oldest virgin in America," the associate in question responded, "If you were the only man—I ***would*** be."

Humour can suggest that you're comfortable with the situation—and if you ***are***, terrific. It can also have the effect of letting men know that they're behaving badly, without giving them a formal dressing-down.

SMART HUMAN TRICK . . .

Female summer clerk at a large firm. The first day she's at the office, a partner walks in, introduces himself, and says, "Hey, you got any—Chapstick?" He puckers his lips. The summer clerk is appalled. She tells him, calmly, "I'll check, and I'll send it to you in the interoffice mail if I find any." He leaves. She goes to the firm's supply room, and gets a large container of Elmer's glue. She makes up a dummy label for the glue that says, "Economy sized Chapstick. Instructions: Apply liberally to lips and hold closed for thirty seconds." She sends him the glue through the interoffice mail. He treats her with respect for the rest of the summer, becoming one of her biggest fans.

SMART HUMAN TRICK . . .

Highly successful businesswoman. Her boss gives her a pair of brass balls for Christmas, with a note saying "Have these so you can stop cracking mine." Her response? "I didn't know you had any."

i. If the offender is somebody you can avoid, avoid them.

If you're in a sufficiently large office that you don't have to see a person who says things that upset you, then avoid them. If it's a colleague who's part of a group with whom you hang out, if you ***stop*** hanging out, there's no problem saying to another person in the group, "I'm sorry, X really bothers me." And then offer to get together with the others. The fact is, if the rest of the group doesn't have a problem with the behavior that bothers you, there's nothing you can do about it. But if it's really that offensive, you'll find more people on your side than you think.

j. If all of these techniques fail and you're truly being made to feel uncomfortable: it's time for step two.

Start taking notes—***always*** have what happened, where and when, ***in writing***—and save any offensive e-mails, cartoons, notes to you. And consider telling somebody outside of the employer with whom you feel comfortable, like your career services director, to avoid having everything boil down to a "he said, she said" matter. Consider telling someone else in the firm—a recruiting coordinator, office manager, mentor, hiring partner, managing partner, ***somebody*** in authority—about the behavior. It's important to talk to someone you trust about the ramifications of pursuing the matter further, and see how you feel about that. I've talked with people who've done a great deal of soul-searching, and let the matter drop, and with others who've pursued lawsuits. That's a decision only you can make, and as I mentioned before—we're not going there, in this book!

4. If somebody else at the office tells you that they're being harassed, you *cannot* keep that news to yourself. There is no such thing as a comment about sexual harassment that's "off the record."

If a colleague shares with you a problem they're having with harassment, they're likely to say, "Please don't tell anybody." This is a confidence that you, unfortunately, ***have*** to violate. That's because once ***you*** know about it, the employer is "on notice," and that has legal ramifications. As one recruiting coordinator said, "I sometimes have associates and summer clerks come to talk to me, and the way they're talking suggests that they're going to tell me about some harassing behavior. I always stop them and say, 'If you go any further, I'm not going to be able to keep this between us. I'll ***have*** to report it.' They usually tell me anyway, but I think it's important for them to know that this is one secret I simply cannot keep."

CHAPTER TEN

Being Your Own Career Coach And Living The Life You Want.

You do the work you do for one reason and one reason only: to make your life as happy as it can be. I don't mean that you'll take joy in every moment of every day. Please! We do lots of things in our lives to facilitate ***other*** things we want to do. If that weren't true, we'd never put away a penny for retirement (it's more fun to spend it all right now!). You probably wouldn't have gone to law school. Surely it's more fun to be on the beach in Hawaii than it is to be agonizing through Civil Procedure. But you do some things as an investment in your life and your future.

Nonetheless, you've got to be able to look at what you're doing and say, is this getting me where I want to go? If I'm not loving it right this moment, can I see how it ***will*** enrich my life at some point soon? ***Is this an investment worth making?***

What we'll talk about in this chapter is how to enrich your work—and therefore your life—now and in the future. We'll talk about balancing your work and your life outside of work. We'll discuss how to take evaluations and criticism and use them to propel your career forward. We'll talk about how you negotiate for more money. We'll spend some time on identifying opportunities to make yourself into a superstar in your career. And we'll wind up talking about what to do if you hate your job. If you're not liking it, it's possible it's not the right place for you—and we'll discuss how you make an exit. After all, it's your ***life***. Make it the one you ***want*** to live!

A. BALANCING YOUR WORK AND YOUR LIFE OUTSIDE OF WORK. STOP LAUGHING!

1. Your career is a marathon—not a sprint. If your work is your whole life, you'll burn out. *Fast.*

As Denver's Anne Stark Walker says, "At the end of the day, at the end of your career, you are not going to wish that you'd spent more time at the office. Work is only one aspect of your life. Don't let your hobbies and loved ones fall by the wayside during these early years. Believe it or not, your work and career will be enhanced if you can manage to maintain a healthy balance in your life." Carlton Fields' Eric Adams adds, "You ***have*** to decompress. You ***have*** to be passionate about something else—your community, your church, basketball—outlets outside of work let you manage your stress."

You may be thinking, "Hah! That's easy for ***them*** to say. They don't have ***my*** job." Well, if it was ***easy*** to balance, there wouldn't be about a jillion books out there about balance and spirituality and blahdiblahdi-blah. It's not easy. But it's really, really important. And if you lose sight of it, you're going to be miserable. Your work, no matter what it is, can ***never*** give you everything you need out of life, and you can't give it "everything" in return. As Jackson & Kelly's Monika Hussell says, "Don't make your work your life. Rather, develop your life to incorporate your work."

2. Balancing your career and your life is always a challenge—not just at the beginning!

As Georgetown's Abbie Willard says, "You'll always be juggling balls in the air. You'll feel guilty whether it's elder care, child care, a relation-ship—there are always competing demands on your time." Georgetown's

Beth Sherman adds that "There's always a deal to be done, a document to file—there's always ***some*** demand on your time."

It's true that as your expertise grows, you become more efficient at work. But it's ***never*** easy to achieve the balance you want. As Abbie Willard says, "Nobody knows that formula!" Make a point of working on balancing your life from the beginning, taking baby steps. Carve out time for yourself bit by bit. It's not selfish. It's just a matter of taking a long-range view of your life, and what will serve you not just now but ***forever.***

3. **If you're starting your career pulling in six figures, you've got a special challenge when it comes to balance. But it's not an *insurmountable* challenge (and psst: if you do great work, you've got a *lot* more bargaining power).**

You're probably wiping the tears of laughter from your eyes about the concept of "balance" if you're starting your career with a silver spoon in your mouth. Heck, ***I'm*** laughing, and I'm not even a ***lawyer.*** As I write this, I've been sitting at my computer for sixteen hours a day for the last five weeks straight, and before that, I spent twelve hours a day on the phone interviewing people. For chrissakes, I don't feel like I'm writing a book. I feel like I'm hatching eggs! So I'm down with how ridiculous the idea of balance can seem when you're under tremendous career pressure. The senior partner at one firm sneered, "Who do they think they ***are*** asking for ***balance*** with these salaries? They should have thought about that before they took the money." It's true that for everything you get, you sacrifice something else. But if you're at a big firm—or anywhere else that wants to work you to death!—you can't sacrifice your life. If you burn out, you'll quit and your firm absolutely doesn't want you to do that.

Large firms go on and on about the investment they have in new associates, and they're coming to realize that if they burn you out, they lose on that investment. So things ***are*** changing. A number of firms are giving new respect to part-time lawyers, and at some large firms they even make partner on a part-time basis. (As I've noted elsewhere, 'part-time' in law is what would be full-time anywhere else—like thirty-five to forty hours a week. But it's still better than really long hours.) Some firms give an extra week of vacation for billing so many hours. And many times, individual partners are appalled when you have to work long hours on something, and they recognize and reward hard work on their own initiative. A lawyer at one large firm talked about having a colleague quit and having to pick up the departing lawyer's work. Because of it, he billed 300 hours in one month. The head of his department came up to him holding his time sheet and said, "Dang! Big grief! Why was your month so crazy?" The lawyer told him what had happened, and the department head responded, "You need to not work that hard in future. You need to delegate." Soon after that, the managing partner called him in to see that he wasn't burning out. I've mentioned elsewhere in the book the story about the associate who'd been burning the midnight oil on a case, and her supervisor told her at Thanksgiving, "See you after New Year's." He gave her the rest of the year off in recognition of her efforts.

In addition, no employer truly wants you to be a night-and-day drone. Not really. As Hofstra's Rebecca Katz-White says, "Even big firms want you to be well-rounded, play a round of golf with a client, be able to go to lunch and discuss something other than the case you're working on."

Now it may be that you're working for a real flesh-eating lawyer who laughs at the concept of balance in ***any*** form. Maybe your firm isn't set up for it. A lawyer at Goulston Storrs reflected that a firm needs to deliver in three areas in order to be able to offer balance to its lawyers: "First, the law firm has to have a critical mass of decision makers who because of age, experience, or other reasons understand the difficulties of balancing work and family and who support that balance, men and women alike; second, the firm needs to be able to assess and evaluate productivity as clients do—that is, on timeliness and quality of work, not on 'face time' or other 'internal' considerations; and third, the firm needs to deliver the tools for working parents to work from home or elsewhere, such as laptop computers with remote dial-in access. Without any one of these, a true balance of work and family becomes difficult if not impossible."

If your firm isn't like that, then you're going to have to fight for balance. The ***best*** way to do that is to turn in top-quality work and impress people, because then you've got a bargaining chip. If your work is great, they'll want to keep you, and they'll be willing to negotiate in "balance goodies" to keep you happy and keep you there. Negotiate to coach Little League on Wednesday afternoon or do Habitat for Humanity on Saturdays, only to be violated for true emergencies. Georgetown's Abbie Willard says that more and more associates are negotiating deals like this. And ***clever*** employers are taking them up on it.

Ultimately, if your employer won't listen to any plea for balance no matter ***how*** good they think you are, you've got a few choices. One is that you can grin and bear it for as long as possible. No matter ***where*** you work, things tend to be out-of-balance in the beginning. They usually improve, but if they don't improve much, you may have to consider other alternatives. One would be to get off the partnership track. Go part time. Be a staff attorney or do contract work. It may be that you won't get the sexiest work, but you're giving up something to get something else. And there's always the option of leaving. As we talk about in the section "What To Do If You're Hating Your Job," you shouldn't make that option A for a whole bunch of reasons, but the option is always ***there***.

4. Don't expect your employer to balance your life for you!

As Emory's Carolyn Bregman says, "If you're willing to work 100 hours a week, few employers will turn you down. ***Think*** about where you want to be down the road!" George Washington's Jim Lovelace agrees, saying that "It's easy, particularly in a town like Washington, to get into the habit of working late nights and weekends as a new associate, even if you don't have to. If you're new in town, your life revolves around your work. But you ***have*** to claim time for yourself. Otherwise, people ***expect*** you to be in—you'll get assignments from people just because they figure you're always there on Saturday! If you develop a sense of balance, you'll ultimately get more respect."

5. OK, you know you *have* to balance your life. What should you do?

The short answer is: whatever floats your boat! Here are some ideas for you:

a. If you've got kids, work for a partner who has kids as well.

"You'll have an easier time balancing your life if you work for someone who has balance in ***theirs***," says Jim Lovelace.

b. Talk about your personal life with your colleagues from time to time.

As a lawyer at Goulston Storrs points out, "If you make yourself human in their eyes and show that you 'have a life,' they'll be more apt to help you out when you get busy and understand when you need time off."

c. Set up "dates" with your loved one and keep them.

Paul O'Donnell, a former *Newsweek* staffer, left the magazine to work at an Internet start-up where he works beaucoup hours. He says, "If you have kids, arrange for a babysitter who gets paid whether you go out or not. If you're single, buy expensive tickets to a concert, or reserve a table at a fancy restaurant. What this does is to raise the cost of blowing off real life." Along the same lines, Pepperdine's Carol Allemeier says, "Make Friday night 'date night' with your significant other, even if it only means popcorn and a video. Saturday morning is always for the kids. Sunday morning is family time. Attend a networking event once a week. Life gets very busy and it's often difficult to set limits for yourself the further you get into a new job. Set them right from the start! A new job is a new beginning."

d. Exercise!

Everybody tells you to do that. But it's a great idea. I have a stationary bike, one of those recumbent ones, plopped right in front of the TV in the living room. I hop onto it every morning for an hour while I watch the news and my husband is getting ready for work. It couldn't be easier. But it doesn't matter whether you use my idea or do anything else to get your heart pumping. Feeling better physically makes you feel better mentally, too. It's worth it!

e. Try to keep your work at work.

I know that there's a huge temptation to take a laptop home—and sometimes, especially if you have kids and want to be home while they're awake, it's a better option than any other. But you don't want work to creep in and invade every one of your waking hours ***outside*** the office. As Florida State's Stephanie Redfearn says, "To the extent you can do your work ***at*** work, do it, and keep your home for your home life."

f. **Develop a pace that suits you, particularly if you're at an employer who doesn't have 'face time' issues and your supervisor is down with it.**

Wake Forest's Bill Barrett says that when he was practicing law, he'd come in at 7:30 in the morning, take an hour and a half for lunch with partners, and then work until 4:30. He'd leave for dinner and come back from 7 until 9 or so at night. He says, "This kind of rhythm worked for me, because I didn't overstress working with big blocks of time. Everybody has a set-up that works for them. Find out what your best set-up is. If you're at a firm where you're more free to set up your own schedule—that's true at a lot of small firms—nobody will care when you show up as long as the clients' work gets done and you make your billables."

g. **If you're at a large firm, take advantage of the huge resources they have, inside and out.**

As Carlton Fields' Kevin Napper advises, "You're in a wonderful situation at a big firm, because of the huge resources. If you want to get appointed to bar association committees, get involved in local politics, arts organizations, you name it, partners can easily get you in. Every large firm has well-connected partners. What you do in the community is not just good for business. It's ***fun***. I'm on the board of a local community radio station. I like radio! I'm on the board of an old historic theater, because I like film. You don't join ***everything*** for business development. It's good for balance!"

h. **Get involved with community/civic organizations, like Habitat for Humanity.**

Not only will you be doing good—you'll do well. Community activities are classic revenue generators. What you do ***outside*** of work can affect what you do ***at*** work. If you coach a soccer team, go listen to new talent night at nightclubs, coach Little League, get involved in the Red Cross or Jaycees—those are fertile grounds for reaping clients. I talk a lot about that in the "Hidden Opportunities" section toward the end of this chapter. My point is, your work and your life don't have to diverge completely. One can feed the other—and you can enjoy yourself at the same time!

i. **Take classes *other* than CLEs—and expand your horizons.**

As a lawyer at the Justice Department points out, "Speaking a foreign language, traveling, having a hobby or other interests not only makes your resume more interesting and enhances your well-being, but the non-legal skills you develop may be useful to you in your career in ways you can't foresee."

j. **"Call your mom once a week!" says Colorado's Tony Bastone.**

6. **If you want to do pro bono work, be prepared to sacrifice your own time for it.**

There's no question that if you don't find that your work feeds your soul as much as you wish it did, pro bono work can help you counterbalance that. And it may be that your firm is serious about it when they say that they place a strong emphasis on pro bono work. Some firms, for instance, view pro bono cases as a means of helping new litigators get their feet wet. But look around you to see how your employer views pro bono work. ***Every*** firm will applaud your pro bono efforts if you're still turning in lots of billables. If they're just paying lip service to it, doing pro bono is ***still*** a great idea—but as Dickinson's Elaine Bourne says, "You've got to be prepared to sacrifice your time for your values!"

7. **It's time to par-tay! You need to take vacations. Draw a line in the sand (on Maui, or Tahiti, or . . .) and stick to it!**

The amount of vacation time you get "in theory" is meaningless if you don't take it. ***Everybody*** needs to recharge their batteries! Eric Adams says that "People brag that they don't take vacations, but they burn out. Everybody does if they don't take time off." St. Thomas' Michelle Fongyee agrees, saying, "I didn't take any vacation days for my first five years in practice. I was afraid to schedule it! But you know what, the firm wasn't afraid. It was just me. They'll work around you." Furthermore, as Jim Lovelace points out, "If you never take vacation, you breed false expectations in your bosses. All of a sudden, false emergencies start cropping up. If you start to forego vacations when there's not really an emergency, people think that you'll ***always*** put off vacations for them. You've got to draw a line in the sand—and stick with it." One lawyer told of how when she was a junior associate, she made plans to fly to the New Orleans Jazz Festival with friends. She was working on a case, and her partner told her, "It's a bad idea to go." That partner's boss, the managing partner, told her, "Oh, go ahead and go." She didn't know what to do. She thought maybe it was an emergency, and she should stay at the office. All of her friends went, except for her. She quickly realized that it wasn't an emergency at all. She said, "The truth is, very few things are true emergencies. Tell them 'this is how I'm reachable,' and go!"

So—how do you go about taking vacations? Here's some advice . . .

a. Give people as much advance notice as you can.

If you're getting married or going to your grandparents' 50th anniversary celebration, let your employer know the minute ***you*** know what the date is.

b. Recognize your billable requirements come first.

If you're at a firm, you've got to do your work if you expect to be able to take a vacation. As one lawyer commented, "Maybe your firm's policy is that you get four weeks of vacation a year. But if you've been billing only twenty hours a week, you'd have to have chutzpah to take your four weeks." The expectation is that you're getting your work done ***around*** your vacation time. Make sure that's true if you expect to be able to get away!

c. Know when you can take a break.

There's no set period of time that you have to work before you take a vacation, but from what I heard, as a rule of thumb you shouldn't take any vacation time before you've been with an employer for six months. Having said that, ***everybody*** knows that emergencies come up, and that you may have to take time off for those. But those aren't vacations!

d. Buy travel insurance!

That's Gail Peshel's advice, and it reflects the fact that you never know when you might need to get your money back. Michelle Fongyee adds that "Even when you go on vacation, you need to be professional and check in, or at least be where they can reach you if there's an emergency. You might not have told the managing partner where that one particular document is!" In extreme situations, you might have to cut your vacation short or take a laptop with you. But as Jim Lovelace points out, "If you're working for decent people, they'll tell you to leave and enjoy yourself, they'll answer your e-mails—with the assumption that you would, and will, do the same for them!"

e. Don't wait until the end of the year for your vacation.

As Jim Lovelace points out, "You don't know if you'll have the time then. When New Year's comes, it's a 'use it or lose it' proposition. No one will remember that you billed 3,000 hours last year and give you double vacation the following year!"

B. USE EVALUATIONS AND CRITICISM TO PROPEL YOUR CAREER FORWARD.

The thought of being evaluated probably makes your skin crawl. That's understandable. Evaluations are far more likely to focus on things you're ***not*** doing well than things you're getting right. They're a font of criticism, and who likes ***that?***

Well, I'm not telling you that an evaluation is something that's organically likeable. But if you prep yourself appropriately, you can use evaluations to identify yourself as a star in the making, even if the evaluation is heavily negative. "What?" you're thinking. "That's not possible!" Sure it is. It may not be obvious, but a lot of what's going on in an evaluation is this: Do you have what it takes to become great? You're probably thinking that your "raw material" is your oral advocacy skill or your writing ability, but that's only partially true. What really determines if you get ahead is whether or not people view you as capable of taking direction to hone the skills you have. ***Nobody*** graduates from law school as a fully-functioning professional. You need to be able to respond to guidance in order to get there. And the place where people are most able to gauge your ability to do that is when you're being criticized, whether in an evaluation or anywhere else. There's an old quote that goes, "It's not until the tide goes out that you can see who's not wearing a bathing suit." When people are patting you on the back for your great grades or passing the bar or doing a good job—that's the easy part. But it's not where people judge you the most. It's when they're telling you, "Here's something you need to improve . . . " or "You don't do this as well as you could." ***That's*** where they'll make up their minds about you. In this section we'll talk about how you handle a situation where you're under fire so that you come out making people think even more of you than they did before. It ***is*** possible. And you're going to do it!

Incidentally, what we'll be focusing on here are evaluations. I talked about handling feedback in general in the "1,640-Hour Interview" chapter on summer clerkships. Go back and read that. In a way, getting feedback on every project—and handling it well—is a microcosm of evaluations. Let's get started!

1. What you need to do before—and in between—evaluations

a. As soon as you start, ask for a copy of the criteria on which you'll be reviewed—including how bonuses are determined.

It's ***crucial*** that you know ahead of time how it is that you'll be evaluated. Why? It's hard to aim for a target you can't see! I've reproduced some sample evaluation forms in Appendix B at the back of the book. Take a look at those. I think you'll be surprised by what you see. As Chicago-Kent's Stephanie Rever Chu says, "What surprises people is that they're being evaluated on things they didn't anticipate. At a large firm, you're judged on your oral skills even if you don't spend time in court. And you're evaluated on relationships with attorneys and staff." It's fairly obvious that if you spend a substantial amount of time on research and writing assignments that you'll be evaluated on your research and writing skills and billables. But they'll also look at your ability to meet deadlines, and your willingness to take on work and to work late. As Valparaiso's Gail Peshel points out, "It's easy to be wrong about the review criteria. You may think it's billables whereas it's actually the files you close."

You also want to pay attention to bonus criteria. The basis on which your employer awards bonuses tells you a lot about what they really value. If they talk pro bono but they reward straight billables, you'd be foolish not to pay attention to that. (I'm not saying not to do pro bono—I'm just saying, pay attention to what your deal is!) If they include pro bono, recruiting activities, or administrative functions in bonus considerations—that's good to know, too.

As you gain more experience with your employer, you'll find that the evaluation criteria will change. They'll expect you to take on more responsibility. Keeping an eye on what you're supposed to be doing, at every step along the way, will ensure that you're never caught off-guard.

b. If your employer doesn't have set review criteria, sit down and agree with your employer on what they ought to be.

As Golden Gate's Susanne Aronowitz says, "Sit down with your employer and settle on what your review criteria will be, if they don't have set reviews. Set some goals, so that you'll be able to say, 'Over the next six months this is what I'll be reviewed on—my ability to handle projects, my writing skills,' maybe later on client development and supervisory skills. Agree on them ahead of time so they seem fair to you!"

c. If you've been at work for six months without a review, ask for one.

As William & Mary's Fred Thrasher points out, "There aren't any exams at work. At school, at the end of the semester, you have some idea of how you're doing. But at work, if you're not reviewed, you don't. If you go for six months without anybody mentioning a review, ask for one!" One lawyer talked about going into his supervisor's office after six months and asking, "Isn't it time for me to be reviewed? I've been here for a few months. I want to know how I'm doing." The supervisor responded, "You're doing great! If something was wrong, believe me, we'd let you know." The lawyer comments, "I was relieved, but asking was the ***safest*** thing to do. Silence can go both ways!"

d. Keep track of your accomplishments and *every* compliment you've received on your work, written or oral. *Close* track.

I gave you this advice in the "Getting Organized" section, and here we are toward the end of the book, and gee—it's ***still*** good advice. There are two reasons for this. Number one, it's good for your resume. I know you've just started ***this*** job, but you always have to keep one eye toward the future. And number two, as American's Matt Pascocello points out, "You can't assume that they know what you've done!"

So what do you want to chronicle? You need:

1. Every project on which you work (and resolutions of cases you handle if you're a litigator);
2. Any special matters you handle (*e.g.*, recruiting, administrative works, helping with articles or speeches, writing your own articles or speeches, pro bono [especially if your employer values it]);
3. Any time you stepped up to the plate to help somebody else (*e.g.*, staying for the weekend at the office to help others with a closing or any other pressing matter);
4. Any interim feedback you receive, both written and oral. Jot down comments that are made to you about your work, whether it's from partners, colleagues, clients, or secretaries.

What you want to do is to keep all of this material in a notebook or folder, so that when you go into your evaluation, you have support material with you. You're not being defensive when you do this; you're being smart.

SMART HUMAN TRICK . . .

Junior associate at a large firm. He writes a memo for a securities partner, and when he gets it back, he sees that the partner has written on it: "I couldn't have done better myself." When a mid-level associate sees this, he says, "That's a kiss from God. Take it into your review with you!"

e. *Actively* seek out opportunities to get the experience on which you'll be judged. If you're unsuccessful, document your attempt.

When you're reviewed, particularly at a large firm, you'll be judged according to how you are progressing in comparison with "your class"—that is, people with the same amount of experience as you. Many times new lawyers are stung by being told that "You're behind your class." Don't let that happen to you! I've already told you to be familiar with the review criteria. Take those criteria and ***ask*** for the opportunity to do the work you're supposed to be doing at your "level." That way, you can't possibly be criticized for not having that experience. If you asked for it and you were turned down, you've done everything you could do!

SMART HUMAN TRICK . . .

Mid-level litigation associate, large firm: "Sometimes, especially as a woman, you might find that you're not getting the juiciest work. You're put on cases where you can't develop. No hearings or client contact, no depositions. At review, they'll tell you, 'You're behind your class,' and deny you a bonus or a promotion. 'Your work product is wonderful but you haven't done A and B and C.' They're weeding you out of the system! What I do is to make a point of going to my partners three times a year, and ask for involvement, so I don't get burned at evaluation time. I know what they're going to evaluate me on, and I make sure I ask for those experiences. I keep track of the experience I get and the experiences I ask for and don't get, and I take that with me into my reviews. During one review, my partner said, 'You've had less deposition experience and you've gone to fewer hearings than other people in your class.' I pulled out my notepad and said, 'On this date I asked you for this and this and this and instead of being given those, I was assigned to these other cases. I am not yet in charge of my caseload. I'm not a rainmaker yet. I get the cases to which I'm assigned. On this date I approached Partner X looking for practical experience, and when you found out you were angry about it.' His jaw just dropped to the floor. After that, he made sure I got the opportunities I needed."

f. Don't assume that everyone with something good to say will tell your reviewers.

It's easy to think, "Well, partner so-and-so loves me, I'll look great in my review." That's only true if that particular partner's opinion is included in the review! As Matt Pascocello points out, "In lots of firms, the practice is for reviewers to send out surveys to partners, asking for feedback about you. Some respond and some don't. You can't count on the responses!" So if someone has loved what you've done, go before your evaluation and ask discreetly if they've filled out a review for you. You want as many arrows in your quiver as you can get.

g. Always keep your finger on the pulse of how you're doing. Evaluations should not be a surprise!

When you get reviewed, they shouldn't say anything to you that comes as a shock. As Harvard's Mark Weber says, "A review time should never be the time when you sit there with your mouth agog!" As I recommended in the feedback section in "The

1,640-Hour Interview" chapter, you need to get feedback on everything you do. If you spot problems along the way, you can correct them before they turn into a bad review. Don't let your evaluation be a cold splash of water!

h. Before you walk into your review, tell yourself things that will make the review *easier*.

In his book *Emotional Intelligence At Work*, Hendrie Weisinger tells you to prepare statements ahead of time to tell yourself in stressful situations. "I'll ask for specific examples of what I need to improve on," "I'll learn from criticisms I get how to be a better lawyer," "I've done good work," "I'll remember positives as well as negatives." If you make a point of telling yourself comments like this, you can make sure that your reactions ***in*** the review are appropriate.

2. How to handle yourself during the review. Take a deep breath . . .

a. Remain calm.

Remember, people can't see how you feel. They only see how you behave. A review is a stressful situation for ***anybody***. Your reviewers themselves aren't happy when they're being reviewed, either. But nobody has to know how you really feel. Take deep breaths. No matter what they say, I'll show you how to handle it. To the extent you can—relax!

b. Remember that what you're hearing are learning tools, not personal judgments.

Any time you receive criticism, whether it's in an evaluation or anywhere else, remember that the ***only*** way to improve is to take the kernels of truth in criticism and make changes in what you do! Yes, it stings. But if you never in your life took any criticism well, you wouldn't be feeding yourself or dressing yourself or making your bed, let alone doing a good job at work. Put criticism in ***perspective***. It's hard to accept when you're hearing it, but criticism really does make you better. As one lawyer commented, "Criticism is designed to make you better. It's not there to break you down as a lawyer!" Remember that when you're on the spot!

c. **Remember that what's going on isn't a search for the "truth." It's a collection of perceptions about you. *Important* perceptions.**

If you get a review that says, "Your writing skills are not up to par," that doesn't mean that there's anything wrong with your writing skills. What it's really saying is, "The work product that you've turned in to us here at the office isn't what we expected." It says nothing about what you're personally capable of accomplishing or what you might do in future. It's got no predictive value. It's just a snapshot of someone's opinion ***right now***.

As I've mentioned elsewhere in the book, my hobby is writing screenplays. My dream is to win an Oscar for best original screenplay. My wonderful mentor, Stewart Bronfeld, has taught me well when it comes to taking criticism. When he criticizes anything I write, he says, "I don't get this. And remember, if I don't get it, you're wrong." So I've learned not to be defensive or say, "But here's what I meant . . . ." It doesn't matter. What's on the written page matters. What other people ***perceive*** matters.

One of my scripts got into the hands of a director in Hollywood, and he called me to talk about it. He started out by saying that he liked the script, and then said, "Would you be willing to make a few changes to it?" I said, "Absolutely!" He went on to make suggestions, large and small, for *forty-five minutes*. I took copious notes, with frequent "Mm-hmms" and "I see's." My husband Henry stood by, dumbfounded, listening to me taking this and looking at the notes I was writing. At the end of the forty-five minutes, I thanked the director for his input and told him I'd make the changes and get the script back to him within a week. When I got off the phone, Henry asked, incredulously, "How could you ***take*** that for forty-five minutes? Why didn't you defend yourself?" I responded, "Why? This isn't about whether or not my script is 'good' or 'bad.' This guy is telling me what ***he*** thinks, and if he wants to direct it, then he gets what he wants!" Henry was still not totally buying it, and I said, "Listen. What's going on when he's talking to me like that is that he's asking himself, 'What would it be like to work with her? Would she give me the changes I want or would she whine and complain and make my life difficult?' Because if he doesn't want to work with me, there are a million other writers and a stack of scripts on his desk three feet thick. He's doing me a ***favour*** telling me what he doesn't like. At least he cares enough to do ***that***!"

I'm not pretending I'm some tower of strength. But I've been writing scripts for so many years and had so much rejection that I've learned to put these things in perspective. You don't have to go through that much pain to learn the same thing! Take it from me. If you put criticism in perspective, it's really not bad at all.

d. You need to know the source of any negative comments.

Evaluations are different from employer to employer. Some reviewers sign their comments, and others don't. Some reviews are totally oral, whereas at others, the reviewers will read to you from evaluation forms.

Everybody agrees that no matter whether the reviews are oral or written, you ***have*** to know the source of negative comments. As Georgetown's Beth Sherman says, "If you don't know who said what, there's no accountability and no way for you to respond. You need the opportunity to sit down with people who say things about you, good ***and*** bad. Otherwise you suspect everybody, and you don't know which projects you've done well and which you haven't!"

It may be that you ask to see the written reviews, and the reviewer won't show them to you. Not a good sign! As the partner at one firm says, "If an attorney won't let you see the review, probably you didn't want to see it in the first place." Reassure the reviewer that you're not worried about what's said about you—you ***want*** to improve, and that means hearing everything, good, bad, or ugly. It's worth a shot!

e. **When you hear criticism—and you will—don't whine, complain, challenge, get defensive, or cry. If you do—you're through.**

The reason I gave you the "self-talk" to use before you walk into an evaluation is that you're going to ***need*** it. Remember—they're watching you closely to see how you handle criticism. It's one of the toughest challenges you face as a new lawyer. Stay calm and collected. Hamline's Vince Thomas says, "Remember the three R's: reserved, respectful, responsive." The hiring partner at one large firm advises that you "Show them that you ***get*** it, that you understand there's an issue and you want to ***improve*** it. If you've done some good projects, bring them in with you, and when they criticize you about something else, pull out your good projects and say, 'I did well here—what did I do wrong over here? Did I go too far or not far enough?' Show them that you care and that you want to do better! If you react poorly, you're done. Even if you're right, who ***cares***? It's all about perceptions." Hodgson Russ' Adam Perry adds, "When you get criticized, soak it up and enjoy it. There's always a way to isolate and get rid of someone who's defensive."

CAREER LIMITING MOVE . . .

In response to a verbal lashing about poor billable hours from a managing partner at a major New York firm, a first year associate offered the following defense: "But Sir, I think the real problem is that my skills would be better utilized doing rainmaking."

SMART HUMAN TRICK . . .

Mid-level associate, large West Coast firm: "My performance evaluations as a litigator were getting so that I knew I wouldn't make partner. It wasn't as though they were saying 'Get rid of this guy,' but there would always be some criticism about my not being aggressive enough, that I was too nice and laid-back to be a big firm litigator. I took the hint and asked for a transfer to corporate. In my next review, it was partially litigation and partially corporate. The leaders from both departments were there, so my brand-new corporate partner heard all the old criticisms. It was like a grand jury indictment! My new boss heard everything the old bosses said, a lot of petty, horrible stuff. I was horrified, but I didn't cry, I didn't get angry, I didn't throw a tantrum. I **wanted** to, but I didn't. I didn't squirm or fidget. When the old boss was done, I said calmly, 'I'm sorry they feel this way, this is what I did, I can understand their perspective, I'd like to point out that they did say good things about X and X and X.' Immediately after the review, my new section leader said to me, 'I thought you handled that review extremely well.' The way she said it, I could tell that she thought **more** of me for the way I handled it. It minimized what they said. Sometimes in your life you'll get unfair criticism. If you think it'll address the substance of your work or damage your career, then address it. If not, be elegant. Don't respond to carping. You want people to be able to say of you: 'He's a class act.'"

f. Don't ever, ever, *ever* whine, "But I did my best."

Doing your best matters to your mom and to God. It doesn't matter in reviews. If you screwed something up, the ***last*** thing you want to say is "Well, I did my best." Great! You did your best, and you got it ***wrong***! The bottom line is, if you didn't get it right, you ***didn't*** do your best. You're capable of getting it right. Law isn't rocket science. Remember the line from the Sean Connery/Nicholas Cage movie *The Rock*. My friend Jody does a killer imitation of Sean Connery responding to Nicholas Cage's protest "But I did my best." "Your *best?"* Connery says. "Your *best?* Losers whine about their best. Winners go home and **** the prom queen."

g. Acknowledge and summarize the criticism you get.

Take responsibility for what you've done right away. That way, you won't sound defensive. "Yes, you're right, I missed that deadline."

Summarize what the reviewer said, so that you avoid misunderstandings. If you say, "I want to make sure I have this right. You're saying that I didn't take enough initiative on X . . . " you're giving them an opportunity to revise any criticism. If you're going to take criticism and use it to improve yourself, you need to make sure you have it exactly right.

h. Recognize the differences between the genders when it comes to communication.

As South Carolina's Phyllis Burkhard explains, "When a male partner is conducting a year-end review and asks, 'How do you feel about your job?' he may not be asking what the woman associate is hearing. For men, this is a 'How's it going?' kind of question, to which the response is, 'Oh, it's great' or 'I've really enjoyed my work on XYZ case.' To women, 'How do you ***feel*'** connotes a question about their emotional reaction to the job. They pour out their likes and dislikes (particularly frustrations about the time pressures, lack of organization of assignments, and the like), and the partner looks increasingly perplexed and uncomfortable. Women leave the interview and say to their female colleagues, 'I could tell he didn't like what I was saying, but he ***asked*** me! I wasn't going to lie about it.' The partner considers the women at the firm as whiners, raising all of these issues for no reason." So don't view your review as the place for a general dump session on your employer. Focus on what you did, what they have to say about what you did, and save your more general complaints for other venues. (I talk about handling "culture" issues in the "Getting Off On The Right Foot" chapter. Take a look at that!)

i. Always ask the reviewer for ways you can improve—even if you get praise!

Maybe your review will be one long handshake. "Well done! Well done!" That's terrific. Even if it's not a love fest—especially if it's not a love fest!—you need to ask the reviewer for ways to improve, and ***write them down***. Criticism is meaningless if you can't take it and turn it around. If you ask for advice on improving, you're showing that you're taking criticism exactly the way you ***should*** take it, and the reviewer will take that as a huge positive. Also, for your next review, you can show how you've improved on what you were told last time around—and again, that kind of initiative is applauded!

j. If the criticism is unfair, tell the reviewer you'd like the opportunity to correct the record or explain your side of the story.

It may be that some of the criticism you get is flat-out unfair. Maybe the person who criticized you was just a jerk and is taking a strip of flesh from you just to be vindictive. One junior associate told me about a project he'd done where the assigning attorney asked him for cases in the jurisdiction supporting a particular proposition. He told him not to use Lexis or Westlaw, just do book research. It turns out there was an opinion that was too new to appear in the books, and it wasn't until a couple of weeks later that it showed up in a pocket part. In his review, the assigning attorney criticized the associate's research skills. Well, for pity's sake, that's just not fair, and it shouldn't be allowed to stand.

But you have to be ***careful*** about lashing out at unfair criticism. Instead, ask the reviewer if you can get together later in the day or perhaps tomorrow to go over the problem. ***Don't***—I repeat, ***don't***—express your feelings right there. You need some time to cool off and absorb what was said and get your thoughts together. When you get back together, have in writing your defense. And be sure to acknowledge any element of the criticism that was accurate, so you don't sound like you're being a whinybaby. Remember, this is about perceptions. You need to correct perceptions that aren't fair, but don't make the problem worse by the way that you go about it!

3. The morning after: What to do when the evaluation is over

a. You can—and will—pick yourself up.

It doesn't matter how bad the review was, or how angry you

are, or how unfair it was. They're just words. Check yourself for cuts and bruises. You won't find any. They're just people's perceptions, and you can change those. As one of my favourite sayings goes, you can't control being knocked down, but you ***do*** control getting up again. You'll get over it!

b. If the review was oral, immediately write up a memo summarizing what was said.

One senior associate recommended that "If you get an oral review, send a memo back, saying, 'For my own career development, I want to make sure that I interpreted your comments accurately . . . ' and then repeat whatever they said. Firms try to protect themselves with oral rather than written evaluations. If the legal market turns bad, old reviews that were good will magically turn bad, and they'll deny it."

c. Change any negative perceptions of you!

Nobody's picture of you is beyond repair. Yes, first impressions count. But they don't count for ***everything***. You know in your own life that you've changed your mind about people. It's always possible. ***Listen*** to what's said of you in evaluations, think about how you can go about changing negative perceptions, ***do it***, and make sure the people who criticized you ***know*** that you're doing it. If you're accused of not getting your work done on time and not following up, then "Work as hard as you have to to make your deadlines, and leave copious e-mail and voice mail messages asking if there is 'anything else you can do,'" advises Denver's Jennifer Loud Ungar. If you're told that you don't exhibit leadership skills, then take on a co-chair position in a bar committee and invite your critic to one of the meetings. One lawyer told of how the managing partner had said in her review that "I mixed with staff members too much, that I needed to lunch with senior associates and partners." "After that," she says, "I organized lunches every week with the firm, inviting partners and associates I liked, and the firm even ***paid*** for it! It was a great compromise. They saw me eating lunch with lawyers, and I still got to eat lunch with the people I ***wanted***

to eat lunch with pretty frequently. It was just that what they ***saw*** changed a ***lot.***"

d. **Seek out people who criticized you in their evaluations, and thank them. And no—I haven't lost my mind.**

Remember—the point of the whole exercise is to make yourself a better lawyer. People who criticize you are helping you do that. Don't vilify them. ***Thank*** them. Apart from anything else, they'll be blown away by your intestinal fortitude. Very few people have the guts to thank their critics. Be one of them!

SMART HUMAN TRICK . . .

Female associate at a large firm. She'd been used to general praise, but at one particular evaluation, a partner for whom she'd done no work contributed his perception that she didn't take initiative and she worked too slowly. He had no rational basis for either comment. She said nothing at the evaluation, but as she says, "I was just **seething**. Afterwards I sat down with my mentor, and using choice words, I told him about it. I finished up by saying, 'What should I do about the son of a bitch?' He looked at me and said, 'Today, don't do anything. Calm down. Tomorrow morning, walk the hallways and find him, and thank him for taking the time to make those comments in your evaluation. And **smile** when you say it. Tell him that you want to be the best lawyer you can be and that you value his advice, and in the future when he sees areas where you can improve you hope he'll tell you directly.' I couldn't believe it. I said, 'But he's **wrong**.' He said, 'It doesn't matter. What he told you tells you how he **sees** you. He's powerful. If you're smart you'll try to change his impression. If you approach him you'll totally disarm him. **Especially** because he says you don't take the initiative.' I wasn't happy about it, but I went away and thought about it and realized I didn't have anything to lose." She laughs when she describes her critic's reaction: "He was totally in shock. He couldn't **believe** I'd taken it like this. He was speechless. The effect was unbelievable. He turned into one of my biggest fans, and I heard through the grapevine that he was saying glowing things about me behind my back. What's ironic is that nothing had really changed. Not really. My work was the same as it always was. But the way he perceived me did a one-eighty."

C. Upping The Ante: How To Make *Thousands* More Than You Thought You Would

Don't tell me. Let me guess. You're going to work for a medium-to-small firm—maybe even a sole practitioner—and you're not happy with the money you've been offered. Or else you've heard about small firm salaries, and even though you think that's the direction you're going, the money issue makes your blood run cold. What should you do? What ***can*** you do? What I'm going to do in the next few pages is to give you the basic strategies that could well line your pockets with more scratch than you expected.

From the outset, you need to know that money is a tricky issue. There aren't any guarantees that you can get more than you were offered. But you ***might*** be able to. There is one common situation where you absolutely positively can't ask for more money, and that's when you're starting your career with a large firm. If your starting salary is in the six figures, for the sake of your physical well-being, do ***not*** ask for more money. Most large firms lose money on new associates who are paid anything more than $50-65,000 a year to start. If you're making double or triple that and you ask for more, they'll kill you. And they'd consider it justifiable homicide. Don't go there. (Having said that, there's talk that large firms may think of going to an individual-negotiation pay structure, where there's none of this everybody-gets-the-same-starting-salary idea. Kind of like baseball players. But we aren't there ***yet***.)

So if you're at a small to medium-sized law firm, you have a shot. What do you need to do to make more money? I've got a simple, three-point plan for you.

Step One: Knowledge is power.

You need to know as much as you can about what the market will bear. The National Association for Law Placement puts out very comprehensive statistics (you'll find them at your career services office) that tell you how much different kinds of law firms pay, in different geographic areas, not just as starting pay but several years out into the future, as well.

Why is this important? Two reasons. For one thing, if you find that the range for a small firm in the area where you're going to live is $30-35,000, and you want $65,000, unless you've got some very clear, very incriminating Polaroids, you're probably not going to get it. On the other hand, you might learn that the employer you're considering is at the low end of the scale. If so, you know—and you can assume that *they* know—that there's wiggle room. You've got negotiating power before you ever enter the room.

Step Two: Recognize that in the absence of other considerations (which we're going to talk about in a minute), you have limited negotiating power as a new lawyer.

When you are talking about a small-ish firm looking at *you,* as an untested lawyer, here's what they're seeing. "When you start, it will take you four hours to do a memo that years down the road you'll be able to knock out in twenty minutes. Much of your early time is written down or written off," says Emory's Carolyn Bregman. Quinnipiac's Diane Ballou adds that "When you start, you don't know anything. They can't send you out alone, you have to tag along, and they can't charge for you. And if you're going to work for just one person, bringing you on is a quantum leap no matter *how* much you get."

So don't get hung up on what you're coming to the table with, just because of your J.D. If you want more, you've got to *offer* more. Which leads me to . . .

Step Three: Answer the question "What's in it for me?"—or encourage them to overlook that question entirely.

Let's say that a small firm, Smith & Jones, offers you $35,000 a year as a new associate. And let's say that this is bang in the middle of the range for your geographic area. You want more. How do you go after it? You have three choices. You can bring more to the table, you can ask for "non-dollar-figure" compensation, or you can negotiate up-front for down-the-road increases.

Before we discuss what these are, remember that asking for more money is not without risk. They may be open to your ideas, with the idea in mind that they want you to be happy working for them. Or they might be resentful that you brought it up at all. Make your approach *gentle* and watch for signals telling you to negotiate further—or retreat. And *always, always, always* stress to them that you are *grateful for the opportunity* to work with them, the money issue aside!

So—let's talk about options for squeezing out more pay:

1. **What else can you offer them? There are many possibilities, Including:**

   Consider negotiating for a cut of business you bring in. This is a particularly easy sell, because if you don't bring in more business, you don't make more money. It's a no-lose proposition for the employer.

   - Offer to write a firm newsletter, as a means of gaining publicity, clients, and keeping their presence visible.
   - Offer to give seminars to a key audience for them: be it the elderly (for estate planning work), investment clubs (for tax work), and the like.
   - Offer to set up and maintain a firm home page, if you've got that kind of skill.

   Any one of these would be viable options for earning more money. What you want to be careful about is any work you decide to do on the side. One lawyer told me about a woman who was doing contract work (it's basically freelance lawyering) for several small firms. One of them made her an offer to join them as an associate. She wasn't thrilled with the offer, but took it anyway—and maintained some of her contract work. The firm found out, and the managing partner went nuts and fired her. So be aware that if you'd rather do extra work elsewhere than negotiate for more money from your employer, you should do it openly. Obviously you can do things like tutoring law students and bar examinees, and there are other kinds of freelance work—like web page design, database management—that are unlikely to offend any law firm employer. In fact, it might shame them into paying you more, out of guilt that you've got to moonlight to pay your bills.

2. "Non-dollar-figure" compensation.

This is a bit of a misnomer, because what you're really asking for here *does* have a monetary value. But since you're not saying, "I want another $3,000," it doesn't *seem* the same. It's somewhat the same psychological trick that's going on when you go to a casino, and instead of betting with money, you're betting with chips. It doesn't seem like money that way. Well, you're using that same principle when you negotiate for non-dollar-figure compensation. You can ask for things like:

- Paid parking.
- Reimbursement for car expenses, if you're expected to travel in your own car.
- Paid lunches.
- A 401K plan.
- Insurance (or alternatively, if they're offering you insurance and your spouse's policy covers you, ask for the money they'd have spent on it to cover you).
- If you haven't taken the bar yet, a bar review course.
- Professional fees.

You get the idea here—you're asking for small things in a non-monetary way to soften the blow.

3. Negotiating now for down-the-road increases.

If the prospects for getting a higher salary look dim—or you try and strike out—consider negotiating for fixed-period increases in the future. Quinnipiac's Diane Ballou suggests that "If you take a job at $28,000 now, you can ask for a reevaluation at three months, six months, nine months, with a chance to make more money then." As she points out, "This gives them a chance to get to know you and like you and need you, and your chances will be better as a result."

Actually, your chances of getting a big raise are ***much*** better if you can bite the bullet and negotiate after you've worked with them for at least a few months. Especially with a small organization, they may quickly find that they can't remember how they functioned without you, and that gives you leverage you didn't have at the outset. You'll also be able to say that you progressed with your work product, your writing skills, and perhaps your business development ability.

Step Four: What to do if your bid for more money fails.

Trying to negotiate for more money at the outset is ***fraught*** with risk. You may alienate an employer who was otherwise willing to welcome you with open arms, but now feels that you are selfish and ungrateful. And you may be resentful that they don't value your time more than your paltry salary suggests. What do you do? ***Fuhgedduhbadit. Pretend you never asked in the first place.*** You've got to approach your job with enthusiasm, an air of appreciation and an obvious desire to learn, no matter *how* much money you make. Rest assured that you'll have ***plenty*** of opportunities to ask for more money once they've had a chance to actually discover for themselves how valuable an addition to the firm you prove to be—and you'll be able to look back on your early, lean years as the learning experience that they are!

D. As Will Rogers Said, "Even If You're On The Right Track, If You're Sitting There, You'll Get Run Over." Take Hidden Opportunities To Make Your Career Take Off Like A Rocket.

If you follow the advice throughout this book, you'd have a hard time ***avoiding*** success. Figuring out the culture, manifesting the right qualities, doing top-notch work on time, cultivating a mentor, getting involved in activities outside of work—people will ***stumble*** over themselves to be associated with you. What I'm going to do here is to highlight some of the qualities that I've already talked about in depth throughout the book, and focus on your long-term career as opposed to the job you've got right now. It may be that you spend your entire career with this employer. If so, that's great. What we'll talk about will make sure you always get great work and move quickly up the ranks. If you decide to move on, what I'll tell you will help you nail a great job the next time around!

1. **Remember: Nobody has a vested interest in your career except for *you.***

If you're going to make it to the top, it'll be under your own steam. You can make it a lot easier on yourself—we'll talk about exactly how to do that—but the fact is, you've got to keep your eyes open for opportunities all the time. They're there, all right. But other people are unlikely to point them out to you. You've got to find and go after them yourself. What you should do is to imagine yourself as a steerage passenger on the Titanic. As you know, most of the steerage passengers drowned; most of them stayed below decks, as they'd been instructed, until all of the lifeboats had cast off. Many of the steerage passengers who ***did*** survive refused to cool their heels down below. They found their way through the Titanic's byzantine stairways onto the upper decks, and made their way onto the lifeboats. If you want great work, if you want a great career, don't wait for instructions and guidance. Get after it!

2. **What to do at the office to get the best work.**

   a. **Do top-notch work on time to generate buzz about yourself.**

   I've already told you how to do great work, how to meet deadlines, all of those things. The benefit to doing great work is that your supervisors talk to each other, and if you give them exactly what they want, that's what they'll say! As Georgetown's Beth Sherman points out, "Getting great work in a firm is a matter of word of mouth. 'X did great work for me,' 'Oh, I want him, too.'"

   b. **Identify powerful people, and cultivate them.**

   In the "Getting Off On The Right Foot" chapter, I talked about the importance of identifying powerful people and making yourself known to them. You don't want to be a toady suck-up, but you ***do*** want to be savvy about cultivating the power base at work. As Quinnipiac's Diane Ballou says, "Find out who's on the Boards of Directors for different activities. Find out what activities they're involved in, which sports they like. If you like the same things, volunteer to do what they do. Don't fake an interest, but if you've got the same ones, take advantage of that!"

c. **Getting great work is *not* a matter of "being in the right place at the right time." It's a matter of saying the right things to the right people.**

When something good happens to somebody, you'll often hear it attributed to "being in the right place at the right time." When it comes to getting great work, ***you*** can take active steps to make sure ***you're*** the one in that enviable position. It's ***not*** entirely a matter of luck. The fact is, if you want the best assignments, go to the people doing the work you want and ask to help out. That kind of enthusiasm is always appreciated—and rewarded. As Missouri's Gerald Beechum says, "Let people ***know***. Don't closet yourself. Tell them what you want!" Carlton Fields' Jason Murray advises you to "Be aggressive about it. Tell people you want to work for, 'Please keep me in mind if you need help. I've got some time.' And ***make*** time for them." Dewey Ballantine's John Ragosta says, "Express an interest in new areas. Request 'the next GATT case that comes into the office.' Stake out territory and volunteer to help anyone who needs help in that area. It will make you the expert in the areas of ***your*** choosing." A partner at Waller Lansden says, "I really like to see associates volunteer to take work in a particular area or for a particular client. I like it if an associate comes to me and says, 'I've never handled an IPO before and I hear you're starting one. Can I help?'" One real estate partner said, "I like what I do. It's cool. If someone was interested in what I do, I'd love that. I'm delighted when someone wants to come to a closing with me. ***Ask***. Don't get preoccupied with whether it's billable or not. Take an interest in it and you'll be amazed how much interest people will take in you."

d. **Listen to the whispers. See who the superstars are at the office. Emulate them.**

I told you this in the "Getting Off On The Right Foot" chapter. There's no better way to figure out what goes over big in your office than by seeing who gets the right whispers—"he's on his way up," "she's a star"—and do what they do.

e. Don't overlook mentors!

As I talked about in the "The 'People' Part of Work" chapter, mentors can have a huge impact on your career. Even though you can't ***make*** people be your mentor, absolutely take the steps to make yourself "mentor-able" by people with clout at the office. As Miami's Marcy Cox says, "Good work is not the most important thing. Having somebody powerful rave about your work ***is***. They'll spread the word about you."

f. Determine a niche for yourself, in terms of business development or expertise.

What do people at the top of any organization do? They look ***outwards*** to figure out how to bring in business. Depending on the size of the organization you join, that may or may not be possible; as a new associate at a large firm you're not likely to be able to solicit a Fortune 500 client unless your daddy is the Chairman of the Board. But you ***can*** take steps that prove your business savvy, and you ***will*** get noticed for it. The two likeliest avenues are to establish an expertise niche for yourself, something no one else in the firm does, or to target a particular kind of client.

How do you do this? Keep up with what's going on in the news. Think organically about what your organization does, and what areas are logical expansions of that. If you practice real estate law, it may be that no one in your firm is familiar with the Fair Debt Collection Practices Act, and that's a niche you can fill.

Look at your own talents, contacts, and background to see if those suggest business opportunities for your employer. For instance, one law student I talked to had been an architect for twenty years before law school, and in that capacity he had developed working relationships with many contractors. There's a fertile business development opportunity for him. Another law student, a Korean-American woman, lamented the fact that many Korean business owners who attended church with her family weren't happy with their non-Korean-speaking lawyers. There's her niche. At the firm Davis Wright Tremaine there's a junior associate who "targeted Oregon wine growers as clients. He began by convincing a partner in the Hospitality Practice Group that it was a good idea, and then finding out what resources he had in the firm." Needless to say, this guy is viewed as a star. One corporate associate at a huge New York City firm distinguished himself by targeting Internet-based businesses as clients. He began attending Internet trade shows, determined the bars where Internet entrepreneurs hang out and started frequenting them (now ***there's*** a tough assignment), and in general talked the talk and walked the walk. He's made substantial headway in luring them as clients.

3. Don't look at your job. Look at your c*areer.*

If you look at what you do as part of a ribbon stretching into your future, you'll behave differently than if you just consider this particular job a way station. This job is the foundation for what you do in the future, whether it's here or anywhere else. You've got to keep constant vigilance to make sure that you're gaining the skills and expertise that will serve you magnificently no matter what you do. As St. Louis University's Wendy Werner says, "Jobs aren't permanent—but skills ***are.***" Wake Forest's Bill Barrett adds, "You're ultimately working for yourself. The skills you acquire, the contacts you make, are ***vital.***"

a. Look at your resume frequently, and focus on activities that will strengthen it.

If you keep a periodic eye on your resume, it will remind you that you're not just working at a job—you're developing a career.

b. Keep track of every single project you work on, and every activity in which you get involved.

Keep them in a folder so that you can add them to your resume, and so that you always have them at your fingertips in case you need to talk about your experience. ***Quantifying*** what you've done, with specific examples, sounds much more impressive than "I was a litigation associate."

c. Expand your horizons.

You have no idea where you'll find your next professional passion, but you certainly won't find it if you don't keep your eyes open! As Harvard's Mark Weber says, "If there's a seminar that intrigues you—go! If there's a specialty you're interested in—read about it! If there's a partner whose work you want to do—solicit it!"

d. Make a name for yourself—starting *now*.

There's nothing that says that you have to wait to become an expert. You can launch your rise to fame ***right now***. It's not difficult. Get to know what's going on, and then make your contribution. Go to CLEs that interest you. Give speeches at the bar association and civic groups. Give seminars on something that interests you. Write a summary of key decisions in your favourite area and e-mail them to others in your firm, or in your specialty outside of your firm. Write articles for trade publications, local publications, relevant websites. Get involved in the bar, in smaller sections where you can have more of an impact. As Hofstra's Caroline Levy says, "You rise through the ranks faster and you get known faster." She advises you to "Join committees that interest you. If you're interested in matrimonial law, join the committee. Volunteer to do a report. Do a good job, and people will remember and respect you. Don't join things in name only. Get involved!" A partner at one firm talked about a new associate who wanted to do franchise law. "He joined bar groups, learned who the players were, found out who the in-house lawyers were, went to CLEs. He developed his niche that way."

Get involved in the community. Habitat for Humanity, Junior League, Jaycees, Rotary, Kiwanis, YMCA. As Florida State's Stephanie Redfearn points out, "It's great for your firm because your name is associated with your firm's name. It's good to give back to the community, but it's also nice for your firm to brag about you. It helps both your and their perception in the community—and it doesn't hurt client development, either!"

Does this sound like work? Yep. Distinguishing yourself from the masses ***does*** take work. But choose the activities that you enjoy, and it won't ***seem*** like work. You'll be developing a reputation and having fun at the same time!

e. Recognize that a lot of the things you do for your own reputation are also *excellent* sources of client development.

Many of the activities I just talked about are wonderful client development tools. If you're at a large firm, the idea of client development is some distance in the future. But you can start developing those skills ***now***. And if you're at a smaller private employer—your client development years are more immediate.

When you're in law school, it's easy to think that client development is like being a car salesman—it's some kind of sleazy glad-handing. Nope! It's a matter of letting people get to know you and like you, and they'll make the leap to trusting you with their business. So if you get yourself known, it doesn't just help your reputation—it's good for yours (and your firm's) pocketbook, too!

Chicago-Kent's Stephanie Rever Chu points out that "Depending on the clients you want to attract, look at community activities that will get you in touch with those constituencies. If you do estate planning and tax work, look at doing presentations at senior community groups and nursing homes. If you have a family law practice, talk to brokers with high net worth clients who may get divorced, and go to lunch with them periodically." Think ***strategically*** when it comes to getting to know people who could potentially become clients. Lewis & Clark's Lisa Lesage asks, "Are you fluent in sign language? One new lawyer I know gets business from the deaf community because ***he*** is." One new lawyer expanded her firm's business by volunteering to help write the instruction manual for local paramedics, to inform them of their legal responsibilities. Their families started to come to her firm for their legal work.

The junior associate at one medium-sized firm knew the firm wanted to expand its real estate practice. He scouted out who the major real estate brokers were in the surrounding counties, and recommended to the partners that they let him open an office across the street from the most successful real estate brokers in the area.

They agreed. With his proximity to their office, he often ran into the brokers at the local coffee shop, the little park next door, and walking in and out of work. As they chatted they got to like him and started pushing work his way. Now, as a second year associate, he's pulling in almost two hundred thousand dollars a year (he obviously—and providentially—negotiated for a cut of the business when he asked to open the new office!).

Wake Forest's Bill Barrett suggests being visible in the community by "Volunteering with organizations to help them with articles and bylaws and other formalities. Look for places that aren't deluged with lawyers. As a new lawyer I talked about legal issues to the local AARP chapter, and got lots of estate planning work that way. You have to view being a lawyer with a small firm as building a practice, which is a business—not just having a job."

Kentucky Public Defender Sarah Madden points out that community involvement "Isn't just something that's good on your resume, and it's not just a good networking tool. If you move to another city, in another state, and they ask you what you're bringing to the table—it's got to be more than education and personality. 'I'm active with the JayCees, the Red Cross, I can bring those people to you.' You can do community work for the best reasons—or the most selfish reasons."

E. What To Do If You're Hating Your Job. Don't Turn Into A Boiled Frog!

1. It's not a man-eating tree of Madagascar. It's a *job*. You have the ultimate power: To leave.

You make compromises in every single aspect of your life. If your inner child tells you that you have to love every moment of your life, then spank your inner child. You're a grown-up, and if you don't know better, you'll be miserable ***forever***. You exercise so that you'll improve the quality of your life as you get older. You eat right for the same reason. Anybody who tells you that "a munchy, crunchy celery stick is just as delicious as a Dorito" is shagged in the head. And when it comes to your work, you balance long-term goals with short-term rewards. What you're doing ***right now*** and what you want to get out of it long-term have to balance what you sacrifice for them.

The problem is that it's very easy to slide down the scale of sacrifice until you're giving up ***way*** too much for what you're getting in return. You don't notice it because it happens so seductively. You take a job because the money is great or because it means security or because you're worried you won't get anything else. You do what you're not crazy about for the promise of doing more interesting work later on. You work long hours figuring that at some point it's got to get easier. Things aren't quite right, but you don't pay attention until . . . when? It's like the story about the frog in the bathtub. If you try to put a frog into a bathtub of boiling water, it'll jump right out. But if you put a frog in a bathtub of warm water and slowly drip in boiling water, one drip at a time, the frog will boil to death without noticing it.

I'm not in the habit of quoting my own scripts. Which means, of course, that that's exactly what I'm about to do. In one of my movie scripts, the main character has had an awful, dead-end job doing mindless work for the twenty years she's been out of school. One of the other characters asks her, "How did you ever do ***this*** job for twenty years?" She responds, "I didn't do it for twenty years. I just never did anything about it today . . . and it turned into twenty years."

So it's a delicate balance. You ***always*** have to make sacrifices. And at the beginning of your career, you do have to pay your proverbial "dues." But what if you're going overboard? The dues paying has to stop sometime—and sooner, rather than later! As lawyers at Markowitz Herbold point out, "You are in control of your future and when you realize that you aren't happy, satisfied, and fulfilled, do something, anything, to make it better." In this section, we'll identify exactly what it is that's really bugging you, and we'll look at your alternatives. Maybe you can tweak things at work—or maybe you'll have to quit. If you ***do*** leave, we'll talk about doing it the right way.

The bottom line is—I don't want you to be a boiled frog. I want you to be happy. Let's get on with it!

2. Everybody hates *something* about their job. Let's identify what's bugging you!

Sometimes I get e-mails from summer clerks and new lawyers, and they say things like, "I hate my job." When I ask, "Why?" they'll respond, "I just ***hate*** it. I hate ***everything*** about it." Clearly that's not true. There's no job in the world that's entirely despicable. (Well . . . maybe.) By the same token, there's no job in the world that's entirely delightful in every way. In order to fix what's broken, you've got to identify the offending parts. As Georgetown's Abbie Willard says, "You can't just say, 'I just hate it.' Otherwise, how do you fix it? You can go to your next employer and hate that, too!" Valparaiso's Gail Peshel adds, "Think specifically about what it is that you hate. Maybe it's not the entire thing. If you have a knee-jerk reaction to your employer, 'This is awful, I never want to practice law again'—it may be that in a different practice area or at a different firm, you might be perfectly happy." NYU's Gail Cutter notes that "It's easy to get so stressed out that you jump at the first 'out.' The 40th time a head hunter calls, you give in. And why? 'I hate my boss'? 'I hate real estate'? 'I hate the firm'? 'I hate the practice of law in general'? You've got to figure it out before you make a move!"

a. Figuring out what it is that's sticking in your craw—if the source of your unhappiness isn't obvious.

1) Rate your activities like you'd rate a movie.

   I think this is a wonderful idea! It's from Vermont's Pavel Wonsowicz. He says, "Don't pull the ripcord too fast when you start feeling dissatisfied with your work. Figure out ***why*** first. When I was practicing law, and I started to get unhappy with it, I kept a daily journal. I rated everything I did like a movie. I gave four stars to what I loved, and one star to what I hated. I analyzed what was good and bad about every day. It helped me figure out what talents I wanted to use, and what it was I really disliked."

2) If you've only been at work for a few months, face the possibility that what you're feeling is just 'sophomore slump.'

It's entirely possible that you don't hate your work. Boston University's Betsy Armour recounts that as a recruiting director at a large firm, "New associates were pretty ebullient for the first six months. It was around February, after six months, that the reality would sink in. The first three to six-month mark—it suddenly hits you, the profound nature of your career commitment." She attributes this to the fact that "It's hard to break out of that 'nine-month' mode from school. There are no new semesters, no summer vacations. 'Depression' might be too strong a word, but it's a sinking feeling. It can, and does, happen. Don't worry about it—it will pass." If you call some of your buddies from school, you'll find that they're suffering from much the same thing. And it feels good to commiserate with someone going through the same feelings you're experiencing!

3) Ignore your feelings immediately after a bad review.

One career counselor I spoke with said that "There's an amazing correlation between being told 'You're not progressing at the rate we expected' and suddenly thinking that your life's work is in civil rights instead of working at a corporate firm." Discount what you think when you're still stinging from a bad review. Maybe it did open your eyes to the fact that what you're doing isn't in line with your values. Or maybe you're just hurt, and you're striking back in the easiest way.

4) Talk out what you think about work, *out loud*, to yourself.

As Hofstra's Diane Schwartzberg comments, "You're smart! In your heart, you ***know*** what's up. Listen to what you say!"

5) Go to an outside career counselor, or go back to your career services director at law school.

As I've pointed out before, when you graduate, it's not a divorce. If you're not enjoying yourself at work, give your career services director a call. Trust me, it's not going to be the first "yikes" phone call (s)he's ever received! All career services folks are experienced in counseling people about jobs, and they're an excellent sounding board when you're not liking it but you can't figure out why. Alternatively, you can go to an outside career counselor. They're all over the country, and you'll find them in the phone book. The bottom line is, when you're vaguely unhappy, it helps to talk it out with somebody else to figure out what's up!

3. Solving the problems you *can* identify. Psst: It often means you don't have to quit to get what you want.

Once you've identified what's wrong, you're most of the way home. We'll see that different kinds of problems demand different kinds of solutions. As a rule of thumb, you can change the work; you can't change the people; and you can maybe change the hours. Now—let's be a little more specific!

a. Sometimes you have an epiphany.

Sometimes something at work will just make it painfully obvious that you've got to make a change. In a way, you've been given the gift of certainty. If you get hit over the head, you don't have to question whether or not you're doing the right thing in making a change.

EPIPHANY . . .

Female associate at a large East Coast firm. She has three young children. Her husband works at home so she can devote herself to her job. She works very hard and travels frequently. In her eighth year with the firm, her mother becomes seriously ill. The associate offloads her work onto colleagues so she can go and see her mother. She sits by her bedside for the last week of her life. She returns to work, and has a review for potential partnership three months later. She is told: "Maybe next year you'll make partner, but clearly your priorities are not in the right place."

EPIPHANY . . .

Large firm. A big case comes up which will need heavy staffing for two years, with lots of travel. The firm brings together the second and third year associates, asking for volunteers. Nobody raises a hand. The senior partner says sternly, "If you're single and you don't have family obligations, we expect you to volunteer first." A woman raises her hand and says, 'How will we ever **not** be single if we take this assignment?"

EPIPHANY . . .

Large firm. Junior associate working in the firm's conference room with another junior associate and a senior partner. The phone rings. The other junior associate picks it up, and says, "Yeah. Yeah. Good. Yeah." He hangs up, and says to the senior partner, "I'm sorry. I can get back to work now." The senior partner asks, "What was that about?" And the other junior associate says, "It was my wife. She called with the results of her biopsy." They go on working with no further comment.

b. Somebody made a comment, and it scared the living daylights out of you.

A lawyer at one firm said that when he was shown into his office for the first time, the managing partner gave him a catalog, and told him to pick out his desk. "Pick carefully," he said, "because you're going to be sitting behind it for thirty years." At another firm, a senior associate commented to a new associate, "Well, it's five o'clock. Only fifteen hours left until 8 a.m."

In those situations, you may ask yourself: Geez, is he ***joking***? Instead of pushing the panic button, go and talk to someone you trust—a mentor, the recruiting coordinator, another junior associate—and ***ask*** them about what you heard. As one partner commented, "Sometimes people make stupid comments without expecting ***anybody*** to take them seriously. If you're going to make a career decision over something somebody said, ask first to see if it's true!"

c. You're just working too hard.

In general, law is a pretty time-demanding profession. But there's demanding—and then there's ***demanding***. If you're working at a huge employer where you're making big money, I've pointed out a jillion times in this book that that means long hours. But there are other employers who demand some serious hourage, too. No matter where you work, if you're going to trial, you're going to be burning the midnight oil. And some employers go over the edge and take the concept of long hours to a whole new dimension. One junior associate said that "When I came here, they sold me on the whole 'family-friendly' thing. What a stinking pile of pony loaf ***that*** turned out to be. You wouldn't believe what goes on here. What they mean by 'family firm' is that if you're in the hospital, it's OK for a family member to answer the phone and take work notes for you. No joke. It really happened. A woman here was in the hospital the day her first child was born, and she's lying there having just given birth when her partner calls to give her work, telling her to fax it back to the office when she's done! And they mean that it's suitable for you to take three days off when your mother dies. Your ***mother***! Again, a true story."

Even if your employer isn't anywhere near that bad—gosh, I certainly ***hope*** it's not!—long hours can wear you down. They can be suffocating. One lawyer commented about a friend who's a junior associate at a very large firm. She said, "He makes tons of money, he just bought himself a new Jag. It's beautiful, but the guy's working all the time. I saw it, and I said, 'It's great. When are you going to drive it?' It's an expensive paperweight!"

Beyond the hours themselves is their unpredictability, and the lack of control you might have over them. If you're in a position where someone can walk into your office at five o'clock and say, "I need this by eight tomorrow morning," that's a blow to your autonomy that's hard to put into perspective.

If you just don't want to work the crazy hours, I can't blame you. It's your ***life***. If the hours are killing you, here are a few ideas to consider:

1) Try to work from home for at least part of your hours.

   It may be that with a laptop and dial-in potential, you don't have to be at the office all the time. If you have kids at home, that might be a possibility.

2) Squash big hours into fewer days.

   You might consider working sick hours during the week in order to keep your weekends free. If your employer doesn't have strict 'face time' on weekends, that might work for you.

3) Go part-time.

   A ***few*** firms will allow you to do this from the start—and at some, you can even be on the partnership track as a part-timer. At many firms, you've got to "prove your worth" before they'll be flexible about it, and have at least a year or two under your belt going full-tilt. But it's worth a try. Remember, as I've pointed out before, 'part-time' in law often means thirty-five to forty hours a week. So your part-time schedule will be what your non-professional friends consider full-time.

4) A staff attorney or contract attorney position.

   You'll work fewer hours, with less prestige, less dough, and projects that aren't as sexy. If the hours are your problem—it's a possibility to consider.

SMART HUMAN TRICK . . .

Early in 2000, Jimmy Lee was the hard-charging head of investment banking at Chase Manhattan. He worked 17-hour days. He had six cell phones constantly busy, and he put together billion-dollar deals for top-drawer clients like AT&T and General Motors. He was making $20 million a year. In an unheard-of move, he ceded some of his power so that he could spend more time with his family. As he told *Newsweek Magazine*, "In the power alleys of Wall Street and the East Coast, it's not manly to admit that work/family is an issue. In fact, the manly thing is to say, 'I don't have a life and I'm proud of it.'" But Lee had an epiphany one day when he was on a business trip to the West Coast and got an urgent phone call from his oldest daughter, a high school senior. Fearing the worst, he took the phone call. It turned out she was calling to say that she'd been accepted at his alma mater, Williams College. It suddenly hit him that he wasn't there to hug her at an important moment in her life. He started thinking: "Where did the year go? . . . I had not gone to one parent-teacher conference at her school. I didn't know any of her teachers' names. I just wasn't involved." He thought about his youngest daughter, and realized he didn't even know what grade she was going into. That led him to ratchet back on his work.

d. You're feeling incompetent.

Welcome to the club. ***Every*** new lawyer feels incompetent. Heck, a lot of experienced lawyers feel incompetent, too—at least once in a while. This isn't something to quit your job over. It's something to live through as best you can, because it ***will*** go away—sooner rather than later. As Golden Gate's Susanne Aronowitz says, "If you're a lawyer, you've always been an over-achiever, you've always had the answers. It's hard to be a new lawyer and not know things. Staring up at the learning curve is hard! You feel out of place. You need to have the patience to hang in and develop confidence. Once you have some successes under your belt, you'll enjoy it!" It's definitely a case of "This too shall pass." As lawyers at Proskauer Rose put it: "Nothing is as bleak as it seems when revisited a day, a month, a year later."

e. Your employer has broken promises to you.

Don't quit. ***Talk*** to them about it first. When they let you down again, ***then*** quit. As Georgetown's Marilyn Tucker suggests, "If you were promised assignments in a particular area and that promise doesn't materialize, make the problem known to your assigning partner, mentor or associate committee chair." Bring it up in a tactful way. Say, "When I came here, you promised that I would get to do X and X. I want to be a good soldier and a team player, and I enjoy working here, but I really do want to do X. How can I go about it?"

Whatever you do, don't put people on the spot in public! One lawyer told me about a meeting of all of the associates at his firm with the firm's management committee. A lateral hire got up and said, "What about all the promises you made to us at X & X about the partnership track?" The lawyer says, "You could see the partners squirming. They were ***so*** angry. This guy should have dealt with the issue in private. He certainly didn't foster any good will that way."

f. The work is at odds with your values.

Doing work you believe in is one of the core elements of being happy with your job. As Chicago's Suzanne Mitchell says, "If you're an ardent right-to-lifer, you're not going to be happy at the ACLU!" If you believe you're doing the right thing, just about every other problem fades into the background. Money, hours—they take a back seat to the satisfaction of doing something you believe in. I've talked to lots of attorneys at the Justice Department, and they all say that being able to get up and say their name, followed by "and I represent the United States of America" is a thrill they never get over.

Prosecutors in general believe in what they do. So do lawyers at legal aid and other public interest jobs. So do lots of lawyers in private firms. One health care lawyer I talked to said she felt great about helping people feel better through her work.

If you're a new lawyer and your values don't mesh with those of your employer, you've got a couple of options. You can take on pro bono projects to feed your soul if your day job doesn't. If you're truly at odds with the clients your employer represents—I mean, you're not just neutral, you find them abhorrent—you're probably going to have to vote with your feet. Regardless of why you took the job, the fact remains that you deserve a happy life. And if you took the job for the wrong reasons—well, you learned your lesson. You'll never do ***that*** again!

In ***very*** isolated circumstances, you might be able to convince your firm to let you opt out of certain projects on a "conscientious objector" basis. As one lawyer put it, "You don't want to seem morally superior to the person who brought in the client. Some attorneys won't tolerate it. Others will take it seriously. But you have to have an ***excellent*** reason. It was a gun manufacturer and your mother was killed by a gun, something like that." It's a real political hot potato, but you might be able to carry it off. As a general rule, you've got to anticipate that if you just don't agree with the clients (or causes) you represent, you'll have to make the change—because they won't.

g. You're bored.

If you go to a prosecutor's office or a judicial clerkship or legal aid, boredom isn't a problem—stress is! But if you go to a law firm, you're unlikely to find everything you do as a new attorney exceptionally stimulating. A number of senior attorneys told me that in the beginning, the work you do as a lawyer—particularly at a large firm—can be tedious. You get some good stuff, but there's a fair amount of tedium. It's part of the job.

There are several ways to solve this problem. First of all, as Loyola's Pam Occhipinti advises, "Don't just do the work that's handed to you! Identify what you ***want*** to be doing, and seek it out!" Even at the very largest employers, initiative is rewarded. Seek out the partners you want to work for, the projects you want to do, and volunteer!

Another option is to look at things you can do to supplement your work that ***are*** exciting. Community involvement, writing articles (if writing flips your switch), leadership in the local bar, public speaking—you can spice things up ***a lot*** if you look around.

If you really just find the subject matter boring, maybe you need to switch specialties. If you're at a large employer, you've got to be subtle about it. I address this whole issue in a minute, under the heading "Switching specialties—Doing it right." If you're at a small firm, it might be more difficult—what you want to do might not come in the door! But it's ***possible***. One way to do it is to become an expert and start soliciting the work you want, yourself! I've talked with more than one lawyer who took it on themselves to write articles, go to CLEs, ***give*** CLEs, develop an expertise, and start bringing in business of their own, doing what they ***want*** to do. It's an excellent way to storm ahead in your career—and get work you don't consider boring!

h. You heard somebody bragging about their job, or you read about somebody in a magazine article who seems to have it made.

As one lawyer commented, "You go out drinking Friday night, everybody you go drinking with is making six figures and you're not. Suddenly, you hate your job. Or you listen to somebody talking about the exciting project they're working on, and you think, 'What am I? A ***loser***?'" The fact is, when people are bragging about what they do or how much they make, you have precisely ***no idea*** what their job is really like. You only know what they're ***saying***. If you're going to make a move, make it on the basis of intelligence that's better than that. Call your career services director from law school and ask to talk to alums who do what this person does. Get a better picture of what it's like, and what sacrifices you have to make to do that same job. I'm not saying that there's no way it's better than what you've got. But there's a substantial possibility that the reality isn't quite the same as the rosy picture people paint when they're hanging out drinking beers. The later it gets, the rosier the picture gets. Check out the facts before you jump!

i. The closer you get to your initial goal, the more meaningless it seems.

When you start work, it may be that you look at the person way ahead of you—the district attorney, the partners, the general counsel—and you think, "That's where ***I'm*** going, Baby." And then the longer you're there, you start thinking—hmm. I'm not so sure. I heard a wonderful quote about law firms that goes, "Becoming a partner in a law firm is like winning a pie-eating contest, where the prize is more pie." If you look at what partners do at your law firm, and you don't like it—well, then you've disqualified one long-term goal. If you don't like the idea of generating business, partnership just isn't for you. That doesn't necessarily mean you should jump now—as I talk about in a minute, you've got to get ***some*** experience under your belt before you make a move—but it does tell you a lot about the direction in which you want your life to head.

j. You're not making enough money.

If this is what's getting to you, it may be that you've got a legitimate beef—or it may be that the headlines in the newspapers have left you feeling that everybody in the world is making a hundred fifty grand a year except for ***you***. That's just not true. Most people ***don't*** work at firms that pay that kind of money, and as you've seen throughout this book, that kind of salary demands a quart of blood in return. Nobody's ***giving*** it away.

You also have to realize that, if you're at a small firm, studies show that within five to six years out of school, you're just about on par with your brethren at large firms. As John Marshall's Bill Chamberlain puts it, "There is a pot of gold a little later on. Don't be too short-sighted!"

But in the meantime, if you work at a small-to-middling firm and you want to try to make more scratch from the start, take a look at section C of this chapter, called "Upping The Ante." It'll tell you what you need to know about negotiating for more scratch!

k. You hate your boss.

It happens. Not everybody is everybody else's cup of tea. If you hate your boss, at least initially try to follow my advice in Chapter 8, "Dealing With Jerks, Screamers, And Other Dwellers Of The Nether Anatomy." It talks all about handling difficult bosses. If you like the work, then it makes sense to try and find a way to deal with Supervisor Torquemada.

If you just can't work things out, what you do depends on the size of your employer. If it's a small employer, you've pretty much got to vote with your feet. It's their gig. There are other jobs you'll enjoy. If it's a large firm, don't flush the baby with the bathwater. It's entirely possible that there are other people you'll enjoy working for, and you should look into that. I go into that in some detail below, under the topic "Switching specialties—Doing it right." It's unfortunate how many associates jump from big firms just because they hate their particular boss or their particular specialty. One career services director told me about two phone calls she received one day, from two different associates working at the same large firm, on two different floors. One of them called and whispered, "You have to get me out of here. I ***hate*** it here. This is the ***worst.***" The other called in later in the day, and said breezily, "I was just checking in. Thanks so much for turning me on to this place! It's ***great.*** They're ***wonderful*** here." Same firm, different planets! Don't write off the whole place because you happen to work for a jerk!

1. **You've got family elsewhere, and you miss them.**

   I'm the wrong person to tell you to stay with a job that keeps you away from people you love. In my book—which is this book, I guess—people first, work second. If you're at a large employer with several offices, see if you can transfer. Your reason is one that anybody can understand. And if it's a small shop—sayonara. They'll understand. And if they don't, it's ***still*** a good reason to go.

4. "In-house" moves you can make to improve your life *without* quitting your job.

It may be that you don't have to take the drastic step of quitting in order to get what you want. You need to see if you can't tweak your current job—and you need to think about what else is out there!

a. Switching specialties—Doing it *right.*

If you're at a large firm or a government agency, don't quit without plumbing the idea of changing departments. Even if you're at a firm that says you can't change, on the Q.T. people will tell you that you can. The fact is, they've got a big investment in you, and they'd rather switch you to something you like than lose you altogether—***as long as*** you're doing good work. And if you've been following the advice in the rest of this book, I trust that that's ***exactly*** what you're doing!

Be ***discreet*** about the way you go about switching, however. You don't want to burn bridges with the people you're working with now, and you don't want to come off as a dilettante. One recruiting coordinator suggests that you "Talk to only one or two people whom you trust—people who ***don't*** have big mouths—and say, 'I'm not necessarily happy. I might want to change sections.' Don't go to your section head first—if they hear that you're not happy, they'll cut you off from good assignments! Go to someone ***else*** in the firm, outside your section. ***Then*** go to the most senior person in the firm you feel comfortable talking to. Say, 'I want to change sections and ideally I'd like to change here.' You have more leverage than you think you have, as long as you're doing good work. They ***want*** to keep you happy!" Another senior partner agrees, saying that "If you thought you liked securities, and nine months out you decide you want to do communications, do it! They don't want to pay a 25% headhunter fee. But be sensitive to the way you broach it! 'I'd like to litigate, and I thought regulatory was that, but it's not.' Not 'Joe's an a*****e.' If he is, no one's surprised. Confine your comments to the subject area. If someone works for me and wants to switch, I'm not happy about it, but I'm OK with it. It's better than losing them!" Another partner at another firm adds "You can go to the partner you want to work with, and say, 'I'd love to work with you, I've learned so much from you.' Take the initiative. Don't just leave the firm because you don't like the partner you're working for. Say 'I think this is what I want.' Take on small projects. You can't say, 'I'm really bored with what I'm doing and I want out,' even if it's true. If you seem negative, they'll say, 'Huh. What makes you think ***I'd*** want you?' Proactivity makes you feel better and stronger!"

b. See if you can add a dimension to your job that will make it more enjoyable.

The most obvious addition that comes to mind is doing pro bono work. If you can squeeze in the time, you might find that a pro bono project you believe in changes your whole attitude about your work in general. Also, see if you can't help generate business that you'd like to work on. You'll rocket your career forward if you do!

 SMART HUMAN TRICK . . .

Junior associate, starts her career with a firm, joins a department in which she has no interest. She wants to do Intellectual Property work, but the firm doesn't get enough of that to give her a steady diet of it. She gets involved with the IP Law Committee of the local bar. She gets hooked up with programming, cowrites an article for someone, starts bringing in clients. "It totally changed the direction of my career!" she comments.

c. *Gently* voice your discontent before you decide to leave.

This is risky. After all, it's complaining, and with some employers, if you say you don't like something, they'll say, "There's the door." But much more often than not, they'd rather try to accommodate you than face the prospect of losing you. As one lawyer put it, "It's cheaper to retain than retrain."

So instead of nailing down another job in secret, consider voicing your concerns—gently. "I was hoping that at this point I would be doing more of X and X with my work—are there prospects of that?

How can I go about doing it?" One lawyer told me about a friend at the firm who hated what she was doing, and got another job without mentioning her discontent to her boss. When she walked in to quit, the managing partner said, "We had a new project coming in, and we were hoping to give it to you." It was ***exactly*** the kind of work she'd wanted to do—and she lost out on it.

5. How long do you have to stay—Before you can go?

I'm not talking here about situations where you're facing harassment or ethical problems. Instead, we're talking about situations where you're just not liking the job all that much. How long do you have to stay?

You hear all different opinions about this. In theory, you can leave any time you want. The downside risk is having future employers question your judgment. As Susanne Aronowitz says, "It's common sense. You can't hop every three weeks or you'll have no credibility." Dickstein Shapiro's Paul Bran says, "You can use a dating analogy. If you're married and divorced in four months, good luck explaining it to your next date! You need a year or two to sound convincing to your next employer." A recruiting coordinator echoes that, saying, "If you've got four jobs in four years on your resume, that tells me everything I need to know about you. You make snap decisions. And maybe it's not the workplace that's the problem—maybe it's you." Another lawyer pointed out that "It takes at least a year to form enough of an impression on people at work that they'd say, 'We'll always take you back.'" Colorado's Tony Bastone says that "As a rule of thumb, try to stay with your first job a couple of years. After a year and a half, head hunters will start coming after you."

And of course the traditional mark is two years, and the reason for that, as Dennis Kennedy explains it, is that "It takes about two years of practice to feel as though you're getting the hang of things!"

So where does that leave you? Using your own judgment based on how much you hate it—and what other opportunity is waiting for you. As Georgetown's Marilyn Tucker says, "If you've been there less than a year and you just hate it, you can't stand the people and you don't want the subject matter, cut your losses and the firm's—they're pouring resources into you for nothing. In the short term they'll be annoyed but in the long term they don't want to waste money for nothing in return." Don't wring your hands, figuring that you'll never be happy. A change of environment can make a huge difference. As Emory's Carolyn Bregman says, "Firms are different from each other. And firms in general are different from DA's offices or government agencies or corporations. A slight change can make a big difference in your life." Similarly, if you've got a once-in-a-lifetime opportunity staring you in the face, you can't afford to wait the regulation two years. Whether it's working for a baseball team and you love baseball, or it's a dot-com and that's your dream, sometimes you have to roll the dice and go!

6. Check and see whether the grass really is greener before you leave your job.

I've said before that every job comes with its sacrifices. It may be that the sacrifices associated with another job will suit you better than the ones you're making right now. But for gosh sakes check that out ***before*** you make a move!

a. If it's another kind of law you want . . .

Go to CLEs on the other specialty. Talk with alums from your school (call your career services director to find them) and get an accurate snapshot of what practicing that kind of law would really be like—and how it would be different from what you're doing now. If it's a practice area that's in your office, hang out with lawyers in that section and ***listen*** to them. Check out NALP's book *The Official Guide To Legal Specialties,* which profiles lawyers doing just about everything. Get an idea of what you're in for before you make a switch, so that the move you make is an ***intelligent*** one.

b. Maybe you want to dump law all together

It's possible. As the partner at one firm points out, "You may find that the things you hate are everywhere in law. Maybe you're just not a lawyer." That's a pretty grand assumption. As I talked about in my *Guerrilla Tactics For Getting The Legal Job Of Your Dreams* book, being a lawyer can be so different in different settings. A large firm versus a small firm versus a government agency versus a trade association versus a corporate legal department . . . they're all different. But if none of them flip your switch, then research another industry the way you'd research any job. Find people who do what you want to do, and talk to them. Call the alumni director of your college or university to find people whose brains you can pick. Go to trade industry functions. Subscribe to magazines in the area. Read profiles of people who do what you think you want to do. Visit web sites and message boards where people post stuff about what you want. (If you want to go to a dot-com, the message board to check out is at F***edCompany.com.) Go to seminars about it. As Georgetown's Marilyn Tucker says, "People spend more time looking for a car than they do thinking and researching what they do with their lives! We make assumptions—what it'll be like, based on what we think we knew in law school. People make that mistake all the time. It's better to get a contact from your law school and talk to them for their perspective. 'Sounds interesting' isn't enough to make a life decision on!"

7. Leaving—Don't burn your Bridges!

If you've made the decision to leave your employer, it might be tempting to pull a Dennis Miller and just say, "I'm ***outta*** here!" But of course, you shouldn't do ***that***. Here's what you ***should*** do:

a. Keep your head in the game as long as you're still at the office—and before you've found something else.

As Harvard's Mark Weber says, "It's easy to let your work falter when you've decided to leave. Don't let that happen! It's easier to find a job while you still have a job. It can spiral. Make sure you get the job done. It can take longer to transition than you think!"

b. Keep your job search discreet.

Emory's Carolyn Bregman reminds you to put "Please keep my inquiry confidential" in any letters you send out. And apply for online jobs from your home computer. Your employer will be really steamed if they hear about your job search because somebody called from another employer looking for you. And Duke's Jill Miller advises, "Don't ever let partners catch you reading the Job Goddess' *Guerrilla Tactics* book—they will definitely get the hint that you are not altogether committed to the firm's partnership track!" (Sorry. I *had* to include that quote.)

c. **Don't use employer resources looking for a job.**

As Carolyn Bregman points out, "As soon as you're out, they'll check your phone and Internet usage." It wouldn't look seemly to have a lot of your job search calls made from the office, especially if you're on billable time. Use a cell phone, and use your home computer for your job search. And—duh—no job-hunting letters on firm stationery.

d. **Leave on good terms. You don't know what the future holds!**

Everybody I talked to stressed the importance of leaving bridges intact when you go. As Akin Gump's J.D. Neary explained, "Number one, your firm may merge with your old firm. And number two, the grass may not really be greener—you may want to come back. We've had lawyers do that. You can't do it if you've burned bridges!" Another lawyer comments that "If you make a stink or you're a cancer in the office before you leave, if you let your displeasure be known—it doesn't serve you! It's truly amazing how you can come full circle and be back in the same office or have to call on them for business. Handle it graciously!"

e. **Mend any hard feelings before you leave.**

If you're jumping ship, now is the time to patch up relationships with people in the office. Shake hands. Get over it. Find ***something*** pleasant to say. Remember that the moment you leave the office is the last time people will see you. You want to be remembered as pleasantly as possible. You never know the circumstances under which you'll see—or need—them again!

f. **Be careful about what you say in your exit interview.**

As Carlton Fields' Eric Adams says, "Leave on a good footing! Only communicate criticisms that can help the employer. Don't say,

'I work too hard' or 'I don't like so-and-so'—that doesn't help anyone. Probably the best thing to say is, 'I'm not leaving. I'm just giving you a potential referral source.'" Florida State's Stephanie Redfearn advises that you say, "I've learned a lot but now I want to do X."

Note that the ***reason*** you're leaving will have a lot to do with what you can say. If you're leaving for a personal reason—your spouse got transferred, your family is far away—nobody's going to take issue with that, and you can say, "Gee, I'd love to have stayed, but. . . . " You'll be an out-of-state referral source. Similarly, if you're going in-house to one of the firm's clients, they'll be ***thrilled*** to have you on the "inside." But if you're going to the firm across the street—it's a touchy situation. Be ***very*** diplomatic about it, and avoid saying anything disparaging—either to people at the office you're in now, or at your new employer.

Small firm, looking to expand, hires a guy coming from a very large firm in a nearby city. They have a series of interviews, and invite him to an office outing right before his start date. He comes to the outing and shakes hands with everybody, fits in well. The firm changes its letterhead in anticipation of his arrival. He shows up for work for his first week, and nothing's wrong. He's doing fine and he seems to be happy. The second week—he's a no-show. The firm is frantic. They call home—no answer. They're completely at a loss as to what happened. Finally, in desperation, they call his old firm to see if they've heard from him. The receptionist calmly says, "Oh, he's here right now. I'll put you through." The guy casually comments, "Actually, I never quit this job. I thought I'd try it out to see if I liked it with you better. I didn't. So I decided to stay here."

8. After you leave, keep those bridges intact!

When you've left an employer, the temptation is to let down your guard. To tell people, "Well, here's what really happened. We went out drinking one night, and Fred wound up in a French maid's outfit . . . ." Don't dish the dirt on your previous employer. As I've already pointed out, you have no idea when you'll work with them again—or when you might be useful to each other. As the recruiting coordinator at one large firm says, "It perturbs me when I hear people badmouthing us after they leave. Just say, 'It wasn't a good fit.' If you badmouth your old firm, the people you work with now will think, 'Gee, what's he going to say about ***us*** when he leaves ***here***?'"

In addition, as Harvard's Laura Share Kalin advises, "Stay in touch with people you've worked with." You're still part of a community, and it may be that keeping up with developments at your old employer has an influence on your career.

Incidentally, now you've got the chance to see who really was your friend, and who wasn't. Remember I told you that people you work with are your colleagues first, and your friends second? Once you've left the office, you're testing those friendships. You'll find that there really are people you keep as friends throughout your life, and the rest? Well, there's nothing wrong with having friendly colleagues while you work together.

9. What if leaving isn't *your* idea? What to do if you're asked to leave.

Getting canned really bites. Believe me, I know. I've been fired from every job I ever had. (Kind of makes you feel good, doesn't it? Seeing as you're reading a book about how to ***keep*** your job. Thank God it's not ***my*** advice you've been reading!) When they tell you to get lost, there's no question that it hurts like hell. But hard as it seems to believe when it happens to you, the sun's going to go on shining. You'll find other jobs. As Abbie Willard puts it—and I just love this—"You've been released to the Universe!" Quinnipiac's Diane Ballou reflects that "It always happens for the best. There's some reason, some perception that's against you. If you stayed, ***something*** would have happened. You ***always*** wind up better off."

The key thing to do when you've been asked to leave is to go with your head held high. No disparaging comments, no foul language, nothing like that. Gail Peshel says that she saw a press conference with a guy who'd been released by the Green Bay Packers, and his only comment was, "Thanks for the opportunity to fulfill a dream." Well, you might not be leaving a dream job, but you've got to have the same classy attitude. If you can't think of any other good reason to do it, do it because it'll have just the effect you ***want*** it to have on people. If you are nice, if you smile and seem remarkably unbothered, you'll make them think, "Gee, I wonder if we did the right thing?" They'll feel guilty for doing something so terrible to somebody so nice. If instead you whine and bitch and badmouth them, they'll think, "Good riddance. Thank God ***she's*** out of here!"

Here's some advice from Diane Ballou for handling a firing, lay-off, release to the Universe, or any other words you want to use for it:

a. If your employer has an EAP (Employer Assistance Plan), use it when you're laid off.

You can get therapy through an EAP, and when you're heartbroken about your job, it's a great idea. You'll quickly figure out exactly what happened so that you can ensure it doesn't happen again. Afterwards, you see all the signs on the wall; it's just that they'd been printed in invisible ink. See if the employer has outplacement or will pay for it. If they don't, go to your career services office for advice.

b. Don't sulk around the office before you leave.

Don't do it. Be classy about it. It's a small community, and you want a good reference.

c. Don't leave e-mails and voice mail for everyone in the office saying "So-and-so is an idiot."

Lean on friends from outside of work for support; don't say anything negative to anybody in the office. Remember: this is the dividing line between friends and colleagues. You won't be able to tell who your friends are until after you've left. While you're still there—painful as it is—be discreet.

d. Don't delete things from your computer. It's theft. And it's petty.

As Anna Davis points out, "You'll come back into contact with these people. There are too many chances they'll impact your future employability."

e. As soon as you leave, go into lockdown mode.

Put on a voice mail to give yourself a chance to get yourself together. Send a simple e-mail to people who try to contact you—"Thanks for your call, I'm getting myself together and I'll be in touch." Remember that when some people contact you, they want reassurance: "If they got rid of her I could be next." You've got think of yourself ***first*** right now.

f. The hurt will pass.

Remember, if you're asked to leave your job—this too shall pass. If you're lucky, being asked to leave a job is the worst thing that will ever happen to you. You'll go on to your next job, you'll do everything that's in this book, and you'll be a ***smashing*** success. Keep your eye on ***that*** prize!

APPENDIX A

INTERNET RESEARCH RESOURCES

Basic background information:

Dun & Bradstreet's Companies Online:	http://www.companiesonline.com
Hoover's Online:	http://www.hoovers.com/

Figuring out if companies are public or private:

http://www.stockhouse.com/

Financial Information:

CNN's Stock Quotes:	http://cnnfn.com/markets
Bloomberg Personal:	http://www.bloomberg.com

Legal Information:

Federal Register & Code of Federal Regulations:	http://law.house.gov/7.htm

Current News:

Newspages:	http://www.individual.com/
Industry Journals:	http://amcity.com/
Time:	http://www.time.com

People:

Yellow Pages Online:	http://www.yellowpages.com
Big Yellow:	http://bigyellow.com
Findlaw:	http://www.findlaw.com
Martindale Hubbell:	http://www.martindale.com

Guides:

New York Public Library's "How To Find Company Information":
http://www.nypl.org/research/sibl/company/companyinfo.html

Federal Information:

Cornell's Legal Institute: http://www.law.cornell.edu/

This web site provides access to:

- United States Code (U.S.C.). You can search for code sections via Keyword, Citation, Popular Name, or via Title through a Table of Contents. Full text of the code section is provided.
- U.S. Constitution
- Code of Federal Regulations (C.F.R.). You can search for sections via a Table of Contents, Citation, and Keyword. Keyword searching is connected to the popular GPO search engine.
- Federal Rules of Civil Procedure
- Federal Rules of Evidence
- U.S. Supreme Court Opinions. The full text of U.S. Supreme Court Opinions from 1990 onwards is available at this site, as is the Court's Calendar and its Schedule of Oral Arguments. Opinions can be searched via Party Name, Date of Decision, and Keyword.

Federal Courts Finder: http://www.law.emory.edu/fedcts/

Maintained by Emory University's School of Law, this site maintains and provides links to decisions from all the federal Circuit courts. At sites maintained by Emory, the full text of decisions from 1995 onward is available. They can be searched by Date, Party Name, or Keyword. You can access decisions from the following federal courts:

- Court of Appeals for Armed Forces
- Court of Federal Claims
- Federal Circuit
- D.C. Circuit
- 1st-11th Circuits

GPO Access: **http://www.access.gpo.gov**

Maintained by the Government Printing Office, this site provides access to a wealth of government information. Links to federal Executive agencies, including the Census Bureau, FDA, and NLRB, are provided as are links to the U.S. Congress and various other government publications, including:

- Code of Federal Regulations
- Federal Register: The full text of the Federal Register from 1994 onwards is available here. Updated daily, the current issue's Table of Contents is listed and provides hyper-text links to the text of the document. Archived issues can be searched by Date or via Keyword with the GPO Access Search Page.
- United States - Government Manual.
- Weekly Compilation of Presidential Documents

House Internet Law Library: **http://law.house.gov**

Changes are underway at this web site, so it may be temporarily disabled, but it is presently maintained by the House Information Resource Center. It provides the full text of the United States Code (U.S.C.), which is searchable via Keyword. It also provides links to: International Laws, including the laws of Canada, France, Mexico, and the United Kingdom, U.S., and other International Treaties, including NAFTA and NATO. Attorney Directories, including the U.K. and E.E.C.

Oyez, Oyez, Oyez: **http://oyez.nwu.edu**

Developed and maintained by Northwestern University, this site is intended to provide access to leading constitutional cases in the United States. Consequently, coverage is selective rather than comprehensive. This site is known for its archive of oral arguments made to the U.S. Supreme Court. To listen to these arguments, you will need Real Audio on your computer. You can search for cases via keyword, party name, or citation. In addition to U.S. Supreme Court cases, this site also provides access to information about all Justices of the United States Supreme Court as well as a virtual tour of the United States Supreme Court.

Thomas: http://www.thomas.loc.gov

Maintained by the Library of Congress, Thomas provides a great deal of information about the U.S. House and Senate. It can be searched via Keyword, Date, Committee, Number, or Sponsor.

Access to the full text of the following is available:

- Pending Bills (text, status and summary available)
- Recently Enacted Public Laws
- Congressional Record (current and archived)
- House & Senate Committee Reports
- Roll Call Votes
- House & Senate Directories

White House: http://www.whitehouse.gov

This site is maintained by the White House Web Team. It is searchable by keyword, and provides the full text of:

- Presidential Press Briefings
- Presidential Radio Addresses
- Executive Orders

State Information:

Findlaw: http://www.findlaw.com

This site was developed by the Northern California Law Librarians, this site provides extensive links to legal resources available on the Internet. The full text of documents can be retrieved, and boolean searching via Keyword is available. Findlaw utilizes the Law Crawler search engine. At Findlaw's state sites, you will find an alphabetical arrangement of hyper-text links to all fifty states. Links are available for:

- Primary Materials (codes, cases and regulations)
- Area Law Schools
- State Government Information
- State Bar Associations

Washlaw: http://washlaw.edu/uslaw/statelaw/

Developed and maintained by Washburn University's Law School, this site provides links to legal resources from all fifty states. Searching is by keyword. States are arranged in alphabetical order. You can obtain the following information on each state:

- Legislative
- Courts
- Statutes
- Rules of Court
- State Agencies
- Local Government
- Congressional Districts

Municipal Code Corporation: http://municode.com

This site is a commercial site that requires fees for the retrieval of full text documents. However, it does provide keyword searching via Folios and retrieves a citation and an abstract to various city and county codes. States are organized alphabetically and codes/ordinances are then listed under the appropriate state. Hyper-text links then allow the user to access Folios and use keyword searching.

Secondary Materials:

Hieros Gamos: http://www.hg.org

Produced by Lex Mundi, this site allows keyword searching. It retrieves both full text and abstracts. It provides access to:

- Legal Guide for Foreign Countries, including the European Union
- Law Journals
- Global Bar Directories
- Directories of Experts

Findlaw: http://www.findlaw.com

In addition to providing primary source materials for the federal and state governments, this site also provides extensive access to secondary sources, including:

- CLE programs
- Directories of Consultants & Experts
- Electronic Law Journals
- U.S. Law Schools

U.S. Law Firms

www.inet-asst.com/legallinks.html
Huge selection of links to useful sites.

www.lawinfo.com
Legal forms, discussion boards, and lots more.

www.catalaw.com
Catalog of law and government; tons of topics

http://law.about.com/newsissues/law/index.htm
Current events, big trials, rulings, legislation

www.asiarecipe.com/tibveg.html#dalai
The Dalai Lama's dumpling recipe

APPENDIX B

SAMPLE LAW FIRM EVALUATION FORMS

Associate Performance Evaluation For New Associates

EVALUATOR: ______________________________ DATE: ____/____/____

ASSOCIATE: ______________________________

1. **WORK CONTACT WITH ASSOCIATE**
Indicate approximately how many hours you have worked with the new associate:
____

2. **PERSONAL EFFORT**
Works hard; capable of and willing to make a sustained effort; readily accepts assignments; shows initiative; responds positively to criticism; developing firm loyalties and a quality workplace.

☐ Outstanding Performance	☐ Needs Improvement
☐ Highly Effective Performance	☐ Needs Much Improvement
☐ Competent Performance	☐ Not Observed

Comments:

3. **ANALYTICAL ABILITY**
Identifies and focuses on critical issues; capable of in-depth and complete analysis of problem; distinguishes material from immaterial; uses imagination and creativity in solving problems.

☐ Outstanding Performance	☐ Needs Improvement
☐ Highly Effective Performance	☐ Needs Much Improvement
☐ Competent Performance	☐ Not Observed

Comments:

4. **WRITING ABILITY**
Writes clearly, concisely and persuasively; uses words precisely with correct grammar and citation form; has good attention to detail.

☐ Outstanding Performance	☐ Needs Improvement
☐ Highly Effective Performance	☐ Needs Much Improvement
☐ Competent Performance	☐ Not Observed

Comments:

5. **ORAL COMMUNICATION**
Articulates clearly; participates effectively in office or client meetings; effective in oral court, administrative or negotiating presentations/sessions.

- ☐ Outstanding Performance
- ☐ Highly Effective Performance
- ☐ Competent Performance
- ☐ Needs Improvement
- ☐ Needs Much Improvement
- ☐ Not Observed

Comments:

6. **JUDGMENT**
Provides sound balance and practical legal advice in relation to affected interests of clients; recognizes degree of gravity of problem and develops appropriate response; recognizes problems that require instant action; is sensitive to ethical considerations.

- ☐ Outstanding Performance
- ☐ Highly Effective Performance
- ☐ Competent Performance
- ☐ Needs Improvement
- ☐ Needs Much Improvement
- ☐ Not Observed

Comments:

7. **PRODUCTIVITY; ABILITY TO UTILIZE TIME AND PRIORITIZE PROJECTS PROPERLY**
Organizes work priorities; works efficiently and systematically; avoids wasting time; completes work on time; works well under pressure.

- ☐ Outstanding Performance
- ☐ Highly Effective Performance
- ☐ Competent Performance
- ☐ Needs Improvement
- ☐ Needs Much Improvement
- ☐ Not Observed

Comments:

8. **FIRM ECONOMICS AND ADMINISTRATION**
Demonstrates appreciation of firm economics (time reports, billing, budgeting time); contributes to firm administrative goals, including recruiting.

- ☐ Outstanding Performance
- ☐ Highly Effective Performance
- ☐ Competent Performance
- ☐ Needs Improvement
- ☐ Needs Much Improvement
- ☐ Not Observed

Comments:

9. RELATIONS WITH ATTORNEYS AND STAFF

Deals effectively with attorneys and personnel at all levels in a pleasant and professional manner. Works well with others, assisting them in common goals and firm projects; returns phone calls promptly and responds to attorney requests on a timely basis.

☐ Outstanding Performance ☐ Needs Improvement
☐ Highly Effective Performance ☐ Needs Much Improvement
☐ Competent Performance ☐ Not Observed
Comments:

10. OVERALL PROFESSIONAL EVALUATION; PROGRESS WITH FIRM

Indicate your evaluation of the new associate's overall performance and progress.

☐ Outstanding Performance ☐ Needs Improvement
☐ Highly Effective Performance ☐ Needs Much Improvement
☐ Competent Performance ☐ Not Observed
Comments:

11. Would you like to work with this associate again?

☐ Yes ☐ No
Comments:

12. Is the associate well-suited for the area of practice to which he or she is currently assigned?

☐ Yes ☐ No
Comments:

New Associate Quarterly Evaluation

NAME OF NEW ASSOCIATE: ______________________

NAME OF EVALUATOR: ______________________

EVALUATOR'S PRACTICE GROUP: ______________________

Following are definitions of the ratings used in this form:

(O) Outstanding: The Associate's performance in this area is consistently characterized by exceptionally high quality and excellence.

(G) Good: The Associate's performance in this area is characterized by initiative and high quality, exceeds the requirements and expectations of the Assignor.

(A) Average: The Associate's performance is generally acceptable, meets the requirements and expectations of the Assignor and has no deficiencies.

(B) Below Average: The Associate's performance in this area is less than acceptable, exhibits certain weaknesses, or requires improvement in order to bring the Associate's level of performance up to the standards of quality of the Firm, but is capable of improvement.

(U) Unsatisfactory: The Associate's performance in this area fails to meet the needs or expectations of the Assignor and/or exhibits major deficiencies.

Please evaluate the performance of ______________________ on the following points:

	O	G	A	B	U
RESEARCH AND ANALYTICAL SKILLS:	☐	☐	☐	☐	☐

Comments:

	O	G	A	B	U
RESOURCEFULNESS:	☐	☐	☐	☐	☐

Comments:

	O	G	A	B	U
TIMELINESS:	☐	☐	☐	☐	☐

Comments:

	O	G	A	B	U
CLARITY & ORGANIZATION OF PRESENTATION:	☐	☐	☐	☐	☐

Comments:

PERFORMANCE IN CONTACT WITH CLIENTS, WITNESSES & OTHERS: ☐ ☐ ☐ ☐ ☐

Comments:

OVERALL EVALUATION: ☐ ☐ ☐ ☐ ☐

Comments:

GENERAL COMMENTS

A. If you had additional work to be performed by an Associate, would you:

☐ Affirmatively seek out this Associate

or

☐ Accept this Associate if the matter were assigned

or

☐ Prefer to have a different Associate do the work.

B. If this Associate expressed an interest in joining your Group, how would you respond?

☐ Very interested and eager

☐ No strong feeling

☐ Would prefer that this Associate join another group

C. How would you rate the usefulness of the work product (e.g., was it suitable for the purpose for which the assignment was made; could it be used in a brief or opinion letter without substantial rewriting; was it a competent job upon which others in the firm could rely)?

D. Please describe any particular strengths or weaknesses which you feel are materially related to this Associate's potential as a lawyer and which are not fully set forth above.

____________________ ____________________

EVALUATOR DATE

Associate Evaluation For First Three Years of Employment

ANNUAL EVALUATION OF ______________________________

for the year preceding (month, year) ______________________________

Evaluator: ______________________________

Extent of Contact: ☐ Extensive ☐ Moderate ☐ Light

INSTRUCTIONS: Check the box opposite the rating which most accurately reflects your evaluation of the Associate in each category.

EVALUATION

I. PROFESSIONAL:

A. **Quality of Legal Work** — What is the caliber of the work which this Associate produces on a consistent basis?

Rating: ☐ Excellent ☐ Needs Improvement
☐ Good ☐ Poor
☐ Satisfactory

B. **Judgment** — Within the framework of this Associate's experience, how do you rate the ability of this associate to make sound decisions on his or her own, as well as know when to consult other laywers when appropriate?

Rating: ☐ Excellent ☐ Needs Improvement
☐ Good ☐ Poor
☐ Satisfactory

C. **Profitable Work** — How do you rate this Associate's ability to complete matters entrusted to him or her efficiently and profitably?

Rating: ☐ Excellent ☐ Needs Improvement
☐ Good ☐ Poor
☐ Satisfactory

D. **Respect** — Does this Associate engender the respect of both clients and other lawyers?

Rating: ☐ Excellent ☐ Needs Improvement
☐ Good ☐ Poor
☐ Satisfactory

Comments:

II. PRACTICE SKILLS:

A. **Organization**

Rating:

- ☐ Excellent
- ☐ Good
- ☐ Satisfactory
- ☐ Needs Improvement
- ☐ Poor

B. **Adherence to Office Procedures**

Rating:

- ☐ Excellent
- ☐ Good
- ☐ Satisfactory
- ☐ Needs Improvement
- ☐ Poor

C. **Following Instructions**

Rating:

- ☐ Excellent
- ☐ Good
- ☐ Satisfactory
- ☐ Needs Improvement
- ☐ Poor

D. **Communications** — How does this Associate keep Directors and clients advised of matters which he or she is handling?

Rating:

- ☐ Excellent
- ☐ Good
- ☐ Satisfactory
- ☐ Needs Improvement
- ☐ Poor

E. **Responsibility** — Does this Associate willingly and successfully accept responsibility of matters?

Rating:

- ☐ Excellent
- ☐ Good
- ☐ Satisfactory
- ☐ Needs Improvement
- ☐ Poor

Comments:

III. PERSONAL

A. **Maturity**

Rating:

- ☐ Excellent
- ☐ Good
- ☐ Satisfactory
- ☐ Needs Improvement
- ☐ Poor

B. **Attitude**

Rating:

- ☐ Excellent
- ☐ Good
- ☐ Satisfactory
- ☐ Needs Improvement
- ☐ Poor

C. **Loyalty to Firm**

Rating:

- ☐ Excellent
- ☐ Good
- ☐ Satisfactory
- ☐ Needs Improvement
- ☐ Poor

D. **Acceptance by Peers**

Rating:

- ☐ Excellent
- ☐ Good
- ☐ Satisfactory
- ☐ Needs Improvement
- ☐ Poor

Comments:

IV. MISCELLANEOUS

A. **Overall Evaluation**

B. **Comments and Suggestions**

Evaluation of Associate

NAME OF ASSOCIATE: ______________________________

PRACTICE GROUP: ______________________________

NAME OF EVALUATOR: ______________________________

To assist the Evaluation Committee in evaluating the performance of ________________, we ask that you complete this form and send it to ______________________ no later than ________________. While written comments are helpful and encouraged, comments must accompany all unsatisfactory reviews and should indicate the specific areas of improvement you feel are desirable or the specific reasons why this Associate's performance was unsatisfactory.

The firm realizes that it is not feasible or practical to set forth in a form all facts underlying an evaluation of an Associate's performance. The intent of the form is to record in concise fashion the most important aspects of and reasons for an evaluation. If, however, you are experiencing any problems with, or if you have any questions or concerns about, an Associate's performance, you should record them.

Following are definitions of the ratings used in this form:

(O) **Outstanding:** The Associate's performance in this area is consistently characterized by exceptionally high quality and excellence.

(G) **Good:** The Associate's performance in this area is characterized by initiative and high quality and exceeds the requirements and expectations of the Assignor.

(A) **Average:** The Associate's performance is generally acceptable, meets the requirements and expectations of the Assignor and has no deficiencies.

(B) **Below Average:** The Associate's performance in this area, is less than acceptable, exhibits certain weaknesses or requires improvement in order to bring the Associate's level of performance up to the standards of quality of the Firm, but is capable of improvement.

(U) **Unsatisfactory:** The Associate's performance in this area fails to meet the needs or expectations of the Assignor and/or exhibits major deficiencies.

I. LEVEL OF KNOWLEDGE

A. How familiar are you with the work of ______________________________?

- ☐ Very familiar (worked extensively with Associate)
- ☐ Familiar (a number of or lengthy assignments)
- ☐ Somewhat familiar (few or brief assignments)

B. How many projects has this Associate done for you? ________________

Describe briefly (e.g., memos, research, pleadings, oral arguments), especially some significant projects:

	O	G	A	B	U
II. PROFESSIONAL SKILLS					
A. **Comprehension:** The Associate's ability to understand complex legal and factual issues.	☐	☐	☐	☐	☐
Comments on Comprehension:					
B. **Analytical Skill:** The Associate's ability to appreciate the significance of facts or legal authorities and to make perceptive analyses of legal problems.	☐	☐	☐	☐	☐
Comments on Analytical Skill:					
C. **Research Skills:** The Associate's ability to locate all relevant legal authority efficiently.	☐	☐	☐	☐	☐
Comments on Research Skills:					
D. **Reliability:** The Associate's ability to consistently produce high quality work.	☐	☐	☐	☐	☐
Comments on Reliability:					
E. **Judgment:** The ability of the Associate:					
1. To perceive and take into account the "real world" effects of actions, statements and positions.	☐	☐	☐	☐	☐
2. To assign priorities correctly to various tasks.	☐	☐	☐	☐	☐
3. To seek guidance or instruction from other attorneys when appropriate.	☐	☐	☐	☐	☐
4. To engender confidence in his/her work product and results.	☐	☐	☐	☐	☐
5. To exercise overall judgment appropriate to the task (such as choosing from a number of possible courses or solutions or knowing when research has proceeded far enough.)	☐	☐	☐	☐	☐
Comments On Judgment:					
F. **Creativity:** The Associate's ability to make an insightful, thoughtful and perceptive contribution to a project and its solutions (as contrasted with perfunctory or superficial contributions).	☐	☐	☐	☐	☐
Comments on Creativity:					
III. COMMUNICATION SKILLS					
A. **Writing:**					
1. Precision	☐	☐	☐	☐	☐

	O	G	A	B	U
2. Persuasiveness	☐	☐	☐	☐	☐
3. Completeness	☐	☐	☐	☐	☐
4. Organization	☐	☐	☐	☐	☐
5. Overall writing ability	☐	☐	☐	☐	☐
Comments on Writing Ability:					
B. Speaking					
1. Articulation	☐	☐	☐	☐	☐
2. Persuasiveness	☐	☐	☐	☐	☐
3. Organization	☐	☐	☐	☐	☐
4. Overall speaking ability	☐	☐	☐	☐	☐
Comments on Speaking Ability:					

IV. APPROACH TO PRACTICE

	O	G	A	B	U
A. Effort: The ability and willingness of this Associate to:					
1. Accomplish tasks in a timely and thorough fashion.	☐	☐	☐	☐	☐
2. Work effectively under pressure.	☐	☐	☐	☐	☐
3. Accommodate pressing needs and inconvenience own schedule.	☐	☐	☐	☐	☐
Comments on Effort:					
B. Efficiency: The value of the Associate's contribution to projects in relation to the time charged.	☐	☐	☐	☐	☐
Comments on Efficiency:					
C. Initiative: The Associate's ability to work independently under appropriate supervision and/or seek guidance in appropriate situations to achieve assigned objectives.	☐	☐	☐	☐	☐
Comments on Initiative:					
D. Promptness: The Associate's reliability in meeting deadlines.	☐	☐	☐	☐	☐
Comments on Promptness:					
E. Thoroughness: The Associate's attention to detail in analysis, research and written work product (as contrasted to a casual style which overlooks errors or issues).	☐	☐	☐	☐	☐
Comments on Thoroughness:					

	O	G	A	B	U
F. **Management of Assignments:** The Associate's ability to delegate and appropriately supervise other attorneys, paralegals and clerical staff.	☐	☐	☐	☐	☐
Comments on Management:					
G. **Motivation:** Whether the Associate is self-motivated (as contrasted to requiring frequent prodding).	☐	☐	☐	☐	☐
Comments on Motivation:					
H. **Realization:** Whether the full amount of the Associate's time could be billed to the client or required write-offs.	☐	☐	☐	☐	☐
Comments on Realization:					

V. INTERPERSONAL SKILLS

	O	G	A	B	U
A. **Client Relations:** The Associate's ability to interact effectively with and inspire confidence and trust in clients.	☐	☐	☐	☐	☐
Comments on Client Relations:					
B. **Interactions:** The extent to which the Associate:					
1. Works harmoniously and effectively with his or her seniors, peers and subordinates.	☐	☐	☐	☐	☐
2. Interacts effectively with opposing counsel and others outside the office.	☐	☐	☐	☐	☐
3. Accepts well and responds to criticism fully.	☐	☐	☐	☐	☐
Comments on Interaction:					
C. **Practice Development:** The Associate's potential for attracting new clients and/or for attracting additional work from existing clients (through professional ability, interpersonal skills, community/civic involvement or otherwise).	☐	☐	☐	☐	☐
Comments on Practice Development:					

VI. GENERAL COMMENTS

A. If you had additional work to be performed by an Associate, would you:

☐ Affirmatively seek out

or

☐ Accept if the matter were assigned to him or her

or

☐ Prefer to have a different Associate do the work.

B. Please give details if, to your knowledge, this Associate either has been contacted directly by, or specifically requested by, existing or new clients to represent them.

Details:

C. Would you expect that in the immediately foreseeable future this Associate will be getting work directly from existing or new clients of the Firm

☐ Yes ☐ No

Please Comment:

D. Please describe any particular strengths or weaknesses of this Associate which you feel are materially related to his or her potential as a lawyer and which are not fully set forth above.

Comments:

SIGNATURE OF EVALUATOR ______________________

DATE OF EVALUATION ______________________

Associate Evaluation Form

Associate ______________________ Department ______________________

Year of Hire ______________ Evaluating Attorney ______________________

Year of Graduation ___________ Period of Evaluation ______________________

Amount of work this Associate has done under my supervision or for which I am billing attorney.

☐ Over 250 billable hours

☐ 25 to 250 billable hours

☐ Under 25 billable hours

Approximately ________ non-billable hours

Definitions: In evaluating this Associate, please use the following criteria.

Excellent: Outstanding, showing unique adeptness or quality; unequalled in performance by any of his/her peers. Definite partnership prospect.

Good: Effective, solid work product and performance; work or performance of a level the firm would expect to have appear over its name. Possible partnership prospect.

Marginal: Inconsistent work product and performance; sometimes below the level of what the firm would expect of an associate qualifying for partnership. Not a likely partnership candidate.

Unacceptable: Failing to meet minimum standard quality for the firm; needing immediate correction. Definitely not a partnership prospect. Termination should be considered.

1. **Quality of Performance**

	Excellent	Good	Marginal*	Unacceptable*	Comments
a. Thoroughness and accuracy of research	☐	☐	☐	☐	
b. Factual and legal analysis	☐	☐	☐	☐	
c. Creativity in solving problems	☐	☐	☐	☐	
d. Willingness and ability to make sound decisions	☐	☐	☐	☐	

* Specific comments and suggestions must accompany a check in this category.

	Excellent	Good	Marginal*	Unacceptable*	Comments
e. Acceptance of and discharge of responsibilities	☐	☐	☐	☐	
f. Clarity of written work and oral presentations	☐	☐	☐	☐	
g. Documents and properly maintains files	☐	☐	☐	☐	
h. Presents work in final form	☐	☐	☐	☐	
i. Kept me advised of his/her progress	☐	☐	☐	☐	
j. Ability to meet deadlines	☐	☐	☐	☐	
k. Willingness to take on additional work	☐	☐	☐	☐	
l. Working relationship with evaluating attorney and other members of the firm	☐	☐	☐	☐	
m. Capability to work without supervision	☐	☐	☐	☐	
n. Ability to get along with subordinates (including secretarial, administrative and support staff)	☐	☐	☐	☐	

* Specific comments and suggestions must accompany a check in this category.

2. **Write-Offs:** If you were billing attorney for this Associate's work, did you have to write off any significant amount of billings for reasons that reflect a deficiency in the Associate's work? If so, please explain.

3. **Client Relationships:** If the Associate had significant client contact, did he/she:

a. Generate confidence in the quality of his/her work? ☐ Yes ☐ No

b. Keep you and/or client advised of the status of the matter? ☐ Yes ☐ No

c. Demonstrate creativity in solving the client's problem? ☐ Yes ☐ No

4. **Professional/Business Development, Training and "Firm Citizenship":** Please indicate what, if any, activities this Associate has engaged in to develop professionally and to contribute to the overall success of the Department and the Firm. Identify any deficiencies or areas for improvement.

5. **Overall Rating**: Based on the criteria set forth on page one, how would you rate this Associate's performance during this evaluation period?

☐ Excellent ☐ Good ☐ Marginal ☐ Unacceptable ☐ Too Early To Tell

6. **Partnership Potential:** (For Associates in their third year and beyond.)

   Considering this Associate's time with the firm, do you believe he or she is progressing satisfactorily toward eligibility for becoming a partner? Bear in mind that some of the criteria for eligibility include:

a. Unimpeachable integrity and ethics.
b. Superior legal ability, based upon opinions of partners qualified to judge by direct personal experience.
c. Assumption and discharge of responsibility for matters on his or her own, to the satisfaction of the client, and of the firm.
d. Willingness to cooperate and work effectively with other lawyers of the firm.
e. Demonstrated ability to carry a full share of the firm's professional and administrative work load.
f. Potential for developing and maintaining favorable client relationships.
g. Exercise of initiative in participating in professional, community, and other activities to widen contacts and develop personal and professional growth.

☐ Probable ☐ Not Probable ☐ Uncertain

Check specific areas which need improvement:

☐ a ☐ b ☐ c ☐ d ☐ e ☐ f ☐ g

7. **Additional Comments:** Please be specific regarding areas where the Associate should be complimented or areas which need improvement:

Personnel Review Committee
Partner Comment Form

Associate: ______________________________________ Class: __________

Partner (print name): ______________________________________

Note to Partners: This Form is intended to elicit your views on the suitability of the above associate for partnership, taking into account various factors which ultimately bear on that decision. These forms are confidential and will not be available to associates.

SUMMARY OF CONTACT AND VIEWS

☐ No contact, or contact too limited to have views concerning partnership. (If so, you need not complete the balance of the form.)

☐ Have views concerning partnership.

- ☐ Based upon direct contact
- ☐ Based upon views of other partners

Duration of Contact	Type of Contact	Time of Contact
☐ Extensive	☐ Legal	☐ Current
☐ Moderate	☐ Administrative	☐ 1-2 years ago
☐ Limited	☐ Casual or Social	☐ More than 2 years ago

PART A: PARTNERSHIP ASSESSMENT

A. Considering his or her level in the firm, do you believe this associate is demonstrating present or potential suitability for election to partnership in the following areas (which are not set forth in any particular order of importance)? Please provide details, including any deficiencies noted.

1. Professional skills (analysis, writing, oral communication, negotiating, judgment)

   ☐ unable to evaluate this area

2. Do you know of any matter which in your judgment will limit this associate in his/her effort to become a partner in the Firm?

B. Are there any other aspects of this associate's partnership suitability not mentioned above that you wish to comment on?

C. Please compare this associate's potential or suitability for partnership with other associates at the same or comparable level and/or in the same practice group or specialty.

D. Overall suitability for partnership compared to others at the same or comparable level and/or in the same practice group or specialty (check one):

☐ Very suitable; top candidate

☐ Suitable; no significant problems noted

☐ Neutral or undecided on candidacy

☐ Negative on candidacy; need to be convinced

☐ Not suitable; cannot support

E. If you have views on this subject, please indicate whether you believe this associate should initially be considered for general partner or special partner. If you do not support this associate for partnership but believe he or she should be considered for a counsel position, please explain your reasons.

F. I would like to be interviewed regarding the foregoing:

☐ in lieu of filling out this form

☐ in addition to my comments above

Note: If you have had substantive and frequent contact with the above-named associate during the past year, please complete Part B of this form.

PART B: ASSOCIATE EVALUATION ASSESSMENT

A. Please rate this associate's performance in the areas noted below in comparison with the performance of other associates with comparable experience. The ratings should be on a scale from 5 to 1 using the following guidelines:

5 = Outstanding performance (reserved for truly exceptional cases)
4 = Very good performance (superior to norm for associates)
3 = Satisfactory performance (the norm for associates)
2 = Performance below the norm for associates
1 = Poor performance (well below the norm for associates)

If your contact with the associate has been insufficient to permit a rating in any category noted below, please mark "N/A" next to that category. If the preponderance of ratings are 5's or 4's, please be sure to respond to paragraph 3 below.

_________ Understanding Problems and Analytical Reasoning

_________ Writing Ability

_________ Research Ability

_________ Accuracy and Thoroughness

_________ Creativity

_________ Initiative

_________ Responsibility and Conscientiousness

_________ Maturity and Judgment

_________ Overall Evaluation

B. Please indicate the nature of the associate's performance in the following categories by placing a check in the appropriate column. If you have had not opportunity to observe the associate's performance in any category listed, please mark "N/A" in the "Performance is Acceptable" column next to that category.

	Performance Indicates STRENGTH	**Performance is ACCEPTABLE**	**Performance Indicates MINOR DEFICIENCY**	**Performance Indicates SERIOUS DEFICIENCY**
Ability to Work with Other Lawyers	______	______	______	______
Ability to Work with Clients	______	______	______	______
Response to Criticism or Suggestions	______	______	______	______
Meeting Deadlines	______	______	______	______
Ability to Withstand Pressure	______	______	______	______
Ability to Work with Minimum Supervision	______	______	______	______
Efficient Use of Time	______	______	______	______
Other (Specify): ______	______	______	______	______

C. Please identify any legal skills, areas of substantive legal knowledge, work habits, or other factors on which you recommend that this associate concentrate to advance her or his professional development. Such constructive suggestions should be made for every associate, including those whose performance has been highly rated in response to the previous questions.

D. Please indicate whether you would be willing to work with this associate again:

☐ Definitely

☐ Possibly (depending on which other associates were available)

☐ No

☐ Other (Specify):

Signature ______________________

Date ______________________

Associate Evaluation Form

NAME OF ASSOCIATE: ______________________ DATE: ____________

EVALUATOR: ______________________________________

KEY

E = Excellent

S = Satisfactory

N = Need Improvement

W = Without Sufficient Information to Evaluate

I. PROFESSIONAL SKILLS

Criteria	E/S/N/W	Evaluator and Associate Comments
1. RESEARCH SKILLS Is this associate accurate, complete and efficient in his/her research?		
2. WRITING ABILITY Does this associate demonstrate effective communicative skills in writing pleadings, briefs, legal documents, correspondence?		
3. SPEAKING ABILITY Does this associate express himself/herself well to others, *e.g.*, clients, attorneys and the Court?		
4. ATTENTIVENESS TO DETAIL Is this associate attentive to detail in his/her analytical and communicative skills?		
5. TIMELINESS Does this associate meet deadlines or inform the lead attorney of the need for additional time sufficiently in advance of deadlines?		
6. RESPONSIBILITY Is this associate assuming lead responsibility for and handling major legal problems?		
7. INITIATIVE Does the associate show imagination or initiative in following through on assignments, exercising his/her own independent judgment in defining the legal issues, exploring alternative theories, strategizing a matter or moving it along effectively?		
8. TENACITY Does this associate seem reasonably aggressive, tenacious and dedicated to serving the client's needs?		

Criteria	E/S/N/W	Evaluator and Associate Comments
9. MOTIVATION Is this associate motivated to practice to the best of his/her ability and does he/she strive to improve his/her ability?		
10. ANALYTICAL ABILITY Does this associate demonstrate imagination, creativity, practicality and awareness of the economic considerations in the approach to issues and problems?		
11. COMMUNICATION OF STATUS Does this associate keep the responsible attorney updated on the status of assignments and deadlines?		
12. RELIABILITY—DEPENDABILITY Is this associate someone you would depend or rely on?		
13. EFFECTIVENESS Is this associate's legal work technically accurate and case approach effective in achieving high quality results?		
14. PROFESSIONAL GROWTH How has this associate responded to previously identified areas needing improvement or otherwise learned new skills?		
II. PERSONAL — A. Intrafirm		
15. ABILITY TO HANDLE PRESSURE Is this associate's behavior and efficiency severely affected when working under pressure?		
16. MATURITY/SENSITIVITY Does this associate exhibit maturity, and sensitivity in his/her relationships with and understanding of others?		
17. JUDGMENT In the context of his/her experience, is this associate able to make sound decisions on his/her own and does he/she consult with other firm members when appropriate to do so?		
18. DISSEMINATION Does this associate attempt to maintain an awareness of current legal issues and problems of other firm members, and does he/she volunteer suggestions, information and research that may be known to him/her?		
19. ACCESSIBILITY Is the associate willing to assist and answer questions from paralegals, clerks and other associates?		

Criteria	E/S/N/W	Evaluator and Associate Comments
20. PRACTICE MANAGEMENT Does the associate manage his/her practice so as to enable him/her to assist others in time of need?		
21. ORGANIZATION Is the associate able to effectively manage his/her time, balance competing demands and prioritize wisely?		
22. FIRM RELATIONS Does the associate maintain appropriate and supportive working relationships with other attorneys and staff?		
II. PERSONAL — B. Extra-firm		
23. CLIENT RELATIONS Does the associate inspire confidence in clients, appreciate clients' needs and generally establish a good working relationship with clients? Does the associate invest time to maintain and enhance existing client relationships? Does the associate, through demeanor and appearance, project him/herself as a professional who inspires client confidence?		
24. ECONOMIC EXPECTATIONS Is the associate performing up to the economic projections made for that associate in terms of billable hours, fees collected, clients generated?		
25. EFFICIENCY Does the associate use his/her time efficiently?		
26. FINANCIAL MANAGEMENT Is the associate aware of the financial aspects of case management including client disbursements and appropriate billing? Does the associate take into account the payment history of a client in budgeting time and expenses on cases?		
27. FIRM ADMINISTRATION Is responsibility delegated to the associate with respect to firm administration and does this associate demonstrate a willingness to participate in this aspect of the firm?		
28. CLIENT DEVELOPMENT Does the associate participate in activities designated to enhance firm reputation and/or generate new business? To what degree and of what effectiveness? Does associate actually bring in new business?		

Criteria	E/S/N/W	Evaluator and Associate Comments
29. ETHICS Does associate handle matters in an ethical manner, also making sure to properly investigate potential conflicts, disqualifications and otherwise abide by the Canons of Professional Responsibility?		

IV. GENERAL CONSTRUCTIVE COMMENTS

This associate's major strengths are:

This associate should attempt to improve:

General comments (you may wish to complete this after you have reviewed the associate's self-evaluation):

RATED BY: ______________________________ DATE: ______________

(Signature)

A copy of this Associate Evaluation of my performance has been given to me and discussed with me on this date.

ASSOCIATE: ______________________________ DATE: ______________

(Signature)

Associate's response, if any, to this Evaluation:

ASSOCIATE: ______________________________ DATE: ______________

(Signature)

Associate Evaluation

Associate's Name: ______________________________

Law School Class: ______________________________

Date of Hire: ______________________________

Evaluating Partner's Name: ______________________________

Degree of Contact with Associate: ☐ Extensive ☐ Occasional ☐ Slight

RATING SCALE: 1-10

10 **Outstanding** — well above average; showing unique adeptness, or quality; unequalled in performance by most associates at that level of experience; SPECIFIC COMMENTS MUST ACCOMPANY A RATING IN THIS CATEGORY.

8 - 9 **Very Good** — distinguished work; better than you would anticipate from an average attorney at this attorney's level.

6 - 7 **Good** — solid work product or performance; characteristic of the work quality you should expect from an attorney at his/her level. (This should be the average grade for lawyers at our firm.)

4 - 5 **Satisfactory** — Fair work, requiring somewhat more supervision than you believe should be necessary for an attorney at this attorney's level; neither displaying particular merit nor containing any serious defects; needs improvement.

2 - 3 **Marginal** — requires substantially more supervision than should be necessary.

1 **Unsatisfactory** — below average; failing to meet minimum standard of quality. **SPECIFIC COMMENTS MUST ACCOMPANY A RATING IN THIS CATEGORY**.

NR **No Rating** — insufficiently observed to form an opinion; too soon to tell.

I. LEGAL SKILLS: **Rating 1-10**

A. **Writing Ability**: (Ability to express thoughts in clear, concise, well-organized and grammatical prose.) Considers: memos, letters, briefs, agreements, etc. __________

B. **Oral Communication**: (Ability to express thoughts in clear, concise,well-organized, and grammatical speech.) Consider: both informal (intra-office meetings and presentations, informal meetings with clients, etc.) and formal (hearings, depositions, trials, formal client presentations, etc.) __________

C. **Advocacy Skills**: (Ability to formulate and persuasively advocate positions to advance client's cause.) __________

D. **Research Ability**: (Ability to uncover all evidence relevant and material to any case and organize such information in an orderly manner.) Consider: legal research document review and interpretation, witness interviews, client interviews, etc. ___________

E. **Technical Knowledge**: (Capacity to comprehend, retain and properly apply previously addressed legal principles and to constantly master new principles to improve one's skills.) ___________

F. **Quality and Thoroughness of Work**: (Ability to produce a work product that is complete, accurate, and of high quality.) ___________

G. **Intelligence**: (Ability to think and reason clearly.) ___________

H. **Problem Solving/Creativity**: (Ability to analytically determine source of the problem, obtain pertinent data and devise a practical, workable solution.) ___________

I. **Judgment**: (Ability to make sound decisions independently; understands priorities, understands the interrelation of legal and practical issues.) ___________

II. WORK HABITS:

A. **Independence**: (Ability to work well with minimum of supervision. Ability and willingness to take a matter and run with it without constant aid and comfort from a partner.) ___________

B. **Confidence**: (Do you go to this associate when an important task absolutely and positively has to be done right and on time?) ___________

C. **Management/Efficiency**: (Ability to manage caseload and deliver superior work product in a timely, cost-effective manner. ___________

D. **Productivity**: (Total volume of quality work produced.) ___________

E. **Industry/Persistence**: (Willingness to work as long and hard as necessary to achieve assigned or desired goals; having the necessary self-discipline to pursue a task to appropriate conclusion.) ___________

F. **Attitude**: (Cooperative with other attorneys and support staff; ability to accept constructive criticism.) ___________

III. CLIENT RELATIONS:

A. **Client Relations**: (Commitment to serve clients, to keep them well informed of status and progress of matters; ability to hear and understand what the client needs and to direct one's work toward meeting such objectives on a timely basis; inspires confidence.) ___________

B. **Business Development**: (Understands the necessity of attracting new clients and additional business from existing clients and is willing to do what needs to be done to accomplish those goals. ___________

IV. PERSONAL QUALITIES:

A. **Professional Presence**: (Projects the image of a first-class professional who instills confidence and commands attention and respect.) ________

B. **Human Relations**: (Skillfully getting along with people, enjoying their camaraderie and considerate and supportive of others; this includes lawyers, support personnel, clients, etc.) ________

C. **Courtesy and Tact**: (Polite attention given to others; including staff, clients, and fellow lawyers, both within and without the office.) ________

D. **Team Player** ________

OVERALL RATING ________

V. GENERAL ASSESSMENT:

A. Special strengths:

B. Suggested areas for improvement:

C. Set forth any positive or negative comments related to you by others outside the firm which you consider to be relevant to the associate's evaluation:

D. Please address overall opinion as to associate's progress, possible reassignment and long-term prospects. Do you prefer to continue working with this associate?

E. Do you believe that this associate should be terminated now or in the near future? If so, please explain.

________________ ________________________________

DATE SIGNATURE OF RATING PARTNER

RETURN THIS FORM TO ______________________________ BY __________ IN THE ENCLOSED SELF-ADDRESSED ENVELOPE. FORMS RETURNED VIA INTEROFFICE MAIL MUST BE SENT TO ______________________ IN SEALED ENVELOPES MARKED "CONFIDENTIAL."

APPENDIX C

CONTACT INFORMATION AND OTHER BOOKS TO CHECK OUT

Lisa L. Abrams / NALP, *The Official Guide To Legal Specialties* (Harcourt, 2000)

If you're still in school and you're wondering what's "out there," this is the book to check out. Very accessible information about a whole bunch of specialties, and day-in-the-life insights into what it's like to practice in different areas.

Guerrilla Tactics For Getting The Legal Job Of Your Dreams— by—well, me—Kimm Walton.

How crass is this? But I'd be an idiot not to recommend a book I think you'll enjoy. Let me put that another way. If you like this book, you'll like that one. If you're still in school and looking for a job, *Guerrilla Tactics* will help you get it!

Hendrie Weisinger, *Emotional Intelligence At Work*

Very smart stuff about how when it comes to getting ahead at work, facts don't count as much as feelings do.

Roger Fisher and William Ury, *Getting to Yes*

THE classic book on negotiating tactics. Everybody recommends it, and it's a 'must-have' in your professional library.

Ronna Lichtenberg, *Work Would Be Great If It Weren't For The People*

A funny and scary-right book about dealing with people at the office.

NALP's Attorney Development and Evaluation Committee, *Beyond the Nuts and Bolts of Associate Evaluation: System Development and Process*

Very practical information on how you, as a lawyer, are going to be judged at a law firm. This book contains sample evaluation forms for new associates, senior associates, partners, and contract attorneys. Eye-opening stuff.

Paul Lisnek, *Practice Made Perfect*

In *What Law School Doesn't Teach You . . .* I didn't talk about handling negotiations or depositions or juries or opening statements or any of those kinds of issues. But in his paperback *Practice Made Perfect*, Paul Lisnek does talk about them, in a very engaging and easy-to-read style. I strongly encourage you to grab a copy! You can get it by calling 1-800-847-7285 (in Illinois, 312-248-5600).

Bill Bryson, *Lost Continent* and *Notes From A Small Island*

These have nothing to do with law whatsoever. But Bill Bryson is the funniest man on Earth, and these two books are spit-milk-through-your-nose funny. When you need a break from whatever stresses you out, dig into these books and you'll quickly forget whatever's bugging you.

Bill Barrett

Bill Barrett knows everything there is to know about using the Internet to find jobs. Check out his website, at www.internships-usa.com.

Sharon Abrahams

Sharon Abrahams is a business etiquette guru. She conducts private, small group, corporate and public seminars in business etiquette skills. She can enhance your already decent manners—or change a frog into a prince! For more information, contact her at pook@mediaone.net or at 954-610-7780.

Debra Strauss

Debra Strauss is the author of *Behind the Bench: A Guide To Judicial Clerkships* (Harcourt, 2001). Everything there is to know about judicial clerkships—Debra Strauss knows it! She also has a website: www.judicialclerkships.com, the clerkship source with information and advice for students, a forum for law clerks to share their clerkship experiences, programs for law schools and centralized services for judges.

The National Directory Of Legal Employers

38,000 Great Job Openings For Law Students And Law School Graduates

The National Directory Of Legal Employers includes a universe of vital information about one thousand of the nation's top legal employers—in one convenient volume!

The National Directory Of Legal Employers includes the name of the hiring partner. The starting salary. How many people the firm intends to hire over the next year, and the criteria they'll use to choose successful candidates. The *Directory* also includes the specialties each firm practices, how the firms view their working environments, their achievements, their major clients, and their plans for the future.

Author: The National Association for Law Placement (NALP)
ISBN: 0-15-900454-3
Price: $39.95
(1,573 Pages, 8-1/2" x 11")

Beyond L.A. Law:

Stories Of People Who've Done Fascinating Things With A Law Degree

Anyone who watches television knows that being a lawyer means working your way up through a law firm—right?

Wrong!

Beyond L.A. Law gives you a fascinating glimpse into the lives of people who've broken the "lawyer" mold. They come from a variety of backgrounds—some had prior careers, others went straight through college and law school, and yet others have overcome poverty and physical handicaps. They got their degrees from all different kinds of law schools, all over the country. But they have one thing in common: they've all pursued their own, unique vision.

As you read their stories, you'll see how they beat the odds to succeed. You'll learn career tips and strategies that work, from people who've put them to the test!

Author: The National Association for Law Placement (NALP)
ISBN: 0-15-900182-X
Price: $17.95
(192 Pages, 6" x 9")

CALL TO ORDER: 1-800-787-8717
ORDER ON-LINE: www.gilbertlaw.com

America's Greatest Places To Work With A Law Degree

And How To Make The Most Of Any Job, No Matter Where It Is!

With *America's Greatest Places to Work With A Law Degree* you'll find out what it's really like to work at hundreds of terrific traditional and non-traditional employers—from fantastic law firms, to the Department of Justice, to great public interest employers, to corporate in-house counsel's offices, to dozens of others. You'll learn lots of sure-fire strategies for breaking into all kinds of desirable fields—like Sports, Entertainment, the Internet, and many, many more. You'll discover the non-traditional fields where new law school graduates pull down six figures—and love what they do! And you'll get hundreds of insider tips for making the most of your job, no matter WHERE you decide to work.

The bottom line is, no matter what you like, there's a dream job just waiting for you. Discover it in *America's Greatest Places To Work With A Law Degree.*

Author: Kimm Alayne Walton, J.D.
ISBN: 0-15-900180-3
Price: $24.95
(776 Pages, 6″ x 9″)

Guerrilla Tactics For Getting The Legal Job Of Your Dreams

Regardless of Your Grades, Your School, or Your Work Experience!

Whether you're looking for a summer clerkship or your first permanent job after law school, this national best-seller is the key to getting the legal job of your dreams.

Guerrilla Tactics for Getting the Legal Job of Your Dreams leads you step-by-step through everything you need to do to nail down that perfect job! You'll learn hundreds of simple-to-use strategies that will get you exactly where you want to go.

Guerrilla Tactics features the best strategies from some of the country's most innovative career advisors. The strategies in *Guerrilla Tactics* are so powerful that it even comes with a guarantee: Follow the advice in the book, and within one year of graduation you'll have the job of your dreams . . . or your money back!

Pick up a copy of *Guerrilla Tactics* today . . . and you'll be on your way to the job of your dreams!

Author: Kimm Alayne Walton, J.D.
ISBN: 0-15-900317-2
Price: $24.95
(572 Pages, 6″ x 9″)

The Best Of The Job Goddess

Phenomenal Job Search Advice From America's Most Popular Job Search Columnist

"Should I wear my wedding ring to Interviews? How can I get a job in another city? I was a Hooters girl before law school — should I put it on my resume?" In her popular *Dear Job Goddess* column, legal job search expert Kimm Alayne Walton provides answers to these, plus scores of other, job search dilemmas facing law students and law school graduates. Her columns are syndicated in more than 100 publications nationwide.

The Best Of The Job Goddess is a collection of the Job Goddesses favorite columns—wise and witty columns that solve every kind of legal job search question! If you're contemplating law school, you're a law student now, or you're a lawyer considering a career change—you'll enjoy turning to the Job Goddess for divine guidance!

Author: Kimm Alayne Walton, J.D.
ISBN: 0-15-900393-8
Price: $14.95
(208 Pages, 4-1/4" x 9")

Proceed With Caution

A Diary Of The First Year At One Of America's Largest, Most Prestigious Law Firms

Prestige. Famous clients. High-profile cases. Not to mention a starting salary exceeding six figures.

It's not hard to figure out why so many law students dream of getting jobs at huge law firms. But when you strip away the glamour, what is it like to live that "dream"?

In *Proceed With Caution*, the author takes you behind the scenes, to show you what it's really like to be a junior associate at a huge law firm. After graduating from an Ivy League law school, he took a job as an associate with one of New York's blue-chip law firms.

He also did something not many people do. He kept a diary, where he spelled out his day-to-day life at the firm in graphic detail.

Proceed With Caution excerpts the diary, from his first day at the firm to the day he quit.

Author: William F. Keates
ISBN: 0-15-900181-1
Price: $17.95
(166 Pages, 6" x 9", hardcover)

CALL TO ORDER: 1-800-787-8717
ORDER ON-LINE: www.gilbertlaw.com